VIOLENT GEOGRAPHIES

VIOLENT GEOGRAPHIES

Fear, Terror, and Political Violence

edited by

Derek Gregory
and Allan Pred

Routledge
Taylor & Francis Group
New York   London

Routledge is an imprint of the
Taylor & Francis Group, an informa business

Routledge
Taylor & Francis Group
270 Madison Avenue
New York, NY 10016

Routledge
Taylor & Francis Group
2 Park Square
Milton Park, Abingdon
Oxon OX14 4RN

Printed in the United States of America on acid-free paper
10 9 8 7 6 5 4 3 2 1

International Standard Book Number-10: 0-415-95147-X (Softcover) 0-415-95146-1 (Hardcover)
International Standard Book Number-13: 978-0-415-95147-0 (Softcover) 978-0-415-95146-3 (Hardcover)

Library of Congress Cataloging-in-Publication Data

Violent geographies : fear, terror, and political violence / edited by Derek Gregory and Allan Pred.
    p. cm.
    Includes index.
    ISBN 0-415-95146-1 (hardback : alk. paper) -- ISBN 0-415-95147-X (pbk. : alk. paper) 1. Political
violence. 2. Ethnic conflict. 3. Terrorism. 4. War on Terrorism, 2001- I. Gregory, Derek, 1951- II.
Pred, Allan Richard, 1936- III. Title.

JC328.6.V58 2006
303.6--dc22
                                                      2006014049

Contents

1   Introduction   1
    Derek Gregory and Allan Pred

2   Bare Life, Political Violence, and the Territorial Structure of Britain
    and Ireland   7
    Gerry Kearns

3   "An Unrecognizable Condition Has Arrived"   37
    Anna J. Secor

4   Cosmopolitanism's Collateral Damage   55
    Eric N. Olund

5   Refuge or Refusal   77
    Jennifer Hyndman and Alison Mountz

6   Imperialism Imposed and Invited   93
    Jim Glassman

7   Spaces of Terror and Fear on Colombia's Pacific Coast   111
    Ulrich Oslender

8   Fatal Transactions   133
    Philippe Le Billon

9   The Geography of Hindu Right-Wing Violence in India   153
    Rupal Oza

10 Revolutionary Islam   175
    Michael Watts

11 Vanishing Points   205
    Derek Gregory

12 Groom Lake and the Imperial Production of Nowhere   237
    Trevor Paglen

13 Targeting the Inner Landscape   255
    Matthew Farish

14 Immaculate Warfare? The Spatial Politics of Extreme Violence   273
    Nigel Thrift

15   The Pentagon's New Imperial Cartography   295
     Simon Dalby

16   Demodernizing by Design   309
     Stephen Graham

17   The Terror City Hypothesis   329
     Mitchell Gray and Elvin Wyly

18   Banal Terrorism   349
     Cindi Katz

19   Situated Ignorance and State Terrorism   363
     Allan Pred

Contributors   385

Index   387

Introduction

Derek Gregory and Allan Pred

Political violence takes many forms, and in this collection we have all tried to respond to its contemporary versions in different ways. As a group, we work with different theories, we analyze different materials, and we write in different voices, so this is not a manifesto. Neither is it a gazetteer, because no single volume (not even a library) could encompass the violence that animates our world. Some of the places and events we write about will be familiar; others will not; and many more, including some that haunt the headlines every day, are absent. But our aim is neither to provide some grand theory of political violence nor a comprehensive rendering of its varied instances and implications. This is simply a collective attempt to work through some of the ways in which a critical geographical imagination can illuminate the spaces through which terror, fear, and political violence are abroad in the world. Here we want to draw out a number of themes that run through the collection.

The immediate provocation for our project was a twin series of responses to the murderous events of 9/11. On one side, there were those who reduced the attacks on the World Trade Center and the Pentagon to a barbarism that passed all understanding. Any attempt at explanation was vilified as exoneration. Terrorism was located beyond the boundaries of civilization and lodged in the pathologies of those who hammered so destructively at its gates. The cry was soon taken up by others, who dismissed any opposition to the sovereign powers of the security state as "terrorism," and who enlisted the rhetoric of the "war on terror" as a means of legitimizing and intensifying their own apparatus of repression. On the other side, there were those who proposed a purely technical or instrumental response to 9/11, drawing on political technologies (that were also geographical technologies) to profile, predict, and manage the threat of terrorism as an enduring mode of late-modern government. The emphasis was on geographies of risk assessment, on geospatial data management and modeling, and on the vulnerability of biophysical and built environments to terrorist attack.

These two approaches were closely connected; in fact, the one was an inverse of the other. Where the first drew its energies from a more or less "popular" geographical imaginary, reproducing its publics through an assiduous dissemination of prejudice, the second offered an "expert" solution framed by the privileges of a supposedly objective science. Where the first directed attention toward the deviant "others" scurrying away in the interstices and beyond the bounds of "our" spaces, the second was focused firmly on protecting our own spaces: "homeland security." One conjured up wild spaces, the other safe spaces. As one commentator put it shortly after 9/11, the world's wild zones and safe zones collided over New York City (a global cartography that, as Simon Dalby shows, draws a red line right through the "war on terror").

1

We regard both responses as crucial failures of a geographical imagination, and one of the purposes of this book is to explain why: to expose the assumptions they make and the consequences they have. But the book has a larger purpose too. It is at once an intellectual and a political project in which we try to signpost other avenues of analysis that ultimately, we believe, lead to more effective and more just interventions in contemporary landscapes of terror, fear and political violence. For that reason, these chapters are not circumscribed by 9/11. Most have been touched by it in one way or another, many deal directly with the multiple geographies that swirl around it, but none takes the events of September 11, 2001 as the prism through which all political violence must now be refracted. On the contrary, one of the central assumptions that runs through the book is the need to be sensitive to the fractured histories of violence, predation, and dispossession—as material fact, as lived experience, and as resonant memory—that erupt so vividly time and time again in our own present. Thus Gerry Kearns shows how political violence in Ireland is inseparable from a colonial past that continues to haunt its post-colonial present, and argues that its contemporary political struggles are in part a struggle over the very terms in which that history is to be understood. Trevor Paglen shows how the modern production of vast tracts of Nevada as secret sites for military testing trades on a history of colonial dispossession, in which the Shoshone were placed beyond the perimeter of the American state and consigned to a "black world" where almost anything could be sanctioned. At the end of the nineteenth century the Spanish-American War gained much of its popular support in the United States through widespread revulsion at the concentration camps established in Cuba by the Spanish colonial regime; and yet after the war, as Derek Gregory shows, the United States leased Guantánamo Bay as a naval station where, since 9/11, it has reactivated a series of thoroughly colonial dispositions to establish its own war prison. The "war on terror" draws on more than a colonial past, however, and Eric Olund reveals how its racialized violence repeats in displaced and distorted form in the biopolitical strategies pursued by the United States during the First World War. And Matthew Farish shows how it continues to draw on tropes that were established in the bipolar world of the cold war. History is neither a narrative of progress nor a parade of discontinuities, then, and seen thus 9/11 becomes neither an inevitable consequence of U.S. foreign policy nor a cataclysmic event that changed the whole world.

Many of the chapters map the imaginative geographies through which political violence works. They take the cartographies of fear on which it feeds and show how these representations are never merely mirrors held up to somehow reflect or represent the world but instead enter directly into its constitution (and destruction). Images and words release enormous power, and their dissemination—or, for that matter, suppression—can have the most acutely material consequences. Thus Farish shows how Area Studies emerged in the United States as a way of localizing American militarism: the original objective was to diagnose distant dangers that were supposed to inhere within particular regions. As it turned out, Area Studies often provided much more nuanced accounts than its progenitors expected, but this has not silenced demands for caricatures that can masquerade as characterizations. Glassman provides a particularly vivid example where, since 9/11, the United States has planed away the diverse political geographies of the Philippines, Indonesia, and Thailand to render them "uniform places of Islamic terrorist threat." Glassman sees this as an attempt to revivify the United States' imperial objectives in South East Asia, but he is no less sensitive to the opportunistic deployment of a parallel logic by the region's own security states. Caricatures are not, of course, a monopoly of the political Right. Philippe Le Billon shows how advocacy campaigns against so-called conflict commodities like diamonds or oil often trade on imaginative geographies that read violence directly out of places of origin. Hegel's ghost thus makes its ghastly reappearance as Africa is constructed as synonymous with primitivism and violence, its diamonds stained with blood, whereas Canada is celebrated as the pure and peaceful North, its diamonds untainted by violence. Campaigns like these do not really dispel the fetishism of commodities, as Marx called it, because they hide the exploitative and exclusionary histories that have accreted around them. Instead, they substitute a fetishism of place that licenses its own violence against independent, small-scale diggers and miners.

The imaginative geographies that Farish, Glassman, and Le Billon describe are more than popular prejudices. They spiral through the state apparatus, the military, the market, and even the academy. But if they are to have maximum effect then the ligatures between power, politics, and the production of public spheres (transnational and domestic) assume a crucial importance. Simon Dalby provides an incisive critique of the ways in which the geopolitical abstractions of American "tabloid realism" are currently being deployed by some commentators to advance a new military imaginary—a "new map" for the Pentagon—so that the United States' unified combatant commands can be reconfigured and redeployed on behalf of "the core" to subdue the dangerous spaces of the so-called "gap." This is not the logic exposed by Glassman, though it is no less disingenuous and dangerous, but what these projects (and others like them) have in common is the calculated mobilization of popular geographical prejudices for a public audience in order to (re)direct public policy and, ultimately, to re-make the world through military violence. Their mappings are simplistic, but this is their strength as well as their weakness: they provide a geopolitical equivalent of the sound-bite that so often captures the public imagination.

Both Michael Watts and Nigel Thrift pay scrupulous attention to the mediations between representation and materialization through the crucial junction term of practice, though they elaborate this in radically different ways. Watts insists that revolutionary Islam be treated as a deeply serious political project whose imaginative geographies of Euro-American modernity cannot be dismissed as so many irrational rejections of "freedom" (as the White House and Downing Street seem to think). Dalby makes much the same point: tabloid realism cannot entertain the possibility that Muslims and millions of others might resist the incursions and interventions of the global North. In the case of revolutionary Islam, Watts shows that those rejections are not the product of superstition and ignorance. This is a radically hybrid project, he argues, whose critique of colonizing modernity is derived from readings of European radical philosophy as well as Islam. It has been hardened in the crucible of corrupt and secular nationalisms, and its hideous violence is wired to the spectacular display of death now made possible by modern technologies. Thrift is keenly interested in the mobilization of those technologies too, and in the mass of witnesses summoned by them, and he urges us to attend to the ways in which radically new imaginaries of violence (his focus is on suicide bombing) have been made possible through their framing by the media but also by a deliberate aesthetics of violence and a calculated assessment of the affective landscape to which it is directed.

Now landscape is more than a metaphor, and several other chapters explore some of the ways in which the sheer physicality of landscapes can become saturated with political violence. We know that "landscape" is a freighted term and that its cultural formations do significant ideological work. Contemporary deconstructions of "the lie of the land" have shown that aestheticized landscapes typically produce their effects by artfully concealing the very work—the embodied labor—that has been invested in their production. But landscapes can embody other traces of blood, sweat, and tears, and sometimes these are not hidden at all. They are deliberately written on the face of the earth to inspire fear on the faces of those who inhabit them. Thus Ulrich Oslender shows how paramilitary and military violence in Colombia uses visible signs of its passage—destroyed houses, abandoned villages, graffiti—as a communicative strategy to create a "space of death" from which people will flee in terror, while Rupal Oza argues that in India the right-wing project of *Hindutva*—the construction of a purely Hindu nation-state—has proceeded in part through the forcible occupation, marginalization, and erasure of Muslim spaces from the landscape. In both cases, as in so many others documented in these pages, the state is actively complicit in the production of fear, terror, and violence.

When people flee violence in its different forms, however, seeking to escape famine, poverty, or war, they often find that they are trapped in new spaces of exclusion. Beyond the explosive war zones in Afghanistan, occupied Palestine and Iraq, so Jennifer Hyndman and Alison Mountz argue, and connected to them in innumerable ways, "a quieter, geographically more distant and dispersed war against refugees is taking place." As they reveal in grim detail, affluent states now routinely fortify their borders against the threat of unwanted peoples, often the surplus residue of their own neoliberal and military adventures, and the physical architectures that are involved—walls, fences, detention centers and the like—depend on a dense armature of spatio-legal strategies. In fact, political violence is inseparable from the law's own violence. Several chapters show how this works through the proliferation of spaces of exception, where "normal" laws are suspended and liberties and protections are withdrawn from particular groups of people. Hence Kearns's demonstration of the multiple ways in which the British excluded the Irish from politically qualified life, reducing them to a bare life that, so he argues, is at the very heart of the colonial project. Similarly, Paglen's "black world" is more than a cartographic silence (though it is that): it is also "a legal nowhere" where laws do not apply and things can be done in secret. In his account Groom Lake (Area 51) emerges as a veritable laboratory of exception, where, "by producing nowhere in the testing sites of Nevada the U.S. rehearses its ability to *reproduce* nowhere. Elsewhere."

This sense of the *seriality* of exception, of the indistinction between law and violence being reproduced at countless replicant sites, runs through several other chapters. In modern Turkey, law and violence constantly fold into one another in a limitless zone of indistinction from which there is seemingly no escape for the poor, marginalized and disadvantaged. A state of emergency prevails in the south-eastern provinces, but according to Anna Secor's painstaking reconstruction many Kurdish migrants find that it precedes them to Istanbul. There too the violence of the state is everywhere, punctuating their lives at roving military checkpoints that can appear anywhere at any time, and yet also nowhere: formless, amorphous and in the shadows. In much the same way, Olund suggests that "the United States' spaces of racialized violence can occur anywhere"—Chicago's O'Hare airport, the Macedonian border (the site of an "erroneous rendition"), or the U.S. Naval Station at Guantánamo Bay—and Gregory's recovery of the circuits between Guantánamo, Abu Ghraib, and the detention and interrogation centers and "black sites" within the global war prison traces this geography of dispersion and dissimulation in detail. Like many other contributors, Gregory's view of space is an active, operative one. He understands these sites as *spacings* through which the indistinctions between law and violence fold in and out of the cages where those who have been placed outside the sphere of the human are confined and tortured.

These chapters and other like them confound the usual distinctions between "us" and "them." They show that terror and torture are not the exclusive property of others, but inhabit the central structures of our own societies too. For that reason, they extend far beyond the integuments of political and military power, and several chapters disclose the pervasive *intimacy* of terror, fear, and violence in our contemporary world. It is vividly present in the wretched experiences of Secor's Kurds or Oslender's Afro-Colombian communities, and Stephen Graham sees this as a calculated strategy of the contemporary war machine. Modern war, so he suggests, is increasingly focused on degrading ("contra-functioning") the infrastructure that makes everyday life possible. The strategy of engineering system collapse has become central to the American and Israeli militaries, for example, and as Graham's case studies from Iraq show with a visceral clarity, it can reduce civilian populations to bare life just as effectively as making them the direct targets of military violence. Mitchell Gray and Elvin Wyly repatriate this devastating logic to the United States through their "terror city hypothesis." This model shows how the infrastructural dependence of everyday life has become saturated by a pervasive discourse of risk and fear, and Gray and Wyly suggest that this extraordinarily volatile combination works to militarize urban policy, planning, and development and to provide new arenas of capital accumulation. Its toxic effects do not end there. Cindi Katz argues that ordinary insecurities now so comprehensively inhabit everyday life in American cities that troops on the street and security screens around major buildings are taken for granted. She doubts that most people are made any safer as a result of these stylized performances of security—a sort of street theater—that she sees as tacit invitations to accept the militarization of everyday life as normal and even desirable. These invitations are embossed by imaginative geographies of the dangerous other, a capillary sense of alien infiltration and circulation, so that what Katz calls "banal terrorism" is enlisted in the service of a no less banal (and no less effective) nationalism: "terror is mobilized to solidify a porous nation." Allan Pred agrees with Katz's assessment, and his satire on the Homeland Security Advisory System is a devastating indictment of the ways in which the Bush administration has manufactured fear in a calculated dissemination of what he calls "situated ignorance" in order to deflect attention from its own failings ("weapons of mass distraction") and to legitimize its military adventurism and political repression.

But we do not end with a simple plea for what Donna Haraway calls situated knowledge to replace situated ignorance and its attendant prejudices, half-truths, and lies. Part of her manifesto was a call to reach out from our different positions, to engage in conversations with others in different situations and to enter into solidarities with them, not so much as to overcome our limitations and partialities as to recognize them for what they are. What can emerge from this, too, is a developing sense of what we share as well as what divides us, and, above all, a principled refusal to exclude others from the sphere of the human. This is vitally important work, but so too is an engagement with the *politics* of fear, terror and violence. For us, given our locations, this takes place within the academy—through the elaboration of studies like those presented in these pages—but it neither begins nor ends there. It involves public address (and response) as an ethical and intellectual responsibility, it involves the fostering of a critical public culture as an indispensable part of any genuinely democratic politics, and it involves showing how political violence compresses the sometimes forbiddingly abstract spaces of geopolitics and geo-economics into the intimacies of everyday life and the innermost recesses of the human body.

2

Bare Life, Political Violence, and the Territorial Structure of Britain and Ireland

Gerry Kearns

When civilian deaths from high-altitude bombing are treated as collateral damage, when people are held without charge and abused in pursuit of evidence in a war on terror that sets aside international law and human rights, then, truly some lives are being treated as if they were either not worth living or not worth protecting. This is the world that Giorgio Agamben has described as the "state of exception." The United States and the United Kingdom are acting in the world as sovereign powers in just the way he described as the exercising of the right to deny to some persons proper political status, reducing them to a sort of "bare life" where their very biological existence continues at the sufferance of the sovereign or its agents.[1] Exceptional measures threaten to become the norm, yet the forces of colonial hubris and civilizational arrogance now abroad recall earlier times.

The colonial state has repeatedly made bare life the basis of sovereignty. Agamben has argued that political communities are formed by exclusion, not inclusion; the sovereign being the agent with the right to exclude.[2] Agamben sees the concentration camp as the clearest example of these acts of exclusion that are at the basis of the modern state. At least as good a case might be made for colonialism as the *nomos* of modernity. The colonial state claims sovereignty without granting citizenship. In the colony the inhabitants are primarily the objects of a sovereign power, rather than its subjects. It is striking that the camp itself first emerges within colonialism. Bare life, then, is at the heart of colonialism. This is nowhere clearer than in the administration of famines in colonies. Where there is a conflict between the economic purposes of colonialism and the mere biological survival of the indigenous peoples, it is all too easy for the colonial power to persuade itself that the general interest is best served by letting people die. The use of famines as a form of social and economic engineering represents a particularly pernicious form of biopolitics. It conceives of society as possessing a materiality embodying both economic and biological laws.[3] However, rather than managing these interactions to enhance the vitality of the social body, they are manipulated to enhance the economic value of local resources for the external metropole, even at the expense of "letting die" many of the people indigenous to the colony. The self-other dialectic here pits the colonizing self against a colonial other who is conceived as making undue demands upon resources earmarked for export. The colonizing self must be defended against its colonial other. In this way, colonialism gives a particularly vicious twist to the more commonly recognized discourses of deviance.[4]

Where people are constituted as objects by a colonial power, as mere biological life and not as political subjects, then, standard democratic forms of expression are closed to them. Some may turn to violence as one of the few avenues of resistance open to them. Others, in an ironic reversal of the reductions implicit in bare life, may use their own bodies, and mortality, as a weapon. Being told, in effect, that they survive at the sufferance of the colonizer, they may risk life to reclaim their own right to let die. The theatricality of their own deliberate decision to risk or even give up their life, by hunger strike or suicidal attack, draws attention to the lack of respect accorded that life by those who could treat it as collateral damage in a war to make the world safer for the colonizer, or as an acceptable casualty of some Malthusian rebalancing of the relations between food and population. Ghassan Hage has argued that the suicide bombers, learning from the occupier that their life is worthless, achieve a symbolic significance for their lives through their death.[5] These associations between colonialism, bare life, and terrorism become sedimented into the relations between peoples of different places and political traditions through the essentializing of identities as an eternal Manichean politics of difference.

Figure 2.1 shows a mural from the Shankill district of Belfast. In the ever more minutely segregated working class districts of this city, murals have been important as territorial markers and as expressions of, even a policing of, community identity.[6] This mural, in a Protestant or Loyalist area, shows Oliver Cromwell and features his

Figure 2.1 A mural from Shankill Parade, Shankhill, Belfast, photographed April 2002. Photograph: Dr. Jonathan McCormick, Northern Ireland Mural Directory, used with kind permission.

Roundheads killing a Catholic. They have the flag of St. George but also one of the flags under which march the Orange Order. The inscription to the left is a quotation from Cromwell: "Catholicism is more than a religion. It is a Political Power therefore I'm led to believe there will be no peace in Ireland until the Catholic Church is Crushed." This is precisely the sort of Manichean vision that sustains essentialized identities. Cromwell is shown as having an allegiance with the Orange Order, formed 150 years after his battles in Ireland and adopting as its flag what was purported to be the standard of William III, who fought the Battle of the Boyne some 50 years after Cromwell's invasion. Furthermore, the statement by Cromwell is not to be understood as relating to his own time and to his own political project but as being true for all time. Similar ahistorical conflations are shown in nationalist murals. Figure 2.2 is a mural from the Catholic or Republican part of the city of Derry. It shows Raymond McCartney, who, in 1980, went on hunger strike in the Maze (or Long Kesh) prison, near Belfast. The mural also shows one of the women who endured hunger strike at that time. Below the mural are the names of the ten hunger strikers who died in the same prison in 1981. The gaunt image of the woman, in particular, recalls the famous illustrations of the famine victims in the *London Illustrated News*, such as the image of the woman begging in Clonakilty from February 1847. The man is Christ-like in appearance. The hunger-strike can easily recall Christ fasting in the desert and the long tradition of Christian fasting and self-mortification. The images are painted in black and white giving them the documentary feel of the engravings of the *London Illustrated News* and of the photographs in a newspaper. The conflations suggest that the Republican prisoners were suffering as the Irish did in the Famine, at the hands of barbarians who would have crucified Christ. The British government, the mural suggests, let the hunger strikers die, just as their predecessors had presided over the mortality of the Famine. This indifference to Irish life is presented as a stable characteristic of the British, and their relations with the Irish people are, by implication, at all times purely colonial.

This chapter tracks continuities of, echoes of, and appeals to histories of violence that ever frame the question of terrorism. It begins with the colonial taking of the land in Ireland and the treatment of the majority of its inhabitants as something much less than political subjects. It then considers the episode of the Great Famine and what Irish opponents of British rule concluded from their observations of British behavior. It goes on to look at how justice was administered in Ireland and at the suspension of civil liberties this entailed. In addition, the chapter considers the use of political violence against British civilians by Irish nationalists. The conclusion offers some brief reflections upon what the Northern Ireland peace process might offer more generally for addressing the legacy of colonial violence.

The Territoriality of Imperialism

Violence has been central to the making and remaking of modern states. The medieval arrangement of territories and governments included city-states alongside fragmented regal domains. Many feudal monarchs received taxes from dispersed holdings. The consolidation of this patchwork into the modern nation-states system

Figure 2.2 A mural from Rossville street, Bogside, Derry, photographed August 2000. Photograph: Dr. Jonathan McCormick, Northern Ireland Mural Directory, used with kind permission.

owed much to new practices and costs of warfare.[7] Territorial contiguity was now vital to the coherence of the state. As states gradually changed, from being the territory of the monarch, to becoming the political expression of some notion of "the people" (however socially and economically circumscribed at first), so we can begin to speak of the emergence of the demotic or nation state in Europe.[8] In this new arrangement, distinct peoples were to inhabit distinct coherent territories. This placed the marches, or borderlands, of countries under particular scrutiny. Under feudal monarchs, the marcher lords of the borderlands, between England on one hand and Scotland and Wales on the other, had enjoyed considerable autonomy. Not without stiff, though crushed, local resistance, Wales was incorporated into an English state by act of treaty in 1278, Scotland into a British one with the Act of Union of 1707. Scotland and Wales were annexed and passed from being independent states, to being constituent parts of a larger entity. Things went differently in Ireland.

English monarchs tried, as in Scotland and Wales, to establish a stable tax regime in what they considered their Irish domain. However, resistance in Ireland meant that by the fifteenth century, the English writ, with its ban on intermarriage between English and Irish, only ran within the English Pale, a strip of land about sixty miles wide along the southern half of the east coast of Ireland. In 1488, this was actually marked out as a ditch around the English parts of the four counties of Dublin, Kildare, Meath, and Louth. After a rebellion of 1534, Ireland was subject to a series of reconquests. From 1534 to 1922, Ireland was administered by a British official, answerable to the Crown, and the British army was garrisoned in Dublin. The English tried to extend their power outside the Pale in two ways. First, they required local Gaelic lords to surrender up to the English monarch their title to their lands in order to have it regranted to them as an act of English sovereignty. Second, where local lords proved recalcitrant, military intervention was followed by plantation. Lands were taken and given to new English (in the Midlands in the 1550s,[9] in Munster in the 1580s, in Connacht in the early seventeenth century) or to English and Scots settlers in the comprehensive plantation of Ulster in the first third of the seventeenth century.

The bloodiest of the many reconquests was that by Oliver Cromwell in 1649–50. After taking Drogheda, Cromwell ordered every tenth Irish soldier killed, and together with civilians, some four thousand were killed After Wexford was captured, two thousand, including women and civilians, were killed. With this defeat, the Irish were to go, in Cromwell's words, to "Hell or Connacht." Irish who had not risen in revolt in the 1640s could move to the province of Connacht or the county of Clare and, if they had been landowners, they would acquire there a diminished property.[10] Even within Connacht, they were, in the colorful phrase of a later traveler, "forbidden to appear within ten miles of the Shannon, or four of the sea, and, if they evaded the stringent passport system which was established, they were doomed to death without trial, although it was said with truth that certain parts of [Connacht] did not contain 'wood enough to hang, water enough to drown, or earth enough to bury a man'."[11] All rebel Irish had to leave Ireland, forfeiting their lands. Some fifty thousand of the poor or defeated Irish were sent out to the Caribbean as indentured labor.[12] The vacated lands were assigned to Cromwell's soldiers and then to English speculators, or adventurers. The legal reallocation was complete on paper by 1659 but only a proportion of the transfers had been effected, although there were enough of these to give rise to nearly eight thousand claims for unjust confiscation when, in 1660, the monarchy was restored under Charles II. Very few of these claims were settled although many tenants simply stayed put and now paid rent to English and Protestant landlords, rather than to Irish and Catholic, ones. Smyth suggests that between 1641 and 1654, from an Irish population of perhaps two million, half a million Catholics either died or emigrated, and perhaps one hundred thousand Protestants.[13] In 1641, Catholics had owned three of every five Irish acres, and by 1691, they had but one.[14] The seventeenth century saw the most dramatic reallocation of land in the history of the country with perhaps four acres in every five changing hands.[15] By the eighteenth century

Catholic land ownership was largely confined to Galway and South Mayo; but even that was to be eroded.

Protestant control of the English crown was confirmed in the late seventeenth century with an oath of allegiance, used since 1689, in which the monarch promises to sustain "the true profession of the gospel and the Protestant reformed religion established by law."[16] In Ireland, this Protestant supremacy was codified by a set of Penal Laws passed by a subordinate Protestant Parliament in Ireland, and designed to constrain the political and economic rights of Catholics who were excluded from the franchise, from public office, from many of the learned professions, and who were not to hold land on tenures exceeding thirty-one years, to have a horse worth more than £5, to possess arms or ammunition, or teach their children to read and write. To take part in the economic or political life of Ireland, an individual had to swear that they found the Catholic rite of the mass to be "superstitious and idolatrous."[17] Catholics who were found to have illegal weapons would, upon a second offense, be subject to *praemunire*; that is, the person would have no protection under the monarch's writ, their possessions would be taken, and they could be imprisoned at the monarch's pleasure.[18] Catholics were forbidden to live within five miles of certain corporate towns. There were sixty-one separate statutes or amendments between 1588 and 1759; fifteen in the 1690s and twelve in the first decade of the eighteenth century.[19] In 1703, the Catholic share in ownership of the land of Ireland was one acre in seven, and by 1776 one in twenty.[20]

Catholics in England were likewise subject to religious terror with the penalty of *praemunire* for: anyone convicted a second time of maintaining the supremacy of any spiritual or ecclesiastical authority over the English monarch (upon a first offence, all goods were forfeited),[21] a first conviction for the offense of maintaining in any way the authority of the Pope or of refusing to swear an oath to the religious supremacy of the English monarch,[22] a first conviction for bringing into England any articles blessed by the Pope,[23] and for a first conviction for sending money abroad to support Catholic seminaries.[24] After 1585, it was high treason, punishable by hanging, drawing and quartering, for any Jesuit priest to be found in England. All these laws were equally adopted by the Irish Parliament at Elizabeth's instruction. In England, too, Catholics were excluded from the professions, from government office, and from holding commissions in the army or navy.[25] In England too, at various times Catholics and Protestant Dissenters were territorially restricted, as in the Five Mile Act of 1665, which forbade them from living in incorporated and chartered towns.[26] In England, however, the penal laws touched mainly upon the civic rights of a minority, in Ireland, they reduced the economic rights of a majority. In Ireland, as the constitutional historian Erskine May put it, "the Reformation was forced upon an unyielding priesthood and a half-conquered people."[27] It was, in short, a tool of imperialism.

All of this was nothing less than religious terror and while in other European countries Protestants and Catholics treated each other equally badly, or even worse, in no other place did the religion of a minority oppress a majority in such a fashion. There is also being elaborated here a spatial technology of imperialism that would be exported to North America.[28] Virginia, for example, was established as a plantation, and the taking of land by the expulsion of native peoples to points further west was intrinsic to British and then American imperialism.[29] Colonialism was always a violent rearrangement of property and persons.[30] There is also in this Irish case, the categorization of one group within the country as noncitizens and, should they assert rights (to bear arms, or affirm their religion) that others are allowed, they are, in Agamben's term, "banned," stripped of all protection under the law.[31] In this way, the violence of colonial war and repeated reconquest, was formalized as a succession of new orderings of property and territory. Even though the penal laws were enforced only unevenly, and in the half-century following 1778 were gradually dismantled, they produced a minority Protestant ascendancy in Ireland and they oversaw a transfer of resources from Catholics to Protestants.

Biopolitics

Michel Foucault described the way mercantilist policies became biopolitical through the discovery that there might be ways that the state could manage the biological life of its citizens.[32] The state now concerned itself with issues of birth, marriage and death and government now included the attempt to regulate these through social policy, taxation policy and environmental regulation. Of course, the direction of biological life was intrinsic to slavery but mercantilism developed the idea that the state might have a sort of property interest in its population. The state might take an interest in reducing mortality through sanitary regulations and promoting the public health. The state might take an interest in managing fertility through the way welfare systems might influence people's decisions about marriage and childbearing.

In England, this gave the poor law system a quite new purpose. Instead of being primarily about the support of the indigent and the disciplining of the work-shy, it had now to recognize its consequences for the rate of reproduction of the poor. Malthus argued against those who believed society to be perfectible.[33] The poor, he argued, would always breed themselves into poverty until checked by sickness or hunger. According to Malthus, "the general laws of nature repress a redundant population."[34] The equivalence between population and food supply was often effected through "vice" (such as civil war, or the exposure of infants), or through epidemics, but in extreme cases "gigantic inevitable famine stalks in the rear, and with one mighty blow levels the population with the food of the world."[35]

In this sense, any doles given to the poor ran the risk of deferring God's regulators, subverting the divine purpose of harmonious nature. Malthus notes that some wealthier people may be "prevented from marrying by the idea of the expenses that they must retrench."[36] In England, the apprenticeship system and the condition of live-in service institutionalized prudent late marriage for some of the poor. In England, at least, "the preventive check to population [...] operate[d], though with varied force, through all the classes of the community."[37] Even so, the use of the poor law to subsidize wages or to sustain the unemployed was an almost unmitigated evil. The prudent laborer would delay marriage until he had accumulated savings rather than turn to the parish for the support of his children. However, precisely this urge to independence was threatened by the English poor laws, which were "strongly calculated to eradicate this spirit."[38] Malthus would have liked to see, as he explained in the first edition of his essay, "the total abolition of all the present parish-laws,"[39] but upon mature reflection decided that "the relief given by the poor-laws [was now] so widely extended, that no man of humanity could venture to propose their immediate aboli-tion."[40] Even in the first edition, he recognized that there might be some who could not work: "for cases of extreme distress, county workhouses might be established, supported by rates upon the whole kingdom, and free for persons of all counties, and indeed of all nations. The fare should be hard [... in these] places where severe distress might find some alleviation."[41] From these ideas sprang the famous Poor Law Amendment Act of 1834 that created districts in each of which was to be a work-house, now to be the only way that relief could be delivered to the able-bodied poor.[42] For those who could work, conditions in the workhouse were to be so repugnant (separation of the genders, the breaking up of families, minimal diet) that they would appear to the poor as the case of lesser eligibility should any waged work be avail-able. In this way, the state was regulating, in Agamben's phrase, the bare life of its citizens, dealing with them not as political subjects but as biological objects.[43] It was doing so while denying that any such direction was involved, for with Malthus we see the "naturalizing" of society (what Harvey terms "biocentric" thinking),[44] placing its fundamental structures beyond human intervention in the realm of nature: "though human institutions appear to be the obvious and obtrusive causes of much mischief to mankind, yet in reality they are light and superficial."[45]

Ireland was treated as an exception. In the first place, British commentators did not see among the Irish, that moral spirit that made poverty and dependence so repugnant to the English laborer. In the eighteenth century, Ireland lacked a poor law system comparable to the English. Although Malthus did not discuss Ireland in the *First Essay*, in the *Second Essay* he was brief though explicit: "[i]f, as in Ireland, Spain, and many countries of the more southern climates, the people are in so degraded a state, as to propagate their species without regard to consequences, it matters little whether they have poor-laws or not. Misery in all its various forms must be the pre-dominant check to their increase."[46] Unlike the Protestant north of Europe, in these Catholic countries, there was little hope for a preventive check. In Ireland, the potato plus Catholicism had done their worst: "the cheapness of this nourishing root, and the small piece of ground which, under this kind of cultivation, will in average years pro-duce the food for a family, joined to the ignorance and depressed state of the people, which have prompted them to follow their inclinations with no other prospect than an immediate bare subsistence, have encouraged marriage to such a degree, that the pop-ulation is pushed much beyond the industry and present resources of the country."[47]

To speak of a "redundant" population and to propose institutionalizing them in workhouses (soon called "bastilles" by poor people) was to raise fears among the poor who rightly read this as the claim that they did not really have a right to live, or did not lead lives worth living. In the eighteenth century, Jonathan Swift had already satirized indifference to Irish lives in a pamphlet, *A Modest Proposal*, that advised the Irish poor to rear their children as foodstuffs. Swift parodied the reduction of life to questions of profit and loss and extended this logic to the horrific suggestion that, in these terms, the only value of the lives of the babies of the poor would be as meat. His targets were several, but prominent among them were Irish landlords: "I grant this food will be somewhat dear, and therefore very proper for landlords, who, as they have already devoured most of the parents, seem to have the best title to the children."[48] Opponents of the New Poor Law saw it as the "repressor of populations and murderer of babies."[49] In the most famous of these pamphlets, the anonymous author, echoing Swift, claimed that the New Poor Law would take one-quarter of English, and all after the first-born of Irish children, and kill them humanely, for its designers had perfected "the art of committing murder without the infliction of Pain, and which is to be effected by gradually mixing with the air breathed by the infants during their first sleep, a sufficient quantity of a deadly Gas, for converting that sleep into the SLEEP OF DEATH!"[50] While the severe treatment of unmarried mothers was certainly claimed to have led some to smother babies they could no longer care for, and the workhouses were clearly so destructive of family life that even inanition would not drive some into their clutches, the nightmarish vision of child-murder presented in critical pamphlets went unrealized. This moral line was not then crossed. The Irish, however, were to learn the nice distinction between sins of omission and those of commission.

In European countries, food shortages were periodic consequences of bad weather or plant diseases. By the eighteenth century, there was a standard set of responses. Food was moved from regions of sufficiency to those of need. Human use of grain took precedence over feeding animals, or brewing and distilling. Domestic consumption precluded export. These policies required that the government direct how grain should be used. There were three reasons why this did not happen in Ireland during the period of the potato blight from 1845 to 1852. First, the promotion of free trade policies in Britain focused on precisely this commodity and culminated in the repeal of the Corn Laws in 1846. The momentous repeal was indeed aided by the claim that, unfettered, grain would flow inexorably where it was most needed, Ireland.[51] Second, the triumphant Malthusian ideology suggested that unearned doles of food would demoralize the Irish poor at a time when the British were trying to bring them under the reformed poor law; workhouses, lesser eligibility and all. Third, the Irish were seen as particularly recalcitrant and many believed that only a famine could engineer the necessary restructuring of Irish agriculture away from peasants and potatoes toward proletarians and pasture. The blight produced a famine that was taken as a "providential" act of God.[52] Indeed, one government economist, Nassau Senior, according to the report of Benjamin Jowett, said "that he feared the famine of 1848 in Ireland would not kill more than a million people, and that would scarcely be enough to do much good."[53] In April 1847, he had decided that the failure of the potato crop left two million Irish people without food. Instead of feeding them through out-relief, which he said would create three million paupers and lead to insurrection in Ireland through the consequent demoralization of the population, he insisted that he would "rather encounter all the miseries that will follow the rejection" of the proposal.[54] Of course, those miseries would be visited more directly upon the Irish small farmers than upon the English economist.

As the famine progressed, the social engineering of the outcome became more explicit. Food relief was monopolized by the British state, taking into its own stores grain bought with foreign charity. All relief was to be administered through a poor law system that would reform the Irish. Starving men were set to hard and often pointless labor with their meal being proportionate to their effort. Starving families had to give up all but a quarter-acre of land to qualify even for this relief.[55] The famine was an acceptable tool of economic restructuring. The small-scale peasant farmers were to be "cleared" from the land. Their capital was used up in paying rent until they were then forced to sell all but a postage stamp should they apply for poor relief. If rent were not paid, they could be evicted and their "cabin" pulled down so that they could not return. This is precisely the proletarianization described by Mike Davis as central to British policy during the administration of late-nineteenth century colonial famines.[56] This "making of the Third World" was a new round of primitive accumulation, or what David Harvey has called "accumulation by dispossession."[57] It happened early in Ireland, with all the violence and indifference that would ever of be its hallmarks.

Should the Irish escape to Britain, they would not be relieved on the same terms as British poor people on the move.[58] Instead, they could be returned to the most accessible Irish port and there left to shift for themselves. The British government refused to allow that the Irish poor who fled to British cities were legitimately a charge upon the imperial purse. The famine was an Irish problem.

The charity of the British was challenged by their perception of the Irish as bringing calamity upon themselves through their culture and religion, and bringing disease into the heart of British cities through their filthiness.[59] In Ireland, the desperate and starving peasants haunted the streets of every town and city. There was no avoiding the catastrophe, and contemporaries spoke of the murder of Irish people through deliberate British neglect.[60] Those charitable souls not content to allow the British state to measure the quality of their mercy sent missionaries to the west of Ireland and, there, language almost failed them.[61] These issues of representation have serious consequences. The Irish, it would appear, could not be represented as what Agamben has termed "politically qualified life," that is as people with rights.[62] Disqualified from representing themselves politically, they could not, in turn, be represented as political subjects. At best, they were represented as biological objects, as bare life. The degradation of poverty and starvation produced images of the Irish that were ironically complicit with their representation as mere animal life. In this context, they could be objects of charity but never subjects who had a right to put their own case. They were moralized about rather than listened to. In 1848, Charles Trevelyan, who was largely responsible for the administration of poor relief in Ireland, wrote to his colleague at the Treasury, Charles Wood, in precisely these terms: "[t]he great evil with which we have to contend is not the physical evil of the famine, but the moral evil of the selfish, perverse and turbulent character of the people."[63]

Readers of the *Times* had been told, by an Irish correspondent, as early as Christmas of 1846 that, in Skibbereen (Cork), for example, "[t]he poorhouse is full to overflowing, and the guardians are weekly obliged to refuse admission to the famishing creatures that throng around the doors; though the general impression among the poor is that admission to the workhouse is equivalent to a sentence of death."[64] Yet, a correspondent from England was sure that the remedy for Ireland was "to toil for food, not to get it by begging."[65] Another Irish correspondent, a Justice of the Peace wrote, also of Skibbereen, that a "mother, herself in a fever, [...] was seen to drag out the corpse of her child, a girl about 12, perfectly naked, and leave it half covered with stones."[66] Another English correspondent wrote contemptuously that it "is to Irish landowners and not to us, the munificent and hated Sassenachs, that the inconclusive gentlemen of Cork and Kilmina should address their ungrammatical epistles."[67] One journalist for the *Times* reported from Ireland that a woman had collapsed in the street in Skibbereen and when carried back to her "cabin" indicated there a pile of straw under which lay "the mangled corpses of two grown boys, a large portion of each of which had been removed by the rats."[68] The *Times* editorialized against the pricks of human conscience ("it will sometimes cost an effort not to throw a trifle into the mendicant's cap")[69] suggesting that only the discipline of a proper poor law could help the Irish. This gap between reports from Ireland and cogitations in England was created by religious and economic doctrines that encouraged many English to consider certain Irish lives not worth the living. Ireland, for many English was, in the resonant but somewhat later phrase of Francis Galton, "overcrowded by a population for whom there was no place at the great table of nature."[70]

The taking of Irish resources into British hands was, I have already suggested, achieved through the colonial reduction of the native Irish to the status of fugitives in their own land. This, in turn, left their interests to be represented by those who had colonized them. It is sad but not surprising that these irresponsible rulers should perceive their recalcitrant subjects as the authors of their own misery and, armed with Malthus and a providential Protestantism, they convinced themselves that the Irish had brought down upon themselves a death-dealing famine. Their lack of empathy with Irish lives enabled them to be understood as bare life and left to the vagaries of Dame Nature. The Irish Catholic bishop, John MacHale, was surely right to conclude that Ireland would never have suffered either the famine mortality (over 1 million, or one in every eight persons living in 1845) or the famine emigration (a further 1.5 million) to anything like the same extent "had she the protection of a native parliament."[71] The priorities of the British government were not answerable to the wishes of the poor people of Ireland and the consequence gave the lie to the claim that Britain could legislate in the best interests of its Irish subjects. The violence of the penal laws resurfaced as the indifference of political economy.

This violence was born of Irish resistance to British colonialism and of the measures, conceptual and physical, taken by the British to assert and justify their rule. This is why over the three-quarters of century of British rule remaining for most of Ireland, there was the evident paradox of a society in Britain that was becoming demonstrably less violent, both in crime and in punishment, administering Ireland at the point of a gun and under the shadow of the hangman's rope. As Townshend notes in his study of violence in Ireland, the persistence of violence must be taken as a clear indication of "the limitations of political talk."[72] The penal laws had largely been dismantled in the late eighteenth century and many of them had been in practical abeyance for some time previously but when Ireland was coerced into political union with Britain in 1801, the British monarch and the majority of lords and commoners in Parliament baulked at incorporating Catholics as full citizens, despite earlier assurances to the contrary. Then, the experience of the Famine showed that British administrators would put the requirements of free markets before the lives of Irish people.

Trevelyan took his place alongside Cromwell in the Pandemonium of British colonialists coruscated in history and song. Resistance to the British continued in many forms, cultural as well as political. Violent resistance was increasingly organized through secret societies, terrorizing landlords as part of a campaign to get control of the land, or plotting rebellion, or attempting to raise such terrorist havoc in Ireland and Britain that the colonialists would decide that retaining their Irish territories was simply not worth the trouble. Responding to these conspiracies, the British introduced to Ireland suspensions of civil liberties, a secret service within the police force, and a battery of military and penal measures that had no parallel in Britain.[73] Throughout the remainder of the period of British control, Ireland remained, in Agamben's terms, a "state of exception," a place where normal liberties were suspended. Both the insurgents and the administration used bodies and lives to make their points. In the absence of genuine political talk, there was little else they could do.

The Body in Law

Agamben argues that the notion of bare life "as a new political subject is already implicit in the document which is generally placed at the foundation of modern democracy: the 1679 writ of *habeas corpus*."[74] The argument is that by requiring the state to produce in court the body of arrested persons, the regulation placed the physical body at the heart of justice, underlining the fact that in being a subject, and even a citizen, one was surrendering up to the sovereign the right to determine the life or death, freedom or confinement, of one's body. The writ was clearly reciprocal for if the monarch had to produce the body, then, also the monarch could require the presence of the body in court to answer any charge brought against that person. The writ of the monarch ran only as far as people would submit to the requirement of *habeas corpus*, would, or could be compelled to, submit to custody if summoned. In return for this submission, the modern monarch would bring the body to court and there test the legality of confinement against a body of law interpreted by magistrate, judge or jury. In this sense, May described the writ as "unquestionably the first security of civil liberty."[75]

There are three other features of the treatment of the body in law that are important here. First, there is the treatment of convicted persons. Second, there is role of juries, and thus the judgment of peers in validating detention, conviction, and sentencing. Third, there is the abridgement of rights under emergency conditions. Over the nineteenth century, there was a gradual diminution in the violence of punishment. From the last decade of the seventeenth-century to the middle of the eighteenth, some 187 offenses had been added to the list of capital crimes.[76] By the early nineteenth century, the revulsion of the people demoralized the application of the law: "[m]en wronged by crimes, shrank from the shedding of blood, and forbore to prosecute: juries forgot their oaths and acquitted prisoners, against evidence: judges recommended the guilty to mercy. Not one in twenty of the sentences was carried into execution."[77] The number of capital offenses fell from 220 at the start of the nineteenth century, to a little over 100 in the 1830s and down to just four in 1861 (murder, treason, arson in royal dockyards, and piracy with violence). In the case of Ireland, government had also to consider the effect of executions on the state of Irish public opinion. Those hanged for political crimes, and even for crimes against property or the propertied, were quickly revered as martyrs. In 1803, when Robert Emmet was beheaded, a legend of some forty years later has women rushing forward to take away the *memento mori* of blood-stained handkerchiefs.[78] The whole iconography of Catholicism with its pictures, relics, and processions was easily mobilized around the republican dead. The transatlantic conspiracy of Fenianism was perhaps only made visible and thus corporeal through a series of diasporic funerals that began in 1861 with the translation of the remains of Terence Bellew MacManus from San Francisco to Dublin via New York and Cork.[79] In 1916, when the leaders of the revolution were executed, the *Catholic Bulletin*, a magazine that had opposed physical force republicanism until then, published a series on their lives that led to its cover and editorial being censored by the British administration in Dublin.[80]

Republican martyrdom asserted the spiritual superiority of a people who would give their lives where their opponents risked nothing in dealing out capital punishment.[81] The British understood this. Executions would amplify rather than deter republican conspiracy. When, in 1867, a police sergeant was killed during the rescue of some Fenians in Manchester, the death penalty seemed inevitable. Even though it was never established who had fired the shot through the lock of the armored van, three men were tried for conspiracy to murder. Even before their trial concluded, the nationalist press referred to them as martyrs.[82] The British decided that the families could not be given the bodies of William Allen, Edward Condon, and Michael O'Brien and they were retained inside Manchester prison, the remains being destroyed by quicklime.[83] This was an extreme punishment for Victorians set great store by the treatment of the remains of those they loved. 'Ghost' funeral processions were held in Manchester, in London, in Liverpool, in Leeds, in Glasgow, in Newcastle, and in Ireland at Dublin, Cork, Kanturk, Limerick, and Middleton, and in the United States, at New York.

In the nineteenth century, very few Irish republicans were executed for treason. Instead, either for treason, or more commonly for treason felony, they were expelled from Ireland or Britain, or given sentences of penal servitude in a British prison, or were exiled to penal colonies overseas. In each case the treatment of the rebel's body was the signifying act.

In banning people from residence at home, the law made them fugitives in their own land, and exiles overseas. The numbers involved were hundreds rather than the millions who fled the famine or who later emigrated in hope of economic or political betterment. Yet these exiles gave other emigrants an opportunity to make sense of their absence from home as politically or economically enforced exile. They fostered a "Greater Ireland" overseas for the republican cause.[84]

The treatment of Irish political prisoners was a further way their bodies were placed in question. Seán McConville argues that in the main, the Irish insurgents of the second half of the nineteenth century were treated no worse than other convicts.[85] There are three qualifications to this. First, the Irish insisted that they were political prisoners and not mere convicts. The motives of their actions were not avarice or vice and thus they should not be degraded in the way that were people who had lost character (I return to this claim below). Second, the risk that the Irish would be sprung from jail by determined comrades, aided by sympathetic turnkeys, as all too real, and this meant that they were kept under conditions of extreme security. At various times, this meant that for years many of them were wakened every hour of the night for positive identification. For many more of them, it meant solitary confinement and a regime of silence. These were cruel and unusual punishments that sent some mad, as McConville documents. Finally, several of them were indeed treated with exemplary sadism. In an English prison in 1869, Jeremiah O'Donovan Rossa was kept over a month restrained with his hands and feet cuffed behind his body.[86] Daniel Reddin, who was lame, had his legs burned with hot irons to test for malingering and claimed that, after electrocution to the genitals, his vomit was cleaned up with his own face.[87] Both these sets of claims were first made to prison authorities, while the pair was still in custody, and had only worse treatment to fear from exaggeration. It is striking that the worst treatments were not only medically sanctioned but were administered by doctors testing for malingering. Most of the prisoners complained of cold and hunger yet "the unvarying diet of brutes"[88] was intended to be part of general prison discipline, symbolizing, in Agamben's term, the reduction of the subject to "bare life."

Execution, exile, and incarceration were each presented by the British as the automatic and perfectly reasonable response to the criminal acts of the Irish. Prisoners of conscience occupy a strange position in the penal system. One of the tenets of passive resistance is that one places one's body in the way of the violence of the state in order to affirm a higher law. There is no question that many of the republican prisoners intended revolution. Few ever fired a shot in anger and most arrests were pre-emptive. The British did not want to create martyrs but they did want to deter men of property from joining, even leading, rebellion. Treason, earned execution, but for many Irish rebels actual treason was an ambition rather than an achievement. Sedition was a lesser charge that covered the sort of plotting the majority had engaged in but as a mere misdemeanor, rather than a crime, it involved no reduction in the status of the subject. When John Mitchel was brought to trial on May 20, 1848, he was tried for the novel offence of treason felony (rushed through Parliament on April 22, 1848).[89] This new crime need involve no more than encouraging others to prepare to deprive the English monarch of some part of its territories of powers, and conviction could involve deprivation of property and transportation, and in Mitchel's case it did. To advocate a British republic, for example, was now technically illegal. The offense had to be tried in the county where it had occurred. Thus Mitchel had to be tried in Dublin since it was there he had published his insurrectionary articles and given his revolutionary speeches. His friend, John Martin, noted that Mitchel was being charged with "uttering sentiments held and professed by at least five-sixths of his countrymen."[90] Juries for political trials in Ireland were characteristically 'packed' with loyal Protestants. Catholics could not be trusted to convict even on the basis of the evidence. They had to be excluded from the administration of justice and, in Mitchel's term, were thus not citizens but rather "slaves" in their own country.[91] The administration of justice in Ireland bore testimony to the refusal that underlined the republican cause. It was not until the 1880s that, with Gladstone, the British government tried seriously to redress the causes of this alienation. Until then, and even after, since partial remedies do not undo the convictions of experience, the writ of the English monarch in political matters was in essence a colonial one.

Finally, the territorial separateness of Ireland was repeatedly reinscribed through special regulations or the suspension of rights that applied in Britain. In 1807 food was short in Ireland. There were struggles in the countryside over the payment of rent and there was the threat of French involvement in an Irish insurrection. Introducing a new set of repressive measures, Arthur Wellesley (soon to become the Duke of Wellington) said "stronger measures were necessary than what the ordinary laws afforded."[92] He proposed an Insurrection Act under which magistrates in prescribed districts could impose a curfew and an Arms Act under which in these same districts all guns had to be registered and all pikes surrendered. These special measures were usually of limited duration; in this case seven years. But they were repeatedly reintroduced. From 1807 to 1846, there were sixteen Acts restricting ownership of weapons in Ireland. Acts for preserving the peace through proclaiming districts were passed not only in 1807, but also in 1813, 1822, 1824, 1833, 1834, 1847, 1850, 1852, 1853, 1854, 1855, 1856, 1870, 1871, 1873 and 1875.[93] In England and Wales, the writ of *Habeas Corpus* was suspended during part of the revolutionary wars with France and then again during Luddite disturbances in 1817. In Ireland, suspensions were granted by the British Parliament in 1800, 1802–5, 1807–10, 1822–4, 1848–9 and 1866–9. What we see here with the restrictions on arms, the possibilities of curfew, and the permission of arrest without charge or subsequent trial is the application of varieties of centralized martial law repeatedly to various parts of Ireland. Nasser Hussain has examined how this politics of the emergency becomes the logic of colonialism.[94] The liberal regime declares these to be exceptional acts but faced with anticolonial resistance they accept them as norms. During the first half of the nineteenth century, "Ireland was governed under 'ordinary' English law for only five years."[95]

In these ways the Irish colonial body was territorialized, marked, constrained, exiled, or placed outside the normal regime of liberal justice. In one sense, these exceptions show the violence that was shielded by the consent of normality. In another, this violence prepares the ground for, and is in turn fed by, political actions that render violence a goal and not just a sad consequence of resistance. These actions try to make societies ungovernable by inducing the ruled to withdraw consent from a sovereign who has lost control over the use of violence in society. Indeed, Max Weber defined a state as "a human community that (successfully) claims the *monopoly of the legitimate use of physical force* within a given territory."[96] By acting violently in ways that yet received popular assent, the Irish insurgents of the second half of the period 1848–1922 intended to show that the British state had lost that monopoly in Ireland. Seeking to delegitimize the violence of the insurgents and present it as a sign of Irish primitivism, the British came to call this violence "terrorism."

Terrorism

In the early nineteenth century, states were as likely as persons to be called terrorist. The Jacobins of 1793 were understood as terrorists because they used the state's monopoly on violence to create a climate of fear among the populace. The term was also used more generally as, for example, when the *Times* wrote of the Sultan of Turkey as about to "pursue his plans of reform, but only by the most complete terrorism"[97] or when it claimed of Portugal that "the public acts of Government are all marked with the stamp of subversion and terrorism."[98] The years 1815–1860 saw forty-seven references to terror, terrorism, or terrorist in the *Times* and twenty-two of these referred to terrorist states, sixteen to France alone, yet references to terrorism in Britain or

Ireland were almost always to individuals or to institutions. British elections were not run by secret ballot and the varieties of intimidation practiced upon voters were regularly termed "terrorist," as when, at an election in High Wycombe, Benjamin Disraeli accused his opponent of terrorism whereas, countered Colonel Grey, it had been Disraeli who "had hired a parcel of drunken brawlers to follow him [Grey] in his canvass,"[99] or where George Grote spoke of the "private terrorism" practiced by landlords who determined how their tenants should vote.[100] The main institutions accused of terrorism were organized religions. When Protestant bishops instructed their clergy to boycott nonsectarian education in Irish schools, this was described as "a complete system of terrorism."[101] There was only one occasion where the British state was described as terrorist, and the context, being colonial, is significant. In 1857, the executions that followed a rebellion of the Indian soldiers were horrific with rebels being strapped to the mouths of cannons and blown to pieces. The reporter in India for the *Times* commented that "[t]error is no doubt a powerful engine in suppressing turbulent populations, but its use is always accompanied by violent shocks which injure the terrorist, and a reaction is sure to supervene."[102]

It is clear that the majority of these references to terrorism are metaphorical. The Terror directed by Robespierre, however, was much more than mere intimidation. It was the creation of a climate of fear so that people would not dare imagine rebellion since they could not know whom to trust, while the penalty for sedition would be summary execution; thousands were executed and over two hundred thousand arrested.[103] After the example of the Jacobins, early-nineteenth-century terrorism was an action of a state against a people. Only the government could authorize the extensive and unpredictable violence that brought true terror. Terrorism was when a government made war upon its subjects. Metaphorically, general intimidation could be termed terrorism. Increasingly, this term was used to describe rural violence in Ireland, especially associated with the Land War in the 1880s. In the *Times*, the articles mentioning "terrorism" or "terrorist" peaked in this decade. There were about 300 such articles in the 1870s and again in the 1890s, but in the 1880s there were 976, of which 824 featured Ireland.

When the Russian nihilists used dynamite to kill Tsar Alexander II (1881), they gave birth to a new world in which a terrorist became almost always an individual using violence against the state to spread fear amongst the people. Dynamite brought this change because it inevitably risked indiscriminate killing.[104] Now the terrorists made war upon the people in order to force a government to surrender. The *Times* editorialized that with the placing of bombs in railway tunnels (and later, waiting rooms, gasworks, police stations, and prominent public buildings such as Scotland Yard), new depths of infamy had been plumbed, "by spreading indiscriminate ruin among masses of innocent and irresponsible people."[105] The *Times'* contempt was reserved for the coward who would kill unknown persons while not being "willing to take his life in his hand." An anonymous Liberal M.P. wrote to the *Times* that the explosions in London, Liverpool and Glasgow, meant that the constraints on liberty allowed in Ireland should be extended to Britain especially given the "presence among us of the *American-Irish* and the *Irish* themselves in such large numbers in our great cities."[106] The first explosion had been in 1867 when, in an attempt to spring the Fenian, Ricard O'Sullivan Burke, from Clerkenwell prison, a barrel of gunpowder was detonated against the wall of the prison yard. Although the wall did not come down, over four hundred houses were damaged, six people died, and over one hundred were injured.[107] Reprisals against Irish people living in Britain followed. Despite the fact that the intention was clearly to breach the prison wall, the *Times* was sure that the aim of the Fenians was "to create a terror throughout the United Kingdom, and such is their unscrupulous ferocity that with a large class of the community they may so far succeed."[108]

The Fenian bombing campaigns of the period 1881–6 defined for the British a domestic figure of the individual terrorist that almost entirely displaced the earlier notion of state terror. There are three ways this connected with the treatment of the Irish as bare life.

First, a sense that the Irish were fugitives in their own land was cherished most strongly among emigrants in the United States. If the Irish were excluded from effective citizenship, then, constitutional nationalism was a vain diversion and armed rebellion all that could work. It was true that propertied Catholics received the vote after 1829, but Irish M.P.s were a small minority at Westminster and when they tried to raise the question of the Repeal of the Union between Ireland and Britain, they were listened to with ill grace or, more commonly, hooted down in the mother of all parliaments. Seeking a more direct route to independence, the Fenian Brotherhood was an American organization aiming to raise money, men, and materiel for an invasion of Ireland. For Britain, the moment of greatest danger was probably late in 1865 when a good share of the soldiers of the British Army stationed in Ireland were either sworn members of, or sympathetic to, the Irish Republican Brotherhood (the Irish and British wing of the conspiracy). The I.R.B. had been very successful in recruiting among the Irish in the British Army. There was also in Ireland at this time a good number of Irish-American soldiers trained and hardened by five years service in the American War between the States. In Dublin, in September 1865, the offices of the main Irish republican newspaper, the *Irish People*, were raided and all its correspondence and business papers seized. Before the end of the year, most of the army regiments with large numbers of Irish soldiers had been removed from Ireland.[109] In February 1866, *habeas corpus* was suspended and some 1,260 persons were taken into custody. Of these, 145, when questioned, said that they were from the United States.[110] After months, in most cases, or years, in some, the vast majority of those detained were released, without charge, on bail, or, on condition they signed a commitment to keep the peace in future. In total, 298 of the prisoners released without charge were required to depart Britain and Ireland for America. These people might consider that they had tried traditional conspiracy and that given the military odds, and the efficiency of the British spying system, new ways of rebellion had to be found. For many of these people, dynamite was the classic weapon of the weak.[111] They also believed that they had a special responsibility, for their cousins in Ireland had "neither the means, the resources, nor the opportunity to strike England a fatal blow."[112]

In the second place, the Famine left a complex legacy. In one sense, the Irish in America had evaded the famine, leaving behind those too poor to quit, too poor to live. Moreover, in America they found themselves hyphenated to a past and a current circumstance that was somewhat shameful. They knew that their fellow Americans, when they "see a 'Mick' or 'Pat,' ignorant or otherwise degraded, they rail or sneer at

him and not at the tyranny which, with diabolical ingenuity, made him thus."[113] The
Irish-Americans recoiled from their memories of famine Ireland: "I have seen more
sickening sights than any beheld on the battle-field; the ghastly skeletons of what
were once God's creatures, fair and comely, and strong, shrivelled into skin and bone
from starvation, and piled in heaps, with a little straw for a shroud, waiting to be
pitched into a common hole, 'unwept, unhonored, and unsung;' this was death–this
was murder."[114] They wanted to have come from a better place than they had, so that
they might be proud of themselves in ethnic America. They had also learned from
James Fintan Lalor, and later from John Mitchel, that in any place where the social
contract did not secure the physical survival of the people, "[s]ociety stands dissolved."[115] Catholic Irish-Americans were also sustained in this belief by at least some
of their bishops. Love of country and respect for its government should go together,
but, as Archbishop John Hughes of New York pronounced at the first great Fenian
funeral, that of Terrence Bellew MacManus: "[i]f that government should degenerate
into oppression and tyranny, then would come the love of country but not its government."[116] With no other recourse, the Irish could then invoke the justifications offered
by Thomas Aquinas for the "just war," helpfully summarized for them by Hughes in
his sermon: that they had reason to believe they were in danger for their lives and
were attacking those intending harm to them, that they acted with the support of
their population, and that their intention was to restore or establish a fair society.[117]

The third reason why the "dynamitards" were funded and largely recruited from
the United States relates to the testimony and risks of the rebel body. After six years
in prison, Rossa was offered release on condition he left Ireland and Britain for
America. He was minded to accept but when told that American Fenians wanted
him to hold out for a complete pardon he commented, somewhat sarcastically: "By
jove they *are* spunky … I have met hundreds of men who would die for Ireland and
have often lamented my own deficiency in this respect. I could never work myself up
to more than a resolution to risk life."[118] For many, donating money from America
was encouraging other people in another place to take and to risk life. In another
sense, the body of Rossa was a priceless exhibit in itself. This was the man who had
goaded the British to try to break him, and there he was among them, a witness to
indomitable Irishry. He had grown up in Skibbereen, in terms of press coverage the
epicenter of the Famine. His family had been evicted and the children had been sent
to live with different relatives. When his father died during the Famine, Rossa took
over his job, at first directing a road-building gang and then visiting the poor who
had applied for parish relief.[119] Whenever he was criticized, for drinking, or financial
irregularity, or reckless rhetoric, there would always be those for whom he was "the
greatest living martyr of the cause of Irish independence."[120]

In December 1875, Rossa sent a letter to one of the most prominent Irish nationalist newspapers in the United States, the *Irish World* of Brooklyn. He proposed that,
just as the American War of Independence had been preceded by the actions of skir-
mishers who harried the British, so the long-awaited conflict between Britain and her
Irish enemies from Ireland, Britain and America, might be preceded by the harrying
of British commerce and administration by men armed with little more than dynamite and convictions. The response was immediate. From Vermont, came a rejection
of windy rhetoric since "a small amount quantity of dynamite is far more persuasive

than any amount of blatherskite."[121] Another sent $5 "to be presented to John Bull in the shape of Greek fire or powder and lead."[122] A woman wrote: "[i]f we cannot do the fighting, we can encourage those who can."[123] One contributor testified: "Ah yes, we remember the slaughter of '47 and '48 by England's artificial famine and her poor-house soup. Though only a boy at the time, I shall never forget the cruel jeers of ruffian gentry and shoneens then. Enclosed are $2 to hasten the day of vengeance."[124] Another woman recalled: "I was in London when Clerkenwell was blown up, and from the scare that seized England, I firmly believe that event led to your release more than anything else. If England feared a repetition of similar things in the prison where Irish prisoners are confined, she would consider it too expensive to be keeping them."[125] One supporter urged that "[a]gainst England, we must use unhesitatingly all means of destruction, and, as John Mitchel says, 'seize, if possible, the very fires of hell and fling them in her face."[126] An ex-prisoner offered $1 by "way of paying for entertainment received in Richmond, Kilmainham and Belfast in '66."[127] The fund became a way that the Irish nation in America could become known unto itself, since Rossa printed their names, where they were from in Ireland and whom they wanted to see among the contributors. It would be, he thought, a "kind of census of the Irish in America."[128] In the four months May to September 1876, ten thousand individual contributions were noted by name in the *Irish World*. By February 1877, $23,00 had been raised, and by 1880, $90,000.[129]

Two significant differences between nationalist thinking in Ireland and among Irish Americans reveal the character of this form of terrorism. First, the revolutionary movement in Ireland and Britain at the time abjured these tactics. Second, when part of Ireland achieved a qualified form of independence, in 1922, very few Irish-Americans came back to live there.

The Irish in Britain and Ireland judged that attacking public buildings in Britain may create mayhem but was not likely to eject the British from Ireland or to ameliorate the condition of Irish people in Britain and Ireland. The chief alternative to this strategy came from one of the few leading Fenians who was not required to leave for America, Michael Davitt. Davitt recognized that merely ending British rule would not of itself create a better society: "[t]he people have never been told the kind of Ireland we should have if the making of it depended on the Nationalists, or how the Nationalists proposed to grapple with any of the burning social and political questions which would demand solution if the country were freed to-morrow."[130] Davitt instead directed his attention to the land question. He judged that the peasantry had most to gain from independence and thus he followed Lalor in making the land question the focus of the national struggle. Violence had its place in this struggle but it was targeted at landlords who charged above what was judged to be a "fair" rent. It was very different to the necessarily imprecise targeting of the dynamitards.

The thousands who funded the dynamite campaign were willing to target an abstraction—"Britain" —with violence because they believed Britain was responsible for their own experience of violence. They wanted vengeance rather than delivery. They were also distant from the consequences of their actions and did not face the inevitable hostility of British neighbors. They saw neither the appeal to direct material benefit with which Michael Davitt wished to infuse nationalism, nor did they appreciate the power of the appeal to public opinion that Charles Parnell was to use so well. They were also unable to appreciate that circumstances might change; that the reforms of the 1880s and 1890s must necessarily change the grounds for violence. If sovereignty has been grounded on the assertion of the sovereign's right over bare life, then, terrorism claims back the right to reply to violence with violence. It is, as Gregory says, a most "uncivil war."[131] It is a fight against civilians who are defenseless and have not accepted the risks of soldiering. The terrorists were not really external to the society they attacked; many of them had lived in Britain for a time and nearly all had relatives and friends who were permanent residents there. It was a war that fetishized violence within a Manichean logic that held the people it claimed to represent as hostages against the violent reprisals of the state it had taken up arms against. The terrorists had to claim that the objective interest of all people of Irish descent lay so clearly in antagonism toward Britain that reprisals against Irish people were the product, not of the terrorism itself, but of this inevitable primordial struggle. Thus, provoking reprisals could actually be presented as an unmasking of the true nature of British rule and even as essential to the education of the Irish people.

Townshend comments that physical-force republicanism has been sustained by more than the emotional and intellectual appeal of republican ideology, rather it rests upon "an inheritance of communal assumptions validating its methods as much as its ends."[132] Those communal assumptions have been in part at least nurtured by experience of colonialism. The British have seen Irish violence as a mark of primitivism and yet had themselves actively pushed the Irish out of the very political realm in which they might find alternatives to violence. Being left with little else, some among the Irish attempted to turn their supposed unruly violence from a mark of their disgrace into a weapon of resistance. This perhaps shares something with the neurosis described by Fanon as wanting to "find value for what is bad."[133] We can see the consequences of this history of political violence in some modern Irish identities, in the zero-sum game of sectarian struggle expressed by many of the murals of Belfast and Derry, and in the various standoffs through which the peace-process in Northern Ireland has stumbled. Frayling believes that "each community in Northern Ireland is imprisoned by its memories, and because those memories are held in isolation, they cannot be healed, and the communities are unable to face the future together."[134]

Yet, there is a peace process and important steps away from violence have been, and continue to be, taken by former terrorists on both sides. The civic spaces of Northern Ireland have been shattered by road blocs, army searches, petrol bombs, car bombs, warnings of car bombs, swaggering sectarian marches, punishment beatings of neighbors, sectarian and reprisal killings, "peace walls," and increasing religious segregation. Yet the civilians who live in those spaces largely believe that the worst of the nightmare is over. The final section of this chapter considers how the history outlined above bequeathed a set of communal assumptions that framed the tragedy that followed attempts to redress the gross unfairness in the treatment of the Catholics of the province. It offers some reflections on how the grip of the Manichean logic can be challenged and steadily undone; how political talk can be fostered so that people are not treated as bare life and are not drawn in consequence to physical violence.

Making Irish and British Territories Anew

The campaign of Davitt and Parnell in the 1880s did not, of course, achieve independence for Ireland. Even the land reforms helped middling rather than the poorest farmers. The larger farmers got reduced rents, the smallest farmers did not secure a viable peasant proprietorship (in this they faced not only political but economic obstacles).[135] It is also true that Gladstone failed to deliver Home Rule for Ireland and thereby redress what he saw as the injustice of earlier British rule. The point about these injustices is that they continued to have effects. The revolution of 1916 (at whose head was the old dynamitard, Thomas Clarke), and more particularly the manner of its suppression, reinvigorated nationalist opinion in Ireland. The majority of Irish M.P.s sent to Westminster in the election of 1918 were nationalists (Sinn Féin won 73 out of 105 Irish seats, with 46.9% of the popular vote). In the face of a guerrilla war and weary after five years bloody conflict in Europe, the British government sued for peace. The refusal of the majority of Protestants in the North-East of the island to contemplate living under majority Catholic rule resulted in the largest possible number of counties (six) with yet an aggregate Protestant majority being constituted as Northern Ireland. Neither the rights of Protestants in the Republic nor those of Catholics in Northern Ireland were properly respected after partition. Although, the Catholic nature of the Republican state was never to be palatable to its Protestant residents, they did not form an economic underclass in the way the much larger minority of Catholics did in Northern Ireland. In the 1960s the civil rights movement in the United States inspired Catholics in Northern Ireland to demand equal access alongside their Protestant neighbors to jobs, housing, and the franchise. The condition of Northern Ireland was an international disgrace and the Labour government of Harold Wilson in the early 1970s tried to force Unionist politicians in Northern Ireland to rectify the inequalities. This was unacceptable to Unionist politicians and to a Protestant working class that saw the province as a zero-sum game in which every gain by a Catholic was something taken from them. The Protestant working class, a largely Protestant police, and a sort of Protestant militia, targeted Catholic areas in Belfast with violence. In 1969, this violence was such that the British army was sent in to protect Catholics.

This was the context in which Irish terrorism began again. A new Provisional Irish Republic Army (IRA) sought to use the crisis to educate Catholics to their view that only the re-unification of the island could protect them.[136] Thus the material and civil rights agenda was displaced in favor of escalating the situation to the point where the province would be ungovernable. Ironically, the Catholic Church, and Irish-Americans, had less difficulty with the purely nationalist Provisionals, than with the somewhat Marxist Official IRA. With the British army increasingly difficult to reach, the IRA bombed softer targets. With the leadership of the IRA increasingly difficult to reach, Unionist paramilitaries killed in a purely sectarian fashion. In 1971 internment without trial (the suspension of *habeas corpus*) began, at first predominantly for republicans. British intelligence was poor and this early sweep gathered in many people who had long since ceased to have any connection with insurrectionary republicanism. Then followed the years of the "dirty war" in which torture and other abuses of human rights were deployed in the search for firmer information about those involved in republican or loyalist paramilitary action.[137]

From 1976 the British aimed to treat the IRA prisoners as common, rather than political, prisoners. The struggle now shifted to the prisons, as it had for Irishmen in earlier times. In 1976 the blanket protest began with prisoners refusing prison uniform. In 1978 the "dirty protest" began with prisoners refusing to slop out and instead smearing the walls of their cells with excreta. In 1980 the first hunger strikes started. They ended with some concessions but these were not implemented in an honest manner and the second set of hunger strikes, which left ten hunger strikers dead, began in 1981. The year also saw 118 deaths outside prison walls, 54 of them civilian. The hunger strike gave the republican struggle new martyrs to set alongside Fenians such as Rossa and the members of the Irish Republican Brotherhood executed after the 1916 revolution.[138] Many of the leaders of the IRA spent a lot of time in prison between the mid-1970s and the mid-1980s. There was intense debate among the prisoners, both theoretical and practical, about the value of violence.[139] Raising the question of what independence was for, led some republicans to ask whether the social goals of republicanism required independence for their pursuit. As Patterson suggests, this tension between a United Ireland as an end in itself or as a means to an end is ever present in republicanism.[140] From 1987, the Provisional IRA, through its political arm, Sinn Féin, began to involve itself with the electoral process. All during this time, murders, bombings, and reprisals failed to bring the British to accept that they should abandon the Protestants of Northern Ireland to the mercy of a united Ireland.

Michael Ignatieff is sure that terrorism has never succeeded in changing a political regime.[141] If so, why is it so tempting? If we look at the recent terrorism in Northern Ireland, we can see three reasons. First, where groups can point to a history in which the lives of some part of society have been treated as expendable, they can assert the essential inhumanity of the regime and the necessity for even violent change. Irish history can show the colonialist use of religious division to suppress a majority and take from them anything resembling equality of opportunity, and, then, the appeal to political economy to enforce a major restructuring of the economy at the expense of the rural poor. In modern cases, the treatment of people as fugitives in their own land through various forms of apartheid and land-dispossession in South Africa and Israel/Palestine, or the dismissal of local lives as collateral damage in shock and awe bombings would be comparable cases. Second, where the state proves willing to act in a brutal fashion to sustain improper privilege, terrorists will recruit easily. Internment without trial and other ways that republicans were stripped of the basis of citizenship revealed the British state asserting as an exception what a certain reading of Irish history could show to be almost a norm. Allowing republicans to die on hunger strikes showed toughness but also was easily seen as callousness. Today, terrorists will be recruited by practices that strip people even of the rights owed to prisoners of war under the Geneva Convention. In the third place, terrorism is attractive because nothing else seems available.

How should people respond to terrorism? Ignatieff is certainly right that as much as possible should be done within the rule of law and that all exceptional powers should be time-limited and subject to both judicial review and legislative scrutiny. It is a distressing feature of recent British legislation that it abandons the practice of time-limited emergency powers and makes antiterrorism laws permanent features of our legal system.[142] The recent experiences in Ireland suggest other lessons. First, it is important to engage with insurgents' readings of history. The Provisional IRA, for example, saw Northern Ireland through a broadly Leninist theory of imperialism in which the colonialism of the seventeenth century continued as the exploitation of Irish labor by British capital in the twentieth. This reading of the economy of Northern Ireland was capable of empirical challenge. The ownership of capital by transnational corporations did not fit easily into this picture and it was important for the peace process that, while Secretary of State for Northern Ireland, Peter Brooke stated in a public speech, of November 1990, that "the British government has no selfish strategic or economic interest in Northern Ireland."[143] It is likewise significant that after discussions between Martin Mansergh and people associated with the Thirty Two County Sovereignty Committee (the political wing of the Real IRA), the Irish Attorney General gave a detailed response to their case for a united Ireland suggesting that the state of Northern Ireland accumulated legitimacy with time and that there were now so many reciprocal treaties between the Republic of Ireland and the United Kingdom that the twenty-six county state was also now a legitimate political entity.[144] Indeed, the historical scholarship of Martin Mansergh, with his emphasis on shared histories and traditions across territorial and sectarian boundaries, is itself a significant contribution to a peace process.[145]

Second, inequities and the legacies of injustice need to be addressed. The Unionist veto of civil, social, political, and economic equality of opportunity for Catholics was basic to the creation of the conditions for terrorism in the 1970s. Something like a Truth and Reconciliation Commission is necessary so that people can bury their dead and try to live with their killings. It is also clear that parity of esteem is an important requirement for self-confident peace. Here, much remains to be done in Britain and Ireland. It was important that in a referendum, the people of the Republic of Ireland decided to amend their constitution and remove their claim to the six counties of Northern Ireland. It is useful that Prince Charles has spoken of wanting to be a defender of all faiths and not just of *the* faith, as British coins used to announce the monarch. Yet, the disestablishment of the British state has perhaps further to go even than the de-Catholicization of the Republican one.

Third, in situations of civil conflict where the partiality of the state is precisely in question, it would be most helpful if international observers and even armed forces were as involved as possible. In Northern Ireland, the British government could have accepted United Nations' assistance in the late 1960s instead of allowing itself to rely upon a sectarian police force and sometimes on an only mildly less sectarian army. Every mistake made in circumstances like this makes the path to peace that much steeper. International scrutiny of prisoners would make it more difficult to abuse them and also more difficult for exaggerated accounts to serve as recruiting agents. Britain has a poor record in this regard both in Ireland and in other colonies.[146] It is vital that, humbled by this recognition, it supports actions of the United States only in strict accordance with the best traditions of constitutional government. At present, many U.S. commentators, particularly the so-called neoconservatives, wish to place U.S. foreign policy beyond any extra-U.S. constraints, legal or military.[147] In contrast, international law exists to prevent powerful nations from treating people outside their borders as mere bare life. The history of the relations between Britain and Ireland shows how easily asymmetries of power breed violence. This history also illustrates how readily such violence engenders as a response violent and sectarian communal traditions that are distressingly resilient.

Acknowledgments

I am grateful to David Butler, Mary Gilmartin, Millie Glennon, Mike Heffernan, Nic Higgins, Phil Howell, Nasser Hussain, Steve Legg, Denis Linehan, John McCormick, John Morrissey, Mick Muldoon, David Nally, Simon Reid-Henry, Willie Smyth, Gerard Toal, Andy Tucker, and Hannah Weston for their advice. I am especially grateful to Derek Gregory and Paul Laxton for their detailed comments and to John McCormick for generously allowing me to use two from his amazing collection of photographs of Irish murals. Thanks to the Department of Geography and NIRSA, NUI Maynooth, for support as a Visiting Research Associate. I am grateful to the ESRC for research support to fund data collection, to Millie Glenn for research assistance, and to the University of Cambridge for sabbatical leave.

Notes

1. Giorgio Agamben, *Homo sacer: Sovereign power and bare life* (Stanford: Stanford University Press, 1998 [1995]).
2. Derek Gregory, *The colonial present: Afghanistan, Palestine, Iraq* (Oxford: Blackwell, 2004), 62.
3. Michel Foucault, "On governmentality," *Ideology and Consciousness* 6 (1979): 5–21.
4. Foucault, *"Society must be defended": Lectures at the Collège de France, 1975–76* (New York: Picador, 2002 [1997]).
5. Ghassan Hage, "'Comes a time we are all enthusiasm': Understanding Palestinian suicide bombers in times of exighophobia," *Public Culture* 15 (2003): 65–89.
6. Neil Jarman, *Material conflicts: parades and visual displays in Northern Ireland* (Oxford: Berg, 1997); Jonathan McCormick and Neil Jarman, "Death of a mural," *Journal of Material Culture* 10 (2005): 49–71.
7. Victor Kiernan, *State and society in Europe 1550–1650* (Oxford: Blackwell, 1980).
8. Philip Bobbitt, *The shield of Achilles: War, peace and the course of history* (London, Penguin, 2003 [2002]).
9. John Morrissey, *Negotiating colonialism* (London: Historical Geography Research Group, 2003).
10. Peter Beresford Ellis, *'Hell or Connaught!': The Cromwellian colonisation of Ireland, 1652–1660* (London: Hamilton, 1974).
11. Arthur Bennett, *John Bull and his other island*, vol. 1 (London: Simpkin, Marshall, Hamilton, Kent & Co., 1890), 59–60.
12. Sean O'Callaghan, *To hell or Barbados: The ethnic cleansing of Ireland* (Coolleen, Kerry: Brandon Books, 2000).
13. William J. Smyth, "Semi-colonial Ireland," in Alan R. H. Baker (ed.), *Home and colonial: Essays on landscape, Ireland, environment and empire in celebration of Robin Butlin's contribution to historical geography* (London: Historical Geography Research Group, 2004), 53–65, 62–63.

14. J. G. Simms, *The Williamite confiscation in Ireland, 1690–1703* (London: Faber and Faber, 1956), 195.
15. Louis M. Cullen, "Catholic social classes under the penal laws," in T. P. Power and Kevin Whelan (eds), *Endurance and emergence: Catholics in Ireland in the eighteenth century* (Dublin: Irish Academic press, 1990), 57–84, 63.
16. Available at http://www.worldfreeinternet.net/parliament/oath.htm; accessed November 1, 2004.
17. 3 William and Mary, c.2 (1691). An act for abrogating the oath of supremacy in Ireland and appointing other oaths, sec. 5.
18. 7 William III, c.5 (1695). An act for the better securing the government, by disarming papists, sec. 3; William Blackstone, *Commentaries on the laws of England, vol. IV* (London: Butterworth, 1825) 125–26.
19. The list is available at: http://www.law.umn.edu/irishlaw/chronlist2.html; accessed November 1, 2004.
20. Simms, *Williamite confiscation*, 160.
21. 1 Elizabeth I, c.1 (1559). An act for restoring to the Crown the ancient jurisdiction over the State, ecclesiastical and spiritual, and abolishing all foreign power repugnant to the same; 1 Elizabeth, c.2 (1559). An act for the uniformity of common prayer and divine service in the Church and the administration of the sacraments.
22. 5 Elizabeth I, c.1 (1563). An act for the assurance of the Queen's royal power over all states and subjects within her dominions.
23. 13 Elizabeth I, c.2 (1571). An act against the bringing in and putting in execution of Bulls and other instruments from the See of Rome.
24. 27 Elizabeth I, c.2 (1585). An act against Jesuits, seminary priests and other such like disobedient persons.
25. 3 James I, c.5 (1605). An Act to prevent and avoid dangers which may grow by Popish Recusants.
26. 17 Charles II, c.2 (1665). An act for restraining Non-Conformists from inhabiting in Corporations.
27. Erskine May, *Constitutional history of England since the accession of George the Third*, vol. III, 3rd ed. (London: Longman Greene and co., 1871), 70.
28. Nicholas Canny, *The Elizabethan conquest of Ireland: A pattern established* (Hassocks: Harvester Press, 1976).
29. Donald W. Meinig, *The shaping of America: A geographical perspective on 500 years of history. Volume 1. Atlantic America, 1492–1800* (New Haven, CT: Yale University Press, 1986); *The shaping of America: A geographical perspective on 500 years of history. Volume 2. Continental America 1800–1867* (New Haven, CT: Yale University Press, 1993)
30. Nick Blomley, "Law, property, and the geography of violence: The frontier, the survey, and the grid." *Annals of the Association of American Geographers* 93 (2003): 121–141; Cole Harris, "How did colonialism dispossess? Comments from an edge of empire," *Annals of the Association of American Geographers* 94 (2004): 165–182.
31. Agamben, *Homo sacer*.
32. Foucault, "On governmentality."
33. Thomas Robert Malthus, *An essay on the principle of population, as it affects the future improvement of society. With remarks on the speculations of Mr Godwin, M. Condorcet, and other writers* (London: J. Johnson, 1798).
34. Ibid., ch. 17, para. 9.
35. Ibid., ch. 7, para. 20.

36. Ibid., ch. 4, para. 9.

37. Ibid., ch. 4, para. 15.

38. Ibid., ch. 5, para. 13.

39. Ibid., ch. 5, para. 25.

40. Malthus, *An essay on the principle of population: A view of its past and present effects on human happiness; with an inquiry into our prospects respecting the future removal or mitigation of the evils which it occasions,* 6th ed. (London: John Murray, 1826), Book IV, ch. VIII, para. 2.

41. Malthus, *Population* [1798], ch. 5, para. 27.

42. J. A. Field, *Essays on population and other papers* (Chicago: University of Chicago Press, 1931) 268; 4 and 5 William IV (1834) c.76. An Act for the amendment and better administration of the laws relating to the poor in England and Wales.

43. Agamben, *Homo sacer.*

44. David Harvey, *Justice, nature and the geography of difference* (Oxford: Blackwell, 1996), 120.

45. Malthus, *Population* [1798], ch. 10, para. 5; Chris Hamlin and Kathleen Gallagher-Kamper, "Malthus and the doctors: political economy, medicine, and the state in England, Ireland, and Scotland, 1800–1840," in Brian Dolan (ed.), *Malthus and medicine* (Amsterdam: Rudolpi, 2000), 115–40.

46. Malthus, *Population* [1826], book IV, ch. VIII, para. 24.

47. Ibid., book II, ch. X, para. 38.

48. Jonathan Swift, A *Modest Proposal for preventing the children of poor people from becoming a burthen to their parents or country, and for making them beneficial to the publick* (Dublin: J. Roberts, 1729), para. 12.

49. Josephine MacDonagh, *Child murder and British culture* (Cambridge: Cambridge University Press, 2003), 98.

50. Anon., *Book of murder; vade-mecum for the commissioners and guardians of the New Poor Law throughout Britain and Ireland, being an accurate reprint of the infamous essay on the possibility of limiting populousness by Marcus, one of the three, with a refutation of the Malthusian doctrine,* 2nd ed. (London: John Hill, 1838 [1833]), 2.

51. Peter Gray, *Famine, land and politics: British government and Irish society 1843–50* (Dublin: Irish Academic Press, 1999).

52. Peter Gray, 'Potatoes and providence': British government responses to the Great Famine," *Bullán: An Irish Studies Journal* 1 (1994): 75–90.

53. Cecil Woodham-Smith, *The Great Hunger: Ireland 1845–9* (London: Hamish Hamilton, 1962), 375–76.

54. Gray, *Famine, land, politics,* 280.

55. Christine Kinealy, *This great calamity:The Irish famine, 1845–52* (Dublin: Gill and Macmillan, 1994).

56. Mike Davis, *Late Victorian holocausts: El Niño famines and the making of the Third World* (London: Verso, 2000).

57. Harvey, *The new imperialism* (Oxford: Clarendon Press, 2003), 144.

58. David Feldman, "Migrants, immigrants and welfare from the Old Poor Law to the Welfare State," *Transactions of the Royal Historical Society* 6 (2003): 79–104.

59. Gerry Kearns and Paul Laxton, "Ethnic groups as public health hazards: The Famine Irish in Liverpool and lazaretto politics," in Esteban Rodríguez-Ocaña (ed.), *The Politics of the Healthy Life: An International Perspective* (Sheffield: European Association for the History of Medicine and Health, 2002), 13–40.

60. Kearns, "Educate that holy hatred: Place, trauma and identity in the Irish national-ism of John Mitchel," *Political Geography* 20 (2001): 885–911.

61. Chris Morash, *Writing the Famine* (Oxford: Clarendon Press, 1995).

62. Agamben, *Homo sacer.*

63. John O'Beirne Ranelagh, *A short history of Ireland* (Cambridge: Cambridge University Press, 1994 [1983]), 117.

64. *Times,* January 2, 1847, 3d.

65. *Times,* January 4, 1847, 3e.

66. *Times,* December 24, 1846, 6c.

67. *Times,* December 29, 1846, 5b.

68. *Times,* December 31, 1846, 8a.

69. *Times,* January 8, 1847, 4b.

70. Francis Galton, *Hereditary genius: An enquiry into its laws and consequences* (London: Macmillan, 1869), 356.

71. James S. Donnelly, Jr., *The Great Irish Potato Famine* (Thrupp, Glos, UK: Sutton, 2001), 244.

72. Charles Townshend, *Political violence in Ireland: Government and resistance since 1848* (Oxford: Oxford University Press, 1983), ix.

73. H. Walker, "The tendency towards legislative disintegration," in J. H. Morgan (ed.), *the New Irish Constitution* (London: Hodder and Staughton, 1912), 388–411.

74. Agamben, *Homo sacer,* 123.

75. May, *Constitutional history,* vol. III, 11.

76. Ibid., 393.

77. Ibid., 394–95.

78. Marianne Elliott, *Robert Emmet: The making of a legend* (London: Profile Books, 2003), 136.

79. William D'Arcy, *The Fenian movement in the United States, 1858–1886* (Washington DC: Catholic University of America Press, 1947).

80. *Catholic Bulletin* 6 (December 1916).

81. Paige Reynolds, "Modernist martyrdom: The funerals of Terence MacSwiney," *Modernism/Modernity* 9:4 (2002): 535–559.

82. *The Nation* (November 9, 1867).

83. Patrick Quinlivan and Paul Rose, *The Fenians in England, 1865–1872: A sense of insecurity* (London: John Calder, 1982).

84. Adrian Mulligan, "A forgotten 'Greater Ireland': The transatlantic development of Irish nationalism," *Scottish Geographical Magazine* 118:3 (2002): 219–34.

85. Seán McConville, *Irish political prisoners, 1848–1922: Theatres of war* (London: Routledge, 2003).

86. Jeremiah O'Donovan Rossa, *Irish Rebels in English Prisons: A record of prison life* (New York: P. J. Kenedy, 1882).

87. McConville, *Irish political prisoners,* 189.

88. Ibid., 282.

89. John George Hodges, *Report of the trial of John Mitchel for felony, before the Right Honourable Baron Lefroy, and the Right Hon. Justice Moore, at Commission Court, Dublin, May, 1848* (Dublin: Alexander Thom, 1848), 2.

90. John Mitchel, *The crusade of the period: And Last conquest of Ireland (perhaps)* (New York: Lynch, Cole and Meehan, 1873), 296.

91. Mitchel, *Jail journal 1876* (Poole: Cassell, 1996), 25.

92. *Times,* July 10, 1807, 2d.

93. Taken from the list of British Parliamentary Papers relating to political crimes and offenses in Ireland available at http://www.bopcris.ac.uk/browse/eppiLCSH/69_3.html; accessed November 10, 2004.

94. Nasser Hussain, *The jurisprudence of emergency: Colonialism and the rule of law* (Ann Arbor: University of Michigan Press, 2003).

95. Townshend, *Political violence*, 55.

96. Max Weber, 'Politics as a vocation' [1919], in Hans H. Gerth and C. Wright Mills (eds), *From Max Weber: Essays in sociology* (New York: Oxford University Press, 1946), 77–128, 78.

97. *Times*, September 18, 1826, 2a.

98. *Times*, April 3, 1828, 2c.

99. *Times*, November 10, 1832, 3b.

100. *Times*, April 25, 1833, 1c.

101. *Times*, March 20, 1833, 1e.

102. *Times*, January 17, 1859, 7a.

103. Keith Michael Baker, *The French Revolution and the creation of modern political culture. Volume 4: The Terror* (Oxford: Pergamon Press, 1994).

104. Walter Laqueur, *No end to war: Terrorism in the twenty-first century* (London: Continuum, 2004).

105. *Times*, November 1, 1883, 9b.

106. *Times*, December 30, 1884, 6b.

107. Quinlivan and Rose, *Fenians in Britain*, 90.

108. *Times*, December 14, 1867, 6e.

109. R. V. Comerford, *The Fenians in context: Irish politics and society 1848–82* (Dublin: Wolfhound Press, 1985).

110. National Archives of Ireland, "Habeas Corpus Suspension Act," 3 volumes plus index. Volume I has been typed into three volumes of its own, but the other volumes are only in manuscript: CSO ICR – II; shelf 3|754|11; vol. 3 was 12, and index volume was 13.

111. James Scott, *Weapons of the weak: Everyday forms of peasant resistance* (New Haven, CT: Yale University Press, 1985).

112. "Report of D. O'Sullivan on his mission to Ireland," in *Seventh National Congress, F. B., Proceedings of the Senate and House of Representatives of the Fenian Brotherhood in Joint Convention at Philadelphia, Pa., November 24, 25, 26, 27, 28 & 29, 1868* (New York, 1868), 38.

113. *Ireland and America, versus England, from a Fenian point of view. A lecture delivered by Brig. Gen. J. L. Kiernan, U.S.A., in the principal cities and towns of the West* (Detroit, 1864), 6.

114. *Oration delivered by Lieut.-Colonel W. R. Roberts, at the great Fenian demonstration, in Jones' Wood, New-York, on Tuesday, July 25th, 1865* (New York: Office of the Trades Advocate, 1865), 12.

115. James Fintan Lalor, "A new nation" [1847], in Lillian Fogarty (ed.), *James Fintan Lalor: Patriot and political essayist: Collected writings,* 2nd ed. (Dublin: Talbot Press, 1947 [1918]), 7–25, 10.

116. *Irish American*, September 21, 1861, 2e.

117. Thomas Aquinas, *Summa Theologica*, [1273] Part II, Question 40.

118. McConville, *Irish political prisoners*, 247.

119. *Cork Examiner*, June 30, 1915, 8b.

120. *Irish People*, February 10, 1872, 5a.

121. *Irish World*, March 18, 1876, 5b.

122. Ibid., March 25, 1876, 5c.

123. Ibid., April 8, 1876, 5c.

124. Ibid., April 8, 1876, 5d.

125. Ibid., April 15, 1876, 5d.

126. Ibid., April 15, 1876, 5d.

127. Ibid., April 15, 1876, 5f.

128. Ibid., April 22, 1876, 5d.

129. McConville, *Irish political prisoners*, 333.

130. Denis B. Cashman, *The life of Michael Davitt, with a history of the rise and development of the Irish National Land League* (Boston: Murphy and McCarthy, 1881), 104–5.

131. Gregory, *Colonial present*, 36.

132. Townsend, *Political violence*, ix.

133. Franz Fanon, *Black skin, white masks* (New York: Grove Press, 1967 [1952]), 197.

134. Nicholas Frayling, *Pardon and peace: A reflection on the making of peace in Ireland* (London: Society for Promoting Christian Knowledge, 1996), 131–32.

135. Paul Bew, *Land and the national question in Ireland, 1858–82* (Dublin: Gill and Macmillan, 1978), 223–25.

136. Ed Moloney, *Secret history of the IRA* (London: Allen Lane, 2002).

137. Peter Taylor, *Beating the terrorists?: Interrogation at Omagh, Gough and Castlereagh* (Harmondsworth: Penguin, 1980); Martin Dillon, *The dirty war* (London: Hutchinson, 1990).

138. Eamon Collins, *Killing rage* (London: Granta Books, 1997), 210.

139. Richard English, *Armed struggle: The history of the IRA* (London: Macmillan, 2003).

140. Henry Patterson, *The politics of illusion: A political history of the IRA*, 2nd ed. (London: Serif, 1997 [1989]).

141. Michael Ignatieff, *The lesser evil: Political ethics in an age of terror* (Princeton, NJ: Princeton University Press, 2004).

142. Clive Walker, *Blackstone's guide to the anti-terrorism legislation* (Oxford: Oxford University Press, 2002).

143. Richard English, *Armed struggle, a history of the IRA* (London: Macmillan, 2003), 269.

144. John Mooney and Michael O'Toole, *Black operations: The secret war against the Real IRA* (Ashbourne, Meath, Ireland: Maverick House, 2003), 143.

145. Martin Mansergh, *The legacy of history for making peace in Ireland: Lectures and commemorative addresses* (Douglas, Cork, Ireland: Mercier Press, 2003).

146. Mark Curtis, *Web of deceit: Britain's real role in the world* (London: Vintage, 2003); Curtis, *Unpeople: Britain's secret human rights abuses* (London: Vintage, 2004).

147. Kearns, "Naturalising empire: Echoes of Mackinder for the next American century?" *Geopolitics* 11 (2006): 74–98.

3
"An Unrecognizable Condition Has Arrived"
Law, Violence, and the State of Exception in Turkey

Anna J. Secor

I enter this chapter on law, violence, and the state of exception through the door of a poem, a poem I have "found" in the translation of a 2003 focus group interview with a 27-year-old Kurdish man who migrated from southeastern Turkey to Istanbul in 1994.[1] The speaker is a refugee from the violent conflict that has wracked Turkey's southeastern provinces since the mid-1980s. The clash between state security forces and the PKK, a militant Kurdish group with a Marxist-Leninist philosophy, led to the loss of an estimated thirty thousand lives and the displacement of at least one million people.[2] Around 3,500 villages suspected of harboring PKK were evacuated and burned by the Turkish military during the height of the conflict in the 1990s. The official "state of emergency," declared in 1987, was finally lifted in 2002 from the last of the sixteen southeastern provinces, though the state continues to maintain a heavy security presence in the region.[3] In the narrative to follow, the speaker refers to being asked to be a "guard." The village guards were Kurdish residents recruited by the state to help fight the PKK. These local recruits, in combination with the security forces, were called "Special Teams." Many of those who lived in Turkey's southeast found themselves caught between the PKK and the Special Teams, forced to choose sides, spend time in jail, or flee.

An Unrecognizable Condition

> We came to Istanbul because our village was burned.
> They came to the village. They killed the men.
> They killed a husband and wife and took the baby,
> later we asked where.
> The PKK came and made this situation.
> We saw them.
> If we said we didn't see them it would be a lie.
> I saw many
> and in 1994 the last thing that could not be overcome came:
> They said, "You will be a guard or else
> you must abandon the village
> at once. If you don't go

we will drop a bomb here," they said, "we will drop a bomb," they said.
What is that?
We entered the battle; we went there with the wrongness.
In a village near the city, bombs were dropped all over the village,
rockets.
They called the police station,
"Hey, you are hitting our village!" they were saying;
"No," they said,
"there are PKK there; we are hitting them," they said, "not you."
But two or three houses were hit.

We went back to the village to see the village,
not a rock remains on top of a rock.
I mean there is nothing except for concrete.
Everything made from the earth and the stone was burned.
When we come again after 1994,
we go and see the village, we don't recognize the village.
An unrecognizable condition has arrived.

If it is left, if the state gives permission, with my own effort,
from the stone and the earth there I would try to make something.
But they say to you, "Okay, return to the thing, but you will be a guard."
Do you become a guard?
In that case you make at least two enemies.
The enemy that is in the mountains is one;
the soldiers that will oppress you are two.

They come to check on the Special Teams.
They come to the houses at night.
During the day you are required to provide hospitality.
After that, again they return to the village,
in official dress.
They say, "Last night I came to your house, you
gave food and this and that to me.
In your house there is this kind of door, the window is like this," they say.
I mean they sat so long they surveyed everything.
They took photos.
Later tomorrow they come to your house.
They take out of their bag and leave
a bomb.
They say, "This bomb is yours."
Even if you say it isn't yours they say it is.

At that moment seventeen of our relatives were in jail.
Seventeen!
My older brother lay in jail for seven years,
They say to you, "This gun is yours."
The people have one crushing, two crushings, three crushings.

Now they say go to the village.
Nobody will go there.

In that place, when our fathers entered the door,
we greeted them with a ready posture.
We waited on them.
We served tea.
But now, here,
if you say to your younger sibling, "Bring tea,"
"Go get it yourself," they say.
Get it yourself, they say!
Why?
Because the respect and love of that place stayed there.

We came to escape the oppression in the village.
But in Istanbul still
you start to talk
you are sitting in a coffee shop
the police come.
"Where are you from? Okay come along, let's take a look."
Where are you from?
I'm from Mardin, from head to toe.
I will be looked at as though I am suspicious
from head to toe.

A man comes, he swears, says you are a terrorist.

I won't go to the coffee shop,
I will go someplace where nobody will see me.

The unrecognizable condition: It is not only the transformation of the village, where under the state of emergency no order remains, no rock on top of a rock, but also life in the city, in Istanbul, that is unrecognizable. Even the rules that once governed familial relations, no longer obtain. Barış—let us name him this, it means peace—is from Mardin, one of the provinces of southeastern Turkey over which the state of emergency had been in force. His poem is one of incarceration, the enclosure of the subject, its transformation into the direct object of violence. His narrative not only unfolds the field of violent authority within which his migration, his life, has been captured, but also shows how the grip of the state of emergency continues to be felt in the city. In this chapter, I will argue that we can understand Barış's situation as one of abandonment before the law. He is banished within the state. He is accused, and always already guilty, subject to the mythical violence of the law over naked life. His only space is a space of invisibility.

When I refer to abandonment, to banishment, I am drawing on the idea of the "ban" as developed by Georgio Agamben (1998). For Agamben, the ban refers to the state of exception, a state in which one's relationship to the law is defined by its suspension. The subject who is banned is included within the law by the sheer force of his exclusion from it. When the state of emergency was put into force over the provinces of Turkey's southeast, this territory was not merely excepted from the "normal" state of law, but at the same time was *interiorized within* state power precisely through its definition as a zone of exception. In its abandonment before the law, this territory and its population become subject to the unbound sovereign power of the state. Agamben argues that the sovereign exception—that is, the exception that arises from the ability of sovereignty to operate outside its own law—does not just distinguish inside from out, but "traces a threshold (the state of exception) between the two, on the basis of which outside and inside, the normal situation and chaos, enter into those complex topological relations that make the validity of the juridical order possible" (Agamben 1998,19). In this ordering of space, the sovereign decision does not create a simple diagram of "spaces of the law" and "spaces without the law," but rather it creates a pervasive zone of indistinction. Agamben calls this zone of exception "unlocalizable"—it permeates and overflows the spaces where the law operates in its various modes. The state of emergency of Turkey's southeast does not represent an isolated case, a case from which those ostensibly outside can remain inured. As Walter Benjamin wrote in 1940, "The tradition of the oppressed teaches us that the 'state of emergency' in which we live is not the exception but the rule" (Benjamin 1968a, 257).

What does it means to live under a state of emergency that is also the rule? Unfolding from the "unrecognizable condition" of Barış's poem, my argument traces the everyday imbrications of violence and law. What is released by Barış's poem, and through the argumentation of this paper, is the spatiality of a state of emergency that is at once diffuse and ordered. Nicholas Blomley, in his work on law, property, and violence, shows how the spatializations of the frontier, the survey and the grid operate to legitimize and found the violence of property law (Blomley, 2003). "Space," he writes, "gets produced, invoked, pulverized, marked and differentiated through practical and discursive forms of legal violence" (Blomley 2003, 135). I argue here that the police operate at the frontier of state power, creating and maintaining a threshold zone of exception, a zone that in its lack of fixity becomes impossible to leave behind. I reflect upon this problematic of space, law and violence by tracing the ways in which differentiation collapses, zones of indistinction spread, and the spaces of law are turned inside out. As this tale unravels, we find the figure of the police, with their distinct mix of violence and law, repeatedly breaking to the surface, agents of guilt and abjection authorizing real and imagined spaces of lawlessness and law. When at last we turn to the question of justice, we find it fleeing the scene—and, interestingly, taking the "State" idea with it.

Istanbul, a vast metropolis of approximately 12 million inhabitants, is ringed with ever widening squatter settlements, apartment complexes, and gated communities. Since the 1950s, migrants from Turkey's rural areas have streamed into the city in search of work and schools. Today, with migrants comprising over 60 percent of the population, Istanbul has become a city marked both by the intermingling of peoples and by the reinforcement of lines of inclusion and exclusion, of spatialized regimes of difference and control. For example, Taksim is a commercial area in the central district of Beyoğlu that has become a major commercial and entertainment center since the 1990s. It is not only a site of consumption and *flanerie*, but also a space where protests and public celebrations are staged. Taksim is, as I have argued elsewhere, the space that best encompasses the imagined public sphere of Istanbul. Yet, at the same time, it is also a heavily policed and exclusionary arena (Secor 2004b). Furthermore, the expansive fabric of Istanbul is transected by differences that comprise a mosaic of neighborhoods, many of which are segregated not only by class, but along ethnic (Kurd-Turk), religious (Alevi-Sunni, secular-religious) or regional (place of origin, *hemşehri*) lines (Güvenç and Işık 1996; Işık and Pınarcıoğlu 2001). Across the city's topography of both movement and fixity, the urban matrix of difference and control is constantly being reconfigured through the everyday practices of Istanbul's diverse inhabitants.

While Barış's story is that of a Kurdish[4] migrant in Istanbul, I am interested not only in Kurds but in the relations of all those who, through their marginality, encircle the center of power and the law in Turkey. Of course, this is almost everyone, in one way or another. This chapter is but one fragment of a study that involves group interviews with men and women, rural-urban migrants, Islamists, poor folk (in Turkish vernacular, the victimized sector, *mağdur kesim*), Alevis (members of a Muslim religious minority), unionists, and others. I draw specifically on seven focus group interviews, each conducted in Turkish, lasting about two hours, and involving seven to ten participants who did not previously know each other. In all groups, participants were from lower socioeconomic status groups, though they ranged from lower to lower-middle class.[5] Two of these groups (conducted in 2003), one with men and one with women, were with Islamists—that is, those who are active in associational and political activities organized around the principle of Islamicization of society. Although Islamists have gained political power in Turkey through the electoral system, they remain at the same time poised in counter-distinction to "the state"—that is, to the secular center of Turkish sovereignty comprised of the military, police, and secularist elites. Despite the inclusion of some insights from these two focus groups with Islamist participants, this chapter does maintain a focus on the Kurdish situation, drawing from five focus groups conducted with Kurdish participants, one with men (conducted in 2003) and four with women (2001). Among the participants in these groups, a minority were Kurdish Alevis. The group interview presents an opportunity to follow the socially embedded circulation of discourse. These stories are told, not just to me, but to a group of strangers who share certain dimensions of identity, such as gender, religiosity, ethnicity, and class.

I will insist that the Turkish case is not exceptional. The Turkish Republic is a democracy that, since its transition in 1946–1950, has been disrupted by three coups d'etat (in 1960, 1971, and 1980). When the 1980 military junta returned the state to civilian rule in 1983, they also initiated a new constitution, which not only contained illiberal anti-labor and anti-terror legislation, but also institutionalized the role of the military in government. Through the body of the National Security Council, comprised of civilian leaders and top military generals, the military once more effected a change in government in 1998, when the Islamist party, then leading the ruling coalition, was forced from power in what has become known as a "virtual coup." Military intervention in government, vaguely worded anti-terror legislation and documented human rights abuses (such as torture in prisons and illegal detentions) continue to soil Turkey's democratic record. Although Turkey's bid for European Union (EU) membership has spurred some important changes in Turkey's penal code, many argue that these reforms have not gone far enough to protect Turkish citizens from the vagaries of the state's security apparatus and justice system (Amnesty International 2004).

It is not my point to condemn the Turkish state, to present it as outside some norm of democratic governance. Certainly, the official state of emergency that bore down upon the southeast for fifteen years, the evacuation of villages and the creation of a displaced people, shows us how the "state of exception" orders space, territory and populations. But the argument I present draws widely on states of exception that have been declared in other times and other places. To understand the everyday struggles of ordinary people in Turkey today, I will ramble across the writings of Kafka, Benjamin, Agamben and Taussig, not stopping to reinforce the boundaries of time and space between them. Not only is Turkey not alone as a space ordered by the state of exception, but as I write this I am daily observing the suspension of law under conditions of war in the United States. This is a state of exception that seeps into the American everyday with new legislation that strips us of our political being, presenting us to the pure force of the law as "enemy combatants," naked, always already guilty, and without the possibility of redemption. This is a state of exception that permitted the torture of Iraqi prisoners by U.S. soldiers at Abu Ghraib prison and the indefinite detention of American citizens and noncitizens without communication or counsel at Guantánamo Bay and elsewhere (see Gregory, 2004). These are not issues that belong to Turkey; this is the tradition of the oppressed.

The Guilt Context of the Living

> *Law condemns, not to punishment but to guilt. Fate is the guilt context of the living.*
>
> (Benjamin 1978a 308)

In Kafka's *The Trial*, K. finds himself arrested upon waking in his room. As he protests his innocence, the warders explain to him that the officials of the Law do not search for crime within society, but simply are drawn to the guilty. When K. objects that he doesn't know this Law, and that it probably exists only in the warders' heads, he only worsens his case, for "he admits that he doesn't know the Law and yet he claims he's innocent" (Kafka 1968, 6). Guilt, as Agamben argues, does not require an act of transgression, but instead marks the condition of being included through exclusion, of being held in relation to something from which one is excluded. In his words, "*Guilt refers not to transgression, that is, to the determination of the licit and the illicit, but to the pure force of the law, to the law's simple reference to something*" (Agamben 1998, 27; emphasis in original). Agamben's ideas about the relationship between guilt and law draw upon the work of Walter Benjamin, who writes in his essay on "Fate and Character" that guilt finds its place not in the religious sphere, but in the sphere of law, where punishment ultimately depends not on morality, or even actions taken and not taken, but on misfortune and fate.

"Last year I went to Tünceli [in the southeast]," explains Gizem, a thirty-six-year-old woman who migrated to Istanbul in 1992, "and every two kilometers there was a checkpoint. When we didn't show our IDs, when we objected, saying 'I am not an anarchist,' when I said I was just going to my own village, they said, 'Then you will stay here.' Their power was shown. Our sin, our guilt is being Kurdish." This is the power to control the movement of subjects even *as the operation of law itself moves*. It is the power to mark passage with the ritual checking of identification cards, the power to hold subjects in a relationship of guilt. This is the power of the law under the state of emergency. Michael Taussig, in his fictionalized ethnography, *The Magic of the State* (1997) calls forth *spatial* passage as the elementary, *ur*-form of ritual. He suggests that while the rite of passage that transpires in passing through police barricades is in one sense a purifying transition from a potentially criminal status, at the same time these passages can also be seen as polluting, declaring all who pass to be suspect, tainted with guilt. He writes, "We remember the man in 'plain clothes' seated with his silver pistol out of sight pointing towards the traffic. To pass by this man is not necessarily to be cleansed or relieved of the strange guilt that being a member of a modern state seems to imply" (Taussig 1997, 148–149). Guilt is not relieved by the passage allowed, but instead is instantiated in the check point. The subject is not purified, but instead is called forward as an already marked subject of guilt, of law.

While the state of emergency sets up road blocks, barriers, and regular check points, in the city the "check point" becomes dispersed; it is potentially everywhere, and no longer localizable. Barış describes being checked by police when he is sitting at the coffee shop in Istanbul and asked by police to show his state-issued ID card that reveals his origins. This is a story told again and again by Kurdish migrants in Istanbul, both men and women, young and old. In the following dialogue, which is telescoped in places for brevity, young women who recently migrated to Istanbul, having been asked to discuss what citizenship means to them, describe their experiences at the "check point," the threshold of the law, which is everywhere in their daily lives:

H----: The police come, saying that my name is Kurdish on my ID card they take me under house arrest. Although Taksim is a political space [*mekan*], they say, "You're suspicious, come! Your name is Kurdish, you're from Dersim [older name for Tünceli], and you're a student, so you must definitely be a participant!" I mean you are potentially guilty. At school the teachers did this. This happened while I was sitting at a café in Taksim. Why must I live this? I don't want to be a Turkish citizen.

Gül: I have also lived this […]. When you pass by the door they ask for the ID. When they asked me I said, "Why didn't you ask the ones that came before me but you ask me for my ID?" He said in a very rude way, "Are you going to show it or not?" […] You are dark and you are Kurdish […].

Afet: Our friend speaks the truth. My uncle's daughter, because she is an Alevi, they arrested her and the friends she was with. Seven years in the Kartal prison, she has a deformed arm. They make separations. Our friend speaks the truth.

Kumru: […] The police come and take you and look at your ID. You are from Mardin but here it is written, citizen of the Turkish Republic. Despite this you are a Kurd and potentially guilty. Even in Mardin at a sewing and embroidery class while I was talking with a teacher, when I said I was a Kurd she was like, "How can you be a Kurd? Kurds are like cannibals but you aren't like that." […]

Fidan: Everyone says that they don't accept Alevi girls as police.

A twenty-three-year-old student who migrated to Istanbul in 1992, H---- is unusual in Turkey for having a given name that is recognizable as Kurdish, despite the laws regarding naming that have for the most part prevented Kurdish children from being given Kurdish names. This mark intensifies her abandonment before the law; H---- finds herself subject to suspicion in all arenas of her life. For her, the public arena of Taksim is both a political space and a space where IDs are often checked where the law comes into force, where guilt is assessed. For Gül, a thirty-year-old French teacher, it is her appearance, her darkness that she feels marks her as Kurdish, marks her as one whose ID will be checked. Once again, as in Gizem's story above about resisting showing her ID in the southeast, the power of the law juts revealingly into sight in this interaction. There is no choice; like Kafka's K., one is advised not to protest innocence before the law, but to accept the stain of guilt and the rituals of purification that are required. Further, Afet, a thirty-four-year-old woman who has been working as a house cleaner since she came to Istanbul in 1991, reminds us that the state of exception overflows the Kurdish conflict. She connects to the other women's stories through experiences that revolve more around Alevi identity than Kurdishness, but likewise reflect a relationship of inclusion through exclusion. The promise of citizenship in the Turkish Republic is seen to be betrayed, even devalued, by the experience of being held in a state of abandonment before the law, a relationship of guilt. (But what of the deformed arm? We will return to the question of torture in a later section.)

Kurdishness as a mark signifying guilt is portrayed in these focus group discussions as emanating from the conflict in the southeast, passing through the state, and entering into the everyday interactions that constitute the spaces that Kurdish migrants inhabit in the city. For example, Vahide, a thirty-one-year-old piece-worker who was born in Istanbul, describes how she sees herself reflected in the gaze of neighbors:

> Because of the clash in the southeast the Kurds are now a shit nation; it's like that, isn't it? According to state politics, it is like that. Naturally, this is reflected in things. No matter how often I say hello to my neighbor across from me, if I say good morning, even if we drink something together, if she is a Turk, when a soldier dies in the southeast she frowns and takes an attitude as if I am the guilty person.

Made into a "shit nation," dirty and guilty, Kurdish identity becomes the guilt-mark of the state of exception whereby, as a Kurdish man put it, "they always see you as against the state." This condition does not remain confined to barricades in the southeast, or even to the "check points" that become diffused through the city. The guilt-mark comes to mediate interactions of everyday life.

Those who are abandoned by the law, and who are therefore guilty, are "exposed and threatened on the threshold in which life and law, outside and inside, become indistinguishable. It is literally not possible to say whether the one who has been banned is outside or inside the juridical order" (Agamben 1998, 28–29). It is easy to see that Kurdish refugees from the state of emergency in the southeast move within this liminal zone where law and life collapse into one another, where guilt defines their fate—not because they have committed a crime, but because they stand before the pure force of the law. But it is not only Kurds who find themselves in this relation; this state of exception in fact describes the rule. Indeed, focus group participants recognized that contact of any kind with the police threatens to turn *you* into the guilty party. As one man explained, "When we were passing there a fight broke out. People watch, they follow the fight. Why? Because if you separate the men, you will be the guilty one. You will be written up. Men are scared. Men are scared to separate them because there is no justice here."

Guilt inheres in the relationship between the individual and the law. In Althusser's (1971) famous allegory of interpellation, the policeman calls from behind, "Hey you, there!" and the one who is hailed *knows* it is (s)he who is hailed, and turns. Althusser denies that this knowing is related to guilt—but perhaps that is because Althusser associates guilt with crime. If instead we understand guilt as fate in a Benjaminian sense, the constantly recurring moment of interpellation becomes infused with the guilt relation between the law and its subject. Held in the gaze of the police, she who is hailed and turns both becomes interpellated as the subject of law and, in that act, condemned to guilt. In the following section, I turn to the question of the relationship between law, violence, and the police.

The Violence of the Law and the Ignominy of the Police

> 'You are terrorists. You are feeding terrorists with your business.' They took us to the police station, to the torture... After that they stripped me, put a draft on my chest, and my daughter they made stark naked. 'Why do you have the desire to speak Kurdish?' they asked. They took my culottes, and there was piped water flowing. My daughter they put on the hook. They didn't put me there but they put my daughter on a Palestine hook. That piped water flowing was like ice.

Her words charged the air of the conference room where we met. The speaker is Semiha, a fifty-year-old woman who migrated from Batman in 1996, as she tells of her own and her daughter's torture in the Kurdish southeast. Torture in Turkey is an open secret; it is known to occur in the prisons, and maintains a diffuse presence within police stations in the southeastern provinces and beyond. As Talal Asad (2003) points out, while public rituals of torture may no longer be necessary for the maintenance of sovereign power, the rise of disciplinary power does not require the end of torture, but only that it become a hidden aspect of policing. Torture is now "exceptional," catalyzed within that zone where the enforcement of law fuses with its own suspension, and the human becomes one with the monstrous (Gregory 2004).

In the focus groups with men, police encounters are frequently portrayed as being bound up with violence. For example, in the group of Islamist participants, Tarık, a forty-two-year-old taxi driver who migrated to Istanbul from Turkey's Black Sea region, reported being taken by the police and asked about a man whose name he had never heard before:

Tarık: Police come and intimidate, they will take you to the police station. If you are taken what will happen? There should be nothing, there are laws, but to what extent are there laws? [...] I don't know this man. The guy [policeman] hits me saying, you will know this man, where is this man! I don't know, I am hearing his name from you, how am I supposed to know this man? It's like this, look, the relationship between the state and the citizen...I was taken to Gayrettepe [prison]... They say there is no torture, this was four years ago, but there was the height of torture.

Ahmet: We all know the fame of Gayrettepe.

[laughter]

Why laughter? Perhaps because torture is both secret and famous, both beyond the limits of legality and the foundational violence of its own shrouded order. "There are laws," he says, but at the same time, "to what extent are there laws?" Here the law operates and is negated in one breath within the spaces of police. This is the terrain into which I now enter, a terrain marked by famous secrets and the lawlessness of the law, an abandoned zone where we may seek the nature of police violence and its connection to questions of law and guilt.

To understand the relationship between law and violence, I turn once again with Walter Benjamin. In his essay, "Critique of Violence," Benjamin describes the origin of law as "violence crowned by fate" (Benjamin 1978b, 286). Fate, as discussed above, refers to the guilt that inheres in the relationship between the individual and the law, as well as the misfortune that attaches to being caught, being *accused* by the law. For Benjamin, this violence that fate completes is twofold, consisting both of the violence of lawmaking—that is, the violence that founds the law as power—and the violence of law-preserving, administrative violence that seeks to uphold the law and to prevent the emergence of (new) lawmaking violence, that is, violence with the potential to found new law.

For Benjamin, in the police we find a lethal cocktail, a "spectral mixture" of lawmaking and law-preserving violence. Benjamin argues that the "ignominy" of police authority "lies in the fact that in this authority the separation of lawmaking and law-preserving violence is suspended" (Benjamin 1978b, 287). The violence of the police floats free from the constraints that bind lawmaking and law-preserving violence, the constraints that call upon the former to create a just order and the latter to refrain from setting itself new ends. The police institution thus operates outside of legal ends and means, outside of the critical evaluation to which the law is subject, and at the constitutive limits of the state. Benjamin writes, "The assertion that the ends of police violence are always identical or even connected to those of general law is entirely untrue. Rather, the 'law' of the police really marks the point at which the state, whether from impotence or because of the immanent connections within any legal system, can no longer guarantee through the legal system the empirical ends that it desires at any price to attain… Its [police] power is formless, like its nowhere tangible, all-pervasive, ghostly presence in the life of civilized states" (Benjamin 1978b, 287). Police violence marks out a "law" that is beyond law, a nervous laughter, an internal exception that is diffused throughout the spaces of the state.

For Taussig, drawing on Benjamin, the police are not only ghostly "but rotten as well, the abject realm of the phobic object; spectral putrefaction in blue uniforms and brass buttons, neatly pressed khaki shirts, dark reflector glasses and bulletproof vests" Taussig 1997, 121). I am reminded of how, in *The Metamorphosis*, Gregor Samsa, as the monstrous vermin, embodies the guilt and debt of his family, but the father is also transformed, as he comes to wear his tight-fitting blue uniform even in the house, though it becomes irredeemably filthy, "covered in stains and gleaming with its constantly polished gold buttons" (Kafka 1972, 41). As Benjamin writes in his essay on Kafka, "Filth is the element of the officials" (Benjamin 1968b, 114). The abjection of the police refers us back to the indelible stain of guilt that spreads before the law and, I would argue, becomes the marker of the police as well. If the police assign guilt with their gaze, their hail, the so-called guilty also come to dread the police and their unholy spaces. Indeed, for the Kurdish women participants, stories of torture were part of a wider imaginary in which police and police stations become vortices of violence, of a "law" that founds itself and operates out of bounds. The violence of the police is both familiar and a threat made only more menacing by its half-glimpsed form. As Ceyden, a twenty-five-year-old student who has lived most of her life in Istanbul, explained:

> When you go to the police station, you don't say you are from Sivas, or that you are Kurdish, because you are afraid of what will come down on your head. And you feel so many things. That the moment they noticed that you are a Kurd, that you are an Alevi, immediately they would take you to some room down below and interrogate you.

In Ceyden's fantasy of what will happen the moment they gaze upon her as a Kurd, as an Alevi, contact with the rotten power of the police confers the stain of the guilt inscribed through the marks of her unacceptable difference. What we can understand as the abjection of the police, the soiling quality of contact with police or entrance into the police station, arises from this injection of violence and law, of state power, into the embodied forces of the police.

The spatiality of police, and of policing, takes shape in part through the mark of guilt and abjection that inheres within everyday encounters. Marked on the bodies of both police and those they hail, policing becomes something that one cannot escape, cannot leave behind within the abandoned spaces or territories that are already governed as "other"—here, the territories of Turkey's southeast. Instead, the ordinary Istanbul coffee shop, the neighborhood police station (*karakol* in Turkish, literally "black arm"), the public square of Taksim—the very ordinariness of these spaces is shot through with the possibility of a "check point," which may take the form of a request for papers, an interrogation, perhaps detention, maybe worse.

Yet the spatiality of police is not simply one of tactical mobility and the infiltration of space. Through its very fluidity and indefiniteness, policing works to mark out territory and to create spatial regimes of power and control. In a brief look at the genealogy of capital in relation to police, Pasquale Pasquino (1991) follows Foucault by relating modern ideas of policing (dating from the late eighteenth century) to an earlier conception that associated police with the extension of order and the creation of the public. The police, argues Pasquino, come to establish as their domain that which escapes other techniques of order:

> This no man's land [that escapes feudal order] is beginning to be perceived as an open space traversed by men and things. Squares, markets, roads, bridges, rivers: these are the critical points in the territory which police will mark out and control. The prescriptions or regulations of police are instruments of this work of formation, but at the same time they are also products of a sort of spontaneous creation of law, or rather, a demand for order which outreaches law and encroaches on domains never previously occupied, where hitherto neither power, order nor authority had thought to hold sway. (Pasquino 1991, 111)

Like Benjamin, Pasquino situates police at the limits of existing order. The police operate to guarantee the aims that the legal system fails to achieve, to exert control and to hold territory at the outer limits of state power. This is the zone of indistinction that the poor and the marginal find themselves inhabiting *everywhere and anywhere* in the city of Istanbul. Within this territory and its fantasy, its gathering thunder-heads of violence and half-glimpsed topography, it is impossible to tell if the law is being either broken or upheld, whether chaos or the normal order reigns, whether we are outside, within, or below the police station. As the narratives of Barış, Semiha, Tarık, and Ceyden attest, the zone of indistinction is marked by violence and the threat of violence, law and lawlessness. It is a violence that with one hand preserves the order of the state, while with the other hand it founds its own unbounded every-day law, exerting itself over what Pasquino calls the "open spaces" that evade all other control. Once again, it is the state of exception that holds us before the law, captured within the force of its no-longer-applying.

Justice and the State

Within this morass of violence and abjection, of abandonment and guilt, how will we find a glint of justice? For Derrida, justice is the experience we cannot experi-ence (Derrida 1990); for Drucilla Cornell it is the good that eludes our grasp (Cor-nell 1990). The relationship between violence, law and justice was taken up in the mid-1980s by Robert Cover, who jolted scholars of jurisprudence by reminding them that legal interpretation takes place within a "field of pain and death" (Cover 1986, 1601; Cover 1983). Cover sought to theorize the impact of violence on the prospect of attaining justice through law, a project which has since been taken up by others who have searched for a path to justice through, or perhaps against, the violence of law (Minow, Ryan, and Sarat 1992; Sarat 2001). Yet for Benjamin, because violence is implicated in the nature of law, law itself must appear in an "ambiguous moral light" (Benjamin 1978b, 287). Indeed, he argues, violence is not diminished with the found-ing of the law, since what is founded is a rule of law alloyed by violence. For Benjamin, the mythical violence of lawmaking cannot produce justice, only power. Justice can only arise from a different kind of violence altogether, the *divine violence*, messianic and revolutionary, that dissolves law and destroys state power.

In Turkish, one of the words for justice is *hakkaniyet* (used among the Islamist women in this study), which has as its root the Arabic-originating word *hak*, mean-ing right or justice. It is also a name of God. Unlike the word "justice," with its roots in the Latin *jus*, law, *hakkaniyet* does not imply law. In Turkish, we therefore do not need to struggle to separate the idea of justice from law, but instead are immediately confronted by its relation to right and to God. Yet *hak*, with all its nuances of mean-ing, does seem to return us to law, to looking around at the door of the state. As one woman put it in the group of Islamist participants, "We want everything to be taken care of by the state and God."

Under everyday conditions of extremity, where do the traces of justice adhere? For focus group participants, justice was clearly elusive, and yet at the same time in its failure, in its lack, it was associated with the idea of the state. Injustice, at least, seems to fall within the domain of fate, rather than religion. In the words of Mahmut, a twenty-three-year-old participant in the group of Islamist men: "Facing the state, justice does not pass between you." He went on to explain:

Now if something happens to me, if I get up to look for my rights, one in a thousand times when you are up against a difficulty do you go to a state office. I say to everyone, Allah, who thinks of the state office? There will be Kemal Ataturk [on the currency] in your pocket, everyone will do your bidding, otherwise, go and come back in a month.

Not only does Mahmut point out that the last place he would look for his rights (preserving the Turkish idiom, *hakını aramak*) would be in a state office, but he further asserts that it is only through money that any good would possibly come of such a trip. There is an irony in that, despite his dismissal of the state, Mahmut seals his point by invoking Kemal Ataturk, the founder of the Turkish republic and icon of the secular state, whose face appears on all the bills of the republic. *What really matters* comes into circulation as the medium of exchange, currency marked by the state as it trades in the commodity of justice.

The unevenness of so-called justice and the impossibility of claiming rights under conditions of poverty were alluded to in all of the focus groups. In discussions of courts and the law, participants regularly pointed out that, in the words of Tarık, "what happens depends on whether you are powerful and have money, or if you are poor. If you have fallen behind with your bread money, then you can't struggle for rights, with the law." In the group of Kurdish men, Barış concluded: "There are no human rights in Turkey. There is no value given to people. Value is given piece by piece. For example, you are well, your situation is good—*and then* the state will also own you. Help will come." Piece by piece—like coins, like body parts, right and justice are exchanged. It is once again a question of inclusive exclusion; as disowned members, phantom limbs, the poor are not "owned" by the state, but rather held within a relationship of permanent exception.

The focus group discussions portrayed the relationship between justice, law, and the state as fraught and unfulfilled. In the group of Islamist women, as they were discussing their dissatisfaction with the laws that restrict the wearing of headscarves in public spaces, the following dialogue took place:

Arzu: Maybe we don't like what the state understands as justice.
Ceren: The state's men make the law. I mean, if there is a state, the laws are made within the state. Citizen's rights, law, can everything be asked from the state?
Moderator: I am asking you.
Belgin: But as I see it, it is the work of the state. The state must be just. The meaning of the state is justice, as I see it.
Ceren: The state determines justice.

This dialogue captures the paradox of the relationship between the state and justice, for at the same time as the state (law) determines justice, its own legitimacy rides on whether it can be judged to be just. These women do not subscribe to a Hobbesian view that only just laws are law, but they do expect justice from the state at the same time as they mark its failure. For Arzu, a thirty-seven-year-old housewife who wears the full body veil (*çarşaf* in Turkish), it is possible to say that the state's secularist understanding of justice is simply not hers, while Ceren and Belgin (also housewives who wear the headscarf) continue to work around the problem of how to demand justice of the state, how to address the state's injustice while at the same time understanding the state as that which defines the contours of right.

Justice, floating beyond reach, tethered only most tenuously to the state, to law, seems to recede. Not only that, but it takes the idea of the State with it. While at times focus group participants declared that the state was everywhere, at other times they declared it was nowhere—especially when they were looking for their rights. Consider the following narrative, shared by Adil, a thirty-one-year-old taxi driver from Sivas, in the group of Kurdish men:

> I had an accident. I hit a Mercedes. Okay, I was speeding. I got out. Well the man got all over me. He was extremely drunk. The police came. What were we going to do? The police came from [the Istanbul district of] Maltepe and one of them was the man's son. He entered the fray and then we lost the true situation. Afterwards I didn't drive, I mean, I still don't like to drive. The man's car was his company car... State, state, there is no state, I mean.

Here, the police are beholden only to their personal relationships with the wealthier members of a community. They are, as usual, both the law and those who operate outside the law. What is particularly interesting in this story, which itself is common enough in its indictment of police injustice, is the way Adil resolves his narrative in the dissolution of the state. Within the zone of exception, when one is abandoned by the law, the state too recedes. Thus, in the group of Islamist women, Havva, a forty-two-year-old housewife, is able to suggest that the traffic police are not part of the state "because at that moment, the police eat the money. I mean, acting as the state, they commit a crime." In other words, the police demand payment of motorists, and pocket it for themselves; the money of the poor is consumed, food for parasitic bodies. Once again the police break to the surface of the everyday, operating as law outside law, the other side of state power beyond the state.

In the central fable of *The Trial*, "Before the Law," the door of the Law stands open. The "man from the country" who, in the fable, has sought out the door, is surprised to find himself forbidden to enter. He had assumed that the Law should be accessible to every man at all times. He is forbidden to enter the door of the Law, yet the door exists for him and with his death is closed. The Law is an open door with a beautiful light streaming through. It is there to hold you in abeyance, in suspension, in a state of being beholden. But the Law is not a space to be entered; it is the threshold at which we live out our lives, prohibited. It is neither hidden nor waiting beyond the threshold; it *is* the threshold. "Where do you find your rights to be most constrained?" asked Ayla, in one of our focus groups. "At the door of justice," Fatima responded. Justice is the threshold at which the state of exception, the ban, comes into effect.

Conclusion: Which Way Out?

Yael Navaro-Yashin argues that in Turkey, the state-as-fetish survives its deconstruction; despite the cynicism with which it is regarded, despite its multiple crises, the state survives as a fantasy in "the everyday life practices of people outside the centers of official power" (Navaro-Yashin 2002, 134). But at the same time as this may be so, it seems that the state also dissolves within the abject mixture of violence and law through which its spaces are ordered. If we consider Fatima, the woman who finds her rights most narrow at the door of justice, in relation to Kafka's man from the country, perhaps we can say that the (wo)man from the country has, today, in Turkey, gotten wise. She recognizes the ban that holds her at the threshold of the law, free and not free, included through her exclusion. But even then, where will she search for her rights? One answer is the Koran, but for Kafka, Benjamin and Agamben, it is not just profane law that is in crisis, but all law that has ceased to signify, that has been reduced to the "zero point of its own content," as Gerschom Scholem put it in his letter to Benjamin on Kafka's *The Trial* (quoted in Agamben 1998, 51). Benjamin's response to this crisis was both messianic and revolutionary, looking forward to the real state of emergency that will forever displace the endless cycle of mythical, law-making violence.

Less apocalyptically, it seems to me that the only way to respond to the violence of the law, and the law of violence (as the State idea recedes, shame-faced, into the folds of its cloak) is with loud bells, bright lights, and theatrical gestures that boldly reveal the state of exception for what it is—the everyday dissolution of citizenship, of right, of political life. Perhaps, then, to return to where we began, this is where poetry comes once more into play. Legal scholar Marianne Constable makes a surprising move at the end of her essay on law, violence and justice in relation to the work of Robert Cover. Where we might expect a last appeal to God or politics, instead she writes, "The poet, unlike the agentic state, may still remind us of our need for justice…We must find the call for justice where we can—in the language of the poets and the silences of law and legal scholarship" (Constable 2001, 96). I do not want to suggest that "the poets" occupy a privileged position with regard to truth or justice or anything else, but I do think I understand what Constable is calling for. It is the eruption of language, the evocation of emotion, the expression of suffering, of political and ethical aspiration, of loss, that may offer us a glimpse of at least the tailfeathers of an idea of justice, an idea of right beyond what we have known. I would like to find a way out of the endless hall of mirrors that the state of exception sets up, the endless division of outside from inside, chaos from order, and the swallowing of each new "exception" within the rule, the absorption of all within a permanently cross-hatched space of violence, guilt and abandonment. I cannot propose a route out, but I can pronounce the poetry that crackles in the voices of those, like Barış, who have suffered and who have considered their suffering, at the threshold of the pure force of the law. It is not, of course, enough. Poetry is not a way out; it is, perhaps, a way in.

Acknowledgments

A previous version of this paper was presented at the workshop on "Law, Landscapes and Ethics" at the International Institute for the Sociology of Law, Onati, Spain, held June 9–12, 2004. I would like to thank the organizers and participants of that workshop for their comments. I am also grateful to participants at the University of North Carolina, where I presented a similar version of this paper in the Department of Geography. My deepest gratitude goes to Derek Gregory, for both inspiration and wisdom, and to those who made this work possible in Istanbul. I alone am responsible for the content of this chapter.

References

Agamben, Giorgio. 1998. *Homo Sacer: Sovereign Power and Bare Life*. Stanford, CA: University Press.

Amnesty International. 2004. Turkey: Injustice continues despite welcome reforms. AI Index: EUR 44/014/2004 (Public). Available at http://www.amnestyusa.org/countries/turkey/news.do; accessed May 13, 2004.

Althusser, L. 1971. *Lenin and Philosophy and Other Essays*. New York: Monthly Review Press.

Asad, Talal. 2003. *Formations of the Secular.*, Stanford, CA: Stanford University Press.

Benjamin, Walter. 1968a. "Theses on the philosophy of history." In *Illuminations*, pp. 253–64. New York: Schocken Books.

Benjamin, Walter. 1968b. "Franz Kafka: On the tenth anniversary of his death." In *Illuminations*, pp. 111–140. New York: Schocken Books.

Benjamin, Walter. 1978a. "Fate and character." In *Reflections*, pp. 304–311. New York: Schocken Books.

Benjamin, Walter. 1978b. Critique of violence. In *Reflections*, pp. 277–320. New York: Schocken Books.

Blomley, Nicholas. 2003. "Law, property, and the geography of violence: The frontier, the survey and the grid." *Annals of the Association of American Geographers* 93 (1): 121–141.

Constable, Marianne. 2001. "The silence of the law: Justice in Cover's 'field of pain and death'," in A. Sarat (Ed.), *Law, Violence, and the Possibility of Justice*, pp. 85–100., Princeton, NJ: Princeton University Press.

Cornell, Drucilla. 1990. "From the lighthouse: The promise of redemption and the possibility of legal interpretation." *Cardozo Law Review* 11: 1687–1714

Cover, Robert. 1983. "The Supreme Court, 1982 Term – Forward: *nomos* and narrative." *Harvard Law Review* 97: 4–68.

Cover, Robert. 1986. "Violence and the word." *Yale Law Journal* 95: 1601–1629.

Derrida, Jacques. 1990. "Force of law: The 'mystical foundation of authority'." *Cardozo Law Review* 11: 920–1045.

Global Internal Displacement Project. 2003. State of emergency in southeastern Turkey: Severe restriction of human rights (1987–2002). http://www.idpproject.org (accessed May 12, 2004).

Kafka, Franz. 1968. *The Trial.*, New York: Schocken Books.

Kafka, Franz. 1972. *The Metamorphosis*. New York: Bantam Books.

Gregory, D. 2004. "The angel of Iraq." *Environment and Planning D; Society and Space* 22: 317–324.

Güvenç, M., and Işık, O. 1996. "Istanbul'u okumak: statü-konut mülkiyeti farklılaşmasına iliskın bir cözlümleme denemesi" ["Reading Istanbul: A trial analysis concerning status-property differentiation"] *Toplum ve Bilim* [*Society and Science*] 71: 6–60.

Işık, O., and Pınarcıoğlu, M. M. 2001. *Nöbetleşe yoksulluk: Sultanbeyli örneği* [*Rotating poverty: The example of Sultanbeyli*]. Istanbul: İletişim Yayınları.

Minow, Martha, Ryan, Michael, and Sarat, Austin, Eds. 1992. *Narrative, Violence and the Law: The Essays of Robert Cover*. Ann Arbor: University of Michigan Press.

Navaro-Yashin, Yael. 2002. *Faces of the state: Secularism and public life in Turkey*. Princeton, NJ: Princeton University Press.

Pasquino, Pasquale. 1991. "Theatrum Politicum: The genealogy of capital – police and the state of prosperity," in G. Burchell, C. Gordon and P. Miller, Eds., *The Foucault Effect: Studies in Governmentality*, pp. 105–118. Chicago: University of Chicago Press.

Sarat, Austin, Ed. 2001. *Law, Violence, and the Possibility of Justice*. Princeton, NJ: Princeton University Press.

Sarat, Austin, and Kearns, Thomas R. 2001. "Making peace with violence: Robert Cover on law and legal theory," in A. Sarat (Ed.), *Law, Violence, and the Possibility of Justice*, pp. 49–84. NJ: Princeton University Press.

Secor, Anna J. 2004a. *Ethnography, poetry and translation*. Paper presented at the Annual Meeting March 15-19, 2004, of the Association of American Geographers, Philadelphia.

Secor, Anna J. 2004b. "'There is an Istanbul that belongs to me': Citizenship, space and identity in the city." *Annals of the Association of American Geographers* 94 (2): 352–368.

Spivak, Gayatri Chakravorty. 1992. "The politics of translation," in Michele Barrett and Anne Phillips (eds.), *Destabilizing Theory: Contemporary Feminist Debates*, 177–200., Stanford: CA: Stanford University Press.

Taussig, Michael. 1997. *The Magic of the State*. New York: Routledge.

Notes

1. Elsewhere, I have written about the poetic and politics of ethnography (Secor 2004a). In that paper, I show how the act of translation can allow language to erupt in evocative and affecting ways. The "found poem" is a poetic form that involves taking texts that are already there, removing them from their prosaic context, and presenting them in a poetic light. Ethnography and translation operate upon texts in similar ways. In this poem, I have allowed the rhetoricity of Turkish to disrupt the surface of English grammar and form (see Spivak 1992). I have also chosen to drop a few lines and, in one place, switched the order of two lines for effect.

2. These numbers are, of course, contested. The Turkish government's Parliamentary Research Commission estimated the displaced to number almost four hundred thousand, while the U.S. State Department reported around one million displaced people in 2001. Human rights organizations estimate the number of displaced people to be around four million people (Global Internal Displacement Project 2003).

3. On July 19, 1987, the "state of emergency" was declared for the provinces of Bingöl, Diyarbakır, Elazığ, Hakkari, Mardin, Siirt, Tünceli, and Van. These provinces had been under martial law since 1980. Adıyaman, Bitlis, and Muş were included under the authority of the official state of emergency as neighboring provinces. Later, when Batman and Şırnak became separate provinces, they were also included within the state of emergency region. The state of Emergency Regional Governor's Office held martial law-type authority, with the ability to exile residents, censor the press, limit assembly and evacuate settlements. The security presence was also felt through regular roadblocks, curfews, and identity checks (Global Internal Displacement Project 2003).

4. When I refer to Kurdish participants, I am referring to those who have identified themselves as Kurdish. When I refer to a participant as "non-Kurdish," this is to indicate that the speaker has not self-identified (at least not to me) as Kurdish. I prefer not to simply call these participants "Turkish" because Turkish has both civic and ethnic connotations; the Kurdish participants are Turkish too. Furthermore, the category "Turkish" masks a wide range of ethnic identities, from Balkan to Caucasian. I should further emphasize that I see these identities as relationally constituted (see Secor 2004b).

5. Kurdish participants were identified through informal networks in Istanbul. Islamist participants were identified through a survey of 4005 Istanbul residents as part of the NSF funded project, "Reshaping Civil Society: Islam, Democracy and Diversity in Istanbul," BCS-0137060.

4

Cosmopolitanism's Collateral Damage

The State-Organized Racial Violence of
World War I and the War on Terror

Eric N. Olund

> Wolf Blitzer, CNN Anchor: ...We understand that there have been more bombings, more explosions unfolding. May, tell our viewers what you are seeing and what you are hearing right now.
>
> May Ying Welsh, Journalist, Baghdad: ...The Foreign Ministry right now, which is just a few blocks away from me, is up in smoke.... But perhaps an hour ago, an hour and a half ago, they bombed a complex associated with the Ministry of Planning and the Council of Ministers. And I saw with my own eyes how that building just went up, and a huge shockwave came off of it. It shook the building I was in....It was a really terrifying experience, I can tell you.
>
> And also, I mean, none of these building are just standing there by themselves. Civilians do live around these buildings. There are residential pockets near all kinds of buildings that are targets in the city. So from the first two nights of the bombing, which were relatively light, they had 37 civilian casualties. I don't know what the civilian casualties are going to be like now.
>
> Wolf Blitzer: May, let's talk a little bit about some of those buildings that you now see have been bombed...
>
> —CNN live interview, March 21, 2003[1]

The terrorist attacks of September 11, 2001 handed President George W. Bush the perfect opportunity and excuse to extend U.S. power in the world through unilateral, preemptive military action at the cost of untold thousands of lives, as well as to extend the power of the executive branch of the federal government at home at the expense of the civil rights of both foreign nationals and U.S. citizens. Racialization has been integral to this process; the nonwhite status of Afghanis and Iraqis has not only made the invasions of their countries politically possible but has legitimated their deaths as acceptable "collateral damage." Along with the studied, callous ignorance within the United States toward their lost lives, this disregard has also encouraged the targeting in the United States of people of Middle Eastern and South Asian descent for harassment and worse.

Such violent racializations are nothing new in the United States, and I want to offer a historical comparison that points to some ways this process of racialization has developed at the federal level to justify intervention abroad and repression at home. Several familiar specters haunt Bush's so-called "War on Terror," perhaps the most commonly noted being the McCarthyist suppression of dissent in public culture that has only recently begun to fade as the public has wearied of the administration's theory that repeating a lie often enough makes it true, and the reprise of World War II internment camps at Guantánamo Bay, which at this writing have suffered setbacks which the administration has been more adept at side-stepping. Silencing and internment serve the same ultimate purpose, to normalize the American body politic in order to purify its republican agency at home and abroad. This normalized American body politic—the body biopolitic—is also the body of U.S. sovereignty, and "We the People" are the subject of two very different political rationalities, one seeking to exercise power to ensure the flourishing of American society at large, and the other seeking to exercise power, including the right of death over life, for its own sake.[2] Silencing and internment serve to keep these two rationalities as close together as possible to consolidate "the will of the people," suppressing dissent and removing physical threats.

Yet if the state simultaneously ensures the life of its constituent people and ensures its own sovereignty, how can it exercise the right to kill its own members that may pose a threat? How does the government of the United States *justify* domestic repression, even in wartime? Michel Foucault locates modern racism in this very contradiction between killing and promoting the life of the people. "What in fact is racism?" he asks. "It is primarily a way of introducing a break into the domain of life that is under power's control: the break between what must live and what must die."[3] He continues, "Racism also has a second function. Its role is, if you like, to allow the establishment of a positive relation of this type: [...] 'The very fact that you let more die will allow you to live more.'"[4] He concedes that this is in fact the relation of war itself and that this in itself is not new. What is new is that "racism makes it possible to establish a relationship between my life and the death of the other that is not a military or warlike relationship of confrontation, but a biological-type relationship [...] something that will make life in general healthier: healthier and purer."[5]

By identifying groups within a given population that are less productive, their elimination will ultimately strengthen the body biopolitic. This is the cold logic of the Nazi extermination camp, but how does this square with the logic of individual rights upon which U.S. sovereignty and republican freedom is based? For even the internment of Japanese-Americans while the United States was fighting Nazism, egregious and hypocritical as it was, fell short of its full ironic potential in one crucial respect— Jews (and Gypsies, gays and lesbians, the disabled, and many others) were sent to the camps to be killed, while Japanese-Americans were released from the camps once the war was over. The internment camps would seem to be unthinkable today, yet Guantánamo Bay belies such wishful thinking. How is it that "Gitmo" can exist and, qualitatively speaking, be even worse than the WWII internment camps as a site of not only indefinite imprisonment, but torture and death for its Middle-Eastern detainees, some of whom are U.S. citizens and thus participants of U.S. sovereignty?

Guantánamo Bay lies at the violent extreme of a very long continuum of racialized internment and suppression at the other end of which lie trivialities of drugstore patriotism such as "freedom fries." But the fact that so many in the U.S. support the War on Terror yet are so reluctant to think of Guantánamo as a space of racial violence sponsored by their own government and so ultimately themselves suggests that there has been a shift in the operation of racism over time. The United States, after all, began as a colonial slave-holding society, and the extermination of Native Americans and the enslavement of African-Americans were widely accepted in times past. While the nascent U.S. relationship with Native peoples was predicated on stealing their territory, African-American slaves were an integral part of U.S. society as a productive labor source. In short, African-American labor was slave labor not because it was valued less than white labor in the abstract (after all slave labor by definition has no exchange value) but because it was valued *as black* labor, as *qualitatively* different from white labor. Foucault's account of modern racism focuses on the quantitative aspect of productivity generally conceived, but American racism also involves a residue of the qualitative aspect of productivity that has persisted to this day to considerably complicate the calculations of our exchange-based society. The United States has *always been* a multi-racial society, and so the task is not to assume that subordinate races have always been slated for elimination in the logic of biopolitics, but on the contrary to account for their differential value and how the U.S. government has managed race and even used racial difference for productive ends as it has become increasingly biopolitical.

For this reason I look to World War I for a historical comparison with the War on Terror. The groundwork for the modern interventionist state apparatus in the United States was laid in the early twentieth century, and World War I gave particular impetus to this project.[6] Integral to this process was the rapidly changing geography of race brought about by the Great Migration of African-Americans to northern cities accompanied by vast numbers of immigrants arriving from Eastern and Southern Europe. What I find compelling about the comparison is how startlingly similar statutory and policy responses to war on the part of the Wilson and Bush administrations, responses that were far more similar to each other than to those of other wartime presidents, nonetheless starkly illustrate changes in the management of racism over time. While racism was strategic in governing the population during the Progressive Era, in our time racism has shifted to an object of governance in and of itself, and this poses the peculiar challenge of taking right-wing antiracism seriously. I am certainly not arguing that George W. Bush is not racist; my point is that he and his allies have recuperated the civil rights agenda to redefine and regulate racism for their own purposes in the so-called War on Terror. This is in contrast to Woodrow Wilson, who as an unapologetic racist, felt no need to contest what racism was, and he used it effectively. Such a comparison is valuable because as a moment of national vulnerability, wartime tends to lay bare the tensions and contradictions that undergird nation and citizenship and provide an opportunity for their rearticulation.

"Just" War

When Woodrow Wilson asked the 65th Congress for a declaration of war he said, "We have no quarrel with the German people. We have no feeling toward them but one of sympathy and friendship. It was not upon their impulse that their government acted in entering the war."[7] He went on to personify the enemy as Kaiser Wilhelm, who had "put aside all restraints of law or of humanity."[8] He advised "that the Congress declare the recent course of the Imperial German Government to be in fact nothing less than war against the Government and people of the United States."[9] Eighty-four years later George W. Bush stood before the 107th Congress to declare, "The enemy of America is not our many Muslim friends; it is not our many Arab friends. Our enemy is a radical network of terrorists, and every government that supports them."[10] Their leader, Osama bin Laden, has the sole purpose "to plot evil and destruction."

Yet while bin Laden was easily recognizable as "the" face of terrorism (for terrorism must be singular even as terrorists in the plural must remain formless), he, unlike the leader of a nation-state such as the Kaiser, proved unlocatable. One year and over three thousand dead Afghani civilians later, the president appeared before the United Nations to make his case to visit the War on Terror on Iraq. He told the world,

> ...our greatest fear is that terrorists will find a shortcut to their mad ambitions when an outlaw regime supplies them with the technologies to kill on a massive scale. In one place—in one regime—we find all these dangers, in their most lethal and aggressive forms, exactly the kind of aggressive threat the United Nations was born to confront....By breaking every pledge—by his deceptions, and by his cruelties—Saddam Hussein has made the case against himself.[11]

Bush's metonymic sleight of hand went well beyond the proximity of "terrorists" and "Saddam Hussein" in the text of his speech. His substitution of bin Laden with Hussein as the new individual face of terror was enabled by the common geographical and anthropological conflation by many in the United States of Middle Easterners, South Asians, Arabs, Muslims, and terrorists. Nonetheless such a conflation begins to fall apart if faces are given to civilian casualties, and so Bush offered the obligatory clarification, "The United States has no quarrel with the Iraqi people; they've suffered too long in silent captivity." But while the eventual capture of Hussein deprived the War on Terror of its new figurehead, the more recent insurgency has offered a replacement—the "killer named Zarqawi who's ordering the suiciders inside of Iraq."[12] At the Rose Garden puppet show with Iraqi interim Prime Minister Iyad Allawi held eighteen months and fifteen thousand dead Iraqi civilians after the invasion, Bush declared, "The war for Iraq's freedom is a fight against some of the most ruthless and brutal men on Earth."[13] Indeed, "As enemies of tyranny and terror, the people of Iraq and the American troops and civilians supporting their dreams of freedom have been the target of acts of violence."

Such a "distinction...between friend and enemy" is the crucial political moment in any declaration of war,[14] but one that is particularly fraught for leaders professing the values of liberal democracy, even if it is a "fighting creed."[15] Carl Schmitt's infamous criterion of political action emphasized defining the enemy, but for Wilson and Bush defining friends was equally important for this served to circumscribe the enemy and prepare the enemy's people for assimilation to liberal democracy. Wilson's declaration seems more clear-cut in that it was a case where "one fighting collectivity of people confronts a similar collectivity."[16] However Bush's was not a formal declaration of war against a nation-state but a declaration of war against terrorism—against a tactic rather than an entity—that knows no geographical or temporal limits. Yet whether in a war to end all wars or a war without end, the racializations that divide U.S. society complicate the task of defining friends as much as enemies, and in a geographically isolated, plural nation this distinction applied to the world at large rebounds upon the territory of the U.S. body politic. Racialized spaces such as the Middle East that entice the United States to such deadly intervention fold into U.S. territory through the presence of similarly racialized people.

The Body Cosmopolitic

Wilson explicitly included naturalized German immigrants as friends in his war address.

> We shall happily still have an opportunity to prove that friendship in our daily attitude and actions toward the millions of men and women of German birth and native sympathy who live among us and share our life, and we shall be proud to prove toward all who are in fact loyal to their neighbors and to the Government in the hour of test. They are most of them as true and loyal Americans as if they had never known any other fealty or allegiance.[17]

Yet throughout his presidency Wilson was adamantly opposed to hyphenated Americanism.

> For my part, I think the most un-American thing in the world is a hyphen. I do not care what it is that comes before the word "American." It may be a German-American, or an Italian-American, a Swedish-American, or an Anglo-American, or an Irish-American. It does not make any difference what comes before the "American," it ought not to be there, and every man who comes to take counsel with me with a hyphen in his conversation I take no interest in whatever....I am not quarreling with those affections; I am talking about purposes. Every purpose is for the future, and the future for Americans must be for America.[18]

Despite his frequent disclaimers, Wilson excoriated German-Americanism more than any other hyphenism after the outbreak of hostilities in Europe. That race and nation were synonymous in "Old Europe" was a basic assumption of Wilson's and so racial loyalty signified to him divided national loyalties. The "German-" of German-American was seen as a national descriptor then as opposed to the less politically-loaded ethnic descriptor it is usually seen as today. While German-Americans as racially kindred to Anglo-Saxons were largely given the privileges of whiteness that Irish- and Italian-Americans had to fight for,[19] they nonetheless retained a racialized ascription and identity as "Teutons" that became more menacing as early as the 1890s as German *Kultur* came to be labeled "Prussianism" and equated with militarism and autocratic governance.[20] *The New Republic* pointed out the consequences of this construction of "German stock:" "We cannot say that the German in Europe is brutal, amoral, servile, and expect his kin in this country to acquiesce in our opinion or even cherish friendly feelings toward us. Yet we did say such things. Our intellectual leaders set the pace in this folly, and the rest of us followed according to our ability. And then we felt aggrieved over the recrudescence of Germanism among us."[21]

This take on the "German race" was widespread. Even Wilson's nemesis Theodore Roosevelt joined in, ranting, "The professional German-Americans...represent that adherence to the politico-racial hyphen which is the badge and sign of moral treason."[22] In 1915 the president lectured a group of immigrants who had just taken the oath of citizenship,

I certainly would not be one even to suggest that a man cease to love the home of his birth and the nation of his origin—these things are very sacred and ought not to be put out of our hearts—but it is one thing to love the place where you were born and it is another thing to dedicate yourself to the place to which you go. You cannot dedicate yourself to America unless you become in every respect and with every purpose of your will thorough Americans. You cannot become thorough Americans if you think of yourselves in groups....the man who goes among you to trade upon your nationality is no worthy son to live under the Stars and Stripes. My urgent advice to you would be, not only always to think first of American, but always, also, to think first of humanity. You do not love humanity if you seek to divide humanity into jealous camps.[23]

Nonetheless as Wilson continued to make clear, people of German or of any other origin could be good American citizens, and since the U.S. tradition of republicanism locates sovereignty in the people, American agency in the world is nothing if not cosmopolitan.

We are the mediating Nation of the world. I do not mean that we undertake not to mind our own business and to mediate where other people are quarreling. I mean the word in a broader sense. We are compounded of the nations of the world; we mediate their blood, we mediate their traditions; we mediate their sentiments, their tastes, their passions; we are ourselves compounded of those things. We are, therefore, able to understand all nations; we are able to understand them in the compound, not separately, as partisans, but unitedly as knowing and comprehending and embodying them all. It is in that sense that I mean that America is a mediating Nation. The opinion of America, the action of America, is ready to turn, and free to turn, in any direction. Did you ever reflect upon how almost every other nation has through long centuries been headed in one direction? That is not true of the United States. The United States has no racial momentum. It has not history back of it which makes it run all its energies and all its ambitions in on particular direction.[24]

That such a diverse people could consent to its own government legitimated a special role for the United States in spreading republican freedom and liberal democracy.

Other countries depend upon the multiplication of their own native people. This country is constantly drinking strength out of new sources by the voluntary association with it of great bodies of strong men and forward-looking women out of other lands. And so by the gift of the free will of independent people it is being constantly renewed from generation to generation by the same process by which it was originally created. It is as if humanity had determined to see to it that this great Nation, founded for the benefit of humanity, should not lack for the allegiance of the people of the world.[25]

Wilson was strongly influenced by Walter Bagehot, the Gladstonian editor of *The Economist* in the mid-nineteenth century who proposed that parliamentary democracy, "government by discussion," arose through natural selection.[26] For Bagehot this made Great Britain the fittest nation on Earth, but for Wilson evolution had passed the torch on to the United States. "The American Revolution was the birth of a nation; it was the creation of a great free republic based upon traditions of personal liberty which theretofore had been confined to a single little island, but which it was purposed should spread to all mankind."[27]

This role the United States had taken on was to be in the service of peace, hence his policy of neutrality in the first years of the so-called European War. Wilson told his audience of newly naturalized immigrants in his 1915 address, "You are enriching us if you come expecting us to be better than we are." He continued,

> See, my friends, what that means. It means that Americans must have a consciousness different from the consciousness of every other nation in the world. I am not saying this with even the slightest thought of criticism of other nations....The example of America must be a special example. The example of America must be the example not merely of peace because it will not fight, but of peace because peace is the healing and elevating influence of the world and strife is not. There is such a thing as a man being too proud to fight. There is such a thing as a nation being so right that it does not need to convince others by force that it is right.[28]

Despite his commitment to peace, Wilson's understanding of cosmopolitan republican agency could justify entering the war just as easily as neutrality. When the United States did eventually declare war against Germany, he told Congress, "Our object now, as then, is to vindicate the principles of peace and justice in the life of the world as against selfish and autocratic power, and to set up among the really free and self-governed peoples of the world such a concert of purpose and of action as will henceforth insure the observance of those principles."[29] As Wilson famously put it, "The world must be made safe for democracy. Its peace must be planted upon the tested foundations of political liberty."[30]

The Bush Doctrine

George W. Bush had much the same to say for his War on Terror. "The advance of human freedom—the great achievement of our time, and the great hope of every time—now depends on us."[31] This mission is as important within the country as it is in its international action. "As we defend liberty and justice abroad, we must always honor those values here at home. America rejects all forms of ethnic and religious bigotry. We welcome the values of every responsible citizen, no matter the land of their birth."[32] Like Wilson's new citizens who looked forward to their contribution to the American experiment rather than backward to their native prejudices, Bush's new citizens take on the responsibilities of citizenship in a democracy whose messianic cosmopolitanism has a particular source: "And we will always protect the most basic human freedom—the freedom to worship God without fear."[33] Wilson shared Bush's evangelical Christianity and his assumption that America's mission is to spread freedom and democracy as part of God's plan. Immigrant America is God's agent on Earth, as though it were the "new creation" described by Paul in the New Testament "where there is neither Greek nor Jew."[34] As converts to Christianity are reborn into the body of Christ through baptism, so too are immigrants to the United States reborn into the body of the nation through the oath of citizenship.

While Bush certainly makes known his religious preferences, the logic of Christian cosmopolitanism secularized does expand his scope of civic inclusion, and to dismiss it as mere hypocrisy is to miss its political effects. "The Islam that we know is a faith devoted to the worship of one God, as revealed through The Holy Qu'ran. It teaches the value and importance of charity, mercy, and peace."[35] Muslims contribute to the cosmopolitan agency of the United States in the world. "We respect your faith.

It's practiced freely by millions of Americans, and by millions more in countries that America counts as friends. Its teachings are good and peaceful..."[36] It also allows him to put religion in a continuum of difference with race: "Every faith is practiced and protected here, because we are one country. Every immigrant can be fully and equally American because we're one country. Race and color should not divide us, because America is one country."[37] This slippage between race, nationality and religion took a particularly grotesque turn in his first declaration of war.[38] "The United States respects the people of Afghanistan—after all, we are currently its largest source of humanitarian aid..."[39]

Never mind that the actual terrorists were Saudi nationals; and, lest there be any mistake, that religion and race are not to be conflated along with different nationalities, the U.S. Congress offered this "finding of fact" in the beginning of the USA Patriot Act, which it passed at the Attorney General's request shortly after the attacks in order to give the executive branch carte blanche to conduct the War on Terror:

> Arab Americans, Muslim Americans, and Americans from South Asia play a vital role in our Nation and are entitled to nothing less than the full rights of every American.[40]

This awkward juxtaposition of religion and race assimilates one to the other even as it seeks to distinguish them.

Axes of Evil

Such cosmopolitan, democratic legitimacy necessarily makes outlaws of Osama bin Laden, the Taliban, and Saddam Hussein, as it did Kaiser Wilhelm. If, according to Wilson, "...the menace to...peace and freedom lies in the existence of autocratic governments, backed by organized force which is controlled wholly by their will, not by the will of their people,"[41] then, according to Bush, "Al Qaeda is to terror what the mafia is to crime. But its goal is not making money; its goal is remaking the world—and imposing its radical beliefs on people everywhere."[42] While the United States respects Afghanis, "we condemn the Taliban regime," that is, the "radical network of terrorists, and every government that supports them." When it came time to invade Iraq, Bush found his justification in the words of a U.N. weapons inspector: "The fundamental problem with Iraq remains the nature of the regime, itself. Saddam Hussein is a homicidal dictator who is addicted to weapons of mass destruction."[43]

A free people taking out an illegitimate government by this definition cannot be conquest. Echoing Wilson's frequent claims that in going to war "We have no selfish ends to serve....We desire no conquests, no dominion,"[44] Bush told the United Nations, "Free societies do not intimidate through cruelty and conquest."[45] Because the United States is a diverse people consensually comprising a nation, its sovereign motives cannot be impeached. By definition its foreign interventions are only against illegitimate governments to liberate the peoples those governments or dictators have effectively conquered. In this sense, the geography of Westphalia is limited to what the U.S. government deems "legitimate" nation-states, and those people who live outside this realm are liable to be racially targeted for violent "liberation." And to suggest that this liberation is, in fact, conquest is tantamount to treason; Ann Coulter could not have said it better when Democratic Senator Zell Miller of Georgia shouted at the 2004 Republican National Convention, "Nothing makes this marine madder than someone calling American troops occupiers rather than liberators!"[46]

E Pluribus Unum

This cosmopolitan, democratic legitimacy for U.S. geopolitical sovereignty is internally a fractious thing, something Bush recognized when he claimed he wanted to be "a uniter and not a divider." By this logic, the United States' strength as an example of a racially diverse people exercising *republican* freedom abroad can be a weakness in exercising *democratic* freedom at home. There is an important conflation in American political discourse of these two freedoms. The first freedom is that of a corporate people, a nation free from foreign domination. Much is made of the etymological relationship of "nation" to "natal" with the singular racial history this implies, but the words of Wilson and Bush on the United States' cosmopolitan agency would appear to belie this conventional, "European," sense of nationhood. After all, while we don't choose our parents, immigrants do choose the United States. Yet Wilson did have a definite sense of the appropriate complexion for this cosmopolitanism. "We come from all the great races of the world. We are made up out of all the nations and people who have stood at the center of civilization."[47] These "civilized races" were, of course, white, something a U.S. president could never explicitly say now.

The second freedom is that of the individual citizen with claims of right against the state, including, ideally, the right to have one's say in choosing the government. In 1917 there was no pretense that this was universal in a concrete sense. African-American men were effectively prevented from voting in southern states under Jim Crow laws, and women of any race had no constitutional right to vote at all. Wilson was a relatively late convert to women's suffrage, and, while he was a professor at Princeton University, he told a student, "I do not believe in it, but I never argue against it, for there *are* no logical arguments against it."[48] But despite his eventual support for voting rights in the abstract, it would not be up to the federal government to actively enforce such rights for decades to come, especially for black men at the state and local levels. "Civil liberties" as we call them now had to be earned and exercised appropriately[49]—a notion still with us as Bush alluded to in welcoming "responsible" immigrants.

The conflation of republican and democratic freedoms is a crucial transfer point for the American political rationality of race in that it not only elides the distinction between the nation within and without but also the obvious inconsistencies internal to both. The slippage between illegitimate foreign government, nation, race, and immigrant is a vector of suspicion that can go every which way. German-Americans fell under suspicion because of the actions of the Kaiser, while Pakistani-Americans are now harassed because Afghanistan and Iraq were invaded, in turn because of the actions of Saudi immigrants back in the United States. Thus the proliferation of hyphenated Americans seems to re-energize the proliferation of racialized enemies at home and abroad, strengthening our republican legitimacy abroad while weakening our civil liberties and democratic participation at home. Among fundamental biopolitical categories by which the existence of biological life has come to be politicized, race has been the most prominent in territorializing the nation-state inside and out, and this spatial process inevitably involves the imposition of violence. We can't seem to do without race in defining our enemies even as we continually seek to abolish it as a discriminatory basis for the exercise of citizenship.

Wilson sought to exclude any racially-marked persons as citizens for fear of disunity while touting cosmopolitan intervention abroad. George W. Bush has also been quite reticent about using hyphenated terms; I have been unable to find any instance of him using the term "Muslim-American" in his speeches—but what is telling is that his one use of "Arab-American" occurred in one of his incoherent ad-libs, betraying how unconsciously assimilated hyphenism has become. As the earlier quotes suggest, Bush does occasionally specify the contributions of Muslim- and Arab-Americans *as such*, and the U.S. Congress showed no qualms at all about using such terms in the Patriot Act. This is a remarkable political change when you consider the anti-hyphenism prevalent during the identity politics of the Reagan presidency. Over the past twenty years, the right wing has made its peace with a (very) weak form of multiculturalism, begun to valorize race and ethnicity beyond whiteness, and has explicitly adopted antiracism in its pursuit of racist public policy and warfare.

States of Exception

The Wilson administration's handling of race in World War I is a useful comparison in illustrating what I mean by the current objectification and negotiability of antiracism. I have already discussed how German-Americans were not solicited *as* German-Americans by the government. As anti-German hysteria was whipped up in advance of the U.S. entry into the war, political parties refused any explicit appeal to the German-American vote during the 1916 election campaign, particularly as Wilson sought to neutralize the potential threat of a unified Republican Party and the possibility of the still-popular and rabidly nativist Roosevelt heading the ticket.[50] Irish-Americans faired slightly better, but both parties were clearly pro-British despite Britain's blockade and "the unwarranted use of the American flag for the protection of British ships."[51] Despite this official neutrality, the U.S. Ambassador to Great Britain, Walter Hines Page, wrote in private correspondence that "we Americans have got to …hang our Irish agitators and shoot our hyphenates and bring up our children with reverence for English history and in the awe of English literature."[52]

Wilson continued to insinuate the disloyalty of German-Americans, but never directly by name. When he accepted the Democratic nomination in September of 1916, he told the delegates,

> The seas were not broad enough to keep the infection of the conflict out of our own politics. The passions and intrigues of certain active groups and combinations of men amongst us who were born under foreign flags injected the poison of disloyalty into our own most critical affairs, laid violent hands upon many of our industries, and subjected us to the shame of divisions of sentiment and purpose in which America was condemned and forgotten….I am the candidate of a party, but I am above all things else an American citizen. I neither seek the

favour nor fear the displeasure of that small alien element amongst us which puts loyalty to any foreign power before loyalty to the United States.[53]

Attempts during the preparedness campaign by German-American organizations to express their support of neutrality and opposition to aid to the Allies according to Wilson's own criterion of "America First," led only to more innuendo against the community. "Ethnic politics" were seen as a threat to republican unity and freedom as the country went to war and would require the suppression of democratic rights and freedoms at home.[54]

Domestic Repression During World War I

Wilson was famously intolerant of dissent, and he assumed that anyone who disagreed with his policies was disloyal to the United States. In his war address, the president warned that German agents had infiltrated the country to "[fill] our unsuspecting communities and even our offices of government with spies and set criminal intrigues everywhere afoot against our national unity of counsel, our peace within and without, our industries and our commerce."[55] Any such disloyalty would "be dealt with with a firm hand of stern repression; but," he had to qualify, "if it lifts its head at all, it will lift it only here and there without countenance except from a lawless and malignant few."[56]

Shortly after, Wilson issued an executive order that required German non-citizens to register and subjected them to the possibility of summary arrest: "an alien enemy whom there may be reasonable cause to believe to be abiding or about to aid the enemy...or violates any regulation promulgated by the President...will be subject to summary arrest...and to confinement in such penitentiary, prison, jail, or military camp."[57] His Attorney General, Thomas W. Gregory, meanwhile, worked with Congress to pass the Espionage Act, which gave the Postmaster General the ex parte power to censor the mails, and authorized other provisions for surveillance and summary arrest that concentrated power in the executive.[58] One skeptical representative asked during debate on the floor, "Suppose a man is sawing wood in his own cellar or, being of an inventive turn of mind, is working at some contrivance, and the man next door gets it into his head that a German spy is working in that cellar. Is there anything in this bill which protects that man against arrest upon the mere suspicion of his neighbor?"[59] The reply from the bill's sponsor was a flat "no."

The bill's opponents' fears were confirmed as Wilson's veiled rhetoric and his cabinet members' more overt enforcement actions encouraged so-called superpatriots to harass people of German origin, whether citizens or not. While nonnaturalized Germans were targeted by statute as "enemy aliens" for registration, surveillance, exclusion from zones of "military sensitivity" (including all of the District of Columbia), internment camps, and deportation, German-language papers were harassed by postmasters at all levels, and German-Americans were frequent targets of accusations of disloyalty resulting in frequent arrests and interrogations,[60] such as a northern man with a German surname who was arrested in Florida for violating the Espionage Act when he exclaimed, "Damn such a country as this," during an unexpected cold snap.[61] Superpatriot groups such as the American Defense Society (headed by none other than Theodore Roosevelt) took the spirit of the law into their own hands by pursuing a drive to eliminate not just individual Germans deemed dangerous, but the traces of German language and culture altogether. One tract they circulated was worthy of present-day characterizations of the Taliban as it described Germans as "the most treacherous, brutal and loathsome nation on earth...The sound of the German language...reminds us of the murder of a million helpless old men, unarmed men, women and children; [and] the driving of about 100,000 young French, Belgian and Polish women into compulsory prostitution."[62]

African-Americans on the other hand were rarely targeted under the Espionage Act despite fears that German agents were working in the black community to spread unrest and encourage draft evasion with promises of "social equality" in the event of German victory.[63] Such attention was unnecessary for African-Americans living in constant fear of lynching, which was on the increase during the Progressive Era as racism became ever more violent and institutionalized after the end of Reconstruction. Wilson allowed his cabinet secretaries to segregate federal departments, but even more egregiously, he refused to acknowledge lynching as a racially-motivated crime. It took the "lynching" of Robert Prager, a German immigrant, in Illinois on April 5, 1918 for Wilson to even publicly acknowledge the issue.[64] Although Prager was an immigrant, he had applied for citizenship but had yet to acquire it. When a rumor started to circulate among his coworkers that agents of the Kaiser had stolen dynamite in a plot to blow up the coal mine in which they worked, they began to suspect Prager. He was put into protective custody, but the miners broke him out of jail and paraded him to a tar-and-feather ceremony; the situation escalated despite his claims of innocence, and Prager was hanged from a tree.[65] When Wilson finally publicly responded to issue of mob violence, all he could bring himself to say was,

> No man who loves America, no man who really cares for her fame and honor and character, or who is truly loyal to her institutions, can justify mob action while the courts of justice are open and the governments of the States and the nation are ready and able to do their duty.[66]

While Wilson attempted to limit the exercise of popular sovereignty, African-Americans were placed in the ban of state law because of their race and German-Americans were beginning to find themselves there as well, and their grievances could only be addressed at the federal level as deracialized citizens. And while it was the ambiguous whiteness of German victims of mob violence that materially provoked a federal response to lynching, Wilson's Americanism required that their ethnicity play no role in the content of that response. *Racism* was not political at the level of national citizenship; it was merely a fact of bare life, a residue "reserved to the States respectively, or to the people."[67]

The federal response that racism did lead to was singularly perverse. Instead of recognizing that the domestic conduct of the war including the Espionage Act enabled the violence of the superpatriots, Wilson and his allies came to a decision that the Espionage Act was not strong enough to prevent it. The federal government needed even more power to suppress dissent for the sake of unity and keep German-Americans and immigrants, as well as the Irish- and African-Americans, socialists,

Wobblies, and anarchists in line and keep *them* from provoking the superpatriots to vigilante justice. In May 1918 the Espionage Act was amended by the passage of the Sedition Act, which prohibited any criticism of the war and further concentrated power in the executive.[68] Racial harassment under these provisions did not end with the armistice; it continued into the Red Scare of 1919–1920, and for some, such as African-Americans, actually increased.[69] Racism was a tool which enabled the federal governance of the people of the United States even as race was disavowed in defining their citizenship.

Domestic Repression During the War on Terror

A great many of the measures taken during World War I are with us again. The equation of dissent with disloyalty, the curtailment of judicial review, and the harassment of racial groups assumed responsible for the existing state of war have all been hallmarks of the War on Terror some ninety years later. What is different now is that the racialization of citizenship has a minimum level of acceptability. Nonwhiteness is coming to be valorized in specific, limited ways as politicians actively court "the Latino vote" or answer to their "African-American constituency." During the Progressive Era, there was little debate over what racism was; people simply disagreed on whether it was good or bad. Now with only a few exceptions racism as such is a sin even in the eyes of the right wing, and "racist" is almost uniformly regarded as a dishonor. The public debate now is over the content of racism, what it actually is, and with the current supposed ambiguity of the term, the handling of racism by the federal government has shifted from a strategy of disavowal to its constitution as an object of management.

I have already shown how President Bush has articulated a vision of cosmopolitan republican agency for the United States in the War on Terror remarkably similar to Wilson's for World War I. Yet for the current administration, Arab-American and Muslim-American citizens and others whose origins lie far from Northwestern Europe are solicited as such. Their contributions to the polity are not sublimated but, theoretically at least, absorbed intact, protected and even celebrated. While the demands for the acknowledgment of race in the federal guardianship of citizenship are much the same as they were over eighty years ago, that they are now being acknowledged is different, and this has important implications for the domestic conduct of war.

Much attention has been given to the Patriot Act of 2001 which passed with little debate in Congress six weeks after the 9/11 attacks.[70] Largely authored by then-Attorney General John Ashcroft, the law is similar to the Espionage Act in that it concentrates enormous power for surveillance, detention, and deportation in the executive at the expense of due process and judicial review. It is important to note that unlike the Espionage Act, which was a fiercely debated response to the specific exigencies of a well-defined war that was a long time coming, the Patriot Act includes a wish-list from the FBI for increased power that had been previously rejected by Congress before the terrorist attacks reduced it to a state of cowardice. It also drew upon and explicitly strengthened a trio of 1996 acts requested by the Clinton administration that served as a dress-rehearsal in Democratic drag for Bush's management of racism.[71] These laws provided numerous enhancements of discretionary power, drastically limited judicial review for illegal immigrants and prisoners, and criminalized any association with groups deemed "terrorist" by the secretary of state.

What is more illuminating than the content of the Patriot Act itself are the guidelines for its enforcement by federal officials. The Justice Department Civil Rights Division's "Guidance Regarding the Use of Race by Federal Law Enforcement Agencies" (June 2003) flatly prohibits racial profiling for "routine or spontaneous activities in domestic law enforcement" and permits the use of race only to aid in identifying a specific suspect.[72] But this prohibition becomes more like a mandate when it comes to "national security" or "the integrity of the nation's borders."

> The Constitution prohibits consideration of race or ethnicity in law enforcement decisions in all but the most exceptional instances. Given the incalculably high stakes involved in such investigations, however, Federal law enforcement officers who are protecting national security or preventing catastrophic events (as well as airport security screeners) may consider race, ethnicity, and other relevant factors to the extent permitted by our laws and the Constitution. Similarly, because enforcement of the laws protecting the Nation's borders may necessarily involve a consideration of a person's alienage in certain circumstances, the use of race or ethnicity in such circumstances is properly governed by existing statutory and constitutional standards.

The department claims it holds the use of race to the "strictest scrutiny" according to the Constitution, but consider the example the guidelines site as a permissible use of race:

> U.S. intelligence sources report that terrorists from a particular ethnic group are planning to use commercial jetliners as weapons by hijacking them at an airport in California during the next week. Before allowing men of that ethnic group to board commercial airplanes in California airports during the next week, Transportation Security Administration personnel, and other federal and state authorities, may subject them to heightened scrutiny.

Gone is any statutory distinction between citizen and alien, their vanishing point forming not only a racialized state of exception by which a person is removed from the protection of the law, but a *space* of exception in which racial violence becomes acceptable—racial violence that is not racist because by this particular rationality, the evil of racism, its definition, is the discrimination on the basis of race against somebody who is a legitimate participant in U.S. sovereignty, and a passport is no necessary indication of this legitimacy. It is a category error to speak of "racism" occurring at the airport security checkpoint, Guantánamo Bay or even Abu Ghraib, spaces of racial violence in which this participation that comes with citizenship is suspended.

This distinction between citizen and alien has been further eroded in practical governance by John Ashcroft's arrogation of the powers of summary arrest and indefinite detention of citizens as "enemy combatants," not to mention the apparent implicit endorsement of torture by then White House Counsel Alberto Gonzales, Ashcroft's eventual successor. Ashcroft indefinitely detained at least two U.S. citizens, Yaser Hamdi and Abdullah al Muhajir. Hamdi was captured in Afghanistan and alleged to have aided the Taliban, but he was not captured in combat, and the certification papers for his enemy combatant status only state that he "resided" in Afghanistan.[73] Al Muhajir was arrested at Chicago's O'Hare airport upon his return from Afghanistan under suspicion of having trained with al Qaeda. Al Muhajir's case has been the more prominent one in the news, and on June 10, 2002, Ashcroft puffed out his chest for the press and crowed,

> I am pleased to announce today a significant step forward in the War on Terrorism. We have captured a known terrorist who was exploring a plan to build and explode a radiological dispersion device, or "dirty bomb," in the United States....Yesterday, after consultation with the Acting Secretary of Defense and other senior officials, both the Acting Secretary of Defense and I recommended that the President of the Untied States, in his capacity as commander in chief, determine that Abdullah Al Muhajir...is an enemy combatant who poses a serious and continuing threat to the American people and our national security. After the determination, Abdullah Al Muhajir was transferred from the custody of the Justice Department to the custody of the Defense Department.[74]

Despite the fact that the U.S. Supreme Court has held in *Hamdi v. Rumsfeld* (2004) that the legal designation of enemy combatants is by statute applicable to either enemy aliens or U.S. citizens captured abroad while actually engaged in combat against the United States, its purpose is not to punish but to detain only until the cessation of hostilities to prevent the combatants from physically rejoining the fight, and furthermore U.S. citizens still have habeas rights to contest their imprisonment.[75] Hamdi was released in October 2004 to the government of his native Saudi Arabia, while Al Muhajir's detention has been upheld thus far in the U.S. Court of Appeals for the Fourth Circuit, which cited *Hamdi*.[76] Interestingly the executive order that established indefinite detention for al Qaeda suspects specifically excludes U.S. citizens,[77] yet when Ashcroft's message was toned down by administration officials, the concern was for fearmongering over dirty bombs rather than due process.[78] Instead the administration has argued that the "necessary and appropriate force" language of the Authorization for Use of Military Force Joint Resolution of 2001 (AUMF) under which the order was issued authorizes the internment of citizens.[79]

As noted before, President Bush's order issued November 13, 2001 under the AUMF entitled "Detention, Treatment, and Trial of Certain Non-Citizens in the War Against Terrorism" is explicitly limited to non-citizens. The order allows the secretary of defense to hold suspected al Qaeda members who have "engaged in, aided or abetted, or conspired to commit, acts of international terrorism, or acts in preparation therefore, that have caused, threaten to cause, or have as their aim to cause, injury to or adverse effects on the United States, its citizens, national security, foreign policy, or economy; or has knowingly harbored one or more individuals described [above]."[80] There are no limits to the duration of detention, trial—should one even occur—is by military tribunal whose decision is subject to review by the defense secretary, and "the individual shall not be privileged to seek any remedy or maintain any proceeding, directly or indirectly, or to have any such remedy or proceeding sought on the individual's behalf, in any court of the United States, or any State thereof, any court of any foreign nation, or any international tribunal."[81] The clause "Any individual subject to this order shall be...treated humanely, without any adverse distinction based on race, color, religion, gender, birth, wealth, or any similar criteria" puts no limitation on who will be detained to begin with.[82] It is an order which nakedly imputes guilt by association and strips detainees of all civil liberties.

But as the Abu Ghraib scandal shows, the definition of "humane treatment" is very much up for grabs when the individual's detainment in such spaces is *already* racially determined. Khaled el Masri is only one recent example of how capricious such targeting can be (the very definition of terrorism). A German citizen of Lebanese origin, Masri was detained by Macedonian border guards as his tour bus was stopped and accused of being a terrorist. He says he was transferred to the custody of U.S. officials and he believes he was flown to a prison in Afghanistan, "where he said he was shackled, beaten repeatedly, photographed nude, injected with drugs and questioned by interrogators about what they insisted were his ties to Al Qaeda."[83] He says he was imprisoned for five months without charge before being released.

> Mr. Masri's lawyer, Manfred R. Gnjidic, said he suspected that his client was swept into the C.I.A.'s policy of "renditions"—handing custody of a prisoner from United States control to another country for the purposes of interrogation—because he has the same name, with a slightly different spelling, as a man wanted in the Sept. 11 attacks. The policy has come under increasing criticism as other cases have come to light recently.[84]

That the United States' spaces of racial violence can occur anywhere, whether at O'Hare, a Macedonian border checkpoint, a naval brig in Charleston, or the more prominent places of Guantánamo Bay and Abu Ghraib Prison, is legitimated by the United States' republican agency, exercised on behalf of and by a "free people."[85]

The "enemy" alien "combatants" held at Guantánamo and other installations with no civil rights include people forcibly drafted by the Taliban and even children, yet President Bush referred to them en masse as "bad people" and Secretary of Defense Donald Rumsfeld labeled them "hard core, well-trained terrorists."[86] Yet such accusations of "terrorist" that have traditionally been reserved for non-citizens have been leveled not only at U.S. citizens such as Hamdi, al Muhajir, but at countless others as the Bush administration brazenly racially profiles "terrorists" in its domestic surveillance activities. By its definition this is not racist; merely by being suspected of terrorists these people are excised from the U.S. body politic and the protection and valorization citizenship affords. Racism can only be a personal failing that may be reflected in law as a violation of civil liberties of those deemed already worthy of citizenship. By this definition the racial targeting of those not worthy by virtue of being suspected as terrorists cannot be racist, and accusations of racism are indignantly brushed aside.[87]

Conclusion

Foucault defined governmentality as "the relationship of the self to the self." Writ large on the U.S. body biopolitic with its multiracial complexion, the relationship of the national citizenry to itself necessarily has become fraught by race in a new way. A compulsion to deny racism has arisen differentially across most of the political spectrum, and so racism has become a negotiable object of governance. During the Progressive Era racism was an undisputed tool of governance even as anti-hyphenism deracialized citizenship at the federal level. Access to citizenship had its racial criteria, but its exercise once achieved could only be unmarked by race, thus implicitly white. Following the expansion of federal power, the civil rights movement, and the rise of multiculturalism, racism is now a contested object of governance in that its characterization as "racist" continuously disputed. U.S. citizens are encouraged to hyphenate themselves and are protected in doing so, so long as they remain "white enough."[88]

Yet as these racial boundaries of citizenship have folded in upon themselves, the more extreme abuses formerly reserved for racialized non-citizens when perpetrated by the federal government—surveillance, summary arrest, and indefinite detention without judicial review—are now nakedly imposed upon citizens who happen to be Arab- or Muslim-Americans, even as their citizenship status offers the Bush administration cover to deny that its activities are racist. Race as a national vector of reproduction has emerged from the state of nature to become politicized at the very source of U.S. sovereign legitimacy, the political participation of the individual citizen. It has confounded any easy geographical distinction between domestic and foreign territory as the multi-racial representative republic that is the United States intervenes anywhere it wills to spread freedom and democracy to racialized subjects of tyranny, and remove racialized persons regarded as threats to the same, sequestering them and subjecting them to extremes of violence and torture. Such a cosmopolitan pursuit will have its collateral damage, but by this logic of biopolitical sovereignty the fact these casualties are almost exclusively non-white cannot be described as racist, especially when the U.S. military proudly displays the overrepresentation of African- and Hispanic-Americans in its ranks.

The contrast with that other biopolitical category, sexuality, is telling—queer Americans are welcomed to participate in popular sovereignty as long as they remain desexualized. But rights claims based on explicit recognition as gay and lesbian citizens are being fiercely resisted, and much the same political spectrum that espouses the contribution of racial diversity to U.S. cosmopolitan agency is fighting to keep republican sovereignty resolutely heterosexual.[89] Such have been the changes in the American biopolitical state, with its decidedly untranscendental notion of citizenship. Woodrow Wilson eventually stopped receiving African-Americans at the White House in 1917, abandoning even the pretense of recognizing lynching as an affront to a racialized group productive of U.S. sovereignty. But nearly a century later, while George Bush calls for a constitutional amendment to ban gay marriage, resists any expansion of hate crimes legislation, and imprisons thousands of Arabs at Guantánamo Bay, the president makes sure to mark Eid ul-Fitr on his calendar.

Notes

1. Ellipses mine. Transcript available at http://transcripts.cnn.com/TRANSCRIPTS/ 0303/21/lol.03.html,. accessed January 8, 2005.

2. My point is not that the U.S. federal government has always been a normalizing force or that all members of U.S. society have been able to participate in popular sovereignty. Rather I want to take seriously the notion that in contrast to Foucault's France, where the political rationality of biopolitics or governmentality detached itself from raison d'état over time, in the United States the right of sovereignty has

always been a product of "the People," regardless of the limits to who has counted as "the People." In short, in France sovereignty discovered the people, while in the United States the people discovered sovereignty. In Foucault's governmentality, work sovereignty is something to be countered because of its entrenchment in European political theory, while in mine it is something to be explained precisely because in the United States European theories of sovereignty always have been countered with a popular and institutionally and geographically decentralized understanding of state power.

3. Michel Foucault, *Society Must Be Defended: Lectures at the Collège de France 1975–1976,* trans. David Macey (New York: Picador, 1993), 254.

4. Ibid., 255.

5. Ibid.

6. For a sustained, albeit institutionalist argument, see Marc Allen Eisner, *From Warfare State to Welfare State: World War I, Compensatory State Building, and the Limits of the Modern Order* (University Park: Pennsylvania State University Press, 2000).

7. Woodrow Wilson to 65th Congress, Washington, April 2, 1917, in Albert Shaw (ed.), *The Messages and Papers of Woodrow Wilson* (New York: The Review of Reviews Corp., 1924) 1:378.

8. Ibid., 373.

9. Ibid., 376.

10. George W. Bush, "Address to a Joint Session of Congress and the American People," available at http://www.whitehouse.gov/news/releases/2001/09/20010920-8.html, September 20, 2001.

11. George W. Bush, "President's Remarks at the United Nations General Assembly," available at http://www.whitehouse.gov/news/releases/2002/09/20020912-1.html, September 12, 2002.

12. George W. Bush, "President Bush Salutes Soldiers in Fort Lewis, Washington," available at http://www.whitehouse.gov/new/release/2004/06/20040618-1.html, June 18, 2004.

13. George W. Bush, "President Bush and Prime Minister Allawi Press Conference," available at http://www.whitehouse.gov/news/releases/2004/09/20040923-8.html September 23, 2004.

14. Carl Schmitt, *The Concept of the Political* (Chicago: University of Chicago Press, 1996), 26.

15. Charles Taylor, "The Politics of Recognition," in Amy Gutmann (ed.), *Multiculturalism: Examining the Politics of Recognition* (Princeton, NJ: Princeton University Press, 1994), 25–74: 62.

16. Schmitt, *Concept of the Political,* 28.

17. Wilson to Congress, *Papers,* 382.

18. Wilson in St. Paul, September 9, 1919, *Papers,* 2:846.

19. Matthew Frye Jacobson, *Whiteness of a Different Color: European Immigrants and the Alchemy of Race* (Cambridge, MA: Harvard University Press, 1998), 46–48.

20. Jörg Nagler, "Victims of the Home Front: Enemy Aliens in the United States during the First World War," in Panikos Panayi (ed.), *Minorities in Wartime: National and Racial Groupings in Europe, North America and Australia during the Two World Wars* (Oxford: Berg Publishers, 1993), 191–215: 194.

21. "Americanization," *The New Republic* 5:65 (1916): 322–323: 323.

22. Frederick C. Luebke, *Bonds of Loyalty: German-Americans in World War I* (DeKalb: Northern Illinois University Press, 1974), 174.

23. Wilson at naturalization ceremony, Philadelphia, May 10, 1915, *Papers*, 1:115–116.

24. Wilson to Associated Press, New York, 20 April 20, 1915, *Papers*, 1:110–111.

25. Wilson at naturalization ceremony, *Papers*, 1:114–115.

26. John Wells Davidson, "Wilson in the Campaign of 1912," in Earl Latham (ed.), *The Philosophy and Policies of Woodrow Wilson* (Chicago: The University of Chicago Press, 1958), 85–99: 94; Walter Bagehot, *Physics and Politics* (New York: Alfred A. Knopf, 1948), 163.

27. Wilson to Daughters of the American Revolution, Washington, October 11, 1916, *Papers*, 1:122.

28. Wilson at naturalization ceremony, *Papers*, 1:117.

29. Wilson to Congress, *Papers*, 1:378.

30. Ibid., 1:381.

31. Bush, "Address to Congress."

32. George W. Bush, "Remarks by the President at Iftaar with Ambassadors and Muslim Leaders," available at http://www.whitehouse.gov/news/releases/2003/10/20031028-9.html, October 28, 2003.

33. Ibid.

34. Colossians 3:11.

35. George W. Bush, "President's Message for Ramadan," available at http://www.whitehouse.gov/news/releases/2001/11/20011115-14.html, November 15, 2001.

36. Bush, "Address to Congress."

37. George W. Bush, "President Promotes Compassionate Conservatism," available at http://www.whitehouse.gov/news/releases/2002/04/20020430-5.html, April 30, 2002.

38. It is important to note that this was not a formal declaration of war as provided for in the U.S. Constitution, according to which only Congress has the power to issue a declaration of war. That the lessons of Viet Nam seem to have worn off is indicated by the fact that nowhere in official discourse is there any reference to "the conflict over terror."

39. Bush, "Address to Congress."

40. 115 *Stat.* 272, Sec. 102.

41. Wilson to Congress, *Papers*, 1: 378.

42. Bush, "Address to Congress."

43. George W. Bush, "President Outlines Iraqi Threat," available at http://www.whitehouse.gov/news/releases/2002/10/20021007-8.html, October 7, 2002.

44. Wilson to Congress, *Papers*, 1: 381.

45. Bush, "Remarks at the United Nations."

46. "Excerpt from Keynote Speech," *New York Times*, September 2, 2004, 6.

47. Wilson in St. Paul, *Papers*, 2:845.

48. Raymond B. Fosdick, "Personal Recollections of Woodrow Wilson," in Latham, *Wilson*, pp. 28–45: 34–35.

49. Paul L. Murphy, *World War I and the Origin of Civil Liberties in the United States* (New York: W.W. Norton, 1979), 32–50.

50. Cited in Luebke, *Bonds of Loyalty*, 157–198.

51. Secretary of State William Jennings Bryan to Ambassador to Germany James W. Gerard, February 10, 1915, *Papers*, 1:223.

52. Cited in Luebke, *Bonds of Loyalty*, 157.

53. Wilson to Democratic National Convention, September 2, 1916, *Papers*, 1: 310.

54. Luebke, *Bonds of Loyalty*, 157–198.

55. Wilson to Congress, 379–380.

56. Ibid., 382.

57. Proclamation of Alien Enemy Regulations, April 6, 1917, *Papers*, 387.

58. *Stat.* 217 (1917).

59. *Congressional Record* 55 (65th Congress, Session 1, May 2, 1917, 1696).

60. Luebke, *Bonds of Loyalty*, 199–266; Murphy, *Origin of Civil Liberties*, 119.

61. Luebke 247.

62. Luebke, 216.

63. Mark Ellis, *Race, War, and Surveillance: African Americans and the United States Government during World War I* (Bloomington: Indiana University Press, 2001),105; Theodore Kornweibel, Jr., *"Investigate Everything:" Federal Efforts to Compel Black Loyalty During World War I* (Bloomington: Indiana University Press, 2002), 54–55.

64. I use the term "lynching" advisedly since it is too easy to lose the specificity of the lynching of African-American men. Nevertheless Prager was targeted because of his ethnicity.

65. Luebke, *Bonds of Loyalty*, 3–26

66. Wilson, Denunciation of Lynching and the Mob Spirit, 26 July 1918, *Papers*, 1:507.

67. U.S. Const, Amend X.

68. 40 *Stat.* 553 (1918).

69. Ellis, *Race, War, and Surveillance*, 183–227; Kornweibel, *"Investigate Everything,"* 270–276.

70. See H.R. 3162, *Congressional Record* 137 (107th Congress, Session 1, October 23–26, 2001).

71. The Antiterrorism and Effective Death penalty Act (AEDPA) 110 *Stat.* 1214; the Prison Litigation Reform Act (PLRA) 110 *Stat.* 1321; the Illegal Immigration Reform and Immigrant Responsibility Act (IIRIRA) 110 *Stat.* 3009.

72. Available at http://www.usdoj.gov/crt/split/documents/guidance_on_race.htm, accessed September 15, 2004.

73. *Hamdi v. Rumsfeld* 542 U.S. 507 (2004) p. 19. Britain's House of Lords has gone farther by finding the Blair Government's Anti-Terrorism, Crime and Security Act of 2001, which in terms of the indefinite detention of foreign terror suspects without charge is substantially similar to the USA Patriot Act, to be inconsistent with the European Convention of Human Rights, which is given effect by Britain's Human Rights Act of 1998.

74. "Transcript of the Attorney General John Ashcroft Regarding the transfer of Abdullah Al Muhajir (Born Jose Padilla) To the Department of Defense as an Enemy Combatant 06/10/02," available at http://www.usdoj.gov/ag/speeches/2002/061002aftranscripts.htm.

75. *Hamdi*, 13 & 1.

76. "Court Gives Bush Right to Detain U.S. Combatant," *New York Times*, September 10, 2005, 1.

77. "Detention, Treatment, and Trial of Certain Non-Citizens in the War Against Terrorism," available at http://www.whitehouse.gov/new/releases/2001/11/20011113-27.html, November 13, 2001.

78. "After a 'Dirty Bomb' Explodes," *New York Times*, June 11, 2002, 1.

79. 115 *Stat.* 224.

80. §2(a)(1).

81. §7(b).

82. §3(b).

83. "German's Claim of Kidnapping Brings Investigation of U.S. Link," *New York Times*, January 9, 2005.

84. Ibid.

85. It is no small matter that it is African- and Hispanic-Americans whose race is valorized as military fodder.

86. Human Rights Watch, "United States: Guantanamo Two Years On" (January 9, 2004), available at http://hrw.org/english/docs/2004/01/09/usdom6917.htm, accessed September 16, 2004.

87. This chapter was written prior to George Bush's political troubles in the autumn of 2005 during which public support for the Iraq invasion and occupation has fallen below 50 percent according to most polls (for a summary of all the major polls, see http://www.pollingreport.com/iraq.htm). This has been due in part to the efforts by activists such as Cindy Sheehan, a white mother of a U.S. soldier killed in Iraq, to raise awareness of *American* lives lost in the war—the cost in Iraqi lives remains largely irrelevant in public discussion.

88. Lauren Berlant, *The Queen of America Goes to Washington City: Essays on Sex and Citizenship* (Durham, NC: Duke University Press, 1997), 207.

89. The spectacle of both George W. Bush and John Kerry condemning same-sex marriage while trying to appear non-homophobic during the 2004 election campaign very clearly showed the limits of diversity acceptable in mainstream American politics. And to be clear, despite the very legitimate equity issues at stake, or more precisely because of them, I am making no claims for the desirability of forms of state recognition that privilege one type of relationship at the very real expense of others, such as legal marriage—gay or straight.

5

Refuge or Refusal
The Geography of Exclusion
Jennifer Hyndman and Alison Mountz

Where the threat of persecution or violence exists, the exclusion of people from spaces that are safe is a dangerous political act. The twentieth century saw the creation of the political refugee with the ratification of the 1951 *Convention Relating to the Status of Refugees* and its 1967 *Protocol.* The latter extended the geographic scope of the convention beyond Europe after WWII to all world regions with no time limit. Nation-states are, however, currently reconfiguring their policies toward potential refugee claimants. With the implementation of policies that favor state security over human security, governments are slowly eroding international commitments to protect by undermining the chances for potential refugees to reach sovereign territory and make claims. This chapter focuses on the increasingly restricted mobility of those fleeing violence and persecution while recognizing that those seeking protection are not so different from impoverished migrants: so-called economic refugees seeking more secure living arrangements. We detail some of the tactics being employed to further the agenda of exclusion. Because of these tactics, asylum seekers increasingly arrive with the assistance of human smugglers, having traveled in groups known to policymakers as "mixed flows." We aim to address broader, pressing questions at hand regarding the changing practice and geography of sovereign power. Whether the twenty-first century will answer the humanitarian questions opened by its predecessor by ushering in the end of the era of the refugee remains to be seen.

States have long constructed migrants as vectors of insecurity and terror, particularly at border crossings. To address this "problem," states have created "spaces of exception" to their own laws:

> The stadium in Bari into which the Italian police in 1991 provisionally herded all illegal Albanian immigrants before sending them back to their country, the winter cycle-racing track in which the Vichy authorities gathered Jews before consigning them to the Germans... or the *zones d'attentes* in French international airports in which foreigners asking for refugee status are detained will then all equally be camps.[1]

Giorgio Agamben theorized these spaces as central to the changing operation of sovereign power, in which states of exception and geographies of exclusion figure centrally.

In the fall of 2004, a *Herald Tribune* headline read, "EU to study transit sites in Libya for immigrants."[2] The article outlined a proposal by Italy and Germany to assess the claims of asylum seekers outside of the European Union before they arrived *in*

EU Offshore Processing of Asylum Seekers

Figure 5.1

Europe. (Figure 5.1) This proposal is but one expression of what has been referred to as "regional solutions" for asylum processing, whereby refugee claims are dealt with 'close to home', *outside* the destination countries. Sweden, France, the Netherlands, Germany's Green Party, and the UN refugee agency meanwhile voiced concerns. Rather than call attention to Libya's role as a human rights pariah in the international community until recently, they objected to the fact that the country was not even a signatory to the 1951 Refugee Convention nor the 1967 Protocol—the bare legal framework that provides protection to those fleeing violence and persecution.

These spatial tactics of exclusion correspond to a discursive war on refugees in public discourse. The double function of processing asylum seekers and detaining enemy combatants in Guantánamo Bay highlights the spatial integration of and increasingly blurred distinction among suspected criminals, terrorists, and refugee claimants. Since 9/11, but starting well before, migrants have come to stand in for all that threatens state security and welfare, particularly in the industrialized countries of the Organization for Economic Co-operation and Development (OECD). This dominant discourse that criminalizes migrants—both asylum seekers and economic migrants—allows governments to popularize and maintain more restrictive asylum processing measures at the cost of the human security of threatened and displaced persons. In July 2004, the number of asylum seekers in the EU reached its lowest level since 1997.[3]

These trends might all be considered part of the "architecture of enmity": "Architectures of enmity are not halls of mirrors reflecting the world—they enter into its very constitution.... . They inhabit dispositions and practices, investing them with meaning and legitimation, and so sharpen the spurs of action."[4] The discursive construction of barriers that make movement more difficult correspond with exclusionary geographic practices that make the employment of the smuggling industry more likely.

This chapter explores the "architecture of enmity" currently under construction on the part of core immigrant and refugee-receiving nation-states. We argue that dispossessed refugees and other poor people on the move are experiencing a fundamental shift in their relationship to states. We contend that this shift is taking place in the name of the security of states too quietly, and at the risk of human rights, personal security, and the mandate of refugee-receiving states to protect those fleeing persecution. By articulating the geographical trends taking place around the globe, we demonstrate that rather than ad hoc, reactive measures, states are assembling a *revanchist* architecture of enmity against undocumented migrants and potential refugee claimants.[5]

We attempt to lay bare the projects enacted to protect state security in the name of human security. By invoking the question—refuge or refusal?—we challenge the fundamental yet contradictory objectives of states that are at once signatories to the Convention and Protocol and yet expanding border enforcement abroad. We see a key connection between the shifting geography of policing efforts and the shifting geography of the interdiction, processing, and detention of refugee claimants. Articulated in sequential fashion, the geography of the *revanchist* project emerges. The current security crises are leading to lasting legislative changes through which the reaction to crisis will stay with us. As Agamben argues, over time, states of exception become the rule.

We develop these arguments by contemplating two specific strategies that states are pursuing to fortify the border. The first is the safe third country agreement signed between Canada and the United States that promises to reduce refugee flows, especially to Canada. By restricting the mobility of refugee claimants and requiring them to file for asylum in the first country in which they land, the agreement aims to deter those contemplating sanctuary in North America. The second is a trend toward the creation of stateless spaces in extra-territorial locales where states hold migrants in legal ambiguity as a mechanism of control. After discussing these two trends, we explore the motivations that underlie and connect this concerted war on refugees. Ultimately, we critically examine these trends with the hope of looking back on these patterns in search of a way forward.

Security: Another Brick in the Wall

Migration is often represented as the "dark side" of globalization.[6] The events of 9/11 have only magnified fear of "the other." From the perspective of states, asylum seekers and undocumented migrants embody insecurity by testing the porosity of political borders. Walls to restrict such movement are being implemented in the name of national security, though one might argue that it is state sovereignty that is equally at stake. The observation of Max Weber almost a century ago that the close connection between the state and the use of violence has not always been the case appears more remarkable now in a political context where state-sponsored detention [in the absence of crime], exclusion, and deportation of migrants is commonplace and naturalized through state discourses of security.[7] While the state may have a monopoly on the use of force and violence, its application has been delegated to new border agencies, privatized to contractors at airports and prisons (and in Iraq), and exported to locations where pre-emptive measures prevent migrants from infringing on sovereignty framed as security risks.

While critics and proponents debate "security for whom?" in relation to the cement wall being erected in the Israel/Palestine territories, a number of less visible but nonetheless exclusionary walls are being erected in and by Europe, North America, and Australia. This multiplication of fortresses is disquieting in light of unprecedented political and economic integration, particularly at the extra-state scale of the EU and the North America Free Trade Agreement (NAFTA). Where territory was once seen to be the prime guarantor of security, "places no longer protect, however strongly they are armed and fortified…. threat and security have become now, essentially, *extraterritorial issues that evade territorial solutions.*"[8] Sovereign territory has been cast as the target of foreign insecurity with exclusion of the *étranger* its prime tactic.

The foundation for the newest "wall" can be found in the plethora of safe third country agreements. Since 1990, over two hundred refugee claimant readmission agreements have been concluded between EU countries, central and eastern European countries, and other nations around the world, both developed (Australia) and developing (Indonesia).[9] One recent accord was implemented between Canada and the United States on December 29, 2004. The North American Safe Third Country Agreement like many in Europe requires that asylum seekers file a refugee claim in the "country of first presence." If they arrive at the land border, they will be turned back to the country from which they have come, with exceptions for minors and those with family in the destination country.

The Safe Third Country Agreement not only reduces the number of asylum seekers coming to Canada, but shrinks spaces of refuge in North America. In Canada, the *number* of refugee claims has fallen dramatically *without* the Agreement in place, through the implementation of tighter entry requirements on visitors to the United States since 9/11. The agreement will do little if anything, however, to improve the *integrity* of claims assessed, that is to assist those in genuine need of political protection. Administratively, it appears to be a strategic plan by a government keen to control costs associated with processing refugee claims. Politically, at first glance, it seems a fair-minded policy that promises to enhance national security. Its primary objective, however, is exclusion from Canadian territory. Geographically, the agreement is likely to divert legal flows of asylum seekers to Canada into more criminal underground channels of cross-border traffic, as prospective claimants in the United States will now need to employ a smuggler to enter Canada.

The more dramatic geographical dimension of the agreement is its application *only to the land border* between Canada and the United States, not to airport, ferry terminals, or inland offices that receive asylum claims. Hence, the challenge for prospective claimants is how to access these application points, while avoiding the official land border crossings. The agreement, created as one piece of a broader security agenda, is likely to generate greater insecurity along the U.S.-Canada border as transnational smuggling outfits capitalize on passengers wishing to reach strategic access points to Canada's refugee determination system by whatever means possible. There is little question that the agreement acts as an invisible but restrictive wall to keep refugee claims and claimants out: during the first six months of implementation, refugee claims made to Canadian ports of entry along the land border declined by 50 percent.[10] Tighter visa regulations on citizens of countries that produce large numbers of asylum seekers are also in place in Canada and the United States. These extra-territorial measures exclude migrants before they land in Canada or the United States. As border enforcement becomes more harmonized in North America, acceptance rates for asylum claims in both Canada and the United States have also fallen since 2001. The United States registered a 49 percent approval rate in 2002, down from 57 percent in 2001. Likewise, Canada's approval rate fell to 44 percent from 58 percent in 2001. Acceptance rates in both countries dropped even further in 2004.

Former Minister of Citizenship and Immigration Canada, Denis Coderre, explained that the agreement would curb asylum shopping and abuse of the refugee determination system in a humanitarian manner. "Canada and the United States have the same commitment to refugee protection and the same international obligations."[11] The United States and Canada do not, however, share the same policies and practices for determining refugee claims nor do they have the same outcomes in terms of who gets in. Refugee claimants themselves reject this argument by "voting with their feet." Canada receives far more asylum seekers moving north from the United States than does the United States receive those traveling south. In 2001, Canada received 13,497 refugee claimants from U.S. territory. The reverse rate is estimated at a "few hundred" per year.[12] Substantial differences in Canadian and U.S. asylum jurisprudence, policy, and practice mean that the effects of the agreement are likely to be differentiated along lines of gender, sexuality, nationality, race, and class.[13] For example, jurisprudence and the hearings process for refugee claims based on gender-related persecution and sexual minority status vary widely between the United States and Canada. A broader interpretation of persecution in Canada translates into a greater likelihood that claims based on homosexuality and domestic violence will be accepted.

The United States was, to employ another example, not safe for Maher Arar, a Syrian-born Canadian who was deported to Syria by the United States to face a year of imprisonment and torture. He was not a refugee claimant but a Canadian citizen, yet was refused passage from JFK airport in New York en route with his family to his home in Ottawa. He was instead sent to his country of birth where he had not visited in more than a decade, a place in which he had not completed military service and would therefore be detained by authorities. This raises the question of safety for those without the protection of the Canadian Government who find themselves in the United States.

The U.S. refugee program has also been shaped by foreign policy and national security concerns to the detriment of asylum seekers. The cold war period was characterized by U.S. admissions policies favoring migrants escaping communist rule, while finding ineligible those who originated from countries allied with the United States.[14] In relation to Central American migrants for example, acceptance rates for asylum seekers from Nicaragua have been far higher than for their Guatemalan and Salvadoran counterparts. Refugee policy in the United States has long been tied to ad hoc foreign policy objectives,[15] whereas Canadian policy is more an expression of obligations under international refugee law. In terms of 2003 adjudication patterns, Canada's overall acceptance rate for refugees was slightly higher than that of the United States, 41 percent versus 37 percent. For Colombians fleeing a four decade old civil war, however, it was 81 percent in Canada versus 36 percent in the United States.[16]

Canada is geographically distant from most of the world's current refugee-producing countries. It shares a land border only with the United States, and has relatively few air links compared to its southern neighbor. Geography can thus act as a major deterrent to refugees seeking protection on Canadian territory. The Agreement, along with other restrictive measures designed to thwart the arrival of asylum seekers, conveniently exploits Canada's geography to lessen the perceived burden of receiving refugees.[17] This agreement is but one of many that together fortify borders and acts of sovereignty through exclusion.

Transnationalization of the Border

In somewhat quieter fashion, states are also fortifying walls abroad vis-à-vis the extension of borders into nonsovereign, noncontiguous territories. By pushing policing and interdiction farther afield, nation-states operate in ambiguous locales where the legal status of persons being detained or processed remains unclear. These are spaces that are stateless by geographical design, characterized not by the absence of the state, but by the assignment of degrees of statelessness to those who occupy such spaces.[18] Like safe third country agreements, the spatial tactics associated with this trend to push would-be refugee claimants away from sovereign territory curb access to the rights that accompany landing. Three such strategies include the intensification of interdiction abroad, the practices of detaining and processing refugee claimants in remote locales (either within or beyond sovereign territory), and the creation of stateless spaces in airports. Mapping the contours of this trend in these three forms, each located successively closer to sovereign territory, reveals an extended pattern of control.

In their efforts to fortify state security and regulate undocumented migration, therefore, receiving states are transnationalizing the border. Some tactics are more reactive, including detention and expedited removal.[19] Other spatial devices are more proactive, such as diverting ships to nonterritorial islands to prevent migrants from reaching sovereign territory, creating stricter requirements for transit visas, imposing carrier sanctions on commercial companies that transport migrants with false documents, training airport and border personnel to profile migrants, strengthening border security systems, entering safe third country agreements,[20] and implementing protection in regions of origin.[21] Stateless spaces render people legally and literally out of place vis-à-vis these practices of exclusion. The strategic use of geography to suppress smuggling and to diminish state commitments to protection is central to each of these enforcement tactics.

States have become particularly creative in their interdiction practices abroad and have enhanced these measures in times of crisis. In a post-9/11 security context, such strategies correspond increasingly with the discourse of leaky borders and fears of terrorist threats. States extend their reach into ambiguous extra-territorial locales by sending civil servants abroad. The exercise of sovereignty is thus changed through the emergence of a global constellation of formal and informal enforcement practices for migrants. Airline liaison officers and immigration control officers police so-called hot spots construed as crisis points where human smugglers recruit and traffic clientele. Held in remote geographic locations, migrants often face restricted access to asylum programs. As such, geography is structured creatively to grant only partial access.

States are not only interdicting but increasingly also detaining and processing migrants abroad. In the case of the EU proposal to process all asylum seekers closer to regions of origin, EU interior and justice ministers debated five processing centers to be set up in Libya, Tunisia, Algeria, Morocco, and Mauritania. The uninterrupted stretch of North African shoreline from the border of Côte d'Ivoire and Mauritania in the West to the eastern border of Libya where it meets Egypt provides a convenient catchment area for processing asylum seekers before they arrive in the EU. The proposed geography of asylum would enable off-shore processing directly south of the EU.

This is not a new strategy. In 2002 Britain proposed transit sites—or "international asylum centres" —in Albania, Croatia, Iran, Morocco, northern Somalia, Romania, Russia, Turkey, and the Ukraine for asylum seekers.[22] Across the Atlantic, the United States has long used Guantánamo Bay—a U.S. naval base leased from Cuba—as an off-shore site for asylum processing, and now for interrogating alleged terrorists, known as "enemy combatants." Such terminology conveniently avoids calling detainees prisoners of war under humanitarian law that would furnish minimal legal safeguards.

The Australian government has led the way in what may be the most original yet retrograde means of repelling and excluding asylum seekers from its shores. In 2001 the Australian government began enacting what has come to be known as "the Pacific Solution." (Figure 5.2) At that time, Prime Minister John Howard's government won an election on the issue of border protection after he refused to let the Norwegian ship, The Tampa, dock in Australia after its crew had rescued 433 asylum seekers from a sinking transit ship off Western Australia.[23] The Iraqi and Afghan asylum seekers onboard The Tampa were instead diverted to Christmas Island and other relatively poor South Pacific islands, such as Nauru. Nauru was promised significant Australian foreign aid in return for accepting asylum seekers. This offer raises the issue of whether one's refugee protection obligations codified in international and domestic legislation can be traded with other nations in exchange for aid, loans, or promises of foreign investment, just as governments trade carbon dioxide emissions.

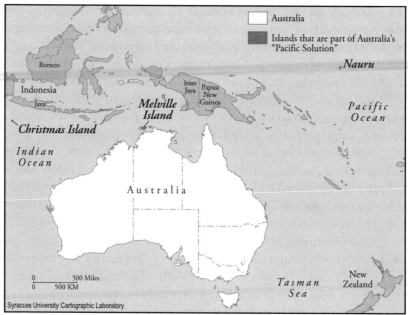

Australia's "Pacific Solution"

Figure 5.2

In November 2003, the arrival of fourteen Kurds in an unsafe Indonesian fishing boat seeking asylum on Melville Island, part of Australia's north coast, drew an unprecedented response. The Howard government voted quickly to separate Melville Island—and four thousand other islands—from Australia for migration purposes. Furthermore, the new law was *retroactive,* excluding the Kurds from claiming refugee status. This legislation contradicts Australia's obligations under the 1951 Convention. Refugee protection under international law is thus being undermined by the national legislation of signatories like Australia.

Stateless spaces come into being when governments perceive, capitalize on, or construct conditions of crisis at which point civil servants activate networks and policymakers and legislators ease the sharing of information, alter legislation, and take other drastic measures in the name of security. Remote interdiction and detention and safe third country provisions each attempt to fix migrants in space: to dwell on points of transit as though a flow might easily be stopped if refugee claimants and those who are merely *potential* refugee claimants could be held closer to their regions of origin.

Another tactic that dwells on sites of transit entails the design of stateless rooms in airports. Stateless rooms are cropping up all over Europe as frontline immigration officers isolate migrants in place either before they exit the airplanes carrying them to their destinations, by demanding their documents while on the aircraft, or once they have entered airports. Through careful microgeographic articulation, spaces within airports are produced as nonsovereign. On a global scale, those seeking asylum and those seeking work are increasingly finding themselves lost in this new policy; in Augé's nonplaces, the spaces between states.[24] In London's Heathrow International Airport, Paris's Charles de Gaulle's International Airport, and in smaller airports across Europe, civil servants from refugee-receiving countries work the "international zones." Like the military bases of Guantánamo Bay and Woomera, these zones are not yet France, not yet the United Kingdom, but ambiguous sites that are neither here nor there.[25] These are paradoxical locales: simultaneously included and excluded, at once England and not-England. Those geographical struggles that occur within sovereign territory correspond with the extra-territorial strategies detailed earlier. The refugee crisis moves into sovereign territory, which in turn is converted to nonsovereign territory.

Detention in remote camps in the Australian outback has been a major deterrent for those seeking refugee status, many of whom protested against the conditions of captivity at centers like Woomera and Baxter by stitching their lips closed. Likewise, in the United States, undocumented migrants are held in small numbers in county jails where they quietly await deportation.[26] As we connect the movement of policing abroad to new, more remote policing and detention practices at home, the reterritorialization of state practices emerges. The cumulative, collective effect of these strategies harkens a powerful, proactive, transnational set of state practices wherein civil servants extend the web of enforcement with each step farther away from—and simultaneously deeper into—sovereign territory. By isolating migrants in remote locations, states restrict access to territories where they might make refugee claims or take up residency illegally.

Articulated sequentially, these trends suggest an exclusionary series of maneuvers on the part of nation-states to exercise control. Agamben argues that the conditions of crisis at work in ambiguous geographical locales—states of exception—ultimately become the rule by the extension of their power over the entire population. Guantánamo Bay and Woomera were militarized, not-national, contested sites long before they came to house refugee claimants remotely where advocacy and legal recourse remained unclear. Stateless rooms in airports represent the mobilization of these in-between points of transit within sovereign territory, into space that is at once sovereign and not sovereign; once sovereign, and now not sovereign.

Refuge or Refusal?

So why have we pulled together these geographical trends of fortress-building and statelessness, and what sense can we make of them? We decided to co-author this essay as a result of the alarming correspondence between trends that we were studying simultaneously from somewhat distinct locales. Our separate research excursions into safe third country agreements and stateless spaces dovetail and raise alarming questions about states' Janus-faced approach to asylum seekers: acknowledging international legal commitments but generating nonsovereign spaces of exception to them. Those fleeing spaces of political violence in their home countries are consistently conflated with those who represent a security threat elsewhere, creating new spaces of political violence in the form of exclusion, detention, and the suspension of civil and human rights.

While violent conflict in Iraq, Afghanistan, Gaza, and the Sudan displaces thousands and the news shrieks across the airwaves of the Western world, a quieter, geographically more distant and dispersed war against refugees is taking place. It is the silent nature of these conflicts that we find most troubling: that these phenomena remain quiet to those citizens on whose behalf states are presumably acting, that they remain quiet among those protesting the world's more publicized wars. It is also misleading to frame these changes as "war" because it is precisely their coming into being in a mode rather unlike war, but instead beneath the radar, that is cause for alarm. Potential refugees suffer as the public is distracted by more pressing, more overtly violent wars in Iraq.

Why do these silences persist? To be sure, the conflation of categories of people on the move has confused refugee issues. Refugees are conflated with terrorists; economic migrants with refugees. Most researchers agree that collectively, the population that employs smugglers comprises what are referred to as "mixed flows" of economically and politically motivated refugees. These mixed flows contribute to the conflation of refugees with economic migrants. Furthermore, public discourse about refugees has been so influenced by the discourse on security and border enforcement that it has grown increasingly difficult in the years that followed the terrorist attacks of 2001 for refugees to reach sovereign territory, and for anyone to advocate on their behalf. James Scott argues that state practices are enacted most effectively in the locales where they face the least resistance.[27] Such is the case in the remote sites of detention and processing and in the more dynamic sites of interdiction where the journeys of potential refugees are abruptly truncated.

Collectively, the state practices outlined in this chapter suggest the stance of a body at war with migrants. People in search of protection and those who advocate on their behalf feel that they too are at war. The current "war on terror"—promulgated by the United States and extended to Iraq with the assistance of a small "coalition of the willing"—only added momentum to these trends and may perhaps serve as a retrofitted explanatory narrative for the outrageous geographies of exclusion being produced. The rise in anti-immigrant and anti-refugee discourse preceded the terrorist attacks in the United States in 2001, as did attempts to harmonize the Canada-U.S. border, as did the deployment of immigration control officers abroad.

We do not employ the term "war" lightly. But this particular war remains silent not only because of the pitch and dimension of other wars, but because of its geography. And this geography lies, fundamentally, at the centre of the reconfiguration of states. Central to this reconfiguration is the state of exception which is making it possible to disembody "the refugee" in public discourse and, in corresponding fashion, to erase the refugee from the immigrant-receiving Western state.

With small strategies implemented by small numbers of people backed by large legislative shifts, states are rewriting the geography of their relationships with potential refugees in daily practice and underscoring these geographical moves with legal weight. Australia legislated excision of some four thousand islands that constitute its sovereign territory *for the purposes of migration*. How could a state's exceptional space—that of not-Australia—be any clearer?

This geographic war also remains silent because of the embeddedness of crisis conditions and the articulation of the "irregular," undifferentiated migrant in public discourse. Wealthier states tighten control over entry in order to keep irregular migrants at bay. What, other than the state of exception, is the irregular migrant? Alternatively stated, who—exactly—is imagined to be the normalized, "regular" migrant who crosses borders during optimal conditions? This is the migrant whose mobility the state facilitates in an orderly fashion. But only a handful of the wealthy destination countries have immigration programs for "regular" migrants. Many make space for a small number of refugees in keeping with their international obligations under the Convention and Protocol, but do little more to add others to their societal mix. As migrants and refugees exercise their own agency to move among economically disparate regions of the world, anti-immigrant and anti-refugee sentiments sharpen in public dialogue in the United States, England, and Australia through the criminalization of migrants and refugees in popular media. It is the conflation of discourse with geography that enables the noisy crisis of the war on terror to become the normative, quieter war on refugees.

The contemporary geography of refugees corresponds with Giorgio Agamben's state of exception, wherein the state of crisis becomes the norm. Building on Agamben's work, Prem Kumar Rajaram and Carl Grundy-Warr argue that the placement of Australian islands outside of its migration zone "has effectively placed the entire Australian nation-state outside the migration zone" (2004, 47). This erasure of the figure of the refugee vis-à-vis the blurred expansion of sovereign territory makes possible Agamben's state of exception through geography.

Geopolitical Failures: Containing Human Displacement

The question remains how to activate a culture of resistance in light of daily developments to wall off Europe, North America, and Australia from migrant "invasions" and how to repatriate the stateless spaces that create legal limbo for migrants. Zygmunt Bauman reminds us that "there are no local solutions to global problems."[28] Containment as a strategy of managing forced migration does not work. Throughout the 1990s, donor governments and their UN counterparts tried a number of experiments to assist people displaced by conflict in their home countries, keeping them literally within the conflict zones that dispossessed them of their livelihoods. This set of tactics was neatly packaged by the UN refugee agency as a refrain on the "right to return" [home] through "preventive protection." Preventive protection and preemptive security measures to protect the state, such as those espoused by the United States after 9/11, are not so different. Both are part of a realist geopolitical framework that needs to be systematically analyzed for its logical and political shortcomings.

The record of "safe havens" as safe spaces for people who are in their home countries but displaced by conflict, violence, and/or persecution is mixed. While UN Operation Salaam into Northern Iraq after the first Gulf War was arguably a success, it was succeeded by a number of less effective 'zones of protection' in Somalia, Rwanda, and Bosnia-Herzegovina. The establishment of safe cities inside the borders of Bosnia between 1992 and 1995 was at best a crisis measure that precipitated more harm than good when the countryside was ethnically cleansed. In July 1995 the lesson of slaughter in Srebrenica was both tragic and instructive: despite the presence of Dutch peacekeepers under UN auspices, more than seven thousand boys and men were killed in this designated "safe city." Militarized sanctuaries are precarious at best.

The current euphemism, "protection in the region," is little more than an extension of this containment strategy. To protect people forced to flee their homes inside conflict zones or in camps situated in poor adjacent countries is simply conventional geopolitical practice where the self-interest of states shapes asylum policy and migration management. Where protection in the region is untenable, as in the case of Kosovo, reluctant temporary protection has become increasingly common. Of course, such temporary solutions are explained by precisely the state of exception that Agamben finds central to the sovereign policing of the modern-state. Like their corresponding policies, these geographies are not necessarily designed to last, but somehow they do.

"Refugee warehousing," another expression of protection in the region, refers to the long-term residence of displaced persons in camps outside their home countries.[29] The issue is a pressing one for the UN refugee agency when donors tire of funding such arrangements. Somali refugees in Kenyan camps; Palestinians in Syria and Lebanon; Afghans in Iran and Pakistan—all represent chronic, long-term displacement in camp-like conditions. Such camps are always only temporary solutions in the mandates and policies of UN agencies and their member states, yet camps often persist for ten years or longer, particularly in the developing countries close to conflict. During the 1990s the world experienced more violent civil wars than ever before. Forty-four countries, or 25 percent of the world's states, were at war, generating human displacement both within national borders and across international boundaries. The median length of civil conflicts is now eight years, which means that many refugees fleeing persecution or violence may be displaced from their home countries for a decade or more.

Camps do not represent a "durable solution," to borrow the United Nations rhetoric that describes three permanent solutions to camp life and refugee status more generally: (1) voluntary repatriation (if political/security circumstances allow); (2) local integration into the country in which the camp is situated (if the host government will oblige); or (3) resettlement to a safe third country, normally to the United States, Canada, Australia, New Zealand, or one of several European, especially Nordic, states. In the absence of options one and two, option three will remain the highly sought after, if largely illusory, geography for people who are otherwise "out of place." As Agamben and others remind us, the state of emergency or exception that camps represent is almost always justified by its "temporariness."[30] "Refugees... are a sitting target for unloading the surplus anguish."[31] In camps, refugees are at least a contained problem. The closer they get to the borders of North America, Europe, and Australia, the less sympathetic governments in these countries become, revealing a geo-optics of asylum that parallels a geopolitics of containment.

Migration as a Security Strategy: Absent or Present?

Migration and refugee flows always highlight the contradictory, even ahistorical projects of states. Politicians, demographers, economists, and law enforcement authorities alike laud some migrants while deploring others, often in an effort to resolve or advance the social dilemmas and agendas of the day. Like border harmonization projects in North America, "Fortress Europe" was under construction long before

9/11, strengthening the perimeter of the continent whilst dissolving its internal borders. As in Canada and the United States, EU member states struggled to mitigate the irruption of their colonial pasts and strengthen national security measures whilst importing immigrants to fill niches in the labor market and build a dwindling population at large.

Jan Karlsson, co-chair of the Global Commission on International Migration, recently highlighted a radical reality: Europe needs between 50 and 70 million migrants for labor market purposes over the next twenty years. He laments that politicians rarely discuss such demands or support higher levels of immigration for fear of losing political support.[32] Demetrious Papendemetriou, President of the Migration Policy Institute, a Washington, DC think tank, added that the United States has 10 million undocumented migrants working in its midst without whom American prosperity would suffer. Yet the militarization of the U.S.-Mexico border continues unabated, while the U.S.-Canada border also becomes less porous.[33]

As we write this chapter, Spain has publicly admitted its need for more migrant labor.[34] It has the lowest birthrate in Europe; as its prosperity grows, fewer people are willing to do manual labor. The new Socialist government has proposed offering amnesty to those undocumented migrants who can prove they have held jobs during the past year. Nonetheless, Spain is under pressure from the rest of Europe to invest heavily in patrol boats, helicopters, night-vision scopes, and heat-seeking cameras to monitor the Strait of Gibraltar, a major crossing point for migrants from Africa. One might ask how to distinguish those fleeing persecution and violence from those seeking employment. Spain has an international obligation to the former and an economic need for the latter. A better question would be how to administer these mixed migration flows given the needs of the nation-state? The public is more likely to support controlled, legal migration over what appears to be disorderly, undocumented migration. In the absence of legal avenues to move, however, migrants will take more clandestine routes.

While beyond the scope of this chapter, one aim of engaged research must be to test unfounded assumptions; prove that migration is not synonymous with terrorism and insecurity; and persuade the public of this. "[W]hat is really striking about our present predicament is not the deployment of knowledge in the service of power, but quite the reverse: the strategic uses of ignorance as a weapon of warfare."[35] The criminalization of migrants, specifically the category of asylum seeker, is a case in point: "the bodies of asylum seekers and refugees are the very media through which the 'war on terror' is normalized into the 'the war at home.'"[36] And yet ironically, the state of exception that governments employ to exclude, detain, and deport make it possible to disembody "the refugee" in public discourse. There is no question that refugee claimants represent mixed flows, that is, a mix of both *bona fide* and not-so-genuine refugees. Nonetheless, the rendering of the asylum seeker as dangerous to society or a threat to state security has become commonplace in dominant media and government discourse on migration; it is deemed better to exclude just in case than to risk and be sorry.

The pilot processing camps proposed by the EU are acute expressions of defensive sovereignties and the securitization of migration on the part of several member states. The camps constitute quasi-legal spaces of exception premised on extraterritorial practices of interception. Australia, by excising its four thousand islands, has created the most obvious exceptions to the rule of law, forcing Nauru, New Zealand, and Indonesia to pick up the pieces. The North American Safe Third Country Agreement represents a different architecture of enmity, a fortification to exclude the dangerous other whose exclusion fortifies the sovereignty of the states involved. But the exception is at work at home too, where migrants sit in detention in the United States following drastic changes that consolidate federal power with the Department of Homeland Security, enable expedited repatriation, and affect *all* noncitizen residents.

This defensive posture of refusing entry "signals no new strategy regarding the refugee phenomenon—but the *absence of strategy*.... they [refugees] are prime targets on which the anguish generated by the suddenly revealed 'personal safety' aspect of existential insecurity can be condensed, unloaded and dispersed."[37] Such patterns and politics of exclusion will continue to produce images of the menacing other and the migrant-as-security-breach, and embolden efforts to wall off wealthy countries from poorer ones. We have delineated an architecture of enmity and state tactics that render undocumented migrants and refugee claimants "out of place." Ad hoc measures performed in the name of state security can no longer be construed as an absence of strategy, but rather as a strategic presence: exceptions that violate human security.

Acknowledgments

Part of this chapter was written at the Helen Riaboff Whiteley Center in Friday Harbor, Washington. The support and hospitality of the center and its staff were most appreciated.

Notes

1. Giorgio Agamben, *Homo Sacer: Sovereign Power and Bare Life,* translated by D. Heller-Roazen (Stanford, CA: Stanford University Press, 1988), 174.
2. Julie Dempsey, "EU to study transit sites in Libya for immigrants," *International Herald Tribune,* p. 1, September 24.
3. Dempsey, *International Herald Tribune,* 1.
4. Derek Gregory, *The Colonial Present* (Oxford: Blackwell, 2004), 20; cf Michael Shapiro, *Cartographies of Struggle: Mapping Cultures of War* (Minneapolis: University of Minnesota Press, 1996)
5. Neil Smith, *The New Urban Frontier* (London and New York: Routledge, 1996).
6. Robyn Lui, "Governing Refugees," *e-borderlands journal,* available at http://www.borderlandsejournal.adelaide.edu.au/vol1no1_2002/lui_governing.html.
7. Max Weber, *Politics as a Vocation,* trans. by H. H. Gerth and C. Wright Mills (Philadelphia: Fortress Press, 1968, c1965).
8. Zygmunt Bauman, "Reconnaissance Wars of the Planetary Frontierland," *Theory, Society & Culture* 19(4): 81–90: 82, 2002.
9. S. H. Legomsky, "Secondary Refugee Movements and the Return of Asylum Seekers to Third Countries: The Meaning of Effective Protection," *International Journal of Refugee Law* 15(4): 567–677 (2003).

10. Canadian Council for Refugees. "Closing the Front Door on Refugees: Report on Safe Third Country Agreement 6 months after implementation," available at http://www.web.net/~ccr/closingdoor.pdf, August 2005.

11. Citizenship and Immigration Canada. "News Release: Minister Coderre Seeks Government Approval of Safe Third Country Agreement", available at http://www.cic.gc.ca/english/press/02/0226%2Dpre.html, 2002.

12. David Matas, "Safe at Third?," RIIM paper #03-05 (2003) in Commentary Series, available at http://www.riim.metropolis.net/frameset_e.html.

13. Robert Lidstone, "Geography as Deterrent: The Canada-United States Safe Third Country Agreement and Declining Refugee Protection in Canada," unpublished manuscript, Department of Geography, Simon Fraser University, 2005.

14. L. Hassan, "Deterrence Measures and the Preservation of Asylum in the United Kingdom and United States," *Journal of Refugee Studies* 13 (2), 184–204.

15. See Douglas Massey, Jorge Durand, and Nancy Malone, *Beyond Smoke and Mirrors: Mexican Immigration in an Era of Economic Integration* (New York: Russell Sage Foundation, 2002).

16. Marina Jimenez, "Last-ditch Bid for Canada's 'Wide Open Spaces'," *The Globe and Mail*, 21 December, 2004.

17. Lidstone, "Geography as Deterrent."

18. Alison Mountz, "Stateless Spaces: Refugees, Irregular Migrants, and the Shifting Geography of Enforcement," *International Migration Review* (forthcoming).

19. Michael McBride, "Migrants and Asylum Seekers: Policy Responses in the United States to Immigrants and Refugees from Central American and the Caribbean," *International Migration* 37(1): 289–317: 30.

20. Audrey Macklin, "The Value(s) of the Canada-US Safe Third Country Agreement," Caledon Institute of Social Policy (2004) available at http://ssrn.com/abstract=557005; Jennifer Hyndman, "Securing States or Refugees? The Canada-US Safe Third Country Agreement" Conference of the Canadian Association of Geographers, Moncton, May, 2004.

21. Canadian Council for Refugees, "Impacts of the Current Canadian Border Policy" available at http://www.web.net/~ccr/borderimpacts.html.

22. Human Rights Watch, "An Unjust 'Vision' for Europe's Refugees," June 17, 2003, available at http://hrw.org/backgrounder/refugees/uk.

23. Graeme Hugo, "From compassion to compliance? Trends in refugee and humanitarian migration in Australia," *GeoJournal* 55: 27–37; Suvendrini Perera, "What is a Camp...?" *e-borderlands journal* vol. 1, no. 1 (2002), available at http://www.borderlandsejournal.adelaide.edu.au/vol1no1_2002/perera_camp.html.

24. Marc Augé, *Non-Places: Introduction to an Anthropology of Supermodernity* (London and New York: Verso, 1995).

25. Perera, "What is a Camp...?"

26. Mark Dow, *American Gulag: Inside US Immigration Prisons* (Berkeley and Los Angeles: University of California Press, 2004).

27. James C. Scott, *Seeing Like a State: How Certain Schemes to Improve the Human Condition Have Failed* (New Haven, CT and London: Yale University Press, 1998).

28. Bauman, "Reconnaissance Wars of the Planetary Frontierland," 84.

29. Merrill Smith, "Warehousing Refugees: a denial of rights, a waste of humanity," *World Refugee Survey 2004*, Washington, D.C.: Immigrant and Refugee Services of America, 2004.

30. Agamben, *Homo Sacer: Sovereign Power and Bare Life,* 18; Gregory, *The Colonial Present*, chapter 7.
31. Bauman, "Reconnaissance Wars of the Planetary Frontierland," 85.
32. Jan Karlsson, "The emerging migration-management paradigm," Ninth International Metropolis Conference, Geneva, September 28, 2004
33. Demetrious Papademetriou, "Amnesties and regularization programs: what has been learned over the last twenty years," Ninth International Metropolis Conference, Geneva, October 1, 2004.
34. Marlise Simons, "Under Pressure, Spain Tries to Close and Open Door," *The New York Times,* October 10, 2004.
35. Felix Driver, "Editorial: the geopolitics of knowledge and ignorance," *Transactions of the Institute of British Geographers* 28: 131–132.
36. Perera, "What is a Camp...?"
37. Bauman, "Reconnaissance Wars of the Planetary Frontierland," 8.

6

Imperialism Imposed and Invited
The "War on Terror" Comes to Southeast Asia
Jim Glassman

Introduction

The Bush administration's response to the catastrophic loss of life in the terrorist attacks of September 11, 2001 has been nothing short of catastrophic. The loss of civilian life in the U.S. attack on Afghanistan that followed exceeded the loss of life on 9/11, and the subsequent use of 9/11 as an implied pretext for the removal of Saddam Hussein's regime and the U.S. occupation of Iraq has led to yet greater numbers of civilian dead, along with dangerous instabilities throughout the Middle East. Moreover, the effects of 9/11 and the U.S. response to it have not been confined to the Middle East and Central Asia but have rippled to other corners of the world, indicating the deeply interconnected character of contemporary geopolitical economic processes and the continuing, enormous impact of U.S. foreign policy in the era of "globalization."[1]

This centrality of U.S. foreign policy ventures to the lives of people around the world is, of course, nothing new, and some have argued that the U.S. response to 9/11 looks as if it might mark the beginning of the end of an era in which the U.S. government was able to exercise unquestioned imperial leadership—at least within the capitalist world.[2] Yet in another sense, the events that have followed 9/11 manifest a tenacity to U.S. imperial power in which the remnants of U.S. hegemony are deployed in still meaningful—if ultimately antediluvian—fashion.

U.S. policies in Southeast Asia illustrate perhaps better than policies anywhere else in the world this complex process of decay. Southeast Asia was once the scene of perhaps the most intensive—and portentious—U.S. imperial venture of the twentieth century, the Vietnam War. The subsequent U.S. withdrawal of troops from Vietnam was followed by an economic transformation that brought the majority of former Southeast Asian allies more fully under the sway of Japanese and Chinese capitalists. The loss in 1992 of rights to the Clark Air Field and Subic Bay Naval Base in the Philippines seemed to place an exclamation mark at the end of the sentence proclaiming the demise of U.S. hegemony in this corner of the world.

Yet post-9/11 events have seen a significant, if strained and contested, revival of the U.S. imperial project in Southeast Asia, a revival threatening interconnected processes of democratization and demilitarization in the region. These processes of democratization and demilitarization, as I will show, have arguably been kicked into reverse through a U.S. attempt to refurbish hegemony in Southeast Asia. The fact of this reversal is itself testimony to the continued influence of U.S. foreign policy in world affairs and thus to the fact of continuing imperial power. But, on the other hand, the ways in which that imperial power has been exercised manifest both its limits and the ways in which local realities, upon which imperial power is imposed, are shaping the decay of U.S. hegemony.

In this chapter, more specifically, I argue that the Bush administration's post-9/11 ventures in Southeast Asia are anchored in a project that is entirely distinct from the terrorist attacks of 9/11 or its agents and are thus being imposed in a fashion that reflects more about U.S. imperial ambitions than about terrorist organizations within the region. Yet this U.S. imposition depends in part upon the opportunistic cooperation of various Southeast Asian elites in packaging locally-rooted conflicts as exemplars of the global terrorist threat in order to take advantage of the climate created by the U.S. response to 9/11.

This interaction of U.S. and Southeast Asian elite ambitions produces a complex, heterogeneous geography of conflict on the ground in Southeast Asia, one that illustrates well the challenges of the U.S. attempt to reconstruct hegemony. I will explain this heterogeneity by noting the distinctive ways in which U.S. imperialism is being mediated by the contexts of social struggle in the Philippines, Indonesia, and Thailand.

The Philippines: Military Machinations and Neocolonial Residues

Shortly after 9/11, U.S. government officials announced that the Abu Sayyaf Group (ASG)—operators of a terrorist racket on the southern Philippine island of Basilan, just southwest of Mindanao—had links to al-Qaeda and would become a focus of U.S. global anti-terrorism efforts. Prior to this, ASG had primarily gained media exposure through small-scale violent acts such as kidnapping for ransom, and occasional execution of, Catholic priests and foreign tourists.

To understand the strains involved in portraying ASG as a threat requiring massive deployment of military force to the region—as well as to understand some of the strange political and military contortions that were to follow this deployment—it is necessary to note briefly the historical geography of social struggles in the southern Philippines. Long the most Islamized region of the Philippines, and also the region with some of the highest levels of poverty (in spite of significant natural resources), the region has also been the most distant from Manila's rulers (be they Spanish, American, or Filippino) and the one most susceptible to separatist struggles.[3]

The most recent phase of struggle in the south developed at the same time leftist activity against the Marcos dictatorship was rising, with the formation of the Moro National Liberation Front (MNLF) in 1971. A nationalist front, the MNLF has been based in Mindanao and has struggled for greater regional autonomy, based in Islamic identity, within a broader framework of struggle against military dictatorship.[4] While the MNLF is the largest of Mindanao's insurgent groups, and the one with the strongest connections to the Philippine left, the late 1970s saw the emergence of a group more committed to struggle for an Islamic state, the Moro Islamic Liberation Front (MILF).[5] Some MILF members have reportedly received training in al-Qaeda camps in Afghanistan, as well as with Indonesian Islamist groups that received similar training.[6] Yet, like the MNLF, the MILF has an indigenous base of social support in Mindanao and operates independently of these international networks.[7] The MNLF and MILF have constituted the most important regional opposition to leaders in Manila, and, with the fall of the Marcos dictatorship, the 1990s regime of President Fidel Ramos had, in fact, been able to move—if haltingly—towards some resolution of regional conflicts by carrying out negotiations with them.[8]

Against the backdrop of these major political maneuvers, the appearance on the scene of ASG in the early 1990s was a barely-noticed event. In a semi-chaotic context where many different criminal and small-scale terrorist organizations operate alongside (and perhaps sometimes in connection with) insurgents, ASG was seen as little more than a group of bandits—in fact, Philippine President Gloria Macagapal-Arroyo characterized ASG as "a money-crazed gang of criminals" prior to 9/11.[9] Indeed, on the Philippine Left, ASG was widely suspected to have been a creation of the CIA and/or Philippine intelligence, formed to further splinter and undermine the Moro insurgency.

Such views, of course, are not easy to fully substantiate, yet interestingly enough, in this case their plausibility is buttressed precisely by the claims emanating from the U.S. government after 9/11. If ASG is indeed a Philippine extension of al-Qaeda, then its "link" with the CIA is straightforward, since it is well known that the CIA provided training for al-Qaeda operatives in Afghanistan. The possibility, then, that ASG operatives have been known to U.S. and Philippine intelligence since their arrival in Basilan and have been at least tacitly allowed to operate cannot be dismissed.

In addition to this, many local activists and community members in Basilan testify to events that imply Philippine military collaboration with ASG leaders and tolerance of ASG operations.[10] Such accusations were largely the province of the Philippine and international Left until July 2003, when a "mutiny" by Philippine military officers brought to the fore parallel charges from the Right. The mutineers accused senior Philippine military officers of selling weapons to Islamic separatist groups in the south and staging bombings in Davao City so that they could receive more U.S. military assistance in the name of fighting the "war on terror."[11]

Again, such charges are difficult to completely prove or disprove, but what they highlight is something more important to the present argument. Specifically, the extension of the "war on terror" to the southern Philippines has been out of proportion to the actual threat of the insurgent forces in the region and has created a gravy train of military expenditures that encourage corruption at the highest levels of the Philippine government. Indeed, U.S. military aid to the Philippines increased from $2 million in 2001 to $80 million in 2002–03, and the U.S. government pledged a total of $100 million in security assistance to the Philippines after 9/11.[12] Moreover, the response to the supposed ASG threat has included joint military operations that have no clear purpose in relation to the terrorist threat, since the Philippine military itself already has considerable experience in fighting the southern insurgency and doesn't very likely need U.S. troops to assist in a struggle that has not in recent years shown any signs of spinning out of Manila's control.[13]

In this context, the most plausible explanation for expanded U.S. military operations in the Philippines is that 9/11 has provided a convenient pretext for the expansion of operations that are favored on grounds independent of any terrorist threat from groups like ASG. As I will show, in fact, the U.S. military has forthrightly stated its desire for renewed access to the Philippines for reasons that have nothing to do with the struggle in Mindanao. Its ability to gain such access on the basis of the 9/11 pretext is, in part, a function of the U.S. government's continued influence in Manila.[14] Such influence stems in part from colonial and neocolonial legacies, as well as from the ongoing dependence of the Philippine elite—and the minimally successful economy they sit astride—on foreign direct investment from the West and access to U.S. markets (including for labor migration). Yet the role of these elites in endorsing the expansion of joint U.S.-Philippine military exercises cannot be overlooked: 9/11 not only provided U.S. elites with a pretext for reassertion of a neocolonial presence, it also provided Philippine elites who have battled against widespread nationalist sentiment in their own country with the opportunity to sell collaboration with the U.S. government as a project in the national interest.

Indonesia: Sub-Imperial Projects and Regional Military Alliances

In Indonesia, the situation is substantially different from that in the Philippines and has necessitated a different form of engagement between U.S. and Indonesian elites. In particular, there is little possibility for the U.S. military to gain permanent basing rights anywhere in the archipelago, given fierce nationalist opposition to this in Indonesia. The goal then is rather to insure tight and supportive relations between the U.S. military and the Indonesian military (TNI). The fact that most TNI members are Muslim, and that the overwhelming majority of Indonesians are as well, makes the use of post-9/11 rationalizations of U.S. actions as a response to Islamic terrorist threats a much more delicate matter in Indonesia than in the Philippines.

It is against this background that I want to consider the U.S. project of rekindling ties with the TNI while playing up the threat to Indonesia putatively presented by al-Qaeda-connected Jemaah Islamiyah (JI). As with ASG, uncertainty and speculation surrounds JI and the nature of its operations. Indeed, even though JI operatives have been tried in Indonesian courts and found guilty in the October 2002 bombing of a Bali nightclub, there is still suspicion as to the possible involvement of people within the Indonesian military.[15] I do not intend to try to pronounce on such uncertainties, but fortunately there have been detailed reports on JI by the International Crisis Group (ICG). The reports provide a useful picture of aspects of JI's operations, a picture that would substantiate its credentials as a terrorist threat within Indonesia. At the same time, as I will indicate, the reports make it impossible to cast the JI threat in the Manichean and selective terms that are central to the "war on terror." Moreover, the way that the United States and TNI response to the JI threat is being played out conforms less to a legitimate project for undermining JI's influence than to a very different project of the TNI (with backing from the U.S. military) for subduing regional rebellions such as those in Aceh and West Papua.[16]

The ICG's reports on JI make several crucial points. First, JI is not an organization that is unique or has come into existence *de novo*. Rather, JI is part of a broader political Islamist tendency that dates back to the Darul Islam rebellions of the 1950s [17] Second, JI is not merely a terrorist organization created out of al-Qaeda's global aspirations. Indeed, the ICG states unequivocally that "JI is not operating simply as an al-Qaeda subordinate" and that "[v]irtually all of its decision-making and much of its fund-raising has been conducted locally," while its focus "continues to be on establishing an Islamic state in Indonesia."[18] Moreover, as an embedded part of the Indonesian social and political landscape, JI has built itself around Islamic schools that are an integral part of Indonesian culture.[19] Third, precisely because it is embedded in a social and political landscape that is pervasively Islamic, JI is not a simple, unified, or regionalized phenomenon. Since Islam mediates and articulates virtually all political positions taken in Indonesia, the sharing of a broadly Islamist agenda has not resulted in uniformity of opinion among self-identified JI members.[20] Beyond this, even if JI is considered to be a coherent organization with a clear identity, it is scarcely singular or unique, and the ICG reports indicate the existence of a large number of other Islamic Indonesian organizations with overlapping agendas.

Fourth, and finally, just as the ICG reports show that JI is not a distinctive, isolated, or homogeneous organization standing apart from the rest of Indonesian society, they show that JI is by no means a straightforward antagonist of the TNI or Indonesian elites. ICG investigations, in fact, found that JI members have worked on the side of the TNI in its struggle against Acehnese rebels, attempting to woo and utilize defectors from the Acehnese independence movement, Gerakan Aceh Merdeka (GAM).[21]

Moreover, links to the TNI are not exclusive to JI members in Aceh or Sumatra. In Poso and Maluku, TNI has supported the military organization *Laskar Mujahidin*, which has links to the army in Maluku.[22] Furthermore, TNI has regularly cooperated with, and included among its ranks, various *preman* (criminals, thugs), who have connections to government intelligence.[23] Indeed, as ICG reports note, connections to the Indonesian military appear central to JI's operations since these connections allow them access to large caches of weapons.[24] In short, the organization that is being portrayed internationally as the core of an Islamic terrorist threat to Indonesia is not only integrated into Indonesian society (even if not representative of the desires of most Indonesians) but is connected with the very organization now being charged with fighting it, the TNI.

In this context, it is not especially surprising that the "war on terrorism" in Indonesia seems to have shown little in the way of success on the internal security front. Even after the Bali bombing and the increased backing from the U.S. military that this helped legitimize, the TNI has seemingly been unable to curtail high profile terrorist activities, including the August 2003 bombing of the Jakarta Marriott, the September 2004 bombing outside the Australian embassy, and another bombing in Bali in October 2005.

While Indonesian intelligence has not been able to eliminate terrorist activities even under the heightened state of emergency imposed in the "war on terror," the TNI has used national security rhetoric to legitimize stepping up its operations in West Papua, playing on domestic fears about separatism in the wake of East Timor's independence. For example, in November 2001, Indonesian security forces murdered Papuan independence leader Theys Eluay.[25] Subsequently, the TNI sent more troops into the province and reversed many of the slight modifications in policy introduced under the Wahid regime in order to reduce political tensions.[26] During 2003, moreover, TNI actions indicated the continuing will of the Indonesian government to suppress independence forces by any means necessary. For example, according to the Indonesian National Commission on Human Rights, in April, seven West Papuan civilians were killed, forty-eight tortured (with an unspecified number claimed to have been raped), and seven thousand forcibly evacuated from their homes in Wamena, near the border with Papua New Guinea, when Indonesian troops searched the area for weapons allegedly stolen from the TNI by members of the Papuan independence movement.[27]

Meanwhile, the TNI also used national security rhetoric to legitimize waging an intensified war on the GAM. Beginning in May 2003, the TNI launched a "shock and awe" campaign against the GAM and its supporters, sending in thirty thousand troops and another thirteen thousand police and paramilitaries to take on the GAM's five thousand fighters.[28] The campaign continued throughout 2003 and into 2004, with appalling results, including hundreds of civilian casualties, the forced evacuation of at least one hundred thousand people during the first three months of martial law alone, and the burning by Indonesian forces of as many as five hundred schools.[29] In the wake of the devastation caused in Aceh by the December 2004 *tsunami*, moreover, the initial response of the TNI was to continue attacking suspected GAM supporters, even when GAM had honored a cease fire declared in order to facilitate relief operations.[30]

The situation in Aceh, fortunately, was at least temporarily transformed in the months following the *tsunami* by the international attention that attended relief operations, and in August 2005 a peace accord was signed between the GAM and the Indonesian government.[31] Nonetheless, the situation in Indonesia remains deeply shaped at present by the U.S. "war on terror." Moreover, whatever the precise realities of JI's threat to Indonesian security, the "war on terror" has seemingly done little to undermine the possibility of terrorist actions in Indonesia, while at the same time its supportive approach to the TNI has created a climate in which it is easier for the TNI to embark on newly intensified rounds of state terrorism in outlying regions.

Thailand: Accommodation and Renewed Militarism

Thailand's position as a U.S. ally in the "war on terrorism" was solidified after the arrest in Ayutthaya of reputed JI operations leader Hambali, in August 2003, the culmination of a renewed security alliance-building process that took several years. Immediately after 9/11, various senior Thai military officials seemed to be pushing for an escalation of military activities against criminal gangs in predominantly Islamic southern Thailand—in the name of anti-terrorism. Increasingly, these officers have gained the support of Prime Minister Thaksin Shinawatra in approaching southern Thailand as an international terrorism problem, implementing martial law in the South since the middle of 2003 and arresting several Islamic figures on questionable grounds to show commitment to the U.S. agenda for the region.[32] Moreover, military violence in the South greatly intensified during 2004, with the burning of twenty schools by the separatist group "Bersatu" on January 4, the Thai military's slaughter of more than one hundred alleged Islamic separatists on April 28, and the horrendous Tak Bai massacre of October 25, in which more than eighty civilians were killed by the Thai military.[33]

Yet, even with the arrest of Hambali and the intensified militarization of the regional conflict with Islamic groups, Thailand's participation in the "war on terror" has been a hesitant and sometimes indirect undertaking for the current regime, and Thaksin's government appears to have been egged on into participation for some time before the arrest of Hambali, including via promises of a free trade agreement (FTA).[34] Indeed, in spite of substantial prodding from the Bush administration and its close collaboration with U.S. intelligence, Thailand has participated in the "war on terror" more surreptitiously and in a somewhat different fashion than have the Philippine or Indonesian governments.[35]

To understand this form of participation it is necessary to note the orientation of the current regime and the complexities of its relationship with other forces in Thailand. Thaksin's Thai Rak Thai (TRT, Thai Love Thai) party came to power in early 2001 on a populist and putatively "nationalist" platform that has wide support because of the impacts of the economic crisis and the International Monetary Fund (IMF) structural adjustment program imposed by the previous government. During TRT's first year in power, Thaksin's faction consolidated its position and put into place a series of spending measures that modestly boosted the fortunes of some groups hurt by the crisis and the IMF program.[36] Having consolidated his position, Thaksin began during 2002 to reshuffle the governing coalition and to move the party more firmly in the direction of not only his own interests but those of dominant political and economic elites that provide crucial backing for TRT.[37]

Of particular significance in this regard has been the change in relations between TRT and popular organizations that supported it during the election campaign. TRT had made various promises to such organizations, including Thailand's broad umbrella network for popular struggles, the Assembly of the Poor (AOP), and during 2001 relations between TRT and AOP were basically amicable. Yet by 2002 TRT leaders had decided that the AOP and other popular organizations made demands that TRT was unable or unwilling to accommodate, including demands for abandonment of various energy-generating projects such as the Pak Moon dam in Northeast Thailand and a gas pipeline from Malaysia that would run across Southern Thailand. Thus, during 2002 Thaksin asked foreign donors that supported Thai NGOs connected with the AOP to suspend their support, while simultaneously bringing fifty-three former military officers into his cabinet as special advisors on security issues, a warning to popular organizations that state relations with "civil society" groups were returning to their modal, antagonistic orientation.[38] This antagonism was confirmed in violent fashion during December 2002 when police attacked Southern protestors against the Thai-Malaysia gas pipeline during a mobile cabinet ministers meeting in Hat Yai.[39]

Yet Thaksin's actions did not openly invoke terrorist threats of the sort being advertised in the Philippines or Indonesia. Rather, they were couched in fairly conventional rhetoric about the "national interest." What began to give the break with popular organizations more of the aura of the "war on terror," however, was the contemporaneous development—clearly noted by popular organizations for its implications—of another high profile war: TRT's "war on drugs."

In this war, Thaksin aggressively made use of the political atmosphere created by the U.S. "war on terror" and the Homeland Security campaign to weaken sources of opposition to TRT. In late 2002, he announced that the governors of each of Thailand's seventy-six provinces would be required by early 2003 to submit lists with at least thirty suspected drug dealers known to live in their provinces. The stated purpose was to eliminate Thailand's methamphetamine and opium industries, but it also appears that one of the major goals of the campaign was actually to weaken the financial base of some of the provincial political bosses who have long been a thorn in the side of Bangkok-based political leaders.

Whatever the precise reasons for the campaign, it had a bloody outcome. As the governors began putting together their lists, a spate of killings occurred. The government claims that most deaths were cases of one drug dealer killing another to insure that they would not be named by investigators. Some are acknowledged to have been extra-judicial executions of suspected drug dealers by police, and many more such extra-judicial executions may have occurred than are actually acknowledged. Overall, by the time the three-month campaign was completed at the end of March 2003, at least 2,637 people had been killed, leading to condemnation—from both Thai and international organizations—of the Thai government's failure to recognize basic human rights.[40] Thaksin shrugged off such criticism, and, in any event, he could rest assured that no substantive condemnation would issue forth from the U.S. government, given his favorable relationship with the Bush family and given that the Bush administration would be in an especially poor position to criticize an ally for human rights violations. Indeed, though the U.S. State Department did officially raise concerns about Thailand's human rights record during the "war on drugs" as well as in relation to the military campaign in the South, Thaksin has dismissed these concerns without the Bush administration taking any action.[41]

Notably, it was only *after* Thaksin had already reinvigorated the Thai national security state in 2002–2003—for purposes that are clearly his own—that his government began to participate more openly and aggressively in the "war on terror" in the South. This more open participation has no doubt pleased both the U.S. government and Thai military elites who have lobbied for such participation, and whose interests are arguably more directly served than are Thaksin's by the intensification of military activity.[42] It is even possible to conceive of Thai royalists and military leaders as having played U.S. military interests against TRT factions that have been less enthused about military activity in Southern Thailand in order to prod Thaksin into a more overtly aggressive stance. As Duncan McCargo and Ukrist Pathmanand note, the military and royalist networks that had crystallized since the 1980s around former military leader and Prime Minister Prem Tinsulanond found their fortunes in decline relative to those of Thaksin and TRT by 2001.[43] While the Thai military was already cooperating quietly with U.S. "war on terror" activities prior to 2003,[44] the arrest of Hambali and the lure of an FTA created a context in which Thaksin—whether enthusiastically or under pressure—could jump on the "war on terror" bandwagon and more readily silence criticism from within the ranks of TRT supporters.

Whatever the precise dynamics, through its general turn against popular organizations and its re-engagement of a cold war-era style of authoritarian politics, Thaksin and TRT leaders have now placed the Thai government fully within the ranks of the authoritarian states that are part of Washington's anti-terrorism alliance. The purposes of such a shift arguably have had little if anything to do with the terrorist threat announced in Washington, and TRT in fact made little of such a threat before 2003–2004. But the need of elites for an authoritarian state that violates basic civil liberties in the name of the national interest and international security has clearly provided a crucial part of the context in which TRT is able to launch its own "war on terror."

The Bush Administration and Southeast Asia: Fighting Hegemonic Decline

The diverse political landscapes of the Philippines, Indonesia, and Thailand have been rendered uniform places of Islamic terrorist threat in Washington, D.C. through the construction of "the war on terror." Even the rather cursory overview provided here of the divergent interests at work in these places and the less-than-straightforward evidence of a unified Islamic threat should suggest that such rendering is a certain kind of ideological feat. What drives this homogenizing and simplifying performance is something quite other than Islamic terrorism. To understand this, it is important to examine projects of the Bush administration, and of the U.S. government more generally, that were announced long before 9/11.

The basics of the Bush administration's agenda in Southeast Asia were articulated long before 9/11, and in ways illustrating that the project is entirely independent of alleged Islamic terrorist threats. One way to discern this is to scan the Project for a New American Century (PNAC) report, "Rebuilding America's Defenses."[45] PNAC is well-known as a bastion of the sort of neoconservative thinking that has animated the Bush administration's domestic and foreign policies, and has been supported since its inception in the 1990s by well-placed figures such as Dick Cheney, Donald Rumsfeld, Paul Wolfowitz, and the President's brother Jeb. The report on "Rebuilding America's Defenses" was authored by Donald Kagan, Gary Schmitt, and Thomas Donnelly and published in September 2000, before Bush became president.

Basing their arguments on the assumptions that the United States currently has a "historic opportunity" as "the uniquely powerful leader of a coalition of free and prosperous states that faces no immediate great power challenge," yet is inhibited in exercising such leadership by the fact that its "military forces limp towards exhaustion" for lack of governmental commitment, the authors went on to outline a vision for rebuilding the military in ways that would enable the United States to capitalize on this historic opportunity.[46] Crucially, in this vision, the geographic locus of strategic competition has shifted, not to the Middle East but to East Asia.[47]

Expanding on this point, the authors suggested that "despite increasing worries about the rise of China and instability in Southeast Asia, US forces are found almost exclusively in Northeast Asian bases."[48] The authors thus recycled the cold war notion of a threat from China that demands substantial military attention to

Southeast Asia. Consequently, while they asserted the need to maintain U.S. military bases in South Korea and Japan (Okinawa), they also asserted the need for expansion of the U.S. military presence in Southeast Asia, where, they noted, "American forces are too sparse to adequately address rising security requirements, particularly since the withdrawal of its troops from the Philippines in 1992."[49] Moreover, the authors argued, "the East Timor crisis and the larger question of political reform in Indonesia and Malaysia highlight the volatility of the region," which "has long been an area of great interest to China."[50]

Notably absent from the report was any serious analysis of the ways in which China might actually be a threat to regional stability. Furthermore, though mentioning "instability" and "volatility" in Southeast Asia, the PNAC report nowhere made any point of a specifically *Islamic* or *terrorist* threat to regional stability. Rather, in spite of pre-9/11 recognition that political Islamist and terrorist organizations exist throughout the region, the threats foregrounded by the PNAC report were far more conventional, and therefore demanded a fairly conventional U.S. military response—namely, more high-tech weaponry and deployment of large numbers of U.S. troops.

That these PNAC visions of the U.S. role in Southeast Asia were not idiosyncratic can be seen by briefly noting two other, contemporaneous reports, the first, a year 2000 Rand study on China, the second, a mid-2001 Council on Foreign Relations (CFR) study on Southeast Asia. The Rand report, authored by Richard Sokolsky, Angel Rabasa, and C. R. Neu and entitled "The Role of Southeast Asia in US Strategy Toward China," was researched under the auspices of Rand's Project AIR FORCE division and can be taken (like the PNAC report) to represent the thinking of many neoconservatives. The CFR report, authored by an independent CFR task force with twenty-seven members and entitled "The United States and Southeast Asia: A Policy Agenda for the New Administration," can be taken to represent to a greater extent the consensus opinions of both "conservatives" and "liberals" in Washington, DC. Both reports were issued before 9/11 and both converged on similar propositions regarding the need to reorient U.S. foreign policy in East and Southeast Asia.

The Rand study argued that China's "geopolitical ambitions will play a crucial role in shaping the future of Southeast Asia and the US military posture in the region."[51] Yet the report also noted that China has a strong economic interest in maintaining favorable economic relations with Southeast Asian countries and a limited military capacity to seriously threaten those countries at present.[52] In light of this, the main source of a potential direct Chinese military threat to Southeast Asia, as the authors saw it, would be through the gradual escalation of a conflict such as the dispute (primarily with the Philippines) over the Spratly Islands.[53]

Significantly, though the Rand authors did their best to find Southeast Asian voices that stated concern over China and a demand for a U.S.-organized regional security project—fundamentally, by limiting their interview sources to defense ministers and conservative military analysts—their conclusion was rather that most Southeast Asian countries do *not* see China as an immanent and serious military threat and would prefer to engage China's leaders constructively, even with regard to territorial disputes like those over the Spratlys.[54] Nonetheless, by the end of the report, the authors managed to turn what might be a logical inference of limited need for U.S. military presence into an argument that the U.S. military will need to take a leading role in the region and should develop a policy of "congagement" that gradually builds U.S. military forces in the region in such a way as to both constrain Chinese ambitions and prevent its leaders from feeling encircled.[55]

The Rand authors placed a special emphasis on restoring military relations with the Philippines, building on the 1999 Visiting Forces Agreement to bring back naval and air forces, as well as developing stronger military relations with Malaysia, Indonesia, and Singapore.[56] In the case of Indonesia, it was argued that "Indonesia's democratic evolution since the fall of Suharto has opened a window of opportunity for closer military-to-military ties with the Indonesian armed forces (TNI)."[57] Notably, the task of securing U.S. relations with Indonesia was seen to demand that the TNI successfully suppress regional uprisings in places such as Aceh and West Papua, since the separatist movements in these places "threaten to destabilize Indonesia's fragile political transition and perhaps unleash a process of fragmentation."[58] Beyond the major states of insular Southeast Asia, the authors also recommended building broad security alliances throughout the region—what they called a "portfolio approach"—so as to limit the possibility of losing access to military facilities from a change in relationships with any one particular country.[59] As with the PNAC report, the Rand authors placed virtually no emphasis on regional terrorist threats, and internal security matters such as those occupying Indonesia and the Philippines were, in fact, seen as problems that prevented Southeast Asian governments from adopting the kinds of outward-looking military policies the U.S. military would prefer of its allies.[60]

The CFR authors reached remarkably similar conclusions. At the outset, they were concerned that the U.S. government deal with "the aftershocks from the economic crisis and rising political turmoil" that were making for "fractious polities, fragile economies, and a loss of investor confidence" in places such as Indonesia and the Philippines, as well as stimulating an "undercurrent of rising political Islam in the archipelagic countries."[61] Yet despite this brief mention of Islam and internal political turmoil, the major recommendations of the report foregrounded the same kinds of outward-looking security projects as the PNAC and Rand studies. "The highest American priority," the authors stated, "should still be assigned to maintaining regional security through the prevention of intra-regional conflict and domination by an outside power or coalition."[62] The accusing finger, here, pointed rather quickly at China: "The United States should pay close attention to other extraregional actors, carefully monitoring Chinese behavior in Southeast Asia and expanding coordination with Japan and Australia."[63]

The CFR report did highlight other objectives besides containment of China, including promoting "market-oriented economic reform, technology-driven development, and measures for poverty alleviation," as well as more ambitious goals like taking "active steps to promote social stability and the rule of law and to foster an environment that diminishes the forces of ethnic and religious-based separatism and extremism in the region."[64] Yet, in the same breath, the report argued for rekindling the U.S. military's relationship with perhaps the major regional force fanning the flames of ethnic and religious-based separatism: "The United States must cease hectoring Jakarta and instead do its utmost to help stabilize Indonesian democracy and the Indonesian economy, as well as to re-engage Indonesia's army."[65] That these goals might be incompatible was observed in a dissenting opinion written by several of the task force members, but nonetheless the CFR report ended up essentially arguing for a variant of the same project pushed by the neoconservatives: increased U.S. military presence in the region to strengthen U.S. economic opportunities and contain potential Chinese expansion, including through the ever-important project of protecting sea-lanes and shallow-water gas pipelines.[66] As with the Rand study, this demanded taking advantage of the Voluntary Forces Agreement to expand the U.S. military presence in the Philippines and resuming military training and cooperation with the TNI in Indonesia.[67]

In short, then, across the relevant policy spectrum in Washington it is evident that relatively consistent and coherent U.S. imperial objectives for Southeast Asia were articulated well before 9/11 offered an opportunity to hasten their implementation. That these objectives have remained central since 9/11 is both clear from the conduct of U.S. policy and from subsequent policy statements. As to the conduct of policy, among many other activities that could be mentioned, the U.S. government's response to the Indian Ocean *tsunami* shows very clearly the will to re-establish a regional military presence for reasons independent of Islamic terrorism. In the immediate aftermath of the *tsunami,* the Bush administration offered a miserly $35 million in relief aid before being embarrassed into upping the offer. Yet it quickly deployed naval and air forces to the region, including sending ships to Aceh and troops to U-Tapao airbase in Thailand, in the name of providing humanitarian relief.[68] By whatever means available, the U.S. government seems intent on legitimizing a constant expansion of its military presence in Southeast Asia; the pretexts may shift, but the project remains the same.

As to policy statements, a December 2004 policy document issued by the National Intelligence Council (NIC) of the Central Intelligence Agency (CIA) highlights the continued U.S. obsession with a "rising China"—and, in this case, India.[69] The NIC's "Mapping the Global Future" presents four possible scenarios for the world in the year 2020. The first two, corresponding to the issues discussed in the PNAC, Rand, and CFR studies discussed above, are: (1) a more globalized but Asia-centric world in which China and India are increasingly powerful ("Davos World"), and (2) a world in which the United States checks these rising Asian powers ("Pax Americana"). The third scenario is one that foregrounds an Islamic threat—the development of a transnational "New Caliphate." The fourth scenario is international disorder, "Cycle of Fear." Yet the rise of such a transnational Islamic threat is seen largely as transitional and conditional, unlike the challenge presented by China and India that are seen as of longer-term significance. As the NIC report puts it, "The collective feelings of alienation and estrangement which radical Islam draws upon are unlikely to dissipate until the Muslim world again appears to be more fully integrated into the world economy."[70] This seems an altogether less dramatic and earth-shaking scenario than "Davos World": "Rising Asia will continue to reshape globalization, giving it less of a 'Made in the USA' character and more of an Asian look and feel. At the same time, Asia will alter the rules of the globalizing process…Asia looks set to displace Western countries as the focus for international economic dynamism—provided Asia's rapid economic growth continues."[71] A "New Caliphate" may (or may not) be a short-term possibility and an inconvenience as far as the CIA is concerned, but "Davos World" (with an Asian face) is the world-transforming event with which U.S. planners are most concerned.

Conclusion

The "war on terror" has provided an opportunity for U.S. neoconservatives to implement an agenda for Southeast Asia that was agreed upon by U.S. elites across the policy-relevant spectrum since before 9/11. The agenda is that of a challenged imperial power whose hegemony in East and Southeast Asia has been in decline and that hopes to restore that hegemony through re-emphasizing its military capabilities. It is an agenda that is broad and uniform in its basic goals, but given the differing realities on the ground in various areas of Southeast Asia, it has different manifestations, these reflecting among other things the diverse projects of Southeast Asian elites.

In all of the contexts discussed, the immediate impacts seem to have included an increased foothold for authoritarian, militarist politicians and policies, this being reflected in the 2004 electoral victories of Arroyo in the Philippines (a possibly fraudulent victory against a right-wing populist candidate) and Susilo Bambang Yodhoyono (SBY) in Indonesia—SBY having been Megawati Sukarnoputri's head of security for Aceh—within a field of exclusively right-wing Indonesian political parties. Meanwhile, Thaksin's TRT has continued to consolidate its seemingly unassailable position, winning re-election in early 2005, perhaps benefiting from some public support for the idea of cracking down on drug dealers and other threats to "national security." Yet the specifics of particular national campaigns being carried out under the cover of U.S. imperial policy have varied, reflecting specific national and historical contexts as well as the aspirations and activities of particular elite groups and the popular organizations that (in these instances weakly) oppose them.

Insofar as the U.S. "war on terror" legitimizes a general resurrection of the national security state, it offers an opportunity for every elite group in the world to participate in the retrenchment of human rights in the name of the "national interest"—provided the elites in question do not run afoul of Washington.[72] As such, the "war on terror" threatens to have an impact well beyond the direct impact of U.S. military interventions or direct support for local militaries. In Southeast Asia, there is great potential for this unsavory outcome as the United States makes a last ditch effort to reassert its historical position of preeminence against the rise of perceived competitors like China. Certainly, the avoidance of such a dire outcome will depend on the ability of people in the region to collectively resist the latest elite onslaught—including the onslaught of nationalist and national security rhetoric that shields authoritarian actors and their projects from the popular scrutiny they so richly deserve.

Notes

1. Noam Chomsky, *Hegemony or Survival: America's Quest for Global Dominance* (New York: Henry Holt, 2003); Derek Gregory, *The Colonial Present: Afghanistan, Palestine, Iraq* (Oxford: Blackwell, 2004); David Harvey, *The New Imperialism* (Oxford:

Oxford University Press, 2003); Chalmers Johnson, *The Sorrows of Empire: Militarism, Secrecy, and the End of the Republic* (New York: Henry Holt, 2004); Retort, *Afflicted Powers: Capital and Spectacle in a New Age of War* (London and New York: Verso, 2005).

2. Gabriel Kolko, "The coming elections and the future of American global power," *Counter Punch* 12/14 March 2004, available online at http://www.counterpunch.org; Immanuel Wallerstein, *The Decline of American Power* (New York and London: The New Press, 2003).

3. Syed Serajul Islam, "The Islamic Independence Movements in Patani of Thailand and Mindanao of the Philippines," *Asian Survey* 38, 5 (1998): 441–456; James F. Eder and Thomas M. McKenna, "Minorities in the Philippines: Ancestral Lands and Autonomy in Theory and Practice," in Christopher R. Duncan, ed., *Civilizing the Margins: Southeast Asian Government Policies for the Development of Minorities* (Ithaca, NY: Cornell University Press, 2004), 56–85.

4. Lela Noble, "The Muslim Insurgency," in Daniel B. Schirmer and Stephen Rosskamm Shalom (eds), *The Philippines Reader: A History of Colonialism, Neocolonialism, Dictatorship, and Resistance* (Boston: South End Press, 1987), 193–199.

5. Islam 1998, 449–450; Eder and McKenna 2004, 73.

6. International Crisis Group (ICG), "Indonesia Backgrounder: How the *Jemaah Islamiyah* Terrorist Network Operates" (Jakarta/Brussels: ICG, December 11, 2002), available online at http://www.icg.org; International Crisis Group (ICG), "Jemaah Islamiyah in South East Asia: Damaged but Still Dangerous" (Jakarta/Brussels: ICG, August 26, 2003), 6, 16–17, available online at http://www.icg.org.

7. Islam 1998; Lily Zubaidah Rahim, "The Road Less Traveled: Islamic Militancy in Southeast Asia," *Critical Asian Studies* 35, 2 (2003): 209–232.

8. Islam 1998; Eder and McKenna 2004, 74–78.

9. International Peace Mission, "Basilan: The Next Afghanistan?" Report of the International Peace Mission to Basilan, Philippines, March 23–27, 2002, 10, available online at http://www.focusweb.org.

10. International Peace Mission 2002, 15–17; International Solidarity Mission, "Behind the 'Second Front'," unpublished Report of the International Solidarity Mission Against US Armed Intervention in the Philippines, July 24–31, 2002, 24, 27–29.

11. Naomi Klein, "Stark Message of the Mutiny: Is the Philippine government bombing its own people for dollars?" *The Guardian* (UK) August 16, 2003; John Roberts, "Military mutiny in the Philippines: A sign of deeper political tensions," World Socialist Web Site (http://www.wsws.org), July 31, 2003.

12. Klein 2003; William Arkin, *Code Names: Deciphering U.S. Military Plans, Programs, and Operations in the 9/11 World* (Hanover, NH: Steerforth Press, 2005), 184–186.

13. Arkin 2005, 185; International Peace Mission 2002, 1, 17.

14. John Roberts, "Philippine president renews her pledge of loyalty in Washington," World Socialist Web Site (http://www.wsws.org), May 28, 2003; James Tyner, *Iraq, Terror, and the Philippines' Will to War* (Lanham, MD: Rowman & Littlefield, 2005).

15. John Roberts, "Bali bombing trials leave key questions unanswered," World Socialist Web Site (http://www.wsws.org), July 24, 2003.

16. In June 2004, the Indonesian government deported ICG's director in Jakarta, Sydney Jones, indicating perhaps the degree to which the ICG's reports were damaging

to the credibility of Indonesian government claims about the "war on terror." See John Aglionby, "Bad Habits are Back," *Guardian Unlimited*, June 4, 2004, avaliable online at http://www.guardian.co.uk/elsewhere/journalist/story/0,7792,1231378,00. html; ICG, "ICG Indonesian Deportation Order Indefensible," available online at http://www.crisisgroup.org/home/index.cfm?id=2791&l=1&m=1.

17. ICG, "Indonesia Backgrounder," 2–3, 7, 21, 25; ICG, "Jemaah Islamiyah," 2, 12–14, 22-23.

18. ICG, "Jemaah Islamiyah," 1; cf. 15.

19. ICG, "Indonesia Backgrounder," 3, 25; ICG, "Jemaah Islamiyah," 26-27.

20. ICG, "Indonesia Backgrounder," 2, 3–4.

21. ICG, "Indonesia Backgrounder," 7, 8, 9, 11.

22. ICG, "Indonesia Backgrounder," 19–20.

23. Cf. ICG, "Jemaah Islamiyah," 25.

24. ICG, "Indonesia Backgrounder," 23, 25–26; ICG, "Jemaah Islamiyah," 25.

25. International Crisis Group (ICG), "Indonesia: Resources and Conflict in Papua" (Jakarta/Brussels: ICG), September 13, 2002, available online at http://www.icg. org.

26. ICG, "Indonesia: Resources and Conflict in Papua;" International Crisis Group (ICG), "Indonesia: Ending Repression in Irian Jaya" (Jakarta/Brussels: ICG, September 20, 2001), available online at http://www.icg.org.; International Crisis Group (ICG), "Dividing Papua: How Not to Do It" (Jakarta/Brussels: ICG, April 9, 2003), available online at http://www.icg.org.

27. John Roberts, "Investigations announced into alleged Indonesian atrocities in West Papua," World Socialist Web Site (http://www.wsws.org), December 3, 2003.

28. Peter Symonds, "Indonesia launches 'shock and awe' military offensive in Aceh," World Socialist Web Site (http://www.wsws.org), May 22, 2003.

29. International Crisis Group (ICG), "Aceh: How Not to Win Hearts and Minds" (Jakarta/Brussels: ICG, July 23, 2003), available online at http://www.icg.org.

30. John Roberts, "Indonesian army steps up war in Aceh," World Socialist Web Site (http://www.wsws.org), January 5, 2005.

31. ICG, "Aceh: A New Chance for Peace," (Jakarta/Brussels: ICG, August 15, 2005), available online at http://www.icg.org; John Roberts, "Indonesia signs shaky peace deal with Acehnese separatists," World Socialist Web Site (http://www.wsws.org), August 20, 2005.

32. Pasuk Phongpaichit, and Chris Baker, *Thaksin: The Business of Politics in Thailand* (Chiang Mai: Silkworm, 2004), 234–236; Shawn Crispin, "Security—Thailand's War Zone," *Far Eastern Economic Review* March 11, 2004, available online at http://www.feer.com.

33. Pasuk and Baker, *Thaksin*, 238; Crispin 2004; *The Nation* (Bangkok), "Tak Bai crackdown: Global outrage as grim details emerge; PM shows no remorse," October 28, 2004.

34. Kevin Hewison, and Garry Rodan, "Closing the Circle?: Globalization, Conflict and Political Regimes," Southeast Asia Research Centre Working paper no. 63, May 2004, City University of Hong Kong, p. 15, available online at http://www.cityu.edu. hk/searc.

35. Garry Rodan, and Kevin Hewison, "Neoliberal Globalisation, Conflict and Security: New Life for Authoritarianism in Asia?", paper presented at the conference 'The Post-Cold War Order and Domestic Conflict in Asia', Department of Sociology, National University of Singapore, 29-30 July 2005.

36. Jim Glassman, "Economic 'Nationalism' in a Post-Nationalist Era: The Political Economy of Economic Policy in Post-Crisis Thailand," *Critical Asian Studies* 36, 1: 37–64; Pasuk and Baker, *Thaksin*, 99–133.

37. Glassman, "Economic 'Nationalism'," 55.

38. Kevin Hewison, "The Politics of Neo-Liberalism: Class and Capitalism in Contemporary Thailand," Southeast Asia Research Centre Working paper no. 45, May, City University of Hong Kong, available online at http://www.cityu.edu.hk/searc.; Glassman, "Economic 'Nationalism'," 54–58; Pasuk and Baker, *Thaksin*, 144–149; Duncan McCargo, and Ukrist Pathmanand, *The Thaksinization of Thailand* (Copenhagen: Nordic Institute for Asian Studies Press, 2005): 129, 151.

39. Glassman, "Economic 'Nationalism'," 56–58; Pasuk and Baker, *Thaksin*, 146–147.

40. Pasuk and Baker, *Thaksin*, 162, 164–166.

41. Hewison and Rodan 2004, 16.

42. Crispin, Shawn W. "Thai-U.S. Relations Fray on Terror – Washington is Said to Seek Quick Arrests of Suspects; Bangkok Eager for Caution," *The Wall Street Journal*, 6 February 2003, A14.

43. McCargo and Ukrist 2005, 130–131.

44. Raymond Bonner, "Thailand Tiptoes in Step with the American Antiterror Effort," *The New York Times*, June 8, 2003, 1, 29; Thitinan Pongsudhirak, "Behind Thaksin's war on terror," *Far Eastern Economic Review*, September 25, 2003, 29.

45. Donald Kagan, Gary Schmitt, and Thomas Donnelly, "Rebuilding America's Defenses: Strategy, Forces, and Resources For a New Century," Report of the Project for a New American Century, September 2000, available online at http://www.newamericancentury.org/publicationsreports.htm.

46. Kagan et al. 2000, 1.

47. Kagan et al. 2000, 2–3.

48. Kagan et al. 2000, 4.

49. Kagan et al. 2000, 18.

50. Kagan et al. 2000, 18–19.

51. Richard Sokolsky, Angel Rabasa, and C. R. Neu, "The Role of Southeast Asia in US Strategy Toward China" (Santa Monica, CA: Rand, Project AIR FORCE division, 2000).

52. Sokolsky et al. 2000, 16–19.

53. Sokolsky et al. 2000, 19–24.

54. Sokolsky et al. 2000, 29–62.

55. Sokolsky et al. 2000, 61-62, 77–79.

56. Sokolsky et al. 2000, 34, 73, 75.

57. Sokolsky et al. 2000, 73.

58. Sokolsky et al. 2000, 67, 77.

59. Sokolsky et al. 2000, 74.

60. Sokolsky et al. 2000, 39, 49.

61. Council on Foreign Relations (CFR), Independent Task Force, "The United States and Southeast Asia: A Policy agenda for the New Administration" (New York: Council on Foreign Relations, 2001), 6, 15.

63. CFR 2001, 12, cf., 17–18, 56.

64. CFR 2001, 10, 51.

65. CFR 2001, 11; cf., 20–21, 53.

66. CFR 2001, 17, 22, 29–30, 38–39, 66.

67. CFR 2001, 22–23, 46, 54.

68. Bill Van Auken, "Powell declares tsunami aid part of global war on terror," World Socialist Web Site (http://www.wsws.org), January 6, 2005; K. Ratnayake, "Under the guise of 'humanitarianism', US marines land in Sri Lanka," World Socialist Web site (http://www.wsws.org), January 12, 2005.

69. National Intelligence Council (NIC), "Mapping the Global Future: Report of the National Intelligence Council's 2020 Project," Washington, D.C., December 2004, available online at http://www.foia.cia.gov/2020/2020.pdf.

70. NIC 2004, 81.

71. NIC 2004, 28.

72. Rosemary Foot, *Human Rights and Counter-terrorism in America's Asia Policy*, Adelphi Paper 363, International Institute for Strategic Studies (Oxford and New York: Oxford University Press, 2004).

7

Spaces of Terror and Fear on Colombia's Pacific Coast

The Armed Conflict and Forced Displacement Among Black Communities[1]

Ulrich Oslender

> These people fled without knowing where they were going nor why. What drove them on was just an elemental desire to run away.
>
> — Czeslaw Milosz (1955), *El poder cambia de manos*

The U.S.-led "war on terror" has many ramifications. Two weeks after his re-election in November 2004, President George W. Bush paid a four-hour visit to his Colombian counterpart Alvaro Uribe. In the scorching heat of the beautiful colonial town of Cartagena on Colombia's Caribbean coast, Bush pledged continued support to Uribe's hard-line approach to fighting narco-trafficking and the country's forty-year internal conflict by promising to ask Congress for a renewal of the support provided by Plan Colombia, a massive drug eradication program launched in 2000 that aims to achieve a reduction of 50 percent in illegal coca cultivation over six years. Of the plan's $7.5 billion total budget, the United States has committed $3.93 billion to Colombia between 2000 and 2005, 80 percent of which is used for the Colombian military, police, and aerial fumigation campaigns. Since its implementation, analysts have heavily criticized Plan Colombia as a militarist plan that will contribute to the destabilization of the conflict zones and to further degradation of the already precarious human rights situation in the country.[2]

In fact, large parts of these funds have been directly channeled into stepping up a military campaign against Colombia's insurgency, especially the country's largest and most powerful guerrilla group, the Revolutionary Armed Forces of Colombia (FARC). In the aftermath of 9/11 and tapping into global concerns over terrorism, the Colombian authorities have pursued a discursive strategy that links the FARC to illicit crop cultivation and drug trafficking, redefining in the process the guerrillas as "narco-terrorists." The aim has been to discredit the guerrilla's political project and conveniently cover up the social and historical roots of the country's ongoing internal conflict. Yet, Uribe's "war on terror" against leftist guerrilla groups employs its very own terror strategies. National and international NGOs

The Pacific coast region in Colombia.

continuously denounce the practice of arbitrary mass arrests, targeted killings of trade unionists and social movement leaders, the continued collaboration between the armed forces and right-wing paramilitary groups, and rampant impunity for crimes committed that have created an environment of fear throughout Colombian civil society.

In this chapter, I want to let this changing context of Colombia's internal conflict "touch ground" by examining the specific ways in which terror and fear have become threaded into the conduct of everyday life in a region that, until ten years ago, was considered a peace haven, excluded from the cartography of political violence in Colombia. By doing so, I want to stress the terrorizing impact of wider (national and global) geopolitical strategies on local populations in a specific setting, thus also questioning the moral high ground of U.S. interventionism, which is largely responsible for the increased militarization of Colombia's internal conflict. Specifically, I will analyze the spaces of terror and fear that Colombia's black communities have become exposed to in the Pacific coast region, only a decade after progressive legislation granted collective land rights to these communities. Although territorially empowered through Law 70 of 1993, tens of thousands of black peasants and fishermen have since been forced off their lands due to the escalation of the armed conflict in the Pacific region.

Whereas numerous studies now exist on forced displacement in Colombia in general, only very little attention has been paid so far to the ethnic variable and to the specific Afro-Colombian experience of this phenomenon.[3] There is the danger that the "invisibility" of black populations in Colombia, a historically grounded strategy of discrimination and exclusion by the nation's dominant classes, is now extended, however consciously or not, to the studies of displacement, in spite of recent inclusionary official discourses of multiculturalism and pluriethnicity.[4] To counteract this trend and to stress the differential Afro-Colombian experience of forced displacement, I will pay particular attention in this chapter to the strategies of resistance and survival that black communities have developed facing the terror unleashed by the various armed actors in the Pacific coast region.

Constitutional Changes, Multiculturalism, and Black Rights

Colombian society faced a deep crisis in the 1980s. The ubiquitous and explosive mixture of leftist guerrilla movements, right-wing paramilitary groups (often openly aided by the armed forces), wide-spread corruption, and the all-pervasive influence of the illicit drug trade had brought the country to the brink of chaos. As an attempt to diffuse tensions within a framework of broader and more inclusive political participation, a new constitution was passed in 1991. Although not directly aimed at the country's ethnic minorities, it also declared the nation to be multicultural and pluriethnic, incorporating a number of inclusionary mechanisms for indigenous groups and Afro-Colombians. Of particular interest to the latter, who make up some 26 percent of the country's population, it paved the way for a 1993 legislation (known as Law 70) that would grant black communities in the rural areas of the Pacific coast region collective land rights over the territories they had been traditionally inhabiting for centuries.[5]

This region covers an area of around 10 million hectares between the borders with Panama and Ecuador and extends up to 160 kilometers from the Pacific coastline to the foothills of the Western Cordillera. Some 80 percent of the region is covered in tropical rain forest, considered to contain one of the world's highest levels of biodiversity, which has attracted considerable international attention.[6] Topographically isolated from the interior of the country through the Western Andean mountain chain, the region has been characterized by its physical and economic marginalization in relation to Colombia's interior. Approximately one million Afro-Colombians live in this region today (about 93% of the area's population, the remainder being 2% indigenous communities and 5% *mestizo* migrants). These are mainly descendants of enslaved Africans who were forced to work the alluvial gold mines in the region during colonial times.[7] The majority lives today in the urban centers of Quibdó, Buenaventura, Tumaco, and Guapi, but it is important to highlight that some 40 percent still live in small hamlets along the myriad rivers that criss-cross the region. For hundreds of years, these communities have maintained distinct cultural traditions, a fact that was finally recognized in national legislation.

As a result of Law 70, collective land titles have been issued to black communities over almost five million hectares, i.e., 50 percent of the Pacific coast region. These lands, although used by Afro-Colombians for hundreds of years in accordance with their traditional production practices, had until then been considered as *baldías*, or state-owned, allowing national and foreign companies to exploit them through timber-felling and mechanized gold mining that wreaked havoc on the environment. Law 70 was partly seen as a way of protecting rural black communities and their lifestyles from such predatory extraction practices. To such an end regulatory decree 1745 of 1995 made provision for these communities to organize in community councils to administer the collectively titled lands as territorial and environmental authority.[8] The ecological significance of these rural black territorialization processes has recently also been recognized at international level with the prestigious Goldman Environmental Prize 2004 for a prominent Colombian black activist.[9]

De-Territorialization and Forced Displacement

Yet, ten years later, the positive effect of the favorable political opportunity structure, provided through the constitution of 1991 and Law 70 of 1993, is being eroded by the escalation of Colombia's internal armed conflict in the Pacific coast region, resulting in unprecedented levels of displacements and effective de-territorialization of rural black populations. In the mid-1990s the conflict sharpened considerably with right-wing paramilitary organizations moving into the northern Chocó Department to dispute the territorial control of the FARC. Under the pretext of combating FARC guerrillas in the municipality of Riosucio on the Atrato River, the military and paramilitary groups launched a coordinated attack in the region at the end of 1996, spreading fear, terror, and chaos among local residents. Testimonies of survivors, who were hiding for days submerged in the rivers with the water up to their necks,

Figure 7.1.   Murindó, in the mid-Atrato basin. Learning to live with the armed groups (here army soldiers). Photo: MARTíN GARCíA/ Archive EL TIEMPO, Bogatá – Colombia (with permission).

talk of the "night of terror" of December 20, 1996, when heavy-armed paramilitaries entered the town of Riosucio at about 5 a.m., kicked down doors, tore people out of their beds, and, with a list in hand, started to kill. Many others disappeared during this "tragic dawn." Witnesses also noticed how towards 8 a.m. helicopters of the national air force began to systematically bomb the surroundings of the attacked villages, killing many survivors who were hiding in the rivers among reeds.[10]

As a result, and fearing for their lives, some twenty thousand Afro-Colombians fled from their villages and rivers in the coming weeks and months. This massive exodus marked the beginning of a model that has been reproduced on countless occasions throughout the Pacific region. Through threats, massacres, and the spreading of terror among local populations, paramilitaries and guerrillas dispute territorial control, with local peasants caught up in the cross-fire, stigmatized as supporters of one group, and, hence, eliminated by the other. And for many communities the presence of armed actors among them has become an everyday reality (Figure 7.1). I should stress that for the purposes of my argument I am not interested here in distinguishing between the various motives and histories of guerrillas and paramilitaries (see note 14), but in examining the impact that their respective terror strategies have on local populations, which has led to the forced displacement of over two million people in Colombia, with some 30 percent estimated to be Afro-Colombians.[11] Since 1998 this development has accelerated, with massacres such as in the Naya River in April 2001 of fifty Afro-Colombian and indigenous peasants, followed by the killing of seven fishermen in the neighboring Yurumanguí River. One of the single worst incidents took place in May 2002 in the village of Bellavista on the shores of the Atrato River. The civilian population had sought refuge in the local church during intense fighting between paramilitaries and the FARC. When a gas cylinder bomb,

Figure 7.2. Remains of the local church in Bellavista, where 119 Afro-Colombians met their death during combats between FARC and paramilitaries; May 2002. Photo: Codhes (with permission).

launched by the guerrillas, landed in the church, 119 people died in the explosion. A mass exodus of the remaining local population followed this massacre (Figure 7.2).[12]

It is important, however, to stress that these cases only mark the tip of the iceberg of a painful development towards the de-territorialization of Afro-Colombian communities. Underneath these "spectacular" acts hide the much less visible realities of daily displacements of individuals and families who simply cannot live any longer with the constant threats to their lives in this context of terror. In this way, just as black communities receive their collective land titles, they are expulsed from these very lands. Fleeing violence, massacres, and terror, they abandon their lands, their houses, and their rivers. To paraphrase Czeslaw Milosz, often "without knowing where they are going nor why. What drives them on is just an elemental desire to run away."

These displacements happen in a context of great chaos, panic, insecurity, and uncertainty, often in the most dramatic circumstances and immediate threat to people's lives. As a displaced woman told me in Guapi in December 2004, she and her family had to flee their hamlet when they got caught in the cross-fire between guerrillas and the armed forces:

> It was about half past five [am], I think, we were still sleeping, when we heard the shooting. We immediately grabbed our six children and jumped into our canoe. Our house was right on the riverbank. I passed the children to my husband who was in the canoe already. We lost one of them, the oldest one, who ran away into the woods, because he was afraid. My husband shouted like mad and finally found him. So then we all sat in our canoe and went downstream. But in the middle of the river our canoe turned over. And none of the children knew how to swim. I had a one-month old girl, who I held in one hand, while hanging on to the canoe with the other. One by one we grabbed the other children and put them into

another canoe that was passing. But one was missing, and we looked for her, and I shouted like mad. Another woman was also hanging onto our canoe. She suddenly felt something under her feet. So she let go of her son, who she had in her hand, put him into the other canoe, and dived to see what was under her feet. And it was my little girl, who was already under the water … Then another canoe passed, and the man helped us to get in … Suddenly we heard a big bang, and another one. And then it was just boom, boom, boom … The water was splashing all around us … I don't know if these were grenades … I think the guerrillas were shooting at the soldiers in their speedboats … So we just got to the other side of the river and were hiding there in the woods until things calmed down a bit." (personal interview held December 13, 2004)

For a month she, her family, and neighbors were hiding on the other side of the river, eking out a living as best as they could. When they returned to their houses in their village, they found them badly damaged. The soldiers had apparently set up camp in them and ripped out doors and floorboards to use them as firewood. Pots and pans were missing, and none of their eight chickens were to be seen. Slowly they rebuilt their house and their lives. When six months later, however, the soldiers passed again to warn them of imminent combat with the guerrillas in the region, they took the few things left to them and fled to the town of Guapi.

As this woman's experience shows, forced displacements may be of short distance and duration (to the other side of the river for one month) or of longer distances (to the town of Guapi, possibly for years, or never to return home). Four main cycles of forced displacement can be identified: (1) *short*—to villages along the same river, (2) *intermediate*—to smaller towns at subregional level, (3) *extra-regional*—to the larger cities of the interior of the country (especially Bogotá, Medellín, and Cali), and (4) *intra-urban*—between different neighborhoods within the same city.[13]

Although space limitations do not permit analysis of the complexity of the Colombian conflict in detail, it should be noted that the forced displacement of rural communities has constituted part of the nation-building process in Colombia, going back at least to the civil wars of the nineteenth century and the "classical" period of *La Violencia* in the 1950s and 1960s. It therefore seems useful to put the phenomenon of political violence, if only briefly, in its wider historical context.

A (Very) Brief History of Colombia's Political Conflict[14]

Colombian democracy since the mid-nineteenth century has traditionally been dominated by the Liberal and Conservative Party elites who encouraged strong partisan loyalties as a means to best serve their own interests. Bipartisan clientelist structures and hereditary party identification were mobilized in successive civil wars in the nineteenth century and still constitute one of the outstanding factors of official politics in Colombia today. While the bipartisan oligarchy monopolized wealth and political power in this way, the mass of the people lived in poverty. In the mid-1940s, the popular opposition Liberal candidate for presidency, Jorge Eliécier Gaitán, mounted a challenge that went beyond party politics to confront the class conflict. When he was assassinated during a rally in Bogotá on April 9, 1948, people spontaneously rose up in a collective fury. Violence spread into the provincial cities and the countryside, people once again taking up arms and running virtually amok in a collective slaughter of the worst kind that became known as *La Violencia*. Between 1946 and 1966 some two hundred thousand people were killed in the most atrocious ways imaginable. Liberal leaders began to organize resistance against Conservative attacks, arming peasants and setting up guerrilla enclaves that were to provide protection for the displaced peasant populations. As thousands of Colombians fled their lands and sought refuge in the cities, the complete breakdown of the social order became apparent. Moreover, the criminalization of social protest forced resistance increasingly underground and built the basis for what were to become in the mid-1960s armed guerrilla groups. The most important ones still dominating the national scenario today are the FARC and the National Liberation Army (ELN). Whereas the ELN was heavily influenced by the ideas of the Cuban revolution, basing their strategies on the *foco* theory of guerrilla warfare, the FARC arose in 1964 as a direct response to government and army repression against peasants. FARC's longer-term regional structure of social welfare for peasants explains the deep loyalties to the guerrilla group and their strong support base in many regions otherwise abandoned or neglected by a weak state until today.

The FARC did not at first provide a serious threat to the government and remained up until the late 1970s a relatively marginal guerrilla force. Yet, the continued lack of space for political participation and for legal opposition led to a surge in social and political support for the guerrillas in the 1980s. Under the government of Belisario Betancur (1982–1986), a peace process was initiated that resulted in a military truce in 1984 and the formation of a coalition of left-wing forces, the Patriotic Union (UP), as an attempt to create a political alternative to the armed struggle. Yet, members of the UP were systematically killed in a dirty war launched by right-wing paramilitary forces and radical sectors in the army who were opposed to any negotiations with the guerrilla movements or what they saw to be their political wing. By the early 1990s the UP was practically wiped out, with over three thousand members and activists and two presidential candidates having been assassinated since its formation in 1985. From then on the FARC's military argument came to dominate their strategies, and the mistrust that resulted from this traumatic experience of entering electoral and party politics clearly has its impact today. It is difficult to see the guerrilla demobilize and reintegrate into society, if their prospect is almost certain assassination by right-wing elements in society.

Another factor contributed dramatically to the intensity of the dirty war since the mid-1980s: the illegal drug trade and the massive corruption of all layers of society. As paramilitary forces financed by drug traffickers launched attacks on leftist groups and activists throughout the country, and drug barons ordered the assassinations of state agents and ministers who favored extradition of narco-traffickers to the United States, massive corruption in state institutions and the party apparatus brought Colombia ever closer to the brink of chaos. Police, army chiefs, and politicians were bribed by drug money, as the country drifted from narco-terrorism in the mid-1980s to a narco-democracy in the 1990s, with all layers of society corrupted by the interests of the drug cartels.[15] At the same time, the growing military involvement of the United States in Colombia through Plan Colombia has exacerbated the militarization of the conflict even further.

Forced Displacement as Strategy

The complex nature of the conflict's microgeographies and its real-life articulation can perhaps best be seen through the recent report of the UN High Commissioner for Human Rights that investigated the combat situation and the massacre of Bellavista in May 2002.[16] The report reads like a script of some war movie that Oliver Stone would have been proud to direct. Alas, the 119 "extras" that died on the set were real people who never knew of the part that they were meant to play. In the conclusions to their investigation into the massacre the UN report does not only hold the FARC responsible for having launched the gas cylinder bomb into the church, and the paramilitaries for having used the civilian population as a shield during combat, but it also acknowledges the responsibility of the state in failing to prevent the massacre. The report accuses various government institutions of having failed to react to early warnings issued repeatedly by the local ombudsman about imminent threats of combat in the region between the FARC and paramilitaries. It further accuses the armed forces of cooperation with the paramilitary groups in that they allowed the latter to transport some 250 fighters in speedboats to the conflict zone in spite of them having had to pass three army check points on the Atrato River on the way. Finally, the report calls for an investigation into "the degree of state responsibility in the acting of the paramilitary group."[17]

As this report so clearly illustrates, rural populations caught up in the cross-fire between different armed groups are abandoned by a state whose military, by supporting paramilitary groups, is too often just another agent of terror to local communities. These people frequently see no alternative but to flee from the conflict zones to save their lives. They arrive with little left in the cities, where an inefficient social security system is unable to provide support. Many of them have few options but to beg at traffic lights, where they look painfully out of place, having had to swap their lands, their rivers, and forests for the unknown and chaotic space of the city's concrete jungle. Once again, just as fifty years earlier observed by the revolutionary priest Camilo Torres during the period of *La Violencia*, Colombia's peasants are on the move, leaving behind a devastated countryside.[18] Only that this time not even the cities provide a safe haven for many of these peasants, as the emerging phenomenon of intra-urban displacement shows. As a result of the continuing territorial dispute between the armed actors within the cities, many displaced people are forced to move from one (usually poor) neighborhood to another.[19]

Whereas this description corresponds to a national trend, there are also regional specificities to be observed. New regions are integrated into the country's cartography of political violence that were, until recently, at the margin of the armed conflict. The case of increasing terror spreading through the Pacific coast region, for example, is linked to an intensification of externally induced capitalist projects for the region. The extension of African palm plantations, plans for mega-projects such as the construction of an interoceanic canal (linking the Pacific and the Atlantic oceans), the construction of the Pan-American highway through the Chocó Department (and the tropical rainforests), together with the dramatic expansion of coca-growing in the region, clash with the life projects of local black and indigenous communities.[20] To implement these projects, the collaboration of local populations is required, or, in case of their noncooperation, the cleansing of the territories. In this way communities are subjected to threats, targeted killings, massacres, and individual and collective forced displacement, to then be replaced by a more "adequate" population to play the capitalist game required for the specific economic interests in the region. In other words, paramilitary groups empty the terrains, preparing them for the intervention of a capital ever more thirsty for new spheres of exploitation and appropriation. The forced displacement of local communities can be seen in this context as a strategy of development.[21] As one Afro-Colombian leader pointed out to me:

> The purpose of the forced displacement is precisely to throw people out, to empty these territories that are needed to develop their mega-projects. [...] When our black communities are displaced from a territory, the *mestizos* arrive immediately, with another culture. And then this huge forest, where the community realized their traditional production practices for their survival, this whole forest is destroyed and converted into grazing fields for cattle. Or it is chopped down for African palm trees. This is a different concept of development that they bring with them. (personal interview held in Bogotá, November 24, 2004)

Spaces of Terror and Fear

If forced displacement is a strategy of development, then terror is its tool. Of course, the application of terror as a tool of social control has a long history in Latin American societies. The Southern Cone dictatorships of the 1970s and 1980s based their authoritarian regimes on terror strategies and effectively created "cultures of fear," the legacy of which is still with us in today's political conflicts.[22] In Colombia, for example, the legacy of the technologies of terror of the period of *La Violencia* (1946–1966) has been shown to be very much alive in the massacres committed by paramilitary groups today.[23] The systematic application of terror by armed actors produces a generalized sense of fear among local populations and becomes a weapon and a local strategy in the struggle for territorial control.[24] Thus specific places and entire regions are transformed into landscapes of fear that break dramatically local and regional social relations.

These landscapes of fear are visible, for example, in the traces left behind by armed actors, such as destroyed and burnt houses or graffiti on walls as a stamp of the presence of the armed actors and as a constant underlying threat to local populations.[25] Effectively, these landscapes of fear can be "read" through these traces. They are also manifest in what can be thought of as "empty spaces," such as villages abandoned by their inhabitants fleeing from persecution and massacres. Although local populations sometimes return to their houses after having been displaced, the sense of terror and fear produced remains stamped in people's imaginations and on the landscape for years to come. One night in April 2001, paramilitary forces massacred seven fishermen in the village of El Firme on the Yurumanguí River, which caused the entire population to immediately abandon the village. Three and a half years later, the inhabitants have still not returned, their memories terrorized by this traumatic experience. In the words of the above quoted black activist:

Nobody has since gone to live in the village of El Firme. The psychological trauma was such that people simply refuse to go and live in this village again. They spread out into the other 11 villages along the river … El Firme is a completely empty village today. Many people, when passing by, they say, 'Ah, look, this *was* El Firme'. If one looks at how the weeds have invaded the few buildings that are still left … It's painful to see the conditions, in which this village finds itself today, which was in its time the place that fed everyone in the river Yurumanguí. With fish and seafood, the vital element of our communities … The massacre of El Firme was the most traumatic experience of our people. Never before had they seen human beings being massacred with an axe, the way in which these people were quartered … they were simple fishermen … We concluded that the strategy was to terrorize people in the river, so they would leave. And what better method of terrorism than massacring a group of people in this terrible way. For it to serve as a warning to the rest of the community. (personal interview held in Bogotá, November 24, 2004)

Beyond the mere physiological death, the terror strategy aims at a lasting effect on the memories of the survivors, who may have escaped the massacre, but who are haunted by the shadow of death that sticks to them throughout their lives. Terror thus becomes a communicative strategy that aims beyond the killings themselves to send a message to the survivors. It is this creation of a "space of death," where death is felt not just as a physiological but as a social fact, that constitutes what Taussig refers to as a culture of terror.[26] Beyond the functional effect of displacing local communities from their lands, the psychological effect of the terror strategy leads to a radical change in the ways people individually and collectively perceive, experience and feel about their places of origin, or in other words, to a radical change in the sense of place. Elsewhere, I have shown how this sense of place in the Pacific coast region of Colombia is conditioned by a tropical rainforest environment in which social relations are spatialized along and between river basins to such a point that we can talk of an "aquatic sense of place."[27] By this, I mean the intimate ways in which rural populations in the Pacific region identify with their rivers. These constitute not only the essential infrastructure of transport and mobility but also the source of collective memory and the site of social life that connects and communicates different communities along and between different river basins.

The context of terror, however, abruptly alters this aquatic sense of place and the ways in which locals think about their rivers. As all transport is on the fluvial thoroughfares of the Pacific, the river is now also messenger of death and terror, used by the armed groups for their mobility. A generalized sense of insecurity is thus imposed on the population, and the imagined geographies and the ways in which locals think about and refer to their surroundings are now impregnated by memories of fear. In a focus group session that I led in December 2004 with seventeen women in Guapi who had been displaced from three of the town's surrounding rivers, most women were extremely reluctant at the beginning to talk in detail about their river of origin and the event that caused their displacement. The discussion centered at first around the difficult conditions that they found themselves in, having to re-construct their lives in Guapi.[28] The reluctance to recall their rivers must be seen as linked to their painful memories of what were traumatic experiences for all of them. However, as the meeting went on and I insisted on asking them about their rivers, one woman began to tell her story. This broke the collective silence, and one participant after another recalled the day of their displacement. Somehow strangely disconcerting, these terrifying accounts were accompanied by great laughter, maybe one way of dealing with these haunting memories. Most tellingly perhaps, none of the women considered returning to her place of origin. Even three years after their displacement, the space of death clings on to their memories: "No, I am not going back to my river. When we lived there, at three o'clock in the morning they came and killed three people, right on the river bank, they killed them. They were friends. Right on the river bank. No, I am not going back there." "I am not going back there. And if I have to eat soil here, but I am not going back there."[29]

The experience of terror and fear must be understood here as a complicated set of spaces, emotions, practices, movements, and materialities that work at a range of scales from the body to the microgeographies of the (lost) home, river, forest, and region. And for a deeper understanding of the workings of terror "on the ground", it is necessary to pay attention to the ways in which people deal with situations of terror and how they confront terror in its place through the creation of spaces of resistance.

Spaces and Networks of Resistance

Black communities have resorted to civil resistance against all armed actors, defending themselves with their bare hands and plenty of courage. In some parts they have set up peace communities declaring their neutrality in the armed conflict. Afro-Colombian peasants of the Community Council of the Baudó River, for example, drew up a set of coexistence rules that they painted on the walls at the entrances to their villages, from which they had previously been displaced.[30] These rules dictate that no information is given by locals to any of the armed actors, and even specifies that local girls are not to enter into love relationships with paramilitary or guerrilla fighters. In November 2001 in the location of Pie de Pató these rules were for the first time publicly read out to a column of ELN guerrillas who entered the village and subsequently retreated respecting the villagers' demands.[31]

In another highly visualized act of resistance, five hundred people embarked on a collective journey along the Atrato River in November 2003—including local peasants and fishermen, representatives of NGOs, the Catholic church, the United Nations, and national and international journalists. They protested against the constant forced displacements as a result of the combats between paramilitaries, guerrillas, and the army in the region, and the economic blockade to which the armed actors had subjected the communities along the Atrato River through the installation of illegal checkpoints controlling the movements of merchandise and people. In some areas this situation has increasingly led to a confinement of the local population impeding their mobility. This boat and canoe caravan traveled river downstream for five days, visiting many villages along the way where residents had been confined for months.[32] The caravan was greeted with great joy, music, and dancing in these villages. And although this was only a temporary affirmation of black territoriality, given the continuing confinement and blockade to which local communities are subjected along this river it was a highly symbolic act of self-empowerment (see Figures 7.3 and 7.4).

One of the participants, a local community leader now exiled in Bogotá, had not been in his river for almost a decade. As he told, the overpowering joy he felt on paying a visit

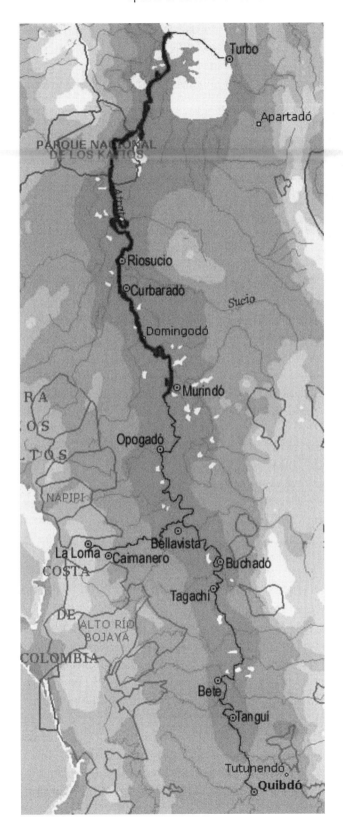

Figure 7.3. Route of the *Atratiando* campaign from Quibdó to Turbo along the Atrato River; November 2003. Map: Project Counselling Service (with permission).

Figure 7.4. *Atratiando*—a 5-day boat and canoe caravan down the Atrato River to protest against the economic blockade imposed by the armed actors along the river; November 2003. Photo: PCS (with permission).

to his river mixed with a nostalgic sadness that he would not be able to return to settle there at his own free will:

> I felt an immense joy and it was as if I was born again. Once again returning to my region of birth, where I grew up. I don't know, I felt a strange pain to just be passing through and not able to go back as it was before. A really difficult experience this … We could go there this time because we were accompanied by a number of international organizations that protected the civilian population in the caravan. But all by my own I wouldn't be able to go there. This is really sad that in order to go to one's territory one has to be protected and body-guarded by other people. Because if they [the armed actors] see you return alone, you will just disappear. (personal interview with community leader from Riosucio; Bogotá November 28, 2004)

Faced with this dilemma, many local communities have decided not to abandon their rivers and territories. Instead, they implement hiding strategies when threatened by an imminent attack of the armed groups. Through constant micromovements within their territories they hide in certain places they know best or flee along particular routes known only to them. The historical experience of runaway slaves and the intimate knowledge of the microgeographies and local spaces combine in this strategy of defense and resistance. A question currently being addressed by Afro-Colombian leaders is to evaluate whether these strategies can be coordinated at regional or national level, for example, to temporarily evacuate entire villages in case of violent incursions. Crucial for this strategy of temporary internal displacement (which corresponds to the first, short cycle of forced displacement discussed above) is the solidarity that exists among black communities along and between the countless river basins.

As the ancestral owners of the territories, we are advancing the proposal of *not* abandoning our territory. That's why we have developed a strategy that we call internal displacement … When a settlement is in risk, we recommend people to move to another settlement along the river where the risk is less … And we need to guarantee the conditions for this kind of displacement to work … When the people of El Firme were displaced due to the massacre in April 2001, the neighboring villages of San Antonio, San José and San Miguel further upstream prepared themselves to receive their brothers. They gave them clothes, we shared the food that we had, and the little space in our houses to accommodate them. That way the displaced suffered less … In this sense our solidarity has been fundamental in resisting in the river. (personal interview with community leader from the Yurumanguí River; Bogotá, November 24, 2004)

To denounce the reality of their terrorized territories, black communities have also created a number of mechanisms. In August 1999 the Association of Displaced Afro-Colombians AFRODES was founded in Bogotá. It works closely with the Consultancy of Human Rights and Displacement CODHES on issues of forced displacement, and denounces human rights abuses with the national government, and national and international NGOs. Transnational alliances are of increasing importance in this context. Although it is at the local and national level that the Colombian conflict will have to be resolved, the role of the international community and the global component of resistance acquire a great strategic value. More than a mere additional option, the participation in globalizing resistance networks becomes a necessity, when local communities feel abandoned by a weak state and its unequal presence in the national territory that cannot guarantee the necessary security for the construction of a life project in their places of origin. Denouncing the state's implication in these acts of political violence at the international level can put significant pressure on the Colombian government. AFRODES has recently opened, for example, an office with a representative in Washington, DC. In particular, Afro-North American politicians, through an ethnic commitment linked to the African Diaspora, have shown great interest in the situation of black communities in Colombia, as demonstrated in a recent solidarity event in Chicago.[33]

At the national level there are also important alliances between Afro-Colombian and indigenous communities that have traditionally cohabited in the Pacific coast region. These relations have been characterized by mutual solidarity links and pacific co-existence. The context of terror, shared and suffered by both groups, now also facilitates an increased collaboration between them. The First Interethnic Meeting of the Naya River in July 2003, for example, is the direct result of the paramilitary incursion into this river in April 2001 and product of a series of preparatory meetings between indigenous and Afro-Colombian activists.

Another Afro-Colombian organization, the Process of Black Communities PCN is one of the most important efforts at coordinating the struggles of black communities at the national level and at giving it coherence in global alliances. A network of some 120 local organizations PCN was founded in 1993, first to impulse the land titling processes on the Pacific coast and increasingly to denounce and organize against the regimes of terror in this region. Their struggles have recently received important international recognition with the bestowment of the prestigious Goldman Environmental Prize onto one of its leaders.[34] PCN has also established important links with the global resistance network People's Global Action (PGA), a convergence space of grassroots organizations, activists, and academics against the neoliberal world order.[35] PGA coordinated, for example, a tour of six PCN members through Europe in 2001 to raise concern about the human rights situation for Afro-Colombian communities with, among others, trade unions and politicians of the European Union. PCN has also made use of the Internet as a tool in their struggle. It allows the rapid spread of information; the "visibilization" of otherwise "invisibilized" protests by the mass media (an important aspect in Latin America, where media are often owned by the oligarchy); urgent action appeals to the international community; and the coordination of collective actions. Breaking with the limitations that the topographic space imposes on the Pacific coast, the Internet is an important means of communication for those voices and opinions that would otherwise not be heard beyond their remote locales.

I want to exemplify this with the text of a message distributed by PCN as an e-mail sent around the world. The message focuses on the tense situation in the Yurumanguí River and is a testimony of the atrocities committed that rarely appear in the mass media. But it is also more than that. It is a way of writing against terror and of constructing the counter-discourses that Taussig calls for in order to oppose terror, or, as I would put it, to confront terror in its place.[36] The narration itself, the message sent out into the world from the Pacific lowlands, is also resistance against the cultural elaboration of a generalized fear among local populations and breaks the silence that terror imposes as strategy of domination. The message is testimony of this necessity, as it states in the introduction, "this, to my friends and to the whole world":[37]

> We are 4000 people who live in the Yurumanguí River, southwest of Buenaventura [...]. This population is entirely of African descent. [...] We want to declare that we have exercised control over this river and its resources for more than 200 years. [...] On 23 of May 2000, through resolution 01131, emitted by the national government, we were given a collective land title over 54,000 hectares, which is administered by the Community Council. But this collective title has become a nuisance for state policies and transnational capital that are just too keen on the wealth of natural resources in our territory. For over a year paramilitary groups [...] have been threatening us with incursions if we do not leave the river. In April 2001, after having massacred 150 people in the upper parts of the Naya River, they entered our river at the village of El Firme, and, with an axe, they hacked to pieces seven members of our Community Council who were fishing. This caused the displacement of 450 people to the port of Buenaventura, and of 600 people along the Yurumanguí River. [...] Now paramilitaries threaten us with an invasion during this Christmas season, and that the members of the Community Council must leave the river, lest our families in the city be killed. We want to inform the whole world that just as our ancestors, who resisted in an organized manner through their *palenques* the invasion, we too will resist politically organized through our Community Council. [...] As a political organization we are ready *not* to abandon our river. For this we are prepared to die with dignity within the territory that our ancestors left behind for us. Río Yurumanguí, December 22, 2001

As this activist so clearly stresses, the Community Council, a judicial figure created through national legislation as territorial and environmental authority, is now mobilized as a space of resistance against the processes of de-territorialization and forced displacement. Despite their struggle being against the seemingly overpowering forces of groups armed to their teeth, many riverside communities have decided to not let themselves be displaced any longer. From their local organizations they mobilize, meet, think about ways of resistance, and put them into practice. To this trend testify the returns of the communities of the Baudó River and Bellavista, the interethnic alliances in the Naya River, and the decision of the leaders in the Yurumanguí River not to give in to the threats of the various armed actors.

Conclusions

The last ten years have seen a constant remapping of the territorialities in the Colombian Pacific region. While territorialization processes by black communities were set in motion through a legislation that finally recognized territorial rights to these communities, the intentionality of this legislation has since been subverted in real life with the escalation of the armed conflict into this region. Law 70 of 1993 pretended to guarantee the sustainability of natural resource exploitation, the conservation of biodiversity, and the protection of Afro-Colombian culture. Yet, the struggle for territorial control between guerrillas and paramilitaries in the Pacific region drives local populations off their lands, producing the very opposite effect of de-territorialization. As a result, we witness the forced displacement of hundreds of thousands of peasants. Whereas no reliable figures exist for the Pacific coast region as such, this conflict has led to over two million internally displaced people in Colombia.

Beyond the usual focus on statistics, humanitarian assistance, and economic implications in the studies of the phenomenon of forced displacement in Colombia, I have stressed the need to instill the analysis with the sense of terror that is experienced in the expulsion zones, where people have to live on an everyday basis with threats, massacres, and selected killings. In particular, I have drawn on the voices of some of the displaced to give a fuller understanding of the spaces of terror and fear that have begun to transform the region of the Pacific coast into landscapes of fear. Yet, at the same time, it is important to stress the many, often creative attempts by local communities to resist the impact of terror and to confront terror in its place.

Such an approach is also a call for a fuller and more critical understanding of the workings of terror and an emphatic engagement with the victims of terror. It encourages us to think about terror in distinct and more nuanced ways than is currently propagated by politicians and the media. Terror and terrorism must be seen as contested terms that take on many forms in different places and conjunctures. It is therefore necessary to stand up against the simplification of the "terror concept" in contemporary dominant geopolitical discourses that define terrorism exclusively as directed against the Western neoliberal democratic state, while at the same time hiding "other terrorisms," including those applied by these very same Western neoliberal democracies. It seems ironic, to say the least, that the "war on terror," led by the United States and its changing allies, actually helps to produce and sustain landscapes of fear and regimes of terror in regions where the West intervenes. The U.S. involvement in Colombia, for example, by directly supporting the hard-line president Uribe and the military that has such clearly documented links to right-wing paramilitary groups, at least indirectly helps to sustain the regimes of terror that these groups impose on rural populations throughout the country.

In such a context, the struggle of Colombia's black communities must transcend the national scenario to create alliances and networks of support and resistance on a global scale. This challenge has been recognized and taken onboard by the Afro-Colombian social movement. Tapping into global environmental concerns over biodiversity preservation and sustainable development, actively participating in global resistance networks such as PGA, and highlighting their struggle with multilateral agencies and international NGOs; all of these activities serve to create a greater awareness of the complex Colombian conflict and the problems facing black communities that should be translated into lasting solutions for these communities. In its own modest way, this chapter intends to be a contribution to this end.

Notes

1. Research for this chapter was made possible through a grant from the UK-based Economic and Social Research Council (RES-000-22-0770). It also benefited from a research grant of the Carnegie Trust for the Universities of Scotland, which partly funded my fieldwork in Colombia in 2003. I have conducted fieldwork in the Colombian Pacific coast region since 1996. My very special thanks to the inhabitants of the town of Guapi and to their community leaders of strong faith and spirit in these difficult times.
2. See, e.g., Ricardo Vargas, "Europa y el Plan Colombia," *Drogas y Conflicto*, Working Document No.1 (April 2001) (Amsterdam: Transnational Institute, 2001).
3. General studies on forced displacement in Colombia include Carlos Alberto Giraldo, Jesús Abad Colorado, and Diego Pérez, *Relatos e imágenes: El desplazamiento en Colombia* (Bogotá: Cinep, 1997), and Ana María Jaramillo, Marta Inés Villa, and Luz Amparo Sánchez, *Miedo y desplazamiento: Experiencias y percepciones* (Medellín: Corporación Región, 2004). Essays on forced displacement among Afro-Colombian communities can be found in the collection by Eduardo Restrepo & Axel Rojas (eds.), *Conflicto e (in)visibilidad: Retos en los estudios de la gente negra en Colombia* (Popayán: Universidad del Cauca, 2004).
4. The argument of the invisibility of black populations in Colombia was first made by Nina Friedemann, "Estudios de negros en la antropología colombiana," in Jaime Arocha and Nina Friedemann, *Un siglo de investigación social: Antropología en Colombia* (Bogotá: Etno, 1984),.507–572. For a similar argument in other Latin-American contexts and the changing nature of this invisibility, see Minority Rights Group, *No longer invisible: Afro-Latin Americans today* (London: Minority Rights Publications, 1995).
5. For aspects of this legislation and the land titling process see Jaime Arocha, "Inclusion of Afro-Colombians: unreachable national goal?," *Latin American Perspectives* 25(3) (1998) pp. 70–89; Libia Grueso, Carlos Rosero, and Arturo Escobar, "The Process of Black Community organizing in the southern Pacific coast region of Colombia," in Sonia Alvarez, Evelina Dagnino, and Arturo Escobar (eds.), *Cultures of politics, politics of cultures: Re-visioning Latin American social movements* (Oxford: Westview Press, 1998),196–219; Peter Wade, "The cultural politics of blackness in Colombia," *American Ethnologist* 22(2) (1995),.341–357; and the special issue of the *Journal of Latin American Anthropology* 7(2) (2002).
6. The Global Environment Facility (GEF) and the United Nations Development Program funded an ambitious biodiversity project in the region in the 1990s. See

GEF-PNUD, *Proyecto Biopacífico* (Bogotá: DNP/Biopacífico, 1993), and Proyecto Biopacífico, *Informe final general* (Bogotá: Ministerio del Medio Ambiente, 1998).

7. For detail on the history of slavery, settlement patterns and production cycles see the seminal monograph by Robert West, *The Pacific lowlands of Colombia* (Baton Rouge: Louisiana State University Press, 1957). See also Norman Whitten, *Black frontiersmen: Afro-Hispanic culture of Ecuador and Colombia* (Prospect Heights, IL: Waveland Press, 1986 [1974]).

8. The experiences of some community councils have been documented in Ulrich Oslender, "The logic of the river: a spatial approach to ethnic-territorial mobilization in the Colombian Pacific region," *Journal of Latin American Anthropology* 7(2) (2002),. 86–117; and in Nelly Rivas, "Ley 70 y medio ambiente: el caso del Consejo Comunitario Acapa, Pacífico nariñense," in Mauricio Pardo (ed), *Acción colectiva, Estado y etnicidad en el Pacífico colombiano* (Bogotá: ICANH, 2001), 149–169. For a wider argument on such an empowering of ethnic groups as "guardians" of fragile ecosystems and the inscription of such a logic in politics of sustainable development and conservationist discourses, see Arturo Escobar, "Constructing nature: elements for a poststructural political ecology," in Richard Peet and Michael Watts (eds.), *Liberation ecologies: environment, development and social movements* (London: Routledge, 1996), 46–68.

9. The Goldman Environmental Prize, considered as the Nobel Prize for the Environment, is given every year to grassroots ecological activists from six geographical regions. Libia Grueso from Colombia's Process of Black Communities won the prize in April 2004 in the category South/Central America. Available at www.goldmanprize.org/recipients/recipientFrameset.cfm?recipientID=132 [all quoted Web pages accessed on August 21, 2005].

10. See Marino Córdoba, "Trágico amanecer," in M. Segura Naranjo (ed.), *Exodo, patrimonio e identidad* (Bogotá: Ministerio de Cultura, 2001),.248–252. The complicity of the Colombian military with paramilitary forces has amply been documented, for example in ONU (Organización de Naciones Unidas), *Informe sobre la misión de observación en el Medio Atrato* (Bogotá: Oficina en Colombia del Alto Comisionado de las Naciones Unidas para los Derechos Humanos, May 20, 2002). See also Human Rights Watch: http://hrw.org/english/docs/2004/01/21/colomb6978.htm.

11. Figures are from the Consultancy for Human Rights and Displacement CODHES, which has monitored forced displacement statistics since 1992 (http://www.codhes.org.co), and from the Association of Displaced Afro-Colombians AFRODES.

12. For an account of this tragedy and the following investigation see the special UN report ONU, *Informe*.

13. For more details on these cycles, see Diego Henao, "Extraños, nómadas y confinados," *Asuntos Indígenas* 4/03 (2003):.20–27 (Copenhagen: International Work Group for Indigenous Affairs: http://www.iwgia.org).

14. This summary section can in no way do justice to the very complex phenomenon of political violence in Colombia, nor to the many excellent studies that have been conducted on it. The following references are a good starting-point for further enquiries into the history of Colombia's conflict. A good introduction can be found in Catherine LeGrand, "The Colombian crisis in historical perspective," *Canadian Journal of Latin American and Caribbean Studies* 28(55-56) (2003), 165–209. For a wide-ranging analysis see the excellent collections by Charles Bergquist, Ricardo Peñaranda, and Gonzalo Sánchez (eds.), *Violence in Colombia: The contemporary crisis in historical perspective* (Delaware: Scholarly Resources Inc., 1992), and *Vio-*

lence in Colombia, 1990–2000: Waging war and negotiating peace (Delaware: Scholarly Resources Inc., 2001). See also the special editions of *International Journal of Politics, Culture and Society* 14(1) (2000) and *Latin American Perspectives* 28(1) (2001). Further seminal studies include Daniel Pécaut, *Orden y violencia: Colombia, 1930–1954* (Bogotá: Editorial Siglo XXI-Cerec, 1987), and Nazih Richani, *Systems of violence: The political economy of war and peace in Colombia* (Albany: State University of New York Press, 2002).

15. From 1986 to 1993 the Medellín drug cartel under the leadership of Pablo Escobar launched a terrorist campaign of total destabilization of the country to press the Colombian government for an end of extradition of captured drug barons to the United States. This period of narco-terrorism was followed by more subtle strategies of corruption of government officials by illegal drug money. In a high-profile judicial process known as *Proceso 8,000*, it was shown how drug money had entered the presidential campaign of the then Liberal candidate and subsequently elected President Ernesto Samper (1994–1998). Samper's whole term in office was overshadowed by this scandal and characterized by a weak and discredited administration.

16. ONU, Informe.

17. ONU, *Informe*, 26.

18. "As in feudal times, the peasants flee to the cities in search of security"; Camilo Torres quoted in Eric Hobsbawm, *Rebeldes primitivos: Estudio sobre las formas arcaicas de los movimientos sociales en los siglos XIX y XX* (Barcelona: Editorial Ariel, 1983 [1959]:264); originally published as: *Primitive rebels: Studies in archaic forms of social movements in the 19th and 20th centuries*, 1959.

19. For the case of Medellín, see Jaramillo et al., "Miedo y desplazamiento,", 37.

20. See Carlos Rosero, "Los afrodescendientes y el conflicto armado en Colombia: la insistencia en lo propio como alternativa," in Claudia Mosquera, Mauricio Pardo, and Odile Hoffmann (eds.), *Afrodescendientes en las Américas: Trayectorias sociales e identitarias* (Bogotá: Universidad Nacional de Colombia/ICANH/IRD/ILSA, 2002), 547–559.

21. Escobar sees a logic in these developments, considering the massive displacements of local populations as the final result of cultural, social and economic processes towards the consolidation of a global capitalist modernity; see Arturo Escobar, "Displacement, development, and modernity in the Colombian Pacific," *International Social Science Journal* 55(1) (2003), 157–167. See also the other articles in this special issue 'Moving targets: displacement, impoverishment, and development' of the *International Social Science Journal* 55(1) (2003). Moreover, I suggest that the massive displacements form part of a global trend towards what I have called "new-geo-economic wars": conflicts that are above all over the access to and control of economic resources, without this necessarily requiring the shifting or redefinition of nation-state boundaries. The recent events in Iraq serve as example: the U.S. military acting, simultaneously and not contradictorily, as a tool of destruction and cleansing to prepare the terrain for the arrival of enterprises with millions of dollars worth of contracts in the "reconstruction plan" for Iraq. For a more detailed elaboration of this argument see Ulrich Oslender, "Construyendo contrapoderes a las nuevas guerras geo-económicas: caminos hacia una globalización de la resistencia," *Tabula Rasa* 2 (2004),. 59–78. Available at http://www.unicolmayor.edu.co/investigaciones/numero2/oslender.pdf.

22. See Juan Corradi, Patricia Weiss Fagen, and Manuel Antonio Garretón (eds.), *Fear at the edge: State terror and resistance in Latin America* (Oxford: University of California Press, 1992).

23. See the excellent studies by María Victoria Uribe, e.g., "Dismembering and expelling: semantics of political terror in Colombia," *Public Culture* 16(1) (2004):. 79–95, or *Anthropologie de l'inhumanité: essai sur la terreur en Colombie* (Paris: Calmann-Lévy, 2004).

24. See Daniel Pécaut, "Configurations of space, time, and subjectivity in a context of terror: the Colombian example," *International Journal of Politics, Culture and Society* 14(1) (2000): 129–150.

25. Such an approach goes beyond the classic humanistic proposal of Yi-Fu Tuan, *Landscapes of fear* (Oxford: Blackwell, 1978). I intend here to establish a systematic relation between fear and landscape in relation to the social space and the embodied practices of everyday life. For a discussion of Tuan's concept in relation to spaces and fear of crime, see John Gold and George Revill, "Exploring landscapes of fear: marginality, spectacle and surveillance," *Capital and Class* 80 (2003): 27–50.

26. See Michael Taussig, "Culture of terror – space of death: Roger Casement's Putumayo report and the explanation of torture," *Comparative Studies in Society and History* 26(3) (1984): 467–497.

27. See Ulrich Oslender, "Fleshing out the geographies of social movements: Black communities on the Colombian Pacific coast and the aquatic space," *Political Geography* 23(8) (2004): 957–985. See also Oslender, "The logic."

28. It is beyond the scope of this chapter to examine in detail the differential gendered experience of terror and forced displacement by women and men. However, it is clear that women carry the great responsibility of having to sustain their children and family, often as widows of murdered husbands. It has also been noted that women adapt more easily to the new urban environment in the place of arrival than men. See the excellent studies by Donny Meertens, e.g., "Facing destruction, rebuilding life: gender and the internally displaced in Colombia," *Latin American Perspectives* 28(1) (2001): 132–148. For a gender perspective on political violence in general, see Caroline Moser and Fiona Clark (eds.), *Victims, perpetrators or actors?: Gender, armed conflict and political violence* (London: Zed Books, 2001).

29. Quotes from focus group session held with displaced women in Guapi, December 16, 2004.

30. The Community Council of the river Baudó ACABA consists of eighty-six communities that were awarded 174,000 hectares of collective lands through Law 70. Some 480 families were displaced from these lands as a result of paramilitary and guerrilla threats. The coexistence rules were collectively set up by the displaced in the departmental capital of Quibdó in August 2001, with first families returning to their lands in October.

31. See El Tiempo, "Manual para días de guerra en el Baudó," Sunday, February 10, 2002, 1–12.

32. For an English-language account of this event visit the Web site of the NGO Project Counselling Service: http://www.pcslatin.org/publicaciones2/16/Blockaded%20communities%20ENGLISH.pdf.

33. From April 25 to 26, 2003 the Association "Chicagoans for a Peaceful Colombia" organized their Second Annual Conference at the DePaul University in Chicago, examining the exploitation of natural resources and the survival of the

Afro-Colombian people. The representative of AFRODES in Washington participated in this conference (http://www.chicagoans.net/conf2003).

34. See note 9 on this prize. See Grueso and others, "The Process," for details on PCN
35. For an argument of PGA as convergence space, see Paul Routledge, "Convergence
    space: process geographies of grassroots globalization networks," *Transactions of
    the Institute of British Geographers* 28(3) (2003): 333–349.
36. See Taussig, "Culture of terror."
37. Message distributed by electronic mail on December 23, 2001; my translation.

8

Fatal Transactions
Conflict Diamonds and the (Anti)Terrorist Consumer*
Philippe Le Billon

Terror, Commodities, and the Politics of Consumption

In 1999, European advocacy groups launched an international campaign calling for consumers "not to support terror."[1] This Fatal Transactions campaign denounced the trade of "conflict diamonds" financing wars in Angola and Sierra Leone, or "terror diamonds" funding Al Qaeda. By superimposing the amputated limbs of war victims on diamond-ringed fingers of brides, or pricing diamonds in deaths rather than dollars, Fatal Transactions campaigners conveyed a powerful message: consuming is killing. Faced with the threat of massive financial losses through a diamond boycott, major diamond industry interests finally acknowledged the problem after years of neglecting or denying the role of the diamonds trade in funding conflicts. To avoid a boycott, the industry stressed that most of the trade had no blood on its hands, that millions of jobs and entire economies were at stake, and that a diamond certification system could remove conflict diamonds from the legitimate diamonds trade.

So-called conflict commodities have financed, to a large degree, about a third of armed conflicts since the end of the cold war (Cooper 2002; Eriksson and Wallensteen 2004; Le Billon 2004). In Cambodia, revenues from timber and rubies financed the Khmer Rouge in the early 1990s as support from China ended (Le Billon 1999). The control of oil fields and diamond mines in Angola became crucial for local belligerents after cold war sponsors and the apartheid South African government withdrew their support in the late 1980s (Hodges 2004). Shortly after the attacks on the World Trade Center and the Pentagon, Al Qaeda operatives were found to have laundered millions of dollars through conflict diamonds from West Africa to evade financial controls (Farah 2001; Global Witness 2003). With U.S. consumers buying about half of the world's diamonds, such "terror" diamonds were likely to end up on American hands unwittingly financing belligerents.

The Fatal Transactions campaign sought to emphasize the point that the conflict commodity trade assumed a major role in financing violent political struggles. War

*Le Billon, P. (2006) 'Fatal Transactions, Conflict Diamonds, and the Anti-terrorist Consumer,' *Antipode* © Blackwell Publishing 2006.

profiteering also had appeared to be a central motivation of belligerents, from African warlords to U.S. politicians and defense contractors (Hersh 2003; Keen 1998; McQuaig 2004; Nordstrom 2004). Curtailing the trade in conflict commodities was thus not only about ending wars and protecting potential victims; it was also about shaming a capitalist system reaping the spoils of war with impunity, and awakening citizens to their responsibility as "terrorist consumers"—that is, individuals bearing indirect responsibility for the perpetuation of acts of extreme violence against civilians through their consumption practices.

Consumption politics has been increasingly recognized as a potent force for change (Daunton and Hilton 2001; Miller 1995). Recent work on consumption and the geographies of commodities stresses the importance of exposing and politicizing structural forms of violence, exploitative labor conditions, or environmental impacts (Hartwick 1998, 2000; Hughes and Reimer 2004; Leslie and Reimer 1999; Nevins 2003). The consumption politics literature, however, also suggests that acting politically through commodities and consumption often entails contradictions, limitations, ambivalences, and unintended effects (Barnett et al. 2005; Bryant and Goodman 2004; Freidberg 2004; Goodman 2005). Consumption politics, as Miller (1995, 33) writes, rests on dialectical contradiction;

> On the one hand, consumption appears as the key contemporary 'problem' responsible for massive suffering and inequality. At the same time it is the locus of any future 'solution' as a progressive movement in the world, by making the alienatory institutions of trade and government finally responsible to humanity for the consequences of their actions.

This contradiction is particularly acute in poor countries affected by conflicts. Conflict trade is often a matter of mere survival for many among the poorest, even if it is also a source of vast profits for some (Collinson 2003). Ending the consumption of conflict commodities may be as much a problem as a solution if it is to further increase the vulnerability of war victims. Economic sanctions, for example, have been widely used to regulate the trade of conflict commodities; but in many cases their drastic humanitarian costs have made them clearly immoral—especially in light of their feeble and controversial political outcomes (Heine-Ellison 2001).

Moreover, the politics of consumption often remain limited in terms of bringing about such "responsibility to humanity," especially so when it is orchestrated through ethical consumption. As Bryant and Goodman (2004, 360) point out, ethical choice frequently represents a process of moral adaptation giving (financially or educationally) privileged consumers the ability "to 'tune in but drop out' of both conventional global economies *and* more demanding forms of resistance to social injustice." There is thus a risk for campaigns to limit themselves to catering for such (privileged) ethical consumption—for example, by helping to develop specialty products of the ethical kind. Achieving broader responsibility than that of the individual consumer and a more radical transformation of production systems also present its own limitations and ambivalences. As campaigners seek to reach into the darkest corners of a complacent industry, they often need to constructively engage with the very businesses and governments that they denounce. As illustrated below, future reforms, rather than accountability for past practices, can thus become the priority.

Reflecting upon ethical consumption practices and their unintended consequences, Barnett et al. (2005, 28) also suggest that the politics of consumption are
not as straightforward as often supposed, because they "often work through registers
that, while outwardly universalistic in their ethical and political claims, are related
to routines of differentiation, discrimination, and distinction." The defetishization
of commodities—one of the main tactics of ethical consumption politics—is particularly vulnerable to such routines. As Noel Castree (2001) notes, deeitishization
narratives remain frequently trapped within the semiotic constructs examined and
shade into an overly simplistic moral denunciation. They are often narrow and essen-
tialize the localities and social relations constitutive of these commodities, such as
"places of origin." Defetishizing commodities also often underplays the positive sides
of production and consumption. Connecting consumers with unethical practices,
in other words, can in such cases prove counterproductive and mostly (re)produce
prejudiced imaginative geographies and agendas (see also, Bridge 2001; Cook and
Crang 1996). Arguably, this risk may be increased as advocacy campaigns rely on
distant perceptions of problems and people, codepend on the mass-media to build
seductive storylines, and outbid each other to attract maximum attention and public
support (Freidberg 2004). Mobilizing such a powerful term as "terror" in consumption politics can prove highly rewarding for advocacy campaigns, for example, in
terms of media interest, but may be ambivalent in terms of its effects on producers,
consumers, and the advocacy campaigns themselves.

The contemporary discourse of the links between oil and terror is an example of
this ambivalence. As the hiking price of gas echoed the blast of bombs in Iraq, the
U.S. oil addiction was denounced as financing and motivating both Al Qaeda terrorists and the US-UK (corporate) invasion of Iraq (Harvey 2003; Jhaveri 2004; Le Billon
and El Khatib 2004; Klare 2005). Following the oil commodity chain from Persian
Gulf oil exports sponsoring 9/11 hijackers to gas-guzzling American SUVs, advocacy
TV ads sought to suggest the schizophrenia of the "terrorist consumer":

> I helped hijack an airplane. I helped blow up a nightclub. So what if it gets 11 miles to the gal-
> lon? I gave the money to a terrorist training camp in a foreign country. It makes me feel safe.
> I helped our enemies develop weapons of mass destruction. What if I need to go off-road?
> Everyone has one. I helped teach kids around the world to hate America. I like to sit up high.
> I sent our soldiers off to war. Everyone has one. My life, my SUV.[2]

These ads ironically echoed those of the US Office of National Drug Control Policy:
using the terror momentum to prop up its own "war on drugs," the ads juxtaposed
pictures of terrorists with that of a teenager smoking a joint and presented the (dubious) links of drugs with terror as "F-A-C-T-S." [3]

These examples suggest that the mobilization of consumption politics via the "war
on terror" is not only about redrawing 'homeland security' around the borders of
the consuming self. It is also about inserting the narrative of terror within everyday
practices, disciplining citizens, and constructing the terrorist "other" through the
consuming self. As part of its Total Information Awareness surveillance program,
the Pentagon sought in 2002 to systematically track consumer purchases, looking for
telltale signs of "suspicious" consumption—such as one-way railway tickets or large
cash withdrawals—matched with biometric data and behavioral models to detect

and identify "*foreign* terrorists."[4] As consumption comes to serve such a project of securitization, not all commodities and services become associated with narratives of terror. Rather, the identity and legitimacy of the trading interests at hand often influence such labeling. In the realm of financial services, for example, Marieke de Goede (2003) exposes how, in the context of the "war on terror," the negative stereotyping of the informal *hawala* money-transfer networks criminalized remittance networks, while implicitly white-washing the involvement of "legitimate" Western banking in financing terrorism and deflecting calls for its much-needed regulation.

Drawing on these debates, I discuss the tactics and ambivalences of a human rights advocacy campaign that sought to mobilize consumers, the diamond industry and governments to stop the financing of belligerents via the diamond trade.[5] Following this introduction, the chapter presents a brief account of the connections between diamonds and violence, and then turns to the conflict diamond campaign and related initiatives, before arguing that a marginalization of the poor and appropriation of ethical space ensued. To sum up, I argue that the conflict diamonds campaign successfully reconnected "violent" spaces of exploitation and "peaceful" spaces of consumption to reform international diamond trade regulation. The campaign had limited and ambivalent effects, however, in terms of corporate accountability and impacts on artisanal mining communities. While reasserting the crucial importance of notifying consumers of their "terrorist" activities, I suggest that redrawing the contours of ethical consumption via discourses of "terror" and racialized images of Africa reproduced spaces and identities of (il)legitimacy supporting dominant corporate interests rather than challenging marginalization processes of Africa(ns) in the diamond industry.

"Diamonds: A Guerilla's Best Friend"?

In the early part of the twenty-first century, diamonds captivated the attention of many conflict analysts and media outlets due to their prominent role in several African conflicts. Easily exploitable (when found in alluvial deposits), highly valuable, and easily concealable, diamonds were represented as a guerrilla's best friend, providing rebel groups the loot necessary to purchase their weapons and the booty rewarding their atrocities (Global Witness 1998; Smillie et al. 2000). In the most well-publicized example, the exploitation and trafficking of diamonds in Sierra Leone and neighboring Liberia generated tens of millions of dollars for armed groups in the 1990s. During the decade-long Sierra Leonean war, the Revolutionary United Front (RUF) rebel movement and (para)military governmental troops were responsible for countless war crimes, including the widespread amputation of civilians used as a terror tactic (Human Rights Watch 1998). In Angola, diamonds provided hundreds of millions of dollars in revenue to Jonas Savimbi's UNITA during the 1990s, enabling the prolongation of an insurrection initiated in the mid-1970s with the assistance of the CIA and apartheid South Africa (Global Witness 1998; Le Billon 2001). Rebellion in eastern Democratic Republic of Congo, and foreign military interventions by regional powers such as Uganda and Zimbabwe were equally tainted by the "lust for diamonds" according to UN investigators (United Nations Secretariat 2001). Even

United Nations peacekeepers, suggested Secretary General Kofi Annan, were not immune to the temptation of the "poisonous mix" of diamonds and greed, alleged to fuel these wars (Crossette 2000).

In addition to financing belligerents, diamonds also provide a means of hoarding, laundering, and transferring funds across borders, because they can easily be concealed, transported, and (to some extent) marketed. Diamonds can thus become a 'currency of choice' for individuals and groups faced by volatile currencies, banking scrutiny, or financial sanctions. For example, less than two months after 9/11, *Washington Post* reporter Douglas Farah (2004) revealed that Al Qaeda operatives benefited from the sales of millions of dollars of "conflict diamonds" mined by rebels in Sierra Leone. Initial reporting confirmed the picture of greedy West African warlords supporting Islamic terrorists. Deals had been conducted in Liberia under the protection of warlord-turned-elected president Charles Taylor. Taylor himself had been an early supporter of the RUF as part of a pan-African revolutionary movement sponsored by Libyan authorities (Sierra Leone Truth and Reconciliation Commission Final Report 2004). West Africa was not only a wild zone endangering the local population, but—as much as Iraq, Afghanistan, or North Korea—a zone of "rogue rule" portrayed as threatening the West. The plot thickened however, with allegations that Charles Taylor had been on the CIA payroll all along to check on Gadhafi (Bender 2004).

The overwhelming majority of these conflict diamonds were jewel-quality, rather than industrial, and intended for mass-consumption, destined to be draped around somebody's neck or slipped around somebody's finger. For long, diamonds had been objects possessed only by the elite and revered for their "magical" powers. Massive diamond discoveries since the late nineteenth century have motivated the industry—and its dominating cartel De Beers—to continually broaden the diamond market through advertising campaigns linking diamonds to love, wealth, eternity, and purity. Close to $500 million per year are spent in advertising by De Beers and its clients to construct "the image of diamonds as a symbol of love, beauty and purity"—often distant from what goes on at the bottom of the pit.[6] Behind these advertisements lie a politics of consumption strongly imbued with class status and aspirations through which the industry succeeded in creating a currently estimated $60 billion world diamond jewelery retail market, half of which is in the United States.

Conflict diamonds were estimated to represent around 3–15 percent of the world rough diamond trade by the late 1990s (Yager 2002). The long-established culture of clandestine trading and "no questions asked" on the part of the diamond industry allowed these conflict diamonds to be purchased by business intermediaries and legally traded in international rough diamonds markets such as that of De Beers or the open market in Antwerp (Vallée and Misser 1997). After being circulated, mixed, cut, polished, and mounted, rough conflict diamonds became virtually indistinguishable from other diamonds. In the eyes of the retailer and consumer, diamonds lost all connections to their place of exploitation, only retaining their commodity characteristics—the four C's: Clarity, Color, Cut, and Carat weight.[7] Yet Fatal Transaction campaigners were pushing consumers to "ask for the 'fifth C'...conflict...before you buy your next diamond" (World Vision 2004).

"Amputation Is Forever": Conflict Diamonds Campaigning

In their first press release, Fatal Transaction campaigners argued that "most people would be horrified to learn that their diamond jewelery had financed the purchase of landmines or guns in one of Africa's brutal conflicts" (Fatal Transactions 1999). Investigative reports, campaigning material, protests at jewelery shops, and widespread reports in the mass media sought to redraw consumers' imaginative geographies of diamonds, replacing "stone" with "people," "dollars" with "suffering," and "desire" with "compassion" (see Figure 8.1). De Beers' well-known advertising slogans proved highly vulnerable to adbusting such as "diamonds are a guerrilla's best friend" or "amputation is forever." As Gavin Bridge (2001, 2169) argues, the diamond exploitation zones "constructed by themes of warfare, pillage, desecration, and ecological and cultural degradation [became] a dystopic horizon from which to critique the insouciance of postindustrial capitalism."

Publicly exposing the links between diamonds and violence was one thing, but curtailing them was (and remains) another. The distinctiveness of diamonds presented both challenges and opportunities to campaigners. As mentioned above, specific characteristics of this commodity—mining accessibility, low weight, high value, low traceability—complicated policing. Yet potential trade regulation reforms were facilitated by its marketing characteristics, as a nonessential luxury good vulnerable to boycott, and by the structure of its industry, with a high concentration through De Beers and the Antwerp market as well as at least two governments—Botswana and Namibia—highly dependent on diamond revenues. Building on these potential leverage points, the Fatal Transactions campaign did not primarily seek to directly

Figure 8.1. "What price for these diamonds?" (Amnesty International, France).

mobilize consumers through a boycott of diamonds. Rather, it used consumer awareness and the *threat* of a boycott to mobilize complacent businesses and governments. This complacency was remarkable given the history of the sector, which included the abuses and violence of British (corporate) imperialism, degrading labour practices, connections with apartheid regimes, and widespread political corruption (Newbury 1989; Vallée and Misser 1997; Worger 1987). The diamond industry thrived throughout much of this tainted history, as most notably demonstrated by the longevity and wealth of its main corporate actor, De Beers. Established in 1888 by British "imperialist" Cecil Rhodes, the company has been under the control of the Oppenheimer family since the early twentieth century. Jonathan Oppenheimer—great-grandson of Sir Ernest Oppenheimer who succeeded in taking control of De Beers—was listed by Forbes magazine as the third richest successor among the world's business magnates, with $3.3 billion (Pitman 2002). In the mid-1990s, about two-thirds of the world's rough diamonds were passing through De Beers' Central Selling Organisation (now Diamond Trading Company). Diamonds from more than twenty countries and worth more than $4 billion were centralized, stockpiled, and sorted in De Beers' clearinghouse in London, before being mixed again in parcels sold at fixed prices to select clients.

The role of diamonds in motivating or financing violence had long been known within industry circles, but public recognition of the problem and action such as the imposition of UN sanctions on conflict diamonds were slow to materialize and impeded by self-interest. As noted by De Beers' Chairman Harry Oppenheimer in the mid-1970s, no other commodity is "less susceptible to dangers from UN sanctions than diamonds" (quoted in Epstein 1982, 20). Faced by anti-apartheid campaigns and the threat of UN sanctions against South Africa and Namibia—where De Beers had major diamond mining interests—Oppenheimer knew that millions of dollars could be smuggled out from these countries in an attaché case, and he believed there would always be buyers.[8] In addition to the ease of smuggling diamonds, effective sanctions also face the difficulty of identifying the origin of diamonds in mixed parcels and the customary tolerance of the industry and importing countries for illicit diamonds—smuggled in order to avoid taxation in producing countries.

Attempts to address the problem of conflict diamonds in Angola in the early 1990s—such as the proposal of a ban on Belgian imports of UNITA diamonds by Belgian MPs in 1993—were initially dismissed using such arguments (Vallée and Misser 1997). Politically, the delay in imposing UN sanctions on UNITA diamond exports was excused by the UN's obligation "to behave impartially between the two sides in helping them to implement the [peace] Protocol … [even if] there were doubts about the sincerity of [UNITA]'s commitment to do so."[9] There was also some resistance on the part of Western politicians favorable to UNITA. Commercially, several producing countries and many companies were also protective of statistical requirements on production figures that could affect their negotiations with major buyers (i.e., knowledge of large stocks potentially weakening their negotiating position on the market). Key importing countries, such as Belgium, were also wary of the possibility that drastic regulations could drive the trade elsewhere, as had occurred in early twentieth century when many diamond-cutting businesses moved from Amsterdam to Antwerp as Dutch unions obtained better working conditions (Epstein 1982).

Momentum to address the problem of conflict diamonds grew in the late 1990s because of a deadlock in peace negotiations with rebel factions in Angola and Sierra Leone, as well as growing public campaigning and media reports on the "terror" aspects of the diamond trade in several African wars, and later on Al Qaeda attacks in the United States. Three initiatives were subsequently pursued. First, the UNITA Sanctions Committee drastically strengthened the implementation of UN sanction regimes through investigation panels "naming and shaming" sanction busters (including the presidents of Togo and Burkina Faso). The Sanctions Committee also lobbied the diamond industry for prompt reforms and sent clear warnings about the consequences of a boycott, citing the example of the fur boycott in the 1980s. The second initiative mobilized the industry and key governments in support of diamond trade reforms through public campaigns, international negotiations over diamond certification of origin (the Kimberley Process), and legislative action. Campaigning NGOs denounced the complicity or inaction of the diamond industry and governments, yet stopped short of calling for a complete diamonds boycott that they perceived as threatening hundreds of thousands of jobs (emphasizing diamond cutters in India), and the diamond-dependent economies of Botswana and Namibia.[10] Nor did campaigners systematically launch judicial processes against corporate accomplices of war crimes and sanction-busting. After initially denying any connection with conflict diamonds, major industry actors championed the creation of an international certification agreement to protect the carefully crafted image of its luxury product from growing media attention to the "terror" aspects of the trade. It seems that part of the industry was more worried about a link between diamonds and "terror" than diamonds and "conflicts," and some campaigners used it to accelerate the momentum in their campaign as the wars in Angola and Sierra Leone were coming to an end.[11] As noted by diamond sector analyst Even-Zohar (2004),

> Conflict diamonds and terror diamonds may have similar connotations, but they are quite different from a consumer perception angle. … conflict diamonds, in all their cruelty, were perceived by the public-at-large as largely an African problem; terrorism, in contrast, is something that hits every consumer at home [USA/Israel]. And al Qaeda represents the worst in terrorism.

The U.S. House of Representative passed the Clean Diamond Act only three weeks after the Al Qaeda story was published in the *Washington Post*. A year later, thirty-eight countries adopted the international Kimberley Process Certification Scheme establishing norms between diamond exporters and importers to prevent the laundering of conflict diamonds.[12]

The third initiative consisted of a set of "peace building" and "fair trade" programs to improve the social conditions, political economy, and governance of diamond mining in conflict-prone countries. Recognizing that the Kimberley Process did not address the concerns of artisanal mining communities, these programs are bringing together industry, governments, civil society organizations, and mining communities to address problems of poverty, corruption, political representation, and violence in diamonds areas (Partnership Africa Canada and Global Witness 2004). The Diamond Development Initiative—founded by De Beers, Global Witness, Partnership African Canada, diamond sector analyst Rapaport, and the World Bank is seeking to "optimize the beneficial development impact of artisanal diamond mining to miners, their communities and their governments" throughout Africa (DDI 2005). In Sierra Leone, projects funded by major international donors—the Peace Diamonds Alliance and Integrated Diamond Management—are seeking to assist communities and the government in managing diamonds and bringing "peace and prosperity" to the population of the Kono region—a key diamond production area of strategic importance for the economy of the war that devastated this country during the 1990s. Well-conceived and attending to most issues perpetuating poverty and risks of renewed conflict, these programs have nevertheless faced numerous implementation hurdles, "the infeasibility of desirable livelihood options in diamond mining communities, ... and the re-emergence of patrimonialism and patronage as key systems of social securitization" (Levin 2005, 5). Most programs are also focusing on artisanal mining, and may overlook and leave unquestioned the role of industrial mining.

This set of three initiatives is often praised as a model to follow when addressing the role of commodities in fueling war (Le Billon 2005; Tamm 2004). Between 1998 and 2003, the UN Security Council had imposed targeted sanctions on imports from Angola, Liberia, and Sierra Leone; the UN had launched high-profile public investigations; and an international certification scheme backed by the industry, advocacy organizations, and the UN General Assembly had come into effect. More than one hundred NGOs had joined the Fatal Transactions campaign to bring about change in the diamond industry, and the public media had extensively covered the issue. Consumer awareness had sharply risen, with British consumer awareness about conflict diamonds growing from 9 to 26 percent between 2001 and 2003, three-quarters of which would have required "conflict-free" guarantees before buying diamonds. In the United States, consumer awareness grew from 7 percent in 2000 to 26 percent in 2003, before falling to 15 percent in 2004.[13] Campaigning and media reports (re)connecting killing fields and shopping malls were not only important in grabbing the attention of the public and industry, they were also broadening the international security agenda into the realm of "conflict" trade by casting a revealing light on the "goodness" of unfettered international trade and the "respectability" of Multinational Corporations MNCs. As discussed below, however, achieving policy reforms entailed much compromise, co-optation, and manipulation.

Marginalizing the Poor, Appropriating Ethics

The seductive power of the conflict diamonds narrative supported the campaign in major ways. As Alex Yearsley (2000), a Global Witness campaigner working on the Fatal Transaction campaign remarked,

> Awareness ... generally relies on our friends in the media. But it also depends on what sort of awareness you want to create ... Global Witness has worked on the issue of timber funding conflict in Cambodia and has not obtained a fraction of the public awareness that has been achieved on the conflict diamond issue.... Basically, diamonds are sexy and logs are not.

Not only were diamonds sexy, but the strength of this message was also the result of its connection with "the repulsive fascination of Africa in the occidental imaginary"

(Amselle 2002). Many people know about the genocide committed in Cambodia, but this knowledge does not compare with the widespread imaginative geography of Africa as the "Dark Continent." Building on prejudice and looking for solutions, the campaign unintentionally created winners and losers through the distributive effects of a racialized discourse of terror. Indiscriminately associating terror with poor young African men, burnishing the "reputable" character of Western industrialized mining, and largely leaving aside state violence were among the ambivalent outcomes of the campaign, its mediatization, and manipulation.

Mediatizing and Marginalizing the Poor

Although key campaigners, such as the NGO Global Witness, had stressed that it did not believe that greed over diamonds was the cause of the war in Sierra Leone and elsewhere, images of pure white stones and greedy African warlords were too sexy a storyline for the media. By 2003, fiction blurred with reality in the James Bond movie *Die Another Day* in which the MI6 agent infiltrates and defeats a diamonds-for-weapons of mass destruction deal that revealed links between North Korea, West African warlords, and key players of the diamond industry. Bond's scriptwriters had consulted members of the Fatal Transactions advocacy group. Some of the advocacy material also played along the lines of neo-Malthusianism and Hobbesian state of nature to describe alluvial diamond diggers, occasionally falling into the trap of subject essentialization:

> A huge number of young men still swarm over the alluvial diamond field… Taken together… there are probably a million African artisanal alluvial diamond diggers. Almost all of them are unregistered and unregulated. These young men, who work for nothing except what they are lucky enough to find—and individually they don't find much—produce ten or maybe twenty per cent of the diamonds that go into the jewellery shops of London, Tokyo, Paris and New York. They are an important part of the diamond industry. But they are potentially dangerous, and over the past decade they have shown just how dangerous they can be.[14]

In many conflict diamond narratives, political leaders, combatants, and miners were often indiscriminately conflated into one single category of "greedy thugs"; even if the status of alluvial diamond diggers as victims and legitimate political agents rightly seeking social change, as well as their social diversity have been documented (Reno 1995; Richards 1996; Zack-Williams 1995). The justified reporting of war atrocities drowned the voices of diggers during the conflict diamond campaign. Among the dissenting voices, several junior western diamond companies cynically sought to justify their involvement with rebel groups as supporting African diggers (as opposed to the large corporate interests working alongside local governments).[15] Campaigners rightly dismissed these claims as shameful pretexts in light of the abuses suffered by these diggers. Even in a post-conflict context, artisanal diggers were largely perceived to be a "problem" standing in the way of a "well-regulated" and largely industrialized sector bringing about peace and prosperity.

Beyond individual miners and artisanal mining communities, the imaginative geographies of conflict diamonds posed a threat to African producers and risked further marginalizing the "legitimate" diamond business on the continent. African diamond producers rapidly identified the risks of such a connection going beyond conflict-affected countries and engulfing them by association (see, for example, Taylor and Mokhawa 2003). With its major mining interests in Botswana, Namibia, and South Africa, De Beers was highly exposed to such a risk. The threat of links between diamonds and terror both called for and provided an opportunity to further distance the pure white stones from the darker side of Africa. The chief target of this move was artisanal diamond mining, which would be displaced through processes of industrialization, mechanization, and selective criminalization/legitimation.

Labor-intensive artisanal diamond mining represents a large share of the industry in places where alluvial diamonds are accessible through minimal capital and technological inputs. Alluvial diamond fields, from this perspective, became the breeding ground for terror and a threat to political order. As a World Bank paper stresses:

> In these countries diamonds are mainly found along river beds. These so-called alluvial diamonds are collected over extended areas by a multitude of *independent* small enterprises and artisans (diggers) using rudimentary technologies. These mining sites cannot be fenced; controls are loose and are frequently ineffective. This is *where* the problem of conflict diamonds arises.[16]

In other words, combining masses of poor people and overly accessible wealth was portrayed as a recipe for disaster. Addressing this threat, in turn, required disciplining this space through land, labor, and capital controls. Such a strategy was, for example, at the base of the consolidation of diamond mining in South Africa or Namibia through the industrialization of exploitation coupled with the criminalization of workers and petty traders. Indeed, diamond mining has a long history of disciplining human labor to an extent rarely found in other industries. Although the physical characteristics and value of diamonds do entail particularly high risks of theft, the risk in itself provides the justification of practices that go well beyond simple security (see, Carstens 2001; Worger 1987). In the process, vast and highly concentrated fortunes were made, most notably that of De Beers.

The artisanal diamond sector being notoriously difficult to tax, many analysts also suggest that industrialized sectors (thereby concentrating revenues through a few corporations) or at least legalized ones (through trade licensing restrictions) are better placed to ensure political stability and "fight terror." Whose interests such policies serve is a controversial issue. Not only does the economic marginalization of artisanal miners and small traders represent a case of structural violence, but fencing out "illegal miners" is also frequently marked by physical violence often embroiling identity politics. In this respect, the criminalization of artisanal miners, in part reinforced by conflict diamond narratives, may have served to justify further violence. For example, after its military victory over UNITA, the Angolan government initiated the violent deportation of tens of thousands of Congolese diamond diggers (many of them from regions straddling the colonial border established between Belgium's Congo Free State and Portugal's Angola). Humanitarian organizations denounced the brutality and health risks of these expulsions. Congolese miners and their families were beaten, publicly humiliated, and denied food and water (Médecins Sans Frontières 2004). Angolan officials routinely carried out body searches—allegedly looking for illicit diamonds—using "one plastic bag or glove for multiple inspections [of vaginal and anal areas, thereby increasing] the risk of transmitting HIV and other sexually transmitted diseases" (Human Rights Watch 2004). Congolese women have been frequently raped, especially after refusing body searches.

The terror of the "cleaning up" and "legalization" process of Angola's diamonds fields echoed the wartime violence of diamond and labor control (see, de Boeck 1999, 2001), with Angolan security forces continuing to abuse and kill artisanal diamond diggers:

> A National Police patrol confronted Tximuanga Jonasse on the banks of the River Cuango, while he was … carrying a motorised pump used by artisanal diamond diggers. After an exchange of words, one of the police shot him at close range in the right foot [and] he subsequently died as a result of the wound, without receiving first aid. As a result … the people from the area … began protesting against the police. When police fired into the air to try to disperse the crowd, one of the police fired a shot that struck Rafael Muangungi in the abdominal area, wounding him fatally. [17]

Such violence, as well as that of dispossession, forced displacement, or child labor, apparently did not qualify as "gross human rights violations" under the Kimberley Certification Scheme. The international scheme only recognized the violence of "rebel movements aimed at undermining legitimate governments" selecting not only which, but also whose violence mattered.[18] Arguably, this narrow definition of conflict diamonds—and its legitimating effect for the rest of the industry—aided the successful conclusion of the Kimberley Process. It nevertheless failed, as a result, to address human rights abuses and unfair wealth distribution within other parts of the diamond industry. As mentioned above, a third phase of the conflict diamond campaign is now supporting (with much less mediatization) a number of "fair trade" initiatives in the artisanal diamond sector seeking to address this gap, with companies like De Beers promoting their involvement and sponsorship (More O'Ferrall 2005).

Anti-terror Branding and Market Appropriation of Ethics

The turnaround of the industry, and most notably that of De Beers, in supporting conflict diamonds reforms not only reflected ethical concerns and new technological solutions to the identification and tracking of the origin of diamonds; this move also clearly reflected self-interested corporate objectives. Previously, De Beers had followed a strategy of denial against claims by a key advocacy group, Global Witness, which had denounced the cartel's complicity in the conflict diamonds trade (Global Witness 1998). This shift in policy in part reflected the growing momentum of the campaign and the fear of a general diamonds boycott—similar to that of the fur industry in the 1970s—if nothing was done. The shift was also opportunistically motivated by commercial and political difficulties in Angola, as well as the adoption of a new corporate policy following a strategic review in 1998, according to which De Beers moved from a horizontal integration strategy of producer and buyer of rough diamonds to one of vertical integration linking its diamond mining interests to jewelery shops. This strategic move allowed De Beers to reduce its huge price-regulating diamond stock, decrease its exposure to U.S. antitrust law, and move from "buyer of last resort" to a potentially more profitable "supplier of choice" through branded diamonds and reduced stocks (Guerrera and Parker 2000). Finally, the campaign was

taking place in the context of record sales of diamonds associated with large marketing efforts linking the turn of the millennium to the purchase of diamonds. An early
and effective consumer boycott could have been devastating, but rough diamond
sales by De Beers grew sharply in 1999 and 2000 despite increasing media coverage
of conflict diamonds (see Figure 8.2).

Beyond the case of De Beers, the connection of diamonds with terror led to an
extensive process of accommodation and appropriation. Like De Beers, the rest of
the industry recognized that luxury goods such as diamonds may be vulnerable to
a consumer boycott.[19] Diamond dependent exporting countries, such as Botswana,
had major economic, social, and political stakes in avoiding a boycott; most favored
strong regulation that would protect this sector.

In contrast to African producers, the imaginative geographies of conflict diamonds
presented "northern" producers with an opportunity. Among them, the Canadian
diamond industry was best placed to secure a premium from the "peacefulness"
and "integrity" of its mining context, as openly advocated by corporate interests
and Canadian politicians (McCarthy 2003). Put bluntly in the words of an industry analyst: "Canada could capitalize on conflict" (Duncan 2000). In addition to the
classic myth-making images of diamonds as symbols of love and desire, Canadian
diamonds were marketed as "pure," "bloodshed free," or "socially conscious" (Stueck
2003). Cast in an icy northern landscape, advertisements suggested that the flawless
purity of Canadian diamonds would guarantee for fiancés that the wedding "promise
arrives pure" through a "Canadian white diamond." This association of the "white"
stone with "white" Canada (both as imagined landscapes and model consumers) easily resonated with the contrasting racist imaginaries of "dark" Africa. Canada (and
more precisely the Canadian "north") was directly associated with purity with such
slogans as: "Purity from the land that defines the word" (Aurias 2005). In the branding
of diamonds from Canadian mines, marketing recast the "fifth C" slogan of human
rights campaigners (C for "Conflict") to C for "Canadian" (Aurias 2005). A survey
of discussions on Internet-based diamond buying forums confirmed that Canadian
diamonds were perceived as offering "the most serious conflict-free guarantee", but

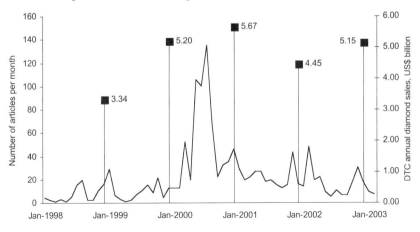

Figure 8.2.   Media coverage of conflict diamonds and De Beers (DTC) diamond sales.[20]

also that many potential buyers were deterred by their high prices.[21] Unsurprisingly (but wrongly to my knowledge), rumors flew in the industry at the time that the Canadian government, industry, and NGOs were orchestrating the conflict diamond campaign for self-interested purposes.[22]

Among major jewelery makers and retailers, Tiffany & Co.—probably the most well known U.S. jewelery company—was quick to distance itself from potentially tainted African stones. The company made it widely known in the sector that it had passed commercial agreements with Canadian diamond producers. It also went public, reassuring its customers that buying a Tiffany diamond was not contributing to war:

> Tiffany & Co. has been sensitive to this problem for some time and has informed its vendors that Tiffany expects them to avoid, rigorously, all commerce in conflict diamonds. You should know that Tiffany & Co. does not have any purchasing operations in Africa and purchases only cut stones from operations conducted outside of Africa.[23]

Ironically, Global Witness (2004, 3) praised Tiffany for being one of the rare retailers to have "outlined its policies to back up the warranty in detail and described how it has strengthened its sourcing procedures and control over its supply chain to prevent dealing in conflict diamonds." Surveying a sample of retailers in the United States—a national market accounting for about 50 percent of worldwide diamond jewellery sales—Global Witness found that most lacked interest and policies on the issue of conflict diamonds and had not trained their salespersons about it. Furthermore, the effects of the conflict diamond campaign on the sensibility of the industry and consumers may not last long. Ironically, the lasting effects of linking diamonds with violence may not be ethical consumption, but rather a stronger dystopian vision of Africa and legitimated position for large "reputable" (Western) companies over smaller local and regional operators.

Consumption and Spaces of Terror

Wars in Angola and Sierra Leone both ended in 2002, before the conclusion of the Kimberley Process Certification Process, largely as a result of military factors. The conflict diamond campaign, however, undeniably strengthened the enforcement of UN sanctions and launched valuable institutional and legislative changes within the diamond industry. The campaign also initiated new ethical dispositions and practices on the part of the diamond industry and diamond consumers, and campaigners are now pursuing this role with regard to artisanal diamond mining. Beyond the diamond sector, the campaign inspired more ethical practices in other extractive industries, notably on the financial transparency agenda. As argued earlier, these successes rested on the powerful conflict diamond narrative of greed and terror, a focus on the most extreme forms of violence committed by non-state armed groups, and a "constructive engagement" buying into the "integrity" discourse of major companies like De Beers and governments such as that of Angola. Through these strategies, the campaign gained vast media coverage, broad consumer awareness, and high-level policy access resulting in tangible reforms.

What was lost through this strategy was a sense of historical accountability for past corporate complicity. Ironically, the De Beers diamond "syndicate" that under priced Sierra Leone's diamonds during the British colonial period was invited by Sierra Leone's government to resume its activities in the country after the end of the conflict (Hart 2001; Sierra Leone State House 2005). The diamond industry successfully insulated itself from the potential financial costs of the campaign, and some even benefited by actively buying into the campaign and constructing the "Anti" Terrorist Consumer market. Prominent corporate interests championed diamond consumption through competing (and complementing) discourses of "prosperity diamonds" reasserting the contribution of the industry to the economy of several African countries (e.g., Botswana, Namibia), or "conflict-free" and "ethical" diamonds based on advertised corporate "integrity" (e.g., De Beers, Rand diamonds) or producing country image (e.g., Canada). While for many campaigners this behavior demonstrated enhanced corporate social responsibility, to others it suggested a corporate take-over and legitimization exercise.

Through its media success, the campaign also informed and reinforced essentializing narratives on violence, actors, and the places of origin of conflict commodities. In the consumer dystopias emerging from these narratives, violence was a purely criminal enterprise driven by "greed," or a senseless attack on "freedom," rather than the outcome of exploitative and exclusionary histories and uneven development.[24] Leaders, combatants, and diamond miners were often conflated into one single category of greedy thugs, overlooking vast differences in identity, motivations, actions, and responsibilities. This connected, in turn, to the justification of state-sponsored "terrorism" against artisanal miners in places like Angola. Places of origin were frequently reduced to jungles, rather than the tailings and scrap yards of past mining ventures. The discourse of alleged greed of the Revolutionary United Front for diamonds, for example, undermines the movement's critique of Sierra Leone's political economy, reducing the conflict to a criminal enterprise and overlooking the role of Britain in creating the country as a dumping-ground for freed slaves and benefiting from a (corrupt) exploitation of diamonds (Campbell 2002, Reno 1995). The perspective of greedy rebels in the bush acting without a cause also silences their individual or collective attempts to "reverse homelessness and social exclusion" through diamond extraction and violence— thereby dismissing in the worst colonial tradition every rebellion as criminal (Richards 2001, 82). As a mirror image of the terrorist consumer, consumer dystopias also constructed rebels and terrorists as "consuming terrorists": depoliticized actors driven by their self-interest and operating within complacent capitalist flows—with their political violence being reduced to economic or criminal violence.

Finally, the terror depicted by the campaign and its mediatization—especially through the Al Qaeda connection—reinforced the rationale of forceful (Western) state intervention, in which terror is both denounced and justified. This is not to say that all these interventions are justified on false grounds or fail to alleviate suffering. There is a major political importance in notifying consumers of their "terrorist" activities and acting accordingly. As illustrated by the case of conflict diamonds, however, once mediatized through the lenses of prejudice and activated by vested political or commercial interests, such calling can obscure grievances while perpetuating spaces of marginalization and violence. As discussed above, while in the eyes of De Beers the Kimberley Process was providing a "wonderful insurance" for the diamond industry, it did little to improve the lot of poor artisanal miners in conflict-affected countries, and in some cases it helped pave the way for violent clean-up operations by government security forces.[25]

The concept of the terrorist consumer is not only about governing consumption in the interest of security. It is also about governing the consuming self along registers of "othering" (see, Barnett et al. 2005), with the mechanistic rejection of participation in conflict trade risks being constructive of the very processes of marginalization that in some cases form the roots of violence. The responsibility of the terrorist consumer—and campaigners and mass media informing them—is thus not only to become an ethical consumer by changing one's consuming practices; it is also about challenging the very definition of the "terrorism" that needs to be rejected via consumption.[26] As this analysis of the Fatal Transactions campaign suggests, balancing material disengagement *from* violence and conceptual engagement *with* violence may lead to a more radical transformation of commodity production and consumption.

Acknowledgments

The author would like to thank for their assistance or comments Karen Bakker, Susanne Freidberg, Michael Goodman, Derek Gregory, Morlai Kamara, Sara Koopman, Estelle Levin, Gilberto Neto, Nancy Lee Peluso, two anonymous reviewers and the participants of the University of California Berkeley's Workshop on Environmental Politics. Funding was received from the Social Sciences and Humanities Research Council, Canada.

References

Amselle, J. L. (2000). "L'Afrique: un parc à themes." *Les Temps Modernes,* http://www.anthropoetics.ucla.edu/ap0901/amselle.htm (accessed April 22, 2004).

Aurias. (2005. The Aurias Difference: The five C's of Canadian Diamonds, http://www.aurias.com/en/difference/five_c.html (accessed April 19, 2005).

Barnet, C., Cloke, P., Clarke, N., and Malpass, A. (2005). Consuming ethics: Articulating subjects and spaces of ethical consumption. *Antipode* 37(1): 23–45.

Bender, B. (2004). "Liberia's Taylor gave aid to Qaeda, UN probe finds." *Boston Globe*, August 4, 2004.

Bridge, G. (2001). "Resource triumphalism: Postindustrial narratives of primary commodity production." *Environment and Planning A* 33: 2149–2173: 2169.

Bryant, R., and Goodman, M. (2004). "Consuming narratives: The political ecology of 'alternative' consumption." *Transactions of the Institute of British Geographers* 29: 344–366.

Campbell, G. (2002). *Blood Diamonds: Tracing the Deadly Path of the World's Most Precious Stones.* Boulder, CO: Westview Press.

Carstens, P. (2001). *In the Company of Diamonds: Kleinzee, De Beers, and the Control of a Town.* Athens: Ohio University Press.

Castree, N. (2001). "Commodity fetishism, geographical imaginations and imaginative geographies." *Environment and Planning A* 33: 1519–1525.

Collier, C. (2000). "Doing well out of war: An economic perspective." In M. Berdal and D. Malone (eds.), *Greed and Grievance: Economic Agendas in Civil Wars* (pp. 91–111). Boulder, CO: Lynne Rienner.

Collinson, S. (2003). *Power, Livelihoods and Conflict: Case Studies in Political Economy Analysis for Humanitarian Action.* HPG report 13. London: Overseas Development Institute.

Cook, I., and Crang, P. (1996). "The world on a plate: Culinary culture, displacement, and geographical knowledges." *Journal of Material Culture* 1: 131–153.

Cooper, N. (2002). "State collapse as business: The role of conflict trade and the emerging control agenda." *Development and Change* 33(5): 935–955.

Crossette, B. (2000). "U.N. chief faults reluctance of U.S. to help in Africa." *New York Times*, May 13, 2000.

Daunton, M., and Hilton, M. (2001). *The Politics of Consumption: Material Culture and Citizenship in Europe and America*. New York: Berg.

DDI. (2005). "Diamond Development Initiative begins. New approach to Africa's diamond problems." Press release from Diamond Development Initiative, August 16, 2005.

de Boeck, F. (1999). "'Dogs breaking their leash': Globalization and shifting gender categories in the diamond traffic between Angola and DRCongo (1984–1997)." In de Lame D and Zabus C (eds.), *Changements au Féminin en Afrique Noire*. Tervuren/Paris: Musée Royal de l'Afrique Central/L'Harmattan, 887-114.

de Boeck, F. (2001). "Garimpeiro worlds: Digging, dying and 'hunting' for diamonds in Angola." *Review of African Political Economy* 28(90): 549–562.

de Goede, M. (2003). "Hawala discourses and the war on terrorist finance." *Environment and Planning D: Society and Space* 21: 513–532.

Duncan, J. M. (2000). "Canada could capitalize on conflict." *Professional Jeweler* June 22, 2000.

Epstein, E. J. (1982). *The Rise and Fall of Diamonds*. New York: Simon and Schuster.

Eriksson, M., and Wallensteen, P. (2004). Armed conflict, 1989–2003. *Journal of Peace Research* 41(5): 625–636.

Even-Zohar, C. (2004). "Bloody Books Can Pain an Industry." January 16, 2004, http://www.tacyltd.com/Ten-Liner_Full.asp?id=52 (accessed August 4, 2005).

Farah, D. (2001). "Al Qaeda cash tied to diamond trade." *Washington Post*, November 2, 2001, A01.

Farah, D. (2004). *Blood from Stones: The Secret Financial Network of Terror*. New York: Broadway.

Fatal Transactions. (1999). *Campaign Launched To Stop Billion Dollar Diamond Trade From Funding Conflict In Africa*, press release dated October 3, 1999.

Freidberg, S. (2004). The ethical complex of corporate food power. *Environment and Planning D: Society and Space* 22(4): 513–531.

Global Witness. (1998). *A Rough Trade: The Role of Diamond Companies and Governments in the Angolan Conflict*. London: Global Witness.

Global Witness. (2000). *Conflict Diamonds: Possibilities for the Identification, Certification and Control of Diamonds*. London: Global Witness.

Global Witness. (2003). *For a Few Dollars More: How Al Qaeda Moved into the Diamond Trade*. London: Global Witness.

Global Witness. (2004). *Broken Vows: Exposing the "Loupe" Holes in the Diamond Industry's Efforts to Prevent the Trade in Conflict Diamonds*. London: Global Witness.

Global Witness and Action Aid. (2003). *Conflict diamonds: How They Affect Your Business*. London: Global Witness and Action Aid.

Goodman, M. K. (2005). "Reading fair trade: political ecological imaginary and the moral economy of fair trade foods." *Political Geography* 23: 891–915.

Goreux, L. (2001). *Conflict Diamonds*. Africa Region Working Paper Series no. 13. Washington DC: World Bank.

Guerrera, F., and Parker, A. (2000). The Changing Face of the Diamond Industry. *Financial Times*, July 11, 2000.

Hart, M. (2001). *Diamond: A Journey to the Heart of an Obsession*. Marble Falls, TX: Walker Publishing.

Hartwick, E. R. (1998). Geographies of consumption: A commodity-chain approach. *Environment and Planning D: Society and Space* 16: 423–437.

Hartwick, E. R. (2000). "Towards a geographical politics of consumption." *Environment and Planning A* 32(7): 1177–1192.

Harvey, D. (2003). *The New Imperialism*. Oxford : Oxford University Press.

Heine-Ellison, S. (2001). The impact and effectiveness of multilateral economic sanctions: a comparative study. *International Journal of Human Rights* 5(1): 81–112.

Hersh, S. M. (2003). "Lunch with the chairman. Why was Richard Perle meeting with Adnan Khashoggi?" *New Yorker*, March 17, 2003.

Hodges, T. (2004). *Angola: Anatomy of an Oil State*. Oxford: James Currey.

Hughes, A., and S. Reimer. (2004). *Geographies of Commodity Chains*. London: Routledge.

Human Rights Watch. (1998). *Sowing Terror: Atrocities Against Civilians in Sierra Leone*. New York: Human Rights Watch.

Human Rights Watch. (2004). "Angola: Congolese Migrants Face Brutal Body Searches," press release dated April 23, 2004.

Jhaveri, N. J. (2004). "Petroimperialism: US oil interests and the Iraq war." *Antipode* 36 (1): 2–11.

Keen, D. (1998). *The Economic Functions of Violence in Civil Wars*, Adelphi Paper 320. Oxford: Oxford University Press, for International Institute for Strategic Studies.

Klare, M. (2005). *Blood and Oil: The Dangers and Consequences of America's Growing Dependency on Imported Petroleum*. London: Penguin.

Le Billon, P. (1999). "The political ecology of transition in Cambodia 1989–1999: War, peace and forest exploitation." *Development and Change* 31(4): 785–805.

Le Billon, P. (2001). "Angola's political economy of war: the role of oil and diamonds 1975–2000." *African Affairs* 100: 55–80.

Le Billon, P. (2004). "Natural resources and the termination of armed conflicts: share, sanction, or conquer?" Unpublished manuscript, University of British Columbia.

Le Billon, P. (2005). *Fuelling War: Natural Resources and Armed Conflicts*. London: Routledge for the International Institute for Strategic Studies.

Le Billon, P., and El Khatib, F. (2004). "From free oil to 'freedom oil': Terrorism, war and US geopolitics in the Persian Gulf." *Geopolitics* 9(1): 109–137.

Leslie, D., and Reimer, S. (1999). "Spatializing commodity chains." *Progress in Human Geography* 23(3): 401–420.

Levin, E. (2005). "From poverty and war to prosperity and peace? Sustainable livelihoods and innovation in governance of artisanal diamond mining in Kono District, Sierra Leone." Unpublished MA thesis, Department of Geography, University of British Columbia.

Marques, R., and Falcão de Campos, R. (2005). *Lundas, the Stones of Death: Angola's Deadly Diamonds*. New York: Open Society Institute.

McCarthy, S. (2003). "Kakfwi comments stir controversy." *Globe and Mail*, September 9, 2003.

McQuaig, L. (2004). *It's the Crude, Dude: Big Oil, and the Fight for the Planet*. Toronto: Random House.

Médecins Sans Frontières. (2004). "Inhumane Treatment of Diamond Miners in Angola Continues" press release dated April 29, 2004.

More O'Ferrall, R. (2005). Presentation by Director of External Affairs of De Beers at the Conference on Integrity and Investment, Addis Ababa, Ethiopia, March 7–8.2005. http://www.oecd.org/dataoecd/11/36/34571080.pdf (accessed May 5, 2005).

Miller, D. (1995). "Consumption as the vanguard of history: A polemic way of introduction." In D Miller (ed.), *Acknowledging Consumption: A Review of New Studies* (pp 1–57). London: Routledge.

Nevins, J. (2003). "Restitution over coffee: Truth, reconciliation and environmental violence in East Timor." *Political Geography* 22(6): 677–701.

Newbury, C. (1989). *The Diamond Ring: Business, Politics, and Precious Stones in South Africa, 1867–1947*. Oxford: Oxford University Press.

Nordstrom, C. (2004). *Shadows of War: Violence, Power, and International Profiteering in the Twenty-First Century*. Berkeley, CA: University of California Press.

Partnership Africa Canada and Global Witness. (2004). *Rich Man, Poor Man. Development, Diamonds and Poverty: The Potential for Change in the Artisanal Alluvial Diamond Fields of Africa*. Ottawa and London: Partnership Africa Canada and Global Witness.

Pitman, J. (2002). "World's richest people: The successors." *Forbes* March 15, 2002.

Raine, G. (2003). "Gas-hogging SUVs aid terrorism, new TV ads say columnist Huffington starts campaign." *San Francisco Chronicle* January 9, 2003.

Reno, W. (1995). *Corruption and State Politics in Sierra Leone*. Cambridge: Cambridge University Press.

Richards, P. (1996). *Fighting for the Rain Forest: War, Youth, and Resources in Sierra Leone*. Oxford: James Currey.

Richards, P. (2001). "Are 'forest' wars in Africa resource conflicts? The case of Sierra Leone." In N. L. Peluso and M. Watts (eds.), *Violent Environments* (pp 65–82). Ithaca, NY: Cornell University Press.

Sierra Leone Truth and Reconciliation Commission Final Report. (2004). http://www.usip.org/library/tc/tc_regions/tc_sl.html#rep (accessed April 15, 2004).

Sierra Leone State House (2005). http://www.statehouse-sl.org/vp-uk-jan20.html (accessed August 4, 2005).

Smillie, I., L. Gberie, and Hazleton, R. (2000). *The Heart of the Matter: Sierra Leone, Diamonds and Human Security*. Ottawa: Partnership Africa Canada.

Stanton, L. (2000). "Ten reasons why you should never accept a diamond ring from anyone." In J. Heintz, N. Folbre, and the Center for Popular Economics *Ultimate Field Guide to the U.S. Economy*. New York: The New Press.(chapter read on the web: http//www.fguide.org/Bulletin/conflictdiamonds.htm last accessed 14 June 2006).

Stueck, W. (2003). "The tundra's icy heart." *Globe and Mail* September 15, 2003,

Tamm, I. J. (2004). "Dangerous appetites: human rights activism and conflict commodities." *Human Rights Quarterly* 26: 687–704.

Taylor, I., and Mokhawa, G. (2003). "Not forever: Botswana, conflict diamonds and the bushmen." *African Affairs* 102: 261–283.

United Nations Secretariat, (2001), *Report of the Panel of Experts on the Illegal Exploitation of Natural Resources and Other Forms of Wealth of the Democratic Republic of Congo*, S/2001/357. New York: United Nations Secretariat.

Vallée, O., and Misser, F. (1997). *Les Gemmocraties: L'Economie Politique du Diamant Africain*. Paris: Desclée de Brouwer.

Wilson, S. (2003). "SUV's and drugs not tied to terrorism," *UCSD Guardian online*, http://www.ucsdguardian.org/cgi-bin/opinion?art=2003_01_23_01 (accessed August 15, 2005).

Worger, W. H. (1987). *South Africa's City of Diamonds. Mine Workers and Monopoly Capitalism in Kimberley, 1867–1895*. New Haven, CT: Yale University Press.

World Vision. (2004). "Why should you care about conflict diamonds." http://www.worldvision.org/worldvision/wvususfo.nsf/stable/globalissues_conflictdiamonds_more (accessed April 22, 2005).

Yager, L. (2002). *Significant Challenges Remain in Deterring Trade in Conflict Diamonds*. Washington DC: General Accounting Office.

Yearsley, A. (2000). "Creating awareness of the role of diamonds and other natural resources in funding armed conflict: the role of NGOs," speech of Global Witness at International Ministerial Diamond Conference, Pretoria, September 2000.

Zack-Williams, A. B. (1995). *Tributors, Supporters and Merchant Capital: Mining and Underdevelopment in Sierra Leone*. Aldershot, UK: Avebury.

Notes

1. Fatal Transactions home page, http://www.fataltransactions.org/intro/index.html, accessed September 1, 2004.

2. SUV stands for Sport Utility Vehicle. Cited in Raine (2003).

3. U.S. President G.W. Bush is cited "When you quit using drugs, you join the fight against terror in America," ONDCP, press release, February 3, 2002; see (Wilson 2003).

4. The program manager, John Pointdexter (a key-figure of the Iran-Contra scandal) quit in 2003 and U.S. Congress sought to remove funds from the program in 2004 (emphasis added), http://web.archive.org/web/20020921161341/www.darpa.mil/iao/TIASystems.htm, accessed August 25, 2005.

5. The chapter builds on fieldwork investigations and participation in policy forums conducted between 1998 and 2004 through projects on war economies for an advocacy group (Global Witness), think tanks (Overseas Development Institute, International Institute for Strategic Studies), and (inter)governmental agencies (World Bank, Foreign Affairs Canada). Interviews with diamond miners and traders, local civil society activists, and governmental officials were conducted in Angola and Sierra Leone in 2001.

6. See "The cartel is not forever," *The Economist* July 17, 2004, 60–62; Guerrera and Parker (2000).

7. See, for example, Associated Press, "Most Diamond Buyers Think about Cost and Quality—Not Bloody African Wars," July 21, 2000.

8. To try to convince me that sanctions against blood diamonds would be ineffective, during an interview in 1999, a De Beers employee placed a rough diamond in the hollow of my hand and declared its value at $750,000.

9. Sir Marrack Goulding, former UK Ambassador to Angola and former head of the UN Department for Peace Keeping Operations, personal communication, October 1999.

10. More radical organizations, however, advocated for a total boycott of diamonds, arguing that the industry as a whole was tainted by human rights, environmental and consumer abuses, including the funding of small arms trafficking, wars fought by child soldiers, slave labour in cutting and polishing industry, the violation of indigenous land's rights (especially the San in Botswana), environmental impacts,

miners' exposure to HIV/AIDS, little resale value, overpricing, and constructed desire; see, Stanton (2000).

11. Interview with De Beers representative, January 2004; see also http://www.amnesty-usa.org/amnestynow/diamonds.html, accessed August 4, 2005.
12. For background information and documents on the Kimberley process, see http://www.kimberleyprocess.com:8080/, accessed August 4, 2005.
13. Poll commissioned by Action Aid, cited in (Global Witness and Action Aid 2003), and Jewellery Consumer Opinion Council.
14. Partnership Africa Canada and Global Witness (2004: 4–5), emphasis added.
15. Interview with the author of the main diamond buyer for UNITA during the mid-1990s, David Zollman, Antwerp, 2001; or "Success for the Kimberley Process may mean starvation for artisan miners," April 15, 2002, http://www.minesite.com/archives/features_archive/2002/April-2002/kimberley150402.htm, accessed May 9, 2005.
16. Goreux (2001), emphasis added.
17. Marques and Falcão de Campos (2005: 50–51).
18. Kimberley Process Certification Scheme, available online http://www.kimberley-process.com:8080/site/?name=kpcs, last accessed August 15, 2005.
19. Interviews with De Beers officials and High Diamond Council, London and Antwerp, 1998 and 2001. For an early discussion of identification issues, see Global Witness (2000).
20. Source: media coverage as estimated from review of English-language newspapers using Lexis-Nexis for the period January 1998 to February 2003; De Beers sales as reported by De Beers Group and industry reports through its rough diamonds sales arm, the Diamond Trading Company (formerly Central Selling Organisation).
21. Survey of Diamondchitchat.com, diamondtalk.com and pricescope.com, August 2005.
22. Interviews with diamond brokers and industry officials, Antwerp, 2001.
23. E-mail received by the author from Tiffany's customer service (September 26, 2003).
24. See the mediatization of the greed argument by director of the Development Research Group at the World Bank, Paul Collier (2000). In later works, Collier spoke of economic opportunities rather than greed and recognized that resource exploitation was a source of grievances that could promote the use of violence.
25. Discussion of De Beers official with the author, January 2004.
26. Consumers should ideally buy "fair trade diamonds" from mining operations maximizing benefits in poor producing countries. Such schemes are being developed in Sierra Leone but are not yet operational, see http://www.peacediamonds.org/home.asp, accessed August 25, 2005.

9

The Geography of Hindu Right-Wing Violence in India

Rupal Oza

Sangh samaj me sangathan nahi, samaj ka sangathan hai (The Sangh is not an organization *in* society, it's the organization *of* society) RSS pamphlet.[1]

A Hindu rashtra can be expected in the next two years… we will change India's history and Pakistan's geography by then. Praveen Togadia, President of VHP (the World Hindu Council).[2]

Introduction

The Hindu Right's political trajectory to power in India has been vested in a particular geography of violence.[3] This is based on the ideological project of *Hindutva*, which considers Hindus to be the original inhabitants of India and Muslim and Christian minorities merely alien invaders. The goal of the Hindu Right is the creation of a pure Hindu *rashtra* or nation-state. The attempt to produce such a nation-state has been accompanied by organized sectarian violence and—the focus of my argument in this chapter—this has been strategically connected to the conversion of public spaces into Hindu spaces. By public spaces I mean both concrete physical spaces such as shrines and mosques where members of the community gather for the collective performance of rituals or leisure and also imagined spaces such as the nation and the public that inhabits these spaces. I examine four instances where the Hindu Right has attempted to convert such public spaces into Hindu spaces. In each case, the strategy has been to discredit Muslim claims to them, and to fill the ensuing cracks and fissures with Hindu symbols and idioms. The result of changing the meanings attached to these spaces is indicative of what Satish Deshpande calls "successful spatial strategies."[4] "Considered as ideologies," he writes, "spatial strategies can be seen as articulating the physical-material and mental-imaginative aspects of social space. In short, successful spatial strategies are able to link, in a durable and ideologically credible way, abstract (imagined) spaces to concrete (physical) places."[5] Thus, when the Rashtriya Swayamsevak Sangh (RSS)[6] claims that it is not one among many organizations *in* society rather it is the organization *of* society, it is an expression of a spatial strategy to organize the entire territorial expanse of the country as Hindu.

The spatial strategies of the Hindu Right are deployed through a discourse of legitimacy whereby Hindus have the sole rightful claim to the nation. This maps a Hindu space onto the national space and attempts to destroy those spaces associated with Muslim presence. The strategy of controlling space in religious nationalism is not new, of course, and Peter van der Veer argues that the "movement and definition of space and territory are central elements in religious nationalism."[7] But the definition and control of space in religious nationalism changes over time. Political and cultural shifts demand persistently new spatial strategies to satisfy the successful grafting of an ideologically constructed pure space over a lived hybrid one. I seek to show, therefore, that modern attempts to construct a Hindu *rashtra* have entailed a dynamic spatial strategy that began by relegating Muslim minorities to the private spaces of their homes and communities; it then placed them at the margins of towns and villages; finally it has sought to erase the landscape of Muslim presence altogether. I trace the arc of this project from the 1980s, but I also show that the project has a long history that can be traced back to a much older construction of Hindus as defenders of the Indian nation against barbaric Muslim invaders. That claim has been significantly inflected by the events of September 11, 2001. In the context of a "war on terror" where the figure of the Muslim terrorist is an already collapsed and laden signifier, the Hindu Right has sought to heighten its legitimacy by claiming that Hindus are also victims of Muslim barbarity. For example, Pravin Togadia, the president of Vishva Hindu Parishad (World Hindu Council), makes the absurd claim that "the Mosque constructed by Babur at Ayodhya 450 years ago by destroying the Ram temple and the September 11th attack on the World Trade Center are symbols of Islamic *jihad*. It is necessary for India, Jews and the Western world to come together and fight Islamic militants."[8] The attack on the Twin Towers in 2001 and the construction of Babri Masjid in the sixteenth century are connected by the unchanging figure of the Muslim perpetrator.

Togadia's statement has particular resonance because it echoes the Islamophobic discourse that emerged in Europe and the United States in the wake of 9/11. Geographically, this Islamophobia divides the world into "us" versus "them." Islamic nations and Muslims become saturated with displaced narratives of instability, violence, mistreatment of women, and theocratic forms of governance, whereas the West is stabilized as the harbinger of peace, freedom, individualism, and democracy. This Islamophobic discourse has its origins in an older tradition of Orientalism. As Said put it, "Orientalism was ultimately a political vision of reality whose structure promoted the difference between the familiar (Europe, the West, 'us') and the strange (the Orient, the East, 'them')."[9] In the Hindu Right's appropriation of this discourse through the figure of the historically unchanging Muslim perpetrator, however, the "West" is not alone. Togadia's statement is an attempt to redraw the boundaries between "us" and "them" such that India is transposed from its prior mapping as part of the Orient to become an ally with the West.[10] Such a geopolitical alliance serves the Hindu Right's own project of internal coherence to build a Hindu *rashtra*. This discourse serves to stabilize a patriotic Hindu "us" against a subversive Muslim "them."

If we are to understand the import of the discourse of the Muslim threat that circulates in different geographies, then it is imperative to understand the political and ideological project of the Hindu Right. To that end, I begin with its genealogy in order to show that spatial strategies have been a central part of its political project since its inception in the 1920s. Then I examine the geography of the project, through four exemplary and successive instances in which the effort to construct a Hindu *rashtra* has entailed the conversion of public spaces into Hindu spaces.

A Genealogy of Hindutva

Hinduism in Colonial and Orientalist Scholarship

Hinduism was traditionally practiced in many different ways because it was characterized by what Romila Thapar calls a conglomeration of sects. Hinduism thus differed from the Semitic traditions by "the absence of a prophet, of a revealed book regarded as sacred, of a monotheistic god, of ecclesiastical organization, of theological debates on orthodoxy and heresy, and, even more important, the absence of conversion."[11] According to Thapar, the consolidation of Hinduism came about in the context of Christian missionaries, orientalist scholarship, and as part of the reform movements that attempted to find parallels with the Semitic religions.[12] These efforts to categorize and designate Hinduism also served the purpose of solidifying boundaries between Hindu and Muslim.[13]

In the mid-nineteenth century the British colonial administration generated intricate classification systems to order the diverse sects and religions in India for effective imperial rule. For this project, classic Hindu texts were used as templates through which to create a taxonomy of castes and sects. The use of these texts led to their designation as the primary authority on all forms of Hinduism. The colonial project also entailed the taking of a census that inscribed the division of the Indian population into a Hindu majority and a Muslim minority. As van der Veer cautions, this division was not a colonial invention "But to count these communities and to have leaders represent them was a colonial novelty, and it was fundamental to the emergence of religious nationalism."[14]

British efforts to govern India employed the tactic of indirect rule, using selected sympathetic "indigenous" elites to govern the regions while retaining ultimate authority at the center. This set in motion what Ayesha Jalal calls the dialectics of centralism versus regionalism and nationalism versus communalism.[15] Representative politics emerged that were framed around Hindu majority provinces and Muslim majority provinces. Muslims were not consolidated into one unified group and, in fact, made alliances that were, for the most part, regionally based. Similarly, Hindus were not unified either, but were described as a conglomeration of disparate sects and traditions with distinctively regional affiliations. The Congress under the leadership of Mohandas Gandhi attempted to resist the communalizing policies of the British by launching "all India" campaigns. The All India Muslim League, however, challenged Congress' claim to represent all of south Asia, and sought to safeguard the interests of Muslims in the subcontinent. Towards the end of colonial rule, it was the Muslim League, under the leadership of Mohammad Ali Jinnah, that made the demand for a separate state of Pakistan that was formalized with the partition of India in 1947.[16]

Orientalist scholars also had a significant impact on the discourse of Hinduism. The roles of scholars such as Charles Wilkins, who translated the Bhagwat Gita, William Jones, who started the Asiatic Society of Bengal, and Alexander Hamilton are well known. A different but equally influential strand of Orientalist scholarship emerged from German scholars, particularly the linguist August Wilhelm Schlegel and Max Müller, who produced a romanticist discourse on India that designated Indian culture as steeped in spirituality and divinity. India's spirituality was set off against Western materialism. This proved to be extraordinarily influential within India, where nationalists and reformers as diverse as Vivekananda, Bal Gangadhar Tilak, Bankimchandra Chattapadhyaya, as well as Jawaharlal Nehru were deeply affected by Orientalist romanticism. In fact, references to India's elevated spirituality continue to recur in the contemporary discourse of the Hindu Right.

The concept of Vedic Aryanism proved to be of particular significance.[17] The Aryans were hailed as a powerful warrior race that had entered India and conquered its inhabitants, the *dasyus*. References to the Aryan race are found in the *Rig Veda*, the oldest and thus supposedly the most authentic texts of Hindu philosophy. The investment in Aryanism by German and British scholars arose from common linguistic and philosophical references within archaic Greek, Latin, and Sanskrit. Indeed, the British Orientalist scholar, William Jones, claimed that "The Sanskrit language, whatever be its antiquity, is of a wonderful structure; more perfect than the Greek, more copious than the Latin... yet bearing to both of them a strong affinity... than could possibly have been produced by accident... that no philosopher could examine them all three without believing them to have sprung from some common source."[18] The common linguistic references led rapidly to efforts to find a common Aryan homeland. Extensive efforts to locate the original Aryan homeland by Max Müller led to frustrated speculations between Europe, India, Persia and eventually to the conclusion that it was "somewhere in Asia."[19]

The construction of Hindus as descendents of Aryans and thus as the original inhabitants of India forms one of the central authenticating claims made by the Hindu Right. One of the most influential ideological figureheads of the Hindutva movement in the 1920s was Vinayak Damodar Savarkar. In his extremely influential book, *Hindutva: Who is a Hindu?*, Savrakar argued that India belonged to Hindus who were descendants of Aryans: "A band of the intrepid Aryans made it [India] their home and lighted their first sacrificial fire on the banks of the Sindhu, the Indus, ...the holy waters of the Indus were daily witnessing [sic] the lucid and curling columns of the scented sacrificial smokes and the valleys resounding with the chants of Vedic hymns—the spiritual fervor that animated their souls."[20]

It is through constructions of this sort that the Hindu Right seeks to legitimize its claim that India belongs to Hindus, and that all those who came to India after—the Mughal invasion and British colonization—are aliens. Consequently, Muslims in India become the "other" and ultimately are made to embody the persistent threat of invasion, sedition, and suspicion. The parallels between the Orientalist distinction between "us" and "them" and the Hindu Right's distinction between "Hindus" and "Muslims" are striking. Within Orientalism, "they" are made to carry an irredeemable otherness that resides in "their" space physically distinct from "our" space, and these distinctions between colonizer and colonized were writ large in the landscapes of the Raj.[21]

The project of the Hindu Right is similarly a narrative of spatial belonging and segregation. But it is considerably complicated by the long joint history of both Hindus and Muslims in India, which has generated material, symbolic, linguistic, and cultural spaces inextricably intertwined that defy easy demarcation as "purely" Hindu or "purely" Muslim.[22] In these syncretic hybrid spaces, the Hindu Right's goal is to create a Hindu *rashtra*, a pure Hindu national space, one not contaminated by signs of the Muslim other. Its challenge is to increase its power and presence from the "Hindu belt" to other parts of the country, but this has been persistently deferred by the growth in Dalit organizing,[23] political opposition from the Congress and the Left parties, along with India's centrist policies. The frustrations induced by this constant deferral goal have been marked by an evolving trajectory culminating in excessive of violence, where the effort is to erase public space of Muslim presence altogether. It is possible to trace this trajectory through successive spatial strategies: nationwide pilgrimages, the Ramjanmabhoomi movement,[24] and the rehabilitated towns and villages after the earthquake that placed Muslims at the margins, through to the pogrom against Muslims in Gujarat in 2001.

The Genesis of the Hindu Right and the Discourse of Territory

The effort to control space and define territory in exclusively Hindu terms has a long genealogy, and I offer here a brief overview of that history. One of the earliest efforts to realize the goal of creating a Hindu *Rashtra* emerged within the context of debates around Aryan migration into India. Towards the end of the nineteenth century, Hindu nationalists formed the Arya Samaj movement that posited a Golden Age of Hinduism in a pristine historic past unsullied by Mughal invasions or British colonialism. In the early twentieth century, the British made a series of concessions to Muslim minorities, and, in response to this, the Arya Samajists formed the Hindu Mahasabha (Hindu Congregation) to foster a Hindu nationalist movement.[25]

Vinayak Damodar Savarkar most forcefully articulated the view of Hindus as descendents of Aryans bound by a common race and culture and, therefore, with a rightful claim to India. He argued that "Hindustan meaning the land of Hindus, the first essential of Hindutva must necessarily be this geographical one. A Hindu is primarily a citizen either in himself or through his forefathers of 'Hindustan' and claims the land as his motherland."[26] In this construction of the nation, race and culture play significant roles. Hindus are bound together by a common blood that ties them into a fraternity. Savarkar insisted that "the Hindus are not merely the citizens of the Indian state because they are united not only by the bonds of the love they bear to a common motherland but also by the bonds of a common blood."[27] Savarkar's understanding of blood brotherhood however was not akin to racial purity. According to Jaffrelot, the "bonds of common blood" for Savarkar did not lend itself to the rejection of the Other.[28] In fact, Savarkar claimed that those who adopted Hindu religion and followed its culture would be "most emphatically Hindus."[29] This paradigm was conditional, however, and applied only to those who converted to Hinduism and would "look on this land as the land of their forefathers, their fatherland as well as their Holyland...."[30] It was here that Savarkar deployed geography to determine his criteria for belonging to the nation. Different sects, religions, and races (*Jati*) could all be part of Hindu India only if they look on India as their *Fatherland* and as their *Holyland*.

> That is why in the case of some of our Mohammedan or Christian countrymen who had orig-inally been forcibly converted to a non-Hindu religion and who consequently have inherited along with Hindus, a common Fatherland and a greater part of the wealth of a common culture...are not and cannot be recognized as Hindus. For though Hindustan to them is Fatherland as to any other Hindu yet it is not to them a Holyland too. Their holyland is far off in Arabia or Palestine. Their mythology and Godmen, ideas and heros are not the children of this soil. Consequently their names and their outlook smack of a foreign origin. Their love is divided. Nay, if some of them be really believing what they profess to do, then there can be no choice—they must, to a man, set their Holyland above their Fatherland in their love and allegiance. That is but natural.[31]

The contemporary accusation that Muslims embody a persistent threat of sedition has its origins in this discourse of belonging. Since almost all Muslims in India have ancestrally been part of India, Savarkar allows them the criteria of common culture but argues that because their holyland is elsewhere, in "Arabia or Palestine," their allegiance to the Hindu nation can never be trusted. In consequence, all Muslims, (and Christians too) are accused of contamination, subversion, and sedition. It is in this geography of belonging and suspicion that the ideological foundations of the modern Hindutva movement were laid. Its practical, organizational base emerged with the creation of the Rashtriya Swayamsevak Sangh.

Rashtriya Swayamsevak Sangh (RSS)

The *Rashtriya Swayamsevak Sangh* (the national volunteer corps) was formed in 1925 in Nagpur by Keshav Baliram Hedgewar.[32] Hedgewar was deeply influenced by Savarkar but his originality lay in adopting Savarkar's ideology of the Hindu nation and operationalizing it through daily rituals and physical training. These prac-tices would be performed in small local braches called *Shakhas*.[33] Often located in grounds attached to Hindu temples, *Shakhas* function as local community centers where young boys gather everyday for ideological and physical training. The *Shakhas* hold tremendous appeal within urban areas because they also serve as "alternative recreational facilities" within overcrowded middle class neighborhoods in cities and towns.[34] The ritualized structure of ideological training with physical fitness is based on the claim that the nation needs to be ideologically prepared for the Hindu *rashtra* and physically prepared to defend itself against invaders.

Madhavrao Sadashiv Golwalkar, who became supreme leader of the RSS after Hedgewar, was responsible for expanding its base by creating links with the tra-ditional Hindu religious community and with Hindus living abroad through the creation of the Vishwa Hindu Parishad (World Hindu Council).[35] Golwalkar drew inspiration from Hitler's ideology of race purity. In his book *We, or Our Nationhood Defined* Golwalkar argues,

To keep up the purity of the Race and its culture, Germany shocked the world by her purg-
ing the country of the Semitic races—the Jews. Race pride at its highest has been manifested
here. Germany has also shown how well nigh impossible it is for Races and cultures, having
differences going to the root, to be assimilated into one united whole, a good lesson for us in
Hindustan to learn and profit by.[36]

These ideological frameworks of purity continue to inform the manner in which
Muslims are constructed as threat through an ideology of racial difference. After Golwalkar, Balasaheb Deoras, who took over as supreme leader, led the Sangh towards
mass recruitment of volunteers. The volunteers in the RSS called *swayamsevaks* are
foot soldiers who bring more members of the community into the fold.

The Sangh experienced its most extensive growth during the 1960s through systematic infiltration of the political, ideological, and cultural apparatus of the country
by setting up branches that work to spread *Hindutva* through education, social, and
economic policy, cultural and religious training centers, labor unions, student and
teacher organizations, and community-based organizations. These organizations
together form the *Sangh Parivar* (Family of organizations).[37] RSS is the umbrella
structure within which all other branches of the *Sangh Parivar* are organized. Among
the more then sixty different organizations, it is the Vishwa Hindu Parishad (VHP)
and the Bharatiya Janata Party (BJP), the political wing of the Hindu Right that are
the most powerful within the *Sangh Parivar*. While the BJP and the VHP have different trajectories and missions, many of its key members were recruited from RSS
cadres and began their careers as volunteers. The BJP-VHP-RSS work in tandem with
each other and assume sole authority to speak for and represent all Hindus, defining
thereby the very terms of what it means to be Hindu in contemporary India.

Despite the intricate organizational dependency, the RSS, BJP, and VHP have
very different roles. The RSS recruits and trains the volunteer base that feeds into
the Hindutva structure. BJP work the political landscape by contesting in the electoral process. Within the triad, it is the VHP's role in Hindutva that has been central
in moving the Hindu Right from its confines within upper-caste and upper-class
politics to a mass organization. In fact, it was with the establishment of the VHP in
1964 that the nationalist Hindutva movement really gained momentum. Basu and
colleagues explain that VHP engages with a new strategy that claims it not only represents, "the vanguard, the politically aware elite within Hindu society (this would
have been, roughly, the earlier RSS claim): it asserts that it *already* includes the whole
of Hindu society as it stands here and now, and that an exact correspondence exists
between its own field and the boundaries of an admittedly varied, pluralistic, differentiated Hindu world."[38] It is by using this framework that the VHP claims to speak
for all Hindus everywhere irrespective of their differences. In this way VHP makes
itself "co-extensive with the phenomenon of mass communalism."[39] According to
van der Veer, the VHP goes beyond the RSS by constructing what he calls "modern
Hinduism" that crafts Hinduism as the national religion of India.[40] He says, it is "In
this way nationalism embraces religion as the defining characteristic of the nation."[41]
With the nationwide processions in the early 1980s, therefore, one sees the deployment of this political and ideological strategy at a national scale.

Hindu Nationalism and Territory

In the 1980s and 90s the Hindu Right initiated new campaigns directed at the masses. Part of this strategy of filling public space with Hindu symbolism was the mass production of stickers, icons, calendars, and so forth that became visible throughout north India. Stuck on cars and scooters, on walls, in homes, and onto school blackboards and books, the Hindu Right became publicly visible in an entirely new way. The simplicity of the images—the hero-god Ram,[42] the yet to be built temple along with the Saffron flag and mother India—consolidated their discourse where images of Ram became synonymous with the Hindu nationalist movement and the VHP.[43] The grafting of Hinduism with the nation was further bolstered by the national television broadcast of the Hindu epics the Ramayana and the Mahabharata in serialized form beginning in 1987, which reached a mass, popular audience so successfully, everyday life came to be divided into before and after the telecast.[44] While the serials were not orchestrated by the Hindu Right, their timing was extremely fortuitous in legitimizing the VHP's public discourse on Hindu nationalism.[45]

More than any of these campaigns however, the nationwide pilgrimages achieved the purpose of integrating Indian territory with Hindu nationalism. The first such pilgrimage was the *Ekatmata Yatra* (pilgrimage of unity or one-ness) in November 1983. The political urgency for this *Yatra* emerged out of what Jaffrelot refers to as the sense of Hindu vulnerability against a threat of being taken over by Muslim conversions.[46] This new set of anxieties emerged in 1981 when about 1000 Scheduled Castes in a village in Meenakshipuram (a district in Tamil Nadu) converted to Islam. The incident sparked concern among Hindu nationalists because a number of Indian Muslims had gone to the Gulf countries for job opportunities available in the 1970s and sent remittances back to India. A discourse of Indian Muslims linked with a pan-Islamic movement in the Gulf states began to gain momentum, fueling suspicion of a larger conspiracy to convert lower caste Indians to Islam. Some reports even claimed that with the conversions, Hindus could become a minority in the country.[47] This discourse of vulnerability was significant because it resonated so strongly with Savarkar's claims sixty years earlier that the loyalty of Indian Muslims lay elsewhere.[48]

The *Ekatmata Yatra* was deliberately constructed as a pilgrimage because it tapped into the significance that pilgrimage holds within discursive Hindu traditions. Van der Veer suggests that a pilgrimage "by definition involves a journey from one's village or town to a sacred center and back, and its performance appears to reinforce the notion of a wider community of believers."[49] It was this larger and discursive "community of believers" that the Sangh sought to draw under a unified umbrella called Hindu. Three pilgrimage routes were planned with the first originating in Kathmandu, Nepal (north) to Rameshwaram in Tamil Nadu (south), the second from Gangasagar in Bengal (east) to Somnath in Gujarat (west), and the third from Haradwar in Utter Pradesh to Kanyakumari in Tamil Nadu. The three routes converged in the center of the country and passed through Nagpur, where the RSS is headquartered. The three major processions were accompanied by forty-seven smaller processions that connected with the larger processions, constructing in effect a web of processions that literally mapped Indian territory as all-encompassingly Hindu. It served to show in extraordinarily powerful ways that different Hindu traditions were nonetheless part of a larger unified Hindu identity. As van der Veer points out that "pilgrimage was effectively transformed into a ritual of national integration."[50]

In the towns and villages along the pilgrimage route, the processions deliberately went through Muslim neighborhoods chanting *"Musalmano Ka ek hee sthan, Pakistan ya Kabristan"* (Muslims have only two places, either Pakistan or the graveyard). The effort clearly was to suggest that Indian Muslims have no claim to the nation. Extensive Hindu Muslim violence followed in the wake of the processions and marked the tenor of a belligerent Hindutva movement where violence against Muslims was to become more excessive and organized.

With the successes of the nationwide processions, the VHP renewed their effort to get the Babri Masjid in Ayodhya opened. The mosque has been built in 1528 by a general of Babar, the founder of the Mughal dynasty in India. The site of the mosque has been contested since the late nineteenth century by Hindu nationalists who claimed that it was built on the site of an ancient Ram temple that had been destroyed. Babri Masjid has since then become the material embodiment of Muslim violence against Hindus. Van der Veer suggests that, "By transforming the mosque in Ayodhya from a local shrine into a symbol of the 'threatened' Hindu majority, however, the VHP [was] instrumental in the homogenization of a 'national' Hinduism."[51]

This transformation of the shrine from a site of dispute to a symbol of Hindu threat began in 1986 when a court in Faizabad ruled that the shrine be opened to the public.[52] From this point on the BJP and the VHP aggressively campaigned for the building of the Ram temple on the disputed site. In response to Hindu organizing, the Babri Masjid Movement Coordination Committee (BMMCC) was formed to represent Muslim interests. The negotiations between the Sangh and Muslim organizations for a resolution to the disputed site ended unsuccessfully on November 6, 1992. One month later, on December 6, 1992, *Kar sevaks* (Temple volunteers), Bagranj Dal activists, and members of the *Sevika Samiti* (women's wing of the RSS) protested and demolished the Babri Masjid. The image of Hindutva activists atop the crumbled structure of the Masjid remains a haunting symbol of Hindutva victory and the public denunciation of secularism.

The demolition of the Babri Masjid resulted in brutal communal violence between Hindus and Muslims across the country. In places like Bombay the police, supported by the Shiv Sena (a political party allied with the Hindu Right), actively participated in the violence against Muslims. In the southern state of Kerela, Abdul Nasar Madani, distressed by the Sangh, formed the Islamic Sevak Sangh (ISS) in direct response to the RSS. Following the destruction of Babri Masjid, ISS participated in violence against Hindus and in 1992, along with the RSS, was banned by the government.

The Babri Masjid—Ram Temple represented a microcosm of the dispute over national space. The victory associated with the forceful occupation of Babri Masjid was nothing short of a symbol for occupying national space. Other shrines throughout India have been sites of dispute since the mid-1980s. Baba Budangiri in Karnataka, for instance, is an old Sufi shrine that has been a site of syncretic Hindu and Muslim traditions for several hundred years. Since the 1960s, the Sangh has been claiming that the shrine was a Hindu temple that was taken over by Muslims.[53] The shrine is significant because it is located in Karnataka, which the BJP and Sangh see as their entrée into extending their influence in the southern states.[54]

The VHP chief Praveen Togadia threatened that the shrine could become "another Ayodhya" at a rally organized on December 6, 2003, the anniversary of the demolition of Babri Masjid.[55]

In response to the infiltration of the Sangh in the south, right-wing Muslim organizations emerged in the 1990s to counter Hindu propaganda. For instance, in Tamil Nadu the Jihad Committee and Al-Umma were formed in the battle over urban space resulting in violent clashes between the RSS front organizations and the Muslim organizations.

The spatial strategies deployed by the Hindu Right in the nationwide *Yatras* symbolized grafting the image of Bharat Mata, and an ideological construction of Hindu *rashtra*, onto national space. With Ayodhya, the spatial strategy shifts so that now those sites and places of significance for the Muslim community are contested through attempts to discredit their validity by alleging the presence of an older (and, therefore, more valid) Hindu structure on the same site. Taking over public sites such as Babri Masjid allows the Sangh to effect two simultaneous moves. The first reconstructs history in such a way that the allegation of Muslim monuments being constructed over Hindu ones is made proof of a Muslim barbarity that remains constant throughout time.[56] The second asserts that public spaces such as mosques, *maidans* (public grounds), and shrines need to be sanitized of Muslim presence such that public space can only be Hindu space.

In essence, this strategy demands that Muslims (and Christians) must publicly demonstrate their allegiance to Hindu symbols (and by extension, the Hindu nation) while withdrawing into the private to practice their religions. During the nationwide *Yatras* for example, Acharya Giriraj Kishore, senior leader of the VHP, proudly claimed that even Muslims and Christians had supported the processions.[57]

Yet, even withdrawing into private spaces was not enough. As the rebuilding of towns and villages after the Gujarat earthquake demonstrates, homes and places of worship of Muslims and Dalits were removed from the core Hindu sections of the towns and rebuilt in the margins. On January 26, 2002, a day usually commemorated for the birth of the Republic, a massive earthquake struck Bhuj in northwestern Gujarat destroying towns and villages and leaving a staggering twenty thousand dead. The relief effort included government agencies, several NGOs, international humanitarian agencies and religious organizations, some directly associated with the Hindu Right. The reconstruction effort entailed building the villages and town demolished in over six hundred affected areas. It is in this reconstruction effort by groups who were either part of the Hindu Right or sympathetic to it that emerged a spatial strategy of erasure and exclusion of Muslim presence.

In his detailed account of the reconstruction effort after the earthquake, Edward Simpson points out that organizations close to the BJP chief minister Narendra Modi's government were given the most publicly visible and thus prestigious sites to reconstruct.[58] In this reconstruction "many villages [were] renamed and new colonies and sub settlements in older villages [were] given distinguishing names and entrance gates to separate them from the settlement of which they were previously a part."[59] The VHP organized reconstruction effort by raising funds through charities affiliated with the Hindu Right in the United States and Britain. With the substantial sum of monies collected, the VHP built a new colony called Keshav Nagar (Krishna's city). The new settlement built atop a hill overlooks salt flats that lead to the border with Pakistan. This village was located at the epicenter and was thus the location that received most media attention. Previously called Lodai, the village had a mixed population of Hindus, Other Backward Castes (OBC's), as well as Muslims and Harijans (Gandhi's term for the untouchable castes). According to Simpson "Keshav nagar, built on the top of a hill overlooking the old village, has been constructed exclusively for caste Hindus and Muslims and others remaining in the old village have had to make do with the evidently inferior houses provided by a Catholic relief organization, once it was obvious that the VHP plans to ignore certain sections of the population."[60]

The attempts to segregate Muslims and lower-caste Hindus reflects an effort to erase from public space the presence of those that do not fit within the schema of a Hindu public space. The reconstruction efforts are small-scale manifestations of intensions of the Hindu *rashtra* at the national scale. In these spaces, upper-caste Hindus occupy the center with access to civic amenities. These spaces are built around temples of Hindu gods; the distant margins reserved for low caste Hindus and Muslims.

Another village at the epicenter, called Dudai, was renamed Indraprastha (city of the god Indra); the reconstruction was organized by Sahib Singh Verma, a former BJP Chief Minister of Delhi. Planned in a similar way to Keshav Nagar, with Muslims and Harijans relegated to the margins, Indraprastha boasts a "Special Study Center" in the center of the village in which are housed nationalist and Vedic literary documents. The central location of the center spatially and ideologically prioritizes Hindu literature and religion.

Each of these plans reveal the attempt to segregate public space such that those occupied by Hindus are sanitized from the contaminating influence of Muslim presence.[61] The new villages spatially represent Hindutva ideology that constructs Muslims not only as marginal but also as dirty and polluted, not only do public spaces within villages have to be erased but even the private space of homes, to which the Sangh wished to relegate Muslims, had to be placed far away so as to minimize contact among Hindus and Muslims.

A year later however, during the Gujarat pogrom, even segregation was not enough, Muslims needed to be permanently removed and signs of their presence erased from the landscape. It has to be said that violence between Hindus and Muslims has accompanied each instance of the Hindutva strategy. After the destruction of Babri Masjid, for example, hundreds of people were killed in Surat in the immediate aftermath with sporadic violence continuing for months thereafter. Since the early 1980s, the Hindu Right has succeeded in generating extreme fear with the threat of violence. But nowhere has this been more pronounced than in Gujarat that has, over the years, become the Sangh laboratory. Gujarat has a long history of sectarian violence—between 1960 and 1969 there were as many as 2,938 instances of violence against Muslims recorded in the state.[62] One of the most brutal examples of violence against Muslims occurred in 1969 when Gujarati Muslims demonstrated in solidarity with Palestinians to protest the destruction of the Al-Aqsa mosque. The Sangh saw this demonstration as evidence that Indian Muslim's loyalty and allegiance lie elsewhere and as proof of sedition. The slow and systematic infiltration of the Hindu

Right in Gujarat led to the BJP winning state power in 1995 such that by the 2001 pogrom there remained little doubt of state complicity in the violence.

The Gujarat pogrom is significant in both the genealogy and the geography of Hindutva violence in many respects. Most obviously, it exceeds other instances in what Tanika Sarkar has described as the macabre "opulence and exuberance" of its violence.[63] While past instances of violence against Muslims by the Hindu Right were brutal, in Gujarat there was an "excessiveness" to the violence. Sarkar documents this excessiveness in terms of the brutality of violence against women's bodies.[64] She points to the ways in which women's genitalia and wombs were specially targeted. As bodies bore the brunt of excess violence, this excess was also etched onto homes, places of business, and, in particular, on mosques and shrines. Given other instances of violence, how does one understand the excesses in Gujarat? I suggest that while the control and occupation of space is fundamental to Hindu nationalism, it remains a frustrated and unrealized goal. Hindu *rashtra* is imagined as a pure space uncontaminated by Muslim presence, however efforts to completely extricate and separate Hindu space from Muslim space have not been entirely realized. Consequently, in the Gujarat pogrom, the effort was made to annihilate visible signs of Muslim presence, to change not only the architecture of the state but the very body politic.

Narratives of the Gujarat pogrom usually begin with the burning of a carriage on the Sabarmati Express on February 27, 2002. The train was returning from Ayodhya when it was stopped at Godhra, a small town just inside the Gujarat border, where one of the carriages was set on fire. Fifty-eight people were killed.[65] A number of those killed in the fire were *Kar Sevaks* (Hindu activists) returning from Ayodhya where they were participating in ceremonies to construct the Ram temple. The fire was blamed on Muslims in Godhra and the Sangh alleged that the fire was preplanned by Muslims. In response to the Godhra incident, the BJP government in Gujarat ordered a closure of all businesses (a *Bandh*). During the *Bandh,* Bajrang Dal activists retaliated by killing Muslims all over the state. The violence, while most vitriolic in the two days of the *Bandh,* extended into months that left two thousand Muslims dead and one hundred and fifty thousand homeless. The geographical spread of the violence encompassed twenty-one cities and sixty-eight provinces all over Gujarat.

The Gujarat pogrom is significant and marks a departure from other instances of violence against minorities particularly because of extensive evidence that points to the preplanned nature of the attack by the Hindu Right. The aftermath of the violence revealed unimaginable brutality and excessive violence in what came to be understood as nothing short of a genocide.[66] It is in this extensive planning and execution that there emerges the blueprint for the annihilation of Muslim presence in Gujarat. If the rural planning orchestrated by the Hindu Right after the earthquake revealed the spatial exclusion of Muslims and lower castes to the margins of Hindu public spaces, then the Gujarat pogrom demonstrated an effort to erase Muslim presence altogether.

Testimonies of informants and survivors of the pogrom claim that months prior to the pogrom, persons claiming to be part of a market survey group began to compile lists of homes and businesses headed by Muslims.[67] These lists then facilitated the organized batches of Hindu activists to specifically attack Muslim homes and businesses while leaving Hindu homes and businesses intact. This extreme planning could only have happened were this information collected and made available to the

Sangh. This paradigm of identifying Hindu and Muslim homes was put into practice a year before during the reconstruction effort after the earthquake when Hindu homes were labeled with auspicious "labh" and "shubh" while the Muslim homes were identified with the number 786, a numerological representation of the first verse in the Quran.[68] In the days after the most intensive violence was over, cities and towns emerged with completely destroyed homes, shops, and restaurants that often stood adjacent to places left untouched.

The pattern of damage revealed the extent to which the attack was systematically orchestrated. Those deployed to attack and pillage were equipped with maps, cell phones, and bottled water. Months prior to the pogrom, weapons, particularly knives and *trishuls* (a three edged knife symbolic of weapons used by some Hindu Gods), were distributed among *advasis* (indigenous peoples). Weapons distribution was sanctioned by a discourse of arming Hindu populations against the imminent danger posed by Muslims in Gujarat. In addition to surveys and weapons the Sangh also distributed flyers asking for a complete economic boycott of Muslim business by the Hindus in the state.

After the pogrom, cities and towns in Gujarat emerged mapped in new ways. Old landmarks, such as a tomb or a small mosque, disappeared to be replaced by paved-over roads dramatically altering the visual geography of the city. In the aftermath it became apparent that mosques and dargas were sites of particularly visceral violence. In total 270 mosques and dargas were destroyed all over Gujarat. In Vasad, for instance, a mosque and darga were completely destroyed by bulldozers leaving no signs of their earlier presence. In Naroda Village, the Noorani Masjid was blasted using gas cylinders. Mosques were often looted, the Korans burnt and, in some instances, urinated upon. In a number of places mosques were also set on fire and "*Jai Shri Ra'*" (Hail to Ram) scratched onto the walls. Saffron flags, to which the Hindu Right pledges its allegiance, were placed on mosques with idols and pictures of "*Hulladiya Hanuman*" (literally, "Riot Hanuman") installed.[69] In Ahmedabad a four-hundred-year old mosque was broken down, and, after installing Hindu idols, *aarti* (a religious ritual) performed. Religious sites are laden with sacred meaning and profound significance for all communities. Their desecration is a particular act of insult and dishonor. The installation of Hindu idols in mosques is about forceful conversion—taking over a mosque to recraft it as Hindu. In a way, these instances were ritualized reiterations of the triumphant demolition of Babri Masjid in Ayodhya.

In addition to the mass desecration of mosques, sites of cultural significance associated with Muslims were also not spared in the attempt to cleanse the space. One of the most brutal instances was the destruction of the tomb of Wali Gujarati. Born in 1667 in Aurangabad, Wali Gujarati is considered the founder of Urdu poetry and wrote in many of his poems about his love for Gujarat. He died in Ahmedabad in 1707, during one of his many visits to the city, and in his honor the people of Ahmedabad built a tomb and conferred on him the title Wali Gujarati. The tomb was located ten meters from the Ahmedabad police commissioner's headquarters. According to eye witnesses, members of Modi's government were present in the destruction of the tomb, after which a saffron flag was placed on the site.[70] In place of the tomb is now a paved road, no sign of the tomb remains. Some auto rickshaw drivers swerve a bit to the left of where the tomb once stood. One of them says, "it wouldn't feel right to go over it. I know other drivers do the same."[71] In the aftermath of Gujarat, the city was remapped, auto drivers of different faiths would take different routes to navigate the city, avoiding Hindu and Muslim dominated areas.

In addition to mosques and shrines, homes in Muslim neighborhood were completely destroyed. In particular was the use of gas cylinders and chemicals to destroy homes and businesses leaving these places so damaged that it was impossible to salvage what remained. Even homes of prominent Muslim members were also not spared during the pogrom. Ahsan Jafri, who was a former trade unionist and Member of Parliament in the Congress Party, was attacked by a Hindu mob while attempting to save people seeking shelter in his house in Gulberg society. He had earlier in the day called the police seeking protection, but no one responded to his calls.

Homes destroyed by exploding gas cylinders damaged the walls and foundations so profoundly that it made them unsafe to inhabit, thereby making it impossible for people to return and reclaim their homes. This was particularly evident in Naroda-Patia, a Muslim neighborhood in Ahmedabad that saw some of the worst destruction and violence. In addition to gas cylinders, the chemical substance to set fire destroyed all traces of forensic evidence. The materials of destruction reveal in themselves a discourse of erasure and annihilation. The aftermath of the genocide generated a different geography in Gujarat. Hindu and Muslim spaces were now completely separated and signs of spatial syncretism removed or converted. What remained therefore, were sanitized, safe, and Hindu public spaces in Gujarat.

The brutality of killing in Gujarat was horrific. Not only were Muslims killed in large numbers, but their bodies were burnt in an imitation of Hindu cremation rituals, denying them, even in death, the possibility of Muslim burial. Muslim women were raped in huge numbers and, in many instances, parents were forced to witness their children being brutalized. Pregnant women were particularly targeted with mobs shouting "kill them before they are born!"[72] Sarkar states that women's bodies were sites of "inexhaustible violence."[73] As with other patterns of sectarian violence, the rape of women is symbolic of community dishonor since women embody the site of regeneration and culture. In one particularly egregious instance, Kausar Bano, from Naroda-Patia, who was nine months pregnant, was caught by mobs; her pregnant belly was cut open and her fetus thrown into a fire, before killing her as well.[74]

The Gujarat pogrom was orchestrated because of the specificity of the political context in which the BJP was in power at the center as well as in the state. This generated the possibility to execute a discourse of "justified revenge" against Muslims without the fear of consequence. Indeed, the state apparatus that had over several years already been infiltrated by the RSS was deployed in specific ways during the execution of genocide. The Human Rights Watch report on the Gujarat pogrom for instance, documents that "in almost all of the incidents…the police were directly implicated in the attacks. At best they were passive observes, and at worst they acted in consort with murderous mobs and participated directly in the burning and looting of Muslim shops and homes …. In many cases, under the guise of offering assistance, the police led victims directly into the hands of their killers."[75] The Chief Minister Narendra Modi, a long-standing member of RSS, directed other departments of the state machinery to support the retaliation by Hindu mobs arguing that the violence against the Muslims was a justified reaction for the train incident at Godhra.

In December 2002, Modi called for early elections in Gujarat and the BJP won 126 of a total 181 seats contested. The overwhelming victory gave sanction to the Hindu Right's vision of Hindu *rashtra* and Gujarat became the Sangh's laboratory that could be replicated in other places. Indeed, Togadia announced with confidence, "The Hindutva lab has started functioning...the BJP has won all the three seats where by-elections were held in Rajasthan."[76] The states of Rajasthan, Madhya Pradesh, and Orrisa all have BJP and their allies in power. The threat of Gujarat as a Hindutva Laboratory that can be replicated in other places therefore, cannot be afforded to be taken lightly in light of these political developments.

Conclusion

I have argued that the Hindutva project has, since its inception, been a spatial strategy crafted in ideological and political terms to construct a Hindu *rashtra*. Efforts to construct this Hindu *rashtra* have entailed progressive occupation and control of public space to recraft it in Hindu terms. These strategies have been accompanied by extensive and increasingly more vitriolic sectarian violence. While the occupation of space is inextricable with religious nationalism, I suggest that the goal of a pure Hindu nation sanitized of Muslim presence remains constantly deferred and never entirely realized. Consequently, the frustrations resulting from an unrealized goal of Hindu *rashtra* lends itself to a pattern of increasing violence and control in an effort to dissuade minority claim to rights within the nation state. From the nationwide yatras that powerfully staked their claim on national space, to the control of sacred shrines, public grounds, and mosques, to reconstructed towns and villages where Muslims and the lower castes were relegated to the margins, to ultimately the effort to erase from the landscape Muslims and the signs of their presence have all entailed an increasing dominion of the Hindu Right over public space. In each instance, the Hindu Right has deployed violence and intimidation through a discourse of revenge and protection. Indeed, the BJP's electoral success after the Gujarat pogrom was testament to the success of their political strategy of fear.

While the BJP, as compared to the RSS and the VHP, is the more public face of the Hindu Right, the success of the BJP from a regional political party to a national party cannot be understood only in terms of the dynamics of electoral politics. BJP's success rests on the political organizing efforts of the *Sangh Parivar* where the discourse of Hindu majoritarianism and Muslim sedition forms a set of core arguments in their efforts to recruit more members into the fold as well fuels their justification for revenge. As a consequence of this complex strategy, in 1998 BJP led government was supported by a coalition of thirteen regional parties. It is the collusion of the Hindu Right at the center and in the states that lends itself to concern for the protection of the rights of minorities in India.

Given the consolidation of power by the BJP during its tenure, it was therefore completely unexpected when it was defeated by the Congress in the 2004 general election. A detailed examination of the elections shows that BJP candidates were voted down in all constituencies on the local and national levels. In Gujarat, their strong base, BJP won with a thin margin of victory. In a radical shift of the political landscape and contrary to every poll that indicated the BJP would return to power, the Congress and its allies formed a coalition with the support of the Left alliance, which had secured the most votes since 1947.[77] The verdict cannot only be read as an anti-incumbency vote. It is a clear indication that BJP and their sectarian politics were challenged. While the defeat of the BJP does not translate into the defeat of sectarianism, it does mean that there has opened, perhaps even conditionally, the political moment where public spaces can be politically redefined in more inclusive and secular terms.

Notes

1. In *Charcha ka Vishay: Mukhya Sutra*, RSS booklet, Delhi. Quoted in Tapan Basu, Pradip Datta, Sumit Sarkar, Tanika Sarkar, and Sambuddha Sen, *Khaki Shorts Saffron Flags: A Critique of the Hindu Right* (New Delhi, India: Orient Longman, 1993), 59. Emphasis added.

2. Togadia's triumphant declaration was in response to BJP's landslide victory in state elections following a brutal pogrom against Muslims in March 2002. Rediff news December 15, 2002, available at http://www.rediff.com/election/2002/dec/15guj13.htm.

3. The Hindu Right here refers to political organizing on the basis of religious difference and is differentiated from the economic Right by their focus on a Hindu sectarian agenda. I owe this point to Ananthkrishna Maringanti. While highly organized, the Hindu right is not entirely coherent and faces opposition from the political left parties in India, dalit communities (people of lower caste), and by a set of internal contradictions because of their predominant focus on upper castes.

4. Satish Deshpande, "Hegemonic Spatial strategies: The nation-space and Hindu communalism in Twentieth Century India," *Public Culture* 10 (2) (1998): 249–283.

5. Satish Deshpande, "Hegemonic Spatial strategies: The nation-space and Hindu communalism in Twentieth Century India," 250.

6. The RSS, which loosely translates to the national volunteer corps, is the structure through which the Hindu Right organizes itself. Later in the essay I explain the genealogy of the RSS.

7. Peter Van der Veer, *Religious Nationalism: Hindus and Muslims in India* (Berkeley: University of California Press, 1994), xii.

8. Quoted in Communalism Combat March–April 2002.

9. Edward Said, *Orientalism* (New York: Vintage Books, 1979), 43.

10. Elsewhere I examine the construction of the geopolitical alliance between India, the United States, and Israel through a shared discourse of Muslim terror. See Rupal Oza (forthcoming) "Contrapuntal Geographies of Threat and Security: US, India, and Israel," *Environment and Planning d: Society and Space.*

11. Romila Thapar, "Imagines religious communities? Ancient history and the modern search for a Hindu identity," *Modern Asian Studies* 23(2) (1989): 209–231: 210.

12. Romila Thapar, "Imagines religious communities? Ancient history and the modern search for a Hindu identity," 218.

13. This is not to suggest that differences between Hindu and Muslim did not exist prior to colonialism, rather my effort here is to point out the genealogy of some of the colonial and orientalist discourses that reappear in the vocabulary of the Hindu Right.

14. Peter Van der Veer *Religious Nationalism: Hindus and Muslims,* 19.

15. Ayesha Jalal, *Democracy and Authoritarianism in South Asia: A Comparative and Historical Perspective* (Cambridge University Press, 1995). 16.

16. The Muslim League's position had been to protect Muslim interests in a unified secular state. In fact in June 1946 the League rejected the offer to carve out a sovereign Muslim state from Muslim dominated areas and advocated for a three-tier federal constitutional system. The Congress, on arguments of expediency and concern for centrality, rejected the League's suggestion. For further information see, Ayesha Jalal, *Democracy and Authoritarianism in South Asia*, 15.

17. Chetan Bhatt *Hindu Nationalism: Origins, Ideologies and Modern Myths* (Oxford and New York: Berg, 2001).

18. Quoted in Edward Said *Orientalism*, 69.

19. Chetan Bhatt, *Hindu Nationalism*, 13.

20. Vinayak Damodar Savarkar *Hindutva: Who is a Hindu?* (New Delhi: Bharti Sahitya Sadan, 1923, reprinted 1989 sixth edition), 5.

21. See Ann Laura Stoler *Carnal Knowledge and Imperial Power: Race and the Intimate in Colonial Rule* (University of California Press, 2002).

22. My attempt here is not to present a celebratory image of mutual co-existence between Hindu and Muslim spaces in India, rather to point to the impossibility of creating pure space. Clearly, both Hindus and Muslims have spaces such as temples and mosques that generate a landscape differentiated on the basis of religion. I am also aware that the attempt to demarcate space within colonialism was also not entirely successful and much more complicated.

23. One of the most persistent countervailing forces in the expansion of the Sangh has been the politics around Other Backward Classes (OBC) and Schedules Castes. OBC's comprise 52 percent of India's population and have been disenfranchised for generations. Efforts to redress the historic inequity have led to strong affirmative action policies and political affiliations on the basis of these identities. For a detailed look at the rise of the Dalit and OBC movements see, Christophe Jaffrelot *India's Silent Revolution: The Rise of the Lower Castes in North India* (New York: Columbia University Press, 2003).

24. Ramjanmabhoomi translates as the movement to liberate the birthplace of Ram (alleged to be at the site on which Babri Masjid was constructed).

25. Christophe Jaffrelot *The Hindu Nationalist Movement and Indian Politics 1925 to the 1990s* (New Delhi, India: Penguin, 1993), 18.

26. Vinayak Damodar Savarkar *Hindutva: Who is a Hindu?*, 2.

27. Vinayak Damodar Savarkar *Hindutva: Who is a Hindu?*, 84.

28. Christophe Jaffrelot *The Hindu Nationalist Movement*, 28.

29. Quoted in Christophe Jaffrelot *The Hindu Nationalist Movement*, 28.

30. Vinayak Damodar Savarkar *Hindutva: Who is a Hindu?*, 129.

31. Vinayak Damodar Savarkar *Hindutva: Who is a Hindu?*, 113.

32. RSS is an exclusively male space and fits within the framework of hetero-patriarchy that serves the rhetoric of virile Hindu men protecting the motherland (Bharatmata) to whom they pledge their allegiance. However, in 1936, the women's wing of the RSS called *Rashtriya Sevikasamiti* was established by offering Hindu women a parallel space to participate in Hindu nationalism. For further information see Paola Bachetta *Gender in the Hindu Nation: RSS Women as Ideologues* (New Delhi: Women Unlimited, 2004).

33. This suggestion to congregate daily is attributed to Sister Nevidita an Irish woman who became a disciple of Vivekananda. RSS is proud of this history and claims

that Sister Nevidita completely adopted the Hindu religion as her own. RSS makes continual reference to Sister Nevidita as proof of their nationalist credentials. See Vinayak Damodar Savarkar *Hindutva: Who is a Hindu?*, 131; Tapan Basu, Pradip Datta Sumit Sarkar, Tanika Sarkar, and Sambuddha Sen *Khaki Shorts Saffron Flags: A Critique of the Hindu Right* (New Delhi, India: Orient Longman, 1993), 16.

34. Tapan Basu et al., *Khaki Shorts Saffron Flags*, 35.

35. Tapan Basu et al., *Khaki Shorts Saffron Flags*, 50.

36. Quoted in Christophe Jaffrelot *The Hindu Nationalist Movement*, 55.

37. The *Sangh Parivar* today consists of approximately sixty different organizations. The Bharatiya Janata Party (BJP) the political wing of the Sangh is focused on organizing and garnering state power through the electoral process. The Vishva Hindu Parishad (VHP) or the World Hindu Council is the cultural/political wing of the Sangh and often consists of the religious leaders that spearhead Hindu doctrine and ideology. The Bajrang Dal is the paramilitary wing of the Sangh and is trained in combat and was in the main responsible for the Gujarat pogrom. Seva Bharti is the service wing of the Sangh that sets up various community service centers. Service to the community is a way to spread the *Hindutva* movement and gather political support. In addition to the political and cultural organizing efforts, the Sangh understood early in its inception that the large labor pool in India was an important arena to organize. Thus the Bharatiya Mazdoor Sangh (BMS) labor union was formed in 1955 and claims to have 7.6 million members. In its mission, BMS clearly states its link to the Sangh: "Bharatiya Culture forms the ideological basis of Bharatiya Mazdoor Sangh" (available at http://www.bms.org/in). In 1991 with India instituting neoliberal policies of economic liberalization and globalization the Sangh created Swadeshi Jagran Manch whose mission is to spread the idea of national self reliance or *swadeshi*. In addition to these, the Sangh has a powerful educational wing that in 2000 changed the National Curriculum Framework (NCF), which sets curriculum for schools all over the country. NCF-2000 seeks to rewrite textbooks, especially those in history, and to infuse it with religious "values" and distort history by presenting the Mughal empire as an invasion of India. Following on this other religions, especially Islam are outside and "alien" to India/ Indians.

38. Tapan Basu et al., *Khaki Shorts Saffron Flags*, 56.

39. Tapan Basu et al., *Khaki Shorts Saffron Flags*, 3556.

40. Peter van der Veer *Religious Nationalism*, 131.

41. Peter van der Veer *Religious Nationalism*, 132.

42. The Ramayana is the epic story of the Hindu god Ram, who is believed to be the seventh incarnation of the lord Vishnu. In the epic, Ram banished from his kingdom in Ayodhya, wages a battle against the demon king, Ravana in Sri Lanka with the aid of a monkey army led by Hanuman to rescue his kidnapped wife Sita. The journey to rescue Sita takes Ram across the length of the country during which he encounters various communities who join him in his mission. Ram's victory and his return to the kingdom Ayodhya is celebrated to this day through various festivals and ends with Diwali, the festival of lights.

43. For further information see Tapan Basu et al., *Khaki Shorts Saffron Flags*, 60. For a detailed examination of the use of these icons and specially Bharat Mata see Lise McKean *Divine Enterprise: Gurus and the Hindu Nationalist Movement* (University of Chicago Press, 1995).

44. For a detailed study of the epics see Arvind Rajgopal *Politics after Television: Hindu Nationalism and the Reshaping of the Public in India* (Cambridge University Press,

2001); for a gendered analysis of the epics see Purnima Mankekar *Screening Culture viewing politics: An ethnography of television, womanhood and the nation in Postcolonial India* (Durham and London: Duke University Press, 1999).

45. Arvind Rajgopal *Politics after Television: Hindu Nationalism and the Reshaping of the Public in India* (Cambridge University Press, 2001).

46. Christophe Jaffrelot *The Hindu Nationalist Movement*, 342.

47. The *Indian Express* published statistics that claimed that Hindus could become a minority by the year 2281 or even by 2231. Quoted in Christophe Jaffrelot, *The Hindu Nationalist Movement*, 342.

48. Christophe Jaffrelot, *The Hindu Nationalist Movement*, 342.

49. Peter van der Veer *Religious Nationalism*, 120.

50. Peter van der Veer *Religious Nationalism*, 124.

51. Peter van der Veer *Religious Nationalism*, 7.

52. A series of political developments directly affected the Babri Masjid issue, among them of most significance were the political debates around Shah Bano and, towards the end of the decade, the agitations around the Mandal commission report that led to BJP's withdrawal of support to the V.P. Singh government. The Shah Bano case involved a 1985 Supreme court judgment that awarded a divorced Muslim woman alimony settlement contrary to Shari'at law. In response, conservative Muslim clerics criticized the government's involvement in Muslim personal law. With the Muslim vote bank at stake, Rajiv Gandhi passed the regressive Muslim Women (Protection of Rights on Divorce) Bill. For further information see, Zakia Pathak and Rajeswari Sunder Rajan "Shahbano," *Signs: Journal of Woman in Culture and Society* 1989, 14(3): 558–582. The Hindu right agitated the Muslim Women Bill by the government and saw this as appeasement to the Muslim community. The opening of the shrine and the decision of the Faizabad court, inturn, was appeasement to the Hindu community.

The Mandal Commission report recommended that 27 percent of all jobs under the direct and indirect control of the central government will be reserved for "Other Backward Castes." In the wake of the announcements, there were extensive agitations by upper caste and upper class students all over India to protest the reservations. The destruction of the Babri Masjid is understood in the context of the caste and class politics that the Mandal Commission report revealed. With the upper-caste vote held hostage the Hindu right needed to displace the political fractures onto another political arena, namely Hindu-Muslim conflict. This displacement allowed them to escape from addressing their upper caste bias while attempting to draw the lower castes and other backward castes on their side by constructing a Hindu versus Muslim divide.

53. Some of the other syncretic Hindu-Muslim sites include the shrine of Ai Mata and Ai Panth in Bilara, Rajasthan. Sila-Khan shows that this site is one of many instances of syncretic Hindu Muslim traditions in India. For further details see Dominique Sila-Khan *Conversions and Shifting Identities: Ramdev Pir and the Ismailis in Rajasthan* (New Delhi: Manahor, 2003).

54. In the last general elections in 2004, the town of Chikmagalur, once a strong Congress constituency and from where Indira Gandhi contested, elected the BJP to power. The Congress Chief Minister S. M. Krishna allowed the BJP/ VHP to hold a large rally in 1992. For further details see Rupal Oza, "Indian Elections: Mandate against Religious Nationalism and Neo Liberal Reform," Guest Editorial. *Environment and Planning d: Society and Space.* Vol 22(5): 633–638, 2004.

55. For further details see, B. R. Srikanth "Another Ayodhya?" *Outlook* 22, December, 2003.

56. For an exploration of the construction of time by the Hindu Right during the Gujarat pogrom see Tanika Sarkar, "Semiotics of Terror: Muslim children and Women in Hindu Rashtra.," *Economic and Political Weekly of India.* July 13, 2002.

57. Peter van der Veer *Religious Nationalism*, 126.

58. Edward Simpson, "'Hindutva' as Rural Planning Paradigm in post- earthquake Gujarat," in John Zavos, Andrew Wyatt, and Vernon Hewitt (eds.). *The Politics of Cultural Mobilization in India.* (Oxford University Press, 2004), 136–165.

59. Edward Simpson, "'Hindutva' as Rural Planning Paradigm in post- earthquake Gujarat," 146.

60. Edward Simpson, "'Hindutva' as Rural Planning Paradigm in post- earthquake Gujarat," 152.

61. Relief organizations associated with the Jama'at-e-Ulama and the Tablighi-Jama'at as well as other organizations were also involved in the rehabilitation effort. However, given that Gujarat was firmly in the hands of the BJP, much of the access to the earthquake region and resources for relief were held by the BJP. Thus while Muslim relief organizations participated, it was the Hindu organizations that had majority say in how and who got rehabilitated.

62. Ghanshyam Shah, "The BJP's riddle in Gujarat: Caste, Factionalism and Hindutva," in T. B Hansen and C. Jaffrelot (eds.). 'The BJP and the Compulsions of Politics in India' in omnibus *Hindu Nationalism and Indian Politics* (New Delhi, India: Oxford University Press, 2004), 245.

63. Sarkar, Tanika, "Semiotics of Terror: Muslim children and Women in Hindu Rashtra, *Economic and Political Weekly of India* vol 37(28), July 13, 2002.

64. Sarkar, Tanika, "Semiotics of Terror: Muslim children and Women in Hindu Rashtra," July 13, 2002.

65. Even as the Hindu Right continued to blame the Muslims in Godhra for the attack, it remains unclear how the carriage was set on fire. An article in the magazine *The Week* cites forensic evidence that casts doubt on the allegation that the fire was or even could have been set from the outside. Anosh Malekar, "Mystery of the Bogie S6 inferno," *The Week*, July 7, 2002.

66. I use the term "genocide" advisedly and with deliberation. I understand it to mean the systematic planned effort to completely annihilate people and the signs of their presence from place. The Gujarat pogrom is proof of this endeavor.

67. See among many others, Human Rights Watch, *We Have No Orders To Save You: State Participation and Complicity in Communal Violence in Gujarat,* vol. 14 no. 3 (C), 2002; *Communalism Combat, Gujarat Genocide,* March–April 2002.

68. Edward Simpson "'Hindutva' as Rural Planning Paradigm in post-earthquake Gujarat" in John Zavos, Andrew Wyatt, and Vernon Hewitt (eds). *The Politics of Cultural Mobilization in India.* (Oxford University Press, 2004), 146.

69. Concerned Citizens Tribunal, *Crime Against Humanity Vol I-III : An Inquiry into the Carnage in Gujarat.*

70. Concerned Citizens Tribunal *Crime Against Humanity Vol I-III : An Inquiry into the Carnage in Gujarat.*

71. Quoted in "How has the Gujarat Massacre affected minority women?" Fact-finding by Women's Panel. Citizen's Initiative, Gujarat. April 16, 2002.

72. Quoted in International Initiative for Justice in Gujarat *Threatened Existence: A Feminist Analysis of the Genocide in Gujarat*, December 2003: 35.

73. Sarkar, Tanika, "Semiotics of Terror: Muslim children and Women in Hindu Rashtra," July 13, 2002.
74. "How has the Gujarat Massacre affected minority women?" April 16, 2002: 10.
75. Human Rights Watch, *We have no orders to save you: State participation and complicity in communal violence in Gujarat,* vol. 14, no. 3 (C), 2002: 5.
76. Available at http://www.rediff.com/election/2002/dec/15guj13.htm.
77. For further details see Rupal Oza, "Indian Elections: Mandate against Religious Nationalism and Neo Liberal Reform' Guest Editorial. *Environment and Planning d: Society and Space,* vol. 22(5), 633–638, (2004).

10

Revolutionary Islam
A Geography of Modern Terror

Michael Watts[1]

How to initiate the revival of Islam? A vanguard must set out with this determination and then keep going, marching through the vast ocean of *jahiliya* [pre-Islamic state of ignorance], which encompasses the entire world. During its course, this vanguard, while distancing itself, somewhat aloof from this all-encompassing *jahiliya,* should also retain contacts with it. The Muslims in this vanguard must know the landmarks and the signposts on the road to this goal....they ought to be aware of their position *vis-à-vis* this *jahiliya* which has struck its stakes throughout the earth. They must know when to cooperate with others and when to separate from them....what characteristics and qualities they should cultivate...I have written *Signposts* for this vanguard which I consider to be a waiting reality about to be realized.

Sayyid Qutb, *Signposts along the Road*, trans. of *Ma'alim fil-Tariq*, 1964

I am going to keep this short and to the point because it's all been said by far more eloquent people than me. But our words have no impact upon you. Therefore I'm going to talk to you in a language that you understand. Our words are dead until we give them life with our blood.

I'm sure by now the media has painted a suitable picture of me. This predictable propaganda machine will naturally try to put a spin on it to suit the government and to scare the masses into conforming to their power- and wealth-obsessed agendas.

I and thousands like me are forsaking everything for what we believe. Our driving motivation doesn't come from tangible commodities that this world has to offer.

This is how our ethical stances are dictated: Your democratically elected governments continuously perpetuate atrocities against my people, and your support of them makes you directly responsible, just as I am directly responsible for protecting and avenging my Muslim brothers and sisters.

Until we feel security, you will be our target. Until you stop the bombing, gassing, imprisonment and torture of my people, we will not stop this fight. We are at war and I am a soldier. Now you too will taste the reality of this situation.

Mohammad Sidique Khan, one of the London bombers, September 2, 2005

In the screaming turbines, the acrid plume across the Manhattan skyline, and the vertiginous collapse of the Trade Towers, the Qutbian signposts shouted out their message. A new vanguard had arrived, draped in the cloak of revolutionary excess,

touting the return of the Caliphate sporting modern garb. A new International— revolutionary Islam—was at hand, carried forth by the stormtroopers of global *jihad*.
And in the wake of New York and Washington, DC came Bali, Casablanca, Barcelona, Madrid, Istanbul, and London. Life through death, religion as war, the ethical
bankruptcy of the commodity world—all concerns of the London bombers and al-
Qaida's "theorist" Ayman al Zawahiri[2] carry the echo of Sayyid Qutb, the philosopher *par excellence* of insurgent, military Islam. Forty years after he had been hung
by Nasser, even Qutb himself might have been surprised by the ferocious political
energies unleashed by the likes of Sidique Khan, a voice at once eloquently modern
and located within the heartland of European multicultural modernity itself.

But what sort of state of emergency—what sort of "space of death"—does revolutionary Islam represent; what sort of politics does this modern form of terror disclose?[3] Terror, said Gershom Scholem to Walter Benjamin, "drives much theorization
into a tumult of totalization."[4] My purpose is not to grant to Islam or the Middle East
a monopoly on terror (by which I mean the deployment of criminal violence, from
above or below, for criminal ends).[5] Terror is, of course, regularly deployed as a term
of abuse by states concerned to discredit or delegitimate the political causes of non-
state groups. States too can be in the business of terror. The War on Terror—now
the War on Violent Extremism and costing the United States over $300 billion to
date—can and does itself deploy criminal violence as a set of tactics (the invasion of
Iraq, said Harold Pinter in his Nobel speech was "an act of blatant state terrorism").[6]
Neither do I wish to spend time arguing that for every Islamist there is a Judeo-
Christian fundamentalism (the neoconservatives have Leo Strauss, they have Sayyd
Qutb). Rather I want to focus specifically on terror made in the name of contemporary forms of militant, revolutionary Islam—without endorsing its violent tactics but
also without either delegitimizing the political claims made by its perpetrators or
seamlessly reading terror into all forms of Islamist politics.

I realize that invoking Islam, revolution, and terror in the same breath is, in some
quarters, something of a provocation, or at least fosters a representation of the Muslim *umma* that is fiercely contested. There are those who would point, quite properly,
to the rapidity with which in the weeks after September 11, 2001—when there was
the possibility of a critical public debate over the role of America in the world, or the
conditions under which political Islam in its insurrectional and militant forms have
arisen, or the nature of terror perpetrated in the name of Islam—the airwaves were
filled to capacity instead with talk of Islamic terror, American crusades, and the cataclysmic struggle between good and bad Muslims.[7] For the neoconservatives, in particular, Islam was not simply premodern, it was modernity's nemesis. In the wreckage
of Ground Zero lay a "clash of civilizations," "the bloody borders of Islam," "Muslim rage," and new threats of "the Green Peril." A titanic struggle over the modern
was being waged. War had been unilaterally declared by the Islamists crowed Daniel
Pipes.[8] In this Manichean world, Muslims appeared as "a nuisance…and always were
a nuisance."[9]

So might a suturing of Islam and revolutionary violence only add to this sorry Orientalist chronicle, conflating the Muslim, the Arab, and the Terrorist, substituting a
wholly unrepresentative—indeed an ideologically ephemeral—strand of contemporary religio-political practice for the complex, varied and heterogeneous firmament

of Muslim belief, practice and political expression? I think not. Those who properly dismiss the notion of Islam as a totalizing cultural system—an essentialist belief, in other words, that Islam is unique among world religions in its capacity to infiltrate fully all aspects of the social and political life believers—must come to terms with the fact that in the spectacle of the collapsing Twin Towers their worst fears of Orientalism were confirmed: by the perpetrators. None of this is to question the insight of Edward Said's *magnum opus* or to lessen the brutal realities associated with a deep Western enmity toward Islamdom in the corridors of trans-Atlantic power. But over the last four years I have been struck by the extent to which many on the Left pass far too quickly over the Islamic constellation—what al-Azmeh calls its historic mutations, social forces and political expressions[10]—in the rush to expose the implacable logic of imperial oil or American militarism.

It must be said that for the Left, September 11, 2001 brought not the ideological clarity of the sort expressed by Samuel Huntington or the American Enterprise Institute but confusion mixed with revulsion: the threats of antipatriotism (even from within its ranks), the grave reluctance to admit "they had it coming," the whispered moral equivalence of casualties (what of Rwanda or the Palestinian *intifada*?), and, at base, a sort of deep schizophrenia: was this not a strike in the name of a modern anti-imperialism or was it grounds for a "just-war" adequate to the horrors inflicted upon the slaughtered innocents? The Left did not know then, and it does not know now, exactly who ordered the attacks on New York and Washington but their actions— and the rhetoric that followed— were instantly recognizable as a form of *modern revolutionary politics*; it was nothing less than a spectacular vanguardist assault on the heart of American capitalism.[11] The cry was "anti-empire," and if I may quote the authority of Mr. bin Laden himself, a mortal blow "struck by almighty Allah" against the "vital organs of America." It was not St. Peter's in Rome that bin Laden attacked, noted Olivier Roy in *L'Islam Mondialise*;[12] "it was not even the Wailing Wall. It was Wall Street." Was this not of a piece with the antiglobalization movement and the struggles waged against the IMF-Treasury nexus and its neoliberal battalions? But who on earth could endorse the reckless destruction of Bamiyan, the grotesque anti-Semitism of the Islamist vanguard, the banning of music and kite-flying, the dreadful misogynism of the *jihadists*, and the very idea of democracy and equality as submission before God? What cosmopolitan Leftist wanted *that*?

Doubtless, there are some on the Left for whom, in any case, my framing of Islamic politics grants revolutionary Islam—whether as a strategy of national liberation or as a call to global Salafism—far too much substance and weight. The brand of militant vanguardism offered by Al-Qaeda or Armed Islamic *Jihad* is, they might say, no more than a sickly excrescence, the psychotic, totalitarian handiwork of a minority network ("a few hundred strong")[13] who operate far beyond the perimeter of what passes as Muslim convention. There are those—Adam Curtis's film *The Powers of Nightmares* is a case in point—for whom Al-Qaeda is a phantom enemy, an illusion fostered by the neocons; there is no al-Qaeda organization says Jason Burke in Curtis's film.[14] The ultimate project of the radical Islamists is to retreat into the privacy of the mosque and the family; radical Islam, says Gilles Kepel, is a "trail of decline," its ideology "diluted" by the global economy.[15] September 11 was, in this account, the death wail of a Muslim terror network that has neither legitimacy nor popular appeal, nor staying power.

This is not my view. I start from the sobering realization that al-Qaida's *political* program —no Muslim, after all, turns to Mr. Bin Laden for theological instruction or exegetical insight—sits quite comfortably with not just the forty-odd percent of Saudis, the 65 percent of Pakistanis, and the 55 percent of Jordanians who "support Osama," but with the many millions who would sanction their political diagnosis.[16] There are perhaps 1.5 billion Muslims. According to Richard Clarke,[17] quoting U.S. intelligence for what it's worth, there might be anywhere from eighteen to forty thousand Islamic insurgents operating under the sign of al-Qaida. But there are, says Clark, "millions" of Muslims who occupy a political and strategic ground largely indistinguishable from that occupied by Mohammed Atta or Sayyid Qutb. This is not laying the blanket of terror over the Muslim *umma*. It is rather a statement of a global discursive shift in which large numbers of believers have come to see Islam as political ideology—as providing the only political alternative to the actually existing postcolonial realities as understood (or perhaps we should say experienced) by the broad swath of Muslims of the Quran Belt: namely secularism as a form of oppression for the community of believers.

Rather I want to pose a paradox: why has the tyranny, oppression, and ruthless austerity of a global neoliberal order in the service of secular American empire generated such a powerful form of resistance (a variant of modern terror), in equal measure ruthless, tyrannical and fanatically single-minded, that draws from the deep well of modern Islam? In addressing the question, Gregory rightly points to this modern form of terror its ideological and geographical coordinates:

> [T]he terrorism of al-Qaeda cannot be reduced to the manipulations of the CIA (or ISI) or the short-lived triumphs of the Taliban....It has its own objectives, and in appealing to hundreds, perhaps thousands, of people around the world, the local and the transnational are woven into its operations in complex and contingent ways.[18]

My task is to show something of the warp and weft of the local and transnational cloth that is modern Islamism, and why one unraveling of it has produced a militant vanguardism. New York, Bali, Istanbul, Casablanca, Nairobi, and Madrid—all these attacks were made in the name of Islam as a political project, perpetrated by globally networked educated moderns for whom the reference point was not the traditional *ulama* and Sufi *tariqas* but the Iranian revolution, the new *jahiliyia* of the modern Brotherhoods, and the compelling ideas of modern Islamic political theorists such as Sayyid Qutb (1906–1966), Hassan al-Banna (1906–1949), Sayyid Abdu'Ala Maududi (1903–1979), Ali Shariati (1900–1977), and Ismet Ozel (b.1944)—to a man as versed in the ideas of Marx, Nietzsche, and Aristotle as in the Sunni or Shi'ite canonical texts. It is surely the dismal Orientalism of the Muslim militants themselves—as much as the crusading mentality of the White House—that must be scrutinized: that is to say as a form of modern utopian thinking, articulated in this case as a radical conservatism, Romantic in its unfailing belief in political restoration echoing the modern ideas of Herder, Heinzen, Morozov, and Schmitt.[19] The modern Muslim intelligentsia and political theorists spoke of a new praxis. They shared an abiding belief that the Islamic project had been left *incomplete*; and that its fulfillment demanded political *restoration*. Not, take note, a simple (and inevitably make-believe) duplication of the original Caliphate, but rather the creation of the *nizam Islami*—an Islamic order with modern resonance. Central to modern Islamism is the desire—quite unlike the theory of government during the classical age of Islam—to hold the state as an agent of responsibility (in the face of any deviations of the existing Muslim community from Islamic principles) and as an instrument of salvation.[20] Indeed, a number of its Islamism's practitioners and recruits are men of impeccable Left credentials, many of whom identified as students two or three decades earlier with Third Worldist *Marxisant* radicalism. Now they spoke—as Paul Lubeck[21] brilliantly outlines—with Hegelian certainty, of "Islam as the future" and of a project to "Islamize modernity": the watchword was *al-Islam huwa al-hall* (Islam is the Solution). To return to the question of Orientalism and its dangers, then, Islam surely is not the same as Islamism or Revolutionary Islam; they are different. But they are not separable either.

Revolutionary Islam (and the deployment of terror as one of its modalities) presumes two implacable realities. The first is that the spectacular assault on the twin pillars of modern American capitalism was made by a revolutionary Islamic *vanguard*. That the attacks, and the subsequent acrobatics of theological self-justification by the vanguard itself represent a grotesque perversion of Islam is true but irrelevant for an understanding of the movement itself. They self-identified as *jihadists*; their murderous and psychotic impulses and sometimes quixotic interpretations of texts cannot obliterate this fact. In making such a claim I understand full well that the contemporary politics of the slum world resemble, as Mike Davis put it, the opiate nightmare of Marx: Hinduism, Evangelical Christianity, and resurgent Islam are the drugs of choice of the laboring poor.[22] But it is only Islam, for now at least, that can claim to provide a political project that is global in reach and ambition, anti-imperialist in thrust, and, in some of its expressions at least, revolutionary in practice. Until such time as an insurgent rainbow coalition of Nigerian, Brazilian, and Korean Pentecostalists launch a vanguard assault against the heart of American capital, we must come to terms with Islam's universalist and transnational ideology, its variegated but nonetheless disciplined organizational structure, and the fact that it has so successfully seized across Islamdom the mantle of political legitimacy from the tattered body of secular nationalism.

The second reality is that political Islam now represents the most powerful anti-imperialist force field confronting military neoliberalism and American empire. The astonishing vitality and political energies contained within and generated by Islamism, derived in large part from the dual-crisis of secular nationalism and of the postcolonial state, is extraordinarily deep. Its *revolutionary* face has been spectacularly successful, by which, as *Afflicted Powers* makes clear, Bin Laden and his "base" cave men not only defeated the imperial state spectacularly, leaving the U.S. economy with a trillion dollar bill and a raft of companies facing Chapter 11, but also after four years of Bush's War on Terror now stand, according to the Institute for Strategic Studies in London, "fully constituted". Al-Qaida has transformed itself from a vanguard organization into a mass movement "with a near unlimited pool of potential operatives."[23] Whether this assessment proves to be true or false (I write in early 2006 when the Bush squadrons talk of al-Qaida as largely smashed), the effective deployment of terror by a Muslim vanguard on the world stage is beyond doubt.[*]

My task here is to understand how and why so many Muslims have come to think politically with their religion—to outline what we mean when we speak of the politics of Islam—and to try and grasp one revolutionary expression of it (capable and willing to deploy terror). At the outset I shall provide a working definition of modern political Islam (or Islamism, I use the terms interchangeably) situating it in on a larger historical canvas. My central concern, however, is the distinctive and multiple expressions of modern Islamism, a mapping (wholly incomplete and partial) of its various currents and intellectual figures, and centrally the form of revolutionary Islam (again gesturing to its organic intellectuals and theoreticians) as one of its expressions. Only then can one plausibly turn to the conditions that haven given rise to the vast force field of modern Islamism and within it, the destructive currents of organized violence. So Islam and Islamism is where I *must* begin. Though it is not where I shall end.

I

> *Every religion is in reality a multiplicity of distinct and contradictory religions.*
> Antonio Gramsci, *The Prison Notebooks*, 1952

If all religions are in the business of propagating their basic ideas across the social field of which they are a part, then to the same extent governing political classes make use of dominant religious ideologies and institutions to legitimate their privilege and power. This surely is no surprise to any student of political economy (or I suppose religious studies). Religions are major repositories of symbolic, cultural, and political capital. Religion—or, to follow Gramsci, *one* iteration of it within a multiplicity—can and do serve, in other words, a hegemonic purpose: it is what Bruce Lincoln calls "the religion of the status quo."[24] Full hegemony of the dominant religion is always incomplete, and within its own ideological orbit (within Islam or Confucianism or Catholicism) there will always be other "distinct and contradictory religions"—"religions of resistance" in Lincoln's terms. There is no unity in their form—they may be militant or pacifist, utopian or nihilist, populist or despotic, ascetic or orgiastic—but they are all defined negatively, by their opposition to the religious status quo (one thinks of Jains, Taoists, Huguenots, and Vodun). For such religions to take on a *revolutionary* role, they must launch a political challenge to the legitimacy of the religious orthodoxy; they must broaden their social appeal and membership, and to do so, they typically come to depend upon a set of material circumstances in which a profound sense of crisis—a declensionist rhetoric is its hallmark—can be plausibly asserted.

Nobody should be surprised, then, by the long history linking politics and Muslim identity (any more than by the claim that Judaism and Christianity began as political movements). As has been noted on many occasions, the Prophet was both the recipient of the Quranic revelation and the founder of the first Islamic political community. The realization of God's will on earth provides the hallucinatory ideal

---

[*] I write two weeks after London police and security agencies arrested 24 militants in the UK who, allegedly, had links to Pakistan-based al-Qaida networks, and intended to detonate 10 airliners with liquid explosives.

in whose shadow Islamic jurisprudence, ethics and political theory all developed.[25] Contemporary Islamic political movements are modern, wide-ranging, and diverse: some emphasize preaching (*dawa*) and social organization from below,[26] some opt for flight and separation, some the ballot box (successfully in Turkey in 1996 and 2003, and in Indonesia in 1999), and others armed insurgency. But they are broadly unified by their advocacy of a political order which makes possible the application of the *shari'a* (Islamic law). They are part of a worldwide Islamic resurgence, and, at the same time, represent a radical challenge to an Islam of the status quo—embracing, it must be emphasized, a vast plurality of political forms, ideologies, tactics, and strategies. Islamism is rooted in the fact that millions of Muslims have been exposed to modern religious ideas outside the confines of traditional Islamic institutions—the *madrassas*, the mystical orders, the ancient brotherhoods—and reared on a diet of reasoning and interpretation (*ijtihad*) rather than imitation (*taqlid*) and the adopted policies of the founding fathers of Islamic jurisprudence. To take one example, to which I shall return, the majority of Pakistani *jihadists* note Zahab and Roy[27] come not from the madrassas but from dysfunctional state schools or private English language schools promising a modern education.

To take another illustration, it was *sawha* preachers like Abdallah al-Hamid in Saudi Arabia—modernists who combined a Wahhabist outlook on social issues with a contemporary Brotherhood orientation to politics, democracy, participation, and civil society—who came to dominate what was customarily posed in the trans-Atlantic policy world as the rigid and austere Wahhabist landscape of the 1990s in the Gulf.[28] In parallel fashion, a public Muslim intellectual like the Syrian engineer Muhammed Shahrur,[29] whose book *al-Kitab wa-l-Quran* has sold hundreds of thousands of copies across the Arab world, draws an analogy between Quranic reasoning and the Copernican revolution. His ideas directly challenge the traditions of Quranic exegesis and Islamic jurisprudence. What is at stake here—and across Islamdom—is the indisputable (if paradoxical) fact that radical Islamism instigates a *democratization*—by which I mean it opens up new spaces for debate and disputation within the circumference of orthodoxy or accepted tradition—of the religion; to return to Lincoln's idea, the notion that the formidable religious habitus of status quo Islam can be contested by lay actors who claim new and different interpretations of key religious texts.[30] Political Islam draws its strength, then, from the collapse or crumbling of a certain sort of religious hierarchy, of an order of religious authority based upon assertions to the unquestioned mastery of religious texts. Even in Muslim states where such Islamic authorities are state-appointed (and state-funded)—for example Saudi Arabia, Iran, Eqypt, Oman—the word of the status quo can be challenged. The new movement's appeal is cross-class, typically male-dominated (democratization only goes so far),[31] and rooted in the discontent of the armies of new migrants and deracinated city poor crowding into the slum-barracks of Baghdad, Cairo, Casablanca, and Jakarta—as well as the ghettos and *banlieus* of the north.

There is no doubt that Islamism is restorative in its impulses: it glances backward to life under the authority of the Prophet and the four successor Caliphs. But at the same time it deploys a distinctively twenty-first-century set of political technologies, ideas, and practices. Its program is to be contrasted with the scripturalist or traditionalist (sometimes called "neo-fundamentalist")[32] movements such as the Taliban,

who do indeed resemble a pure "counter-modernity"[33] —reviled as medieval obscurantism by the Iranian *mullahs* across the border. But even here caution is in order.
As Cole notes, the Taliban too exhibited a firm grasp of modern forms of spectacle,
surveillance, and intimidation. The ground of modern political Islam is still open,
still evolving. Here are its contours sketched for us by a CIA man—a retired vice-
chairman of the agency's National Intelligence Council—not suffering from "intelligence failure":

> Islamism represents the largest, and often the sole alternative to most entrenched authoritar-
> ian regimes today ... violent and peaceful, radical and moderate, ideological and practical....
> a vehicle for numerous Muslim aspirations: a desire to restore Muslim dignity and voice
> in the world, to create a new Islamic identity, to remove present dictatorships, to achieve
> democracy and greater social justice, to restore a moral compass to Muslim society, to
> achieve greater power for the Muslim world, to reject foreign domination, and [to defend]
> the rights of oppressed Muslim minorities everywhere.[34]

We must begin from the fact that political Islam—and its revolutionary vanguard
variant too—is a conspicuously modern phenomenon. But that exactly does *not* mean
that there were no politics in Islamdom until the modern era. On the contrary, and
as with all major religions, the history of Islam reveals movements of reform (*islah*)
and reinterpretation (*ijtihad*), which have served as political and institutional forces
across Islam's entire span.[35] Indeed they were central to the political successes of the
classical age. But the triumphal progress of the Prophet's movement and the territorial conquests by his immediate successors (the "rightly guided" Caliphs) was not
sustained. The idea of an Islamic state, Islam's aspiration to universality, and the message of social justice and equality all, says Malise Ruthven,[36] quickly foundered, in the
years following the Prophet's death, on the reefs of dynastic, sectarian and tribal politics. Civil war, the implosion of the Arab empire, the draining of Caliphal legitimacy,
and deep political fragmentation—these were the factors that contributed to the early
Islam's failure at the level of government and state formation. In Ruthven's[37] account,
the absence of a church or priesthood, early Islamic political authority came to rest
in two lay constituencies: a warrior caste of tribal leaders, for whom Islam served as
a basis for social solidarity, and the *ulama* (the lay interpreters of the law), possessing no executive authority and reliant on external sources of power. In pre-modern
times, he says, Islamic societies were held together by a complex mix of clan, family,
and mystical Sufi brotherhoods.

The Islamic state, seeming bogged down in the local, not only disappointed the
early adherents and their "political imaginary," but was further compromised, of
course, as the Islamic world came under Western colonial domination. As a result,
modernization within Islamdom proceeded along a secular (and technocratic) path
while religion remained under the purview of the *ulama*. Islam never bonded with
the state in the way of Christianity. In Protestant Christianity, says Ruthven, the
struggle occurred within the churches and teaching institutions, while in Sunni
Islam it was driven by secular elites who wished to integrate politics along Islamic
lines. An incomplete "Reformation"[38]—I reserve judgment on whether contemporary radical Islam has affinities with the Puritan saints who helped pave the way for

Lockean liberalism—has long remained a source of weakness. Political Islam turned the weakness into a strength.

Over the *longue durée* of politics within Islam, a distinction is customarily made between the "reformists," offering to renovate from within the traditional ranks of the *ulama,* and "modernists," challenging their monopoly of interpretation. In practice the traffic in ideas between them has been brisk. The origins of Islamic modernism, or what one might call modern reformism, are in large measure reactions to seventeenth-century European imperialisms and Hindu-Muslim syncretisms. But it is within the force field of late-nineteenth-century European empire and early-twentieth-century Ottoman collapse that a distinctively modernist movement comes into being, offering the vision of a modern Islamic state capable of both reviving and refiguring the Caliphate. The ideas of Sayyid Ahmd Kahn (1817–1898), Jamal al-Din al-Afgani (1839–1897), and Muhammed 'Abduh (1849–1905) were crucial. The modernists' watchword was *salaf* —harking back to the pious "predecessors" of Islam's inaugural generations. The Salafists despised the inertia of latter-day Sufism and its cult of the saints, railed against Sufi corruption, and denounced the collusion of the Muslim clerisy with empire. In place of the present, they dreamt of a Muslim world united across the Sunni-Shi'ite divide and within Sunni Islam across the four legal schools or rites. After the First World War, the Salafiyya movement[39] aligned itself with a resurgent Wahhabism in the new Kingdom of Saudi Arabia but its focus was largely religious reform (even if a more political wing contributed, in the 1930s and 1940s, to the nationalist movements in Morocco and Algeria). But already they were confident that the great inheritance of Islamic science and technology could be revitalized by selective use of what the West had to offer in the same fields.

Islamic modernism, in other words, was both multistranded and ambitious. But politically and strategically, it proved unable to mobilize Muslim civil society. It was not until the 1920s and 1930s, and then primarily as an offshoot of a series of pietistic, and in some respects crypto-fascist youth and sporting movements, that a series of innovations finally began to supply the political and organizational framework of the radical Islam recognizable to us in 2006.[40] Perhaps the formative movement in which Islam and modern political organization were linked—and one with filiations to the instigators of September 11—was the Muslim Brotherhood (*Jam'iyyat al-Ikhwan al-Muslimin*), founded in 1928 by Hasan al-Banna,[41] an Egyptian schoolteacher who took his reformed Islam into private mosques and schools to avoid state control. The Muslim Brotherhood was an association serving workers in the British-controlled Suez Canal Zone, which developed into an organization designed to Islamize civil society—schools, clubs, professional associations, social welfare services for the new city districts—in order to seize political power in the name of a modern Islamic state.[42] This is not the place to rehearse the details of the Brotherhood's innovative recruitment, its flexible organization techniques, its secret militias and cell structures, its crypto-communist bureaucratic discipline, or the internal splits and sectarian divisions in the Nasserite period. What matters is its urban, mass character, and the extent to which it irrevocably shifted Islamic governance from the *shaykh*s to the urban professionals, from the trustees of religious tradition to the Western modernizers. It was the idea of Islam as a parallel world within the crucible of the new modern city—a positive set of institutions, keeping the secular state at bay—that was to prove the key to the future.

The Brotherhood was proscribed in Egypt in 1954 and when its members, especially those from the paramilitary wing, emerged from prison during the 1970s they had to rebuild the movement outside of state control and indeed they did to the point where the radical Gamaa Islamiyya joined the flourishing Brotherhood.[43] During this rebuilding, the Brotherhood was fueled by the first storm of post-war petroleum revenues, and especially by the Islamic activists innovative dual strategy to capture the public education system and vital professional associations. By the time of the oil boom proper in the 1970s, which underwrote a huge expansion of state education at all levels, the public schools had become the battlefield on which the *ulama,* the Islamists and the state struggled for control.[44] Wickham has shown how, in Egypt during the 1970s and 1980s it was the professional associations as much as the Brotherhood that became the sites of what she calls "political experimentation.[45] It was the independent Islamic students associations that started the growth which through Islamist outreach, through institutional and interpersonal forms of *da'wa* associated with the independent mosques, grew to include a vast array of social groups that became, in fact in the context of authoritarian and exclusionary politics, a "counter society."[46] Islamists rooted their efforts in local forms of communalism. At moments their organizations seemed to be moving toward genuine countrywide mobilization; at others they fragmented into warring sects. It was from within this political vortex that revolutionary Islam gained strength or, more properly, incubated new and hybrid forms.[47]

In the annals of radical Islam, however, Mawlana Sayyid Abd'l-A'la Maududii (1903–1979) and Sayyid Qutb are arguably the central political figures, or, perhaps, revolutionary Islam's great organic intellectuals and theoreticians.[48] Both were revolutionary vanguardists: one intent on building a modern political party or system from above through an elitist vanguard; the other building a pan-Islamic movement from below, by violence if necessary, through a vanguard of loyal martyrs. Both were ruthlessly modern minds.

Maududii traced his lineage to a noble Delhi family and was schooled by the traditional Deobandist ulema. By the 1920s however, he had broken from the orthodoxy and entered into a modern education against the backdrop of mounting anticolonial agitation, a deepening communalist politics and the rise of the Muslim League in the 1930s. Maududi's ideological position started from what he saw as the elimination of politics from religious life and from the rejection of tradition (what he saw as Sufi latitudinarianism). He was resolutely modernist, weaving modern ideas, idioms, structures, and procedures into an Islamic fabric. It was forged against, on the one hand, Hindu communalism and, on the other, a Muslim League that was, in his view, far too conservative and factionalist. He denounced capitalism and socialism alike (for their secularism, aetheism, and imperialism), but made explicit use of notions of vanguard, revolution, ideology. His close reading of communist and fascist movements were central in his vision of a party that would be an "organizational weapon" to lead from above. Jama'at-I-Islami (the Islamic party), which he founded and lead from 1941 to 1972, is one of the oldest and most influential of the Islamist movements, the first to develop "a modern revolutionary reading of Islam."[49] It has influenced Islamism from Morocco to Malaysia (there are at least eight discrete parties worldwide) and became the self-appointed vanguard of the Islamic revolution. In practice it has failed in its mission and has never captured the masses—in fact, it has always been compromised by its internal paradoxes (revolution as a top down struggle against the secular state, a political party as a holy community, and so on). Yet the legacy of Maududi as a theorist and practitioner of Islam as social action and as a vanguardist political movement to directly take on the secular state is incontestable.

Born to an educated national family in Upper Eqypt, Qutb was educated in a Western-style academy and published poetry and works of literary criticism while working for the Ministry of Education. Qutb became a member of the Muslim Brotherhood during the 1950s but drew upon a wide range of ideas—from al-Banna to the Pakistani jurist Maududi to the European Romantics to the French Vichy collaborator and eugenicist Alexis Carrel—in shaping a political theory of the Muslim vanguard. His revolutionary texts—*Signposts, Islam: The Religion of the Future*, and his massive thirty volume exegesis *In the Shade of the Qu'ran*—were in part drafted in prison where he was tortured and finally executed by the Nasser government in 1966. What Qutb had on offer was a militant, utopian theory of Islamic praxis. He wrote under conditions not too different from Gramsci, but he turned out to be Islamism's Lenin.

Qutb provided the canonical texts for an urban and pan-Islamic insurrection. The frame of reference was not Egypt or national liberation or the Arab world but a utopian "universal revolution." Qutb's twin ideas were jahiliya as applied to the present and the establishment of hakimiya (divine sovereignty on earth). His interpretations of the Q'uran and the hadith (prophetic traditions) actually represented a bold revolutionary program: Islamic opposition to state terror, equality and freedom as common submission before God, the shar'ia as the sole source of sovereignty, the approbation of physical science but a radical disavowal of philosophical science, a moral critique of post-Enlightenment political theory, a rejection of the liberal separation of Church and State, and a formidable critique not simply of the spiritual bankruptcy of the West but of the entire landscape of liberal civilization as "a gigantic lie." Qutb's immediate bequest was a wave of revolutionary affiliates spun off from the Muslim Brotherhood in Egypt: the Islamic Liberation Group, Takfir wa'l Hijra, the Mukafaratiya ("Denouncers of the Kafirs"), the Jund Allah ("God's Soldiers") and Jama'a al-*Jihad*. But his real legacy extends much further afield. The Qutbian program—Marxism and capitalism as terminal states of moral exhaustion, and everything outside of the "house of Islam" as a "house of war"—is immediately recognizable as the stock in trade of many contemporary Muslim terror networks. Islamic *Jihad*, al-Qaida, Armed Islamic Group, the al-Aqsa Martyrs Brigades, the Great East Islamic Raiders Front, the Moroccan Combat Group, and Al-juma'a al-Islamiyya are Qutbist through and through.

Much could be said about Qutb's subtle and nuanced exegesis and his utopian Islamic project. For our purposes, there are three key moments in his political theory of vanguard Islam. The first is the great threat of liberalism to Islam through its ability to sideline religion, to separate it from the political sphere, and from life in general—and in so doing to produce a lifeless materialism devoid of spirituality, a wasteland of dreary blandness deprived of "life-giving values" (is it any surprise that the leader of the Palestinian Islamic *Jihad*, assassinated in 1995, was a disciple of T.S.

Eliot?). The second was the collapse of the Ottoman project in 1924 at the hands of Ataturk in the wake of the First World War, precisely as an exemplar of the liberal incursion into the heart of the Caliphate.[50] Finally, Qutb's political vision required authentication not just by *jihad*, but through an assertive vanguard capable of combating the dangers of jahiliya and the prospect of religious annihilation. By vanguard Qutb meant a cell of renovators holding themselves aloof from kufr (disbelief), and capable of kickstarting both a worldwide assault against all forms of jahili barbarism and the rebuilding of an authentic Islamic society free of "contamination." Qutb's shift from a defensive notion of *jihad* to an offensive vanguard, for whom there was "no real loss in their death since they continue to live,"[51] occurred during the early 1950s following his spell of expatriation in the United States. Upon his return from the "rubbish heap of the West," the task of "purifying the filthy marsh of the world" (a church hop in Greeley, Colorado in which the pastor, doubling as a DJ, played "Baby, It's Cold Outside" seems to have provided Qutb's the raw material for his swampy depravity) could only be waged through *jihad*, through armed struggle, and, inevitably, through acts of martyrdom.

In his prodigious output (some forty volumes of key texts), Qutb has almost nothing of substance to say about the nature of the Islamic state and how shari'a might be applied under modern conditions. Yet his trio of foundational ideas have proven to be enormously influential. Qutb's core vocabulary, despite its rejection of Westernization, was a complex amalgam of Muslim and Western ideas. In many respects they are instantly recognizable to us, a "dialectical responses" to rationalization and Westernization that seek to "abolish, transcend, preserve and transform modernity."[52] His arguments were derived, however, not from an ahistorical reading of the primary texts, as Qutb himself believed, but through a radical rejection of traditional exegesis. By engaging with and assimilating modernist ideas, Qutb sees Islam in aesthetic terms in which revelation is a divine art. True Islam required an existential leap of faith—resting on the recognition that consciousness not knowledge is the ground for Being. Here was a radical agenda for the entire Sunni world, and indeed a decade or so after his death, for the Shi'ite revolution in Iran. A straight (if tortuous) road connects Qutb to bin Laden's founding charter for al-Qaida.[53]

The creed of revolutionary Islam, then, is utterly hybrid.[54] Its tactics and strategies borrow heavily from the Marxist canon: vanguardism, anti-imperialism, revolutionary terror, and popular justice. The political impulse behind the deployment of these ideas is, as we have seen, sometimes global, sometimes local, sometimes inward and separatist, sometimes outwardly assertive to "inflict the maximum casualties."[55] Often it is difficult to separate the two (al-Qaida, lest we forget, is a mongrel offspring of Saudi and Egyptian militant Islam, directed against a worldwide anti-Islamic conspiracy (Zio-Crusaderism) led, it believes, by secularists, Jews and Shi'ites). There is no unified body of Islamist thought and practice, and this holds true *a fortiori* for its most militant or terrorist forms of expression. Nowhere is this clearer than in the recent history of al-Qaida itself: ferocious disagreements among all manner of factions and cells, with ceaseless splitting and internecine strife (the sectarian history of recent North Atlantic revolutionary struggle looks tame by comparison). A map of insurgent Islam anywhere pushes political cartography to the limit.[56] The Algerian Salafist and Brotherhood sects, for example, whose tactics defined the field of armed struggle through much of the 1980s, had morphed into at least nine different armed groups by the early 1990s, each crosscut by its own internal "tendencies" and networked affiliations to internationalist groups in Afghanistan, Pakistan, and the Gulf. The *jihadi* face of Saudi Wahhabism—customarily bundled together under the moniker "al-Qaida on the Arabian Peninsula"—is no less hybrid and sectarian. What they shared was a common modernity and internationalism. In Marc Sageman's inventory of nearly two hundred global Salafi *mujahedin*—recruited from the Maghreb, West Asia, the Caspian, and Southeast Asia—almost three-quarters were college graduates with a secular education, almost half were "professionals," and 70 percent had joined the *jihad* in a country in which they had not grown up.[57] Revolutionary Islam was a veritable rainbow coalition, forged in the crucible of a cold war military internationalism.[58]

The common denominator, across these divides, is the fact that the Islamist intelligentsia was most often the product not of the traditional religious schools but of universities with a curriculum (official or otherwise) centered on Marxism, Third Worldism, and the literature of national liberation struggle. These men took the playbook of Marx, says Olivier Roy, and injected it with Quranic terminology.[59] The reach of political Islam extended well beyond the universities, of course; it was in the slums of West Asian and North African cities that Islamism seized the imagination of a broad swath of urban youth. It revived the project of anti-imperialism, couched now in the language of community decay, state illegitimacy and moral bankruptcy. The vast majority of Muqtada al-Sadr's Mahdi Army in Iraq is drawn from this urban underclass, from the sewage-strewn slums of al-Hayaniyeh in Basra and al-Hurriyeh in Baghdad. It is a signal achievement of the U.S. occupation of Iraq that for a moment in the spring of 2004 it appeared as though it had succeeded in uniting the Sadrist Shi'ites and the radical Sunni Salafists in a single, loose-knit insurgency.*

II

It is tempting, of course, to fold the revolutionary vanguardism of contemporary militant Islam into the longer history of modern terror. The terrorizing and pacification of undefended cities on the nineteenth century imperial frontier was standard procedure for the Great Powers. A century later the devastation of Germany (and Japan) converted a military tactic into a way of life: and in so doing produced a kind of self-anaesthesia. The "lively terror," so much admired by Winston Churchill in the tactics of the British military in Iraq in the 1920s, was inflicted upon thousands of the civilians of Dresden, Frankfurt, and Hamburg and became, said W.G. Sebald in *The Natural History of Destruction*, an experience "incapable of public decipherment."[60] Two centuries of modern state terror, perpetrated by those in power on those who are excluded from power (wherever they may be), is always directed against "enemies of the state," sometimes through singular acts, sometimes through a coordinated

---

* Of course, this was a contingent unity (like Hezbollah and Hamas in the wake of the Israeli occupation of southern Lebanon in July–August 2006) and Iraq (and much of the Middle East) is now expecting a complex refiguring of the Sunni-Shi'ite divide.

series of acts conducted as part of a war or civil conflict. State terror from above, or "enforcement terror,"[61] is what we might call *normalized violence*. Its paradigmatic twentieth century theoretician and practitioner was Robert McNamara.[62]

Revolutionary Islam points to another tradition of modern terror and revolutionary violence—*improvised, spontaneous violence* from below. The vanguard, in this sense, is a concept of impeccably modern provenance, its lineage traced to the revolutionary anarchists in Tsarist Russia, to the Bolshevik *groupuscules*, to the *foco* guerilla movements of postcolonial Latin Americas, to the Weathermen, and Baader-Meinhof. The sentiments expressed by Osama bin Laden's mentor Sheik Abdullah Azaam[63]— "*Jihad* and the rifle alone," "History does not write its lines except in blood" —were born in the salons of Europe. Tactically Hezbollah and the Moroccan Islamic Combat Group speak the language of the European Counter-Enlightenment. The names of the Islamists groups are, as Al-Azmeh[64] reminds us, echoes of those adopted by ascendant modern nationalisms (Renaissance, Salvation, Awakening). The apocalyptic romanticism, the myth of Armageddon, the post-Kantian aesthetics, the figure of the political martyr—all of this is eerily familiar in the beliefs of what bin Laden calls the "blessed group of vanguard Muslims."[65]

The advantage of seeing revolutionary Islam as a return of improvised violence from below is that vanguard Muslims are properly constituted as modern agents. Its great deficiency is that it obscures, or downplays, revolutionary Islam's character and capacities: what makes it different, and what lends it such political gravity and historical agency? One aspect of this contemporary particularity resides in Islam itself. Islam has no monopoly on theocratic violence of course. But this still leaves open the question of how Islam and revolutionary violence is constituted, and from whence it draws its appeal and evidently, in some quarters at least, its theological legitimacy? What symbolic resources—what religious ideas, texts, and concepts—does revolutionary Islam draw upon, refigure, and discursively project? But Islam cannot provide a full account of revolutionary Islam. Instead we must turn to a trio of conditions of possibility that lend revolutionary Islam its almost unprecedented anti-imperialist powers (could Sergei Nechaev or even Che Guevara compare with the global celebrity of Osama's terror?). In shorthand we refer to these preconditions—revolutionary Islam's modern calibration—as: the *virtual*, the *incendiary*, and the *spectacular*.

Let me start from the fact that Mohammed Atta's final message to his eighteen militants to instigate the 9/11 attacks was delivered by e-mail: "The semester begins in three more weeks." Al-Qaida is a modern organization, or more properly it is a modern network with a decentralized, cellular structure. It has no fixed abode, active members operating in virtually every part of the world (it has operatives in at least one hundred countries according to the Pentagon), and its infrastructure is a hard drive. Al-Qaida is "an organizational structure built around a computer file."[66] The virtual qualities of revolutionary Islam grew technologically speaking from the laboratory of the new media, and institutionally from the broad movement originating in the 1970s known as al-da'wa ("a call" or "summons") in which preachers circulated their sermons as part of a mode of political action (its originary point is, once again, Hassan Al-Banna and the Muslim Brotherhood) to bring about political and moral reform. The distribution of underground recordings had created a "supranational focus" evident in the "considerable attention given to. . .the plight of Muslims worldwide."[67] New media, including satellite TV stations, newspapers distributed free on the Internet, news distribution through listserves, chat rooms and text messaging, and the vast traffic in CDs and DVDs, established the means to circumvent state censorship across the Middle East (and elsewhere in Islamdom) and a mediatic architecture capable of sustaining a transnational Arab public sphere.

It is this quite remarkable mediatic transformation within the Arab world that revolutionary Islam has deployed to such extraordinary effect. And this is no less the case for the twenty or so million Muslims in the European Union. Either way, the World Wide Web and the Internet provide the ground for the creation of a virtual umma. They erase the frontiers between dar-al-Islam (the land of believers) and dar-al-Kufr (the land of impiety) facilitating a universal norm backed by the religious might of an internet shar'ia and fatwa system.[68] None of this is to suggest that television images have been eclipsed. My point is that there is now a sort of *jihadi* subculture—massively proliferated since 9/11—and a parallel image-world largely driven by Webcams and the Internet.[69] In seven years the number of terrorist Web sites has grown from twelve to over four thousand; the *jihadi* Web site qal3ah.net (now relocated) had 7,939 registered members in 2003. Yahoo! alone provides a home for over two hundred *jihad* chat groups. Inevitably there are two on-line magazines associated with al-Qaida (Sawt al-*Jihad*, and Muaskar al-Battar) that feature articles for the novice insurgent on kidnapping, terrorist targets, and money-laundering.

Revolutionary Islam contains three levels of virtual community: the message boards (e.g., Al Qal'ah (the Fortress) and Al Sahat (The Fields), the informational hubs (e.g., Global Islamic Media), and the "mother sites" of the vanguard operatives (e.g., Al Faruq (He who distinguishes Truth from Falsehood) and Markaz al-Dirasat wal-Buhuth al-Islamiyyah (Centre for Islamic Study and Research). The mother sites are compelled to move—often several times daily—to avoid capture but they maintain their position by stealing unguarded server space (most recently that of the Arkansas Department of Highways) and sending out e-mails each day to inform the community of new links to a new site address. Virtual Islam operates in a world largely beyond the frontiers of regulation and detection.[70]

By the early 1990s, the sense of an Arabist public sphere contracted under the press of the Gulf War, the Middle East Peace process, and by the unassailable concentration of state power. Yet a decade later a new "Arabist community"[71] had arisen, stoke by the fires of the new media. Islamic *Jihad* or al-Qaida cannot take credit full credit for this, but radical Islam has contributed, in its tactical use of al-Jazeera and the virtual world, to the creation of a profound sense of collective suffering in which Iraq has come to stand for all Arabs and all Muslims, for the belief that the American occupation of Iraq is radically contrary to Arab and Muslim interests.

The virtual life, then, provides vanguard Islam with an instantaneous interconnectedness that permits unprecedented degrees of coordination and decentralized flexibility. A vast virtual community has come into being that feeds on the horrors of the New American Century. The circulation of its propaganda and spectacular images, the capacity to move strategic resources (by some estimates a war chest running to the billions of dollars) and to launder money associated with drugs and the illicit diamond trade have become its hallmarks. These virtual structures hold together an enormously complex constellation of internationalists—first and second generation *jihadists* war-hardened by the struggles in Afghanistan, Bosnia and Chechnya—and local teams of militants. Already the Web has helped constitute what Olivier Roy calls Islamist "franchising"[72] as the never-ending array of new vanguards (the Al-Andalus brigade situated in the land of Tariq ibn Zayad)[73] detonate their home-made bombs in the "brand name" of al-Qaida.

Three years after 9/11, the long inventory of terrorist attacks belies the claims of the Bush men that al-Qaida is on the run (3,500 sympathizers have been detained they say, 75% of the leadership killed). My point is that the vanguard's virtual qualities mark them off, not simply because they deploy satellite telephones, laptops, and encrypted Web sites. What matters is the ways in which such technologies afford a sort of meeting ground for the millions of disaffected Muslims and the universalist aspirations (the global *jihad*) of the Islamic revolutionaries themselves.

The second theme addresses the flourishing secondary market in arms and the global armaments industry more generally. The widespread availability of kalashnikovs and AK-47s—and increasingly more sophisticated weapons—has become the hallmark of the failed postcolonial state. There is no equivalency between the pathetic rituals of authoritarian leaders to disarm civilian groups and the conspicuous ease with which militants can rearm now themselves with even more sophisticated weaponry. What is true for the automatic rifle no less true for the RPG or Stinger missiles. And then, of course, there is nerve gas, anthrax, fissile material, and the like.

In the story of markets, states, and popular arsenals, a number of forces are at work: the collusion between decrepit militaries and illegal marketers, the proliferation of the private arms trade, dumping of outdated arms in an industry marked by constant innovation and a rising rate of destructive power,[74] the multiplication of Internet sites devoted to the construction and employment of high-tech weaponry, and the ever increasing miniturization, portability, and invisibility of explosive (and bioterror) devices of enormous destructive effect. The state has surely lost its monopoly of the control of the means of violence. Let us recall that the operational costs for the Jakarta bombing are estimated to have been $2,000, for Madrid $1,000, for New York/Washington, D.C., perhaps $175,000. Perhaps too much has been made of cyber-terror—the U.S. troops in Afghanistan found engineering software, virtual models of dams, and computerized information on nuclear power plants but no evidence of actual cyberattack's—but the possibilities are real nonetheless, and its attributes are unequivocal: it is cheap, anonymous, varied, remote, and potentially catastrophic. All of this, one could say, has radically democratized the means of destruction. Radical Islam has been one of its primary beneficiaries.

Finally there is the world of images and the question of spectacular politics. It is a measure of the strategic brilliance of al-Qaida that it could chillingly predict the outcome of its actions: an assault on the heart of U.S. empire would elicit an immediate reaction—violent, imperialist, "the maddened beast"—fully confirming for all Muslims across the Quran belt, bin Laden's political diagnosis of America: a rogue imperial state, at heart anti-Arab and anti-Muslim, willing to engage in mass killing of civilians in order to occupy the holy lands, with, of course, the active collusion of a posse of corrupt West Asian puppet states.[75] They also fully understood it would all be televised.

The extraordinary discovery of several al-Qaida hard drives—purchased by a *Wall Street Journal* writer in a Kabul market—confirms the extent to which revolutionary Islam has displayed an uncanny grasp of spectacular politics and the world of appearances.[76] Perhaps more than anything else, the computers disclose the fact that Al-Qaeda "understands that twenty-first century wars are spectacular encounters in which the dissemination of images is a core strategy."[77] They are adept in the fine arts of "spectacular theatrical violence,"[78] acts that simultaneously confirm essential religion convictions and transmit political messages to the world of heretics, infidels, and unbelievers. Bin Laden returned to Saudi Arabia in the mid-1980s, after fighting in the Afghan *jihad*, as a popular hero. But it was his adept use of Saudi media that gives reason to question Prince Bandar's assessment of Osama at the time—he could not "lead eight ducks across the street"—and to mark his development as a very savvy publicity hound.[79] Some of the most ferocious internal struggles within "the base" turned on the extent to which Egyptian cells resented Osama's TV persona—driven by the fact that Al-Arabiya and Al-Jazeera had become his indispensable mouthpiece. Fatwa's are routinely issued as grainy video-recordings; CDs circulate widely and Web sites offer the vanguard leadership exhorting the faithful (see *jihadspun*.net's thirty-six minute video of Osama "preaching" and making threats). Grisly beheadings are now ritually Webcast. Al-Zawahiri and Osama bin Laden's post-September 11 video debriefing (a hybrid doubleness if ever we needed confirmation of "the old new," as Brecht put it), a videography features a poetic Caliphal tableau of rocks, carpets, and religious texts with Osama chuckling over the value of his engineering degree, exulting the martyrs, reflecting on eighty years of Muslim humiliation. Its spectacular power was lost on no one. Just days after the attack, al-Qaida had produced a promotional video— "The Big Job"—including a clever montage of lower Manhattan footage set to rousing victory music. In spite of the massive assault on its operations, the vast industry of cassettes, photos, CD-ROMS, DVDs, and the ever-changing virtual landscape of al-Qaida Web sites, continue to flourish. The measure of radical Islam's spectacular victories in the battle over appearances is the extent to which the US states the constant refrain—"look, we are defeating al-Qaida, there has been no attack on US soil since 2001"—rings so hollow and false. September 11 was a spectacular defeat for which there is no compensatory response within the image world. This spectacle cannot be superseded (embedded journalism? the fake popular toppling of the Saddam statue? leveling Afghani outhouses with laser missiles?). It can only be hidden from view, withdrawn from the public eye in the vain hope that its spectacular power dissipates.[80]

What matters, then, in historical terms is not so much the agents or actions of revolutionary violence: the martyrs, the suicide bombers, the slaughtered children, the looted museums, the ravaged mosques. But the instantaneous circulation and consumption of these images across Islamdom as a spectacle. It is here that the centrality of suicide—individual but increasingly group—to Islamist terror carries a particular weight. The martyr has become part of the spectacle of violence with, apparently, its own appeal. According to research by Eyad Serraj, 25 percent of young people in Gaza "aspire to a martyr's death"[81]—a death that carries a spectacular power. Who could forget the image of Reem Raiyi, the Hamas suicide bomber, with her young son Obida holding an RPG? It is through the spectacular power of revolutionary Islam that so many Muslims around the world came to believe that the war on terror is a war on Islam. Hosni Mubarak's prediction—the Iraq war will "create a hundred bin Laden's"—now seems so chronically inhibited. The occupation of Iraq has become the terrorist's field of dreams.

III

Revolutionary Islam is obviously not the whole story of political Islam. Like other political movements with a utopian cast—twentieth-century guerilla Marxism, for example, or sixteenth-century Protestantism—there are a variety of tactics and strategies employed by Islamists, from armed insurrection to building a parallel civil society to Muslim political parties operating within parliamentary democracy. Islamism is a many-headed religion and operates at many levels—the global *ummah*, reform of territorially defined nation state, the moral economy of the urban neighborhood—and this, in part, explains its appeal, its reach and its astonishing political dynamism and energy. A measure of the fantastic ability to mobilize for essentially modern ends the desire to be part of a transnational and transcendental community is Islamism's vast library—much available on-line—on just about everything: social justice, democracy, gender, human rights, government, banking, pedagogy. And every effort by secular states to suppress or control such activity in the name of freedom or the liberal separation of church and state simply unleashes a firestorm of Muslim protest and opposition.[82] What is incontestable is the extent to which, within Muslim majority states, Islamists are the most organized and effective political presence in relation to, on the one hand, newly-minted neoliberal states offering at best a minimalist packages of services and, on the other, a thoroughly discredited and incapacitated state socialist alternative. The Islamist repertoire conversely is deep, wide-ranging, and disciplined:

"Islamists are very active....their actions include organizing demonstrations, mobilizing civil society against structural adjustment, building and staffing schools, medical clinics and employment centers...demanding charity for the poor, denouncing repression and torture, ...constructing parallel institutions to dispense material, emotional and social support to those marginalized by the relentless march of global neo-liberalism. Hezbollah is the archetypical case and is active in rebuilding of southern Lebanon in the wake of the 2006 UN negotiated cease fire." [83]

Over the last two decades, all of these movements drew enormous strength and ideological legitimacy from one fundamental fact: the existence of an actually existing Islamic alternative to secular national development, that is to say an actually existing Muslim theocracy in Iran. It is impossible to exaggerate the electrifying significance (at the height of the oil boom no less) of the Iranian Revolution in 1979. Here lay an authentic Islamic revolution for and by the people, a bulwark in the face of American empire, and a grand, brilliant political experiment of rule by jurists. Iran provided an imagined community of immeasurable power for all Muslims that resonated across sectarian and political lines. The rise of Ayatollah Khomeini and his mullahs marked a foundational moment in the contemporary Islamist project:

Here was an Islamic Revolution which was populist and anti-imperialist, which had spotted some of the vocabularies and slogans of the left. For some it seemed that unlike the 'imported' ideologies of Marxism or nationalism, is in its political and progressive form, is more accessible to the people, springing as it does form their historical cultural roots. Political Islam acquired many recruits, a political respectability and viability, it became firmly established in the mainstream.[84]

No matter that the revolution obliterated the anti-imperialist Left, resorted to the principle of revolutionary necessity, and deployed the absolute powers of the Islamic State with brutal effect (even if it contradicted Islamic law). It was an exemplar, a blueprint, a home grown alternative. Khomeini's democracy was not an extension of Qutb's radicalism but represented a different revolutionary road altogether,[85] extending the already formidable power of the jurists within Shi'ite theology. Yet a number of its innovations have diffused across the Shi'ite and Sunni mainstreams alike.

How can one grasp the massive proliferation and the broad horizon of appeal of Islamist practice—as its revolutionary iteration in particular—since the 1970s? Why the powerful wave of utopian Muslim militancy? And who were the militant recruits? Liberal analysis typically answers these questions by turning to the disruptive consequences of modernization and rapid urbanization—a "cultural revolution"—upon a tradition-bound *umma*. On the Left, it is the failure of puppet or rogue-states whose subjects act out of Fanonite desperation. My argument turns, rather, on a profound sense of crisis which we term the *crisis of secular nationalist development*—the depth, breadth, and structural character of which has been radically underestimated even on the Left—and the poisonous political-economic conjuncture (oil, primitive accumulation, and cold war geopolitics are its coordinates) that sealed the fate of modern development.

One must begin, however, in the great, sprawling mega-cities of the South—a vast urban archipelago of destitution and disenfranchisement. More than half the world's population now lives in cities, and 95 percent of the projected demographic growth over the next generation will be stored in the desolate wastelands of the developing world's metropoli. Almost half of its urban population are housed in slums: in south-central Asia it is 58 percent, in sub-Saharan Africa the figure exceeds 70 percent.[86] The abject misery of slum life in Mumbai, Jakarta, or Lagos—each holding-pens for populations in excess of ten million—is unprecedented, not simply in virtue of its scale or explosive growth, but by the uncomfortable fact that this vast new proletariat was forged in the white heat of economic recession and neoliberal austerity.[87] Within twenty-five years, the world's slum population could reach two billion, perhaps more.

A planet of slums is the indispensable starting point because the new politics of the Quran Belt—and of the profound crisis of West Asia more specifically—is located in its cities. Islamic cities have always been the theatres in which the complex dialectics of ruler and ruled, man and woman, and space and identity have been performed. In contemporary Cairo, Amman, Kano, and Kuala Lumpur, it is Muslim urban civil society that provides the ether in which an expanding, and contentious, public sphere—debating matters of legitimate rule, modernity, gender equality, social justice, and human rights—now flourishes. In the ten most populous Muslim states (excluding India), already half of the population is urban.

By 2015 the figure will exceed two-thirds. These populations are overwhelmingly under thirty, increasingly literate and educated, and, for the most part, slum-dwellers. One might say that the historical agent of the contemporary Muslim city is the young, part or wholly-educated, unemployed male scraping a marginal living in the shambolic economy of Jakarta's *kampungs*, Istanbul's *gecekondus*, Khartoum's *shammasas*, and Cairo's *baladis*. It is from this incendiary milieu that the fire of political Islam has spread and where the crisis of secular nationalism is most palpable.

Any account of secular nationalism within west Asia must recognize that the modern nation-building project was in some respects still born. The experiences of Ataturk's Turkey, Nasser's Egypt, and Pahlavi's Iran exposed the superficial rooting that secular nationalism had developed within Muslim civil society. Almost always an imposition from above by authoritarian bureaucratic nationalists and praetorian guards,[88] the state was little more than a blunt instrument in the service of third-rate mimesis: modern Western development. If the Muslim royalist states (Saudi Arabia, Jordan, and the Gulf States) more readily accommodated Islam, the legitimacy and solidity of their models of secular nationalism, nonetheless, remained questionable at best. But the brittle political infrastructure associated with these secular nationalisms could not possibly withstand the brutal assault that was unleashed in the wake of the Second World War and, in particular, by the irresistible ascendancy of oil. The 1967 Arab-Israel War and the crisis of import-substitution industrialization began the rot, but it was the great crashing waves of petro-capitalism, neoliberal austerity, and recession (the most primitive of accumulation) that finished the job, finally destroying whatever remained of the tattered social contract between the political classes and the urban poor. Eviscerated too was the very idea of modern secular development. Modernity was, to return to Qutb, a condition of decay, a disenchanted world urgently in need of redemption.

The delicate balancing act of modern development—secular nationalism on the one side and state capitalism on the other—was turned upside down by the contradictions of the petroleum boom of the 1970. On the one side it provided one last gasp of life for the state-led model of development as petro-dollars flooded into state coffers. But on the other the undisciplined and chaotic oil grab that it unleashed—corruption does not adequately capture the variety of ways in which the public purse was raided, and the institutions of the state totally vandalized—quite literally discredited any sense of development as material improvement, democratic deepening and social justice.

The oil boom proved, then, to be a sordid and highly flammable mixture. The quadrupling of oil prices—driven by war, cartelization, and the forces of corporate oligopoly as we saw in our account of blood-for-oil—converted a number of Muslim states into the pathetic spectacle of fully-fledged "oil nations." The rudiments of this transformation are now widely understood. Oil-dependent economies are, in spite of their vast resource wealth, some of the most sordid, chaotic, socially unjust and inequitable of all political economies. As the proportion of GDP accounted for by oil increases, economic underdevelopment, lack of social achievement, state corruption, political violence, and human rights violations grows in equal measure. The petro-dollar catastrophe—the "paradox of plenty"[89] —is one of the few issues on which the IMF, Jeffrey Sachs, the human rights community, the Catholic Church, and the millions of urban poor in Cairo, Karachi, and Jakarta are in full agreement.[90] How else can one interpret the sordid history of Nigeria, to take one example: $400 billion oil dollars over forty years (1965–2004), $50 billion of which simply disappeared, at the end of which average standards of living were lower than at independence in 1960. But the story of Iraq or Iran or Qatar is no different.[91] Building this country said Prince Bandar, "we corrupted $50 billion….So what? We didn't invent corruption."[92] Well, that's alright then.

The oil boom shunted dollars, unimaginable quantities of them (the Saudi's pocketed over $300 billion between 1973 and 1980) directly into state coffers. Fiscal centralization and massive state-led economic expansion, produced not a mean and lean turbo-charged free market, but a flabby, corrupt rentier capitalism. Political classes distributed bloated contracts to clients and patrons, promoting hopelessly ambitious industrial ventures—all in the name of modernization. The construction boom sucked millions of people from the countryside into the ranks of the urban lumpenproletariat just as inflation, land speculation and endemic corruption crippled what remained of the urban moral economy. Oil shocks turned the ossified Muslim monarchies and city-states into spectacles of petro-decadence ("minor" princes, said a Saudi architecture, must have $40 billion palaces.)[93] Petrodollars inserted into pre-oil class structures provided all manner of opportunities for the crass privatization and pillaging of public office. The state itself appeared morally bankrupt and organizationally inept at the very moment that it was forced upon the public imagination. Petro-states were simply hollowed out and eviscerated. The modern oil nation turned out to be nothing more than one big crummy family.

At the same time, non-oil Muslim states were simultaneously transformed by the oil boom. The 1970s shifted vast dollar resources to the Saudi and Gulf States, sucking in millions of workers—over 20 million by some estimates—to labor on stupid construction projects (golf courses and irrigated wheat in the desert wastelands), thereby exposing the platoons of foreign Muslim workers to puritanical and insurrectional Wahabbi-Hanabali doctrines. Pakistani, Indian, Philippino, Afghani, Egyptian, and Tunisian workers were tossed together in a multicultural labor market that served as a world class incubator for popular Islamic radicalism. In equal measure, the region's petro-dollars funded tenticular and multilayered global networks of Islamic associations, charities, banks, mosque, and, as we now know, vanguardist cells across the Muslim world. Bin Laden senior, a Yemeni expatriate contractor and King Saud acolyte, turns out to have been a paradigmatic case of oil wealth at work.

What goes up must come down. And it was the spectacular petro-crash in the mid-1980s (from almost $41 to $8 dollars a barrel between 1981 and 1985) that provided a structural blow to secularism. Collapsing state revenues, expanded public borrowing, and painful debt servicing all began to spiral out of control as each ran headlong into global neoliberalism and the bitter medicine of structural adjustment. The exploding cities of Islamdom—awash with rural migrants, international workers, and unemployable university graduates—plummeted into the terrifying descent to World Bank/Wall Street/Treasury penury. Devaluation, privatization, the elimination of state subsidies and basic needs programs, the withdrawal of state services, and exposure to the advance storm troopers of American capitalism (the fast food chains and low-wage outsourcing) finished what the oil boom had begun.

What, in other words, do the historic experiences of secular national states within the shatterbelt of oil share in common? Dictators, endemic corruption, religious oppression, and a totally failed development. Ataturk, Boumedienne, Nasser, Sukarno, Asad, Hussein: more than anything what this cohort of leaders represented was the deadly association between secularism and suppression, between modernity and immorality, between development and the "nationalization" of Islam.[94] As the secular state withered under the ruthless onslaught of neoliberal reform, and on occasion (e.g., Somalia) collapsed altogether, Muslim civil society, now thickened and empowered by oil revenues and a half century of civic activism, stepped up to the plate.

Running across the wastelands of petro-capitalism and global neoliberalism is the instantly recognizable vapor-trail of cold war politics, and here resides the final episode in the crisis of secular nationalism that incubated revolutionary Islam.[95] The squalid history of territorial scramble for the Ottoman oil fields in the 1920s, the U.S. special relationship with the House of Saud, the Mossadegh coup, the blind support of the Pahlavis, and more recently the establishment of U.S. military bases in the Gulf all played their role. But several new lines of American power were in effect unleashed with the cold war proper: oil as U.S. national security, unquestioned support for Israel, and the Olympian struggle against Communism. Each directly contributed to the irresistible rise of Islamism. The arming and support of the Taliban in Afghanistan is, of course, the most egregious case not because it provided the Soviets with "their own Vietnam" but rather because it trained an entire generation of war-hardened transnationally oriented *jihadists*. To this one must add the unthinkable provocation of the presence of U.S. military bases close to Mecca, the endless humiliation of unlimited and unabashed support for Israel, and the treachery of encouraging a rebellion in southern Iraq in 1991 only to see George Bush senior withdraw troops and have the Shi'ite militants slaughtered by Saddam. The stench of American complicity in the rise of Islamism is simply overpowering.[96]

IV

> Everywhere you could see open graves standing empty as the New advanced on the Capital. Round about stood those who inspire terror, shouting: Here comes the New, it's all new, salute the New, be new like us! And those who heard, heard nothing but their shouts, but
> those who saw, saw certain people who were not shouting.
> So the Old strode in disguised as the New, but it brought the New with it in its triumphal procession and presented it as the Old.
> The New went fettered and in rags. They revealed its splendid limbs.
> And the procession moved through the night, but what they thought was the light of dawn was the light of fires in the sky. And the cry: Here comes the New, it's all new, salute the New, be new like us! would have been easier to hear if everything had not been drowned in the thunder of guns.
>
> —Bertolt Brecht, "Parade of the Old New," 1938

The Old strode in disguised as the New. Brecht was on to something. In revolutionary Islam there is a sort of doubling; the old is to be restored in some way but in a modern guise. No less, the New Modern—barked by the likes of the Project for a new

American Century and the World Bank—is always accompanied by the thunder of guns. The empty graves lay open as the New advances.

To emphasize the world-systemic significance of the Old New in its radical anti-imperialist guise, currently operating under the sign of political Islam, is not to endorse its political project. All manner of atrocities have been thrown up in the name of resisting empire and modernity. I reject the terror of the militants and have little reason to believe that their reading of the texts—the Quran as rocket science as Malise Ruthven put it—can possibly lay the groundwork for cosmopolitan forms of political practice. But neither is it particularly helpful to simply label the vanguardists as "Islamo-fascist" as Hitchens argues[97] or for that matter as renegade anarchists.[98] al-Qaida and its like have no foundation in organic nationalism, racial superiority or charismatic leadership. Their call to arms is at once universalist, multicultural, and internationalist—representing a global *umma*. In any case, I have placed the utopian radical project on a larger canvas of political Islamism, some expressions of which may produce gradualist, nonviolent forms of democratic inclusion—a development signaled both by the large moderate middle-ground of the Egyptian Muslim Brotherhoods, some tendencies within the Iranian clergy, and by a diverse group of progressive intellectuals (Indonesian scholar Harun Nasution, Moroccan philosopher Muhammed Abdel al-Jabri, Eqyptian cleric Gama al-Banna, among them). The relationship of radical and other forms of political Islam to nationalism, capitalism and globalization is always complex and contradictory. A multitude of Muslim voices they may be, but they fit uneasily, if at all, into the category of that name expounded by Messrs Hardt and Negri in *Empire* or *Multitude*.

The revolutionary Islamists have beaten Bush at his own game: faith-based service provision and regime change. Flexible, pragmatic, and disciplined, Islamism is a model of basic needs provision: and what the National Security Strategy calls "effectively acting against emerging threats." One thing, at least, is perfectly clear. The conditions that created the brutal and clinical disassemblage of modern secular nationalist development in the Qu'ran-belt are alive and well. As the new wave of petro-dollars washes across West Asia—according to current estimates,[99] over $160 billion in 2005 for Saudi Arabia alone*—why should we believe that the grim developmental failures of the 1970s are not simply to be repeated (as farce or as apocalypse?). Sayyid Qutb, lest we forget, was not a critic of modernity as such but of post-Enlightenment reason. He fought the atrocities of untrammeled rationalization, Westernization and the "blind action of soulless institutions." Mohammed Atta, we should recall, waxed lyrical in his Hamburg University thesis on the Aleppo *souk*, under siege, in his view, from tourists, fast food restaurants, and ugly hotels. It was the American skyscraper that symbolized for him the shameless greed of those who sought to violate the integrity of the old Aleppo.

Modernity as decay, the endangerment of Islam—the twin foci of Qutbist reaction. It is hard to imagine any circumstances in which these two ideas have been so dramatically confirmed for millions of Muslims as in the last few years along the banks of the Euphrates. Military occupation, the terrorization of Iraqi civilians, the assault

---

* As of the summer of 2006, with oil prices at $80 per barrel, the oil states are once more awash with hundreds of billions of petro-dollars.

on the Najaf cemetery and other holy sites, the degradation and humiliation at Abu Graib, perhaps fifty thousand Iraqis slaughtered—all the horrors of the current phase of America's permanent war—have corroborated, in the most public and spectacular way, the profound truth of the vanguardist assessment of the filth of *kuffar*. Military neoliberalism is now a colossal forcing house for the efflorescence and multiplication of political Islam—and inevitably revolutionary terrorists.

And here resides the truly unwelcome political truth. The Vanguard of Terror has become modernity's opposition—a vicious, spectacular, and effective all at once—that speaks certain truths to the modern in a manner that no language of Reason dares to. As my comrades in Retort put it, "the purer and more asphyxiating the condition of modernity becomes, the more powerful the vanguard's appeal—not essentially as a political tactic, but as a *form of life*."[100] This form of life has mobilized many Muslim insurgents in unprecedented ways. At the end of September 2004, a "routine" month according to the Pentagon, there were 2,368 attacks by insurgents (every province was hit at least once): 799 home made bombs, 664 mortar and rocket attacks, and 272 R.P.G.s.[101] More than half of the Iraqi population live in circumstances in which the 2004 elections could not be safely conducted. As of the summer of 2006, there are almost 40 insurgent attacks in Baghdad alone. "Goodness knows," says Donald Rumsfeld, "it does not take a genius to blow up a building."

V

> We can't kill them [the Iraqi insurgents] all. When I kill one, I create three.
> — Lieutenant Colonel Frederick Wellman, US Army, 2005

I am not sure that Lieutenant Wellman has fully grasped Gregory's insistence that radical Islam reflects how "the local and the transnational are woven into its operations." But perhaps it is a start. If my account suggests anything, it is not only how militant particularism meets up with global flows. It is how this constellation of "complexity and contingency" (Gregory's language again) has produced, for now, a particular sort of certainty: that is to say, a stable and self-reproducing system of terror within the circumference of what passes as American empire and military neoliberalism.

Notes

1. Much of this chapter is the product of long discussions with three comrades—Tim Clark, Iain Boal and Joe Matthews—the product of which is a book, *Afflicted Powers* (Verso, 2005), which addresses the question of terror and Islam directly in chapter 6. A version of this chapter was written in the first instance for that book. I have also benefited hugely from the work of Paul Lubeck and Terry Burke. All errors are, of course, my own responsibility.
2. See Gilles Kepel, *The War for Muslim Minds*. Cambridge, MA: Harvard University Press, 2004, chapter 3.
3. Michael Taussig, *The Nervous System*. London, Routledge, 1994.
4. Cited in J. Rose, *The Question of Zion*. Princeton, NJ, Princeton University Press, 2005, 1.

5. See Fred Halliday, *The Middle East in International relations*, Cambridge University Press, 2005, 246.

6. *Guardian Weekly*, December 16, 2005, p.18.

7. See Mamood Mamdani, *Good Muslim, Bad Muslim*. New York, Pantheon, 2004.

8. Daniel Pipes, *Militant Islam Reaches America*. New York, Norton, 2003.

9. Ernest Gellner, cited in Aziz Al-Azmeh, "Postmodern Obscurantism and the Muslim Question," *Socialist Register* 2003, New York: Monthly Review Press, 46.

10. Aziz Al-Azmeh, "Postmodern Obscurantism and the Muslim Question," *Socialist Register* 2003, New York: Monthly Review Press, 2003.

11. The relation between Islamic radicalism and the spectacle is pursued at length in *Afflicted Powers*, London, Verso, 2004, chapters 1 and 6.

12. Olivier Roy, *L'Islam Mondialise*, Paris, 2002, cited in Clifford Geertz, "Which way to Mecca?", *New York Review of Books*, July 3, 2003, 37.

13. The state stenographers conjure up the magic figure of 0.02% as the unacceptable "radical'" fringe of the Islam community (see United States Institute for Peace: http://www.usip.org). An army, in short, of some 300,000 strong. It is estimated by Peter Bergen, "Backdraft," *Mother Jones*, July-August 2004, 44. that 120,000 militants received military training in Afghanistan alone; Juan Cole suggests that a minimum of 60,000 militants have been trained by Al-Qaeda.

14. Jason Burke has himself written that "al-Qaedism" is however growing stronger by the day! See Jonathan Raban, "The Truth about terrorism", *New York Review of Books*, January 13, 2005.

15. Gilles Kepel, *Jihad: The Trial of Political Islam*. Cambridge, MA, Harvard Universitty Press, 2002, 371; see also Olivier Roy, *The Failure of Political Islam*. Cambridge, MA: Harvard University Press, 1994;

16. Cited in Max Rodenbeck, "Islam confronts its demons," *New York Review of Books*, April 29, 2004, 17.

17. Richard Clarke, *Against All Enemies*. New York, Free Press, 2004

18. Derek Gregory, *The Colonial Present*. London, Blackwell, 2004, 46.

19. See Aziz Al-Azmeh, *Islam and Modernities*. London, Verso, 1996.

20. Laura Guazzone (ed.), *The Islamist Dilemma*. Reading, UK, Ashgate, 1995.

21. Paul Lubeck, Islamic Revival, Working Paper, Centre for International, Global and Regional Studies, University of California, Santa Cruz: available at http://www.ucsc.cigrs.edu.

22. Mike Davis, *Planet of the Slums*. London, Verso, 2005.

23. Peter Bergen, "Backdraft," p.45.

24. Bruce Lincoln, *Holy Terrors: Thinking about Religion after September 11*. Chicago, University of Chicago Press, 2003, 79.

25. Malise Ruthven, *A Short Introduction to Islam*. Oxford, Oxford University Press, 2001, and *The Fury of God*, London 2003.

26. See C. Wickham, *Mobilizing Islam*. New York, Columbia University Press, 2002, 130–131.

27. M. Zahab, and O. Roy, *Islamist Networks*. New York, Columbia University Press, 2004.

28. Wahhabism is a term that has increasingly lost its analytical significance. It has become a synonym for austere, conservative Islam. But Wahhabis (who refer to themselves as *muwahhidun*) embrace a vast array of religious and political dogmas, from *jihadism* to political reform to social reform to so-called *sahwa* "rejectionism" to variants of liberalism. Wahhabism is in any case not the only Muslim denomi-

nation in Saudi Arabia (the people of Hijaz, which contain the holy cities, do not even follow Hanbali law, on which Wahhabism is based). See "Saudi Arabia Backgrounder," IGC, *Middle East Report #31*, Brussels, 2004, 8–12.

29. Shahrur's ideas and the debate around them can be followed at: http://islam21.org.

30. Here the reference is *ijtihad*—a legitimate means of reasoning within Islam that turns on interpretation, creativity and imagination.

31. There is, of course, a vital, expansive debate within Islamist circles over gender and the role of women in the public sphere. See the "Muslim Modernities" Workshop, at UC Santa Cruz: http://www2.ucsc.edu/cgirs/conferences/islam/modernities.html. See also H. Ashfar, *Islam and feminisms*. London, Palgrave, 1999.

32. See Olivier Roy. *Global Islam*. Columbia University Press, New York, 2004.

33. Juan Cole. "The Taliban, women and the Hegelian private sphere," *Social Research*, 70/3, 771–808,

34. Graham Fuller, *The Future of Political Islam*, London 2003, cited in Clifford Geertz, "Which Way to Mecca?". *New York Review of Books*, July 3, 2003, 38–39.

35. Muslims all over the world believe that the Qu'ran is the literal word of God as revealed, over twenty-three years, to the Prophet Mohammed through the Angel Gabriel at the onset of the seventh century. Most of its verses were revealed in direct relation to material and social conditions then confronting the early community of believers. A number of "sciences" (for example, *itjihad* (legal or creative reasoning) which flourished in the ninth and nineteenth centuries) were developed to understand the reasons for, and preconditions of, specific verses, and to understand how in their specific meanings they could be made to speak—based on reason, deduction and prioritization—to the historically changing circumstances in which a community of believers found itself.

36. Malise Ruthven, *A Short History of Islam*. Oxford University Press, London, 2001.

37. Ibid., 10–1.

38. A. A. An-Naim, *Toward Islamic Reformation*. Syracuse, NY, Syracuse University Press, 1996; C. Ernst, *Following Muhammed*, Chapel Hill, University of North Carolina Press, 2003.

39. The contemporary Salafiyya movement is often taken to be identical to Wahhabism (in fact they are rather different) but it has actually reverted from its original political vision to a mainstream "scholarly" form (*Salafiyya 'ilkiyya*), largely apolitical and preoccupied with proper behavior. A distinctive militant wing of Salafiyya—so-called "warrior Salafiyya"—developed out of the Afghan campaigns and is linked to al-Qaida.

40. See Aziz Al-Azmeh, *Socialist Register*, 2003.

41. Al-Banna brought together the Salafist views of Rashid Rida (rejecting the stultifying interpretations of the official *ulama*) with the notion, taken from the Persian Shi'ite al-Afghani, of creating a modern Islam through positive social, political and (if necessary) military praxis. Al-Banna explicitly rejected, however, the colonial conditions with which the Salafists were prepared to coexist.

42. Here al-Banna broke with the Salafiyya: if they sought to "modernize Islam," his project was rather that of "Islamizing modernity." Al-Afghani argued that constitutional government was key to Muslim progress; al-Banna's rallying cry was "the Quran is our constitution."

43. Paradoxically the Brotherhood has changed in the last twenty years to the point where it is now indistinguishable from those political rivals who champion economic liberalism. Its original vision of an Islamic state representing the poor and

excluded has been so diluted that other groups—Gamaa Islamiyya, for example—remains able to represent the poor. Hussam Tammam, "Egypt: Muslim Brothers retreat," *Le Monde, September* 2005, 4.

44. G. Starrett. *Putting Islam to Work*. Berkeley, University of California Press, 1998.

45. C. Wickham, *Mobilizing Islam*.

46. Ibid., 174

47. The double movement between for example, on the one hand the fact that the Brotherhood established itself as an important and unofficial part of the political landscape in the 1980s (and 1990s) and a desire among many rank and file to form a party and on the other the extremism and violence of the revolutionary groups (Takfir wa'l Hijra, the Mukafaratiya, the Jund Allah and Jama'a al-*Jihad*) that exploded onto the political scene in the early 1990s speaks precisely to this process of incubation within a vortex of political Islam.

48. Elizabeth Euben, *Enemy in the Mirror*. Princeton, NJ., Princeton University Press, 1999.

49. S. Nasr, *The Vanguard of the Islamic Revolution*. Berkeley, University of California Press, 1994, xiv.

50. Let us recall that in bin Laden's famous post-September 11 video, he referred to "more than eighty years" of humiliation. This is, in fact, a Qutbist reference: the watershed is Ataturk's submersion in secular modernity and his abolition of the Ottoman Caliphate that promised the "extermination" of Islam.

51. See Paul Berman, *Terror and Liberalism*. New York, Norton, 2003.

52. Roxanne Euben, *Enemy in ther Mirror*, 167.

53. Sayyid Qutb's brother, Muhammed, fled to Saudi Arabia after his brother's death and taught at King Abdul Aziz University. Among those who attended his lectures was bin Laden. And bin Laden's own sometime mentor, Abdullah Azzam, was a friend of Qutb himself.

54. Mamood makes the claim that Maududi and Qutb differ on the grounds that the former wanted an Islamic state and the latter was "society oriented." State centered Islamists he argues generate Islamist political terror. This is a curious claim both because Maududi did not deny, as Mamdani suggests, the possibility of interpretation, and because Qutb is the reference point par excellence for revolutionary Islam (even if the deployment of terror is not sometimes not for the purpose of claiming state power). See M. Mamdani, 60–62.

55. Ayman al-Zawahiri, cited in Marc Sageman. *Understanding Terror Networks*, Philadelphia, 2004, 23.

56. Jason Burke for this reason refers to "a radical internationalist ideology" with no "central hub". See J. Burke, "Think Again: Al Qaeda," *Foreign Policy*, May/June, 2004.

57. Marc Sageman, *Understanding Terror Networks*. Philadelphia, 2004, 70–96.

58. See Mamood Mamdani, *Good Muslim, Bad Muslim*. New York, Pantheon, 2004.

59. Olivier Roy, *Failure of Political Islam*, 3.

60. W. G. Sebald, *A Natural History of Destruction*. New York, Vantage, 2003, 12.

61. This is taken from Fred Halliday, *Two Hours that Shook the World*, New York, 2001.

62. Paul Hendrickson, *The Living and the Dead*. New York, Knopf, 1996.

63. See http://www.religiscope.com.

64. Al-Azmeh, *Islams and Modernities*, 27.

65. See *What does Al-Qaeda Want? Unedited Communiques*. Berkeley, Terra Nova, 2004.

66. Gilles Kepel, *Jihad*, 315.

67. Charles Hirschkind, "Civic Virtue and Religious Reason," *Cultural Anthropology*, 16/1, 2001, 11.

68. Olivier Roy, *Globalized Islam*. New York. Columbia University Press, 2005, 183–184.

69. Lawrence Wright, "The Terror Web," *The New Yorker*, August 2, 2004, 40–53.

70. G. Weimann, *Cyberterrorism*. United States Institute for Peace, Special Report 119, Washington, D.C., 2004.

71. Marc Lynch, "Beyond the Arab Street," *Politics and Society*, 31/1, 2003, 55–91.

72. Olivier Roy, "Al-Qaida brand name ready for franchise," *Le Monde Diplomatique*, September 2004, p.1. See also Jessica Stern, *Terror in the name of God*. New York, Harper, 2003, chapter 9.

73. Sarhane Ben Abdelmajid Fakhet was a Moroccan immigrant to Spain responsible for the Madrid bombings that were perpetrated, he said, in the name of Al Andalus the Arabic name for the portion of Spain that fell to Muslim armies after the invasion by the Berber general Tariq ibn Ziyad in 711.

74. See for example L. Lumpe (ed)., *Running Guns*. London, Zed Press, 2000.

75. In an al-Qaida statement released in the wake of the Madrid bombings, the organization hoped that Bush would win the November election because he acts "with force not wisdom" and "Being targeted by an enemy is what will wake us form our slumber". Cited in M. Rodenbeck, "Islam confronts its demons," *New York Review of Books*, April 29, 2004, 16.

76. Alan Cullison, "Inside Al Qaeda's 'hard drive'," *Atlantic*, September 2004, 55–72.

77. John Gray, *Al Qaeda and What It Means To Be Modern*. New Press, New York, 2003, 76.

78. Jason Burke, *Al-Qaeda: Casting a Shadow of Terror*. London, Tauris, 2003.

79. Jonathan Randall, *Osama: The Making of a Terrorist*. New York, Knopf, 2004, 90–92.

80. This argument is further developed in *Afflicted Powers*, in the first and final chapters.

81. Cited in P. Conesa, The Suicide terrorists, *Le Monde Diplomatique*, June 2004, 1–2.

82. Paul Lubeck, Islamic Revival.

83. Lubeck and Britts, Ibid., 134.

84. Sami Zubaida, *Islam, The People and the State*. London, Routledge, 1989, 56.

85. Like Qutb, Khomeini argues that the legitimacy of sovereignty turns on Allah's exclusive right of legislation, that all law is divine, that Islamic governance resembles the Platonic philosopher-king, and that all secular authority is corrupt and idolatrous. But Khomeini departs radically from the Qutbist model in locating the rule of Islamic law as under the guardianship of jurists (*fuqaha*).

86. *State of the World's Cities 2004/2005*, World Urban Forum, UN-Habitat, Barcelona, September 13-17, 2004; *The Challenge of the Slums*, London, UN-Habitat, 2003. See Mike Davis, *Planet of Slums*.

87. Mike Davis, "Planet of Slums," *New Left Review*, 26, 2004, 5–34.

88. Fred Halliday, *The Middle East in International Relations*, p.75-96.

89. Terry Karl, *The Paradox of Plenty*. University of California Press, 1997.

90. Barnes, S. "Global Flows: Terror, Oil and Strategic Philanthropy," *African Studies Review*, 48/1, 2005, 1–23; Catholic Relief Services. *Bottom of the Barrel*. CRS, London; Christian Aid. 2003. *Behind the Mask: The Real Face of Corporate Responsibility*. Christian Aid, London; CSIS. 2004. *Promoting Transparency in the African*

Oil Sector, Center for Strategic and International Studies, Washington, D.C.; Global Witness, 2004. *Time for Transparency: Coming Clean on Oil, Mining and Gas* revenues, Washington, D.C.

91. See for example, *Follow the Money,* the Soros Foundation, New York, 2005; Transparency International's 2005 *Corruption Index* found that half of the most corrupt states in the world are oil producers. On Saudi Arabia see: http://www.caat.org. uk/information/publications/countries/saudi-arabia-intro.php. The Volker Committee's investigations in the systematic corruption associated with the UN Oil-for Food programs in Iraq between 1996 and 2003 endorsed the deep culture of bribery and theft that operated with the Iraqi state and the UN itself. See http://www.iic-offp.org/documents/Briefing%20Paper21October04.pdf

92. S. Hersch, "King's Ransom," *New Yorker,* October 22, 2001, 36.

93. L. Wright, "The Kingdom of Silence," *New Yorker,* January 5, 2004, pp.48–66.

94. Nikki Keddi, "Secularism and its Discontents," *Daedalus,* summer, 2004.

95. Mamood Mamdani, *Good Muslim, Bad Muslim;* S. Coll, *Ghost wars.* New York, Penguin, 2004; J. Cooley, *Unholy Wars.* London, Zed Press, 2000.

96. In light of this litany perhaps one can begin to grasp the effects of the US occupation in Iraq as described by U.S. soldier Jim Talib in Fallujah: "A few days later a group of [US] Humvees from another unit passed by one of our machine gun positions and they had the bodies of two dead Iraqis strapped to the hood like a couple of deer. One of the bodies had exposed brain matter that had begun to cook on the hood of the vehicle....it was [a] medieval display," cited in Ignacio Ramonet, London, twinned with Baghdad, *Le Monde,* August 2005, 1.

97. Christopher Hitchens, Of Sins, the Left and Islamic Fascism, *The Nation,* September 27, 2001.

98. *The Economist,* "For *jihadist,* read anarchist," August 20, 2005, 17–120.

99. *The Economist,* "A Long Walk: A Survey of Saudi Arabia," January 7, 2006, 11.

100. RETORT, *Afflicted Powers,* London, Verso, 2005.

101. "The Conflict in Iraq," *New York Times,* September 29, 2004, A10.

11

Vanishing Points
Law, Violence, and Exception in the Global War Prison

Derek Gregory

> When one hears about another person's physical pain, the events happening within the interior of that person's body may seem to have the remote character of some deep subterranean fact, belonging to an invisible geography that, however portentous, has no reality because it has not yet manifested itself on the visible surface of the earth
>
> —Elaine Scarry, *The Body in Pain: The Making and Unmaking of the World*

Power, Space, and Visibility

The vanishing points that I seek to identify in this chapter can be brought into preliminary view through three figures and two sites. The three figures are a hooded man, a masked philosopher, and an outlaw president, none of whom is quite what he seems. The two sites are the U.S. Naval Station at Guantánamo Bay and Abu Ghraib prison in Iraq: and neither of these is quite what it seems either.

A Hooded Man, a Masked Philosopher, and an Outlaw President

In the middle of October 2003 Haj Ali al-Qaisi, the former *Mukhtar*—community leader—of al Madifai, a district west of Baghdad, was arrested by U.S. troops on his way to work. He was hooded, handcuffed, and taken to Abu Ghraib prison, where he was asked about Saddam Hussein, Osama bin Laden, and the insurgency. "They wanted me to become their eyes in the region," he said. But he protested that he knew nothing, and he was left to kick his heels in a large tent compound. Ten days later he was taken to Cage 49 in Cellblock 1. There he was interrogated daily, and frequently made to spend the night hanging by his handcuffs from the crossspiece of the bars in his cage. Finally, he was told that he had exhausted the patience of his captors. Forced up on a box, electrodes were attached to his fingers. Again he was asked for names of insurgents, and again he protested that he did not know any. Silence. He could see the flashes of cameras through the rough hood. Then he felt the first electrical shocks: "My eyes felt like fire, my whole body shook; I lost feeling in my tongue and bit it. I fell down; my tongue was bleeding. They took the hood from my face and a doctor came to me. He opened my mouth with his foot and put some water in my mouth and said, 'He is OK. Shock him some more.'" He endured two more sessions before being returned to the tent compound. He says he vomited when he saw the sun. He was released in January 2004 and told that it had all been "a mistake." For some considerable time, Al Qaisi was believed to be the hooded man in the iconic photograph from Abu Ghraib, but it now seems that this was another prisoner who was subjected to similar treatment. According to a terse deposition from Abdou Hussain Saad Faleh, he was forced to stand on a box "with no clothing, except a blanket. Then a tall soldier came and put electrical wires on my fingers and toes and on my penis, and I had a bag over my head. Then he was saying, 'Which switch is for electricity?'"[1]

Some commentators have exploited the uncertain identification of the hooded man to discredit Al Qaisi's testimony and his work for the Association of the Victims of American Occupation Prisoners, while Faleh's testimony—like that of other victims—is shuffled off into an appendix to one of the official investigations. But their voices need to be heard, for the fact remains that the war prison described by victims like these is a far cry from the modern carceral regime described by the masked philosopher, Michel Foucault. It is a strange hybrid. It is not a prisoner of war camp, since its central operation is the continued interrogation of prisoners taken during the "war on terror," most of whom are denied the status of prisoners of war; yet many of its sites are inspected by the International Committee of the Red Cross, required to visit all prisoners held as a result of armed conflict or military violence. Neither is it an ordinary prison, since its inmates have been captured by security forces and placed outside the normal legal process, and the regime to which they are subjected is not an intrinsically correctional one; yet they are subject to stringent surveillance and moved through a hierarchy of spaces depending on their cooperation with their captors. In what follows I suggest that the war prison (like the "war on terror" more generally) can be understood as a dispersed series of sites where sovereign power and bio-power coincide.[2]

It was Foucault who distinguished these two modalities of power, but Italian philosopher Giorgio Agamben claims that Foucault failed to locate the "vanishing point" to which these "perspectival lines" converged, "a hidden point of intersection between the juridical-institutional and the bio-political models of power." In fact, however, Foucault was acutely aware of their contradictory combination, and argued that they coincided within the paroxysmal space of the Third Reich. This is the same constellation identified by Agamben, who describes the point of intersection between the two as the production of bare life—"life exposed to death"—and treats the concentration camp in general and Auschwitz in particular as the paradigmatic space of political modernity.[3] Here I treat the global war prison as neither a paroxysmal nor a paradigmatic but a potential space of political modernity, which is given form and force through a profoundly colonial apparatus of power that the metropolitan preoccupations of Foucault and Agamben more or less erase.

One of the crucial differences between these philosophical projects is that Foucault focused on strategies through which the normal order contains and confines "the outside" (the sick, the mad, the criminal) whereas Agamben focuses on strategies through which "the outside" is included "by the suspension of the juridical order's validity—by letting the juridical order withdraw from the exception and abandon it." This "space of the exception," Agamben argues, is produced through martial law and a state of emergency, which then become the ground through which sovereign power constitutes and extends itself. It is here that we encounter the outlaw president. Three days after the terrorist attacks on the Pentagon and the World Trade Center on September 11, 2001, President George W. Bush declared a National Emergency "by reason of [those] attacks and the continuing and immediate threat of further attacks on the United States." This was followed by a further declaration on September 23, 2001 to deal with "the unusual and extraordinary threat to the national security, foreign policy and economy of the United States" by "grave acts of terrorism and threats of terrorism committed by foreign terrorists." The emergency has been renewed in each subsequent year, and Agamben suggests that Bush "is attempting to produce a situation in which the emergency becomes the rule": in which "provisional and exceptional measures" are transformed into "a technique of government." The cascade of national emergencies did not begin with Bush; he has continued seven previous National Emergencies and declared eight others.[4] But what attracts Agamben's attention, and what distinguishes the double emergencies declared in September 2001, is their proximity to a supposedly new kind of war (the "war on terror") and the legal formularies that have been mobilized around it.[5] Although it has become a commonplace to describe this as a "war on law," however, I seek to show that it is also a war fought through the law ("law as tactic," as Foucault might say). While the Bush administration shows manifest disdain for domestic and international laws, it neither dismisses nor disregards them.[6] This matters because it means that law is a site of political struggle not only in its suspension *but also in its formulation, interpretation, and application.*

Guantánamo and Abu Ghraib

The Bush administration produced two different exceptional geographies to account for—and prize apart—its operations at Guantánamo Bay and Abu Ghraib. In the first case, Guantánamo was construed as a legally constituted space of the exception. It was selected because the Department of Justice believed that the location of the Naval Station—as "foreign territory, not subject to US sovereignty" would militate against any attempt to use federal courts to obtain a write of *habeas corpus* on behalf of enemy aliens held prisoner there. Other legal protections were withdrawn when the President determined that neither al-Qaeda nor Taliban prisoners qualified as prisoners of war under the Geneva Conventions. In the second case, in contrast, Abu Ghraib was declared a crime scene, the incidents there held to be offenses against both U.S. military and international law, and official inquiries were conducted that issued in reprimands, disciplinary actions and (in the case of enlisted soldiers) courts-martial. What happened at Abu Ghraib was glossed as unacceptable but un-American, appalling but an aberration, inexcusable but an exception.

The different meanings of exception that were invoked depend on the articulation of two different space-times. Guantanámo signifies not only an ambiguous space—a grey zone over which the United States claims jurisdiction but not sovereignty—but

also a place of indeterminate time: "As a territory held by the United States in per-
petuity over which sovereignty is indefinitely deferred, the temporal dimensions of
Guantánamo's location make it a chillingly appropriate place for the indefinite detention of unnamed enemies in what the administration calls a perpetual war against
terror."[7] Conversely, Abu Ghraib is made to appear as a precise punctuation in time
and space: the abuse of prisoners was supposedly confined to Tier 1A of the so-called
Hard Site of the Baghdad Central Correctional Facility, and it occurred in a number
of isolated incidents during the night shift from October through December 2003.
One is produced as an exception by being located beyond the law; the other is produced as an exception by being localized within the law.

I want to contest all these partitions by showing that Guantánamo and Abu Ghraib
are connected by the intersections of sovereign power and bio-power that are realized
through a series of spaces that fold in and out of them.

Agamben and Auschwitz

In describing these connections as "foldings," I am using Agamben's topological
vocabulary, but my mapping is guided by two critical considerations. One concerns
the state of exception and extra-territorialization—the volatile geographies produced
through geopolitics and international law—and the other concerns witnessing and
the apparatus of violence. Both arise from Agamben's reflections on Auschwitz, and
while I do not seek to collapse American Empire into the Third Reich I do want to
urge recognition of its proto-fascist potentialities.

Exception and Extra-Territorialization

Agamben's description of sovereign power and the state of exception is almost always
framed by a single state. His brief history of the state of exception in Europe and
the United States is shaped by the exigencies of war, but the emphasis is on suspensions of national law during states of emergency declared by France, Germany, Italy,
Britain, and the United States.[8] In treating the camp as the exemplary locus of the
modern space of exception, Agamben notes that concentration camps first emerged
in colonial spaces of exception in Cuba and South Africa, but he passes over these to
focus on Nazi concentration camps and, in particular, Auschwitz. Yet Auschwitz, like
the other five extermination camps that were dedicated to the horrifying production
of what Agamben calls the "German biopolitical body," *was within Nazi-occupied
Poland*. Agamben has drawn parallels between the legal status of prisoners in these
camps and prisoners in Guantánamo: their situations, so he says, are formally—
"paradigmatically"—equivalent. To adjudicate such a claim, however, and to connect
the metaphysics of power to its material inscriptions, it is necessary to ask how the
state of exception is mediated by the connections between war, military occupation
and *international* law.

Agamben is silent on this question, whereas one of his principal provocations,
the German jurist Carl Schmitt, wrote passionately about war, military occupation,

and international law. He saw an intimate connection between the state of exception within a state's territory and belligerent occupation where, in practice, "the occupied population is subject to the holder of undifferentiated power without even the protection afforded to it indirectly by pure international law, for it is not a legal subject."[9] He knew what he was talking about, given his own complicity with the Nazi regime, but his argument raises a question that is central to any critical analysis of the "war on terror." If the *state* of exception is also a *space* of exception, as Agamben insists, then in these situations surely the exception depends on the articulation of *multiple* spaces of political-juridical violence and an ex-ception, a "taking outside," through the *extra-territorial* inscriptions of colonizing power?

International law is no stranger to the inflections of colonialism and imperialism, and it is scarcely surprising that the perverse and paradoxical spatiality that Agamben attributes to the exception should be compounded by the spatialities of international law. International law is decentered, without a unitary sovereign to ground or guarantee its powers; its provisions are distributed through a congeries of conventions, treaties, and organizations. For this reason, nineteenth-century legal philosopher John Austin famously declared that international law is not really law at all: laws could only be "properly so called" if they were "commands of a sovereign" that made international law merely "law by close analogy."[10] After the Second World War, one of Schmitt's sharpest interlocutors extended this view (though to different ends) to suggest that "'if international law is at the vanishing point of law, the law of war is perhaps even more conspicuously at the vanishing point of international law." And more recently, Lieutenant-Colonel William Lietzau, Special Adviser to the General Counsel of the U.S. Department of Defense, extended even that view to propose that "the global war on terror' is at 'the vanishing point of the law of war."[11] Taken in sequence, these three telescoping perspectives direct the politico-legal gaze through an extended series of vanishing points towards non-places for non-people: sites like Guantánamo and Abu Ghraib.

Witnessing and the Apparatus of Violence

Those visual metaphors raise a second set of questions: what happens when those sites become sights? The question is raised most powerfully by the images from Abu Ghraib, but despite the iconic status of both Guantánamo and Abu Ghraib—or, rather, because of it—we need to remember that these are spaces of both constructed and *constricted* visibility and that most of what happens there continues to be shielded from the public gaze. The images that entered public cultures around the world multiplied with extraordinary speed. They attracted the attention of cartoonists, graphic designers, sculptors and artists, and in the fall and winter of 2004 many of the photographs from Abu Ghraib were displayed at the International Center of Photography in New York and the Andy Warhol Museum in Pittsburgh.

What are we to make of this image-frenzy? Cultural critics have raised myriad questions about the connections between the images and other photographic regimes in the United States but the most urgent centered on the complex affiliations between aesthetics and politics.[12] In this case these are complicated by the fact that both sides in the "war on terror" deploy images as strategic devices, and by the strong sup-position that, had it not been for the minimalist release of the Abu Ghraib images, neither the Pentagon nor the White House would have taken much notice of reports of prisoner abuse and torture. That the images have been aestheticized seems beyond doubt, then, but in many cases and contexts it seems no less clear that they also carry a political charge. And yet, I have come to agree with Mark Danner when he suggests that the photographs eventually came to stand in the way of an adequate understand-ing of what happened. The public gaze was directed towards the images not the pro-cess and policy behind them. Critical attention was focused on acts isolated as a series of stills and frames rather than on the apparatus that produced them.[13]

These concerns intersect with Agamben's reflections on Auschwitz and the ethics of bearing witness. He distinguishes two senses of "witness": one is juridical, and concerns third-party testimony to establish the facts of the matter in a trial, whereas the other derives from first-hand experience that radically estranges its testimony from law that "is solely directed toward judgement, independent of truth and jus-tice." This distinction opens into a lacuna, because those who survived Auschwitz are witnesses in neither sense. They were scarcely third-party observers, but neither can they substitute for the first-hand testimony of those millions who died in the camps. Agamben confronts the absence—"the untestifiable, that to which no one has borne witness"—through the figure of the *Muselmann* (the Muslim), the abject prisoner who moved in the indeterminate shadows of life and death, in a space where 'humanity and non-humanity' constantly passed through each other. He thus reads the *Muselmann* as a "perfect cipher" for the camp itself, the bearer of its secret per-formative geography.[14]

In a passionate commentary, however, Jay Bernstein suggests that what is lost from view, as a constitutive moment in Agamben's itinerary of reductions to bare life, is the complex of institutions, practices and people through which human beings were transformed into *Muselmänner*: the gas-chambers, the guards, the huts, the watch-towers, the railways, the police, the roundups, in short the whole apparatus of vio-lence of the Reich itself.

> At no point does [Agamben's] account veer off from the space of impossible sight to the wider terrain: from the victim to the executioners, to the nature of the camps, to the ethical dis-positions of those set upon reducing the human to the inhuman. Just the inhuman itself fills Agamben's gaze, and hence ours; such is the *pure* desire to bear witness.

Bernstein's concern is that Agamben transforms the act of witnessing into an aesthetic act that re-stages what he calls 'the pornography of horror' through its abstraction. For Bernstein, this aestheticization betrays 'one of the deepest strains in Agamben's thought' by 'suppressing the very ethical space it means to elaborate.' If this is so, then what are we left with? What remains? Bernstein's answer:

> Not the chambers or Auschwitz, not a place or set of practices, not the apotheosis of a com-plex historical trajectory, just the result of it all. With this we can hear the shutter of Agam-ben's philosophic camera snap open and closed. Click.[15]

In order to pre-empt the closure that Bernstein so acutely identifies—"Click!"—it is vitally important to recover the lines of sight (flight?) that converge on these vanishing points and to reconstruct the spaces that fold in and out of the sites of their captivity. Torture derives from the Latin *torquere* meaning to twist, and under the sign of our colonial modernity torture not only twists bodies—piling them on top of one another, shackling them to bed frames, standing them on boxes – but also twists space and time. To explicate this requires in turn the topology of sovereign power, and hence of the state of exception, to be understood as a performance, a doing. Only in this way do I think it possible to show (first) how "Guantánamo" has been produced through a series of juridical divisions, a sort of parsing of legal sentences, and (second) how "Guantánamo" and other spaces were folded into "Abu Ghraib" and beyond. I have briefly reintroduced the scare-quotes to emphasize that neither is reducible to a single space: both are prisons but their cages and bars are not able to contain the practices that are inscribed through them. In explaining why this is the case, I also hope to show that law and violence are not opposed but hold each other in a deadly embrace.[16]

Guantánamo Bay

Critics have described the Bush administration as waging a "war on law", and the president has provided them with substantial evidence. "International law?" he responded to a reporter in December 2003, "I'd better call my lawyer. I don't know what you're talking about by international law."[17] More particularly, it has become common to treat the U.S. prison complex at Guantánamo Bay as a "lawless place"—"beyond the reach of national and international law"; a place where sovereign power has been mobilized "outside the rule of law"; a wild zone subject to "a lawless and prerogatory power," where "the law is effectively suspended in both its national and international forms" and where sovereign power is extended "in excess of the law." Agamben himself describes the state of exception as "a kenomatic state," a vacant space limned by the "emptiness of law."[18] I want to change the landscape these claims bring into view by rattling the chain that yokes colonialism, violence and the law at Guantánamo and then tracing the legal and paralegal production of Guantánamo as a staging-post for the "war on terror." En route, it will become clear that Bush does indeed know what international law is about—and that he has repeatedly called his lawyers.

Colonialism, Violence, and the Law

Colonialism frequently operates under the imprimatur of law, both in the past and the present, and its violent assaults on land, liberty and life are regularly authorized and articulated through legal formularies. The legislative and interpretive fields, the actions of rulers and judges, are thus suffused with violence. If their metropolitan operation "takes place in a field of pain and death," as Robert Cover once presciently observed, then how much more anguished is their colonial mode of address; if their normal powers are "realized in the flesh," as he also remarked, then how much more painful is their emergency invocation.[19]

Guantánamo Bay bears the marks of these ligatures between colonialism, violence, and the law. Its modern history has been shaped by military encounters between three imperial powers—Spain, the United States, and the Soviet Union—and by enduring military occupation. Cubans rose against their Spanish occupiers in 1868–78, 1879–80 and 1895–98. Alarmed by the success of the revolutionaries in the final War of Independence, the Spanish military governor sought to cut off their popular support through a policy of *reconcentración*. Hundreds of thousands of peasants were forcibly relocated into concentration camps, where many of them were left to starve to death. American public opinion was inflamed by these atrocities, but the desire for military intervention was also motivated by thoroughly instrumental economic and strategic interests. In fact, the United States had made repeated attempts to purchase Cuba from Spain in the closing decades of the nineteenth century, and it was only after the last of these offers had been rejected in 1897 that Washington, buoyed by the rising tide of public opinion, found a pretext and in 1898 declared war on Spain. This too was an image war. Photographs of the effects of Spain's counter-insurgency operations heightened public condemnation of its oppressive colonial regime. And, as Daniel Ross wryly observes, "the American prize for its outrage at Spanish concentration camps in Cuba has become the right to run its own camp on the same territory."[20]

When peace was concluded later that year Spain relinquished all its overseas possessions, but Cuba remained under American military occupation for three more years. In 1901 the United States stipulated its conditions for Cuban independence through provisions set out in the Platt Amendment to the appropriations bill in Congress that authorized the continued financing of the occupation. These reserved to the United States the right to intervene in the future "for the preservation of Cuban independence" and, to that end, required Cuba to sell or lease to the United States "lands necessary for coaling or naval stations."[21] Accordingly, Guantánamo Bay was leased from Cuba in February 1903 "for the time required for the purposes of coaling and naval stations" and the United States was permitted "to do any and all things necessary to fit the premises for use as coaling and naval stations only, and for no other purpose." The lease could only be terminated with the consent of both parties or through the unilateral abandonment of the base by the United States. Its central provision read thus:

> While on the one hand the United States recognizes the continuance of the ultimate sovereignty of the Republic of Cuba over the above described areas of land and water, on the other hand the Republic of Cuba consents that during the period of the occupation by the United States of said areas under the terms of this agreement the United States shall exercise complete jurisdiction and control over and within said areas.

The language, as Kaplan argues, imposes a hierarchy between recognition and consent, "rendering Cuban sovereignty over Guantánamo Bay contingent on the acknowledgment of the United States, in exchange for which Cuba agrees to cede sovereignty over part of the territory it never controlled." The lease also locates Guantánamo in an ambiguous space between the "ultimate sovereignty" of Cuba and the "complete jurisdiction" of the United States.[22]

In 1959, following the revolution, the government of Cuba tried unsuccessfully to terminate the lease, and since then it has maintained that the presence of American

armed forces on Cuban soil is an illegal occupation. At the height of the Cuban missile crisis in October 1962, President John F. Kennedy rejected Secretary of Defense
Robert McNamara's proposal that the United States should offer to withdraw from
Guantánamo as a *quid pro quo* for the removal of Soviet medium-range missiles and
bombers from the island. On the contrary, the base's perimeter was strengthened as a
symbolic frontier between capitalism and communism, and Guantánamo remained
under American occupation. In subsequent years, the base provided logistical support
for U.S. military interventions in the Caribbean and Central America. From 1991 to
1994 detention camps were constructed there for 36,000 refugees from the military
coup in Haiti who were denied entry to the United States, and again in 1994–45,
21,000 Cubans seeking asylum in the United States were imprisoned there. The construction of the camps violated the terms of the lease, which allowed the land to be
used only as a coaling or naval station. A prison camp is at best an extra-legal appendix to the original agreement, and yet it became the central mission of the base.

When Kaplan describes Guantánamo as "haunted by the ghosts of empire," then,
she is surely correct. She also suggests that its history reveals "a logic grounded in
imperialism, whereby coercive state power has been routinely mobilized beyond the
sovereignty of national territory and outside the rule of law." Much of that is accurate too; but the base has also emerged through a long process of legal argument,
and it subsists through legal formularies—bundles of memoranda and minutes, acts
and amendments, treaties and the terms of the lease itself—that, taken together, have
produced a legal impasse: a stand-off between the United States (insisting that it has
a legal right to occupy Guantánamo) and Cuba (declaring the continued occupation
illegal). For this reason, it seems necessary to add that the space of Guantánamo also
derives from law at a standstill. It is a zone of indistinction where the legalized and
the extra-legal cross over into one another.[23]

Producing Guantánamo

The Bush administration has made much of the presumptive novelty of the "war on
terror," but the selection of Guantánamo as a prison camp, the designation of its
inmates as "unlawful combatants," and the delineation of a regime of interrogation
do not depart from the templates that shaped the base's colonial history and their
mobilization of legal protocols. In particular, Fleur Johns argues that:

> The plight of the Guantánamo detainees is less an outcome of law's suspension or eviscera-
> tion than of elaborate regulatory efforts by a range of legal authorities. The detention camps
> are above all works of legal representation and classification. They are spaces where law and
> liberal proceduralism speak and operate *in excess*.[24]

For far from the reactivation of the prison camps at Guantánamo signaling the retreat
of law from the field of battle, there was a vigorous debate between the Departments
of Defense and Justice and the State Department over the prosecution of the "war
on terror."

The immediate objective was to place selected prisoners taken during the war in
Afghanistan beyond the reach of any federal district court that might entertain a

habeas corpus petition.[25] Here the ambiguous status of Guantánamo conferred a distinct advantage over other sites that were considered, like the U.S. bases on Midway and Wake, which were included within the federal district of Hawaii. For Guantánamo was "neither part of the United States nor a possession or territory of the United States" and yet the United States exercised "complete jurisdiction" over the base. The reactivation of Guantánamo thus produced precisely the space envisaged in the President's Military Order of November 13, 2001, in which it would be possible to detain and try suspects "for violation of the laws of war and other applicable laws" while simultaneously suspending "the principles of law and rules of evidence generally recognized in the trial of criminal cases in the United States district courts."[26] These provisions, elaborated through a series of detailed memoranda, allowed a convergence between sovereign power and governmentality through what Judith Butler describes as "a law that is no law, a court that is no court, a process that is no process." She sees this as an instrumental, expedient, paralegal tactic, in which both detention and trial are determined by discretionary judgments that "function within a manufactured law or that manufacture law as they are performed."[27]

The imperative of indefinite detention, extending the emergency ad infinitum, jibed against a second objective that interrupted its limbo through the counter-imperative of speed.[28] This is where battle was joined between the Departments of Defense and Justice on one side and the State Department on the other. The first group argued that the "war on terror" had inaugurated a new paradigm that required interrogators "to quickly obtain information from captured terrorists and their sponsors,' and in their view this rendered "obsolete [the] Geneva [Convention]'s strict limitations on questioning of enemy prisoners." That being so—and law officers in the State Department protested that it was not so—interrogations would have to be conducted beyond the prosecutorial reach of both the federal War Crimes Act and the Geneva Conventions. Accepting the advice of Defense and Justice, Bush declared that none of the provisions of the Geneva Conventions applied to al-Qaeda prisoners. He also accepted that he had the authority "under the Constitution to suspend [the] Geneva [Conventions] as between the United States and Afghanistan," and his favored legal advisers outlined several ways in which he might do so. But Bush preferred the simpler expedient of deeming Taliban prisoners to be "unlawful combatants" who did not qualify as prisoners of war under the Geneva Conventions. [29] There are established procedures to determine the status of prisoners taken during armed conflict, but the White House insisted that these were only to be invoked where there was doubt. And in the view of the President's inner circle, there could never be any doubt. [30]

Here was sovereign power at its most naked, and when the first prisoners arrived at Guantánamo Bay in January 2002, it was equally clear that they were to be reduced to bare life. All legal protections had been visibly withdrawn from them. Photographs of their transportation and incarceration at once displayed and reinforced their reduction to something less than human. They seem to have been published "to make known that a certain vanquishing had taken place, the reversal of national humiliation, a sign of successful vindication."[31] The prisoners had been chained, gloved, ear-muffed, and masked throughout their twenty-seven hour flight, and arrived soaked in their own bodily waste. Otherwise, the chairman of the Joint Chiefs of Staff explained, they would "gnaw through hydraulic lines at the back of a C-17 to bring it down." As they slowly shuffled down the ramp in their jumpsuits, one reporter wrote: "[They] don't look natural. They look like giant bright orange flies." Then were led off to their makeshift steel-mesh cages at Camp X-Ray.[32]

A senior CIA analyst concluded that fewer than 10 percent of the prisoners who were transferred to Guantánamo were "high-value" terrorists. Most of them were minor players or indeed wholly innocent people who had been turned in to settle old scores or to receive bounties of thousands of dollars.[33] Yet our horror ought not to be measured by the innocence or guilt of the prisoners—a matter for the very judicial process denied to them—but by the calculated withdrawal of subjecthood from all of them. The legal determinations of the location of Guantánamo Bay worked in concert with the imaginative geographies of the 'war on terror' to produce what Butler calls "a zone of uninhabitability":

> The exclusionary matrix by which subjects are formed requires the simultaneous production of a domain of abject beings….The abject designates here precisely those "unlivable" and "uninhabitable" zones of social life which are nevertheless densely populated by those who do not enjoy the status of the subject, but whose living under the sign of the "unlivable" is required to circumscribe the domain of the subject. This zone of uninhabitability will constitute the defining limit of the subject's domain.[34]

If the prisoners were "bodies that mattered," to continue to speak with Butler, then in Washington measures were being contemplated to ensure that they mattered *only* as bodies: as biopoliticized bare life. Throughout the discussion that follows, it needs to be remembered that the Bush administration repeatedly insisted that prisoners would be treated in a manner 'consistent with' the Geneva Conventions. Such a claim relegates the treatment of prisoners to a matter of policy not law; it is not an acknowledgement that the actions of the United States are *subject to* the Geneva Conventions, and this lexical slippage creates a space of executive discretion (Schmitt's "decision") that would otherwise be (and as a matter of fact *is*) closed by international law.[35]

In fact, as Corine Hegland remarks, "even as the CIA was deciding that most of the prisoners at Guantánamo didn't have much to say, Pentagon officials were getting frustrated with how little the detainees were saying."[36] In the summer of 2002 Alberto Gonzales, then Counsel to the President and now Attorney-General, was busily considering advice from the Department of Justice about the bearing of the Convention Against Torture and Other Cruel, Inhuman and Degrading Treatment or Punishment as implemented by Title 18 (Part I, Chapter 113C) of the United States Code on the conduct of interrogations outside the United States. Under §2340A of the Code 'whoever *outside* the United States commits or attempts to commit torture' or conspires to commit torture is guilty of a criminal offence (my emphasis). This presented the White House with a real prisoner's dilemma, of course, because Guantánamo had been selected as a site of indefinite detention because it was *outside* the United States. But the Department of Justice pointed out that the relevant provisions of the Code defined the United States as 'all areas under the jurisdiction of the United States', including all places and waters 'continental or insular'. And according to the lease the United States exercised 'complete jurisdiction' over the base. Through this contorted legal geographing, Guantánamo was *outside* the United States in order to foreclose *habeas corpus* petitions from prisoners held there and *inside* the United

States in order to forestall prosecutions for torturing them. As Voltaire put it: 'Those who can make you believe absurdities can make you commit atrocities.'

The memorandum also provided an intricate parsing of definitions of "torture" that not only raised the bar at which the conjunction of violence and pain turned into torture but made this threshold the property of the torturer. First, "only the most extreme forms of physical or mental harm" would constitute torture: severe pain that would "ordinarily" be associated with "death, organ failure or serious impairment of bodily functions," or severe mental suffering that produced "prolonged mental harm." This allowed "a significant range of acts that though they might constitute cruel, inhuman or degrading treatment fail to rise to the level of torture." Second, a defendant could only be convicted if these consequences were a known and intended outcome of his or her actions: "Where a defendant acts in good faith, he acts with an honest belief that he has not engaged in the proscribed conduct." If these sophistries were not enough, Gonzales was assured that "criminal statutes" could not infringe on the President's "complete" and "ultimate" authority as Commander-in-Chief over the conduct of war, including the interrogation of prisoners.[37]

This memorandum had been prepared with CIA rather than military interrogations in mind, but the lines were already becoming blurred. In October 2002, the Joint Chiefs of Staff were presented with recommendations from the Joint Task Force charged with conducting Department of Defense/Interagency interrogations at Guantánamo to allow a graduated series of increasingly "aggressive" techniques to be used against prisoners who had "tenaciously resisted" current methods. Category I techniques involved direct questioning, yelling, and deception; Category II techniques involved the use of stress positions, hooding, removal of clothing and forced shaving, and the induction of stress through aversion ("such as fear of dogs"); Category III techniques involved convincing the prisoner that death or severe pain were imminent for him and/or his family, "exposure to cold weather or water," and "use of a wet towel and dripping water to induce the misperception of suffocation." The Department of Defense authorized the first two categories and noted that while all the techniques in the third category may be legally available their approval was not warranted at this time.

If the skeletal list of approved techniques seems unremarkable, even banal, this is the result of two strategic missions. First, the list contained no *limits* on the use of these techniques, and in a remarkably pointed exchange the General Counsel for the Navy, Alberto Mora, urged William Haynes, the General Counsel for the Department of Defense, "to think about the techniques more closely."

> What did "deprivation of light and auditory stimuli" mean? Could a detainee be locked in a completely dark cell? And for how long? A month? Longer? What precisely did the authority to exploit phobias permit? Could a detainee be held in a coffin? Could phobias be applied until madness set in?

Seen thus, Mora insisted, there was no clear line between the approved techniques and torture.[38] Second, the list was concerned entirely with instruments and provided no consideration of their *effects*. Since the end of the Second World War the United States has developed a consistent interrogation protocol that centres on sensory deprivation and self-inflicted pain. According to historian Alfred McCoy, 'the method relies on simple, even banal procedures—isolation, standing, heat and cold, light and dark, noise and silence—for a systematic attack on all human senses.' Early experiments showed that subjects could stand only two or three days of being goggled, gloved, and muffled in a lighted cubicle, while forced standing for 18-24 hours produced 'excruciating pain' as ankles swelled, blisters erupted, heart rates soared, and kidneys shut down. These 'no-touch' techniques leave no marks, but they create 'a synergy of physical and psychological trauma whose sum is a hammer-blow to the fundamentals of personal identity': they deliberately ravage the body in order to 'unhouse' the mind.[39]

In January 2003, Secretary of Defense Donald Rumsfeld withdrew his permission for the use of Category II techniques and convened a Working Group to prepare an assessment of "Detainee Interrogations in the Global War on Terrorism." Its final report was not circulated to those who, like Mora, had been critical of the original recommendations. In effect, the Pentagon was now pursuing what Jane Mayer describes as a "secret detention policy" whose guidelines followed the memorandum of the previous August to the letter. The report found that, because Guantánamo is within the United States for the purpose of title 18, "the torture Statute does not apply to the conduct of US personnel at GTMO." It reaffirmed the inadmissibility of the Geneva Conventions and in reaffirming the ultimate authority of the president made an astonishing reversal of the precedent set by the Nuremberg tribunals: "The defense of superior orders will generally by available for US Armed Forces personnel engaged in exceptional interrogations except where the conduct goes so far as to be patently unlawful." (Remember, those last two words had been eviscerated by the law officers favored by the White House). The report suggested a range of thirty-five interrogation techniques from "asking straightforward questions" and providing or removing privileges through hooding, "mild physical contact" and dietary or environmental manipulation to "exceptional" measures that included isolation, twenty-hour interrogations, forced shaving, prolonged standing, sleep deprivation, "quick, glancing slaps," removal of clothing and "use of aversions" ("simple presence of dog"). Rumsfeld approved twenty-four of them. Although he withheld approval of all the "exceptional" measures other than isolation, however, the list of authorized techniques contained none of the crucial limitations. There was thus considerable latitude for coercive interrogation to slide through cruel, inhuman and degrading treatment into outright torture. If this were not enough, Rumsfeld also accepted that "interrogators [must be] be provided with reasonable latitude to vary techniques" for reasons that included the degree of resistance and "the urgency of obtaining information."[40]

I have no way of knowing how much extra "latitude" that final clause was intended to allow; I simply make two observations. First, testimony from prisoners, soldiers, and interrogators makes it clear that the red lines (such as they were) were repeatedly crossed. There have been consistent reports of enforced nudity; exposure to extremes of temperature; deprivation of adequate food, water, and pain medication; induced disorientation through loud music, strobe lighting, and sleep deprivation; menacing by dogs; prolonged short-shackling in fetal positions; sexual taunting and assault; immersion in toilet bowls to induce fear of drowning; and isolation for months at a time.[41] Second, notwithstanding the techniques proscribed for military intelligence, since March 2002 the CIA had been authorized to use six "enhanced" techniques that included forcing prisoners to stand, handcuffed and shackled, for more than forty hours; forcing them to stand naked in a cold cell for prolonged periods and frequently dousing them with cold water; and simulated drowning ("waterboarding"). The CIA ran its own prison within the GTMO complex (at Camp Echo), but the CIA and the military frequently worked in concert because Guantánamo was the designated operating base for a Joint Interagency Interrogation Facility.[42]

During the summer of 2005, when Senator John McCain proposed an amendment to the Defense Appropriation Bill that would ban cruel, inhuman, or degrading treatment or punishment of anyone in U.S. custody anywhere, Vice-President Cheney insisted that the CIA should be exempt—it required "extra latitude" (that word again)—and the White House vigorously rejected any such measure that would "restrict the President's authority [not ability] to protect Americans from terrorist attack." The bill passed the Senate 90–9 and the House 308–122, but when the president reluctantly signed the Detainee Treatment Act into law at year's end he added a defiant signing statement insisting that he would interpret its provisions in a manner consistent with "constitutional limitations on the judicial power" and his own executive powers to protect national security, and he made it clear that he reserved the right to waive those restrictions in "special situations." Thus the hermeneutic circle—the mutuality of interpretation—was hammered flat until it fitted the Oval Office.[43] But, it turns out that, the Act contained its own catch-22. In March 2006 lawyers for the Department of Justice reminded a district court judge that, under the provisions of the Act, prisoners at Guantánamo only had the right to appeal their designation as enemy combatants—not to seek protection against their treatment there. As Human Rights Watch put it, "The law says you can't torture detainees at Guantánamo, but it also says you can't enforce that law in the courts."[44]

Abu Ghraib

Abu Ghraib had been a vanishing point since its construction by British and Dutch contractors in the 1960s. After the coup that brought the Ba'ath party back to power in 1968, mass arrests, torture, and imprisonment of opponents of the regime resumed, and political prisoners were consigned to Abu Ghraib even before it officially opened in 1970. The prison was under the control of the Directorate of General Security, and was the scene of some of the worst excesses of Saddam Hussein's regime. Within its walls prisoners were routinely beaten, broken and degraded, stripped, chilled, and electrocuted. Thousands were put to death, sometimes two or three hanging from the scaffold at the same time, their bodies buried in unmarked graves.

This history is immensely important, but not because it can be invoked to excuse what happened after the American rehabilitation of Abu Ghraib in the summer of 2003. Far worse atrocities took place there under Saddam Hussein, but it is grotesque to hold up his regime as a standard to judge the ill-treatment and torture of Iraqi prisoners by their American captors. Neither is it important because there is a direct parallel between Saddam's Iraq and Bush's Iraq. Instead, this history matters for the lives it remembers, and for the memories that were reawakened by the reopening of the prison under American administration. After the cruise missiles, the cluster bombs, and the killings I doubt that many people's fears were dispelled by the large sign that replaced Saddam's portrait at the main gate: "America is a friend of all Iraqi people."

The decision to fold the invasion and occupation of Iraq into the "war on terror" produced another series of fraught intersections between violence and the law. On the one side, coalition forces were surprised by the widespread resistance to continued military occupation, and their aggressive counter-insurgency operations served only to intensify the insurgency. The collection of executable intelligence was placed at the centre of this spiral. But the possibilities for interrogation were circumscribed by the President's acknowledgement that, unlike Afghanistan, the Geneva Conventions would be applied to prisoners captured in Iraq. On the other side, therefore, the rapidly improvised detention regime in Iraq exerted extraordinary pressure on the provisions of international law. There were two crucial questions: How far was it possible to "enhance" interrogation methods in Iraq without violating the letter of the law, and, if this provided insufficient "latitude," was it possible to transfer prisoners out of Iraq to other sites under the control of the United States or its allies and accomplices? I treat these considerations in turn. I begin by plotting the spiral of insurgency and counter-insurgency in Iraq, and then I turn to the architecture of an emerging carceral archipelago.[45] Between these two parametric geographies lies the hideous intimacy of the torture chamber, and it is at this vanishing point that I end.

Insurgency and Counter-Insurgency

The insurgency in Iraq has many roots and takes many forms, and its complex, adaptive geography cannot be reduced to a single map. The failure of the occupying powers to comprehend the scale of dislocation and distress brought about by the combination of Saddam, sanctions and war was a major cause. Millions of Iraqis had suffered terribly under Saddam and rejoiced at the downfall of his regime, but thousands had also died as a direct result of sanctions and two U.S.-led wars; there was scarcely a family that had not been touched by America's wings of death too. Shortages of electricity, water, and medical supplies, the breakdown of public order, the economic dislocation and the enforced privatization of the economy all heightened a common sense of grievance, especially in the central and southern regions of the country. Then there were the thousand and one daily humiliations of occupation: the ceaseless surveillance, the armored patrols, the checkpoints, the body searches, the midnight raids, the sheer inability or unwillingness to understand. Time and time again American troops fired on unarmed demonstrators calling for an end to the occupation; civilians were seriously injured or killed when troops opened fire during raids on houses and markets; countless others were humiliated, beaten and even killed at checkpoints. Excuses were offered as explanations; apologies were rare, investigations perfunctory. These were all landmarks of occupation agonizingly familiar from the Israeli occupation of Palestine.[46]

President Bush declared the end of major combat operations in May 2003, but by the summer it was difficult to distinguish occupation from war. In Baghdad there were daily attacks on troops patrolling the streets, and in the so-called Sunni Triangle mortars and rocket-propelled grenades were used to ambush convoys and

attack checkpoints. The coalition launched ever more aggressive military operations in June and July, involving thousands of troops backed by tanks, helicopter
gunships, and aircraft. These massive deployments resulted in the deaths of hundreds
of Iraqis and the detention of thousands more, all of which increased popular resentment of the occupation.[47] The opposition was many-stranded, at once spontaneous
and organized, nonviolent and militarized. As the summer wore on, demonstrations
and riots spread across the Shi'a south, with thousands marching in Basra, Najaf and
other cities to demand an end to the occupation. There was the real possibility of the
opposition turning into a national resistance movement in which Sunni and Shi'ites
would fight side by side. While the Americans were slow to realize this, others were
not. Iraq is part of the heartland of Islam, and the U.S. occupation turned it into a
new field of struggle for political Islam. Abu Mos'ab al Zarqawi, leader of a Salafi
terrorist group with a base in northern Iraq, chose this moment to launch an armed
jihad against both the coalition forces ("the far enemy") and the Shi'a ("the near
enemy") in order to nullify the prospect of a unified, nationalist and above all secular
resistance. In August his group was responsible for two spectacularly deadly attacks:
a massive truck bomb exploded at the United Nations mission, murdering the head of
the delegation and more than twenty other people, and at the end of the month a car
packed with explosives crashed into the Imam Ali mosque in Najaf, murdering more
than one hundred Shi'ites, including the spiritual leader of the Supreme Council of
the Islamic Revolution.[48] That month there were an average of twelve attacks a day on
American forces. This rose to fifteen attacks a day in early September; by the beginning of October there were more than twenty-five a day, and at the end of that month
thirty-three a day. Large areas of Baghdad were declared hostile, and the guerilla war
expanded beyond the Sunni heartland into the north and the Shi'a south. The situation was rapidly sliding out of control.

All of this bears directly on Abu Ghraib, which has been portrayed as a place
of chaos outside the normal order. By the winter of 2003–2004, more than eight
thousand prisoners were crammed inside its compounds. Facilities were poor, and
overcrowding increased the pressures; the detainees seethed with resentment, and
riots and escapes were common. Military investigations and the media reported that
Abu Ghraib was seen by those who worked there as the forgotten outpost, poorly
defended, and constantly rocked by mortar attacks. It was variously described as "a
prison on the brink," a howling chaos, a "hellish place" (for the guards not the prisoners). In short, it was made to appear as a sort of twilight zone where the boundary between order and disorder was constantly slipping away, patrolled by exhausted
and jumpy reservists, outnumbered and ill-prepared for their duties, who labored
under inadequate resources and ineffective supervision. Beyond the perimeter and
its watchtowers, however, the rest of Iraq was descending into chaos too. In response,
the level of military violence was ratcheted up and "pressure increased to obtain
operational intelligence on the enemy's identity, support systems, locations, leadership, intelligence sources, weapons and ammunition caches, and centers of gravity."
It was decided that a more aggressive structure of human intelligence collection and
analysis was imperative.[49]

And so Abu Ghraib was not exceptional at all. It was the gravity of the situation *outside* Abu Ghraib that was used to license the horrors *inside* Abu Ghraib: not because

the prison was "out of place," removed from the surveillant eyes of a high command preoccupied with the insurgency beyond its perimeter, *but because the U.S. military folded the prison into its counter-insurgency operations.* This connection is extremely important, because otherwise the violence of torture obscures the violence of invasion, incarceration and occupation. As our eyes are drawn to the hideous images from Abu Ghraib, they are drawn away from the atrocities committed by the U.S. military in places like Fallujah. As other forms of military violence are marginalized by the "exceptional" violence of torture, so the politico-military project of domination becomes contorted into the image of "liberation."

The Carceral Archipelago

In May 2003, the Department of Defense sent a team to Iraq to assess its detention system. Abu Ghraib had been virtually emptied when Saddam issued a general amnesty in October 2002, and after the war, like most other Iraqi prisons, it was heavily damaged and extensively looted. Only three prisons were operational, with a combined capacity of just five hundred prisoners. At Abu Ghraib two compounds had been totally destroyed and all the others were badly damaged, but two cellblocks were suitable for immediate renovation. Out of the twenty-one sites the team visited, the team considered Abu Ghraib "closest to an American prison." They not only attached a priority to its reconstruction; they also supervised the work. As the new Baghdad Central Correctional Facility, Abu Ghraib was to serve two purposes. It was intended as a temporary prison for criminal prisoners until a new Iraqi government took office and a new prison was established elsewhere. These prisoners began to arrive in June and were confined in tent-blocks rimmed by razor-wire. It was also to serve as the primary place of detention for the U.S. Army's "security detainees," who began to arrive as soon as the renovations of the cellblocks were completed in August.

It was not long before anxious Iraqis gathered at the gates of the prison seeking information about the thousands of men and women who had been arrested by the military. Most met with little success, and petitioners and prisoners became lost in an administrative labyrinth. By then, according to journalist Seymour Hersh, decisions to align detention and interrogation operations in Iraq with those elsewhere in the "war on terror" had been made at the highest reaches of the administration. Vice-President Cheney subcontracted execution to Secretary of Defense Rumsfeld who had the system engineered by his Under Secretary of Defense for Intelligence Stephen Cambone. Rumsfeld's capacity for micro-management is well-known —"the 8,000 mile screwdriver"—but it is extraordinarily difficult to trace the torque. The official investigations that have been made public contain much huffing and puffing about the problems of information flowing up the chain of command—how were they to know? — but provide no rigorous examination of the ways in which reverse flows helped set the conditions for what happened at Abu Ghraib and elsewhere. Those flows include memoranda, directives, and orders, together with more informal understandings, but they also include speeches from the White House, the Department of Defense, and the military that consistently described America's enemies as outlaws, barbarians, and monsters. Is it any wonder that American forces subjected their Iraqi captives to brutal and dehumanizing treatment? They had been told repeatedly that this was a war against Evil incarnate, so that they were not fighting enemies so much as casting out demons. The fate of those imprisoned at Abu Ghraib was not decided by a few rotten apples at the bottom of the barrel: it was the fruit of a vast poison orchard assiduously cultivated by the president and his under-gardeners.[50]

The central strategy for interrogation and intelligence that they devised had three elements. The first was the designation of prisoners. Although President Bush had accepted that the Geneva Conventions would apply in Iraq, their provisions were stretched to the very limit by designating most of the prisoners held after the nominal end of hostilities as "security detainees" or "security internees" (the terms were interchangeable) rather than Prisoners of War. Of the five thousand prisoners in its custody in May 2003, the United States recognized only five hundred as Prisoners of War. "Security detainee" was a technical term of particular significance because it allowed the full protection of the Geneva Conventions to be withdrawn from such prisoners for the duration of the armed conflict where "absolute military security so requires." This determination was invoked in a letter dated December 24, 2003, drafted by the Office of the Staff Judge Advocate and signed by Brigadier-General Janice Karpinski, the officer commanding the 800th Military Police Brigade at Abu Ghraib, in reply to serious concerns about detention and interrogation operations contained in interim reports from the ICRC: "While the armed conflict continues, and where 'absolute military security so requires,' security internees will not obtain full G[eneva] C[onvention] protection."[51]

This provision is contained within Article 5 of the Fourth Geneva Convention. But in its commentary the ICRC makes it clear that this can only be applied "in *individual* cases of an *exceptional* nature, when the *existence of specific charges* makes it almost certain that penal proceedings will follow," and only to those who can be shown to be a continuing threat to security. It is not a catchall clause to allow the prolonged detention of thousands of people for endless interrogation.[52] Yet the letter under Karpinski's signature insisted on the "military necessity" of holding security detainees for their "significant intelligence value," and senior officers regularly repeated the same objectives. In the course of his inspection of detention and corrections operations in Iraq in November 2003, however, Major-General Donald Ryder, the Provost Marshal General, had found that 117 Prisoners of War, 101 "high value detainees," and 3,400 security detainees were still in U.S. custody, and he cited numerous cases "where Iraqis at most expressed displeasure or ill-will" at the occupation "and have been held for several months." The intensifying counter-insurgency rapidly boosted the number of security detainees, even though it was reliably estimated that 85–90 percent of those held were in the wrong place at the wrong time and "were of no intelligence value." Perversely, this increased their vulnerability: their very innocence "made them more likely to be abused, because investigators refused to believe they could have been picked up on such arbitrary grounds."[53] The ICRC describes Article 5 as a "regrettable concession to state expediency," and warns with chilling prescience that "what is most to be feared is that widespread application of the Article may eventually lead to the existence of a category of civilian internees who do not receive the normal treatment laid down by the Convention but are detained under conditions which are almost impossible to check."[54]

The second element in the strategy was to "enhance" methods of interrogation. In September 2003, a thirty-member military team arrived in Iraq to conduct an assessment of "counter-terrorism interrogation and detention operations." With the encouragement and support of the Department of Defense, and Under Secretary Cambone in particular, the team was led by Major General Geoffrey Miller, Commander of JTF Guantánamo. His report recommended an immediate transition from "tactical" to "strategic" interrogation with a focus on the "rapid exploitation" of prisoners for "actionable intelligence." As at Guantánamo, detention and interrogation were to be integrated so that the one would "set conditions" for the other: "It is essential that the guard force be actively engaged in setting the conditions for successful exploitation of the internees." Miller recommended the introduction of "new approaches and operational art" developed at Guantánamo, which elsewhere he called a central "laboratory for the war on terror," and he provided details of the standard operating procedures that had been instituted there. An expert team from Guantánamo worked at Abu Ghraib from October through December "to assist in the implementation of the recommendations' and by November 'the real changes began to show."[55]

By that stage rumors of renewed abuse and torture at the prison were circulating widely in Iraq. Since April the ICRC had made a number of oral and written reports to the coalition complaining of consistent ill-treatment of prisoners and serious violations of international humanitarian law. After twenty-nine visits to fourteen internment facilities between March and November, delegates had seen enough to protest that the methods of physical and psychological coercion, "that in some cases might amount to torture," formed a "standard operating procedure"—a systematic apparatus of abuse—that included beating, stripping and hooding prisoners, the use of prolonged stress positions, photographing prisoners naked, and having them humiliated still further by female guards. Several officers admitted that "it was part of the military intelligence process" to hold prisoners "naked in a completely dark and empty cell for a prolonged period [and] to use inhumane and degrading treatment, including physical and psychological coercion" to "secure their cooperation." In January 2004, Major-General Antonio Taguba confirmed "numerous acts of sadistic, blatant and wanton criminal abuse" so pervasive and repetitive that they were "systemic."[56]

Hersh concluded that "Abu Ghraib had become, in effect, another Guantánamo."[57] According to subsequent investigations, however, the procedures recommended by Miller were intended to be no more than starting-points, and Miller and other senior officers claimed that it was clearly understood that they could not be implemented without modification "because, unlike Afghanistan and Guantánamo, the Geneva Conventions applied in the Iraq theater." The categorization of most prisoners as "security detainees" considerably closed that gap between the permissible procedures, however, and the connections established between the two carceral regimes through Miller's report and the expert team contracted the distance still further. In fact, by September 2003 JTF-7 had decided that the latitude provided for the treatment of security detainees was insufficient. Reverting to the designation of prisoners from the war in Afghanistan, Sanchez argued that "unlawful combatants" were present in Iraq too and that, in accordance with the President's Memorandum of February 7, 2002, they were not entitled to *any* of the protections of the Geneva Conventions. He then authorized twenty-nine interrogation techniques, of which twelve went beyond those described in Army Field Manual 34-52, and five of those exceeded the techniques approved for Guantánamo. CENTCOM viewed these additional methods as "unacceptably aggressive," and in mid-October Sanchez rescinded his directive "and disseminated methods only slightly stronger than those in Field Manual 34-52." Even so, his new memorandum remained as close as possible to the Guantánamo template provided by Miller. Interrogation operations were to be "conducted in close cooperation with the detaining units" and interrogators had to have "reasonable latitude" (again) to vary their techniques depending on both the prisoner and "the urgency with which information must be obtained."[58] In March 2004 Miller was transferred from Guantánamo to assume command of U.S. prison operations in Iraq.

The circuits connecting Afghanistan, Guantánamo, and Iraq were more than words and paper. Interrogators circulated and interrogation techniques migrated from one theatre to another, and it gradually became clear that similar abuses were widespread in both Afghanistan and Iraq. The ICRC reported a consistent pattern of brutality during arrest and transfer in Iraq, and this was subsequently shown to have extended throughout the detention system and to have started before and continued after the torture at Abu Ghraib. One officer and two NCOs testified that "the torture of detainees took place almost daily" throughout their deployment at FOB Mercury, for example, twenty kilometers east of Fallujah, from September 2003 through April 2004. Many of those most closely involved had been attached to Special Services in Afghanistan, where they had witnessed CIA interrogations, and they brought knowledge of those techniques with them to Iraq. These revelations were particularly significant because they showed that torture was not the product of a small number of ill-trained, undisciplined support troops but extended to front-line regiments, including "some of the best-trained, most decorated and highly respected units in the US Army." Special Operations units were active in Iraq too. Task Force 6-26 occupied an Iraqi military base at Baghdad International Airport, for example, designated as Camp Nama, and converted its former torture chambers into "interrogation rooms." There, according to Department of Defense, CIA and FBI witnesses, prisoners were kept in darkness, beaten with rifle butts, stripped naked "and had cold water thrown on them to cause the sensation of drowning." From these and other reports it is evident that Abu Ghraib was no aberration.[59]

The third element of the interrogation and intelligence strategy was to outsource these operations. Inside Iraq the practices I have just described were plunged deeper into the shadows by the use of private contractors. The U.S. occupation would be impossible without twenty thousand contractors undertaking tasks that were once the preserve of the military. They were intimately involved in the preparation and execution of the invasion—Peter Singer calls them "the coalition of the billing"—and the demand for their services soared as the occupation wore on. Thirty contractors were hired for interrogations at Abu Ghraib: the Titan Corporation (San Diego) supplied interpreters and CACI International (Arlington) supplied interrogators. This strategy was more than a matter of outsourcing and profiteering, because it enabled the actions of contractors to be removed from any public ledger where they could be called to account. They were not part of the military chain of command and so were not subject to military justice; the Coalition Provisional Authority also explicitly excluded them from the provisions of Iraqi law. Indeed, no contractors operating anywhere in Iraq have been indicted, prosecuted or punished for anything; the only corporate inquiry into the events at Abu Ghraib was conducted by CACI which, as Singer says, "unsurprisingly found that CACI had done no wrong." (Equally unsurprising, CACI also provides the U.S. government with training videos on ethics). In short, private contractors were—and remain—free to operate in a zone of absolute indistinction between the legal and the extra-legal.[60]

Outsourcing reaches far beyond Iraq. Abu Ghraib was wired to a global network of prisons and detention centers run by the U.S. military, the CIA, and allied intelligence services.[61] In March 2004, the White House wanted to know if it could forcibly transfer prisoners from Iraq so that they could be held indefinitely and subjected to even more extreme methods of interrogation. Forcible transfers are explicitly proscribed by the Geneva Conventions, whose architects had before them the policies of mass deportation and the enforced disappearance of individuals into the *Nacht und Nebel* programs carried out by the Nazis. But this did not deter the legal cartographers in the Department of Justice. Their counter-argument appealed to Iraq's immigration law which, unlike virtually every other law on Iraq's statute books, apparently could not be repealed or suspended by the occupying power. This provided for anyone entering the country illegally (the "foreign fighters" who had joined the insurgency, not the thousands in US Army uniforms) to be imprisoned or deported. It seems unlikely that the drafters of the original law entertained the prospect that these measures could be coincident, but Guantánamo and its replicant sites made it possible for the United States to deport and imprison in a single gesture.[62]

This program dovetailed with a system of extraordinary renditions organized by the CIA. The Clinton administration had authorized the clandestine program after the bomb attacks on the World Trade Center in 1993 but nominal safeguards were attached to the process. Every abductee was supposed to have been convicted in absentia or to have been charged with a criminal offence that would lead to a judicial trial; each rendition required individual review and approval. The Bush administration dramatically expanded the program after 9/11 and removed most of those requirements. The central objective was to shackle indefinite detention to extreme interrogation. According to Jane Mayer, what started as a program aimed at a small, discrete set of suspects was thus widened to include a larger and looser target population of "unlawful combatants" for whom any pretence of judicial process was abandoned. The objective was to put such people "outside the protection of the law" altogether and place them "completely in the power of their captors."[63] It is estimated that one hundred to one hundred-fifty people have been rendered under the revised program and taken to jails in Egypt, Jordan, Libya, Morocco, Saudi Arabia, Syria, and Uzbekistan—all of which have been criticized by the State Department for gross violations of human rights. Equally cynically, the program uses the law to violate the law. Renditions are carried out using civilian rather than military aircraft to take advantage of the Chicago Convention on International Civil Aviation (1944), which makes it unnecessary for non-scheduled, non-commercial civil aircraft to seek permission to pass through the airspace of other states or to land at civilian airports. The aircraft usually belong to a number of shell companies to take advantage of commercial law: "You can set them up quickly," one former CIA agent explained, and "dismantle them when they are exposed." These slippery maneuvers are necessary because enforced disappearances are expressly prohibited under international law, which further imposes on all states an absolute and unconditional ban on transferring people to states where they risk torture. The token gesture of compliance made by the United States is really a sign of utter contempt: it claims to seek assurances about the treatment of those subject to rendition, and US diplomats are nominally in charge of monitoring compliance. But the Director of the CIA, Porter Goss, openly admits that "Once they are out of our control, there's only so much we can do...:" which is, of course, precisely the point.[64]

Some prisoners remain firmly under U.S. control, however, because the CIA also has its own covert prison system that was also authorized by President Bush after 9/11. These so-called "black sites" open and close at different times, and prisoners are regularly flown from one to another for interrogation that exceeds the boundaries of federal and international law. At Abu Ghraib there was a formalized Memorandum of Understanding with the military over the CIA's "ghost detainees" who were held in isolation on Tier 1A of the Hard Site. They were not identified by name or registered and they were moved around the prison to hide them from ICRC delegations. At least one prisoner died in CIA custody at Abu Ghraib.[65] Other black sites have been identified in Afghanistan and Pakistan, in Qatar and Yemen, on the British Indian Ocean Territory of Diego Garcia, in Thailand (which was closed in 2003), at Guantánamo (which was closed in 2004 when federal courts began to exercise jurisdiction over prisoners there), and in the Czech Republic, Poland, and Romania (all of which were closed in November 2005 following widespread outrage in Europe). All these sites are under direct U.S. control where, to take Goss at his weasel word, there is plainly a great deal that the United States can do.[66]

The very language of "extraordinary rendition," "ghost prisoners," and "black sites" implies something out of the ordinary, spectral, a twilight zone: a serial space of the exception. But this performative spacing works *through* the law to annul the law; it is not a "state" of exception that can be counterposed to a rule-governed world of "normal" politics and power. It is, at bottom, a process of *juridical* othering that involves three overlapping mechanisms: the creation of special rules that withdraw legal protections and permit the torture of what Ruth Jamieson and Kieran McEvoy call "juridical others"; the calculated outsourcing of war crimes to regimes known to practice torture; and the exploitation of extra-territorial sites where prisoners are detained and tortured at the pleasure of sovereign power. These strategies are not novel, however, and they did not begin with 9/11. Neither are they exclusively American strategies; the agencies of many other states have been complicit in the process. What is new is the way in which the vanishing points that they so assiduously produce are selectively but deliberately brought into fleeting view—in a calculated gesture of intimidation—and the way in which they reveal the totalizing will to power that lies at the crucial intersections of sovereign power and biopolitics.[67] In all these ways, as Kaplan concludes, the Bush administration has sought to redraw the borders of the law in order "to create a world in which Guantánamo is everywhere."[68]

In fact, the wheel has turned full circle, and Afghanistan has turned into a major hub in the global system of clandestine detention centers. "Prisoner transports crisscross the country between a proliferating network of detention facilities," and this prefigures what two reporters describe as "a radical plan to replace Guantánamo Bay." The intention, so they claim, is to produce a global prison network beyond the reach of American or European judicial process. By the summer of 2005, negotiations were under way to transfer 50–70 percent of the prisoners under the jurisdiction of the Department of Defense at Guantánamo to Afghanistan, Saudi Arabia, and Yemen, where they would be incarcerated in purpose-built jails financed and constructed by the United States. Once again, it was claimed that the State Department would assume responsibility for "monitoring agreements to make sure prisoners were not mistreated." It beggars belief that occasional diplomatic visits announced in advance could be regarded as effective monitoring when so many officers working inside Abu Ghraib claimed not to have known what was happening day after day under their own noses. [69]

Torture Chambers

The renovated cell-blocks at Abu Ghraib (the Hard Site) set the stage for a convergence between the U.S. war machine and the U.S. prison industry. The United States jails over two million of its citizens; around half of those prisoners are African American, and many of them are Muslims: estimates suggest they make up 10–20 percent of the total prison population. Federal and state prisons have long been sites of crucial encounter between Islam and those versions of America that exclude its Muslim 'other'. In this system, racialized brutality and intramural violence are more or less sanctioned, and humiliation and abuse have become ritualized and routinized.[70] As Michelle Brown remarks, prisons are thus "liminal spaces both inside and outside the boundaries of constitutional law." Is it so surprising that two of the ringleaders at Abu Ghraib should have been corrections officers back home? This does not excuse their actions, of course, still less the carceral system that makes them possible. Brown's point is that the ideology of crime and punishment and the prosecution of the "war on terror" are both conducted in a language of retribution that, at the limit, reduces its "object-other" to a pure embodiment of the force of sovereign power: to bare life.[71]

The parallels between the two are indeed close, but the space between them needs to be retained because what happened at Abu Ghraib was more than a foreign replay of the odious domestic regime of incarceration. Abu Ghraib was in the middle of a war zone where the U.S. Army was deploying ever more force and not only failing to suppress the insurgency but also increasing opposition to its occupation. In contradistinction to the triumphant mastery displayed in the photographs of the first prisoners arriving at Guantánamo, therefore, Allen Feldman reads the images from Abu Ghraib as recording "ceremonies of nostalgia" that betray a longing for the power that was so visibly slipping away. Through these rituals, he argues,

> The perpetuators re-acquire, if only in an allegorical idiom, their former sense of mastery and command in a situation that is rapidly lurching beyond their grasp…. [The] hooded and faceless bodies that are being manipulated and posed are merely emblems of a collective, recalcitrant Iraqi body politic that has to be dissected as the treacherous social surface of an occupied Iraq.[72]

This reminds us that the torture chamber is a setting for the aggrandizement of power, and that its affirmation is likely to become more frenzied as it is mocked or threatened. Elaine Scarry suggests that:

> The torturer's questions objectify the fact that he has a world, announce in their feigned urgency the critical importance of that world, a world whose asserted magnitude is confirmed by the cruelty it is able to motivate and justify. Part of what makes his world so huge is its continual juxtaposition with the small and shredded world objectified in the prisoner's answers... It is only the prisoner's steadily shrinking ground that wins for the torturer his swelling sense of territory.[73]

Conversely, as the vortex of insurgency and counter-insurgency intensified, perhaps it seemed to these soldiers and their accomplices that, outside the confines of the cell-block where their command was undisputed, the ground of the U.S. Army was steadily shrinking as the insurgency asserted its own "swelling sense of territory" (and sovereignty). The degradation, humiliation and sheer cruelty were, in their hideous way, a petty reversal of that greater reversal. That the attempts to engorge their enfeebled sense of power played on an elaborately Orientalized fantasy of feminized Arabs and of political militants as products of a failed heterosexuality enables Jasbir Puar to link torture in a metonymic chain that culminates in a climactic assertion of a heteronormative nationalism. "The bonding ritual of the carnival of torture— discussing it, producing it, getting turned on by it, recording it, disseminating the proof of it, gossiping about it— [becomes] the ultimate performance of patriotism." No wonder it is the last refuge of the scoundrel.[74]

Scarry makes another suggestion that helps make sense of the larger canvas that was folded in to Abu Ghraib when she notes that the questions and answers in the torture chamber are "a prolonged comparative display, an unfurling of world maps." This speaks directly to the project of interrogation and intelligence. Some commentators have sought to explain what happened there by blaming it on ignorance: "Soldiers were immersed in Islamic culture," one military psychiatrist wrote, "a culture that many were encountering for the first time."[75] Yet the scenes that were recorded in the cellblocks revealed a display of knowledge as well as power. They combined many of what Arab cultures see as utterly shameful acts in a montage of incandescent horror: "the display of naked flesh; the use of dogs and dog-like treatment in human company; the removal of space between people and forced contact, groveling and prostration; physical and intimate touching by strangers; nudity and sexual exposure before other men; homosexual contacts; the humiliation of men in front of women; filth; enslavement."[76] This was not happenstance. Neither were the techniques invented by the torturers. Written testimony and photographs shows that prisoners' arms were often stretched behind their backs and shackled to the bars in a high-stress position that is known as a "Palestinian hanging" from its use by the Israeli secret service in the occupied territories; it contributed directly to the death of Manadel al-Jamadi in CIA custody at Abu Ghraib. The crucified position into which the hooded man was forced is called "the Vietnam," an extraordinarily painful method studied by the CIA and used by interrogators in South Africa and South America. It strains credibility to believe that such tableaux of intense humiliation and pain—a theatre of cruelty if ever there was one—were nothing more than the artless staging of a handful of reservists from small-town America.

That said, one has to confront the rictus of delight shown on the faces of those hometown, Homeland soldiers. They were not just triumphant; they were exultant. Michael Taussig makes the sharp point that "it is not the victim as animal that gratifies the torturer, but the fact that the victim is human, thus enabling the torturer to become the savage." In other words, torture requires its victims to be less than human, so that the degradation can continue—the specter of "the monster" stalks the torture-chamber—but it also requires them to be human: otherwise sexual gratification is withheld from the torturer. A space that is at once inside and outside the political-juridical order is a space where these doubled subjects can be conjured into being, paraded and subjugated. Here, in the most intimate recesses of the space of the exception, we finally come face to face with the other specter that haunts these splattered cellblocks. For here, in Taussig's vital paraphrase of Benjamin, "mimesis occurs by a colonial mirroring of otherness that reflects back onto the colonists the barbarity of their own social relations, but as imputed to the savage they yearn to colonize."[77]

After Words

Iraqis responded to the images from Abu Ghraib with understandable outrage, and much of their anger was focused on the colonial mirroring that Taussig describes: the Janus-face of occupied Iraq, preaching liberation while practicing degradation. But one of the most telling responses that I have seen comes from the Weblog of "Riverbend," a young Iraqi woman in Baghdad:

> Seeing those naked, helpless, hooded men was like being slapped in the face with an ice cold hand. I felt ashamed to be looking at them—like I was seeing something I shouldn't be seeing and all I could think was, "I might know one of those faceless men…" I might have passed him in the street or worked with him. I might have brought groceries from one of them or sat through a lecture they gave in college… any one of them might be a teacher, gas station attendant or engineer… any one of them might be a father or grandfather… each and every one of them is a son and possibly a brother.[78]

These are haunting words. The practices at Guantánamo, Abu Ghraib, and elsewhere are saturated with a colonial past that is reactivated in our colonial present, and I hope that in making them visible I have helped to undercut the pernicious claim that terror and torture always refer to the actions of others never to ourselves. Seen thus, as Philip Kennicott says, the images from Abu Ghraib are unexceptional: "In different forms, they could be pictures of the Dutch brutalizing the Indonesians; the French brutalizing the Algerians; the Belgians brutalizing the people of the Congo." When we look at these images, he concludes, we should see ourselves because they are *ours*: "Every errant smart bomb, every dead civilian, every sodomized prisoner, is ours."[79] This seems exactly right to me. But Riverbend's anguish suggests another way to see ourselves in these images: for they are also *us*. There has never been a greater need to untwist the separations between "us" and "them" than the present moment of danger. For as the viral "war on terror" proliferates across the globe, and as regimes around the world invoke national security to suppress human rights, we are all, potentially, *homines sacri.* Our vulnerability is differentially distributed—scored by class, gender, sexuality, 'race' and other markers—but it is also *shared*. We could all end up on other boxes in other prisons, arms outstretched and wires attached to our trembling bodies.

Acknowledgments

I am grateful to Matthew Farish, Davis Nally, and Matthew Sparke for helpful comments.

Notes

1. Paola Coppola, "The man beneath the hood speaks out," *Guardian,* September 21, 2005; Donovan Webster, "The man in the hood,"*Vanity Fair,* February 2005; Kate Zernike, "Cited as symbol of Abu Ghraib, man admits he is not in photo," *New York Times,* March 18, 2006; "Translation of statement provides by Detainee 18470," Karen J. Greenberg and Joshua L. Dratel (eds.), *The Torture Papers: The road to Abu Ghraib* (Cambridge: Cambridge University Press, 2005), 526.
2. Cf. Julian Reid, "The biopolitics of the War on Terror," *Third World Quarterly* 26 (2005): 237–52: 241.
3. The central texts are Michel Foucault, *Discipline and punish: The birth of the prison* (London: Penguin, 1977); idem., *The history of sexuality: an introduction* (London: Penguin, 1978); idem., *"Society must be defended": Lectures at the Collège de France 1975–1976* (New York: Picador, 2003),. 260; Giorgio Agamben, *Homo sacer: sovereign power and bare life* (Stanford, CA: Stanford University Press, 1998),6; idem., *Remnants of Auschwitz: The witness and the archive* (New York: Zone Books, 1999); *State of exception* (Chicago: University of Chicago Press, 2005).
4. Harold Relyea, "National Emergency Powers," Congressional Research Service, The Library of Congress, Washington, D.C., September 15, 2005.
5. Agamben, *Homo sacer; State of exception*, 2, 22.
6. Indeed, both neo-liberalism and neo-conservatism work to disparage existing laws and juridical practices (the insistence on the supreme power of the 'unitary executive,' the assault on 'activist judges,' the drive to 'de-regulation') and also to introduce new ones that, inter alia, restrict democratic politics, roll back human rights and reify the market.
7. Amy Kaplan, "Where is Guantánamo?' *American Quarterly* 57 (2005): 831–58: 837.
8. Agamben, *State of exception*, 11–22.
9. Peter Stirk, "Carl Schmitt, the law of occupation and the Iraq war," *Constellations* 11 (4) (2004): 527–36: 530.
10. John Austin, *The province of jurisprudence determined* (edited by Wilfred E. Rumble) (Cambridge: Cambridge University Press, 1995; first published in 1832), 254. It would not be difficult to argue that the United States now seeks to arrogate to itself precisely that sovereign role.
11. Hersch Lauterpacht, "The Problem of the Revision of the Law of War," *British Yearbook of International Law* 29 (1952): 360–82: 382; William K. Lietzau, "Combating terrorism: Law enforcement or war?" in *Terrorism and International Law: Chal-*

lenges and responses, International Institute of Humanitarian Law (2002), 75–84: 79.

12. Susan Sontag, "Regarding the torture of others," *New York Times Magazine*, May 23, 2004; W. J. T. Mitchell, "The unspeakable and the unimaginable: Word and image in a time of terror," *English literary history* 72 (2005): 291–308.

13. Mark Danner, *Torture and truth: America, Abu Ghraib and the war on terror* (New York: New York Review of Books, 2004), xiii, 9, 40, 47.

14. Agamben, *Remnants*, 17–18, 41, 47.

15. J. M. Bernstein, "Bare life, bearing witness: Auschwitz and the pornography of horror," *parallax* 10 (1) (2004): 2–16: 3, 7, 14. See also Catherine Mills, "Linguistic survival and ethicality: Biopolitics, subjectification and testimony in *Remnants of Auschwitz*," in Andrew Norris (ed.) Politics, metaphysics and death: Essays on Giorgia Agamben's *Homo Sacer* (Durham NC: Duke University Press (2005), 198–221: 218 note 4.

16. Cf. "The sovereign is the point of indistinction between violence and law, the threshold on which violence passes over into law and law passes over into violence": Agamben, *Remnants*, 32. This does not exhaust my reservations about Agamben's project. I also want to emphasize the multiple ways in which the reductions of people to bare life are contested: in this case, by the prisoners themselves, and by a host of other actors inside and outside the Bush administration and inside and outside the United States.

17. Philippe Sands, *Lawless world: America and the making and breaking of global rules* (London: Allen Lane, 2005), xii; "President discusses year-end accomplishments in Cabinet meeting," at http://www.whitehouse.gov/news/releases, December 11, 2003.

18. Amy Kaplan, "Homeland insecurities: reflections on language and space," *Radical History Review* 85 (2003): 82–93: 91-9-2; idem., "Where is Guantánamo?" 832; Judith Butler, "Indefinite detention," in *Her precarious life: The powers of mourning and violence* (London and New York: Verso, 2004), 51, 56, 64; Agamben, *State of exception*, 6, 86.

19. Robert Cover, "Violence and the word," *Yale Law Journal* 95 (1986): 1601–1629; Nasser Hussain, "Towards a jurisprudence of emergency: Colonialism and the rule of law," *Law and critique* 10 (1999): 93–115; idem., *The jurisprudence of emergency: Colonialism and the rule of law* (Ann Arbor: University of Michigan Press, 2003).

20. Louis Pérez, *Cuba between empires, 1878–1902* (Pittsburgh: University of Pittsburgh Press, 1983),. 55–56; Ada Ferrer, *Insurgent Cuba: Race, nation and revolution 1868–1898* (Chapel Hill: University of North Carolina Press, 1999); Daniel Ross, *Violent democracy* (Cambridge: Cambridge University Press, 2004), 128.

21. The Platt Amendment was abrogated in 1934, when a new treaty was signed between the US and Cuba, but this did not affect the lease of Guantánamo.

22. Louis Pérez, *Cuba under the Platt Amendment, 1902–1934* (Pittsburgh: University of Pittsburgh Press, 1986); Alfred de Zayas, "The status of Guantánamo and the status of the detainees," Douglas Mc. K. Brown Lecture, University of British Columbia, November 2003; Kaplan, "Where is Guantánamo?" 836.

23. Kaplan, "Where is Guantánamo?" 832, 836; cf. Agamben, *State of exception*, 48, who describes the state of exception as both "an emptiness *and standstill* of law" (my emphasis).

24. Fleur Johns, "Guantánamo Bay and the annihilation of the exception," *European Journal of International Law* 16 (2005):. 613–35: 614.

25. A writ of *habeas corpus* orders a prisoner to be brought before a court to determine whether s/he has been imprisoned lawfully. Congress granted all federal courts jurisdiction under title 28 of the United States Code to issue such writs to release from custody prisoners held by state or federal agencies in violation of the Constitution.

26. Greenberg and Dratel (eds.), *Torture Papers*, 25–8; 29–37. In June 2004, however, the Supreme Court ruled that it had jurisdiction over Guantánamo to hear *habeas corpus* petitions from those imprisoned there. This landmark ruling was subsequently challenged by the Detainee Treatment Act (2005) that, *inter alia*, limited jurisdiction to the validity of the decision to detain a non-citizen as an "enemy combatant": see p. 218. It also reaffirmed that 'For the purposes of this section, the term "United States", when used in a geographic sense, ... does not include the United States Naval Station, Guantánamo Bay, Cuba."

27. Butler, "Indefinite detention," 58, 62; Johns, "Guantánamo Bay" radicalizes this interpretation: for her, Guantanamo Bay is "more cogently read as the jurisdictional outcome of attempts to *domesticate* the political possibilities occasioned by the experience of exceptionalism." The regime at Guantanamo Bay, so she suggests, "is dedicated to producing experiences of having no option, no doubt and no responsibility."

28. Butler says much less about this second imperative, though she does acknowledge that the withdrawal of legal protections from the prisoners and their indefinite detention are effected through their constitution as "less than human": pp. 75–76, 98. Johns is silent on the question.

29. Greenberg and Dratel (eds.) *Torture Papers*, 38–79: 67, 69; pp. 81–117: 102; 129; 134.

30. Kenneth Watkins, "Warriors without rights? Combatants, unprivileged belligerents and the struggle over legitimacy," Occasional Paper, Program on Humanitarian Policy and Conflict Research, Harvard University, Winter 2005; de Zayas, "The status of Guantánamo"; G. H. Aldrich, "The Taliban, Al Qaeda and the determination of illegal combatants," *American journal of international law* 96 (2002): 891–98.

31. Butler, "Indefinite detention," 77.

32. See David Rose, *Guantánamo: America's war on human rights* (London: Faber and Faber, 2004); Derek Gregory, *The colonial present: Afghanistan, Palestine, Iraq* (Oxford: Blackwell, 2004). 66.

33. Tim Golden, and Dan Van Natta Jr, "US said to overstate value of Guantánamo detainees," *New York Times,* June 21, 2004; Michelle Faul, "Gitmo detainees say they were sold," *Associated Press,* May 31, 2005; Kim Sengupta, "Voices from Guantánamo, "*Independent,* March 6, 2006; Tim Golden, "Voices baffled, brash and irate in Guantánamo," *New York Times,* March 6, 2006. A detailed independent review revealed that most prisoners at Guantánamo were arrested neither in Afghanistan nor by U.S. troops but were seized in Pakistan by Pakistani authorities. The Bush administration has dismissed their claims of innocence by characterizing them as well-trained liars but, as Corine Hegland observes, "if a well-trained liar looks like an innocent man, what does an innocent man look like if not a well-trained liar?" See her "Who is at Guantánamo Bay?," "Guantánamo grip," and "Empty evidence," all in *National Journal* 3 February 2006.

34. Judith Butler, *Bodies that matter: On the discursive limits of "sex"* (New York: Routledge, 1993), 3.

35. Nigel Rodley, "Looking-glass war," *Index on Censorship* (2005): 54–61: 55; Butler, *Precarious life*, 80–81.

36. Hegland, "Guantánamo," National Journal.

37. Greenberg and Dratel (eds.) *Torture Papers*, 172–217, 218–222: 202–3. On this basis you wonder how Saddam Hussein could ever be brought to trial for war crimes. For a devastating critique of these and related claims by Bush's lawyers, see Jordan J. Paust, "Executive plans and authorizations to violate international law concerning treatment and interrogation of detainees," *Columbia Journal of Transnational Law* 43 (2005): 811–63.

38. Greenberg and Dratel (eds.) *Torture Papers*, 228; 223; 237; "Statement for the record: Office of General Counsel involvement in interrogation issues," Memorandum from Alberto J. Mora, General Counsel of the Navy to Vice-Admiral Albert Church, Inspector General, Department of the Navy, July 7, 2004.

39. Alfred W. McCoy, *A question of torture: CIA Interrogation from the Cold War to the war on terror* (New York: Metropolitan Books, 2006) pp. 8, 35, 46.

40. Greenberg and Dratel (eds.) *Torture Papers*, 241–85: 265–6; 286–359: 291; 360–65: 365; "Statement for the record: Office of General Counsel involvement in interrogation issues," Memorandum from Alberto J. Mora, General Counsel of the Navy to Vice-Admiral Albert Church, Inspector General, Department of the Navy, July 7, 2004; Jane Mayer, "The memo," *New Yorker*, February 27, 2006.

41. See, for example, David Rose, "How we survived jail hell," *Observer*, March 14, 2004; Severin Carrell, "US guards at Guantánamo tortured me, says UK man," *Independent*, April 24, 2005; "Detention in Afghanistan and Guantánamo Bay: Statement of Shafiq Rasul, Asif Iqbal and Rhuhel Ahmed," Center for Constitutional Rights, New York, July 26, 2004; Guantánamo and beyond; "Testimony of Guantánamo detainee Jumah al-Dossari," Amnesty International, November 7, 2005; Mark Oliver, "'They couldn't take away my dignity'," *Guardian*, November 18, 2005.

42. Dana Priest and Scott Higham, "At Guantánamo, a prison within a prison," *Washington Post*, December 17, 2004; Douglas Jehl, "Classified report warned on CIA's tactics in interrogation," *New York Times*, November 9, 2005; Brian Ross and Richard Esposito, "CIA's harsh interrogation tactics described," *ABC News*, November 18, 2005.

43. Josh White, "President relents, backs torture ban," *Washington Post*, December 16, 2005; Charlie Savage, "Bush could bypass new torture ban," *Boston Globe*, January 4, 2006.

44. Josh White, Carol Leonnig, 'US cites exception in torture ban', *Washington Post* 3 March 2006.

45. Oliver Klemens, Jesko Fezer, Kim Forster, and Sabine Horlitz, "Extra-territorial spaces and camps: judicial and political spaces in the "war on terrorism'," in Anselm Franke, Rafi Segal, and Eyal Weizman (eds.) *Territories: Islands, camps and other states of utopia* (Berlin: KW – Institute for Contemporary Art, 2003), 22–28.

46. Gregory, *Colonial present*, 225–47; Zaki Chehab, *Inside the resistance: The Iraqi insurgency and the future of the Middle East* (New York: Nation Books, 2005). 129–47.

47. Carl Conetta, *Vicious circle: The dynamics of occupation and resistance in Iraq. Part One: Patterns of Popular Discontent* (Cambridge, MA: Project on Defense Alternatives, Commonwealth Institute, 2005); Alistair Finlan, "Trapped in the dead ground: US counter-insurgency strategy in Iraq," *Small wars and insurgencies* 16 (1) (2005): 1–21.

48. Loretta Napoleoni, *Insurgent Iraq: al Zarqawi and the new generation* (New York: Seven Stories Press, 2005), 157–60.

49. Doug Saunders, "US citizen-soldiers terrified, overwhelmed by chaotic Iraqi prison," *Globe & Mail*, May 8, 2004; Scott Higham, Josh White, and Christian Davenport, "A prison on the brink," *Washington Post*, May 9, 2004; Douglas Jehl and Eric Schmitt, "In abuse, a portrait of ill-prepared, overwhelmed GIs," *New York Times*, May 9, 2004; Greenberg and Dratel (eds.), *Torture Papers*, pp. 987–1131: 998.

50. Seymour Hersh, *Chain of command: The road from 9/11 to Abu Ghraib* (New York: HarperCollins, 2004), 59–60. "To fight in the name of humanity does not eliminate enmity; it only makes one's enemy the representative or embodiment of the inhuman": Andrew Norris, "Us" and "Them": The politics of American self-assertion after 9/11," *Metaphilosophy* 32 (2004): 249–72; Gregory, *Colonial present*.

51. http://www.abc.bet.au/4 corners/content/2004/s1143841.htm, June 7, 2004.

52. "Convention IV relative to the protection of civilian persons in time of war," Geneva, August 12, 1949 [full text and commentaries] (my emphases), at http://www.icrc.org.

53. "Report on Detention and Corrections Operations in Iraq," Office of the Provost Marshal General of the Army, November 5, 2003 [the Ryder Report]: 27, 54; Julian Borger, "'Cooks and drivers were working as interrogators'," *Guardian*, May 7, 2004; Douglas Jehl, "US disputed protected status of Iraq inmates," *New York Times*, May 23, 2004.

54. "Convention IV," commentary.

55. Greenberg and Dratel (eds.) *Torture Papers*, 451–59, 1062–66.

56. Ibid., 391–92, 416.

57. Hersh, *Chain of command*, 41.

58. Greenberg and Dratel (eds.) *Torture Papers*, 912, 1035–38.

59. *Leadership Failure: Firsthand accounts of torture of Iraqi detainees by the US Army's 82n^d Airborne Division*, Human Rights Watch, September 2005; Eric Schmitt, Carolyn Marshall, "Before and after Abu Ghraib, a US unit abused detainees," *New York Times*, March 19, 2006. See more generally *Beyond Abu Ghraib: Detention and torture in Iraq*, Amnesty International, March 2006.

60. Peter Singer, "Beyond the law," *Guardian*, May 3, 2004; idem., "War, profits and the vacuum of law: Privatized military firms and international law," *Columbia Journal of Transnational Law* 42 (2) (2004): 521–549. The use of proxies for state violence–mercenaries and private military firms–is a common strategy of distancing the state from the perpetrators of its crimes: Ruth Jamieson and Kieran McEvoy, "State crime by proxy and juridical othering," *British Journal of Criminology* 45 (2005): 504–27: 512–14.

61. Dana Priest and Joe Stephens, "Secret world of US interrogation," *Washington Post*, May 11, 2004.

62. Greenberg and Dratel (eds.) *Torture Papers*, 373–74.

63. *The United States' "Disappeared": The CIA's long-term "ghost detainees,"* Human Rights Watch, October 2004; Jane Mayer, "Outsourcing torture," *New Yorker*, February 14, 2005; *Rendition and secure detention:A global system of human rights violations*, Amnesty International, January 2006.

64. Stephen Grey, "US accused of torture flights," *New York Times*, November 14, 2004; Dana Priest, "Jet is open secret in terror war," *Washington Post*, December 27, 2004; Michael Hirsh, Mark Hosenball, and John Barry, "Aboard Air CIA," *Newsweek*, February 28, 2005; Douglas Jehl and David Johnston, "Rule change lets CIA freely send suspects abroad to jails," *New York Times*, March 6, 2005; Dana Priest, "CIA's assurances on transferred suspects doubted," *Washington Post*, March 17, 2005;

Scott Shane, Stephen Grey, and Margot Williams, "CIA expanding terror battle under guise of charter flights," *New York Times,* May 31, 2005; *Below the radar: Secret flights to torture and 'disappearance,* Amnesty International, April 2006.

65. Josh White, "Army, CIA agreed on "Ghost" Prisoners," *Washington Post,* March 11, 2005; Jane Mayer, "A deadly interrogation," *New Yorker,* November 14, 2005.

66. Dana Priest, 'CIA holds terror suspects in secret prisons," *Washington Post,* November 2, 2005; Demetri Sevastopulo, Guy Dinmore, Caroline Daniel, and Jan Cienski, "Evidence CIA has secret jails in Europe," *Financial Times,* November 2, 2005; Allan Freeman, "EU eyes alleged CIA jails," *Globe and Mail,* November 4, 2005; Josh White, "Prisoner accounts suggest detention at secret facilities," *Washington Post* November 7, 2005; Luke Harding, "Rice admits US mistakes in war on terror after wave of criticism across Europe," *Guardian,* December 7, 2005; "European investigator says US 'outsourced' torture," *Associated Press,* January 24, 2006.

67. Jamieson and McEvoy, "State crime by proxy," 515, 521; John Parry, "The shape of modern torture: extraordinary rendition and ghost detainees," *Melbourne Journal of International Law* 6 (2005): 516–33.

68. Kaplan, "Where is Guantánamo?": 854.

69. Tom Engelhardt, "Into the shadows," at http://www.TomDispatch.com, April 5, 2004; Dana Priest and Joe Stephens, "Abu Ghraib is just the most notorious of a network of detention centers," *Washington Post* May 23, 2004; Julian Borger, "US plans permanent Guantánamo jails," *Guardian,* January 3, 2005; Jonathan Steele, "A global gulag to hide the war on terror's dirty secrets," *Guardian,* January 14, 2005; Douglas Jehl, "Pentagon seeks to transfer more detainees from base in Cuba," *New York Times,* March 11, 2005; Adrian Levy, Cathy Scott-Clark, "'One huge US jail'," *Guardian,* March 19, 2005; Josh White and Robin Wright, "Afghanistan agrees to accept detainees," *Washington Post,* August 5, 2005.

70. Rachel Zoll, "US prisons become Islam battleground," Associated Press, July 14, 2005.

71. Michelle Brown, "Setting the conditions for Abu Ghraib: The prison nation abroad," *American Quarterly* 57 (2005): 973–97: 989. The interpolation of Agamben is mine not Brown's. Her argument turns on the way in which the Hard Site at Abu Ghraib followed the logic of the self-contained "supermax" prison in the United States, where exclusion, segregation and isolation—the removal of all ordinary human interaction – are used as managerial strategies under the sign of "security" (986–88).

72. Allen Feldman, "Securocratic wars of public safety: Globalized policing as scopic regime," *Interventions* 63 (2004):. 330–50: 340.

73. Elaine Scarry, *The body in pain: The making and unmaking of the world* (New York: Oxford University Press, 1987), 36.

74. Jashir Puar, "On torture: Abu Ghraib," *Radical History Review* 93 (2005): 13–38: 28; see also Jasbir Puar and Amit Rai, "Monster, terrorist, fag: The war on terrorism and the production of docile patriots," *Social text* 72 (2002): 117–48.

75. Greenberg and Dratel (eds.) *Torture Papers,* 448.

76. Doug Saunders, "This has disgraced America…," *Globe & Mail,* May 7, 2004.

77. Michael Taussig, *Shamanism, colonialism and the wild man: a study in terror and healing* (Chicago: University of Chicago Press, 1987) pp. 83, 134.

78. Riverbend, "Baghdad Burning," at http://riverbendblog.blogspot.com, April 30, 2004.

79. Philip Kennicott, "A wretched new picture of America," *Washington Post*, May 5, 2004; Geoffrey Galt Harpham, "Inadmissable evidence: terror, torture and the world today," *Chronicle of Higher Education*, October 15, 2004.

12

Groom Lake and the Imperial Production of Nowhere

Trevor Paglen[1]

It's four in the morning, and I'm standing under the metal halide lights of a remote gas station, shivering in the desert cold and staring at a decrepit sign: "Tonopah, Nevada 'Home of the Stealth Fighter'." I've driven seven hours through some of the most isolated country in the U.S. to arrive here, and the black plane on the town's welcome sign speaks to the reason why I've come. Tonopah lies on the northern border of the Nellis Range Complex. Encompassing 3.1 million acres and 12,000 square miles of airspace, Nellis is the largest piece of classified real estate in the Western world.

I head east along the border, turning south on Highway 375 a few hours later. The beginnings of sunrise bring a pink, hazy glow to the emptiness of the Basin and Range, revealing isolated hints of human activity: there's a radar dome on the top of a distant mountain and a trailer bristling with antennae like a giant metal sea-urchin parked in the middle of a dusty valley. Lonely dirt roads lead towards the mountains in the west. It feels like I'm near the middle of nowhere.

The antennas and radars that dot these mountain peaks hint at what lies beyond Nellis' border. The Nellis Range Complex is home to menagerie of secret weapons and secret bases, nuclear craters and poisoned dirt, bombing ranges and doomed cities built for the sole purpose of being annihilated. When military journalists describe these hidden structures and expanses of land as part of the Pentagon's "black world" of secret spending and testing, I'm reminded of another "black world"—the "black world" at the margins of empire: murderous treks up the Congo River, industrial genocide at Birkenau, the fire-bombing of Tokyo, smoldering villages in the Mekong Delta, bloodstained rubble in Nablus, and blitzkrieg in Najaf. When I pull over and step outside the car, there's nothing but silence.

Silence rules the Basin and Range. A deep-down, unsettling silence. No wind, no birds, no insects, no cars. None of the little sounds that whisper in your ears letting you know that you're alive and that the world is in motion. It's the sublime silence that Freeman Dyson once described as the silence of being "alone with

God."[2] And it reigns over the military machinations taking place in these sunken valleys. In a restricted basin somewhere to the west, the Pentagon has built a place without a name, a place that does not appear on any official maps, and as far as the government is concerned, doesn't even properly exist. It's a place that stymies speech, hidden behind denials and official silence by order of the president.[3] But somehow the awesome silence of the Basin and Range seems to shout its aphasiac presence.[4] Some people call it "Groom Lake." I'm almost there.

The Nellis Range Complex is home to some of the most highly-classified projects in the United States, and to the infrastructures that house them. There's the Nevada Test Site, where mushroom clouds filled the skies until they went underground in 1962;[5] the Tonopah Test Range, where a squadron of stealth fighters trained for almost a decade before their existence was revealed to the public; and Creech Air Force Base, which was recently expanded to house the Air Force's squadrons of unmanned Predator drones. And there's the cabalistic place that Francis Gary Powers knew as "Watertown Strip" while he trained for his ill-fated reconnaissance flights over the Soviet Union. It is a secret base near Groom Lake, more popularly known as "Area 51."

Of all the places in the Nellis Range, Groom Lake is probably the most famous, but in a paradoxical kind of way: in popular culture, "Area 51" is famous for the fact that it does not "officially" exist. Publicly available satellite images and photographers with telephoto lenses speak to its presence, but the Air Force refused to acknowledge the base for many years. More recently, they have begrudgingly confirmed the presence of an "operating location near Groom Lake," but nothing more.

Figure 12.1.   Groom Lake Road.

In popular culture, Area 51 signifies government secrecy and cover-up. It's been the setting for stories about crashed UFOs, alien corpses suspended in giant life-support tanks, secret technologies, and conspiratorial plots. And it's been the inspiration for everything from dystopian video games to tacky Las Vegas night clubs. It has been the home of alien spacecraft in the movie *Independence Day*, and the setting for suspicious government experiments in the *X-Files*. Despite the official silence and denial that enshrouds it, Area 51 has become famous. This Air Force "operating facility" has, in fact, become a cliché.

Heading south, I pass Rachel, Nevada (pop. 98): an assemblage of fossilized clichés under a delicate layer of plutonium dust. It's most visible establishment, the Little A'Le'Inn (est. 1990), is a ramshackle testament to the folklore surrounding "America's Most Secret Base"—there's a flying saucer hanging from the end of a chain on the back of an old tow truck, and a sign outside the door: "Earthlings Welcome." A smiling alien on the A'Le'Inn's door looks south towards the radiation-meter at the edge of town, keeping tabs on the amount of radiation the locals are exposed to on any given day.

In defense-industry and aviation circles, you often hear references to the existence of two "worlds," one called the "white" world, and another called the "black" world. The "white" world, according to this taxonomy, involves unclassified research, development and spending. It's out the open. The "black" world, on the other hand, signifies all the work that is being done in secret: the secret weapons, secret bases, secret laboratories, and secret bureaucracies. It's enormous—a whole "world," created by tens of billions of dollars in Pentagon spending (the exact number is, of course, classified, but current estimates put the figure at around $28.0 billion for fiscal year 2006).[6] The black-world consists of massive landscapes, corporations and privately-held firms, workers sworn to lifelong secrecy, engineers, pilots, accountants, mail deliverers, garbage collectors, and truck drivers. It is a landscape produced through secrecy and compartmentalization. And much of this world, immune from public oversight, is hidden behind remote desert mountains just as its budget is hidden in cryptic corners of the ledger.

‡

In February of 1944, Senator Harry Truman noticed that hundreds of millions of dollars were disappearing into mysterious projects. As the chairman of a committee investigating war-profiteering, he was outraged. Trying to track the money, Truman encountered a bureaucratic mobius strip, an economic topology that repeatedly folded in and upon itself, always leading to nowhere. When Truman privately confronted Secretary of War Henry Stimson about his findings, Stimson told him that the funds were going towards the development of a "secret weapon" and that Roosevelt himself had ordered the project kept "most top secret."[7] Truman's committee had discovered the labyrinthine world of the Manhattan Project hidden behind banal-sounding line items in the military budget. Phrases like "Engineer Service: Army" and "Expediting Production" stealthily pointed to a massive undertaking that was masked from congress and hidden from the public.[8]

The Manhattan Project created a hidden world, a world of "secret cities" complete with thousands of workers who were either sworn to secrecy, or unaware of their work's true purpose. Outside but alongside the more conventional workings of the state, the bomb project created its own airplanes, its own factories, its own infrastructures, and its own territories.[9]

The secrecy surrounding the Manhattan Project wasn't new. Governments have always maintained secrets from their peoples and enemies alike. What *was* new about the Manhattan Project was its scale along with its organizing and funding structures—it was the first highly-classified, multi-billion dollar U.S. effort. To build the bomb in secret, the state had to develop ways to undertake such a project without congressional or public oversight. The bomb called for innovative ways to manage a new kind of bureaucracy—one organized around compartmentalization and "need-to-know" access to information. The organizing forms of the Manhattan Project had to manage the thousands of people working on the weapon at any given moment, while restricting knowledge of the project's true purpose to a very small number of people.

When Roosevelt authorized the development of the atomic bomb, he—perhaps inadvertently—established a tradition of secrecy with regards to nuclear weapons that would take on a life of its own. The initial justification for secrecy was to keep Hitler from acquiring the bomb, but by the end of 1944 it was clear that Nazis were nowhere near the weapon.[10] Even through its initial rationale had become moot by late 1944, the tradition of secrecy persisted. It had become in the words of McGeorge Bundy (National Security Advisor to Kennedy and Johnson) "a state of mind with a life and meaning of its own," a tradition that was so ingrained that it was not questioned.[11]

When Truman reorganized the military and intelligence community with the National Security Act of 1947, he established the Air Force as an independent branch of the military, and created the Central Intelligence Agency.[12] Largely immune from congressional oversight, the CIA was charged with collecting and disseminating intelligence, and "[performing] such other functions and duties... as the National Security Council may from time to time direct."[13] These "other functions and duties," which appear almost as an afterthought to the mission of the CIA, would become the basis for a long series of covert operations under the direct control of the president.[14] By 1958, CIA director Allen Dulles plainly stated that since 1947 the intelligence community in the United States had a "more influential position in our government than Intelligence enjoys in any other part of the world."[15] And much of the funding for this new military-intelligence apparatus came funneled through innocuous line-items in military appropriations budgets—the secret funding techniques developed for the Manhattan Project had turned into the Pentagon's "black budget."[16]

In April of 1955, a test pilot named Tony LeVier disguised himself as a hunter and headed east from Burbank, California in an unmarked Beechcraft airplane. He was under orders from his boss, Lockheed's Kelly Johnson, to conduct a survey of dry lakebeds and find "somewhere where we can test this thing in secret."[17] LeVier had just been chosen to be the test pilot for the new U-2 airplane, a commission from the CIA. Known internally as "the angel" for the fact that it could fly many miles higher than anything before it, the plane was designed to overfly the Soviet Union undetected using powerful cameras for CIA reconnaissance.

Figure 12.2. Rachel, Nevada.

After LeVier had explored a number of lakebeds for a testing-site location, Johnson, CIA overseer Richard Bissell, and his Air Force liaison, Osmond Ritland, finally decided on a dry lakebed in the northwest corner of the Atomic Energy Commission's (AEC) Nevada Test Site. It had been an isolated bombing range during the Second World War, but was abandoned in the war's aftermath.[18] The site's remoteness made it attractive. Groom Lake was only accessible by air, and the AEC's security restrictions would cut off access to the site by anyone without prior clearance. Constant nuclear explosions just a few miles away at the Nevada Test Site would keep the curious away. After being informed of the proposal, the Atomic Energy Commission agreed to accept the CIA as its new neighbors and annexed Groom Lake onto the Nevada Test Site.[19]

The effort to build the base, initially dubbed "Paradise Ranch" by Kelly Johnson, had all of the classic cloak-and-dagger elements of a secret CIA operation. Johnson and his CIA handlers created a front company called "C & J Engineering" to build the base, and Lockheed's name never appeared on the project.[20] In turn, C & J Engineering hired Reynolds Electrical and Engineering Co., Inc. (REECo), who had been cleared to work at the Nevada Test Site, to construct the base.[21] When REECo subcontracted some of the work out, one of the bidders warned the company to "watch out for this C & J outfit. We looked them up in Dun and Bradstreet and they don't even have a credit rating."[22] LeVier returned to "the Ranch" in early July to prepare for the U-2 flight tests, and by his own account he "almost fainted" when he saw how quickly the dry lake had been converted to a secret airfield.[23] The hangars, mess hall, mobile homes, control tower, and airstrip had been installed in a matter of months.

On August 4, 1955 the first U-2, a plane without any markings, took flight over the clandestine base at Groom Lake.[24] In only a few months this CIA "angel" was secretly breaking altitude records while hydrogen bombs at the Nevada Test Site lit the skies below. "Paradise Ranch" had become, in the words of Gary Powers, "one of those 'you can't get there from here' places."[25]

In the early days, everything about the site was meant to be temporary. U-2-era pilots lived in mobile homes—there were no clubs, commissaries, or comforts at "Paradise Ranch."[26] But Groom Lake become permanent when the CIA commissioned Lockheed to build yet another spy-plane, this time with a degree of "security... even tighter than on the U-2."[27] Ironically code-named OXCART, this new plane would fly higher than the U-2 and faster than a speeding bullet.[28] OXCART provided the research and know-how for the planes which would become known as the "black-bird family": the CIA's A-12, its Air Force counterpart, the SR-71, and several variations on the two. Compared to the U-2, these supersonic spy-planes required massive infrastructures and support-crews. "Paradise Ranch" had been built to accommodate about 150 people, but the OXCART program would require more than 1,500 at the testing site. The CIA and Lockheed had looked into the possibility of running the program out of a decommissioned Air Force Base, but none existed that could provide the degree of secrecy that the CIA demanded. In September of 1960, major construction at Groom Lake began again. The runway was extended and new hangars, new housing units, and additional warehouse space were installed. Despite contractors working double-shifts, the new round of construction took almost four years to complete.[29] By the time OXCART was ready for its initial tests, Groom Lake had become a state-of-the-art flight facility.[30]

Over the years, the desolate base at Groom Lake became more and more useful as a place where the military and CIA could do things in secret. In the late 1960s, more hangars were added to the base, providing a home to the Air Force's secret squadron of purloined Soviet MiGs.[31] When Lockheed began to build the "stealth fighter" in the late 1970s (one of the most highly-classified weapons since the Manhattan Project)[32] it was a matter of course that Groom Lake would host the testing and development.

Since the public unveiling of the stealth fighter in 1988, only a few singular examples of aircraft have emerged out from under Groom Lake's restricted cloak.[33] But the fact that few operational aircraft have come out from the secrecy of Groom Lake does not mean that the facility is inactive. On the contrary, comparisons of newly acquired commercial satellite photos to declassified Russian satellite images show that the base has expanded considerably since the 1980s, and that it, in fact, continues to expand.[34]

The origin and expansion of Groom Lake follows a theme that can be generalized to much of the Nellis Range Complex itself. It is a space where the temporary has become permanent, where an exception to the rule became the rule itself. The Manhattan Project, conducted secrecy with its war-time "black budget," enacted temporary measures that achieved permanence in the context of the open-ended cold war. The Nellis Range Complex recapitulates the same theme: it was meant to be a short-term practice bombing range for the Second World War, but was reactivated in 1947.[35] Much of the Nellis Complex and the means by which it is funded and organized exist in a kind of suspended animation—a state in which temporary measures have become "permanently temporary." They consist of spaces and bureaucracies created in response to a perceived emergency, as short-term exemptions from normal laws and oversight, but which became permanent by virtue of their continual use and expansion.[36]

Groom Lake doesn't appear on any government maps, but a source on the Internet told me how to find a particular dirt road leading to the base several miles south of Rachel. When I see an intersection matching his description, I take a sharp right turn onto its dusty gravel. This is Groom Lake road, a seemingly endless stretch that feels almost like a river of sand and rocks pulling me upstream towards an unknown and invisible place.

I've been warned that the moment I turn down this road, my car will trigger an array of ground sensors broadcasting my location to a team of armed guards hiding among the hills in the distance. I feel angry, helpless, and creeped-out as I approach the perimeter. The towering mountains and the emptiness of the basin makes you feel very, very, small. You could easily disappear here, swallowed by the Joshua trees and creosote bushes like a helpless surfer caught in a sudden and unforgiving undertow. There's a plume of dust on the horizon—something is moving in the distance.

I turn around a curve and bring the car to a sudden halt. A telescopic surveillance camera stares down at me from the top of a small hill like a microscope bearing down on a squashed bug. To my right, two men in an unmarked pickup sit watching me from a dusty knoll. My heart is racing. A place that doesn't exist

Figure 12.3. Groom Lake Border.

has me in its crosshairs, and I'm terrified. I'm too afraid to open the door of my car, or even zoom my camera onto the faces watching me. Directly in front of me are three signs; signs that rip through the desert silence like a stealth fighter screaming across an empty sky.

The signs stake out invisible borders cutting through this dirt road. One phrase marks the limit of public space: "No Trespassing." Another marks a limit of visibility: "Photography Prohibited." And the third announces that the rawest expression of sovereignty governs the no-mans-land only a few feet away.

USE OF DEADLY FORCE AUTHORIZED

This is a place where the "normal" rules of society don't apply. It's a place where armed and camouflaged men in unmarked trucks have the right to kill you to prevent you from entering. These men are not soldiers, they wear no insignias, and are presumably not subject to the same rules of engagement as their enlisted counterparts.[37] All of the justifications for secrecy, all of the line-items obscured in "black budgets" and all of the conspiracy theories and alien stories aside, in this moment, Groom Lake seems to come down to a simple and brutal fact: "If you try to come in here, or if you even try to take a picture of what's in here, we're going to kill you." Anyone who has ventured towards to the border has felt the same thing. Jim Goodall, stealth-watcher and aviation author, says "the thing that bothers me about Area 51 [is] that a camouflage dude in a white Jeep Cherokee can come up to you, shoot you in cold blood, drag your butt a quarter of a mile inside the perimeter of the base, and throw it out where the buzzards can get to you, and there isn't a government agency or law-enforcement agency in this country that has the authority to go in there and get your body. Even if they could, there's no one who can be held accountable, because the place doesn't officially exist. You might as well be on Mars."[38]

‡

You may as well be on Mars, indeed; you may as well be somewhere that is totally *alien*; you may as well be *nowhere*. Groom Lake is famous for the fact that it does not properly exist, that it is quite literally *nowhere*. And the history of this nowhere is older than the U-2, or even the Manhattan Project. The nowhere of the "black world," of this silent and foreboding place, is as old as the United States itself. In the nineteenth century, it was the nowhere at the margins of empire, the "black world" of American expansion, of indigenous "savages," and of wholesale and indiscriminate death. It was a swath of uncharted land, a blank space on the map, a space in the crosshairs of manifest destiny, a space that stunk of death.

With the exception of an 1820s campaign to trap all the beaver in the area, the native peoples of the present-day Nellis Complex, the Western Shoshone and Southern Paiute, were left alone by whites until the mid-nineteenth century.[39] As emigrants, miners, and prospectors arrived to the area, violence between the Native Americans and whites became common. It was in this context that the Treaty of Ruby Valley was signed in 1863. Declaring "peace and friendship" between the U.S. and the Western Shoshone, the treaty granted the United States certain rights of passage and mining claims throughout the land, but maintained Shoshone sovereignty over the land.[40] The Western Shoshone, for their part, were to ensure that "hostilities and all depredations upon the emigrant trains, the mail and telegraph lines, and upon the citizens of the United States within their country, shall cease."[41] In return, the whites promised to compensate the Western Shoshone for the "inconvenience resulting to the Indians in consequence of the driving away and destruction of game along the routes travelled [sic] by white men, and by the formation of agricultural and mining settlements."[42] But from the beginning the treaty did not extend the same guarantee of safety to the Western Shoshone that the whites themselves demanded. Raymond Yowell, the Western Shoshone Council Chief, describes the signing of the Treaty of Ruby Valley itself the following way:

> They had [the Indians] lined up along that ridge, and the troops were standing there ready with their rifles... They fed the Indians first, before signing the treaty. Before they did that they had the Indians turn over a supposedly bad Shoshone to them, who'd maybe killed some white people or something like that. And so they hung him in front of them first, that morning when they were going to sign the treaty. And then, after he was dead, they cut him down and took him away, and they [the Shoshone] didn't know what they did with him. His relatives wanted the body, but they wouldn't give it to them. Later on, they fed [the Shoshone] a meat that they couldn't recognize. Pretty soon, they figured out that they had cooked the Shoshone that they had hung and fed it to them. That's what they figured.[43]

The violence of "peace and friendship" at Ruby Valley was consonant with the times. Miners were poisoning the land with mercury and cyanide,[44] whites were cutting down trees for fuel, and their cattle were devouring plants that native peoples relied on for food. Local game was frightened off the land.[45] Invading settlers attacked Western Shoshone women, raped mothers in front of their children,[46] and slaughtered native peoples indiscriminately.[47] In the 1860s and 1870s, Nevada's main newspaper, aptly titled *Territorial Enterprise*, advocated for "exterminating the whole race."[48] Expansion, a U.S. variation of nineteenth century imperialism, had created its own "black world." It was a legal nowhere, a dark place where certain people could be killed without consequence. An alien place. A place in the desert where the words and deeds of settlers and newspapers would be echoed in the deranged exhortation of a certain Mr. Kurtz in the African heart of darkness: "exterminate all the brutes."[49]

‡

In the late 1920s, the Navy chose Hawthorne as the site for a massive ammunition-depot, and modern weapons arrived to the area known to the Western Shoshone as Newe Sogobia. To claim the land, President Calvin Coolidge invoked the Pickett Act of 1912, which authorized the president to *temporarily* withdraw public land for waterpower, irrigation, and "other public purposes."[50] With the outbreak of World War Two, the Department of War created many of Nevada's contemporary military landscapes. On October 29, 1940, Roosevelt issued Executive Order 8578 to establish the Las Vegas Bombing and Gunnery Range (that would become the Nellis Range Complex). To do this, he reached into an obscure corner of the law books to invoke the Army Appropriations Act of July 9, 1918—an almost forgotten authority that allowed the president to claim unappropriated public domain lands to create aviation fields for testing and experimental work.[51]

After World War Two, the weapons kept coming to Nevada. In January of 1951, the Atomic Energy Commission went public with its plan to carve the Nevada Test Site out of the Las Vegas Bombing and Gunnery Range and its intentions to begin exploding nuclear weapons at the site.[52] The decision had been made in secret. The site had been chosen from among several locations under scrutiny by the members of Project Nutmeg, the effort to locate a continental site to explode nuclear weapons.[53] Only a brief interval of time separated the announcement establishing the Nevada Test Site from the first nuclear explosion: on January 27, an Air Force B-50D bomber dropped an atomic bomb on a place the white government called Frenchman Flat. If, based on the Treaty of Ruby Valley, the Western Shoshone's Newe Sogobia was still a sovereign nation, then, in this instant, the Indian Wars had gone nuclear.

Part of the justification for turning much of Nevada, or Newe Sogobia, into a massive bombing range was that, at least to the white population, the area was a "wasteland"—it wasn't "good" for anything. And so it didn't matter what was done to it. In hindsight there's a strange irony to all of this. The sense that the land was "valueless" is perhaps the reason that the Treaty of Ruby Valley ultimately ceded sovereignty over the land to the Western Shoshone—the whites didn't bother to take "legal" sovereignty from the native peoples because they couldn't see any reason to appropriate these desert "badlands."[54] The continuing attitude that this land "didn't matter" provided the justification for turning it into a massive bombing range. The Army Air Corps explained that the reason for creating the Las Vegas range where they did was that the land "wasn't much good for anything but gunnery practice—*you could bomb it into oblivion and never notice the difference*" [italics added].[55] Or, to put it another way, you could bomb it into oblivion because it *already was* in oblivion. It already was nowhere.[56]

Throughout the history of white occupation, the places we call Groom Lake and the Nellis Range Complex have inhabited an in-between space; a space in the seemingly-paradoxical position of being both *inside and outside* the state at the same time.[57] A space of indistinction. During the frontier era, the "black world" known to some people as Newe Sogobia was "outside" the U.S. state. But as the United States took and transformed this land, it largely *preserved* the qualities that had made this land an "outside"—laws didn't apply, things could be done in secret and without consequence, the land could be bombed indiscriminately, and so forth. When the United States established much of Nevada as an exclusively military landscape, it was as if the "black-world" of the frontier made a smooth and almost effortless (from the U.S. point of view) transition into the "black-world" of military weapons, testing, and secrecy.

Groom Lake is clearly *inside* the state: it was and is produced by the state, and paid for with taxpayer's money. The state (through a privatized paramilitary force) reserves the right to kill anyone attempting to breach its border. Groom Lake belongs to the state: it's used to develop secret weapons, airplanes, and other clandestine technologies. Now operated by the Air Force, it is synonymous with the state itself. But at the same time, Groom Lake is *outside* the state: the installation is exempt from many laws; it has no "official" name, no verifiable designation, and it does not appear on government maps. It is a space whose very existence is *arcanum imperii*, an official secret. It is exempt from almost all of the conventions and logics that—in theory at least—provide the basis for democratic society. But there is another irony to the inside/outside topology of Groom Lake: the U.S. government cannot produce a legal document demonstrating that they, and not the Western Shoshone, can claim legal sovereignty over the land.[58]

The space encompassing Groom Lake and the Nellis Range Complex is a landscape that has been produced and reproduced, throughout the twentieth century and into the twenty-first, as oblivion, as nowhere: a nowhere in the service of *testing*. Testing next-generation war machines. Testing fighter-pilots' combat skills. Testing hardware stolen from other nations. Testing nuclear weapons. The paradoxical nature of this space—its neither/nor-ness, is a part of an overall testing strategy, a strategy designed to blur the line between the Nellis Range Complex and the places where the "testing" at Nellis will be reenacted "for real." By *producing* nowhere in the testing sites of Nevada, the United States rehearses its ability to *reproduce* nowhere. *Elsewhere.*

The words "test" and "testing" seem harmless. They seem to imply a detached, scientific endeavor that takes place in a controlled laboratory or classroom. We test materials to see if they do what we predict, and test students to see if they've done their homework. The word "test" is ubiquitous among the facilities within the Nellis Range: the Nevada Test Site, the Tonopah Test Range, and one possible name for Groom Lake which is the Air Force Flight Test Center, Detachment 3.[59] The testing that goes on at these places involves making sure that weapons work, ultimately so that they'll work when they're used elsewhere, against other people. Testing weapons means flying them or dropping them in Nevada so that the test can be recreated "for real" somewhere else.

Something strange happens to the morphology of the built environment under these conditions. In the "testing" landscapes of the Nellis Range, the built environments begin to look like distorted versions of the places for which these tests are marked for export. The Nellis Range contains places like "Terrortown"—a mock city used for training Special Forces,[60] facilities like "Korean Airfield"[61] that electronically simulate foreign countries for various war-games, and many other architectural doppelgangers. And there are always more in the making: a new round of facilities at the Nevada Test Site includes a model of the U.S. border, a simulated airline inspection terminal, and a seaport.[62]

But a more abstract kind of testing occurs here as well: the state tests it ability to keep a secret, and tests the extent to which it can operate outside of its own laws. Much effort goes into keeping a facility like Groom Lake and the programs within it hidden. Thousands of people either consent, or are coerced, into maintaining the silence surrounding the facility. If the state had failed to produce a single supersonic spy-plane or stealth fighter, the technologies of state secrecy needed to produce a place like Groom Lake would be in themselves a remarkable achievement. As much as Groom Lake is a place to test weapons and planes, it's a place to produce, test, and reproduce secrecy. And through the testing and reproduction of secrecy, these social and bureaucratic technologies that confound external oversight and inquiry, become improved.

Groom Lake is a testing area, a desert "laboratory of exception," where nowhere is produced, reproduced, and where its efficiency and efficacy are evaluated. And if the architecture of the testing landscapes at Nellis Range serves as a mirror of the places where its weapon tests are exported, then perhaps the nowhereness of Groom Lake works in a similar way. If the built environments like "Korean Airfield" in the Nellis Range are designed to be indistinct from an actual airfield in Korea, then perhaps the *nowhere* of the Nellis Range Complex and *elsewhere* of the eventual targets of its tests are designed to be similarly indistinct. The "black world" of the testing ranges is designed to blur into the "black world" of *elsewhere*. Blurred like one night in 1989 when six stealth fighters emerged from their secret base at Nellis and flew to Panama instead of their local targets. They dropped the first bombs of the Panama invasion.[63] Or blurred on a day in 2004, when the remote crew of an unmanned Predator drone at Nellis learned long after the fact that they had inadvertently participated in the capture of Saddam Hussein. No one had told the remote crew the nature of the mission they had piloted from halfway across the world.[64] Or perhaps the line between nowhere and elsewhere is blurred in an even more fundamental and foundational sense. Perhaps this line has been blurred every day since whites occupied the Western Shoshone land. The black-worlds of Nevada come full-circle and fold into each other when Raymond Yowell, referring to the Western Shoshone and Southern Paiute's continuing struggles with the United States, describes Newe Sogobia as "the most bombed nation in the world."[65]

There's only one place on public land from which you can actually see Groom Lake. To get there, I drive towards the town of Alamo, and then turn off the pavement onto a lonely dirt road. It's about twenty miles through open range, stopping to open and close various dilapidated cattle gates along the way. Eventually, the road starts to incline and patches of snow appear alongside my car. Before long, there's more snow than dirt and I start to worry about getting stuck. I finally see the cattle-spring where I've been instructed to park, and I tuck the car under a tree. For the hike, I fill my backpack with two cameras, a military scanner, a recorder, some snacks, and some extra clothes. I'm not an outdoorsy person, so the two miles up a steep mountainside in several feet of snow is not easy. Trudging up through snow-covered shale, I hear the sounds of fighter-planes racing through the skies. Like many things around this landscape, they're gone by the time you hear them. When I reach the summit, it's nighttime.

From the top of this peak, Groom Lake is about thirty miles to the West, a few miniscule dots of light on the horizon. Lights flickering on and off in various combinations during the hours I spend sitting here. The blinking lights of a plane approaching and landing at the base are too dim and too far away for me to identify. My scanner chirps and gurgles in a language only intelligible to the initiated. Even if I did understand these bits of distorted voices, they would probably not reveal anything more than the pin-pricks of light in the far distance: the fact that something is going on, but nothing more.

‡

A curious thing happened at the end of the cold war. To some, all the justifications for the secret weapons—the "black budgets," the $2.5 billion stealth bombers, the nuclear bombs—were simply gone. Quite suddenly, in fact. Some suggested that all the money saved by militarism could be put into social services, that with the war gone, a significant amount of the hundreds of billions once spent on military activities and procurements could be put into other kinds of programs. There would be a peace dividend, some said—one that would make us more secure financially, physically, and even psychically. Others argued the opposite, claiming that as the world's only "superpower," the United States needed to maintain the size of its military more than ever, particular with new images of bad guys like Manuel Noriega and Saddam Hussein running "rogue nations." A report by the WEFA Group pointed out that if the United States dismantled much of its military, it would simultaneously dismantle a significant part of its own economy.[66] Military cuts did begin to occur in the 1990s, but the "black world" held its own.[67]

As the "evil-empire" began to crumble with the Berlin Wall and the Soviet Union fractured into pieces, some people turned to the Nevada desert in order to understand what had happened during the long cold war. Groups of "stealth-watchers" and "interceptors" formed informal clubs dedicated to "revealing the secrets" of the Nellis Range Complex. Often prompted by rumors of captured extraterrestrial technology at "Area 51," they sought to uncover the facilities, activities, and programs beyond the death-signs of Groom Lake road. Over the years, these amateur geographers[68] developed incredibly sophisticated and specialized techniques for long-range photography, intercepting radio communications, interpreting obscure shapes, and using the Freedom of Information Act to follow up on the most obscure details contained in Air Force press releases and Internet rumors. Through Web sites, public appearances, and popular articles, they became largely responsible for the appearance of "Area 51" on the cultural map, if not the USGS map.

The blurry images, bits of intercepted military traffic, and clips of grainy video that the stealth watchers have collected, depicting the "secrets" of the Range, have a peculiar aesthetic. It's an aesthetic based on the decontextualized fragment, the image that lasts only as long as the blink of an eye, or the flickering light observed from the top of a desert peak. These bits of information almost always fail to signify anything other than the presence of a seductive but inaccessible truth. Perhaps this infinite deferral of "truth," the inability of these fragments to sensibly speak, but whose contours continually promise to provide a reverse-outline of the black world, is what has kept the stealth-watchers interested. The attempts to see and hear Groom Lake captured in the stealth watchers' fragmented photos and recordings cause one to scratch one's head and start to speculate on what these things "could" mean, or to resign oneself to the impossibility of steadfast truth beyond a single stable signifier at the perimeter of Groom Lake: "this place does not exist, but if you try to come in here, we will kill you."

Because there is, in fact, so little to see of Groom Lake, people see different things when they look west from the mountain where I am standing. Some people see a relatively boring military installation that handles classified projects like stealth technology and Unmanned Aerial Vehicles, while others see a giant Potemkin village: a colossal diversion designed to prevent the stealth-watchers from turning their attention to other, more important, secret bases. Staring from this mountaintop, some people see a vast conspiracy, with Groom Lake as the staging ground for an imperial New World Order—an effort to exterminate democracy and impose martial law worldwide. At the most extreme end of conspiracy, some see Groom Lake as an *alien* base, a place from which reptilian extraterrestrials secretly rule a world they have already conquered. A place that is so outside the structures that a democratic government is supposed to take, that its existence can only be explained by the fact that the United States is indeed already under the control of a malfeasant external power.

I spend the rest of the night driving home and arrive back in Berkeley to a morning haze similar to the one I'd found in the desert.

As I walk through campus, the university begins to take on new meanings. I remember that the Bechtel engineering building a few yards away from my own office bears the name of the company charged with managing the Nevada Test Site. I remember that the Lawrence labs in the hills above campus were built, in part, to separate U-235 from gaseous uranium hexafluoride—to produce the heart of an atomic bomb. I remember that the Berkeley campus is named after a man most famous for the lines: "westward the course of empire takes its way." [69]

When I first saw the names and uses of the places in the Nellis Range Complex, it was obvious to me that these places were designed to be indistinct from the targets they simulated. "Korean Airfield" signified and simulated Korea; "Terrortown" did the same for Tehran. Now, as I entered the Geography Department in McCone Hall, it occurred to me that the place where I stood might be as much a part of the "black world" as a secret base guarded by armed men in unmarked vehicles.

Walking into the building that bears his name, I remembered how John McCone's career was inexorably bound to the testing landscapes of Nevada. John McCone, the Under Secretary of the Air Force from 1950–1951, who accused Cal-Tech scientists of being "taken in" by "Soviet propaganda" and attempting to "create fear in the minds of the uninformed that radioactive fallout from H-bomb tests endangers life." [70] A man who later became Chairman of the Atomic Energy Commission (1958–1961), responsible for years of atmospheric nuclear explosions at the test site—tests that killed untold numbers of "downwinders." When he became the director of the CIA from 1961–1965, McCone oversaw the expansion of Groom Lake for the A-12 program. As my own mind instinctively tried to fill the gaps in the classified histories and landscapes of the Nellis Range, I permitted myself the luxury of speculating on the fragments I had seen in the desert. As I stared at a flyer announcing a class on "development" or "area studies" or "geographic information systems"—I really don't remember exactly—an ironic thought occurred to me. I imagined that another McCone Hall might exist: a McCone Hall, named in honor of a former CIA director, near a dry lakebed in the middle of nowhere at a base that doesn't exist. [71]

Notes

1. I'd like to thank Jaime Cortez, Aaron Gach, Jack Paglen, Allan Pred, Praba Pilar, Ananya Roy, and Zhivka Valiavicharska for their extensive comments and help in producing this chapter.
2. Freeman Dyson, *Disturbing the Universe* (New York: Harper Collins, 2001), 128. Rebecca Solnit and John McPhee have both used this quote to describe the silence of the basin and range.
3. In 1995, President Bill Clinton signed an executive order removing Groom Lake from the courts, saying that a discussion of Groom Lake in a court of law could "reasonably be expected" to damage national security. See Phil Patton, *Dreamland: Travels Inside the Secret World of Roswell and Area 51* (New York: Villard, 1998), 268. Since this initial exemption, presidents have signed yearly orders to maintain this prohibition. Available at http://www.whitehouse.gov/news/releases/2003/09/20030916-4.html.
4. This passage borrows liberally from Allan Pred's descriptions of "unspeakable" and "unspoken" spaces and geographies. For Pred, departing from Foucault, the unspeakable consists of the forgotten assumptions, taken-for-granteds, the "absolutely atrocious," and the "literally unsayable"—the silences that structure discourse and everyday life. See Part Two of Allan Pred, *The Past is Not Dead* (Minneapolis: University of Minnesota Press, 2004).
5. For a history of the Nevada Test Site, see Terrence Fehner, and F. G. Gosling, *Origins of the Nevada Test Site* (U.S. Department of Energy, History Division. DOE/MA-0518), 82.
6. Steven Kosiak, *Classified Funding in the FY 2006 Defense Budget Request* (Center for Strategic and Budgetary Assessments, March 23, 2005), available at http://www.csbaonline.org. See also Chalmers Johnson, *Sorrows of Empire* (New York: Henry Holt, 2004).
7. Tim Weiner, *Blank Check* (New York: Warner Books, 1990), 20
8. Weiner, *Blank Check*, 20
9. See, for example, Richard Rhodes, *The Making of the Atomic Bomb* (New York: Simon and Schuster, 1986).
10. McGeorge Bundy, *Danger and Survival* (New York: Random House, 1988), 55.
11. Bundy, *Danger and Survival*, 76
12. Weiner, *Blank Check*, 5
13. Weiner, *Blank Check*, 116
14. For a history of the CIA's secret operations see John Prados, *Presidents' Secret Wars: CIA and Pentagon Covert Operations from World War II Through the Persian Gulf* (New York: Ivan R. Dee, 1996).
15. Quoted in Hannah Arendt, *The Origins of Totalitarianism* (New York: Harcourt, 1976), xx.
16. Weiner, *Blank Check*, 5.
17. Ben Rich with Leo Janos, *Skunk Works* (Boston: Back Bay Books, 1994), 132.
18. Rich, Skunk Works, see also Curtis Peebles, *Dark Eagles* (Novato: Presidio, 1995), 25–27
19. Peebles, *Dark Eagles*, 26.
20. Rich, *Skunk Works*, 120.
21. The name of REECo. has been redacted from the CIA history of the U-2 program. See Gregory W. Pedlow and Donald E. Welzenbach, *The CIA and the U2 Program* (Washington D.C.: Central Intelligence Agency, 1998). See also Rich, Skunk Works, 133 and Peebles, Dark Eagles, 26–27.

22. Rich, *Skunk Works*, 133.

23. Rich, *Skunk Works*, 134.

24. Peebles, *Dark Eagles*, 28. See also Pedlow and Walzenbach, *The CIA and the U2 Program*.

25. Francis Gary Powers and Curt Gentry, *Operation Overflight* (New York: Holt, Rinehart and Winston, 1970), 28.

26. Powers, *Operation Overflight*, 33.

27. Rich, *Skunk Works*, 200.

28. Rich, *Skunk Works*, 201.

29. Peebles, *Dark Eagles*, 58–59.

30. Peebles, *Dark Eagles*, 59.

31. Peebles, *Dark Eagles*, 219–223.

32. Rich, *Skunk Works*, 40.

33. These include an aircraft code-named Tacit-Blue that was revealed in (1996), and Boeing's "Bird of Prey" prototype. See the Federation of American Scientists Web site on mystery aircraft http://www.fas.org/irp/mystery/tacitblu.htm for Tacit Blue. Interestingly, although the "Bird of Prey" was tested throughout the 1990s at the height of "stealth-watching" at Groom Lake, its existence remained largely unknown until its unveiling in 2002. For Bird of Prey, see http://www.boeing.com/news/releases/2002/q4/nr_021018m.html.

34. See Federation of American Scientists report on satellite imagery obtained in 2000 at http://www.fas.org/irp/overhead/groom.htm. For more recent imagery, including the construction of a new taxiway in 2003, see the "info and photos" section of the Dreamland Resort Web site at http://www.dreamlandresort.com.

35. Rebecca Solnit, *Savage Dreams* (Berkeley: University of California Press, 1994), 57.

36. In this way, they share some commonalities with what Georgio Agamben calls the "camp." See Georgio Agamben, trans. Vincenzo Binetti and Cesare Casarino, *Means Without End: Notes on Politics* (Minneapolis: University of Minnesota Press, 2000), 38. If we describe the Nellis Range as a "space of exception," then it is different from Agamben's camp insofar as the Nellis area does not seek to manage life (the primary role of Agamben's camp). Instead, the spaces in the Nellis Range Complex exist to perfect *technologies* of violence; they function primarily to prepare and refine the *means* of domination. But in order to test the means of violent domination, a degree of violent domination is necessarily exercised, collapsing the distinction to a certain extent. Thus, Groom Lake and the Nellis Complex act as a "laboratory of exception"—I point to this dialectic in the "testing" section of this work.

37. According to several authors, the "cammo dudes" work for the EG&G companies' "Special Projects" division, a privately held company that manages many of the operations at the Nellis Range and Groom Lake. See David Darlington, *Area 51: The Dreamland Chronicles* (New York: Henry Holt, 1997), 18.

38. Quoted in Darlington, *Area 51*, 142.

39. Solnit, *Savage Dreams*, 163.

40. Solnit, *Savage Dreams*, 163–164.

41. "Treaty With The Western Shoshoni" (1863). Reprint available at http://www.wsdp.org.

42. "Treaty With The Western Shoshoni."

43. Paul Nellin, *Interview with Raymond Yowell* at http://www.nativeweb.org/pages/legal/shoshone.

44. Solnit, *Savage Dreams*, 169.

45. Solnit, *Savage Dreams*, 167.

46. Solnit, *Savage Dreams*, 167.

47. Solnit, *Savage Dreams*, 167. See also Brigham D. Madsen, *The Shoshoni Frontier and the Bear River Massacre* (Salt Lake City: University of Utah Press, 1995). The Bear River is in Southern Idaho, which is also traditional Shoshone territory.

48. Solnit, *Savage Dreams*, 167.

49. The quote is, of course, from Joseph Conrad's *Heart of Darkness* (New York: Penguin, 1983), 123.

50. David Loomis, *Combat Zoning* (Reno: University of Nevada Press, 1993), 5–6.

51. Loomis, *Combat Zoning*, 9–10.

52. Fehner and Gosling. *Origins of the Nevada Test Site*, 55.

53. Valerie Kuletz, *The Tainted Desert* (London: Routledge, 1998), 71.

54. See Solnit, *Savage Dreams*, 171.

55. Loomis, *Combat Zoning*, 10.

56. Kuletz refers to this phenomenon as "The Wastelands Discourse" (13–14). This echoes Mbembe's point that "colonial occupation commonly claims to deal with 'uninhabited and masterless land.'" Furthermore, colonial occupation takes land that is "deemed to belong to the category of things that have never belonged to anybody... the settler as the person taking possession does not succeed anyone." See Achille Mbembe, *On the Postcolony* (Berkeley: University of California Press, 2001), 183.

57. As such, they demonstrate a spatial ordering that recalls Agamben's topology of sovereignty: "The 'ordering of space' that is, according to Schmitt, constitutive of the sovereign *nomos* is therefore not only a 'taking of the land' (*Landesnahme*)—the determination of a juridical and a territorial ordering (of an *Ordnung* and an *Ortung*)—but above all a 'taking of the outside,' an exception (*Ausnahme*). Georgio Agamben, trans. David Heller-Roazen, *Homo Sacer: Sovereign Power and Bare Life* (Stanford, CA: Stanford University Press, 1998), 19.

58. Instead, the government has argued that it controls the land based on an internally contradictory argument around "gradual encroachment" to which Raymond Yowell, chief of the Western National Shoshone Council replies, "if gradual encroachment is the law of the land, we have gradually encroached it back." See Solnit, *Savage Dreams*, 171.

59. Patton, Dreamland, 175

60. See the Center for Land Use Interpretation CD-ROM. *The Nellis Range Complex.* 2003

61. Center for Land Use Interpretation, *The Nellis Range Complex.*

62. These new facilities are to be used in order to test the effects of a "dirty bomb" at these kinds of locations. Steve Tetreault, "Test Site Takes on Security Role," *Pahrump Valley Times*, June 11, 2004. Available at http://www.pahrumpvalleytimes.com/2004/06/11/news/ymp.html. These facilities are constructed for "defensive" testing, which makes them seem a little less ominous, but it's important to point out that a test for "defensive" reasons can produce the same data as a test for an offensive capacity.

63. Tonopah housed the Air Force's squadron of stealth fighters in secret for almost a decade until 1989, when six of these planes flew south to drop the first bombs in the Panama invasion. Two of the planes actually dropped bombs—the other four were used as back-ups. See Malcom McConnell, *Just Cause: The Real Story of America's High-Tech Invasion of Panama* (New York: St. Martin's Press, 1991), 35.

64. Keith Rogers, "Nellis Crew Helped Nab Saddam," *Las Vegas Review-Journal*, Tuesday, March 2, 2004 at http://www.reviewjournal.com/lvrj_home/2004/Mar-02-Tue-2004/news/23335929.html.

65. Kuletz, *The Tainted Desert*, 72.

66. See, for example, Clemens P. Work, Robert F. Black, and Doug Pasternak, "The High Cost of Olive Branches." *U.S. News & World Report,* vol. 107, no. 23; p. 32. December 11, 1989.

67. See Kosiak. When I say "held its own" I mean that it remained relatively consistent as a percentage of overall Pentagon spending. Classified Pentagon spending is now (FY 2004) at its post cold war high.

68. When I say "amateur geographers" I don't mean to suggest that these people are necessarily hacks. On the contrary, I mean to suggest that these "un-disciplined" researchers and the techniques they have developed to interpret landscapes have a great deal to contribute to geographic thought and epistemology. It is a historical fact that amateurs, precisely because of their lack of academic discipline, have made enormous contributions to the sciences through their ability to see and interpret the world without many of the presuppositions that a "professional" researcher may have.

69. See Grey Brechin, *Imperial San Francisco* (Berkeley: University of California Press, 1999), 317.

70. David Wise and Thomas B. Ross, *The Invisible Government* (New York: Random House, 1964), 192–193.

13

Targeting the Inner Landscape

Matthew Farish

According to its critics, among the most egregious stumbles committed by the Bush administration during its ongoing "war on terror" is the mishandling and even ignorance of public diplomacy. The Pentagon's attempt to establish an Office of Strategic Influence (OSI) to "provide news items, possibly even false ones, to foreign media organizations as part of a new effort to influence public sentiment and policy makers in both friendly and unfriendly countries" was officially shut down in February 2002 after a public furor.[1] A panel put together in 2003 by Congress and the State Department found "shocking levels" of "hostility toward America" in the Arab and Muslim world.[2] The State Department's position of head PR agent for America, when filled, has been occupied by a rapid succession of advertising executives, diplomats, and close acquaintances of the President. One of the latest occupants of the office, Margaret Tutwiler, stepped aside in April 2004, just as a now-ubiquitous set of torture photos from Abu Ghraib prison in occupied Iraq fell into the hands of the *New Yorker's* Seymour Hersh and then the rest of the media.[3] She was eventually replaced by George W. Bush's confidante Karen Hughes, whose forays into the Middle East (where she had never traveled) in the fall of 2005 were greeted with significant derision in both her host countries and in the American press.[4]

Surveying opinion on this latest battle for hearts and minds reveals a strikingly consistent skepticism towards American public diplomacy. Even *Fox News* admitted, in May 2004, that the effort was a challenging one, as represented in the mixed successes of such outlets as the U.S.-funded Middle Eastern television network Al Hurra, actually based in northern Virginia.[5] In the same month, the editor of the similarly U.S.-sponsored Iraqi newspaper *Al-Sabah* quit, citing interference.[6] Early in 2004, the Pew Research Center for the People and the Press reported, as part of its Global Attitudes Project, that discontent with the United States was shockingly high in both Europe and the Middle East.[7] And on the eve of the November 2004 election, a *Christian Science Monitor* report described the continuing inability of American public diplomacy to match image-improvement campaigns with support for reform and civil society initiatives.[8] For daring to raise these issues—albeit in a highly generic way—during the first of three presidential debates, Massachusetts Senator John Kerry was mocked by President George W. Bush, who parlayed Kerry's "global test" phrase into xenophobic material for the campaign trail.

If understanding the events of September 11, as Neil Smith has noted, mandates consideration of terror's "multiple scales," from the intimately local to the sweepingly global, and ultimately, inevitably, to the reassuringly national, then a similar perspective is required for the subsequent American response.[9] Two dimensions of contemporary geopolitics separated by location and scope, public diplomacy and homeland security are united by the appeal to a singular American nation-space, projected abroad and promoted domestically. They also share a concern with the power (and danger) of psychology, or, more accurately, *psychological warfare*. Situated within a universal conflict at times depicted in the terminology of good versus evil, the pairing strikingly resembles an earlier dual campaign with the same aims, namely cold war propaganda operations overseas and civil defense initiatives in U.S. cities and neighborhoods.

Indeed, if there is a recent precedent for the universal and vague scope of the "war on terror" and its resultant domestic anxieties, it is the strange dance that rose out of the ashes of the Second World War some sixty years ago. The cold war also featured a division of the world into two camps and a global search for amorphous enemies, including at home, where narratives of fear, patriotism, and security ran rampant.[10] Similarly, as accusations of un-Americanism and treason surged after 9/11, the importance of a homogeneous patriotism—ironically dependant on particular and narrow norms of expression—to geopolitical moves conducted both inside and outside national boundaries was once again made manifest. Homeland security programs, from color-coded alerts announced at "politically opportune times" to the ill-fated Terrorism Information and Prevention System (TIPS), have become crucial to the formation of a "heartland geography," in which cultural and social distinction is defined in reference to particular *sites* of banal nationalism.[11] But these sites are neither exclusively material nor completely novel in their conception; they are part of imaginative geographies with deeper genealogies.

During the confusing combination of peace-and-conflict known as the cold war, an era marked by threats of atomic apocalypse and stark geopolitical confrontation, the promise of apparently more enlightened and bloodless forms of combat was tantalizing. This would be war that struggled with the "inner landscape" of "national and international psyches."[12] In alliances characteristic of the time, industries combining academic, business, military, and intelligence sectors emerged to develop, advocate, and implement such operations. The consequences of what was quickly dubbed *psykewar* were felt most in the so-called third or developing world, where rival programs escalated minor conflicts and subjected large populations to repeated manipulation attempts. For U.S. planners, psychological warfare was understood, according to an influential 1958 casebook, as the "*planned* use of *propaganda* and *other actions* designed to influence the opinions, emotions, attitudes, and behavior of enemy, neutral and friendly foreign groups in such a way as to support the accomplishment of national aims and objectives." Revealingly, the casebook, whose chief author worked in the Army's Operations Research Office at Johns Hopkins University, treated "military psychological warfare and cold war or peacetime information activities as invoking similar problems."[13]

Like its interdisciplinary counterpart, nuclear strategy, the study of psychological warfare drew from and depended on a staggering range of expertise; it was as much an investigative problem for historians and social scientists as it was for those interested in the technical aspects of broadcasting and propaganda. Indeed, psykewar and theories of nuclear exchange were inseparable, not only because the atomic bomb itself was an obviously psychological device, but also because both targeted abstract populations. And, ironically, some of the most striking evidence for this assertion was literally located within the United States itself. While rarely made explicit, for obvious reasons, it was widely acknowledged that "peacetime information activities" were also useful on American soil, where cold war uncertainties produced public opinion in need of careful and extensive management. Like more recent appeals to the virtues of duct tape, civil defense may have been fodder for satire, but, in the form of publications, traveling exhibits, magazine features, and drills, it also contributed profoundly to the militarization of everyday life.[14] Civil defense was paralleled, of course, by a hunt for slippery subversives within American society, whose detection occasionally required hysteric narratives reaching to the very psyche of the individual in a Cartesian attempt to resolve doubt over who was real (American) and who was not.[15]

Since the ostensible end of the cold war, diplomatic historians and historians of social science have traced the genealogy of American psykewar from its intellectual roots to its execution around the globe.[16] I am concerned in this chapter with the spatial dimensions of these histories—the geographies of "truth" carved out by psykewar and its theorists. As Michel Foucault noted in his 1975–76 lectures at the Collège de France, war produces a form of truth operating as a weapon. To illustrate this claim, Foucault, unsurprisingly, drew overwhelmingly from the early modern period, and made little reference to his own century. And yet in 1953, Edward Barrett, an Assistant Secretary of State for Public Affairs during the Truman administration, and the chief architect of President Harry Truman's Psychological Strategy Board, published a book on persuasion, propaganda, and psychological warfare titled *Truth is Our Weapon*.[17] But how was this weapon fashioned, and then deployed? In beginning to answer this question, I will travel across the contours of the cold war to explain how psykewar worked at various scales, from the planetary prospects of geopolitics to the individual minds and bodies of its targets.

Although I will focus more on cold war principles and policy created for "distant" regions than on the equivalents of today's homeland security initiatives,[18] it is crucial to note that the premises of psychological warfare spilled beyond its foreign objects to infiltrate the banalities of American life, an inevitable failure of containment mirrored in the fears of a more recent time—fears I return to at the end of the chapter. As Nikolas Rose reminds us, the human sciences, notably psychology, "embody a particular way in which human beings have tried to understand *themselves*—to make themselves the subjects, objects, targets of a truthful knowledge."[19]

A Hostile World

During the Second World War and the early years of the cold war, the Earth itself was turned into an object of militarism, a holistic environment for the exercise of American strategy. This space was what the modernization theorist Daniel Lerner, author of the classic study *Sykewar* (1949), aptly labeled "a global arena of national action."[20]

The geographic views fashioning Lerner's arena were a practical manifestation of the much older tendency to see the world as a whole.[21] While never entirely detached from locations or areas, the world map of cold war geopolitics was a more fully realized and systematic version of Halford Mackinder's turn-of-the-century discussions of social explosions reverberating "from the far side of the globe," shocks that were part of a self-regulatory "closed circuit…complete and balanced in all its parts."[22]

In the United States after the Second World War, the term "geopolitics" was almost completely discarded and replaced by a more reasonable science, backed by the authority of an equally sanitized national identity. President Dwight D. Eisenhower summed up this deterministic and discursive shift in a 1954 speech: "The world, once divided by oceans and mountain ranges, is now split by hostile concepts of man's character and nature," two "world camps" lying "farther apart in motivation and conduct than the poles in space."[23] In his statement, Eisenhower not only articulated the binary spatial division at the heart of the cold war, but also affirmed the global character of cold war geopolitics by endorsing the *worldly* nature and aspirations of each antagonist. Eisenhower's imagery was not simply an instance of hyperbolic rhetoric deployed for effect, but a reflection of a much broader geographical condition which linked America to a global space and which held up the Communist camp as an obstacle to a perfect match with that space. Eisenhower's words, moreover, indicate that cold war geopolitics was deeply psychological, a trait that could not be erased by even the most hard-headed of strategists. And because the earth was divided by conduct, or behavior, opponents were not easily bounded in space. Their pervasive and ubiquitous presence (or potential) meant that the world itself became an object of surveillance and a scene of suspicion.

As part of a project of containment that acquired its own militarist global dimensions, the antithetical character of cold war rivalry voiced by Eisenhower was supplemented by an alternative, less conservative theme in American geopolitics: that of *integration*, a clever, positive intermediary between isolationism and stark imperialism. Eisenhower's 1953 inaugural address, for instance, was rife with the rhetoric of international unity, shared faith, and "common dignity." These tropes provided a rationalization for certain forms of American foreign policy in the name of political self-determination and economic liberalization, and forced the concealment of other forms inside the covert methods of espionage and psykewar.[24] What Amy Kaplan has written with respect to the recent invocation of the term *homeland* is equally applicable to this flexible and even contradictory realm of cold war geopolitics, which turned ultimately on the definition of the American nation itself:

> A relation exists between securing the homeland against the encroachment of foreign terrorists and enforcing national power abroad. The homeland may contract borders around a fixed space of nation and nativity, but it simultaneously also expands the capacity of the United States to move unilaterally across the borders of other nations.[25]

Crucially, however, and regardless of whether difference or unity was in favor, a dominant cold war sensibility positioned America at the heart of a *hostile* world—an impulse again on display in a "war on terror" where genuine allies seem scarce. As it rose to global prominence, the United States was, so it seemed, surrounded by antagonists, dangers, and threats. Well before the official commencement of the cold war, Isaiah Bowman had predicted and clarified the geopolitical threats accompanying growing American responsibilities. In his 1943 presidential report to Johns Hopkins University, he argued that "we can not safely limit our future responsibilities to narrow zones of power. No line can be established anywhere in the world that confines the interest of the United States because no line can prevent the remote from becoming the near danger."[26] Assuming this was the case, Bowman and his American counterparts were concerned with two questions: how could the dynamics of this strategic world be accurately represented, and how was security achieved, nationally *and* globally?

In addition to funding research by scholars who moved into policy planning positions, philanthropies backed intellectual gatherings where the bases of these questions were debated. At one such Rockefeller Foundation-sponsored meeting in 1954, Yale's Arnold Wolfers argued that the introduction of "behavioral or psychological aspects" had drawn geopolitical realism away from abstract schema to address "situational components." Generalization, in other words, was no longer drawn from "complex entities such as great powers or empires but could be derived from the study of such abundant simple elements as human demands, expectations, choices, ambitions, fears and reactions to environmental factors, the atoms, ions, and velocities of international politics."[27] Behavioralism, for Wolfers and many others, was simply a step closer to reality, and made verification of this reality easier. And although the unit of analysis may, in one respect, have shrunk drastically from the empire or state to the individual, it was clear that the move back up the chain was not at all impossible.

Across the relatively narrow spectrum of cold war commentary, strategists, and politicians represented the Soviet Union as markedly, irrevocably distinct from the United States—so distinct that in many cases there was little room for negotiation or diplomatic compromise. Rooted in the *foreign* nature of the Soviet Union was a vague, if powerful, threat of an expansionistic Communism, always on the verge of leaking out and ultimately enveloping America. Because of such related geopolitical formulations as the "domino theory," the geographical spread of Communism, no matter how distant, was *always* a danger to American security. Some cases, of course, were more crucial than others. By April of 1950, these theories had reached their apotheosis with National Security Council document 68 (NSC-68), a paper prepared primarily by Paul Nitze, George Kennan's successor as head of the State Department's Policy Planning Staff. Arguing that the Soviet Union desired and required "the dynamic extension of their authority and the ultimate elimination of any effective opposition to their authority," NSC-68 was filled with dramatic, sinister, and active language: the enemy is said to expound "a new fanatical faith, antithetical to our own." By the time President Harry Truman approved it in September, events in Korea had "confirmed the validity of its analysis and conclusions." Kennan, who had never endorsed a global "zero sum game" in which "gains for communism anywhere constituted, to an equivalent degree, losses for the United States and its allies," had been left behind. His original, more particular arguments on containment were distorted, to be sure, but were also taken to their logical cold war conclusions.[28] And cold war geopolitics had become saturated with psychological rhetoric only bolstered by the invocation of the globe as a strategic space, a jigsaw whose parts featured contests for human character, each necessary for national survival.

Regional Intelligence

For many Americans, the spatial extent of the Second World War and the cold war generated significant interest in previously ignored parts of the world. This attention prompted a quest for knowledge that familiarized distant landscapes in the language of military interests. Across the complex networks of military, industrial, and academic research, the systematic study of *areas*, with an eye to their strategic value, emerged during the cold war as a subject of tremendous significance. These regions became testing grounds, delimited and legible places where the ambitions of American militarism and social science could be localized. And psychological warfare was one means—perhaps the best means—to locally test such ambitions.

The anthropologist Carleton Coon, who operated under diplomatic cover in North Africa during the Second World War, stated that "it is probably the secret ambition of every boy to travel in strange mountains, stir up tribes, and destroy the enemy by secret and unorthodox means." Such sentiments, part of a long tradition of masculine adventure travel, were neither novel nor remarkable, and can be found in a variety of period literature.[29] Compact manuals and guides consulted and carried by soldiers and spies, in particular, were updated versions of the "hints" for colonial travelers, enacting a war on regions and their populations in advance of departure, but concurrently gesturing to earlier journeys steeped in violence. "Distant dangers," one aid tellingly titled *On Your Own* noted, "seem most hazardous. Remember this when you go into strange country."[30]

Another anthropologist sent overseas in World War II was Gregory Bateson, who spent much of 1944 and 1945 working for the legendary Office of Strategic Services (OSS) in Asia. Among his duties was the creation of false, exaggerated Japanese propaganda broadcasts in Thailand and Burma. Unlike his wife Margaret Mead, Bateson, who "took part in the communications systems which he helped to create or hoped to disrupt," grew disillusioned with applied anthropology after the war, perhaps because he had participated in much more visceral operations. Yet he seemed to throw himself headlong into his OSS tasks, which also included analysis of raw intelligence, composing papers on intelligence methodology, and even secret rescue missions. Nor did he hesitate to comment on the potential post-war role of the OSS in Asia, arguing that an American neocolonial order could, and should, be maintained by altering attitudes, and not necessarily through the traditional institutions of empire. By studying, encouraging, and shaping "native achievements," rather than imposing an external cultural model and risking the rise of "nativistic cults," the United States could ensure that nations such as India progressed in the appropriate direction. This was the classic psychological warfare approach standardized by the CIA after the war.[31] Indeed, while still in the field, Bateson was able to compose a sobering memo to his OSS boss, William Donovan, just days after the use of atomic weapons on Hiroshima and Nagasaki. For Bateson, the atomic bomb altered the "relation between attack and defense," increasing the likelihood of psychological and economic warfare as those with and without the technology sought to avoid atomic confrontation at all costs. Agencies responsible for the indirect, "peaceful" methods of combat would thus be even more pervasive and powerful after the war.[32]

Whether conducted at home or in the field, Second World War research in social psychology and anthropology was a key precedent for cold war area studies. While experimentalists preoccupied with problems of sensation and perception were participating in "man-machine" engineering research, another set of social scientists sought to comprehend the "national character" of German and Japanese foes. All of these efforts advanced psychological techniques and interdisciplinary approaches while concurrently articulating the relevance of social scientific authority within a democratic society, particularly one engaged in prolonged, global conflict. If nations possessed characters, cultures could then be diagnosed and classified as disordered, and psychology could lead to policy. This was, obviously, a narrow and even anticultural perspective on culture. Militarism allowed psychology to "operate as a weapon system" of the imagination, against "epidemics of irrational emotion and flawed national characters in need of containment or reconstruction."[33]

Given the Boasian critique of scientific racism that defined early twentieth-century anthropology, it was hardly surprising that many American anthropologists, beginning with Franz Boas himself (although he died in 1942), would take issue with Nazism. Several formed a Committee for National Morale (that included Mead, Bateson, Geoffrey Gorer, Ruth Benedict, Clyde Kluckhohn, and George P. Murdock) to promote the utility of interdisciplinary behavioural science even before Pearl Harbor. They and others then joined the rush of social scientists to war-related posts. Benedict, for instance, replaced Gorer as head analyst in the Office of War Information's (OWI) Overseas Intelligence Bureau in June 1943. This division prepared propaganda for enemy nations and distributed more innocuous information to allies and neutral states.[34]

The support of the War Department meant that studies of other cultures, positioned next to ongoing consideration of America's unique attributes, contributed substantially to the solidification of a regionalized world with the United States at its center. Crucially, the cultural foundations heralded in culture and personality research were consistently those of "America," and not "the West." This made sense given Europe's wartime horrors, and the role that America was beginning to play as the locus of a new modernity, but also for practical reasons of geopolitics made manifest by militarism. Far from presenting the placid version of relativism that was much maligned at the time, the psycho-anthropological work conducted during the war advocated a global geography that was certainly divided by culture and politics, but this division was discordant and hierarchical. It emphasized differences and the inherent flaws within other regions—not just those occupied by American enemies. Mead and others were beginning to walk the theoretical and practical tightrope that defined post-war area studies: an opposition to authoritarian forms of rule and persuasion, next to a desire or need to nudge populations towards democratic values, even if undemocratic techniques were required.

In its most simplistic variants, national-character study documented the acquisition by a culture of a singular personality. To create unity and pattern in a world of shifting alliances and heterogeneous populations, an integrated whole had to be created and bounded, at both cultural and global scales, and history had to be deemphasized in favor of timeless categories borrowed from fields such as psychiatry. Recognizing and defining this order meant an increased awareness of one's own pattern. Advocates of this approach focused on cultural anthropology and psychology.

Yet a largely unstated geographical element exerted significant influence as well. Even if certain habits might cut across regional and other differences, such speculation was halted by the geopolitical exigencies of war that favored blocs and states. In this respect Japan, widely viewed as completely homogeneous, was the perfect case study, as it was set apart from the United States through practices of demonization to a greater degree than any other foe.[35] And although Benedict and other innovative theorists such as Bateson were keenly aware that characters were constructed markers of difference depending on stereotypes, they defended these formations as nonetheless significant. They were norms from which one could speak of alterity—without fully comprehending complicity, whether immediately or though military application, in the continuation of essentialism.

But this long-range scrutiny aided by the compilation of various data sources and *not* by personal experience necessarily adopted a detached perspective, more prone to generalization and abstraction than even the most egregious colonial ethnographies. Grounded observation had been replaced by library research, interviews, study of popular cultural sources, and even statistical analysis. Individuals remained blurry and were relatively devoid of agency. These were all common themes in the study of totalitarianism that dominated cold war scholarship on the Communist bloc, and also in theories of psychological warfare working with, but extending far beyond, this same amorphous territory.

Psychwar and Area Studies

Hiroshima did not diminish Margaret Mead's interest in national cultures or in associations with the military. Shortly after the war, she and Ruth Benedict received a grant from the Human Resources Division of the Office of Naval Research (ONR) and, perhaps to limit association with wartime propaganda efforts, set aside the term "national character" for "cultures at a distance."[36] The Research in Contemporary Cultures initiative at Columbia University continued well after Benedict's untimely death in 1948, and was extended into "several successor projects," on Soviet Culture (for the Rand Corporation), and Contemporary Cultures (for the ONR and MIT's Center for International Studies). The ultimate result was a manual, presented first to the ONR in the autumn of 1951 and then published for popular consumption in 1953.[37] In a section titled "Political Applications," Mead noted that the methodology outlined in the manual had already aided in military occupation by facilitating interaction with allies and partisan groups in enemy countries, estimating the capabilities of opponents, and preparing foreign policy documents. All of these tasks required a diagnosis of "cultural regularities in the behavior of a particular group or groups of people that are relevant to the proposed action." Whether issuing propaganda, offering threats of reprisal, or announcing a new regulation, a "specific plan or policy" was consistently the anchor for cultural study, which would be used to predict the success of such plans and policies.[38] Not only did work on national character fail to fade after its flowering in the Second World War, then, but it also proved easily translatable—perhaps after shedding certain softer cultural and psychological elements, and occasionally shifting its spatial boundaries—to a much more widespread and mainstream form of social science.

In October 1950, a diverse group of psychwarriors gathered at MIT's Lexington Field Station, later journeying to Washington to meet with Secretary of State Dean Acheson. This gathering, called Project Troy, was a definitive moment in the creation of psychological techniques for waging the cold war. Although Troy's final report cited the Marshall Plan and other economic initiatives as important precedents, it also called these measures "defensive," and recommended a more aggressive and comprehensive program that could use social science to identify and distinguish "target populations" in the Soviet Union, Europe, and China.[39] Within just the "Cambridge complex" of Harvard and MIT institutes, Troy directly inspired several subsequent progeny, including Walt Rostow's study of Soviet social dynamics, interviews of refugees at Harvard's Russian Research Center, and the establishment of a permanent institute for political warfare at MIT. The last, the Center for International Studies (CENIS), was funded by the CIA and the Ford Foundation, and through the 1950s it "was a place where a wide variety of academic specialists could come together in academic surroundings to participate full- or part-time in classified research and discussions." But as conceived by MIT administrators and Ford Foundation staff, the "ultimate aim" of the CENIS was "the production of an alternative to Marxism."[40]

Unlike the strategists who plotted an impending Armageddon, the behavioral scientists at CENIS and related sites addressed banal forms of conflict. Those intrigued by the psychological and sociological aspects of battle were pushed to the forefront of social scientific research during the Korean War, when all but the most fervent planners resisted talk of atomic applications. Using the premise of an enemy "operational code" of political decision making, teams of advisors from the Air Force's Human Resources Research Institute and the Rand Corporation traveled to the Korean peninsula, where they found another formidable study set in the thousands of Chinese and Korean prisoners of war housed in United Nations compounds. This was "historical" research, but it could also be used to provide intelligence to future psykewar campaigns that would require data on target areas and their vulnerabilities.[41]

Another purveyor of psykewar advice was the Army's Special Operations Research Office (SORO), housed at American University in Washington, DC, and set up in 1957 to assist the preparation of intelligence studies on specific regions. SORO went on to achieve infamy for its role in the disastrous Project Camelot during the 1960s, but in 1958 it also began to produce Psychological Operations Handbooks providing "appeals and symbols of tested persuasiveness for communicating messages to specific audiences in a given country." These audiences comprised various social groups—ethnic, economic, and geographic—who were understood to be differentially susceptible to certain messages and techniques, and diversely opinioned on the subject of American influence.[42] The SORO and its older relative, the Operations Research Office, were essentially attempting to provide *maps* of a region's communications networks, both technical and cultural, that identified locations of weakness to be exploited by American propaganda campaigns. In tandem with the broader area studies movement, then, psychwarriors shared with colonial missionaries the goal of creating new, modern persons in an alien space, but the twentieth-century practitioners of imperial social science were also concerned with molding humans en masse.

Coming Home

During the Second World War, the Office of Strategic Services established an elaborate program of behavioral testing to weed out unsuitable recruits. Assisted by the distinguished social scientists Clyde Kluckhohn, Alexander Leighton, and Kurt Lewin, OSS staff scrutinized the actions of over five thousand candidates in intensive three- or one-day camps in the Washington, DC area. The summary report of this "Assessment of Men" is dense and heavily mathematical, the product of "months of statistical calculation" aided by IBM. It describes a rigorous schedule of tests, interviews, group tasks, questionnaires, and physical activities, including a "map memory" exercise, all intended to shed light on general variables such as motivation, emotional stability, leadership, and initiative. A further series of "special qualifications," including physical ability, observing films and reporting, resistance to interrogation, and propaganda skills were also considered. The aim was to move beyond distinct tests to an "organismic" understanding of the entire personality which, once built up, could be dissected into appropriate segments. What drove the results beyond mere psychoanalysis, the report concluded, was work in anthropology and sociology that had "furnished evidence of the determining influence of different cultural forms, ideological and behavioral."[43]

The OSS Assessment was only a dramatic example of a much broader interest in military psychology and human engineering spurred by the Second World War. Yale's Robert Yerkes, known for his comparative research with primates and his direction of mental testing in World War I, sought greater authority for the applied aspects of psychology that covered every type of military work, from training and morale to equipment design and punishment. Employing the term "engineering" was simply an appeal to the authority of science, an attractive and acceptable means of crossing from animals and mechanisms to humans as subjects of study. Psychology was objective and biological, and could be used "at every stage in the life cycle" to facilitate 'adjustment'— "matching human capacities to the technologies of modern warfare." That the psychological dimensions of hostility were expanded during the cold war was simply viewed as proof of the continued importance of human engineering.[44]

By the late 1950s, psychology and warfare, irrevocably twinned, had penetrated into the smallest of spaces, and bodies and brains had become thoroughly militarized. But as depicted and parodied in popular films such as *Invaders from Mars* (1953), *Them!* (1954), and *Invasion of the Body Snatchers* (1956), although "reds" remained a distinctly alien category, the threat of this Other could no longer be contained within a field of visible externality. Rather, danger emerged from *inside*, producing a problem of indeterminate identities and insecurity. At every interlocking scale of psychological warfare, borders broke down, and overseas operations merged in direction and intent with witch-hunts and civil defense rituals at home—in many cases literally so. Such blurring becomes strikingly cautionary when set next to the contemporary summary with which I began this chapter, even if the efforts of Karen Hughes and other Bush administration representatives are considered bumbling compared to the coordinated, cultured rhetoric produced by the United States Information Agency and other divisions of the cold war public diplomacy program.[45]

Inside the indefinite boundaries of the homeland, moreover, we have recently witnessed another set of school drills, urban simulations, propaganda-heavy press conferences, and, most importantly, calls for the mobilization of minds in the service of American militarism. The legendary Duck and Cover exercises held in schools during the cold war have been replaced by the Ready Deputy Contest, which sent students into their neighborhoods as recruiters, directing families to assemble emergency preparedness kits. The school enlisting the most families received $10,000 and Secretary Ridge as Principal for a day. (The deadline was October 29, 2004, four days before the presidential election.)[46] Meanwhile, the desert town of Playas, New Mexico has been purchased by the Department of Homeland Security as a location for antiterrorism training, while the militarized "empty space" of the Nevada Test Site received $13 million dollars in 2004 for the construction of "mock border stations, a simulated airline inspection terminal and a seaport" to stage the transmission of radiological materials into the country and practice preventative techniques.[47] Fifty years ago, the same landscape was used to demonstrate the effects of atomic weapons on "typical" American housing.[48] The Bush administration has been repeatedly charged with underfunding certain aspects of homeland security—certainly compared to its widespread military operations, but specifically in places such as New York City, a policy that resembles the write-off of certain urban areas as doomed (and dangerous, should their populations spill outward) during the 1950s.[49] And finally, a series of major exercises have simulated biological and other attacks in places such as Seattle and Chicago, where during 2003's TOPOFF 2 the spread of plague was supplemented by a concurrent (staged) explosion and plane crash, so as to involve more response agencies.[50]

These anxious initiatives are a reminder of a similar event in Spokane, Washington, in 1954:

> National Guardsmen were posted at street corners; emergency civil defense and military vehicles moved on the streets; anti-aircraft and machine gunners fired their weapons from the roof tops of several buildings; jet fighter planes and bombers flew over the area.... At 10 a.m., to simulate an attack, a bomber dropped leaflets over the city, saying "This might have been an H-bomb." The bomber missed the target area, and the pamphlets fell on an outlying residential district near one of the theoretical evacuation zones.[51]

Only in noting historical precedents for more recent formations of political violence, then, will we understand the significance of the scientist and cold warrior Lloyd Berkner's 1952 comment that "Our interest in disasters stems not so much from their spectacular aspects, as from the fact of our growing realization that even the worst events can be brought under some measure of control."[52]

Notes

1. James Dao and Eric Schmitt, "Pentagon Readies Efforts to Sway Sentiment Abroad," *The New York Times,* February 19, 2002. As a Fairness and Accuracy in Reporting (FAIR) analysis of the OSI noted, the American government is not permitted to distribute propaganda domestically, "but it's almost certain that any large-scale disinformation campaign directed at the foreign press would have led, sooner or later, to a falsified story being picked up by U.S. media" (see Rachel Coen, "Behind the Pentagon's Propaganda Plan, *Extra! Update* April 2002 (http://www.fair.org/extra/0204/osi.html). A subsequent FAIR advisory noted that while the OSI was disbanded, its responsibilities may have simply been reassigned and spread across other secret branches of the Defense Department, including a "strategic communications" office established in September 2004 to "combine public affairs, psychological operations and information operations." "The Office of Strategic Influence Is Gone, But Are Its Programs In Place?" November 27, 2002 (http://www.fair.org/press-releases/osi-followup.html); Frank Rich, "Operation Iraqi Infoganda," *New York Times,* March 28, 2004; Mark Mazzetti, "PR Meets Psy-Ops in War on Terror," *Los Angeles Times,* December 1, 2004; Thom Shanker and Eric Schmitt, "Pentagon Weighs Use of Deception in a Broad Arena," *New York Times,* December 13, 2004.

2. Steven R. Weisman, "U.S. Faulted on Hostile Image in Arab World," *International Herald Tribune,* October 2, 2003.

3. Christopher Marquis, "Promoter of U.S. Image Quits for Wall Street Job," *New York Times,* April 30, 2004; Ellen Goodman, "Those Images of Abuse Have Hit US Hard," *Boston Globe,* May 6, 2004; Daniel Henninger, "America's Missing Voice," *Wall Street Journal,* May 7, 2004. Hersh's important articles on the subject have been collected in *Chain of Command: The Road from 9/11 to Abu Ghraib* (New York: HarperCollins, 2004).

4. Steven Weisman, "Hughes, New U.S. Envoy, Makes First Diplomatic Effort," *The New York Times,* September 25, 2005; Glenn Kessler, "Hughes Reaches Out Warily in Cairo," *Washington Post,* September 26, 2005, A16; Fred Kaplan, "Karen Hughes, Stay Home! *Slate,* September 29, 2005 (http://www.slate.com/id/2127102/).

5. Peter Brownfield, "Diplomats Look to Cold War Tactics for Help in Arab World," *Fox News* 26 May 2004 (http://www.foxnews.com/story/0,2933,120922,00.html); Ed Finn, "Unhip, Unhip Al Hurra," *Slate,* February 20, 2004 (http://slate.msn.com/id/2095806); Faye Bowers, "Al Hurra Joins Battle for News, Hearts, and Minds," *Christian Science Monitor,* February 24, 2004. It was Al-Hurra that President Bush gave an interview to on May 5, 2004 after the revelations of torture at Abu Ghraib.

6. "Editor of U.S.-funded Iraqi Newspaper Quits," *Toronto Star,* May 3, 2004.

7. See the report of PEW's nine-country survey, dated March 16, 2004 (at http://peoplepress.org/reports/pdf/206.pdf). Among the many columns on this subject, see Paul Krugman, "America's Lost Respect," *New York Times,* October 1, 2004. Intriguingly, few American cultural and economic icons appeared to be suffering; see Simon Romero, "War and Abuse Do Little to Harm U.S. Brands," *New York Times,* May 9, 2004.

8. Howard LaFranchi, "US-Muslim Relations: Hard Choices Ahead," *Christian Science Monitor* November 2, 2004 (at http://www.csmonitor.com/2004/1102/p03s01-usfp.html).

9. Neil Smith, "Scales of Terror and the Resort to Geography: September 11, October 7," *Environment and Planning D: Society and Space* 19 (2001): 631–637.

10. Among the many commentaries in which this comparison can be found, see Robert Kuttner, "Vigilance Needed as Cold War II Grips US," *Boston Globe,* December 3, 2001 (at http://www.commondreams.org/views01/1203-03.htm). Many writers have rued the absence of the cold war's "successful" United States Information Agency (USIA) and its various programs; see, for instance, John Hughes, "A Cold War Tool for the Terror Era," *Christian Science Monitor,* May 5, 2004. One of the more intriguing reprisals of a cold war worldview under the banner of a "war on terror" is the rebirth of the Committee on the Present Danger, which itself had two cold war manifestations. See Laura Rozen, "The Resurrection," *Alternet,* August 25, 2004 (http://www.alternet.org/story/19647).

11. "Mr. Ridge's Red Alert Day," *New York Times,* December 1, 2004; Matthew Sparke, "Outsides Inside Patriotism: The Oklahoma Bombing and the Displacement of Heartland Geopolitics," in Gearóid Ó Tuathail and Simon Dalby, eds., *Rethinking Geopolitics* (London: Routledge, 1998), 198–223; Deborah Cowen, "From the American Lebensraum to the American Living Room: Class, Sexuality and the Scaled Production of 'Domestic' Intimacy," *Environment and Planning D: Society and Space* 22 (2004): pp. 755–771; Michael Billig, *Banal Nationalism* (London: SAGE, 1995).

12. Ellen Herman, *The Romance of American Psychology: Political Culture in the Age of Experts* (Berkeley: University of California Press, 1995), 137, 124.

13. William E. Daugherty, with Morris Janowitz, *A Psychological Warfare Casebook* (Baltimore: The Johns Hopkins Press, 1958), 2, original emphasis.

14. See, in particular, Laura McEnaney, *Civil Defense Begins at Home: Militarization Meets Everyday Life in the Fifties* (Princeton, NJ: Princeton University Press, 2000).

15. See Robert Corber, *In the Name of National Security: Hitchcock, Homophobia, and the Political Construction of Gender in Postwar America* (Durham, NC: Duke University Press, 1993).

16. See, for example, Christopher Simpson, *Science of Coercion: Communication Research and Psychological Warfare 1945–1960* (New York: Oxford University Press, 1994); Walter L. Hixson, *Parting the Curtain: Propaganda, Culture, and the Cold War, 1945–1961* (New York: St. Martin's, 1998); James H. Capshew, *Psychologists on the March: Science, Practice, and Professional Identity in America, 1929–1969* (Cambridge: Cambridge University Press, 1999); Ron Robin, *The Making of the Cold War Enemy: Culture and Politics in the Military-Industrial Complex* (Princeton, NJ: Princeton University Press, 2001).

17. Michel Foucault, *"Society Must Be Defended": Lectures at the Collège de France, 1975–76,* trans. David Macey (New York: Picador, 2003), 15; Julian Reid, "Foucault on Clausewitz: Conceptualizing the Relationship Between War and Power," *Alternatives* 28 (2003): 1–28; Mark Neocleous, "Perpetual War, or 'War and War Again': Schmitt, Foucault, Fascism," *Philosophy and Social Criticism* 22.2 (1996):. 47–66; Edward Barrett, *Truth is Our Weapon* (New York: Funk and Wagnalls, 1953). In a speech to the Institute of Peace on August 19, 2004, National Security Advisor Condoleezza Rice cited the cold war as a model for the "war of ideas" with populations in the Middle East, arguing that "truth serves the cause of freedom." See "Rice: U.S. Using Cold War Techniques in War on Terror" (http://www.cnn.com/2004/ALLPOLITICS/08/19/rice-muslims).

18. I have written at length on these latter topics in Matthew Farish, "Disaster and Decentralization: American Cities and the Cold War," *Cultural Geographies* 10 (2003): 125–148; and "Another Anxious Urbanism: Defence and Disaster in Cold

War America," in Steven Graham, ed., *Cities, War and Terrorism: Towards an Urban Geopolitics* (Oxford: Blackwell, 2004), 93–109.

19. Nikolas Rose, *Governing the Soul: The Shaping of the Private Self*, 2nd ed. (London: Free Association Books, 1999), viii, my emphasis.

20. Daniel Lerner, "American Wehrpolitik and the Military Elite," *The New Leader* (April 26, 1954): pp. 21–22; the quote is from p. 21; Lerner, *Sykewar: Psychological Warfare against Germany, D-Day to VE-Day* (New York: G. E. Stewart, 1949).

21. See Denis Cosgrove, *Apollo's Eye: A Cartographic Genealogy of the Earth in the Western Imagination* (Baltimore: John Hopkins University Press, 2001).

22. Mackinder is quoted in Jonathan Haslam, *No Virtue like Necessity: Realist Thought in International Relations Since Machiavelli* (New Haven, CT: Yale University Press, 2002), 173; see also Paul N. Edwards, *The Closed World: Computers and the Politics of Discourse in Cold War America* (Cambridge: The MIT Press, 1996), 8.

23. Quoted in Herman, *The Romance of American Psychology*, 135.

24. Ann Douglas, "Periodizing the American Century: Modernism, Postmodernism, and Postcolonialism in the Cold War Context," *Modernism/Modernity* 5.3 (1998), 71–98; Leerom Medovoi, "Cold War American Culture as the Age of Three Worlds," *The Minnesota Review* 55-57 (2002): 167–186; Christina Klein, "The Sentimental Culture of Global Integration," *The Minnesota Review* 55-57 (2002): 153–165; the quote is from p. 153.

25. Amy Kaplan, "Homeland Insecurities: Reflections on Language and Space," *Radical History Review* 85 (2003):. 82–93; the quote is from p. 87. "If the attacks of September 11 punctured this delusion of geographical exceptionalism, the anxious nationalization of these events since September 11 simultaneously worked to reassert US exceptionalism while framing Americanism *as* globalism." Smith, "Scales of Terror," 635.

26. Isaiah Bowman, "A Department of Geography," *Science* 98.2556 (December 24, 1943): 564–566; the quote is from p. 564.

27. Arnold Wolfers, "Theory of International Politics: Its Merits and Advancement," in RG (Record Group) 3.1, Series 910, Box 8, Folder 69, Rockefeller Foundation Papers, Rockefeller Archive Center, Tarrytown, New York, 4.

28. "NSC-68," April 14, 1950, in Thomas H. Etzold and John Lewis Gaddis, eds., *Containment: Documents on American Foreign Policy and Strategy, 1945–50* (New York: Columbia University Press, 1978), 385–442; the quotes are from pp. 387, 384; Anders Stephanson, "Fourteen Notes on the Very Concept of the Cold War," in Ó Tuathail and Dalby, eds., *Rethinking Geopolitics* (London: Routledge, 1998), 62–85; the quote is from p. 80; David Campbell, *Writing Security: United States Foreign Policy and the Politics of Identity*, revised ed. (Minneapolis: University of Minnesota Press, 1998), 23.

29. Carleton S. Coon, *A North Africa Story: The Anthropologist as OSS Agent, 1941–1943* (Ipswich, MA: Gambit, 1980), 3.

30. Samuel A. Graham and Earl C. O'Roke, *On Your Own: How to Take Care of Yourself in Wild Country—a Manual for Field and Service Men* (Minneapolis: The University of Minnesota Press, 1943), 148. For more on the political and cultural geography of Second World War area studies, see my "Archiving Areas: The Ethnogeographic Board and the Second World War," *Annals of the Association of American Geographers* 95.3 (2005): 663–679.

31. Virginia Yans-McLaughlin, "*Science, Democracy, and Ethics* "Science, Democracy, and Ethics: Mobilizing Culture and Personality for World War II," in *Malinowski,*

Rivers, Benedict and Others: Essays on Culture and Personality, ed. George W. Stocking, Jr. (Madison: The University of Wisconsin Press, 1986), 184–217; the quotes are from pp. 202–203; David Price, "Gregory Bateson and the OSS: World War II and Bateson's Assessment of Applied Anthropology," *Human Organization* 57.4 (1998), 379–384.

32. Memo, Gregory Bateson to General Donovan, "Influence of Atomic Bomb on Indirect Methods of Warfare," August 18, 1945, RG 263, Entry 15, Box 2, Folder 35, National Archives and Records Administration, College Park, MD, original emphasis.

33. Herman, *The Romance of American Psychology*, 305.

34. David Price, "Lessons from Second World War Anthropology: Peripheral, Persuasive and Ignored Contributions," *Anthropology Today* 18.3 (2002): 14–20.

35. See John Dower, *War Without Mercy: Race and Power in the Pacific War* (New York: Pantheon, 1986).

36. Judith S. Modell, *Ruth Benedict: Patterns of a Life* (Philadelphia: University of Pennsylvania Press, 1983), 292.

37. Margaret Mead and Rhoda Métraux, eds., *The Study of Culture at a Distance* (Chicago: The University of Chicago Press, 1953); see also Eric R. Wolf and Joseph G. Jorgensen, "A Special Supplement: Anthropology on the Warpath in Thailand," *The New York Review of Books* 15.9 (November 19, 1970), at ⟨http://www.nybooks.com/articles/10763⟩.

38. Mead and Métraux, eds., *The Study of Cultures at a Distance*, 397.

39. Simpson, *Science of Coercion*, 8; Allan A. Needell, "'Truth Is Our Weapon': Project Troy, Political Warfare, and Government-Academic Relations in the National Security State," *Diplomatic History* 17.3 (1993): 399–420; the quotes are from pp. 409, 411. Needell points out that Troy also led directly to the creation of the Psychological Strategy Board (PSB), which reported to the National Security Council and included representatives from the CIA and the Departments of State and Defense. On the PSB, see Edward P. Lilly, "The Psychological Strategy Board and its Predecessors: Foreign Policy Coordination, 1938–1953," in Gaetano L. Vincitorio, ed., *Studies in Modern History* (New York: St. John's University Press, 1968), 337–382; and Robin, *The Making of the Cold War Enemy*, 42–43. The Soviet Union also ran a "large and reasonably sophisticated psychological warfare campaign against the United States." See Simpson, *Science of Coercion*, 7.

40. "The Nature and Objectives of the Center for International Studies," August 1953, in AC 4, Box 48, Folder 16, MIT Archives; Needell, "'Truth Is Our Weapon'," 417, 419; George Rosen, *Western Economists and Eastern Societies: Agents of Change in South Asia, 1950–1970* (Baltimore: Johns Hopkins University Press, 1985), 28. In his memoirs, MIT President James Killian recalled the CENIS thusly: "the CIA funding was later to bring into question the freedom of the center's work, even though those of use who knew the individuals involved had complete confidence in their intellectual integrity. I shared in this [funding] decision and came to regret it." James R. Killian Jr., *The Education of a College President: A Memoir* (Cambridge: The MIT Press, 1985), 67. The CENIS dissolved its ties to the CIA in 1965.

41. Raymond V. Bowers, "The Military Establishment," in *The Uses of Sociology*, eds. Paul F. Lazarsfeld, William H. Sewell, and Harold L. Wilensky (New York: Basic Books, 1967), 234–274, especially 243–244; Robin, *The Making of the Cold War Enemy*, 8–10; "Role of Intelligence, Research, and Analysis in Psychological Warfare," in Daugherty, with Janowitz, *A Psychological Warfare Casebook*, 425–430. No specific author

was given for this chapter. But the contributors to the casebook included McGeorge Bundy, Merle Fainsod, Alex Inkeles, and Clyde Kluckhohn, all of Harvard; Daniel Lerner and Lucien Pye of MIT; and Alexander Leighton, then in Cornell's Sociology Department. "Operational code" is drawn from Nathan C. Leites, *The Operational Code of the Politburo* (New York: McGraw-Hill, 1951), a study prepared for the Rand Corporation.

42. Bowers, "The Military Establishment," 246.

43. The OSS Assessment Staff, *Assessment of Men: Selection of Personnel for the Office of Strategic Services* (New York: Rinehart and Co., 1948), 3–4, 30–31, 124, 467; Capshew, *Psychologists on the March*, 111–114.

44. Robert M. Yerkes, "Man-Power and Military Effectiveness: The Case for Human Engineering," *Journal of Consulting Psychology* 5.5 (1941): 205–209; Walter V. Bingham, "Military Psychology in War and Peace," *Science* 106.2747 (August 22, 1947): 155–160; Capshew, *Psychologists on the March*, 48–51, 54, 144–145; Donna J. Haraway, "A Pilot Plant for Human Engineering: Robert Yerkes and the Yale Laboratories of Primate Biology, 1924–1942," in her *Primate Visions: Gender, Race, and Nature in the World of Modern Science* (New York: Routledge, 1989), 59–83.

45. Kaplan, "Karen Hughes, Stay Home!"

46. See http://www.americaprepared.org/rd_rules.html. Ridge, of course, announced his resignation on November 30, 2004, with a decidedly mixed record as Secretary. President Bush's first choice for a successor, former New York Police Commissioner Bernard Kerik, was a spectacular failure, while the second, federal judge Michael Chertoff, oversaw many of the most controversial domestic aspects of the "war on terror" while serving as Assistant Attorney General under John Ashcroft. See Eric Lichtblau and Christopher Drew, "Ridge's Record: Color Alerts and Mixed Security Reviews," *New York Times,* December 1, 2004; William Branigin, "Chertoff Named to Head Homeland Security," *Washington Post,* January 11, 2005.

47. Simon Romero, "In Desert Town, Training for 'Terror Attacks'," *New York Times,* September 26, 2004; Steve Tetreault, "Test Site Gets New Security Mission," *Las Vegas Review-Journal,* June 9, 2004 (http://www.reviewjournal.com/lvrj_home/2004/Jun-09-Wed-2004/news/24066101.html).

48. See Tom Vanderbilt, *Survival City: Adventures among the Ruins of Atomic America* (Princeton, NJ: Princeton Architectural Press, 2002).

49. For two devastating liberal critiques, see Jonathan Chait, "The 9/10 President: Bush's Abysmal Failure on Homeland Security," *The New Republic,* March 10, 2003, and Michael Crowley, "Playing Defense: Bush's Disastrous Homeland Security Department," *The New Republic,* March 15, 2004. See also Amanda Ripley, "How We Got Homeland Security Wrong," *Time,* March 29, 2004 (http://www.time.com/time/archive/preview/0,10987,1101040329-603192,00.html); Jack Newfield, "Bush to City: Drop Dead," *The Nation,* April 19, 2004 (http://www.thenation.com/doc.mhtml?i=20040419&s=newfield); "Nickel and Diming Homeland Security," *Mother Jones* September/October 2004 (http://www.motherjones.com/news/feature/2004/09/08_402.html); John Mintz and Joby Warrick, "U.S. Unprepared Despite Progress, Experts Say," *Washington Post,* November 8, 2004; Mimi Hall, "Terror Target List Way Behind," *USA Today,* December 8, 2004 (http://www.usatoday.com/news/washington/2004-12-08-terror-database_x.htm).

50. Gene Johnson, "Mock Explosion Launches Bioterror Drill," *Washington Post,* May 13, 2003. "A detailed, 200-page scenario has been written for the drill, which offi-

cials said will look as realistic as possible. Stand-ins will portray President Bush, Vice President Cheney and even White House press secretary Ari Fleisher."

51. This summary quote can be found in the Disaster Research Group Folder, National Academy of Sciences-National Research Council Archives, Washington, D.C.

52. "The Common Aspects of Disasters," Box 9, Folder "Speeches and Papers – LVB: AAAS Symposium on Disaster Recovery: St. Louis – 12/27/52," Lloyd V. Berkner Papers, Library of Congress Manuscript Division, Washington, D.C., 7.

14

Immaculate Warfare? The Spatial Politics of Extreme Violence

Nigel Thrift

If "future" becomes a war casualty, it comes not of "losing" or "winning," but in the sheer fact of violence … neither the impact nor the amelioration of violence will make sense if violence is configured only as a physical act. It is in the more intangible realms of the existential—the meaning of existence—that violence takes its definition and its toll. (Nordstrom 2004, 69)

In the twentieth century, the idea of human universality rests less on hope than on fear, less on optimism about the human capacity for good than on dread of human capacity for evil, less on a vision of man as maker of his history than of man the wolf toward his own kind. The way stations on the road to this new internationalism were Armenia, Verdun, the Russian front, Auschwitz, Hiroshima, Vietnam, Cambodia, Lebanon, Rwanda and Bosnia. A century of total war has made victims of us all, civilians and military, men, women and children alike. (Ignatieff 1997, 18-19)

Introduction

The debate continues but, so far as we know, aggression and violence are all but constants of human life. There seem to be few human societies in which these phenomena are not present and do not do their work in one form or another: violence and bloodletting are a key part of humanity's cultural heritage, not an aberration. For example, many commentators have argued that war is a normal state of human affairs and, it has to be said, the evidence so far is markedly on their side. As Carolyn Nordstrom (2004, 43) puts it:

> In the twentieth century alone, over 250 formally declared wars took over 100 million lives. Undeclared wars–political repression, communal violence, and tribal genocide–took millions more; for example, between 50 and 100 million tribal people have been killed by forces and citizens of states in the last century. As we enter the third millennium, one third of the world's

countries are engaged in some form of political violence. In addition, approximately two thirds of the world's security forces routinely violate human rights. Wars today are longer in duration, deadlier, and kill higher percentages of civilians than wars of preceding centuries.

For all that, Georges Sorel's judgment of 1906 in the classic *Reflections on Violence* in large part continues to ring true: "the problems of violence still remain obscure." Part of the reason for this state of affairs is that practices of violence and aggression still tend to be treated as phenomena derived from other phenomena, such as state or nation,[1] rather than as phenomena existing in their own right. In what follows, in order to right this particular ship, I want to take an excerpt from a larger project that I have been engaged on for some time now that is concerned with the phenomenality of violence itself and how that phenomenality is currently being manifested (see Thrift 2005). That may seem a long way off from the dreadful litany of violence to be found in places like Palestine or Chechnya or Tibet or the Sudan or the Congo or …. but it will come as no surprise to find that I will be arguing the opposite.[2]

What do I mean by phenomenality? I mean that which appears, which is prior to ontology in that appearing is more essential than being (Seel 2004). And violence is what I call, following the work of Michel Henry (2003a), an affective auto-revelation. That is, it constantly produces its own affective essence, generates its own affective terms. This means that I want to blur the edges of violence, by arguing that violence is not just the physical trauma of bullet penetrating body or fist impacting jaw or knife rending flesh or, indeed, bomb cutting a swathe through an unsuspecting street (an example to which I will return). Rather, it is a line of flight which is expanding its grip through the invention of new kinds of affective performance.[3]

Why should I take this particular tack? There are four main reasons. First, and most generally, I am concerned to produce a democratic politics which is at the same time realistic about human capacities, and especially their *biological* structuring without, at the same time, imagining that violence should be counted as just a pre-given state of nature (c.f. Thrift 2005). But, I am not willing to become mired in utopian thinking, precisely because that seems to be one of the main determinants of certain kinds of violence and especially the presumption of the right to kill (Weitz 2003). Nor am I willing to become trapped by the kind of sentimental thinking that currently characterizes the affective episteme[4] of Western liberal democracies; for reasons that will become clear below I believe that that particular current of thought has become as much a part of the problem as it is a part of the solution. Second, because I am concerned to demonstrate that violence and aggression are not just negative qualities, as they are so often portrayed. Indeed they may, in certain situations, be positive performative presences. Like Isabelle Stengers (2002), I do not want to automatically renounce all violence everywhere but, also like her, neither am I drawn to it in a way that some on the left have undoubtedly been.[5] Third, because I want to show the crucial determinations produced by space in setting up and breeding certain forms of violence. Spaces do not just provide a context, they provide a medium and a means and a momentum, as well as a measure. Fourth, because I want to argue that there are practicable affective measures that can be taken to combat certain forms of violence. In particular, there is the possibility of working on and stimulating *compassion*, understood as the strongest form of positive passion because it taps into *practical* wells of affect, rather than making affective flourishes that soon run dry (Berlant 2004).

Recently, I have been concentrating more and more of my attention on this politics of affect (c.f. Thrift 2004, 2005).[6] There is no more pressing illustration of the importance of that politics than those contemporary "necropolitical" (Mbembe 2003) arenas that have brought forth such a desperate practice as suicide bombing, a practice I will examine in some detail. These arenas are inhabited by determinate political situations which are difficult to resolve, not least because they are beset by shifting affective fields which can complicate matters immeasurably, habitations of affect which clearly vary in their cultural form, function and range but which all exert their own kinds of power over the situation. Affects that are commonly identified—in Western cultures, at least—by words like despair and anger and fear and hatred[7] produce spaces in which any kind of progress or dialogue becomes difficult, most particularly because they instil a kind of hopelessness: 'violence isn't intended to stop with the crippling of physical bodies. Violence is employed to create political acquiescence; it is intended to create terror, and thus political inertia; it is intended to create hierarchies of domination and submission based on the control of force. As Elaine Scarry writes, it "unmakes the world" (Nordstrom 2004, 61). I would therefore argue that any political strategy for peace and reconciliation (when it even makes sense to consider this as an option) needs to think much more extensively about affect and must explicitly include a politics of hope (rather than simple optimism): only if agonistic parties can locate a different kind of time together can progress be made (Miyazaki 2004).

This chapter is in four parts. The first part briefly contemplates the nature of collective violence. Above all, I will be concerned to show that a certain disposition to violence is probably an indispensable part of being in the world, a necessary accompaniment to dwelling. It is also a biopolitical manifestation, not just because violence is increasingly mixed in with an ability to mark exception by counting "those who do nothing but reproduce their own multiplicity and who, for this very reason, do not deserve to be counted" (Rancière 1998, 121) but also because it is part of the auto-affection of life and must be thought of, therefore, as a signification which is more than the perception of life itself: "to signify means to 'aim into the void' in such a way that no intuition of reality yet corresponds with this target" (Henry 2003b, 40). In other words, to repeat a point made previously, I want to take a quasi-phenomenological approach to violence, but I want to concentrate on those aspects of structures of *appearing* that are too often ignored in that approach, namely aspects to do with violence, discomfort, and a sense of lack of fit to the world as it presents. Such an emphasis on appearing has obvious and inescapable aesthetic dimensions which, I will argue, are particularly applicable to violence in many of its manifestations and need to be faced up to. I will therefore take my cue not just from the biopolitical thinking represented by, for example, Foucault's historical problematology and by Agamben's approach to "radical evil",[8] which can be too heavy-handed, but also from the processual and heavily affective view of life represented by the process philosophy of Whitehead and Zubiri and by the "return to religion" to be found in European philosophy, as represented by authors like Henry, Girard, Žižek, and others.

The second part of the chapter draws attention to one particular kind of violence currently being perpetrated in a whole series of current struggles, namely the rise of

the relatively new violence specialism (Tilly 2003), suicide bombing. This form of violence is considered first of all as a mundane practice in the manner of the sociology of
science. For it is important to understand that forms of violence like suicide bombing
are, in certain senses, everyday practices, backed up by more or less informal support
networks (Knorr-Cetina 2005). But they also have important aesthetic dimensions
which, precisely, are intended to exceed the condition of everyday living by abandoning its relation to life (Bell 2005).

The third part of the chapter considers these aesthetic dimensions and the way that,
when presented to the West, they fall back into a dramatized melodramatic consciousness that forces their violence into a culturally prepared frame of victim and victimizer
that annuls their affective force. Then, in the fourth part of the chapter, I will attempt
to draw some tentative political lessons. I will want to make a distinction between a
politics of pity and a politics of compassion. I will argue that one of the prime political
tasks now is to begin to build up more institutions of compassion and to leave behind
the politics of pity that frameworks like melodrama inculcate. Some very brief conclusions concerning the practicalities of this task round out the chapter.

My main political goal is simple in any case: "to demonstrate that peace may be reinvented as the biopolitical condition of life" (Alliez and Negri 2003, 16), just as long
as, paradoxically, that peace includes a place for violence.

The Ways of Violence

Violence potentially encompasses "a vast range of social interactions" (Tilly 2003,
4). But the classic account of violence is clearly the one provided by Hannah Arendt
(1970). In it, Arendt argues that primal human violence has three major characteristics: it involves the affect of rage, it acts without argument or a counting of the consequences, and it is fast:

> There are situations in which the very swiftness of a violent act may be the only appropri-
> ate remedy. The point is not that this permits us to let off steam—which can indeed be done
> equally by pounding the table or slamming the door. The point is that under certain circum-
> stances violence … is the only way to set the scales of justice right again. … In this sense,
> rage and the violence that sometimes —not always—goes with it belong among the "natural"
> human emotions, and to cure man of them would mean nothing less than to dehumanize or
> emasculate him. (Arendt 1970, 63–64)

No doubt, such a description still fits many kinds of violence: brawls in the street,
many kinds of domestic violence, and so on. But it is easy to argue that collective
violence is often unlike this description, though it may still have elements of it. Collective violence usually involves a range of other affects, it acts with considerable
calculation that nearly always involves some level of planning, and it can take a long
time to build. One of the reasons for this is clearly the growth of institutions that
apply violence selectively and to determinate ends: most especially, the state or various parastatal forms typical of large parts of the world at present (Tilly 2003). A second reason is the related growth of primary means of thinking like race and nation
with their ability to produce not only new forms of identity but also new categories
of other (Weitz 2003). A third reason is the growth of new imaginaries of violence, as

in the reaction to the industrial-scale killing of the First World War that did not just produce revulsion but also fascination and desire (Weitz 2003). These imaginaries have been massively fuelled by the growth of the mass media: though it is a cliché, it is also true that much modern violence presupposes an aesthetic appeal to a mass of witnesses based on firing up a brief commotion somewhere between art and pain (Spivey 2001, Sontag 2003), a point to which I will return at much greater length below. A fourth reason is the growth of mass participation—and complicity—as wars and similar disputes have expanded their orbit, such that 'the boundary between the guilt of the few and the innocence of many blended away' (Weitz 2003, 242). A fifth reason is also pointed to by Arendt—violence "needs implements." Violence is not an appearing that arises just from the human body, traditionally conceived, but from the alignment of the body with all kind of prostheses, whether the prosthesis is a smashed glass or a jet fighter. Indeed, given that this is the case, it is possible to argue that violence is best treated using the same approach as the sociology of science and this is what I will make a cursory attempt to do in what follows. I will argue that violence is an expanding series of practices in which objects—many of them of a sophisticated kind—have a more than incidental place and that, increasingly, violence works to an agenda driven by the requirements of these objects, and not least the affective landscape being produced by the media. A final and related reason is therefore increasingly what might be called the aesthetic dimension, a dimension which has usually been constructed over many centuries of interpretation and counter-interpretation: violence is, after all, *performative* (Whitehead 2004).

A New Form of Violence

So how might we think about these practices of collective violence? I want to trace out the genealogy of one particular practice of violence specialism in some detail, namely suicide bombing and how and why it has impacted on Western liberal democracies (Hage 2003).

In its current form, suicide bombing is a comparatively recent martial development. It seems to have been pioneered by religious organizations like Hamas and Hizbollah who, from 1982, carried out a number of such operations in Lebanon and Israel. Attacks have continued through the 1980s and 1990s, with incidents also taking place in many other parts of the world, including eastern Turkey, Egypt, India, Chechnya (and, by extension, Russia), Uzbekistan, and Sri Lanka. From the considerable number of studies now available, it seems that the bombers form something of a contrast to the ideal of Japanese kamikaze pilots who are sometimes thought of as progenitors. Suicide bombers are predominantly but not only recruited from extremely violent environments in which the act may seem a familiar part of life: "the story of suicide bombing is a story of people driven to extremes. 'Children who have seen so much inhumanity,' El-Sarraj states, "inevitably come out with inhuman responses"" (Rose 2004, 24).[9]

That may well be one of the few things that most (but even here, not all) suicide bombers share in common. Suicide bombers seem to occupy a very wide spectrum of backgrounds and preoccupations. For example, though often portrayed as young, poor, and ignorant, in fact they occupy a large age range—from 15 to 55—are likely to be intelligent, may well be well-educated (as in the use by Hamas of two highly educated British suicide bombers in an operation in Israel in 2003),[10] and are as likely to have job and family as not. Some have been brought up in determinate quasi-military organizations[11] where they may train for martyrdom from an early age, even marching with mock explosives tied to them to familiarize them with the mechanics of the act.[12] Others have not. The reasons that individual suicide bombers may have for choosing their fate are many: they may include revenge, humiliation, or despair mixed with the powerful pull of sacralized causes like religion or nationalism. Indeed, though suicide bombing is often portrayed as an act of religious fundamentalism, most of the time the sacralized cause is as much national as religious.[13]

Gender has also become a significant factor of late. Female suicide bombers have become a staple of some campaigns since their first use by Kurdish dissidents in Turkey in 1996–1999. Women have become routinely involved in the conflict in Chechnya. In Palestine, their use is much more recent, really only dating from January 2002. Reasons for that use are partly contextual: in Chechnya so many young men are in prison that women have become a kind of reserve army. In Palestine, women seem to have been used because they are more likely to get through checkpoints (Victor 2003). But usage is also bound up with the greater media exposure that women can gain: pictures of women "martyrs" (or their children) are likely to produce greater press interest and audience response, a point I will return to below.

Whatever the specificities of background and particular preoccupation may be, the use of suicide bombers has now become institutionalized in some theaters of conflict; for example, in the current hostilities in Iraq coordinated use of suicide bombers has been a constant. But it is also important to note that suicide bombing is usually seen as part of a spectrum of martial activity, and not just as a means in itself.

Suicide attacks are hardly a novel feature of collective conflict. Through history, one of the options open to those engaged in conflict has been self-immolation in the cause of a cause. Clearly, such a practice could be loaded with a lot of affective freight in current circumstances. But, at least to begin with, I want to consider this practice as precisely that and inquire as to how exactly it was able to come into existence as simply a mundane organization of various objects and organizational resources. This is to argue that violence is not just channelled by objects but is, to a considerable degree, created by them.

Suicide bombing has become a weapon in the arsenal of conflict because of a number of mundane developments have made it into a more feasible option than it formerly was. First, because in most of the arenas of conflict in which suicide bombing is used striking at targets has become much harder as these targets have become "target-hardened" through the application of more and more defence and surveillance technologies. But attacks on military and civilian populations in streets and quasi-public arenas like hotels or clubs or markets by relatively small quasi-military organizations using a flexible military technology like suicide bombing are still comparatively easy to make, especially when these organizations cannot easily gain access to other modern weaponry. As one leader of Islamic Jihad in the Gaza Strip (cited in Fields 2004, 155) put it, "We only have that option. We do not have bombs, tanks, missiles, planes, helicopters." Suicide bombers are not only relatively easily constructed but they are also necessarily difficult to defend against, except at massive cost, since their target is the spaces of everyday life.

Second, because of the growth of modern technology, it has become much easier to instigate, plan, carry out, and publicize these attacks—and it is important to point out that most of these attacks are very carefully planned. In particular, it is possible to point to crucial four technologies. First, there is the advent of relatively easily obtainable plastic explosive, which has occurred mainly since the 1980s, explosive that can be combined with nails, nuts, and bolts, or other loose metal, to lethal effect. Second, there is the range of different but easily available means of delivery—from foot or the bicycle, through the car, to the lorry. Third, modern technologies allow much more intense logistical planning. The fax, then the mobile phone, and now e-mail has allowed the planning of most attacks to become much more flexible and opportunistic. In turn, these technologies are surrounded by an envelope of practical knowledge that is widely available and easily passed on to others via the Web. Fourth, modern media technologies have increasingly become "do-it-yourself," involving a wide variety of means for capturing, disseminating, and publicizing "news" of an event like suicide bombing (Gillmor 2004). Through technological change, the media has become a commonly available tool. But "do-it yourself" most certainly does not mean unsophisticated. For example, Hizbollah's channel, Al-Manar TV, based in Lebanon, has grown from a small operation of 120 people in 1997. It now claims to attract 800,000 viewers and can be received via satellite in both Europe and the United States (Reuter 2004).

All this is to ignore the body of the suicide bomber. This body is both a crucial and incidental element of the weapon, transporting explosive in a covert manner. "Unlike the tank or missile that is clearly visible, the weapon carried in the shape of the body is invisible" (Mbembe 2003, 36). One might well argue that a particularly forbidding element of this form of embodiment is that the suicide bomber becomes, in effect, the most expendable part of a hybrid "machinic" complex in which cause, medium and violence are mixed together in complex combinations. Suicide bombers are do-it-yourself cyborgs. In some senses, the bodies of suicide bombers take on the characteristics of machine, becoming the expendable delivery mechanism: subject becomes object, so to speak, and the self is left behind in the final compulsion of the moment, blasted out of existence.

However, in many ways as important as the killings carried out by suicide bombers are the affective resonances of their acts that are based on a particular politics of time and space which denies the power of particular forms of embodiment.

> The body in itself has neither power nor value. The power and value of the body result from a process of abstraction based on the desire for eternity. In that sense, the martyr has established a moment of supremacy in which the subject overcomes his own mortality, can be seen as labouring under the sign of the future. In other words, in death the future is collapsed into the present. (Mbembe 2003, 37)

The manner of death affords the body its signification. But, crucially, that signification will vary according to the apprehensions of the audience that responds to the act since, as Bell (2005, 242) points out, to an extent at least, suicide bombers "remove themselves from the role of explanation" by promulgating a politics of affective sensation as much as discursive opinion.[14] It is these significatory resonances that I want to concentrate on in this chapter, mainly in the context of the effects that are *felt* by Western audiences.[15] Straightaway, I should point out that my concern will not be the reporting biases of the Western media: these seem to me to be obvious enough to need no further comment (e.g., Said 1996). Rather, I want to concentrate on how these acts are affectively framed in the West.

The Aesthetics of Violence

It may seem odd to think of violence in *aesthetic* terms but most violence is not a simple primal force whose existence is its proof. Quite the reverse, most violence comes loaded with all kinds of more or less carefully constructed freight. Let me take one fluctuating aesthetic complex as a particularly relevant example, namely the idea of the noble death. This idea can be found in many cultures over long periods of time (e.g., Cormack 2002; Van Henten and Avemarie 2002), although it is highly variable in its application. For example, in the ancient world, a death involving self-sacrifice was applauded. Even now, military deaths that take this form may be thought of as particularly admirable and may be rewarded by some form of posthumous decoration. However, as many commentators have pointed out, a noble death differs from martyrdom. The idea and practices of martyrdom have been and continue to be contested. Whereas a noble death has often been construed as heroic because it implies fighting against the odds and either winning and staying alive or death in the process of bringing down the enemy, martyrdom has been treated with considerable suspicion. Though martyrologies have continued to multiply in many traditions, still the act of actively seeking out death is often seen as rash and reprehensible.[16]

Perhaps the most obvious current application of the idea of martyrdom is to be found in Islam, although equally it is vital to point out that the phenomenon of suicide martyrdom is hardly specific to Islamic societies: there is a whole Catholic martyrology, for example. But it has certainly been prevalent in Islam of late and has particular roots in the recent history of the Middle East, for example in the children's suicide brigades of the 1980–1988 Iran-Iraq war.[17] Muslim ideas of martyrdom, which some commentators argue underlie the current practices of suicide bombing in a number of the parts of the world, originated in a warrior culture. The ideal was one of active struggle (*jihād*) in which the will to die in the way of God was decisive, so martyrs did not just have to consist of those who died in battle; "So crucial is [that will] that even those who die in shipwreck, childbirth, or pestilence may enjoy the rewards of martyrs in paradise, while those who just happen to die in battle, but whose heart is on something other than God, may not" (Cormack 2002, xiii). However, Brown (2002) documents the impact of colonialism on Muslim thinking, which led to a resurgence of the ideal of actually dying as part of the struggle, in the way of God which is simultaneously intended to fight the colonial oppressor and bring Islam back to life as a forward-looking and confident (rather than defensive and reactionary) religion. Of course, contemporary Islamic thought on the matter of martyrdom is hardly monolithic. Thus, whereas Shiite Islam "presents us with an enduring and dramatic modern case of a system of belief for which martyrdom is a central value" (Brown

2002, 107), one which has left an enduring mark through the Iranian Revolution, the Iran-Iraq war and the bitterness of the Lebanese civil war, other groups have been less concerned to assert such a value (although some Sunni revivalists would also make martyrdom central to their program). Whatever the case, it is important to note that martyrdom may have an *aesthetic* aspect: one must be skilled at dying, there is an art to death, suffering can be redemptive, and so on. But there is massive variation of interpretation. For example, many Islamic scholars would argue that suicide bombing is an abomination. Others would argue that it constitutes an admirable death in, and only in, "war zones." Still others (a few) see it as a legitimate act almost anywhere.

That said, in the West, I think that it is possible to argue that the affective proving ground for understanding violence, noble or otherwise, has chiefly been prepared by Christianity in its many and multiple forms of affinity. What all these forms of Christian sensibility share is an empathy for victims and outcasts.

> In one form or another, all of the world's great religions urge their faithful to exercise compassion and mercy, as does the Judaeo-Christian tradition. But the empathy for victims—as victims—is specifically Western and quintessentially biblical. The burr under the saddle of "Western" culture, the source of its moral uneasiness and social restlessness, is precisely this growing empathy for victims. Most of the West's political innovations are linked to it, and our most deeply held social and moral sensibilities are suffused with it. (Baillie 1995, 19)

Indeed, one could argue that concern for victims has become one of the principal points of the moral compass in the Western world (Stark 2001) and of the Western "trauma culture" that is continually rebroadcast day after day and night after night (Cvetkovich 2003). Even as Western powers become involved in various forms of globalization of (in)civility—confused imperialism, economic hegemony, or environmental degradation—still claims of victim or victimization provide a kind of moral swagger for a West that may (or may not)[18] be losing a Christian heritage but that still cleaves to Girard's (1987, 35) famous saying that "the victim has the last word in the Bible and we are influenced by this even though we do not want to pay the Bible the homage it deserves."

> Even the most vicious campaigns of victimization—including, astonishingly, even Hitler's— have found it necessary to base their assertion of moral legitimacy on the claim that their goal was the protection or vindication of victims. However savagely we behave, and however wickedly and selectively we wield this moral gavel, protecting or rescuing innocent victims has become the cultural imperative everywhere the biblical influence has been felt. (Baillie 1995, 20)

We might interpret this victimology as an affect (a natural, universal emotion) or an aesthetic (of sacrifice) or an ethic (of personal, moral achievement) or simply as the way that the world appears. In truth, it contains all of these different aspects.

In this section, I want to claim that the media reaction to the practice of suicide bombing has gained a particularly important aesthetic dimension in the West through the continued rehearsal of this victimology using the affective frame called melodrama. As I have already pointed out, violence tends to have an aesthetic dimension. In particular, human beings tend to act into the world as though someone were watching and relating to them. But, over the centuries, that "imagined audience" of confreres and compatriots has been expanded by the modern media, most especially through the practices of "news." News is, of course, a relatively recent and carefully constructed commodity. Almost from its inception, news has been an affective form, bound up with the generation of emotional response through the deployment of various practical aesthetics of layout, by-line, story, picture, and so forth. Engaging the reader requires the production of an emotional reaction of some kind: horror, condemnation, surprise, amusement, fear (Marr, 2004). Collective violence is one of the supreme media events, usually following well-worn affective tracklines. For example, it has become a cliché that modern wars are fought out under the gaze of the media—and therefore through the aesthetic conventions of the media—but the fact that it is a cliché does not make it any the less true.[19] Acts of martial self-immolation, like suicide bombing play, to many of the same aesthetic conventions. Many suicide bombings are prepared, at least partially, as media events and are intended to produce particular feelings in audiences, conceived of as such. Very often, suicide bombing is integrally entangled with media presentations of various kinds, from the video of the bomber and his or her family through, in some cases, to film of the act itself, all feeding into an anticipated media response which will have both local and global resonance. The aim is to have an affective impact through the media which will be sufficient to give distant suffering presence. Thus, though suicide bombings are clearly a way of making a statement about a cause, they are also heavily structured by aesthetic conventions that attempt to maximize affective impact. Thus, these attacks are sometimes justified by reference to a romantically inclined political ethos that might even be described as a kind of "art." Thus interpreted, these are events of "sacro-politics" (Berlant 2003) that are meant to be felt by audiences as exceeding the concept, as making a point simply through their excessive character. There is more there there. The existence of the events is the argument. They provide dense and radiant images of the politically saturated which are meant to change wills. Well, in theory.

In other words, what seems certain is that suicide bombing would never have taken on the form it has or have become so popular as a means of delivery were it not for the presence of the mass media. In a number of senses, suicide bombing is served up for the media, and in a number of arenas its impact is as much meant to be a media event as it is a calculated rending of flesh. These attacks, or so I would argue, have more resonance in modern life because they are so heavily mediated, becoming a part of what I will call, following Ohnuki-Tierney (2002), the "militarization of aesthetics."[20] Suicide bombers are not just involved in acts of vengeance. In many cases, they are also enacting wrongs—and the righting of these wrongs. But, as well, their acts are also playing to two intermingled audiences; their own polity, often sympathetic to some of the bombers' causes (if not necessarily the bombings) and a Western audience that tends to be mainly indifferent to these causes, but is vexed by the issue of terrorism's ability to disrupt their everyday lives, to make them vulnerable. It is this audience that I want to concentrate on here.[21]

In the West, suicide bombing figures, at least in part, as an appeal to affect carried out through the "intimate public sphere" of the media, to use Berlant's phrase, which is continually broadcasting images of suffering that conform to a number of aesthetic formats and conventions that I have already begun to touch on. In particular, the Western media can, through deploying particular affective frames, produce determinate affects, and especially dysphoric affects like fear and anger in its audiences (cf. Altheide 2002, Robin 2004). This is particularly true of the dominant mode of communication of these events—the news—which routinely employs a series of "'frames' that simplify, prioritize and structure the narrative flow of events" (Norris, Kern, and Just, 10). Moreover, the news has become increasingly entertainment-oriented as it has had to compete with other formats (Mindich 2004).[22] Though it is possible to make entirely too much of this process—as has already been pointed out, almost from its inception, news has been structured to produce affective response—still the continuing conflation of news and entertainment has allowed certain affective frames to gradually increase their grip on how and what news is presented.

The problem, of course, is that in order for these events to have an impact at a distance, they have to become a part of a language of understated affective media frames that are increasingly used around the world. One of, and very likely the chief of these frames in use currently,[23] *the main shared space of appearance*, is melodrama.

Melodrama was originally devised in the nineteenth century as a dramaturgical device to enliven theater and novels but has subsequently become a nearly ubiquitous means of presenting how events appear and feel in the West, a victimological structure of feeling which can be understood as "a form of the tragic ... for a world in which there is no longer a tenable idea of the sacred" (Brooks 1976, 211).[24] It is an affective genre that now leads its own life and, although it now takes on many local forms, it still has a number of identifiable characteristics: a concentration on the everyday, the featuring of "ordinary" people's experience, a succession of "personalized" moral lessons, and a substantial emotional content, often based around the sheer force of emotions and tending to privilege affects like pain and suffering (Cvetkovich 1992). These characteristics summon a particular subjectivity that sees life as a (melo)drama and trains people to see the world as an interpersonal stage which is motivated by an extensive vocabulary of sentiment that is quite far from the traditional bourgeois self.[25] In other words, in melodrama, it is people who are sick, not the situation (Despret 2004).

In the mass media, the melodramatic consciousness is perhaps best typified by forms like the soap opera (cf. Ang 1982) but it has been consistently colonizing other forms over time, including now the presentation of news and current affairs where it can function to anchor larger than life events by straining them through a familiar technology for handling the disconcerting.[26] The drawback, of course, is that a technology meant to foreground the pain of ordinary events flattens out the pain of extraordinary events by assimilating them to the same means of facing situations, of encountering life. Their excess is domesticated. Scenes of devastation meant to be felt in the gut as horrifically incomprehensible quickly become familiar elements of the screens that populate everyday life.

In the West, in other words, events like suicide bombings figure as part of a continuous feed of news into a sphere that is increasingly used to violence and, indeed, feeds on it as one of its chief sources of stories, against a general affective background that increasingly favors the excessive sentimentality of melodrama: certainly in the West, the capacity to feel the pain and empathy of the victim is becoming one of the central qualifications for personhood, usually enacted collectively in response to certain sacro-political events in mass culture which become iconic and exemplary. The media produce spaces of pain which are undeniable but, equally, function as spaces of entertainment. In particular, we see the remnants of Aristotle's thought in the *Poetics*; "objects which in themselves we view with pain, we delight to contemplate when reproduced with minute fidelity: such as the form of the most ignoble animals and of dead bodies." In other words, the media is a part of the machinery of a melodramatically inclined "subject-forming, habit-forming aesthetics of disaster" (Berlant 2003, 161) that can take in and domesticate almost any violent event. It is as if the affect released by the melodramatic frame makes it possible to avoid thinking: the expressive is enough and introspective forms of judgment (which, ironically, might generate their own disconcerting and menacing emotions) can be put aside. The result is that no one has to see the broken forms in each other. But, as Grossman (2003, 23) puts it: "This is what I want, right now. That we will see the darkness in each other.". In other words, what we need is a kind of euphoria, but one that is also a measure of bleakness, an exuberance that is also sorrowful and that works.

To put it another way, suicide bomber attacks run the risk of being much closer to Western culture than they might at first appear. They simply become a part of a much wider aesthetic genealogy of inhumanity that arises out of the presence of sacro-political imperatives and out of the presence of many socially negated survival populations that "are marked definitionally by their proximity to death and survival, by a sense of being too alive and not alive enough" (Berlant 2003, 167), as sampled by a Western media machine. Though they may become the subject of moments of indignation, they are just as likely to be drawn into a general spectacle of suffering which implies observation rather than action. In other words, they suffer the constant danger of devalorization through becoming part of a formal vestibularity which also typifies the position of large parts of the population of Western liberal democracies in which citizenship depends upon a privatized dream of what is probable beyond the event of identity, rather than the vote and all its paraphernalia (Berlant 2002). Therefore, though they may be terrible, these events are subsumed into a general set of mediatized conventions that, though not avowedly political, have a political effect, both in terms of how the world appears and in terms of the structural position such events occupy.

Spaces of Blame

A character who briefly appears in Boswell's *Life of Johnson* tells of how he has tried to be a philosopher but failed—because "cheerfulness was always breaking in" (Spivey 2001, 7). Rather like that unfortunate, I cannot bring myself to pronounce the advent of Armageddon. Is the outlook entirely bleak? I think not. There are reasons for hope. To begin with, I would make a simple empirical point by directing attention to the people who unselfishly work to the script of a worldly cosmopolitical activism, all the way from the young people who have been witnesses for the International Solidarity Movement through those who devote their lives to the continual groundswell of charitable causes (Gilroy 2004). It is too easy to be cynical about this kind of work that is often low-key and goes on outside the glare of the media or alternatively is surrounded in meaningless media clichés (saints, etc.). After all, many of these workers have suffered solitary and painful deaths. They are the closest to what I would regard as modern-day martyrs.

Then, a body of political thinking is beginning to emerge that has begun to address these problems based around a nascent politics of time and space. In this final section, I want to mobilize this fragile, but still I think viable, "politics of hope" that is both theory and method. In mobilizing this politics of hope, I will attempt to steer clear of the blandishments of an agonized liberalism that would reduce politics to an ethos of multiplying procedures for being nice to one another whilst also trying to avoid the kind of hope that is often generated by right-wing elements, which often relies on moving back to a supposed, but largely mythical, past in which all problems had been solved by virtue.

Why is a politics of hope so crucial to questioning violence? Because violence is so often caught up with hopelessness in its many forms, with a bringing forth of a particular appearance of the world in which the future itself becomes a casualty because any sense of anticipation is deadened; "violence changes the very sense of a meaningful outcome to life's plans" (Nordstrom 2004, 98). Violence is about the death of hope.

> People don't fight or flee war because of the sheer fact of violence. They fight or flee war because of what violence "feels" like.

> And how does violence feel? …it feels like existential crisis, like hopelessness, like loss of the future. It feels like impossible contradictions of resistance within oppression, like the struggle of humanity within terror. Violence is about impossibility, about the human condition and the meaning of survival. This is why wars are fought with bloodletting, why torture takes place, and why neither violence nor war is limited to the physical carnage of the battlefield. (Nordstrom 2004, 58)

A politics of hope involves a double commitment to changing the world. One commitment is temporal.

> Only thinking directed towards changing the world and informing the desire to change it does not confront the future (the unclosed space for new development in front of us) as embarrassment and the past as spell. (Bloch, 1986, 8)

But, at the same time this temporal commitment is no simple utopian-radical millenarianism. Rather, it is a politics of surprise aiming at multiplying moments of hope by pulling the future into the present.[27] It is, in other words, still utopian-radical in its sympathies, but substitutes the question of *temporality* for the question of agency in the belief that it is vital to break from the limitations of "historical" time.[28] So,

> both Bloch and Benjamin draw attention to the character of a hopeful moment. For both, hope is always disappointed. Yet, in Benjamin's view, hope in the present points to its own future moment of salvation. Likewise, Bloch draws attention to unfulfilled hope as 'the repressed, the interrupted, the undischarged on which one can in one and the same act fall back upon while it reaches forward to us in order to develop in a better way' and points to how in this unfulfilled hope, the "corresponding points of the now sparkle and transmit each other" (1998, 29). Both seek to apprehend a moment of hope, in other words, by striking it with a perspective whose direction is opposite to that of the moment. In other words, to borrow Benjamin's expression, the spark of hope flies up in the midst of the radical temporal re-orientation in their own analyses. (Miyazaki 2004, 23)

The other commitment is spatial. For hope is unequally distributed. There are zones of the world in which the circumstances are so unbearable that belief starts to fade that these circumstances will ever come to an end. In part, suicide bombing can be seen as a reaction to the geography of these unbearable spaces, of these spaces of pain. Thus on one side, suicide bombing can be seen as the result of the current proliferation of necropolitical spaces. It is a cliché of modern geopolitical writing that the number of wild spaces outside state control has been proliferating, in part because of the vagaries of late modern colonial occupations of various kinds which tend to be uncertain and fragmentary affairs which, as a result, seem to promote such an extreme militarization of daily life that they produce an accelerated and constant state of violence (Mbembe 2003). On the other side, suicide bombing can be seen as resulting from the wider and wider definition of what counts as a battlefield. In the past, a key illusion of Western audiences has been that wars take place in defined spaces and involve defined combatants: soldiers shooting (mainly) at other soldiers. War does not spill outside these spaces: in other words, war and peace have their own spaces and they do not infect each other. But through the twentieth and into the twenty-first century, the question "where is war"? has become increasingly difficult to answer. Martial violence cannot be parochialized: it takes in many people in many different places. "War itself now spills across the landscapes and cityscapes of prosaic life. The image of the complete battle, separate from the civilian life around it, is antiquated, unreal" (Nordstrom 2004, 58). In other words, elsewheres increasingly do not exist but modern media conventions still attempt to keep them in place so that affective schemas like melodrama can still graze.

To summarize, the affective framing of the general media spectacle prevents populations in Western liberal democracies from forming an idea of the suffering of the unfortunate, even when they may be in close geographical proximity. In certain senses, events like suicide bombings are simply assimilated into a particular media paratext that has already prepared a place for them—meaning that they can only figure in very limited ways as part of an already prepared affective template.

So part of a politics of hope is the necessity of working on the affective episteme of Western populations so that they make connections with the world they currently may lack, and thereby create new entanglements that allow us to be moved in different ways and teach new things to ourselves (Callon and Rabeharisoa 2004). How, in other words, might we turn the politics of hope into a living, breathing presence? It is to this task of affective politics that I want to turn in this final section by mobilizing Arendt's distinction in *On Revolution* between pity and compassion.[29] For, at best, so I now want to argue, Western populations exhibit pity when what is really needed is *compassion*. Of course, there are at least four bystander states to be found in the available Western affective palette (Boltanski 1999; Cohen 2001). The first is that the misery of the unfortunate may simply be *ignored* and inspire no pity whatsoever. A dreadful event registers no claim and inspires only apathy. Another possibility is that those who are more fortunate may demonstrate *a concern for the unfortunate* that does not constitute a politics as such: rather it consists of a benevolent, patriarchal concern. Then there is the exercise of *pity*, an emotion that generalizes in order to deal with distance but, in order to generalize, it becomes eloquent, adding many words, thereby both recognizing itself as emotion and feeling and feeding on what it has conjured up. Pity, in other words, has an aesthetic quality that, in modern times, is best represented by melodrama. By comparison, as an outcome of entanglements that are close to the actors themselves, *compassion* has a practical character and, because it does not generalize, is not loquacious and shows no great interest in boosting emotion for its own sake. As a direct response to the expression of suffering, compassion is not 'talkative and argumentative' (Arendt 1990, 86). It is nonrepresentational and comes from the necessity inherent in the situation.[30] It is local and practical and immanent. It is about making contact without falling back immediately on an abstract contract or a moral certainty. The unfortunate is never just anyone or any category.

The question for me is how we can recover a politics of compassion to bring forth situations of necessity, rather than wallowing in a politics of pity that sounds grand, no doubt feels the victim's pain, but, in its commitment to either relativism (as in genealogical explanations) or transcendence (as in notions of a primal human nature or good will), is too close to current forms of normative affective politics like melodrama to do more than produce a brief ethical hiatus. How can we, in other words, summon life by fashioning a politics of affect which can "keep the condition of life in mind and … make the condition of life count in the organization of behaviour" (Damasio 2003, 165), a goal that was, in all likelihood, affect's original biological function? How can we, to use Arendt's phrase, remain "fully alive"?

Part of this politics, if that is not entirely too grand a word, would be an allegiance to two principles: first, that it is only possible to attain partial justice: to attain complete justice is to destroy another's dream and would itself be unjust; second, that it is necessary to have the courage of one's own ambivalence. It is not necessary to settle.

> Seasoning one's claims with self-irony and modesty, cultivating a tolerance for moral ambiguity, periodically practicing normative self-reticence, building up a resistance to the pleasure of purity, minding your own business, doing what you can to forget to wreak vengeance, defending negative freedom even if there is no such thing, and playing around are the best you can do. But that's quite a lot. (Bennett and Shapiro 2002, 22)

Perhaps, then, all that holiness in the air would begin to dissipate a little and it would no longer be necessary to live death in life. That best, because so fragile yet so powerful affect, *hope*, would return.[31]

I should say straightaway that all I have are a few fugitive and fleeting thoughts about what such a politics would consist of. But one amongst many necessary tasks will be to change the dominant aesthetic of violence and it is this task that I want to concentrate on. What we need is an ethico-aesthetic sensibility that can draw us into the density of the world, can re-sacralize our feeling for human particularity and let us take pleasure in it (a passion for living together), and, at the same time mount a critique of those forces that menace our ability to form human lives. In other words we need to change people's *sense of reality* rather than simply make invocations of commonality or spurious epistemic claims (e.g., about the mediation of overarching political truths). The goal is to fashion a world "whose texture of realness has the particular quality of fullness rather than force" (Curtis 1999, 12). In Arendt's terms that means valuing passions which intensify our awareness of reality, rather than simply valuing the force that passions may exert: "those [passions] that are truly pleasurable have the capacity to intensify our awareness of reality, to make our sense of the real fuller, deeper" (Curtis 1999, 7).

Above all, that means fashioning a shared space of *appearance* that does not squander human particularity and in which, therefore, compassion can thrive. That space will be an aesthetic one in that

> in an appearing world, our sense of reality depends on a mutual aesthetic provocation between actors and spectators—that is, it depends on the urge to see and be seen, to hear and be heard, to touch and be touched in a world of plural others. (Curtis 1999, 20)

All this will seem high-handed and far from concrete situations, even as it strives to articulate an ethic of concrete situations. But I think not. Humanity lies in its entanglements and theory can only go so far. There is always more to address in life than theory can encompass. Some things are always left out, interrupting and demanding a reply (Fortun 2001).

Conclusions

I want to end on a practical political note rather than indulge in the easy moralizing that is a part of the problem and that leads to the production of sanctimonious priests of certainty who just make things worse (Bennett and Shapiro 2002). To end practices like suicide bombing clearly requires the removal of festering injustices that are plain for all to see. Such a removal of the causes of frustration, despair, and general hopelessness surely cannot be denied. Social relations need to be changed (Tilly 2003). But, by itself, that would not, I suspect, be enough, even for the most convinced consensual realist. Other things are required to produce a situation in which, as Badiou (2003, 124) puts it, we can understand emancipatory politics "in terms other than those of the absolute of war."

As I have already argued, that requires the *institution* of *compassion*, rather than pity, through the hard work of peace[32] and a politics of becoming that realizes not only that "a generous ethos emerges when number of constituencies engage actively and comparatively those differences in themselves and others the regulation of which allows them to be what they are" (Connolly 1999, 156)[33] but also, more than this, supports an active change in the commonsense lexicon of alterity so that the other's difference can be located and a generous ethos can begin to emerge in the first place (Gilroy 2004). At least four steps need to be taken.

First, we would have to cast down a long line of Romantic thinking that insists there is a complete system, whether it be industrial capitalism or Western civilization or some other supersaturated global order, that only extreme and heroic sacralized acts of one form or another can transgress and tear down.[34] This "me against the system" logic is both seductive, self-aggrandizing, and gratuitous. Far better a more modest politics of desire something like that described by Lentricchia and McAuliffe (2004, 4), a politics of desire that would

> rest with marginality and the understanding that the world will not be altered by artistic acts. To rest with the minimal hope that ... a different way of seeing might be assumed in

local pockets of culture, might even make a little change here and there. It is the sort of artistic commitment that doesn't eventuate in failure and despair because such desire is a commitment to permanent exile and renunciation of political ambition. Desire for the margins is at peace with its minority status, even as the secular world abandons and scorns it, leaving it free to create beautiful, challenging things. This is not the aim of the transgressive artist who wants so much more.

Second, we would need to continue to work with processes of mediation. Many on the left seem to express a kind of contempt for the kinds of negotiation and mediation programmes mounted by institutions like Harvard Law School. They are slow and sometimes a bit tiresome. But I think that these kinds of intercessions are vital. They are not just palliatives but are the real stuff of constructing the political will to end violence. They require patient mobilization, credible incentives, new kinds of law (Hirsh 2003), and the dogged construction of belief that violence is not inevitable, especially, it might be added, amongst the violent (Ury 2002). They require compromise, understood as the dismantling/untelling of power. But they also require a folding back into the spaces of everyday life, rather than just a concentration on legal formularies.

Thus, third, we would need to give much greater attention to political socialization understood as a basic conviviality[35] and, at the same time, less attention to nostalgia for the unity of identity and a corresponding sense of desire for the return of the one, in whatever form. It seems to me that it is here that one of the great challenges of contemporary political thought arises, in bringing forth systems and subjects that can cope with diversity and disagreement because they subscribe to an ethic of openness to and compassion for the other without falling into the affective quagmire that mistakes empathy for action. Elsewhere, I have pointed out some of the politics now coming on to the horizon that can act to produce new forms of appearance (see Thrift 2004, 2005). For now, I would only want to add that all these forms of politics suggest a long slog. For it is only by changing the subject, which in turn must mean changing the content of taken-for-granted backgrounds of appearing, that we can produce a citizen who wants to reach out because the situation demands it.

Finally, that goal requires a change in the texture of spaces and times. We need spaces and times that take hybridity and connection to be the normal state of appearance but somehow do this more directly than the Western mass media's automatic interpretation/feeling machine will currently allow. This is a move away from the idea of public space towards something rather different, a space of routine orientation towards strangers in which the performative opposition stranger-intimate no longer holds (Warner 2002) and new kinds of world-making can take shape which mould the space and time of public life in other ways.

References

Abu-Lughod, L. (2002). "Egyptian melodrama – technology of the modern subject?" in *Ginsburg, F. D., Abu-Lughod, L., Larkin, B. (eds.), *Media Worlds. Anthropology on New Terrain*. Berkeley: University of California Press, 115–133.

Ahmed, S. (2004). *The Cultural Politics of Emotion*. Edinburgh, Edinburgh University Press.

Alliez, E., and Negri, A. (2003). "Peace and war," *Theory Culture and Society*, 20: 109–118.

Altheide, D. L. (2002). *Creating Fear. News and the Construction of Crisis*. Hawthorne, NY, Aldine de Gruyter.

Alvarez, A. (1971). *The Savage God. A Study of Suicide*. New York, Norton.

Ang, I. (1982). *Watching Dallas. Soap Opera and the Melodramatic Imagi*nation. London, Routledge.

Axell, A. (2002). *Kamikaze. Japan's Suicide Gods*. London, Longman.

Arendt, H. (1970). *On Violence*. San Diego, Harcourt Brace.

Arendt, H. (1990). *On Revolution*. Harmondsworth, Penguin.

Badiou, A. (2003). "Beyond formalization: an interview," *Angelaki*, 8: 111–126.

Baillie, G. (1995). *Violence Unveiled. Humanity at the Crossroads*. New York, Crossroad Publishing Company.

Bell, V. (2005). "The Scenography of Suicide. Terror, Politics and the Humiliated Witness," *Economy and Society* 34, 291–260.

Bennett, J., and Shapiro, M. J. (eds.) (2002). *The Politics of Moralizing*. New York, Routledge.

Berlant, L. (2003). "Uncle Sam Needs a Wife: Citizenship and Denegation," in Castronovo, R., and Nelson, D. (eds.), *Materializing Democracy. Toward a Revitalised Cultural Politics*. Princeton, NJ, Princeton University Press, 144–174.

Berlant, L. (ed.) (2004). *Compassion. The Culture and Politics of an Emotion*. New York, Routledge.

Blank, J. (2001). *Mullahs on the Mainframe. Islam and Modernity amongst the Daudi Bohras*. Chicago, University of Chicago Press.

Bloch, E. (1986). *The Principle of Hope*. (3 vols.). Oxford, Blackwell.

Bloch, E. (1998). *Literary Essays*. Stanford, CA, Stanford University Press.

Boltanski, L. (1999). *Distant Suffering. Morality, Media and Politics*. Cambridge, Cambridge University Press.

Brooks, P. (1976). *The Melodramatic Imagination*. New Haven, CT., Yale University Press.

Brown, D. (2002). "Martyrdom in Sunni Revivalist Thought," in Cormack, M. (ed.) *Sacrificing the Self. Perspectives on Martyrdom and Religion*. New York, Oxford University Press, 107–117.

Callon, M., and Rabeharisoa, V. (2004). "Gino's lesson on humanity: genetics, mutual entanglements and the sociologist's role," *Economy and Society*: 33, 1–27.

Campbell, D., Shapiro, M. J. (eds) (1999) *Moral Spaces. Rethinking Ethics and World Politics*. Minneapolis, University of Minnesota Press.

Cohen, S. (2001). *States of Denial. Knowing about Atrocities and Suffering*. Cambridge, Polity Press.

Conolly, W.G. (1999). *Why I Am Not a Secularist*. Minneapolis, University of Minnesota Press.

Cormack, M. (ed.) (2002). *Sacrificing the Self. Perspectives on Martyrdom and Religion*. New York, Oxford University Press.

Curtis, K. (1999). *Our Sense of the Real. Aesthetic Experience and Arendtian Politics*. Ithaca, NY, Cornell University Press.

Cvetkovich, A. (2003). *An Archive of Feelings. Trauma, Sexuality and Lesbian Public Cultures*. Durham, NC, Duke University Press.

Damasio, A. (2003). *Looking for Spinoza. Joy, Sorrow, and the Feeling Brain*. London, Heinemann.

Davis, J.M. (2003) *Martyrs. Innocence, Vengeance and Despair in the Middle East*. London, Palgrave Macmillan.

Despret, V. (2004). *Our Emotional Make-*Up. Ethnopsychology and Selfhood. New York, Other Press.

Dupuy, J. (2002). *Pour un Catastrophisme Éclairé*. Paris, Editions du Seuil.

Fields, R. M. (2004). *Martyrdom. The Psychology, Theology and Politics of Self-Sacrifice*. New York, Praeger.

Fortun, K. (2001). *Advocacy After Bhopal. Environmentalism, Disatser and Global Orders*. Chicago, University of Chicago Press.

Gillmor, D. (2004). *We the Media. Grassroots Journalism by the People, for the People*. Sebastopol, CA, O'Reilly.

Gilroy, P. (2004). *After Empire. Melancholia or Convivial Culture?* London, Routledge.

Girard, R. (1987). *Things Hidden Since the Foundation of the World*. Stanford, Stanford University Press.

Grossman, D. (2003). *Death as a Way of Life*. London, Bloomsbury.

Hage, G. (2003). "'Comes a time we are all enthusiasm': Understanding Palestinian suicide bombers in times of exighophobia," *Public Culture*: 15, 65–89.

Henry, M. (2003a). "Phenomenology of Life," *Angelaki*, 8: 100–110.

Henry, M. (2003b). *I Am the Truth. Toward a Philosophy of Christianity*. Stanford, CA, Stanford University Press.

Hirsh, D. (2003). *Law Against Genocide: Cosmopolitan Trials*. London, Glasshouse Press.

Ignatieff, M. (1997). *The Warrior's Honor. Ethnic War and the Modern Conscience*. New York, Henry Holt.

Israeli, R. (2003) *Islamiskaze. Manifestations of Islamic Martyrology*. London, Frank Cass.

Jay, M. (2003) *Refractions of Violence*. New York, Routledge.

Khosrokhavar, F. (2002) *Les Nouveaux Martyrs d'Allah*. Paris, Flammarion.

Lamont-Brown, R. (1997). *Kamikaze. Japan's Suicide Samurai*. London, Weidenfeld and Nicolson.

Knorr-Cetina, K. (2005). "Complex global microstructures: the new terrorist microstructures," *Theory, Culture and Society*, 22: 213–234.

Larzillière, P. (2001). "Le 'martyre' des jeunes Palestiniens," *Politique Étrangère*, 66, 937-951.

Lentricchia, F., McAuliffe, J. (2003). *Crimes of Art and Terror*. Chicago, Chicago University Press.

Llobera, J.R. (2003) *The Making of Totalitarian Thought*. Oxford, Berg.

Marr, A. (2004). *My Trade. A Short History of British Journalism*. London, Macmillan.

Mbembe, A. (2003). "Necropolitics," *Public Culture*, 15:11–40.

Mindich, D. T. Z. (2004). *Tuned Out. Why Americans Under 40 Don't Follow the News*. New York, Oxford University Press.

Miyazaki, H. (2004). *The Method of Hope. Anthropology, Philosophy, and Fijian Knowledge*. Stanford, CA, Stanford University Press.

Nordstrom, C. (2004). *Shadows of War. Violence, Power and International Profiteering in the Twenty-First Century*. Berkeley, University of California Press.

Nordstrom, C., and Martin, J. (1992). *The Paths to Domination, Resistance and Terror*. Berkeley, University of California Press.

Nordstrom, C., and Robben, A. C. G. M. (1995). *Fieldwork under Fire*. Berkeley, University of California Press.

Norris, P., Kern, M., and Just, M. (eds.) *Framing Terrorism. The News Media, the Government and the Public*. New York, Routledge.

Nussbaum, M. C. (2001). *Upheavals of Thought. The Intelligence of Emotions*. Cambridge, Cambridge University Press.

Ohnuki-Tierney, E. (2002). *Kamikaze, Cherry Blossoms and Nationalisms. The Militarization of Aesthetics in Japanese History*. Chicago, University of Chicago Press.

Parkin, D. (ed) (1987) *The Anthropology of Evil*. Oxford, Blackwell.

Peluso, N., Watts, M. (eds) (2001) *Violent Environments*. Ithaca, NY, Cornell University Press.

Petersen, A. (1996) *Martyrdom and the Politics of Religion*. Albany, State University Press of New York.

Protevi, J. (2001) *Political Physics. Deleuze, Derrida and the Body Politic*. London, Athlone.

Ranciere, T. (1998). *Politics and Philosophy*. Minneapolis, University of Minnesota Press.

Reuter, C. (2004). *My Life is a Weapon. A Modern History of Suicide Bombing*. Princeton, NJ, Princeton University Press.

Robin, C. (2004). *Fear. The History of a Political Idea*. Oxford, Oxford University Press.

Rose, J. (2004). "Deadly embrace," *London Review of Books*, 26: 21–24.

Said, E. W. (1996). *Covering Islam. How the Media and Experts Determine How We See the Rest of the World*. New York, Vintage.

Salisbury, J. (2004). *The Blood of Martyrs. Unintended Consequences of Ancient Violence*. New York, Routledge.

Scarry, E. (1985). *The Body in Pain. The Making and Unmaking of the World*. New York, Oxford University Press.

Schoolman, M. (2001) *Reason and Horror. Critical Theory, Democracy and Aesthetic Individuality*. New York, Routledge.

Seel, M. (2004). *Aesthetics of Appearing*. Stanford, Stanford University Press.

Sontag, S. (2003). *The Pain of Others*. New York, Vintage.

Sorel, G. (1906/1999). *Reflections on Violence*. Cambridge, Cambridge University Press.

Sosky, W. (2002). *Violence. Terrorism, Genocide, War*. London, Granta.

Spivey, N. (2001). *Enduring Creation. Art, Pain and Fortitude*. London, Thames and Hudson.

Stark, R. (2001). *One True God. Historical Consequences of Monotheism*. Princeton, NJ, Princeton University Press.

Stengers, I. (2002). in Zournazi, M. (ed) Hope, London, Routledge.

Swearingen, J., and Cutting-Gray, J. (eds.) (2002). *Extreme Beauty. Aesthetics, Politics, Death*. London, Continuum.

Thrift, N.J . (2004). "Intensities of feeling: towards a spatial politics of affect," *Geografiska Annaler*, 86: 57–82.

Thrift, N. J. (2005). "But malice aforethought: cities and the natural history of hatred," *Transactions of the Institute of British Geographers*, NS 30, 133-150.

Tilly, C. (2003). *The Politics of Collective Violence*. Cambridge, Cambridge University Press.

Ury, W. (ed.) (2002). *Must We Fight?* San Francisco, Jossey Bass.

Van Henten, J. W., and Avemarie, F. (eds.) (2002). *Martyrdom and Noble Death*. *Selected Texts from Graeco-Roman, Jewish and Christian Antiquity*. London, Routledge.

Victor, B. (2003). *Army of Roses. Inside the World of Palestinian Suicide Bombers*. New York, Rodale.

Vollmann, W. T. (2004). *Rising Up and Rising Down. Some Thoughts on Violence, Freedom and Urgent Means*. London, Ecco.

Wacquant, L. (2004) *Body and Soul. Notebooks of an Apprentice Boxer*. Oxford, Oxford University Press.

Wall, T. C. (1999) *Radical Passivity. Levinas, Blanchot and Agamben*. Albany, State University of New York Press.

Warner, M. (2002). *Publics and Counterpublics*. New York, Zone Books.

Weitz, E. D. (2003). *A Century of Genocide. Utopias of Race and Nation*. Princeton, Princeton University Press.

Whitehead, N. L. (2002). *Dark Shamans. Kanaimà and the Poetics of Violent Death*. Durham, NC, Duke University Press.

Whitehead, N. L. (2004a). "Rethinking anthropology of violence," *Anthropology Today*, 20 (5): 1–2.

Whitehead, N. L. (ed.) (2004b). *Violence. Poetics, Performance, Expression*. London, James Currey Publishers.
Žižek, S. (2003). *The Puppet and the Dwarf. The Perverse Core of Christianity*. Cambridge, Mass., MIT Press.

Notes

1. Lest I be misunderstood at this point, this does not mean that I abjure these other forms of analysis of violence. To the contrary. But I think that it is dangerous to try to reduce violence to simply a sociological or juridical explanation: there is, in other words, a certain agency that I am trying to capture that cannot be indemnified by these kinds of explanation.

2. Thus, I am not going to make a roll call of violence to others: that has been done many times now (see most recently, for example, Sosky 2002; Vollmann 2004) and, in any case, there are reasons to believe that, at least in part, such litanies are complicit with their object, and can degenerate into a gluttony of grief (Spivey 2001).

3. Thus, I will make heavy play of the role of the media, although I do not want to call all applications of force violence, as in Bourdieu's notion of symbolic violence, for example.

4. I am using this word, with its obvious Foucauldian connotations, to signal the palette of affective responses and descriptions that characterizes Western social orders. This episteme will be made up of typical combinations of statements, senses and emotional loadings that are used to generate and describe interactions.

5. One thinks here of Mao's entirely non-Marxian conviction that "power grows out of the barrel of a gun" or Sartre's declaration that "irrepressible violence … is man creating himself" and it is through "mad fury" that "the wretched of the earth" can "become men" (both cited in Arendt 1970).

6. I will be taking my cue from four main sources. First, the work of Abu-Lughod, Ahmed, Berlant, and others on new forms of affective normativity. Second, the work on the construction of mass publics to be found in media studies, especially around staged forms of violence. Third, the work on nearness to the death drive and expiation, as found in work on discourses of pain (Scarry 1985; Spivey 2001). Fourth and finally, the body of work on the performance of violence, as found especially but not only in anthropology (e.g., Nordstrom 2004; Nordstrom and Robben 1992; Nordstrom and Martin, 1995; Whitehead 2002, 2004a, b).

7. Of course, affects like anger and despair and fear vary cross-culturally: for example, some cultures do not have an affect that they call anger and, indeed, it has been argued that anger does not exist in these cultures (although such cultures are often perfectly capable of identifying anger—because they are in frequent contact with people from the West) (cf. Despret 2004). Other cultures may sanction a much greater range of situations in which anger is appropriate than do others (cf. Nussbaum 2001). All we can say is that aggressive behaviour is differently expressed affectively in different cultures.

8. Although I count Agamben's influential work on the state of exception as, ultimately, a theoretical blind alley, so repulsed by sociological modes of explanation that it makes for a casual reductionism that has obvious attractions of the same kind as a flat positivism.

9. All this said, even the Israeli Secret Service has never been able to build a typical profile of a suicide bomber. Indeed, it can be argued that 'the desire to solve the problem is creating it, that burrowing into the psyche of the enemy, far from being

an attempt to dignify them with understanding, is a form of evasion that blinds you to your responsibility for the state that they are in' (Rose 2004, 204).

10. One went to Repton and London University, the other to Cranfield College. One blew himself up killing three civilians, the other's bomb failed to explode. He managed to escape but was found murdered some days later by persons unknown.

11. Organizations that may vie with each other to produce spectacular suicide bombings (see Hage 2003).

12. In some arenas, the bombers are offered a spiritual and a worldly bonus for completing their missions: the delights of paradise and a range of bounties and stipends for their families.

13. The exception is provided by transnational causes like al Qaeda whose members are often culturally heterogeneous. However, it can be argued that al Qaeda is as much a loose coalition of the disaffected as it is a single cause.

14. In her paper, Bell (2005, p. 245) argues that the acts of suicide bombers are shot through with aesthetic considerations. "To violently transform bodies moving into everyday routines into the smoking mangled burnt out wrecks of metal, rubble and body parts. This is the aesthetic task of such acts of terrorism. Whatever the political 'goal' the product is a scene of devastation, a scene and an accompanying series of images over which survivors and commentators will struggle." But I think this kind of account ignores the extent to which the Western media have been able to familiarize these images, a point to which I return in detail in the next section.

15. I do not feel competent to extend my brief to non Western audiences since all of my area studies expertise is concentrated in Southeast Asia.

16. On the case of the power of martyrs in early Christianity, for example, see Salisbury, 2004. It is worth remembering that the Catholic Church has an authorized martyrology. But such a treatment contrasts with a general tendency to define martyrdom with little respect for its historical integrity, as simply pointing to someone who has died tragically.

17. As, for example, in the case of the Iranian boy soldiers who walked through minefields to clear the way for regular troops (cf. Reuter 2004).

18. From Europe, this statement may appear obvious but from the United States less so.

19. Of course, not all wars or suicide bombings do become media events. But I would argue that the media have become an assumed accompaniment to acts of violence to the extent that people increasingly imagine these kinds of violence as if media frames were there. Further, in many cases, it is clear that the act of drawing attention to a cause through the media is a crucial part of the reason for an operation. Many causes struggle to gain media exposure at all and the ferocity of some responses can be explained by this imperative.

20. It has been argued that an aesthetic impulse of sorts may also add fuel to the motives of some participants, many of whom are well-educated and cleave to a kind of expressive-cum-performative impulse, as well as other motives like indignation and revenge. Usually, an analogy is drawn with Japanese kamikaze pilots (Axell 2002; Lamont-Brown 1997; Ohnuki-Tierney, 2002), nearly all of whom were highly educated student scholars who were supposedly caught up in an aesthetic of painful beauty centered on the image of the cherry blossom that was able to express the unresolved ambiguities in their lives. I have some reservations about the individualism of this argument that become more extreme in the context of modern suicide bombing.

21. There is, of course, a very large literature on the specifics of non-Western audiences and of media channels like Al-Jazeera, but I am leaving this aspect for another time.

22. Though there are still exceptions to this rule, for example in France.
23. Notice that I am not claiming that melodrama is the only way in which the world appears: other strategies include genres like the romantic, the humorous, and the rebellious.
24. In what follows, I will concentrate upon how extraordinary events play out in the now extensively melodramatized Western media but it is worth noting that extensive anthropological work suggests that this genre, whilst obtaining a very different reception in other parts of the world, is now becoming general and is having an affective impact that can sometimes be surprisingly similar across many different cultures (cf. Abu-Lughod 2002).
25. Of course, this genre can work upon viewers and hearers in numerous ways but its general affective force is clear enough.
26. One of the stock roles of melodrama is the victim, of course. Another, it might be added, is the martyr.
27. The affinity with certain elements of the temporal politics of suicide bombing should not be downplayed here. But the means is entirely different.
28. Žižek (2003) has a number of very interesting points to make on this project, using the work of Dupuy (2002).
29. Other authors have used these terms in quite different ways (e.g., by reversing their meaning), so it is important to attend to the definitions provided here.
30. Thus, studies of non-Jewish people who helped Jews in the Second World War are unable to account for their actions in terms of general sociological characteristics or political or religious affiliations. Indeed, those interviewed often could not account for their actions in terms of general motives and often argued that they found themselves in situations in which they often had no wish to be as they were brought into contact with hunted individuals who they then could not turn away.
31. Note here that I will not be going down the route of framing the problem in terms of the other, a stratagem followed by so many authors, including highly influential figures like Derrida and Levinas. On the whole, I find this kind of thought entirely too abstract to make any sense of—quite literally.
32. Obviously, this will mean ridding the world of some of the notions of sovereign power that provide one of the key materializations of war and a nominal opposite called peace. But, as I am trying to argue, by itself that would not be enough.
33. As Connolly goes on to point out, this can only ever be a regulative ideal.
34. Such a view can be thought to mimic the world economy because the promise of redemption is also the promise of a reward that is unthinkably great (Swearingen and Cutting-Gray, 2002).
35. I use Gilroy's (2004) term here to signify a radically open sense of "interpersonality," one meant to express what happened to multiculturalism in the absence of any strong identifications like race: the construction of new settings that cannot be easily slotted in to any political scheme.

15

The Pentagon's New Imperial Cartography
Tabloid Realism and the War on Terror

Simon Dalby

Tabloid Realism

Following the September 11, 2001 attacks in New York and Washington the ensuing political crisis was resolved by invoking categories of warfare. Many commentators discussed matters in terms of "global" wars. Numerous discussions of this supposedly new "global" politics invoked geographical language. The apparent violation of the sanctity of the metropolitan center by terrorists, who had penetrated from peripheral places, reprised the long pattern of dividing the world into wild zones and tame zones, areas of civilization in comparison to residual places of barbarism, somewhere vaguely "out there." These colonial geographies of empire were quickly reworked into the new language of the "global war on terror."

But these geographies of danger were frequently less than clearly described. Unless, that is, a specific target was designated, in which cases the practices of representation invoked all too precise target sets for the supposedly guided munitions of the war on terror. The technocratic logic of military representation of targets, weapons, zones and installations in photos, video sequences, as well as various forms of cartography, remove humans and other living beings from view.[1] But as this chapter argues, such "inhuman geographies" also work on the very largest scales in the abstractions of geopolitical discourse.

The popular rendition of the many works of both scholarship and policy advocacy in international politics has become commonplace; their presentation of the world in terms of dangerous places and the ever-present threat of violence part of the increasingly pervasive security culture. In Debrix's terms this didactic tabloid realism "... is composed of fragments of realist geopolitics, American nationalist ideology and cultural reactionism that are loosely put together to propagate shock effects in the public."[2] This genre is a form of geopolitics designed to appeal to a wide public while invoking fear through geography and political *gravitas* in its presentation of the world as a dangerous place in need of American violence. All of which simplify politics and, apparently, connect to the everyday life of many readers.

Above all tabloid realism invokes an American common-sense attitude to the world long familiar to readers of the popular geopolitics in the *Reader's Digest*,[3] and, more recently, to radio talk show audiences who listen to Rush Limbaugh, Mike Savage, and similar commentators. Of particular importance is the reduction of the world into simple geographical categories and identities. Debrix suggests that Robert Kaplan's vision of a bifurcated world in his much cited essay of a decade ago "The Coming Anarchy" is especially noteworthy in the genre. Debrix reprints the following from Kaplan's dystopic text of 1994:

> We are entering a bifurcated world. Part of the globe is inhabited by Hegel's and Fukuyama's Last Man, healthy, well fed, and pampered by technology. The other, larger, part is inhabited by Hobbes's First Man, condemned to a life that is "poor, nasty, brutish, and short." Although both parts will be threatened by environmental stress, the Last Man will be able to master it; the First Man will not. The Last Man will adjust to the loss of underground water tables in the western United States. He will build dikes to save Cape Hatteras and the Chesapeake beaches from rising sea levels, even as the Maldive Islands, off the coast of India, sink into oblivion, and the shorelines of Egypt, Bangladesh, and Southeast Asia recede, driving tens of millions of people inland where there is no room for them, and thus sharpening ethnic divisions.[4]

Kaplan reworks Fukuyama's neo-Hegelianism to draw a distinction between the affluent technologically capable Last Man and a Hobbesian First Man mired in poverty and violence and, maps these very loosely on to contemporaneous specifications of the world into tame zones of civilization and the wild zones beyond.

The Pentagon's New Maps

To deal with those wild zones, in the aftermath of September 11, 2001 the Pentagon has continued to update and modify its command structure. In 2002 the command arrangements incorporated the responsibilities for "homeland" defense into a new geographical combatant command called Northcom, finally arranging matters so that each area of the world now is assigned to a combatant commander.[5] Homeland security effectively means the total surveillance of planet earth by active combatant commands of the U.S. military. Global security has been appropriated and is now defined in military terms by one power even as it invokes coalition activities to legitimate its actions as on behalf of a global collectivity. Now the whole world is a potential battlefield; the global war on terror is, at least in the cartographic sense, just that, global.

Most salient in the contemporary discussions of the military geography of the war on terror is the work of Thomas Barnett, author of the aptly titled *The Pentagon's New Map*.[6] While much of the discussion of the war on terror is structured within a crude register of geographical categories, "The Pentagon's New Map," first published for a wide readership in the March 2003 issue of *Esquire* magazine on the eve of the American invasion of Iraq, explicitly tries to render the world in a cartography of safety and danger.[7] Subsequently the article was reworked into a popular book the following year, which among other things, explicates the argument through an autobiographical narrative of how the ideas in the article were developed.

The basic structure of Barnett's world is one of a divided planet, one in which the majority of the world's population is becoming integrated in the globalized core while the remaining parts live in the nonintegrated gap. Connectivity is the key; those not connected are prone to violence and live under a variety of tyrannies. Those who are connected in the core live in better conditions because connectivity means a substantial degree of freedom to follow one's own course in life. Kaplan's bifurcated world is very similar to what Barnett invokes as the cartography that is needed in understanding the world after 9/11; Barnett's integrated core and nonintegrating gap in the world economy maps neatly onto Kaplan's fears. But contrary to Kaplan's assumption that little can be done, Barnett is clear that the U.S. military has a role to ensure that the First Man is not doomed to his miserable Hobbesian fate. Instead he will be connected into the global economy and given all the benefits and opportunities of modernity available to the Last Man.

Barnett's book is interesting as an attempt to suggest a post-cold war strategic mentality that has far reaching implications for both the American military and the global economy. Its grand strategy for the layperson is presented in tabloid populism terms. Wars of a new type he suggests, ones for which the old Pentagon, designed to protect the American National Security state of 1940s vintage through the cold war, is singularly ill prepared, are already upon the American people; 9/11 simply confirmed the pattern. The Pentagon is so ill prepared precisely because it is still operating on a series of geographic premises that have been rendered irrelevant by the demise of the Soviet Union and the rise of globalization. New maps of the strategic situation are needed. Barnett provides this in a map that divides the world between connected and those that are not (yet) in this happy position of being a Last Man.

The Pentagon's New Map proposes the use of American military force to eradicate the isolated political regimes in the remaining parts of the world from whence threats to globalization emanate. It never quite claims to advocate a war to end all wars, but Barnett argues this is, in fact, a possibility now that globalization has dramatically reduced the probabilities of wars between nation states. It is this premise that links strategy to globalization, military planning to a very different world, one where *pax Americana* combined with the integration of the global economy which has, it seems, the real potential to finally rid humanity of the dangers of major wars between states. But this is not empire Barnett insists; imperial wars are a matter of past misdemeanors on the part of the great powers, not something America indulges in—from Kosovo to Afghanistan, and on to Iraq, American forces bring liberation and the chance to join the global economy, rather than an extension of American rule.

Crucial to all this is Barnett's insistence that America's enemies are no longer major states; China is not the much feared next rival for global hegemony, but rather the latest success story in the global economy that wants to trade rather than build weapons. Small rogue states, mad dictators, and, of course, international terrorists who thrive in such circumstances, are the target for the new American military, one that will have to figure out how to do nation building sooner rather than later. But if the Pentagon still insists on preparing for war against other major states, rather than dealing with the real threats to international security from the gap, then the breakdown of international order that these threaten, might in fact lead to precisely the kind of war the Pentagon is planning.

In many ways Barnett fits the description of tabloid realism. The stories Barnett tells of his struggles to get attention among the Pentagon bureaucrats fit neatly into the tabloid realism genre. So too the reaction to many of the e-mail criticisms that Barnett has received in response to the *Esquire* article where he has been accused of being the secret mastermind behind Pentagon planning for the invasion of Iraq among other things. Barnett's response in the book in joking about his role as Fox Mulder, or the mysterious smoking man of *X-Files* infamy, or likening himself to Tom Clancy's fictional CIA analyst cum action hero Jack Ryan, shows not only a sense of self-deprecating humor, but a clear understanding of the need to link his heroic struggles to get the Pentagon bureaucrats to focus on their new roles as shrinkers of the gap, to the wider readership skeptical of the competence of the military to accomplish many things. Combined with his apparently compulsive blogging activities, Barnett is clearly a man of the people engaged in a nearly single handed attempt to remake the American military so that it can fulfill the American dream of an orderly and peaceful world in which all may pursue life, liberty, and happiness.[8]

Barnett's argument that globalization in the long run promotes democracy suggests that middle classes are key to stable liberal democracies. But globalization's success is not inevitable and may need the application of considerable military force to ensure that disconnected regimes are connected into the global integrated core. Where Europeans may be squeamish in sending their troops to Iraq, there are other potential allies that might be much more suitable for the war on terror that is all about remaking the nonintegrated gap. Writing in the *Washington Post* in April 2004 in the aftermath of the terrorist attacks in Madrid prior to the Spanish election, he heaped scorn on the Spanish for withdrawing troops from Iraq, and suggested that the American strategy needed to look for more appropriate allies with a growing commitment to the global economy. Bemoaning the failure to get India to send 17,000 troops to Iraq, and continued support for a Pakistan that harbored al Qaeda supporters, he suggested that India, China, and Russia are three rapidly integrating states with whom new U.S. strategic partnerships should be built: "When the United States enlists the active support of a China, India or Russia, it gains military partners who won't run at the first sight of blood, argue incessantly over the constitutional rights of "enemy combatants" or see their governments collapse every time the terrorists land a lucky strike back home."[9]

This is not just a repudiation of old Europe, it's a dramatic rethinking of where America might find useful allies in its war on terror. Such arguments for the use of allied troops in pacifying a conquered Iraq suggest an imperial project of global proportions. All of which raises the crucial questions of the geography of violence and the imposition of globalization on those who are not integrated. In short, given the invasion of Iraq, and Barnett's proposed wholesale remaking of societies, it raises the question of empire and the current interpretations of U.S. policy in these terms.

Empire

In among the endless discussions of American empire, whether it is one, should be one, and if so how it might shape global politics, is a debate about the role of military force and what kind of American military is needed to prosecute the so called war on terror. Implicit in most of these discussions, and explicit in just a few, are the unavoidable political questions concerning how the world in which American military power operates is to be described, known, and policed. Geopolitics, literally the way in which the world becomes known and the related arguments for appropriate action in that so-specified world, are at the heart of most discussions of empire. They are also implicitly in the arguments that deny geographical complexity in favor of abstract specifications of George Bush style theological geopolitics and the moral economies of them and us, virtue and evil. The denial of geographical context in favor of a moral canvass nonetheless is a form of geopolitics, one that implicitly asserts that all places operate within a universal set of categories known to those who specify the world in such ways.[10]

While the controversy over in what sense the United States is an empire, and what the consequences of such formulations might be for American foreign policy rages, Barnett flatly denies that the United States is an empire. Falling back on the jargon of a number of earlier studies he has been involved with, he suggests that empires are about "maximal rule sets" which clearly, he thinks, the United States is not trying to impose on the rest of the world. He understands globalization as a process of increasing interconnection to the global economy; a matter of mutual interdependence; a process that he suggests the United States is furthest ahead and from which it benefits most.[11] This process is also inevitably about challenges to traditional cultures and national identities. But he suggests Americans must understand such nationalism as such rather than as anti-Americanism.[12] More specifically he continues:

> Remembering that disconnectedness itself is the ultimate enemy, America can, by extending globalization in a fair and just manner, not only defeat the threats it faces today but eliminate in advance entire generations of threat that our children and grand children would otherwise face. In short, there is simply no possibility of keeping the threat "outside, over there" anymore. If we as a nation accept the logic of globalization's advance, our definition of *us* must include all of *them* who now feel left out of globalization's benefits, as well as all of *them* who would employ all manner of violence to deny its advance. This historical process is neither forced assimilation nor the extension of empire, but the expansion of freedom first and foremost.[13]

Quite how the contemporary operation of international financial institutions, or the shenanigans of Halliburton and numerous other military contractors in Iraq in the aftermath of the 2003 invasion, might qualify as agents of the fair and just extension of globalization is not discussed in Barnett's book. But following the passage quoted above, he goes on in the next paragraph to suggest that "Real freedom exists within defined rule sets that reduce life's uncertainties to the point where individuals can efficiently run their own lives, avoiding the tyrannies of extreme poverty, endemic violence, and talent stifling political repression."[14] This passage is in the context of the denial of America being an empire.

What this all suggests, however, is that Barnett's notion of the rule sets of freedom are very close indeed to Hardt and Negri's discussion of *Empire*.[15] In this interpretation, global capitalism is understood as caught up in the extension of rules and regulations that involve the morphing of sovereignty into a larger system that they call Empire with a capital E. Might Barnett's fascination with globalization, something he claims came from his work with the global investment company Cantor Fitzgerald in a series of workshops in the World Trade Center prior to September 11, not also be traced back to his earlier graduate student career as an expert on the Soviet world and his work as a teaching assistant in a course on Marx? He might deny any such imputation, but the exuberance of Barnett's panegyrics to globalization neatly mirrors Hardt and Negri's retelling of the rise of capital in their idiosyncratic neo-Marxist mode. After all, it is Marx and Engels who penned the best description to date of globalization:

> The bourgeoisie, by the rapid improvement of all instruments of production, by the immensely facilitated means of communication, draws all, even the most barbarian, nations into civilization. The cheap prices of commodities are the heavy artillery with which it forces the barbarians' intensely obstinate hatred of foreigners to capitulate. It compels all nations, on pain of extinction, to adopt the bourgeois mode of production; it compels them to introduce what it calls civilization into their midst, i.e., to become bourgeois themselves. In one word, it creates a world after its own image.[16]

Extinction for regimes that refuse to play by the rules of the global market place is what Barnett argues is necessary; they must become bourgeois, by being convinced of the obvious benefits if at all possible. But if they are not to be induced or convinced, they must be compelled by force, if all else fails, to be free. Such military adventures are the stuff of imperial history, of course, from India to the Sudan in the nineteenth century and in numerous other places since, including Iraq from 1917, when the British "liberated" it, through the early 1920s when the Iraqis violently rejected the occupying "liberators."[17]

Mapping the End of Global Warfare

While none of this is new; indeed these repetitions of imperial history would be farcical if they were not so tragic, especially for the large number of Afghani and Iraqi victims of contemporary violence, what is supposedly new in Barnett's argument is the apparent end of great power warfare. While imperial adventures are a matter of warfare, and recalcitrant regimes in the nonintegrating gap apparently need disciplining, the possibility of doing so is not now complicated by the fear of such military interventions escalating into a superpower confrontation. Nuclear weapons may have imposed a stalemate on the United States and the USSR in the period of the cold war, but the victory of the globalizers, if not the United States in that struggle, suggests to Barnett a new strategic landscape on a much larger scale. Indeed for all the focus on Iraq in the discussion of Barnett's writings, this larger argument he makes is in many ways much more important, and as it unfolds, much more frightening because it assumes that globalization will be an unstoppable force if it can be appropriately accelerated by the use of the American military. This is loosely consistent with the sentiments expressed in the post- September 11 *National Security Strategy of the United States of America* in 2002 where, in among discussions of military capabilities and alliance systems, is a section delineating free trade initiatives and global economic growth as essential to the future of American national security.[18]

While Barnett might be understood in terms of a revived form of grand imperialism, his crucial argument is that technology combined with globalization has

effectively put an end to any prospect of inter-state warfare among the largest powers. His whole agenda in the 1990s was about the fact that the Pentagon had failed
to grasp this new geopolitical situation. As a result, the war planners and weapon
designers were focused on the dangers of the emergence of a new potential rival for
global hegemony, one that looked remarkably like China in many of the scenario
planning exercises in the Pentagon in the 1990s. Thinking in terms of a "bolt from
the blue" Pearl Harbor style surprise attack from a "near peer," and the weapon systems needed for a confrontation in the Pacific, meant that attacks such as the one
launched by al Qaeda in September 2001, were simply not seriously contemplated by
Pentagon planners.

Barnett goes on to argue that, given the threats to the United States and to globalization posed by terrorists who inhabit the nonintegrated gap, a fundamental
restructuring of the U.S. military, at least as significant as that carried out in the
1940s when the United States adapted to its new global role, is needed. More specifically the Pentagon needs to reorganize its forces so that it maintains the ability to
destroy any potential military rivals and also to build a substantial force capable of
doing what was frequently referred to in derogatory terms by the Bush administration as "nation building." Indeed in Barnett's terms the ability of the U.S. military to
destroy the Iraqi military opposition in a few weeks in March and April of 2003, but
its apparent inability to occupy, administer, and reconstruct Iraq after the invasion,
is proof of the need for such a new force.

Calling this force the "system administrators" of an extended globalization may
not be a wise choice of terminology, but peacemaking, institution building service
providers, backed by considerable firepower, is what he claims the new U.S. military
needs. Then it can rebuild states that it has conquered and link them into the benefits of civilization, whereupon they will cease to present a threat to the rest of the
world and the United States in particular. Most non-Americans might understand
this as imperial pacification, because such tasks have long been an important role for
garrison troops in the far flung reaches of many empires. But given the ideological
proclivities of American politicians and the American public to deny their identity in
imperial terms, such terminology will not appear in Barnett's formulations.

Put in these terms, Barnett suggests that the war on terror is not a war without
end, an Orwellian nightmare of perpetual military violence in "Pipelinestan" as well
as elsewhere, as Bulent Gokay suggests,[19] precisely because the gap can be shrunk
quickly if an American grand strategy takes its cue from Barnett and sets about doing
so with a series of demonstration projects, of which Kosovo, Afghanistan, and Iraq
are but the beginning. Other states, (Libya for example?) will quickly see the way the
geopolitical wind is blowing and work out accommodations with the system administrators whose task it is to integrate them into the benefits of civilization. When the
last recalcitrant parts of the gap have been eliminated American forces can assume
the role of global cop ensuring order in a now pacified global neighborhood. Then
victory can be declared. The rivalries that led to disastrous wars in the twentieth century will be a matter of historical curiosity and the system administrators will ensure
that civilization will remain triumphant.

This is, of course, classic grand strategy; it presents a clear mapping of the world,
its dangers to the political order of, in this case American led globalization, and a

practical series of forces, tactics and priorities for military planners, American and other politicians.[20] It renders the apparently disorderly world into a series of places with strategic roles to play, and suggests very clearly where friends might be found, where enemies are to be attacked and how victory is to be accomplished. And victory will be accomplished if the generals have the appropriate forces and the politicians understand that new alliances and complicated bargains with former foes are a necessary part of finishing the job that globalization has started and that al Qaeda and various rogue states threaten to thwart.

Given the arguments above about imperial power and rivalries might this not be seen as simply one more imperial arrangement? Barnett seems to suggest that its global reach makes it a different situation; one in which no external rivals will arise so a universal political arrangement of globalization will not fall prey to the emergence of a rival. This is the crucial assumption which makes the strategy of shrinking the gap by using what coalitions of the willing can be arranged the appropriate priority, rather than planning for the supposedly inevitable emergence of a global military competitor. In short, and in keeping with the geopolitical formulation of wild zones and tame zones that structures so much of tabloid realism these days, this is much more about Fukuyama's Hegelian specification of the end of history than it is about Huntingdon's clashes of civilizations. In Barnett's world there is now only one civilization, one culture that is on the threshold of victory if only its rulers can be made to understand the realities of its contemporary strategic geography.

Empirical objections to Barnett's formulations are obviously many; although he has a ready answer to some of them. What about the crash of the Asian economies in the late 1990s? The answer is local banking practices rather than any fundamental problems with international capital markets or currency traders. Argentina likewise? Oil dependent states in the Middle East are not really interconnected with the rest of the world; their trading is limited to one commodity and they frequently limit external contact to reduce cultural challenges to traditional nondemocratic rule. But dismissing the petroleum producers of the Middle East as unconnected apart from their oil sales is simply wrong, as Saddam Hussein found out after his invasion of Kuwait in 1990, when it became clear the Kuwait economy was offshore in the investment houses of Europe and North America.[21]

Environmental disruptions simply do not get discussed; after all this is a book about globalization and military strategy; the material context for either is not of great import given contemporary technologies. Understanding contemporary wars as new omits the history of imperial rule. It ignores the connections between violence and the control over transport of essential supplies from peripheries to metropoles. These are matters which frequently facilitate opportunistic political violence in poverty stricken areas as well as resistance by local peoples to the disruption of local ways of life by resource extraction industries. More recently the politics of international consumer action around conflict diamonds and the international regulation of many other commodities have highlighted this violent politics.[22]

As a strategic analyst charged with thinking about the future and the needs of the U.S. armed forces, its not surprising that Barnett addresses the future in terms of the role of the military. As a political scientist and cold war analyst plunged into a world of high finance, it is perhaps not surprising that he so took to heart the view of the

world from the top of the World Trade Center that his international financial investment colleagues at Cantor Fitzgerald used in planning their corporate strategies. As a
self-confessed peddler of PowerPoint briefs, rather than a writer of lengthy scholarly
works, it's not surprising that Barnett is willing to hang so much of his argument on
a very flimsy and ill-defined notion of connectivity, and ironically ignore the much
more robust work of international relations scholarship that substantially supports
his case about global integration providing better security outcomes than attempts
at national autarky.[23]

Cartographies of War

Most important of all in putting works such as Barnett's into context is the implicit
assumption that the current crisis is caused by either rogue states or Al Qaeda. When
America was attacked on September 11, 2001, the opportunity to respond in a non-
military way was not even seriously considered.[24] The subsequent war on Iraq, which
the Bush administration falsely claimed was connected to the campaign against Al
Qaeda, alienated allies and caused dissention in the alliance constructed to prosecute
the war on terror, a major strategic error in at least the opinion of former NATO
commander Wesley Clark.[25] In addition to the assumption of war as the appropriate
social response is the cartography of danger that cannot conceive that Al Qaeda and
large parts of the population of the world might object to American interference in
their affairs. After all, Al Qaeda's campaign to rid the land of the two holy places of
infidel interlopers and the comprador elites they arm and support, is also a matter of
claiming noninterference by outsiders.

The problem with the cartography of danger, as with the dangers of all geopolitical
categories is precisely that they include too much and simplify the complex mess of
human geographies into abstract inhuman entities.[26] Thus, once Barnett has drawn
his line between the core and the gap, interventions into the gap are all of a kind;
whether terrorists or sovereign states, drug lords or recalcitrant rulers, because they
are in the gap they are potentially dangerous. Because they are specified as dangerous by Barnett's fantastic cartography they can be targeted. Once again geopolitical
abstraction given the "objectivity" of cartography renders peoples and places ready
for military action.

Tabloid realism usually suggests a pessimism about the world and the difficulty of
managing dangers from abroad. In this respect, Barnett dramatically parts company
from the other grand strategists, the Brzezinskis and Huntingdons and their nostalgia for a simple geography of domestic homogeneity and dangerous external threats.
Barnett will have none of this; his is a blueprint for conquest, a refusal of this pessimism, a call to arms and to the further expansion of American power, in the interest
of all of humanity, of course. In this it is a liberal expansionist coupling of financial
power to military conquest, an imperial impulse once again, but one that refuses the
necessity of what Debrix calls the tabloid realist therapy of ideological conservativism
and securitization in favor of pre-emptive conquest. As such Barnett tweaks the Bush
administration's preventative war policy and simultaneously extends the arguments
of the Project for a New American Century into a new geographic representation.

But he also extends the Pentagon's mandate to a global development initiative, one designed to connect all remaining recalcitrant parts of the world into the circuits of globalization, or in Hardt and Negri's terms, Empire.

In their subsequent analysis of war, in the first section of *Multitude,* which they describe as the sequel to *Empire*, Hardt and Negri note that warfare has become extended both metaphorically and practically into constituting many facets of social life. Wars on drugs, poverty, and many other matters extend the social relations of force and domination, all in the name of the provision of security of course. This is what Orwell feared and why Michael Moore invokes Orwell's language in *1984* in concluding his critique of what is happening in George Bush's America in his movie *Fahrenheit 9/11.*[27] The exceptional powers granted to rulers in times of war have been extended now by the global war on terror, temporary powers of emergency rule extended in a world where high intensity policing and its rationales of producing "security" have merged with low-intensity warfare and counter-insurgency operations. Hardt and Negri claim, in a reversal of Clauswitz's famous axiom, that politics is now the continuation of warfare.

> What is distinctive and new about the claim that politics is the continuation of war is that it refers to power in its normal functioning, everywhere and always, outside and within each society. ... War in other words, becomes the general matrix for all relations of power and techniques of domination, whether or not bloodshed is involved. War has become a regime of biopower, that is, a form of rule aimed not only at controlling the population but producing and reproducing all aspects of social life.[28]

But Hardt and Negri go on to point out that the contemporary American mode of warfare, relying as it does on immense technological sophistication, surveillance, communications, and the overwhelming superiority of air and naval power, a combination of doctrinal and technological innovations usually summarized as constituting a "revolution in military affairs" (RMA), is ill prepared for the policing duties and counter insurgency roles that operating in Somalia, Kosovo, Afghanistan, and Iraq require. The limitations of the RMA are thus very considerable. Here Barnett is onside with Hardt and Negri's critique, because clearly he wishes to dramatically reorganize the U.S. military to include a large component of system administrators who act as the police to ensure that Empire/globalization expands by doing the appropriate nation building to ensure broadband connectivity and hence pacification by integration into the functional core. While Hardt and Negri go on to ruminate about the increasing number of mercenaries and contract employees that these inadequacies in the Pentagon's capabilities require, and then ponder the fact that empires tend to collapse when they no longer rely on an armed citizenry, Barnett suggests reforming the U.S. military dramatically to enable it to carry out its task of extending Empire.

Tabloid Imperialism

Read in these terms Barnett's program is effectively a military manual for the expansion of Empire. In an entirely different vocabulary, Barnett parallels Hardt and Negri's understanding biopower as productive, the condition of Empire and its extension of governance rules neatly parallels Barnett's concern with rule sets. Barnett is unhistorically dismissive of empires as consisting of maximal rule sets that determine how things must be in favor of minimalist global sets that are what globalization is all about.

> America does not shrink the Gap to conquer the Gap, but to invite two billion people to join something better and safer in the Core. Empires involve enforcing maximal rules sets, where the leader tells the led not just what they cannot do but what they must do. This has never been the American way of war and peace, and does not reflect our system of governance. We enforce minimum rule sets, carefully ruling out only the most obviously destructive behavior. We push connectivity above all else, letting people choose what to do with those ties, that communication, and all those possibilities.[29]

But this concern neatly parallels Hardt and Negri's formulation of Empire as the rules and modes of governance that have slipped the traditional bounds of national sovereignty only to become part of a larger territorially unbounded function of rule in Empire.

All of which suggests that Fukuyama and the triumph of liberal ideals is closer to the mark than Huntingdon. Hardt and Negri are delightfully scornful about Huntingdon's clash of civilizations suggesting, in parallel with Barnett's cartography, that Huntingdon got his geography wrong by suggesting that geographically defined regional blocs would vie for power in the future.[30] The fault lines lie not between civilizations but between the periphery of the global economy and the integrated core of Empire where civilization (singular) rules. If one accepts this cartography, then what lies in store is more of what Max Boot terms "small wars," which have historically been very important in the rise of American power.[31] In this sense, too, there is little new here.

Thus Barnett's writing goes beyond the genre of tabloid realism; it is something much more ambitious. It is not a matter of realist pessimism concerning the possibilities of anything but the eternal return of geopolitical conflict. It is nothing less than a manifesto for global warfare to transform the world, for its own good, of course. This is a dangerously seductive ideological vision of the promise of imperial warfare. For that is what the conquest of peripheral places and their incorporation into the political and economic arrangements of the metropolis is in practice. A war to end all wars, but this time with a strategy and in circumstances where civilization really will win over the remaining barbarisms in the periphery. This is closer to tabloid idealism, in the sense of a blueprint for universal peace, a manifesto for final victory, a utopian scheme for which the tools and circumstances are propitious, if only the elites will pay attention to the possibilities for resolute action, which will unfortunately require the spilling of some blood on the way to final victory.

All this also neatly fits into Hardt and Negri's formulation of the current situation as one that invokes two exceptions.[32] Exceptional in the case of political theorist Carl Schmitt who discusses sovereignty as lying in the invocation of emergency measures which are rendered necessary in times of war. But exceptional too in the American sense, where America does not need to abide by the normal rules of human conduct because it is the universal bearer of the promise of the future of humanity. In Derek Gregory's words concerning the invasion of Iraq: "The strategy of the Bush administration was, once again, to present the United States as the world—the 'universal nation' articulating universal values—against 'the enemies of civilization': terrorists, tyrants, barbarians."[33] From this powerful formulation comes impetus for a war on terror, a war to eradicate the regimes, peoples and conditions that breed opposition to Empire.

But as the violence and chaos in Afghanistan and Iraq powerfully indicate, the seductions of militarism need to be resisted by insisting that real people live in the gap/wild zones, people who might be better served by political action and the insistence that peace comes by peaceful means rather than the extension of war as the fundamental social relation of our time. Hardt and Negri are infuriatingly vague on what forms resistance to war as the dominant social relation might take. But clearly the point of thinking through Barnett's logic, in parallel to Hardt and Negri, is to refuse to accept either the cartographies of militarized Fukuyamism or the perpetual pessimism of Huntingdon's clashing spatial entities.

The future will be better served by geographies that are sensitive to the prior disruptions of the non-integrated gap by the depredations of the core, and a mapping that does not elide the long histories of cooperation between the elites of many rogue states and rulers and business people in the core.[34] This is not the Marxist conspiracy that Barnett derides; it is a long historical record sensitive to the lived geographical diversity of humanity that needs to be taken seriously in any analysis of present circumstances.

Above all, the peoples of the world would be better served if the stories of American intervention were told in the practical terms of real histories and real peoples rather than in the abstractions of geopolitics where rich histories and geographies are reduced to flippant comments about rule sets. Challenging formulations such as Tom Barnett's, with their all too convenient cartographic representations of the complex and violent human condition, is a necessary part of the broad task of resisting war as the dominant social relation of our times.

Notes

1. Derek Gregory, *The Colonial Present: Afghanistan, Palestine, Iraq.* Oxford: Blackwell, 2004.
2. Francois Debrix, "Tabloid Realism and the Revival of American Security Culture," *Geopolitics* 8(3), 2003: 151–190; 163.
3. Joanne Sharp, *Condensing the Cold War: Reader's Digest and American Identity.* Minneapolis: University of Minnesota Press, 2000.
4. Robert D. Kaplan, "The Coming Anarchy," *The Atlantic Monthly* 273(2), 1994: 44–76, 1994; Robert D. Kaplan, *The Coming Anarchy: Shattering the Dreams of the Post-Cold War World.* New York: Random House 2000, 24.
5. See W. S. Johnson, "New Challenges for the Unified Command Plan," *Joint Forces Quarterly* Summer 2002:. 62–70.
6. Thomas P. M. Barnett, *The Pentagon's New Map: War and Peace in the Twenty-First Century,* New York: Putnam's 2004.
7. Thomas P. M. Barnett, "The Pentagon's New Map," *Esquire* March 2003:. 174–179 available at www.nwc.navy.mil/newrulesets/ThePentagonsNewMap.htm.
8. See his Web site at http://www.thomaspmbarnett.com/ for near daily updates of the reception of his work and his further plans for spreading the word.

9. Thomas P. M. Barnett, "Forget Europe: How About These Allies? *Washington Post*, April 11, 2004, B5.

10. Gearoid Ó Tuathail, *Critical Geopolitics: The Politics of Writing Global Space.* Minneapolis: University of Minnesota Press, 1996.

11. In an interesting irony relating to this claim, the issue of *Foreign Policy* on the newsstands when Barnett's book was published, contained the magazine's fourth annual "globalization index." According to a combination of economic, personal, technological and political criteria, which appear to be close to Barnett's ill defined notion of connectivity, the United States ranked seventh on the index behind, in order of most connected, Ireland, Singapore, Switzerland, the Netherlands, Finland, and Canada. See "Measuring Globalization," *Foreign Policy*, March/April 2004: 54–69.

12. Barnett, *The Pentagon's New Map*, 123.

13. Barnett, *The Pentagon's New Map*, 124.

14. Barnett, *The Pentagon's New Map*, 124.

15. Michael Hardt, and Antonio Negri, *Empire*. Cambridge: Harvard University Press, 2000.

16. Karl Marx, and Friedrich Engels, *The Communist Manifesto* Harmondsworth: Penguin 1967, 84 (Original publication 1848).

17. As journalist Robert Fisk repeatedly documents. See http://www.robert-fisk.com.

18. *The National Security Strategy of the United States of America*, Washington: The White House September 2002.

19. Bulent Gokay, "The United States against the World: Oil, Hegemony and the Militarization of Globalization," in *11 September 2001; War Terror and Judgment*, eds. Bulent Gokay and R. B. J. Walker, 91–109. London: Frank Cass, 2003.

20. On grand strategy see Edward Luttwak, *Strategy*. Cambridge, MA: Harvard 1987; Richard Rosecrance, and Arthur Stein, eds., *The Domestic Bases of Grand Strategy*. Ithaca: Cornell University Press, 1993.

21. Tim Luke, "The Discipline of Security Studies and the Codes of Containment: Learning the Lessons from Kuwait," *Alternatives* 16(3), 1991: 315–344.

22. See Dietrich Jung, ed., *Shadow Globalization: Ethnic Conflict and the New Wars*. London: Routledge, 2003; Philippe le Billon, ed., "The Geopolitics of Resource Wars" Special Issue of *Geopolitics* 9(1), 2004.

23. Etel Solingen, *Regional Orders at Century's Dawn: Global and Domestic Influences on Grand Strategy*. Princeton, NJ: Princeton University Press, 1998.

24. Simon Dalby, "Calling 911: Geopolitics, Security and America's New War," *Geopolitics* 8(3), 2003:. 61–86.

25. Wesley K. Clark, *Winning Modern Wars: Iraq, Terrorism and the American Empire*. New York: Public Affairs 2003.

26. Mat Coleman, "The Naming of 'Terrorism' and Evil 'Outlaws': Geopolitical Placemaking After 11 September," *Geopolitics* 8(3), 2003:. 87–104.

27. Tom Barnett went to see a showing of Fahrenheit 9/11 in July 2004 after a day briefing policy makers in the Pentagon. He is dismissive of it as "Marxist conspiracy" in his blog of July 8, "I'm called to the Pentagon," available at http://www.thomaspmbarnett.com.

28. Michael Hardt, and Antonio Negri, *Multitude: War and Democracy in the Age of Empire*. New York: Penguin 2004, 13.

29. See Barnett, *The Pentagon's New Map*, 355.

30. Hardt and Negri, *Multitude*,. 33–35.

31. Max Boot, *The Savage Wars of Peace: Small Wars and the Rise of American Power.* New York: Basic, 2002.
32. Hardt and Negri, *Multitude.*
33. Gregory, *The Colonial Present*, 195.
34. Susan Roberts, Anna Secor, and Matthew Sparke "Neoliberal Geopolitics," *Antipode* 35. 2003:. 886–897.

16

Demodernizing by Design
Everyday Infrastructure and Political Violence[1]

Stephen Graham

Everyday Infrastructures as Geopolitical Sites

> If you want to destroy someone nowadays, you go after their infrastructure. You don't have to be a nation state to do it, and if they retain any capacity for retaliation then it's probably better if you're not.[2]

On our rapidly urbanizing planet, the everyday life of the world's swelling population of urbanites is increasingly sustained by vast systems of infrastructure and technology. Whilst often taken for granted, at least when they work, these systems allow modern urban life to exist. Their pipes, ducts, servers, wires, and tunnels sustain the flows, connections, and metabolisms that are intrinsic to contemporary cities. Through their endless technological agency, these systems help transform the natural into the cultural, the social and the urban. Such edifices thus provide the hidden background to modern urban everyday life.

By sustaining flows of water, waste, energy, information, people, commodities, and signs, the vast complexes of contemporary urban infrastructure are the embodiment of Enlightenment dreams of the social control of nature. They are a prerequisite to any notion of modern civilization. And yet, at the same time, the potential for catastrophic violence against cities and urban life has changed in parallel with the shift of urban life towards ever greater reliance on modern infrastructures. The result of this is that the everyday technics, spaces, and infrastructures of urban life—highways, metro trains, computer networks, water and sanitation systems, electricity grids, airliners—may be easily assaulted and turned into agents either of instantaneous terror or debilitating demodernization. In a 24/7, always-on, and intensively networked society, urbanites, especially those in the advanced industrial world, become so reliant on infrastructural and computerized systems that they creep ever closer to the point where, as Bill Joy puts it, "turning off becomes suicide."[3] Given that all of the 'Big Systems' that sustain advanced, urban societies are profoundly electrical, city residents become, in particular, "hostages to electricity" (Leslie 1999). The complex social and technological architectures of cyberspace, for example, "remains an incomprehensible, immaterial, and abstract entity as long as we continue to disregard the physical foundation of the artifacts of the electrical infrastructure."[4]

Urban everyday life everywhere is thus stalked by the threat of interruption: the blackout, the gridlock, the severed connection, the technical malfunction, the inhibited flow, the network not available sign. During such moments, which tend to be fairly normal in cities of the global South and much less so in cities of the global North, the vast edifices of infrastructure become so much useless junk. The everyday life of cities shifts into a massive struggle against darkness, cold, immobility, hunger, the fear of crime and violence, and, if water-borne diseases are a threat, a catastrophic degeneration in public health levels. The perpetual technical flux of modern cities becomes, in a sense, suspended. Improvisation, repair, and finding alternative means of being warm, safe, drinking clean water, eating, moving about, and disposing of wastes quickly become the overriding imperatives of everyday life. Very quickly the normally hidden background infrastructure of urban everyday life becomes, fleetingly, palpably clear to all.

All this means that "tremendous lethal capabilities can be created simply by contra-functioning the everyday applications of many technics."[5] The use of systems and technologies that previously tended to be taken for granted, ignored, or viewed as banal underpinnings to everyday urban life, thus becomes increasingly charged with anxiety. Unknowable risks connected with internationalized geopolitical conflicts are palpably infused into everyday technological artifacts. The post-cold war landscapes of "asymmetric" conflict blur into a transformation of banal technical artifacts of urban material culture into potential weapons causing death, destruction, and disruption.

Of course, such anxieties are not entirely new. Warfare and political violence have long targeted the technological support systems of cities. World War II bombing planners evolved complex methods of destroying transport systems, water infrastructures, and electricity and communications grids. Car bombs, of course, have been the staple of every insurgency and terrorist campaign for at least the past four decades. Nevertheless, it is clear that the sophistication with which everyday infrastructures are attacked and exploited to project lethal power is dramatically escalating.

The most obvious examples here, of course, were the devastating airline suicide attacks of September 11, 2001.[6] In this example, massive cruise missiles were, in effect, fashioned out of just four of the few thousand or so airliners that fly above and between U.S. cities at any one time. Strategic and symbolic targets at the very metropolitan heartlands of U.S. military and economic power were devastated in the attacks and thousands of people were murdered in a few hours—effects beyond the power of the entire Nazi or Japanese regimes during the whole of World War II. As the World Trade Center towers collapsed, destructive power approximating a small nuclear bomb was unleashed. Massive infrastructrure failures across large parts of Manhattan and the eastern seaboard were, in turn, manufactured through the use of everyday infrastructures as weapons.

Of course, the effects of the attacks on the Twin Towers and the Pentagon were also rhetorically manufactured by politicians and the media to produce a sense of generalized and normalized attack on the United States and the Western World as a whole (a precursor, as we shall see, to a massive military assault on Afghanistan and

Iraqi societies and their fragile urban infrastructure systems). But, at the same time, such enormous destruction was engineered through the coordinated use of a few box cutters to turn everyday systems of mobility into catastrophic weapons which, in turn, brought down large swathes of the technical fabric of one of the world's largest and most intensively networked urban corridors. At one level, this was spectacular violence using everyday infrastructures as weapons to destroy or disrupt other everyday infrastructures.

Al-Qaeda's later Madrid train attacks of 2003, the exploitation of the inevitably crowded capsular spaces of Israeli buses by Palestinian suicide attacks in the Al-Aqsa intifada, the London tube and bus bombings on the 7th of July, 2005, and the bombing of Moscow metro cars by Chechyen terrorists in February 2004, have also exploited everyday mobility systems to murderous effect.

Much less recognized, however, over the past few decades, nation states have also developed the capabilities to deliberately target and destroy the basic technical infrastructures of urban life, sometimes with effects even more deadly than even the 9/11 attacks. A core principle of the doctrine of the U.S. and Israeli militaries is to systematically demodernize the entire urban societies of those deemed to be adversaries. It is striking, then, that the innovations underpinning both informal and state terror—to use the words of Timothy Luke—"mobilize assets for attacks that destructively activate the embedded threats of large technical systems, everyday logistics, and civil offensive capabilities."[7]

In such a context, this chapter seeks to focus critically on the strategies, doctrines, techniques, and discourses surrounding state-backed infrastructural warfare. The focus is deliberately placed on state backed infrastructural warfare because it has received much less attention from critical researchers than the exploitation of urban infrastructures by terrorist groups, despite producing much larger levels of immiseration and destruction than even the largest terrorist attacks. Because of its transglobal military power, this chapter centers in particular on the infrastructural warfare efforts of the world's global hegemon: the United States. The discussion that follows falls in to three parts. The first explores the central role of infrastructural targeting within U.S. air power doctrine. Part two follows this up with a brief case study of U.S. state-backed infrastructural warfare in practice. This focuses in particular on the experience, at the hands of the U.S. military and government, of war, sanctions, and war of Iraq between 1991 and 2004. It also addresses the emergence of a state-backed computer networked attack capability in the United States. Finally, in the chapter's conclusion, a brief reflection is made on the geopolitics of forced disconnection, and demodernization, within contemporary war and strategy.

Infrastructural Warfare as a Central Tenet of U.S. Military Doctrine

It should be lights out in Belgrade: every power grid, water pipe, bridge, road and war-related factory has to be targeted [...]. We will set your country back by pulverizing you. You want 1950? We can do 1950. You want 1389? We can do that, too!"[8]

We need to study how to degrade and destroy our adversaries' abilities to transmit their military, political, and economic goods, services and information [...]. Infrastructures, defining both traditional and emerging lines of communication, present increasingly lucrative targets for airpower. [The vision of] airmen should focus on lines of communications that will increasingly define modern societies.[9]

Rather than stemming from informal terrorist organizations, efforts to forcibly destroy everyday urban infrastructures derive overwhelmingly from the formal violence of nation states. Drawing from the traditional, Weberian conception that nation states should legitimately hold a monopoly over organized political violence—a monopoly that is fast unraveling in the post-cold war world—many state military thinkers and theorists have centered since World War II on the massive impacts that can be gained by targeting urban infrastructure.

Befitting its hegemonic status currently, one state, in particular—the United States—dominates such infrastructural warfare. Whilst it would be an oversimplification, it is possible to argue that the geopolitical and military strategy currently being developed to maintain U.S. power as a global hegemon rests on a simple, two-sided idea. On the one hand, develop new technology-based networked mobilities and control and surveillance capabilities to a level which allows attempts at globe-spanning dominance based on a near-monopoly of space and air power (what is being termed network-centric warfare and the Revolution in Military Affairs or RMA[10]). On the other hand, develop the tools and technologies that can disconnect, demodernize, and immobilize adversary societies at any time or place deemed necessary.

Such a transformation in U.S. military doctrine is extremely contested. This is particularly so after the massive urban insurgency in Iraq undermined the power of those, like Donald Rumsfeld, who argued that U.S. air and space power could be ratcheted up to the extent where ground forces would be progressively marginalized. This transformation also involves complex institutional politics within the vast array of military departments, political agencies, and defense and media industry groups involved. Care must also be taken not to exoticize the transformation as science-fiction (as, arguably, Paul Virilio has often done[11]). But the combination of the near informational and infrastructural omnipotence of U.S. forces, and the systematic demodernization of adversary forces (and, often, societies)—particularly those in the key geopolitical target areas of central Eurasia—is a central axiom of the RMA. Such doctrine emerges from the military's quasi-imperial motives of globe-spanning dominance via verticalized, informational power, combined with a self-confessed preoccupation with the minimization of U.S. casualties, regardless of the losses by opposing forces. As Mike Davis argues:

> As US battlespace awareness is exponentially increased by networked sensors, it becomes ever more important to blind opponents by precision airstrikes on their equivalent (but outdated) command and control infrastructures. This necessarily means a ruthless take out of civilian telecommunications, power grids, and highway nodes, all the better, in the Pentagon's view, to allow US Psychological-Operations (or 'PSYOPS') units to propagandize, or, if necessary, terrorize the population.[12]

Underpinning this double-edged strategy is the notion of the "enemy as a system." This was devised by a leading U.S. Air Force strategist, John Warden,[13] within what he termed his *strategic ring theory*. This systematic view of adversary societies builds on the industrial web theorization of U.S. air power strategists in World War II, and provides the central U.S. strategic theorization that justifies, and sustains, the rapid extension of that nation's infrastructural warfare capability. The theory has explicitly provided the basis for all major U.S. air operations since the early 1990s.

"At the strategic level," writes Warden, "we attain our objectives by causing such changes to one or more parts of the enemy's physical system."[14] This "system" is seen to have five parts or "rings": the leadership or "brain" at the center; organic essentials (food, energy, etc.); infrastructure (vital connections like roads, electricity, telecommunications, water, etc.); the civilian population; and finally, and least important, the military fighting force[15] (see Figure 16.1). Rejecting the direct targeting of enemy civilians, Warden, instead, argues that only indirect attacks on civilians are legitimate. These operate through the targeting of societal infrastructures—a means of bringing intolerable pressures to bear on the nation's political leaders. This doctrine now officially shapes the projection of U.S. aerial power and underpins the key U.S. Air Force doctrine document—2-12—published in 1998.[16]

It is important to stress here that such rhetoric is little but sophistry. For, as we shall shortly see, by devastating the infrastructural fabric of modern, urban societies, human life is debilitated, destroyed and killed in very large numbers just as effectively as when people are the direct targets of strategic or carpet bombing campaigns. People die just as certainly and in very large numbers; the means of inducing death are merely changed.

What is more, air power theorists are clearly well aware that this is so. In a telling example of this, Kenneth Rizer, another U.S. air power strategist, recently wrote an extremely telling article in the official US Air Force Journal, *Air and Space Power Chronicles*.[17] In it, he seeks to justify the direct destruction of dual-use targets (i.e., civilian infrastructures) within U.S. strategy. Rizer argued that, in international law, the legality of attacking dual-use targets "is very much a matter of interpretation."[18]

Rizer writes that the U.S. military applied Warden's ideas in the 1991 air war in Iraq with, he claims, "amazing results." "Despite dropping 88,000 tons in the forty-three-day campaign, only three thousand civilians died directly as a result of the attacks, the lowest number of deaths from a major bombing campaign in the history of warfare."[19] However, he also openly admits that systematic destruction of Iraq's electrical system in 1991 "shut down water purification and sewage treatment plants, resulting in epidemics of gastro-enteritis, cholera, and typhoid, leading to perhaps as many as 100,000 civilian deaths and the doubling infant mortality rates." [20]

Clearly, however, such large numbers of indirect civilian deaths are of little concern to U.S. Air Force strategists. For Rizer openly admits that:

> The US Air Force perspective is that when attacking power sources, transportation networks, and telecommunications systems, distinguishing between the military and civilian aspects of these facilities is virtually impossible. [But] since these targets remain critical military nodes within the second and third ring of Warden's model, they are viewed as legitimate military targets […] The Air Force does not consider the long-term, indirect effects of such attacks when it applies proportionality [ideas] to the expected military gain.[21]

More tellingly still, Rizer goes on to reflect on how U.S. air power is supposed to influence the morale of enemy civilians if they can no longer be carpet-bombed.

Figure 16.1.   John Warden's (1995) Five-Ring Model of the stragetic make-up of contemporary societies—a central basis for U.S. military doctrine and strategy to coerce change through air power (Source: Felker, 18=998, 12).

"How does the Air Force intend to undermine civilian morale without having an intent to injure, kill, or destroy civilian lives?" he asks.

> Perhaps the real answer is that by declaring dual-use targets legitimate military objectives, the Air Force can directly target civilian morale. In sum, so long as the Air Force includes civilian morale as a legitimate military target, it will aggressively maintain a right to attack dual-use targets.[22]

In 1998 Edward Felker, an air power theorist, like both Warden and Rizer, based at the U.S. Air War College Air University, further developed Walden's model.[23] This was based on the experience of the 1991 war with Iraq (code-named *Desert Storm)* and drew directly on Felker's argument that infrastructure, rather than a separate "ring" of the "enemy as a system," in fact pervaded, and connected, all the others to actually "constitute the society as a whole" (see Figure 16.2). "If infrastructure links the subsystems of a society," he wrote, "might it be the most important target?"[24]

By constructing linear, and nonlinear models of the first, second, and third-order impacts of destroying key parts of the networked infrastructure of an adversary society, U.S. military planners have started to develop a complex military doctrine underpinning the extension of U.S. infrastructural warfare. This centers on organized, systematic demodernization not just of the military forces of those deemed to

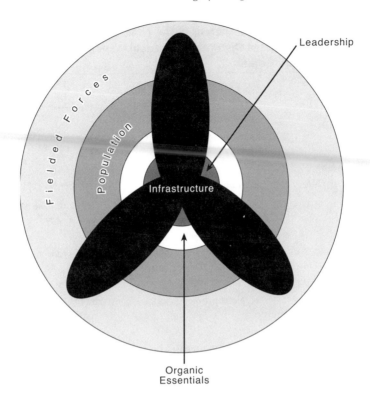

Figure 16.2. 'A new model for societal structure': Edward Felker's (1998, 19) adaptation of Warden's Five-Ring Model (see Figure 16.1), stressing the centrality of infrastructural warfare to post Cold War U.S. airpower doctrine.

be enemies, but of their civil societies as well[25] (see Table 16.1). Indeed, U.S. military analysis here is now concentrating on finding the "tipping points" in critical infrastructure systems that will lead to the nonlinear, spiral effects that will most rapidly induce complete, societal chaos.

In short, the reorganization of U.S. military strategy as part of the shift to "network centric warfare" and the Revolution in Military Affairs centers, crucially, not on territorial mobilizations of industrialized killing machines to extend, or defend, national territory. Rather, it involves a networked, real-time, and meticulously coordinated effort to destroy strategic targets and bring down or destabilize the complex, multifaceted infrastructure and media systems that are seen as the very connective tissue of adversary societies.

This transformation has been backed by recent adjustments in the international laws of war that legitimize and legalize "precision" assaults on dual-use civil infrastructure when "militarily necessary" whilst proscribing the strategic and carpet bombing of cities. As Smith writes, "these changes have been a boon for [US] public relations officers, because, probably, the U.S. is alone in being capable of waging legal warfare on a vast scale because of its near monopoly on [the] precision guided weapons" needed to precisely target dual-use infrastructures.[26]

TABLE 16.1   Patterson's (2000) Analysis of the First, Second and Third Order "Ripple" Effects of U.S. Forces Disrupting Electrical Power Grids during Urban Warfare in an "Adversary Country."

First Order Effects	Second Order Effects	Third Order Effects
No light after dark or in building interiors	Erosion of command and control capabilities	Greater logistics complexity
No refrigeration	Increased requirement for power generating equipment	Decreased mobility
Some stoves/ovens non operable	Increased requirement for night vision devices	Decreased Situational Awareness
Inoperable hospital electronic equipment	Increased reliance on battery-powered items for news, broadcasts, etc.	Rising disease rates
No electronic access to bank accounts/money	Shortage of clean water for drinking, cleaning and preparing food	Rising rates of malnutrition
Disruption in some transportation and communications services	Hygiene problems	Increased numbers of non-combatants requiring assistance
Disruption to water supply, treatment facilities, and sanitation	Inability to prepare and process some foods	Difficulty in communicating with non-combatants

"Bomb Now Die Later": The War on Public Health in Iraq 1991–2004

Whilst the abstract theorization of doctrine and tactics outlined above are reveal-ing, the centrality of infrastructural warfare to emerging U.S. geopolitical strategy can only be fully understood when specific case studies are investigated. By way of example, in what follows, the experience of war, sanctions, and more war in Iraq between 1991 and 2004 is analyzed as a way of illustrating how devastating state-backed infrastructural warfare can be on targeted societies.

The First Gulf War, 1991

> Destroying the means of producing electricity is particularly attractive because it can not be stockpiled.[27]

The Desert Storm bombing campaign was targeted heavily against so-called dual-use urban infrastructure systems, a strategy that Ruth Blakeley has famously termed "Bomb Now, Die Later."[28] Because the reconstruction of these life-sustaining infra-structures was made impossible by the sanctions regime that was imposed between 1991 and 2003, it is now clear that the 1991 demodernization of Iraqi metropolitan life—in a profoundly urbanized nation—created one of the largest, engineered public health catastrophes of the late twentieth century.

Because Iraq's actual military targets were so easily annihilated, it is crucial to realize that what happened in Desert Storm was that a very large percentage of strategic
aerial missions were targeted against industry, power generation, roads and bridges,
rather than military assets. The military planners, and lawyers, behind Desert Storm,
made the most of the unprecedented unevenness of the forces, and the resulting lack
of opposition to allied forces based in the air and in space, in their target planning.

Along with military and communication networks, urban infrastructures were
amongst the key targets receiving the bulk of the bombing. One U.S. air war planner,
Lt. Col. David Deptula, passed a message to Iraqi civilians via the world's media as
the planes started going in: "hey, your lights will come back on as soon as you get rid
of Saddam!"[29] Another, Brigadier General Buster Glosson, explained that infrastructure was the main target because the U.S. military wanted to "put every household
in an autonomous mode and make them feel they were isolated... We wanted to play
with their psyche." [30] As Colin Rowat suggests, for perhaps 110,000 Iraqis, this "playing" was ultimately to prove fatal.[31] Bolkcom and Pike recall the centrality of targeting dual-use infrastructures in the planning of Desert Storm:

> From the beginning of the campaign, Desert Storm decision makers planned to bomb heav-
> ily the Iraqi military-related industrial sites and infrastructure, while leaving the most basic
> economic infrastructures of the country intact. What was not apparent or what was ignored,
> was that the military and civilian infrastructures were inextricably interwoven.[32]

The political rationale of "turning the lights off in Baghdad" generated much
debate amongst Gulf War bombing planners.[33] The U.S. Military's Gulf War Air
Power Survey (GWAPS), completed by the U.S. Defense Department at the formal
end of the war, revealed that:

> there was considerable discussion of the results that could be expected from attacking elec-
> tric power. Some argued that ... the loss of electricity in Baghdad and other cities would
> have little effect on popular morale; others argued that the affluence created by petro-dollars
> had made the city's population psychologically dependent on the amenities associated with
> electric power.[34]

Thus, the systematic annihilation of infrastructure, used by both military and
civilians alike—to disable Iraq's war machine and influence civilian morale—led,
indirectly, to mass civilian casualties, as an urban society was ruthlessly demodern-
ized. "On the whole, civilian suffering is not caused by near misses [collateral dam-
age], but by direct hits on the country's industrial infrastructure."[35]

The prime target of the air assault was Iraq's electricity generating system. During
Desert Storm, the allies flew over two hundred sorties against electrical plants. The
destruction was devastatingly effective;

> almost 88% of Iraq's installed generation capacity was sufficiently damaged or destroyed by
> direct attack, or else isolated from the national grid through strikes on associated transform-
> ers and switching facilities, to render it unavailable. The remaining 12% was probably unus-
> able other than locally due to damage inflicted on transformers and switching yards.[36]

Bolkcom and Pike add that:

More than half of the 20 electrical generator sites were 100 percent destroyed. Only three
escaped totally unscathed [...] The bombing of Iraq's infrastructure was so effective that, on
either the sixth or the seventh day of the air war, the Iraqis shut down what remained of the
national power grid. It was useless.[37]

The surfeit of armed aircraft, combined with a paucity of real targets (and a very
poor or nonexistent enforcement of international law) led to a total overkill in the
process of demodernizing Iraq by bombs. As Bolkcom and Pike admit, in this type
of overwhelming, and totally uneven, aerial onslaught, an extremely wide range of
targets were attacked, not because they needed to be, but because they *could be*. An
ever-lengthening list of targets was sanctioned simply because of the unopposed
air power and ordinance that was available, literally hanging around Iraqi airspace,
looking for things to destroy. Bolkcom and Pike offer the example of al-Hartha
power plant in Basra. First attacked on the first night of the bombing:

The initial attack shut down the plant completely, damaging the water treatment system and
all four steam boilers. During the course of the conflict, al-Hartha was bombed 13 times,
even though there would be little opportunity to repair the power station during a major war.
The final attack bounced the rubble a half hour before the cease fire on February 28, 1991 [...]
Reportedly, the power plant was bombed so frequently because it was designated a backup
target for pilots unable to attack their primary targets [...] The goal of multiple bombings
late in the war was to create postwar influence over Iraq. It is very difficult to repair a power
generator, for example, when the repair personnel have no power.[38]

Another reason for the savagery of the demodernization was a failure to enforce
even the extremely questionable guidelines for infrastructural bombing adopted
in the planning of Desert Storm. These clearly stated that, in the case of electricity,
"only transformer/switching yards and control buildings were to be targets and not
generator halls, boilers and turbines."[39] The reasoning behind this was that it would
take much longer to repair the latter to be reconstructed whilst the former could be
repaired relatively easily, cheaply, and quickly.

Such guidelines were largely ignored, however. The Gulf War Air Power Survey
concluded that "the self-imposed restrictions against hitting generator halls or their
contents was not widely observed in large part because the planners elected to go
after the majority of Iraq's 25 major power stations and the generator halls offered the
most obvious aim points." [40]

It is no surprise, then, that, at war's end, Iraq had only 4 percent of pre-war electricity supplies. After four months only 20–25 percent of pre-war levels had been
attained, a level of supply "roughly analogous to that of the 1920s before Iraq had
access to refrigeration and sewage treatment."[41] The devastation of the generator halls
and turbines would have condemned Iraqi society to a largely nonelectric future for
years to come, even if Western technological and financial assistance had been possible in rebuilding.

The UN Under-Secretary General Martti Ahtisaari, reporting on a visit to Iraq
in March 1991, was clearly shaken by what he had seen. "Nothing that we had seen
or read had quite prepared us for the particular form of devastation that has now
befallen the country," he wrote:

The recent conflict has wrought near-apocalyptic results upon an economically mechanized society. Now, most means of modern life support have been destroyed or rendered tenuous. Iraq has, for some time to come, been relegated to a pre-industrial age, but with all the disabilities of post-industrial dependency on an intensive use of energy and technology [...] Virtually all previously available sources of fuel and power, and modern means of communication are now, essentially, defunct… there is much less than the minimum fuel required to provide the energy needed for movement or transportation, irrigation or generators for power to pump water or sewage.[42]

Even immediately after the war's end, the UN reported that:

Iraqi rivers are heavily polluted by raw sewage, and water levels are unusually low. All sewage treatment plants have been brought to a virtual standstill by the lack of power supply and the lack of spare parts. Pools of sewage lie in the streets and villages. Health hazards will build in weeks to come.[43]

Post-war Sanctions and Bombing, 1991–2003

And so it was to be. The most devastating impact of mass de-electrification was indirect. Iraq's water and sewage systems, relying completely of electrical pumping stations, completely ground to a halt. Prospects of repair, as with the electrical system, were reduced virtually to zero. This was because of the U.S. Coalition's punitive regime of sanctions that were introduced, with the help of UN resolutions, just before the war. As a result, virtually any item or supply required for infrastructural repair was classified, and prohibited, as a dual-use item with military potential—ironically, the very same slippery legal jargon that had legitimized the massive infrastructural destruction in the first place. Here the rhetoric of dual use took another murderous and perverse twist. As Derek Gregory describes in *The Colonial Present*, sanctions planners classified a whole variety of basic infrastructural spare parts, all of which were essential to bringing Iraq's devastated infrastructure into anything like a functioning order as dual use technologies and so proscribed through the sanctions.[44]

As with the clear culpability of U.S. bombing theorists before the massive civilian deaths in Iraq, it is clear that the humanitarian catastrophe triggered by the punitive sanctions was fully known by the U.S. Department of Defense at the time. Now-declassified documents from the U.S. Defense Intelligence Agency (DIA), for example, demonstrate the degree to which the U.S. military was aware of the terrible impacts of the combination of aerial demodernization and sanctions on public health in post-war Iraq. Thomas Nagy has demonstrated that DIA memos in early 1991 clearly predicted what they called "a full degradation of Iraq's water system."[45] The memos argued that a failure to get hold of embargoed water treatment equipment would inevitably lead to massive food and water shortages, a collapse of preventive medicine, an inability to dispose of waste, and a spread of epidemics of disease like cholera, diarrhea, meningitis, and typhoid.

These, in turn, it was predicted, would lead to huge casualty rates, "particularly amongst children, as no adequate solution exists for Iraq's water purification dilemma [under sanctions]."[46] The memo titled "Disease Outbreaks in Iraq," dated February 21, 1991,[47] stated that "conditions are favorable for communicable disease outbreaks, particularly in major urban areas affected by coalition bombing." Despite all this, planners went ahead with the imposition of the sanctions.

By 1999, these predictions had come true. Drinkable water availability in Iraq had fallen to 50 percent of 1990 levels.[48] Colin Rowat, of the Oxford Research Group, has calculated that:

> the number of Iraqis who died in 1991 from the effects of the Gulf war or postwar turmoil approximates 205,500. There were relatively few deaths (approximately 56,000 military personnel and 3,500 civilian) from direct war affects. The largest component of deaths derives from the 111,000 attributable to postwar adverse health effects.[49]

Using a longer time-frame, UNICEF[50] estimated that, between 1991 and 1998, there were, statistically, over five hundred thousand excess deaths amongst Iraqi children under five—a six-fold increase in death rates for this group occurred between 1990 and 1994. Such figures mean that, "in most parts of the Islamic world, the sanctions campaign is considered genocidal."[51] The majority of deaths, from preventable, waterborne diseases, were aided by the weakness brought about by widespread malnutrition. The World Health Organization reported in 1996 that:

> the extensive destruction of electricity generating plants, water purification and sewage treatment plants during the six-week 1991 war, and the subsequent delayed or incomplete repair of these facilities, leading to a lack of personal hygiene, have been responsible for an explosive rise in the incidence of enteric infections, such as cholera an typhoid.[52]

The Second Gulf War, 2003: "Welcome to the Republic of Darkness and Unemployment"

Not surprisingly, the second, even more savage onslaught of aerial bombing that Iraq was subjected to in 2003—organized as it was after twelve years of systematic demodernization and impoverization through sanctions and continued bombing—led to an even more complete demodernization of everyday urban life in the country. This has occurred even though key centralized infrastructure nodes were targeted less extensively than in 1991. This time, the bombing strategy was ostensibly designed to "avoid power plants, public water facilities, refineries, bridges, and other civilian structures."[53] But new weapons, including electromagnetic pulse (EMP) cruise missiles, were used for the first time to comprehensively "fry" dual-use communications and control equipment.

Dual-use systems such as electrical and power transmission grids, media networks, and telecommunications infrastructures were still substantially targeted and destroyed. Media installations and antennae were destroyed by new CBU-107 Passive Attack Weapons—non-explosive cluster bombs that rain metal rods onto sensitive electrical systems and are nicknamed "rods from God" by the US Air Force. In addition, more traditional bombs were used to destroy Al-Jazeera's office in Baghdad on April 8, killing several journalists. This was because the Pentagon considered that the highly successful, independent channel's coverage of the dead civilians that resulted from the bombing was undermining its propaganda (or PSYOPS) campaign aimed at asserting information dominance. As Miller suggests, in current U.S. geopolitical strategy, "the collapse of distinctions between independent news media and psychological operations is striking."[54]

Finally, as in 1991 and NATO's 1999 Kosovo intervention, carbon 'soft' bombs were once again widely used on electricity distribution systems. The resulting fires completely ruined many newly-repaired transformer stations, creating, once again, a serious crisis of water distribution because of the resulting power blackouts.[55] In addition, the old and decayed water pipes in Iraq's main cities often fractured simply through the seismic shocks of nearly explosions. In al-Nasiriyya, Human Rights Watch researchers found that "in many places people had dug up water and sewage pipes outside their homes in a vain attempt to get drinking water."[56] Once again, large numbers of waterborne intestinal infections were, not surprisingly, reported after the war, a direct result of the targeting of electrical distribution systems.[57]

By the end of 2003, it was estimated that another 100,000 Iraqis had died prematurely due to the bombing, insurgency, violence, and disease that had directly resulted from the Second Gulf War.[58] As this latest wave of deaths and misery has unfolded, two points need to be stressed. First, once again, the widespread demonization of Iraqi cities amongst U.S. military and political leaders that has accompanied this latest assault has implied that such cities, and their inhabitants, are somehow unworthy of a modern existence. Iraqi cities have often been described by these people as fundamentally "evil" places, as "terrorist nests" shielding animalistic insurgents worthy of little but U.S. military ordinance.[59] Moreover, as "bare life" unworthy of a modern urban existence, the deaths of Iraqi civilians are rendered of no account in such representations.[60] The numbers killed are not even counted.

Second, it is becoming clear that, even in the narrow terms of the U.S. military, the accumulated and systematic demodernization of Iraq since 1991 has been an absolute disaster. For the "liberating" U.S.-UK forces, who now struggle to control a devastated, immiserated, and desperate country, the almost complete absence of functioning urban infrastructure—a direct result of their savage policies in the preceding thirteen years—has provided ideal conditions for a whole host of ruthless and murderous militias, warlords, and Islamist groups. The very legitimacy and power of such groups stems directly from the premodern and apocalyptic conditions that Iraq's overwhelmingly urban population are being forced to survive in. Thus, even for an aggressive strategy, such as the Bush administration's invasion of Iraq, aimed at accumulating wealth, resources, and capital through war, invasion, and dispossession, the systematic demodernization of whole society's based on the air power theories discussed at the start of this chapter is likely to prove a giant own goal.

Towards Computer Network Attack

According to the Director of the Center for Infrastructural Warfare Studies, William Church, the next frontier of infrastructural warfare will involve nation states developing the capacity to undertake the types of coordinated "cyberterror" attacks that they are so comprehensively mobilizing against through, for example, the homeland security drive within the continental United States. "The challenge here," he writes, "is to break into the computer systems that control a country's infrastructure, with the result that the civilian infrastructure of a nation would be held hostage."[61] Church argues that NATO considered such tactics in Kosovo in 1999 and that the idea of cutting Yugoslavia's Internet connections were raised at NATO planning meetings, but that NATO rejected these tactics as problematic. But within the emerging U.S. doctrine of Integrated Information Operations and infrastructural warfare—involving everything from destroying electric plants, dropping electronic Magnetic Pulse (EMP) bombs that destroy all electrical equipment within a wide area, developing globe-spanning surveillance systems like Echelon, to dropping leaflets and disabling Web sites—a dedicated capacity to use software systems to attack opponent's critical infrastructures is now under rapid development.

Deliberately manipulating computer systems to disable opponent's civilian infrastructure is being labeled Computer Network Attack (or CNA) by the U.S. military. It is being widely seen as a powerful new weapon, an element of the wider "Full Spectrum Dominance" strategy.[62] Whilst the precise details of this emerging capability remain classified, some elements are becoming clear.

First, it is apparent that a major research and development program is underway at the Joint Warfare Analysis Center at Dahlgren (Virginia) into the precise computational and software systems that sustain the critical infrastructures of real or potential adversary nations. Major General Bruce Wright, Deputy Director of Information Operations at the Center, revealed in 2002 that "a team at the Center can tell you not just how a power plant or rail system [within an adversary's country] is built, but what exactly is involved in keeping that system up and making that system efficient."[63]

Second, as with its mirror image—critical infrastructure protection in the cities and urban corridors of the increasingly securitized U.S. homeland—a main focus in such offensive information operations is to find ways of destroying the often commercial software code that makes advanced infrastructures function.[64] This is known as SCADA, or Supervisory Control and Data Acquisition. "One of the terms I've learned from these guys," continued Wright, "is SCADA. Basically, SCADA is the computer control for a power system or railroad, sewer, or water system. We relate more and more on those kinds of systems as potential targets, and sometimes very lucrative targets, as we go after adversaries."[65]

In the U.S. Air Force doctrine document, *Air Force 2025*, Kelly argues that "monitoring will be required of developments in commercial-off-the-shelf (COTS) systems which could be used to attack industrial systems (anti-SCADA programs) [and] financial and communications networks."[66] The driving idea here is to develop the capability of what Kelly calls "a Full Spectrum attack on the adversary's information infrastructure which renders him blind, deaf and dumb, so facilitating the dominant maneuver of US forces."[67] The guiding principle here is that:

> adversary military forces are ultimately an output or peripheral of a weapon system and its sustaining, often civil, infrastructure. Corrupt the sustaining systems and, like a driver deprived on his oxygen supply, the adversary military force may be ineffective. Once the pattern of information-dependent human activities is identified, the information target can be detected and identified, and the data on which the activity is dependent could be intercepted, destroyed, or corrupted by appropriate replacement [...] in peace and war.[68]

In other words, what Kelly's report demonstrates is that the techniques to attempts at the computerized disablement of entire societies—both in peace and war—are not only envisaged by the U.S. military; they were actually under development way back in 1996. Whilst Protocol I of United Nations Resolution 3384 on human rights protection (1975) bans such attempts to disable civilian infrastructures in war, the U.S. military has, as we have seen, repeatedly defended their right to use computer network and physical attacks to disable dams, dykes, and nuclear generating stations.

Third, it is clear that, in the 2003 invasion of Iraq, unspecified offensive computer network attacks were undertaken by U.S. forces.[69] Richard Myers, Commander in Chief of U.S. Space Command, the body tasked with Computer Networked Attack, admitted in January 2000 that "the U.S. has already undertaken computer networked attacks on a case-by-case basis."[70] A National Presidential Directive on Computer Network Attack, (number 16), signed by George Bush in July 2003, demonstrated the shift from blue-sky research to bedded-down doctrine in this area. Illustrating the difficulty of controlling the cascading and multiple-scaled failures of networked systems, however, the US Air Force computer network attack staff considered the complete disablement of Iraqi financial systems using computer network attack techniques. But they "rejected the idea because the Iraqi banking network is closely linked to financial communication network in France."[71] This meant that "an attack therefore might have brought down the ATM machines in Europe as well."[72] "We don't have many friends in Paris right now," one unnamed U.S. intelligence source quipped on the emergence of this decision. "There is no need to make more trouble if Chirac won't be able to get any Euros out of his ATM!"[73]

Conclusions

This chapter has sought to assert the central place of everyday urban infrastructures within contemporary spaces of terror. Whilst long-neglected, banalized, and taken for granted, the everyday technics of urban life are increasingly at the heart of contemporary geopolitical conflict. They are the main targets for catastrophic terror attacks. They are increasingly central in the doctrines of advanced Western and non-western militaries. They are a widespread means of the projection of state terror.[74] There is also increasing evidence that nation states are already actively engaging in low level computer network attacks on a more or less continuous basis.

This chapter suggests that infrastructural warfare thus needs to be placed at the center of any effort to grapple with the post-cold war geopolitical world. This is crucial because the emerging approaches to the projection of state and nonstate terror through everyday infrastructures discussed above remain largely ignored. This is precisely because the everyday technics of urban life continue to be banalized, taken for granted and rendered invisible within the broader domains of human geography and political science.[75] Without constructing critical analytical frameworks that capture the multi-scaled processes through which everyday, local technics become weapons of distanciated terror and violence, some critically important geopolitical trends will inevitably be overlooked. This is made more likely because the intrinsically dynamic global-local logics that surround infrastructural war and terror fall in the interstices

and gaps between a wide variety of academic disciplines. Thus, the analysis of infrastructural warfare must take its place within the forging of a new interdisciplinary
opening: what I have called an explicitly critical geopolitical urbanism or an explicitly critical urban geopolitics.[76]

The analytical questions confronting such a project are many and pressing. For
example, how does the pervasive anxiety now associated with the use of everyday
urban infrastructures in many cities affect the material cultures and politics of threatened cities and societies? How widespread is the practice of computer network attack
in today's world and how damaging are its effects? Does infrastructural warfare herald some major break down in any convincing geopolitical separation of the "insides"
of metropolitan, Western, "core" nations and the supposedly threatening and *othered*
"outsides" of the urbanizing global South? Does the proliferation of infrastructural
warfare techniques in both non-state terrorist activity and the war-making strategies of nation states herald a fundamentally new blurring in the spatial and temporal
demarcations separating zones and times of "war" from those of "peace"?

If this is the case, does the proliferation of infrastructural violence inevitably mean
that "war"—as Phil Agre puts it[77]—is, in a sense now "everywhere and everything"?
Does it automatically follow that war must now be seen as simultaneously "large and
small"? Does contemporary war necessarily have "no boundaries in time and space"?
And does the escalation and globalization of infrastructural war mean that, as Agre
ponders, "life itself is war." Finally, what does the growth of network or infrastructural war across scales of time-space imply for notions of causality, of cause and effect,
given that actions and their impacts are now often so separated in time and space?
How can the continuous accidents and blackouts that afflict all complex infrastructure systems be even *separated* from collapses engineered for political violence or
manipulation? Interestingly, following the widespread fears that al-Qaeda had insti-
gated the massive electricity blackouts in the northeastern United States in 2003—a
collapse actually caused by mismanagement—James Der Derian argued that:

> networked technology provides new global actors the means to traverse political, economic,
> religious, and cultural boundaries, changing not only how war is fought and peace is made,
> but making it ever more difficult to maintain the very distinction of not only accidental,
> incidental, and intentional acts but war and peace itself.[78]

Conversely, are such sentiments being overblown by military commentators and
critical theorists alike? Even after 9/11, are the threats of infrastructural terrorism
in fact being grossly exaggerated, particularly in the West? If so, does such exaggeration allow political and military elites to ratchet-up states of emergency, build up the
edifices of national security, and feed the hungry military-industrial-security-media
complexes that are doing so well out of both "homeland security" and the "war on
terror"? Does the demonization of continuous, invisible, unknowable, and unprov-
able threats allow political leaders to entrench their political positions through the
cynical manufacture and exploitation of cultures of fear and the pervasive anxiety
that the basic materials of a technologized society can be turned into murderous
weapons at any moment and at any location? And does such endless "terror talk" by
political, military, and media elites, stressing the endless vulnerabilities of everyday
living spaces and infrastructures, serve to prop up the aggressive military strategies

of states like the United States and Britain as part of that "war on terror"—strategies that themselves routinely assault the living spaces and everyday infrastructures that sustain life in urban societies that are supposedly the adversaries of the West within this "war."[79]

Without serious theoretical and empirical engagements with the unfamiliar and seemingly bizarre landscapes of infrastructural warfare, addressing such questions can rely on little but conjecture, anecdote and ideology. It is time, then, to launch critical and interdisciplinary research programs so that the use of everyday technics as weapons of war and terror can be addressed with the kinds of sustained and critical attention that is long overdue.

Notes

1. Parts of this chapter are adapted from parts of a paper published in *City* 9(2), July 2005. The author would like to express his thanks to the British Academy for support which made this research possible. Thanks also for comments from Phil Agre, Ash Amin, Zygmunt Bauman, David Campbell, Bulent Diken, and Derek Gregory on an earlier draft.

2. P. Agre, "Imagining the next war: Infrastructural warfare and the conditions of democracy," *Radical Urban Theory* (September 14, 2001), at http://www.rut.com/911/Phil-Agre.html, February 12, 2004: 1.

3. W. Joy, "Why the future doesn't need us," *Wired*, (2000) April, 238–260: 239.

4. B. Carroll, *Seeing Cyberspace : The Electrical Infrastructure is Architecture*, (2001), available at www.electronetwork/works/seeing/versions/html/images/htm, February 17, 2004.

5. T. Luke, "Everyday technics as extraordinary threats: Urban technostructures and nonplaces in terrorist actions," in S. Graham (ed.), *Cities, War and Terrorism* Oxford: Blackwell, 2004, 120–140.

6. S. Graham, "In a moment : On global mobilities and the terrorised city'" City 5(3) (2001): 411–415.

7. Luke, "Everyday techniques."

8. Thomas Friedman, *New York Times*, April 23, 1999, cited in I. Skoric, "On not killing civilians," posted at amsterdam.nettime.org (May 6, 1999). February 16, 2004.

9. E. Felker, *Airpower, Chaos and Infrastructure: Lords of the Rings*, (U.S. Air War College Air University, Maxwell Air Force Base, Alabama, Maxwell paper 14), 1998: 1–20.

10. J. Harris, "Dreams of global hegemony and the technology of war," *Race and Class*, 45(2) (2003): 54–67.

11. P. Virilio, *Desert Screen: War at the Speed of Light*, (London : Continuum, 2002).

12. M. Davis, "Slouching toward Baghdad." *Znet*, available at http://www.zmag.org/content/print_article.cfm?itemID=3150&sectionID=11 (March 26, 2004).

13. J. Warden, "The enemy as a system," *Airpower Journal*, 9 (1)(1995): 41–55.

14. Warden, "Enemy as a system."

15. Felker, *Airpower, Chaos and Infrastructure*, 11.

16. United States Air Force, *Strategic Attack: Air Force Doctrine Document 2-1.2*, (Washington, D.C., US Air Force, 1998).

17. K. Rizer, "Bombing dual-use targets: Legal, ethical, and doctrinal perspectives," *Air and Space Power Chronicles* (January 5,) at www.airpower.maxwell.af.mil/airchronicles/cc/Rizer.html, February 2001: 1.

18. Rizer, "Bombing dual-use targets," 1.

19. Rizer, "Bombing dual-use targets," 10.

20. Rizer, "Bombing dual-use targets," 1.

21. Rizer, "Bombing dual-use targets," 10.

22. Rizer, "Bombing dual-use targets," 11.

23. Felker, *Airpower, Chaos and Infrastructure*, 20.

24. Felker, *Airpower, Chaos and Infrastructure*, 20.

25. C. Patterson, *Lights Out and Gridlock : The Impact of Urban Infrastructure Disruptions on Military Operations and Non-Combatants*, (Washington, D.C. : Institute for Defense Analyses, 2000).

26. T. Smith, "The new law of war : Legitimizing hi-tech and infrastructural violence," *International Studies Quarterly*, 46 (2002): 355–374: 36.

27. C. Bolkcom, and J. Pike, *Attack Aircraft Proliferation: Issues for Concern*, (Federation of American Scientists, 1993), available at www.fas.org/spp/aircraft, 25 February 2004: 2.

28. R. Blakeley, (2003), *Bomb Now, Die Later*. Bristol University : Department of Politics, available at www.geocities.com/ruth_blakeley/bombnowdielater.htm, February 2004: 25.

29. Cited in C. Rowat, "Iraq Potential consequences of war," *Campaign Against Sanctions in Iraq Discussion List*, (November 8, 2003), available at www.casi.org.uk/discuss/2002/msg02025.html, February 12, 2004.

30. Cited in Rowat, "Iraq Potential consequences of war."

31. Rowat, "Iraq Potential consequences of war."

32. Bolkcom and Pike, *Attack Aircraft Proliferatio*, 3.

33. Blakeley, *Bomb Now, Die Later*, 25.

34. T. Keaney, and E. Cohen, *Gulf War Air Power Surveys* (GWAPS), (Washington, D.C. Johns Hopkins University and the US Air Force, 1993, vol ii Part II, ch. 6 p. 23, footnote 53), available at www.au.af.mil/au/awcgate/awc-hist.htm+gulf, 15th February 2004.

35. Bolkcom and Pike, *Attack Aircraft Proliferation*, 3.

36. Keaney and Cohen, *Gulf War Air Power Surveys*, vol, II, part II, ch. 6, pp. 20, cited in Blakeley *Bomb Now Die Later*, 20.

37. Bolkcom and Pike, *Attack Aircraft Proliferation*, 5.

38. Bolkcom and Pike, *Attack Aircraft Proliferation*, 5.

39. Blakeley *Bomb Now Die Later*, 20.

40. Keaney and Cohen, *Gulf War Air Power Survey*, 20.

41. Bolkcom and Pike, *Attack Aircraft Proliferation*, 5.

42. Reported in P. de Cueller, 1991, cited in Blakeley, *Bomb Now, Die Later*, 25.

43. De Cueller, 1991, cited in Blakeley *Bomb Now, Die Later*, 25.

44. D. Gregory (2004). *The Colonial Present*. Blackwell: Oxford, 173–179.

45. T. Nagy, "The secret behind the sanctions : How the U.S. Intentionally destroyed Iraq's water supply," *The Progressive*, (September 1–6, 2001), available at www.progressive.org/0801issue/nagy0901.html, 12 February 2004.

46. Cited in Nagy, "The secret behind the sanctions."

47. Defense Intelligence Agency, *Iraq Water Treatment Vulnerabilities,* Filename 511rept.91, Memo to Centcom, January 18, 1991, cited in Nagy, "The secret behind the sanctions.

48. R. Blakeley, "Targeting water treatment facilities," (Campaign Against Sanctions in Iraq, Discussion List, January 24, 2003), available at www.casi.org.uk/discuss/2003/msg00256.html, 18th February 2004: 2.

49. Rowat, "Iraq Potential consequences of war."

50. United Nations Children's Fund (UNICEF), *Annex II of S/1999/356, Section 18,* 1999), available at www.un.org/Depts/oip/reports, February 17, 2004.

51. Smith, "The new law of war," 365.

52. Cited in Blakeley, "Bomb Now, Die Later," 23.

53. Human Rights Watch, *Off Target: The Conduct of the War and Civilian Casualties in Iraq* (Washington, D.C.: 2003), available at http://www.hrw.org, 18 February 2004.

54. D. Miller, "The domination effect," *Guardian* (January 8, 2004), 24.

55. Human Rights Watch, *Off Target:* 3.

56. Human Rights Watch, *Off Target:* 3.

57. Enders, 'Getting back on the grid,' *Baghdad Bulletin* (June 10, 2003), available at http://www.baghdadbulletin.com, 19 February 2004.

58. Roberts, L., Lafta, R., Garfield, R., Khudhairi, J., and Burnham, G., "Mortality before and after the 2003 invasion of Iraq: Cluster sample survey," *The Lancet* (29 October, 2004):1-8.

59. Graham, S. (2005), "Remember Fallujah: Demonising place, constructing atrocity", *Environment and Planning S; Society and Space,* 23, 1–10: 23, 1–10.

60. Gregory, *The Colonial Present,* 62–63.

61. W. Church, "Information warfare," *International Review of the Red Cross,* 837(2001): 205–216.

62. U.S. Department of Defense, *Joint Vision 2020,* Washington DC (2000).

63. Cited in Church, "Information warfare."

64. S. Graham, (2006) "Constructing 'homeland' and 'target' cities and the 'war on terror," *Int. Jnl. Urb. Reg. Res.* 30, 255–76.

65. Cited in Church, "Information warfare."

66. J. Kelly, *Air Force 2025,* U.S. Air War College Air University, Maxwell Air Force Base, Alabama(1996): 2.

67. Kelly, *Air Force 2025,* 4.

68. Kelly, *Air Force 2025,* 5.

69. D. Onley, "U.S. aims to make war on Iraq's networks," *Missouri Freedom of Information Center,* 2003, available at http://foi.missouri.edu/terrorbkgd/usaimsmake.html, 24th February 2004.

70. P. Stone, "Space command plans for computer network attack mission," *U.S. Department of Defense : Defense Link* (January 14, 2003), available at http://www.defenselink.mil , 22nd February 2004.

71. C. Smith, "U.S. wrestles with new weapons," *NewsMax.Com* (March 13), available at http:/www.newsmax.com/archives/articles/2003/3/134712.shtml, 19th February 2004.

72. Smith, "U.S. wrestles with new weapons."

73. Smith, "U.S. wrestles with new weapons."

74. Space has not allowed, for example, the systematic targeting of Palestinian urban infrastructures by Israeli Defense Forces to be explored in this chapter. See S. Graham, "Lessons in urbicide," *New Left Review,* 19(2003) 63–79.

75. S. Graham, and S. Marvin, *Splintering Urbanism* (London: Routledge, 2001).

76. S. Graham, "Postmortem city: Towards an urban geopolitics," *City,* 165–196, Graham, S. (ed.) *Cities, War and Terrorism: Towards an Urban Geopolitics,* (Oxford: Blackwell, 2004).

77. All quotes from Agre, "Imagining the next war," 2

78. J. Der Derian, "Network pathologies," at *InfoTechWarPeace,* available at http://www. watsoninstitute.org/infopeace/ (2003): 8th October, 2004.

79. C. Katz, chapter 18, this volume.

17

The Terror City Hypothesis[1]

Mitchell Gray and Elvin Wyly

Introduction

Wolf Blitzer: "While terrorists may be eying targets across America, the government may be leaving some places more vulnerable instead of helping them get ready. A city that literally attracts tens of millions of visitors each year is one surprising example. Our homeland security correspondent Jeanne Meserve is here with details. Jeanne?"

Jeanne Meserve: "Wolf, brain dead. That's the phrase that Congressman Ric Keller was using to describe the funding formula for the Department of Homeland Security's Urban Area Security Initiative grants. Keller is upset because Orlando, Florida, in his district, got no money this year while cities like Omaha, Nebraska did."

Ric Keller [video clip]: "Orlando, Florida should get the money because we protect forty-three million tourists every year and so when we go to orange level, our sheriff doesn't say, hey, we're only going to protect our residents. We have to protect everybody and we need significant resources to do that."[2]

September 11, 2001 was simultaneously global and local: the day's victims left behind grieving families not only in New York, New Jersey, and Connecticut, but also in dozens of countries around the globe. Almost immediately, however, a "glocal" catastrophe was nationalized and the American response began to reconfigure key elements of the urban scale. Shanksville, Pennsylvania was soon forgotten as the event became a world-city catastrophe. New York City's tragedy was aggressively nationalized and drafted to provide symbolic flag-draped support for ongoing and new military campaigns and murder in Afghanistan, Iraq, and other settings where cities were invariably portrayed as mysterious terrorist havens appearing as brightly-lit targets on the Pentagon's real-time digital maps.[3] Capital as well as political, legal, and cultural resources were invested in the ideological construction of a suddenly vulnerable American Homeland for which all things have changed. American urbanism entered a new and paradoxical era, at once familiar and uncertain: cold war anxieties of the middle twentieth century were revived and revised in accordance with the elusive spatiality of today's terror. In this new and yet familiar American urbanism, the imaginative construction of risk assumes a central role in the material and discursive dualities of local and global, here and there, us and them. These politics of constructed risk were seized immediately by the Vulcans, the self-named team of neoconservative foreign policy advisers who gave credibility to a presidential candidate who once quipped that he thought the Taliban was a rock band. The Vulcans' prior experience and inspiration came not from the traditional urban laboratories of Presidential power (Wall Street, Capitol Hill, state capitals, and Cambridge, Massachusetts), but from the Pentagon and other fortified nodes in America's gunbelt.[4] At the heart of a powerful neoconservative alliance, the Vulcans mobilized the specter of terrorism to justify an ambitious geopolitical agenda, while their allies in the domestic policy infrastructure quickly learned to exploit the terrorist threat to suppress dissent and to accelerate attacks on the tattered remains of the American welfare state.

In American cities, more and more aspects of everyday life and death now *take place* in the shadow of horror and fear, sustained by the manufactured certainty of uncertainty in an endless American war on terror. A culture of intensified (yet routine and almost mundane) militarization now pervades daily life in America's roster of world cities (see Figure 17.1). In turn, the militarization of urban life helps to reinforce the widespread perception of a new urban vulnerability, providing popular support in America for the expansion of old and new campaigns of horror and war elsewhere in the global urban system.

In this chapter, we develop a conceptual framework to guide research on this new and yet somehow historically comforting variant on the traditional American fear in and of the city. Although our perspective on urban spaces of terror is certainly shaped

Figure 17.1. America's roster of global cities, once celebrated as the pinnacle of American exceptionalism and flexible capitalism, are being reshaped by militarized security measures that are becoming routine, almost mundane. New York Police Department officers standing guard outside the New York Stock Exchange in the wake of an Orange Alert in early August 2004. Photograph courtesy of Spencer Platt/Getty Images.

by the growing body of post-September 11 urban research,[5] our manner of presentation is inspired by an earlier attempt to sort out the urban dimensions of a contested and supposedly new destabilizing process. In the spirit of John Friedmann's 1986 "World City Hypothesis," we propose seven interrelated theses "as a framework for research." As with economic globalization in the 1980s and 1990s, the urbanization of today's wars of and on terror may be too fluid and unstable to fit into what Hank Savitch proposes as a "new paradigm" for cities.[6] Yet the terrorist specter does have similarities with the global investment networks that have inspired so much research: both help us to "understand what happens in the major global cities ... and what much political conflict in these cities is about."[7] It is essential, therefore, to negotiate what Friedmann offered as "a starting point for political enquiry" in the spirit of the original Greek *hupothesis*, a *foundation*. We offer a terror city hypothesis as a proposition not derived from direct experience, but formed and used to explain certain facts. And facts matter in these days of everyday violence and war: Bruno Latour recoils in horror from the social-constructionist language games of the Republican consultant Frank Luntz—the wordsmith who gave us "death tax" to replace "estate tax," and who emphasizes the lack of scientific certainty to undermine efforts to respond to global warming, because, after all, "climate change" can be good or bad, depending on your position. Latour is deeply concerned:

> Do you see why I am worried? ... Have things changed so fast? In which case the danger would no longer be coming from an excessive confidence in ideological arguments posturing as matters of fact—as we have learned to combat so efficiently in the past—but from an excessive distrust of good matters of fact disguised as bad ideological biases![8]

We suggest that the aggressive and entrepreneurial moves of prominent and powerful actors in the American neoconservative movement—in partnership with allies in the defense, technology, and producer services sectors—are reconfiguring ideological arguments and matters of fact by creating a genuinely new urban narrative object.[9] The terror city is a construct that redefines the urban by portraying all cities in terms of their *vulnerability to* terrorism or their *propensity to breed and harbor* terrorists. More than simply the urbanization of post-nine eleven politics, the terror city is a fundamental reconstruction (and co-optation) of theories and methods at the heart of urban studies. It is constructed by strategic planning and political communication, but it is also sustained by the consent of many urbanites who do sincerely believe that everything is different now, and that the war on terror must inform even the most local concerns about crime, property taxes, or the security of visitors to Disney World.

In this chapter, our primary concern is with the particular terror city that refracts the view of urbanites in the United States. Urban terror is by no means new, and it is most assuredly not at its worst in the United States. And yet the explicit urbanization and nationalization of 9/11 have come to represent a singular violation of a sacred American exceptionalism[10]—and thus it is the U.S.-centric construct stripped of so many local conjunctures and contingencies that is so potent in underwriting state-sanctioned horror and violence in cities across the globe. The danger is that the terror city is a matter of concern that is well on its way to becoming a matter of fact. Urbanity is being redefined just as "The Americans and British created facts where there were no facts at all,"[11] and as a senior aide to Bush put it a few weeks before the 2004 election, "We're an empire now, and when we act, we create our own reality. And while you're studying that reality —as you will—we'll act again, creating other new realities, which you can study too, and that's how things will sort out. We're history's actors ... and you, all of you, will be left to just study what we do."[12]

The terror city is constructed by carefully managed perceptions and imaginations of risk.

A single day reinvigorated a unifying, modernist narrative of risk and fear for residents of America's global cities, redeeming the short-attention-span ennui of an ambiguous, disorienting post-cold war political climate. Recall the vertigo of confusion and paralysis apparent in the once-confident sense of American geopolitical purpose that appeared a little more than a decade ago:

> It is the 1990s, and everything is changing. The Cold War order of superpower rivalry, East/West bloc formation, ideological competition, and North/South economic friction has imploded, giving way to that which President Bush once prematurely and optimistically labeled "the New World Order." In this new world order, strange tendencies are emerging. Previously stable territorial formations ... are devolving into unsettling convulsive chaos, while typically unstable extraterritorial flows...are evolving into new coherent tensions.[13]

If Francis Fukuyama was right and history ended after the cold war,[14] it seemed to have crashed to a halt in a particularly confusing landscape of recurrent famines, regional wars, and scattered, escalating atrocities. To be sure, the plight of distant strangers embroiled in horrendous violence (invariably presented as an outgrowth of irrational ethnic or tribal tensions) did provoke deep fears whenever the American media lens transmitted suitably graphic images back home. But the recurrence of collectively disorganized menaces failed to create any sort of shared, coherent, or directed insecurity. Fear was unfocused. When no single source of insecurity could be privileged among the overwhelming barrage of macabre infotainment, fears were manifest as the equivalent of a white noise of unease. Mike Davis reminds us of the "inexplicable anxiety" in the United States in the late 1990s, culminating in the absurdity of the pre-Y2K techno-millennial panic: "There was a diagnostic consensus among social scientists and culture theorists that Americans were suffering from acute hypochondria."[15]

In common parlance, September 11, 2001 changed everything. Everyone from Paul Wolfowitz to Peter Marcuse, Donald Rumsfeld to Norman Mailer, Dick Cheney to Noam Chomsky, agrees that things are different now.[16] Ambiguous, unspecified angst now has an iconographic and material expression in the urban landscape. Two theories are essential in understanding this shift. First, Ericson and Haggerty suggest that Canada and the United States have in recent years become "risk societies" marked by a "focus on danger, and the perpetual doubt that danger is being counteracted."[17] The provision of security becomes an ever more important goal of governance in a risk society, but of course security is intangible, elusive, and open-ended. Risk management becomes a task of measuring and managing probabilities, driving the expansion of scientific analysis, threat assessment, public relations, insurance, and securitization. But any probability distribution that manages temporarily to assuage public and investor fears is immediately shattered once anything happens that was believed unlikely. More resources are invested to attain better knowledge in the hopes of eliminating the possibility of unexpected events: "Collective fear and foreboding underpin the value system of an unsafe society, perpetuate insecurity, and feed incessant demands for more knowledge of risk."[18] Second, the risk society fosters reliance on the "precautionary principle," worst-case scenario planning that distorts the allocation of security resources.[19] The precautionary principle attracts increasing security investments to deter the most heinous low-probability events, drawing resources from all sorts of pressing social investments. Precautionary spending even bleeds resources from other *security* spending, eroding protections against mundane but high-probability risks. There is no way out of this dilemma, but political (and financial) capital can be accumulated through greater security expenditures.[20]

Both of these concepts—the risk society and the precautionary principle—are at the heart of new configurations of state intervention and new blends of political discourse, popular culture, and security policy. Calculations of risk have shifted, and an altered spatiality of danger encourages scenario planning in line with the precautionary principle. The evidence is now undisputed that powerful alliances in the American neoconservative movement seized the fear after September 11 as an unprecedented opportunity to pursue longstanding imperial agendas—while unleashing a sudden round of domestic risk-society realignments. While annual federal defense appropriations approach the half-trillion dollar mark and the new Department of Homeland Security extends its tendrils in a major structural reorganization of the executive branch, state and local governments are caught in the most severe fiscal crisis in more than half a century. In the months prior to the 2003 invasion of Iraq, more than 160 local governments passed resolutions protesting the war in the face of massive cuts in social programs; at one public event an elected official asked Bush to wage war in East Cleveland, Ohio so its crumbling schools and roads could then be rebuilt. One local resolution protested the war because its "cost would be borne by the people of the City of Los Angeles, who rely on federal funds for anti-poverty programs, for workforce assistance, for housing, for education programs, for infrastructure and for the increased demands of homeland security."[21] Cities perceived as vulnerable to terror are colliding with the binding constraints of the precautionary principle amidst recession and unfunded security mandates from above. Some state and local officials, mindful of the local costs, decide on a case-by-case basis whether to follow federal directives when the terror color-coded alert system issues warnings of heightened risks. Others follow the lead of Ric Keller's plea on behalf of Disney World for increased federal funding. And some deploy the new imperatives of security to continue the assault on urban social welfare expenditures.

Perceptions of fear, vulnerability, and exposure are reshaping political discourse as well as physical planning in many cities. Constructions of risk are changing the experience of city life and relations within and among cities. The outlines of a global hierarchy of terror and antiterror are coming into view.

Cities are ranked in shifting hierarchies based on perceived risks of terrorism.

In classical theories of urban systems from the 1960s and 1970s, cities are creatures of economic competition, using innovation to attract growth and investment to climb up the hierarchy.[22] In the 1980s and 1990s, certain features of these old theories were either jettisoned or revised to capture the urban dimensions of globalization—but the emphasis on economic competition was retained and strengthened. Cities came to be seen as the leading edge of the particular type of globalization promoted and often enforced by the United States, and thus any nation-state responding to such pressures invariably opened its cities to ever more complex transnational flows of investment, trade, migration, and communications.[23]

America's reflexive infatuation with globalizing cities is over, at least for those factions of the state leading the reorientation of geopolitical strategy and what is now officially known as homeland security. Cities are now seen as breeding grounds or targets, and sometimes both.[24] The American view of terrorist threats overseas is only implicitly urban, partly because of the continued centrality of the nation-state in diplomacy, and partly due to the nature of complex transnational organizations. And in the case of public pronouncements, federal rhetoric remains geared to the nation-state thanks to the general geographical ignorance of the American electorate. Nevertheless, each day's headlines prompt a resorting of cities and regions across the globe according to real and perceived risks as well as American responses, and cities like Kabul and Falluja become ever more familiar landmarks in the mental maps of average Americans.

On the domestic front, the attempt to map terror's urban system is more explicit, but, of course, always provisional and uncertain. Many institutions have taken an interest in this new, uneasy cartography, but the clearest map yet comes from the Urban Area Security Initiative (UASI), launched by the Office of Domestic Preparedness of the new Department of Homeland Security.[25] The first round of the program applied a formula including population density, critical infrastructure, and "threat/vulnerability assessment" to identify cities for targeted grants "to enhance the local governments' ability to prepare for and respond to threats or incidents of terrorism."[26] The first wave of recipients could thus be regarded as the official roster of America's first-order terror cities: New York City, Washington, D.C., Los Angeles, Seattle, Chicago, San Francisco, and Houston.[27] Almost immediately after its inception, however, UASI became the vehicle for the predictable bring-home-the-bacon imperatives of Congress, creating security budget windfalls (on a per capita basis) for Wyoming, Montana, and scores of small cities. Sustained press coverage and fierce battles among Congressional delegations, Homeland Security staffers, and big-city mayors finally culminated in a revised threat- and population-based formula for Fiscal 2005.[28]

The U.S. terror city hierarchy coexists and interacts with the now-familiar urbanization processes of neoliberal governance and statecraft, but introduces several fundamental differences. First, the mapping enterprise involves intense research and speculation regarding terrorist motives, and thus tends to sideline the celebration of utility-maximizing consumers or heroic entrepreneurs. Indeed, the subtle shifts in meaning and signification that marked the 1990s (e.g., the recasting of diversity as a market opportunity for capitalism) have taken a sharp turn. In an article ironically drafted shortly before September, 2001, Savitch and Ardashev devised a ranking of cities vulnerable to terrorism, and gave "diversity" an ominous connotation that has subsequently proven quite influential:

...urban heterogeneity puts different social groups in close proximity to one another. While social pluralism provides rich synergies, under certain conditions it can be a nesting-ground for terrorist organisations. A sense of relative deprivation sharpens as different groups come into closer proximity. Word gets around more quickly and socialisation proceeds more rapidly in densely packed environments. This kind of environment provides an abundant source of recruitment for potential terrorists.[29]

Second, the hierarchy is inherently unstable and uncertain, and its dynamic character is further complicated by the circulation of hallmark sports events, tourist festivals, trade summits, and other real and perceived targets. The itinerant travel of potential targets introduces an inherently dynamic element to the hierarchy of vulnerability, as demonstrated by the mobile infrastructure of fortified motorcades, clean-swept routes from airports to downtown landmarks, and isolated patchworks of anti-protest "free speech zones" that follow President Bush whenever he visits a city. Third, the unstable domestic hierarchy of vulnerable American cities interacts with the accumulation of new intelligence (some reliable, some not) to create a dynamic sorting of the global hierarchy of perceived threats. In the American geographical imagination, "cosmopolitan" cities can rapidly jump up the terror ranking while sliding down the economic scale (Beirut in the 1980s, Sarajevo in the 1990s, perhaps Beirut again now), and once-obscure places assume sudden prominence. Yesterday's Entebbe is today's Kabul, Quetta, or Falluja.[30] Nevertheless, key domestic elements of the risk ranking are likely to remain comparatively stable: New York and Washington, D.C. are almost certain to remain atop the urban security hierarchy for the foreseeable future.

Sustained debate over the identity and motivation of terrorists is allowing federal officials to create a new form of national urban policy.

Any attempt to evaluate threats to different cities requires some understanding of the thinking of individuals and groups defined as terrorists. In the United States, political traditions of fierce federalism and home rule have always undermined the development of any meaningful framework for a national urban policy.[31] But the recent intersection of urban risk assessment and expanding federal authority seems to have overcome these barriers, allowing unprecedented discussion of Washington's power and responsibility for the fate of the nation's cities. It is axiomatic in this debate that federal authorities have the final word on who the terrorists are; and the new Department of Homeland Security has staked out clear parameters for theorizing and policy analysis. But longstanding contradictions have deepened. President Bush and cabinet members routinely visit nativist American audiences to deliver speeches laden with the rhetorical tropes of irrationality and zealotry to explain the terrorist threat. At the same time, official policy is unequivocal in its recognition of terrorists' rational planning and tactical competence:

One fact dominates all homeland security threat assessments: terrorists are strategic actors. They choose their targets deliberately based on weaknesses they observe in our defensiveness and our preparedness.[32]

Similarly, the National Strategy for Combating Terrorism portrays the threat as "a flexible, transnational network structure, enabled by modern technology and characterized by loose interconnectivity both within and between groups."[33]

Constructing terrorists as strategic, deliberate, and rational is a rather ironic anti-Orientalist move, a militarized postcolonial trope coexisting with firmly-established Western stereotypes of Islamic zealotry.[34] The move requires and justifies corresponding analytical investments in homeland security, prompting a wide-ranging reconfiguration of the federal posture towards individual cities and the entire urban system. The post-September 11 federal transfers to New York City and the Urban Area Security Initiative certainly stand out as the clearest examples of a nascent and deliberate urban policy.[35] Yet the implicit impacts of the federal bureaucracy still dominate. The urban impacts of expanded defense and security expenditures (along with domestic multipliers from new overseas wars) are layered atop the city outcomes of relative or absolute cuts in social welfare transfers in a climate of state and municipal deficits. It remains unclear whether explicit federal commitments under the banner of urban security will end America's longstanding tradition of *de facto* policy through implicit, urban impacts.[36]

The terror city is a microcosm of transnational conflicts with national-level implications.

Terror cities highlight the complexities of intercultural and ideational interaction, exacerbating tensions of identity, difference, and otherness. Global conflicts are reproduced at the local level. Terror networks emerging from the global semi-periphery reach the United States, prompting swift American retaliation across the globe while opening new wounds in cities at all levels of the global terror hierarchy. Terror and antiterror have created a new version of Peter Hall's "City of the Tarnished *Belle Époche*" driven by polyethnic fears of profiling, scapegoating, and retribution.[37]

The predictable result is a selective yet pronounced hardening of ethnic-enclave boundaries in terror cities, as if the urban map began to mimic its unstable yet clearly-marked international counterpart. At the neighborhood scale, pockets of political dissent and cultural difference throw into sharp relief the divided allegiances of faith, ethnicity, nation, and generation. At the regional and national level, these tensions are woven into evolving discourses of immigration, racial and ethnic change, and the insecurities of America's white middle class. It is not unreasonable to expect that the urban landscape will endure at least some increase in polarization as a reflection of North-South and East-West animosities, perhaps with new waves of intraurban white flight that sharpen patterns of segregation by class, ethnicity, and race.[38] Such divisions will grow deeper if the scale and duration of American military engagements begin to affect refugee flows in European and North American cities.

But the terror city has national-level implications as well, suggesting inter-scalar dynamics similar to those observed in the link between neoliberalism and devolution.[39] The terror city hierarchy is based on evaluations of *urban* vulnerability to the transnational spatiality of terror networks, but the political response involves a sharp and pronounced revitalization of the nation-state. As Neil Smith observes, this was a "global event and yet utterly local..." and yet almost immediately this complex transnational event—perpetrators and victims from around the world—was scripted into

a *national* tragedy. September 11 was drafted into service by a "powerful nationalization of grief, anger, and reciprocal terror."[40]

The reactive elements of this change are obvious, as homeland security policy mandates tighter travel restrictions, intensified border policing, and heightened scrutiny
of immigrants, workers, and students. But there are also innovative and preemptive
elements to the change, and part of the work done by the terror city construct is to
pry open new points of entry for city figures moving into the national policy apparatus. Rudolph Giuliani's polarizing legacy of the 1990s (tourists love Times Square,
but many New Yorkers remember the crackdown on dissent and the tough-on-crime
credentials embellished with unapologetic defense of almost every single bullet ever
fired by NYPD officers) was immediately forgotten after September 11. Giuliani
secured an heroic *national* image, and after an ill-considered proposal to extend his
own term in office, he quickly launched Giuliani Partners to offer advice on security, policing, and Times-Square style urban revitalization to big-city majors in Latin
America and elsewhere across the globe. Giuliani Partners might well be considered
the terror-city counterpart to the more traditional style of consulting firm launched
amidst the nation-state rivalries of the cold war (e.g., Kissinger Associates). Nevertheless, those who try to use expertise gained in the terror city are not always able
to achieve the goals of fast policy transfer: Giuliani's one-time police commissioner
(Bernard Kerik) was later dispatched with great fanfare to supervise urban policing
in Baghdad for the Coalition Provisional Authority, but quietly abandoned the effort
after only a few months on the job (before his own nomination for Homeland Security Secretary collapsed in the face of yet another Nannygate and a classically New
York legal dispute over unpaid condo fees).

On the other hand, the terror city narrows the autonomy of many other city-based
officials in their relations with a revitalized federal executive branch. Moreover, the
urban police surveillance tactics developed in response to the wave of globalization
protests that began in Seattle in 1999 have been refined, redirected, and increasingly
federalized. Close federal-local cooperation is now an essential part of preparation
not just for trade talks and political conventions, but also for anti-war rallies and all
other forms of dissent. In October, 2003, the F.B.I. sent a confidential memorandum
to local law enforcement agencies detailing antiwar protesters' Internet organizing
tactics and asking local authorities to report any suspicious activity to federal antiterrorism squads.[41]

The terror city construct is also now providing justification for a broad range of
opportunistic state interventions, while also helping to deflect attention from state
failures and crimes. On the one hand, an ever-broader range of dissenting views and
actions are being recast as terrorist threats. Peaceful demonstrators protesting the
economic violence of neoliberal policy were beaten with batons at the Free Trade Area
of the Americas (FTAA) summit in Miami in October 2003, where Mayor Manny
Diaz applauded the federal-state cooperation in security: "This should be a model for
homeland defence."[42] Miami's police chief described FTAA protesters as "outsiders
coming in to terrorise and vandalise our city," and $8.5 million of the event's secu-
rity costs came directly from the $87 billion Congressional appropriation for the
Iraq invasion.[43] On the other hand, terrorist priorities are now routinely invoked to
explain or masquerade unrelated state scandals. In late 2003 the House Committee

on Government Reform issued a report citing the FBI for extensive use of murderers as informants in Boston for more than three decades. The document offers a macabre inventory of a quintessentially local, urban underworld in 1960s South Boston, but the Bureau's official response is quick to shift the focus from Boston 1965 to New York 2001 or Baghdad 2003: "While the F.B.I. recognizes there have been instances of misconduct by a few F.B.I. employees, it also recognizes the importance of human source information in terrorism, criminal, and counter-intelligence investigations."[44]

As the outlines of the terror city hierarchy become clearer, the new urban system born of transnational vulnerability helps to justify a resurgent, activist and militarist nation-state. Glocalization has accelerated, while shifting from a discursively constructed, aspatial conception of economic empire[45] to a more explicit reassertion of borders and boundaries enforced by military tactics and geopolitical strategy.[46]

A pervasive discourse of risk and fear is changing the purpose, scope, and methods of urban planning.

The mantra that "all things have changed" since September 11 has altered the way cities are seen by many different groups of urbanites—not just national war planners in the Iron Triangle of the Pentagon, Capitol Hill, and Crystal City defense contractors, but also big-city mayors coping with uncertain, fluctuating, and increasing unfunded mandates from above in a time of fiscal disaster, as well as wealthy residents of Chicago's high-rise John Hancock Tower and other elite addresses suddenly perceived as potential targets. But the urban planner seems to have endured the most jarring dislocation. Planners are confronted with an urgent and evolving barrage of demands, many of them suddenly rendering irrelevant the old dichotomies that have shaped the planning profession since the 1960s (e.g., theory/praxis, quantitative/qualitative, economic/cultural, participatory-pluralist/expert-modernist).

The planner's first task, unsurprisingly, was to respond to (or join) the immediate wave of urban futurism. Less than a week after the September 11 attacks, Kunstler and Salingaros concluded, "We are convinced that the age of skyscrapers is at an end. It must now be considered an experimental building typology that has failed."[47] They predicted the end of skyscraper construction and the dismantling of existing structures: no one could feel safe in a megatower again, and they should not, because "[e]very would-be terrorist who is now a child will grow up and be instructed by those surreal, riveting images of the two airplanes crashing into the World Trade Towers."[48] Marcuse and others also suggested the possibility of security-minded dispersal, as residents, state institutions, and "multinational businesses change their spatial strategies in the search for security in more outlying areas."[49] In this way, planners' sudden, urgent attempts to come to terms with new urban fears revived a theoretical and discursive tradition of America's mid-century urbanism:

> As the Cold War deepened, many scientists and political commentators began to suggest that American urban populations were excessive; atomic disasters would simply affect too many people, and too many industrial sites. The most effective and comprehensive solution to this problem ... was a massive program of urban dispersal and decentralization ....[50]

Contemporary urban sprawl, to be sure, cannot so easily be linked to policies of planned dispersal. Yet as a multifaceted spatial expression of complex and often contradictory social forces, the suburban built environment now provides a deep reservoir for intensified insecurities in the "war on terror." Private alarm and surveillance companies and automakers have been quick to revise their marketing campaigns to emphasize security, and Ford went so far as to introduce a new SUV concept car at the 2005 Detroit Auto Show—a "techno sanctuary sculpted in urban armor and inspired by the popular B-cars of congested international hotspots."[51] Ford advises that "As the population shifts back to the big cities, you'll need a rolling urban command center," and the new SYN^{US}—under the slogan "Vaulting Into the Urban Future"—is lampooned by the transportation activist Aaron Naparstek as the "Ford Blade Runner."[52] But, of course, Ford's new SUV should come as little surprise for a commodity "always advertised as a vehicle of war, a machine of escape and velocity in and through the urban jungle," and Eduardo Mendieta is certainly correct to define the SUV as the "vehicle of a violence and destruction that epitomizes a new form of anti-urbanism."[53] If the exuberant Cadillac tail-fins symbolized late-1950s American suburbia, today's icons include the Hummer, the Expedition, and soon, perhaps, the Ford Blade Runner.

Other planning functions are also having subtle effects on the physical fabric of cities. The precautionary principle is intensifying pressures on city planners and architects to minimize risks by adjusting building air intake vents, designing advanced air filters, building structural fortifications around ground-level columns, and designing redundant webs of structural beams to avert the disaster of building collapse.[54] American urban architecture may come to reflect selective adaptations of common Israeli designs, and security systems of all types are selectively hidden or highlighted in order to maximize deterrence.[55] In general, terror cities will include more divisions, separations, walls, and checkpoints—amidst new relations between public and private space, and new criteria for public citizenship and the rights of privacy and private association. In this way, the terror city reinscribes the lessons of the public space literature from the 1990s,[56] where spatial solutions flowered as a direct result of societal failures to deal with inherently social problems: even the strongest spatial fortifications of the most insular terror city in the American Homeland "will never provide real security in the presence of deep social, including international, differences."[57]

Public officials and private entrepreneurs are remaking the internal structure of the terror city with risk-based revaluations of urban space and centrality.

The terror city has reshaped significant parts of the American insurance and risk management industries, installing a militarized analytical perspective on urban space and the built environment. The initial shock of September 11 was seen as cataclysmic for this sector: the attacks were projected to "result in the largest insured loss ever recorded by U.S. insurance companies," prompting Standard and Poor's and other credit rating agencies to place 19 large insurance companies on immediate "credit watch."[58] Predictable calls for federal assistance were couched in terms of the need to assure employers, developers, and investors; within ten weeks Congress had completed its work and President Bush signed the Terrorism Risk Insurance Act (TRIA) of 2002. The legislation requires that insurers provide terrorism coverage, in return for a tiered system of federal backing for claims against the industry above a specified threshold (starting at 90% of claims above $10 billion in the first year).[59] The legislation was intended to provide only a transitional solution, but it is far from clear that unfettered (unsubsidized) entrepreneurial innovation will ever replace corporate welfare and investor socialism.

In the long term, TRIA and related federal interventions will expand the scale and *de facto* policy leverage of the risk management industry—much as regulatory policies in the debt markets has for many years given bond-rating agencies veto power over city spending priorities.[60] Emblematic of the sector is Risk Management Solutions, Inc., a spinoff originally founded at Stanford University in 1988. Now billing itself as "the world's leading provider of products and services for the quantification and management of natural hazard risks," RMS has reoriented many of its models to include terrorist vulnerability. The models are used by more than four hundred insurers, reinsurers, and investors (as well as the Rand Corporation's Center on Terrorism Risk Management Policy) and some estimates suggest that RMS holds half of the market for catastrophe modeling.[61] The firm's methods involve a blend of game-theoretic probability models, adaptations of financial market models (e.g., weather derivatives), geographic information sciences and spatial diffusion models, and expert opinion techniques. In its terrorist risk assessments, RMS ranks potential U.S. target locations based on the known aims and *modus operandi* of known terrorist organizations; of course, Rumsfeld reminds us that there are known unknowns, and then there are unknown unknowns. The RMS model estimates the likelihood of a particular type of attack at a specified location, with stratified probability estimates for the use of conventional, chemical, biological, or nuclear attacks. It then evaluates the capacity of counter-terrorism measures and security procedures at various sites to "disrupt or deter" various modes of attack.[62] The firm's products offer a wide variety of customized maps of event probability and itemized loss severity; examples of model output include detailed maps of downtown San Francisco targets with the highest "utility" for terrorists, building damage footprints from a truck bomb in downtown Chicago, spore deposition densities from an urban anthrax attack, and urban population vulnerabilities to smallpox spread in northeastern U.S. cities.[63]

Private entrepreneurial innovation in risk management and insurance is never far removed from federal research, policy, and subsidy; indeed, the RMS literature gives one the sense that the firm has somehow created less controversial (i.e., less publicly visible) versions of John Poindexter's ill-fated Terror Futures Market and Terror Information Awareness Program. The latest release of the RMS U.S. Terrorism Risk Model now includes "integrated functionality for analysis of coverage provided by" TRIA for certified events, and in February of 2003 the Insurance Services Office of the U.S. announced nonbinding "benchmark rates" for terrorism coverage in what were considered to be the most vulnerable centers: New York, Washington, D.C., Chicago, and San Francisco.[64]

The terror city is becoming an ever more important instrument of capital accumulation.
The commodification of terror and war should come as no surprise. The last three years have seen a remarkable spirit of military and intelligence entrepreneurialism, with innovative erosion of the dichotomies of economics and culture, defensive pro-

tection and offensive pre-emption.[65] Yet many of the most visible signs that seemed to point to immediate profiteering—Bush's pleas for Americans to continue shopping to defy terrorists, no-bid Iraqi reconstruction contracts for Halliburton, the wave of Homeland Security expenditures financed by record federal deficits[66]— are only incidentally urban. The direct role of the terror city in capital accumulation lies on a more subtle level, and must be seen in the context of three decades of geopolitically-conditioned urban and regional restructuring. Even if we set aside the historically-rooted question of the spatial politics of transnational oil markets and domestic fossil fuel consumption,[67] the evidence suggests that subtle changes in economic production and competition in American cities are now interwoven with an endless "war on terror."

First, the unstable yet rapid realignment of the post-cold war domestic regional-industrial network is being reversed and reconstructed. Congress, the White House, and security industry lobbyists have recast the early-1990s policy dilemmas of "defense conversion"—which forced regions and cities to diversify away from heavy reliance on military functions—as irresponsible and dangerous luxuries of a lost era.[68]

Second, new industries, new services, and the critical role of lobbying and communications have privileged cities with particular industrial mixes. Growth-machine elites have been quick to identify and pursue the profit opportunities distinctive to Hollywood's creative industries, Seattle's struggling aviation base, Silicon Valley's software and data-mining preeminence, and New York's financial markets. The Washington, D.C. area is particularly well positioned with its vast federal workforce and a global agglomeration of lobbyists, associations, think-tanks, military policy consultancies, and media strategy consultants. The $87 billion 2003 appropriation for Iraq and Afghanistan allocates $40 million for an Iraq studio for Al Hurra ("The Free One") a U.S.-sponsored news network designed to compete with Al Jazeera; studios were completed in Springfield, Virginia, a suburb on Interstate 95 a few miles south of Washington, DC.[69] Other items in the reconstruction budget are more firmly privatized, as in the case of Creative Associates International, a D.C.-based for-profit company that landed a $157 million contract for "educational reform" in Iraq.[70] Other prominent recipients of the first round of reconstruction contracts include the familiar names of Halliburton, through its Kellog, Brown, and Root subsidiary, as well as Bechtel and Flour; but others (the Research Triangle Institute, the Washington Group International) provide an explicit reminder that much of the "Iraqi" reconstruction expenditures will cycle through America's postindustrial service suburbs.[71]

Third, the spinoff multiplier effects of heightened domestic security are generating new opportunities that seem set to create ever more complex forms of local economic development entrepreneurialism. Steven Brill, creator of a media legacy anchored by *CourtTV* and *The American Lawyer*, is working with a former national security adviser and other partners to create Verified Identity Card, Inc., an enterprise that will offer an EZPass-style security check at airport gates for customers willing to pay and go through security screenings.[72] Among the thousands of homebuilders attending the 2004 International Builders Show in Las Vegas were thousands of displays of ever more sophisticated security cameras, fortified deadbolts, antibiological invasion technologies, and a "Secure Mail Vault" to replace the nostalgic mailbox.[73] Adapting urban economic base theory to a post-September 11 era suggests that cities will face mounting pressures to innovate and profit from (rather than simply sign up to pay for) the constant flood of new products and services mandated by what David Lyon has called "circuits of city surveillance" in "a new global alliance of surveillance states."[74] The city is becoming a *secured and biometrically-monitored* growth machine.

These accumulation opportunities expose significant contradictions. First, the over-reaching of the coalition of military/security industries and the federal government has generated a potent backlash, temporarily uniting right-wing antigovernment conservatives with progressive and radical groups to challenge the presumed tradeoff between security and constitutional rights of privacy and due process. This unlikely alliance has also tapped into a deep vein of consumer resistance. It may be no coincidence that the Pentagon's Terror Information Awareness and Terror Futures Market projects—powerful blends of market forces and information technologies —died in the same year that Congress passed antispam legislation and half of all American households signed up for the Federal Trade Commission's "Do Not Call" antitelemarketing list.[75] It is also instructive to consider how the institutions established in earlier generations to impose market discipline on liberal social-welfare expenditures are gradually becoming more hostile to the unprecedented deficits racked up by neoconservative militarism (witness the decline of the U.S. Dollar and the unease among Asian central bankers and other bond traders buying steadily-devalued U.S. Treasuries that finance the deficit). Second, the realignment exposes new conflicts between cities and other units of local government and higher levels of the state, as the costs required to sustain profit opportunities exceed the fiscal capacity of cities and regions. The nineties saw the growth of a national, domestic prison-industrial urban system as deindustrialized small towns and rural market centers sought to attract state facilities or private correctional contractors; suddenly these cities are vulnerable to the changing priorities of state legislatures unable to afford mandatory sentencing policies for minor drug offenses.[76]

Finally, the comparatively organized urban system of America's cold war war machine[77] has evolved into a far more complicated global network of military-commodity-chains. This system exposed the contradictions between the nostalgic "buy American" streams of conservatism and contemporary flexible specialization global production networks when Duncan Hunter, the conservative Republican chair of the House Armed Services Committee, inserted "buy America" provisions into the Fiscal 2004 Pentagon Budget. Facing a nightmare for Pentagon managers and military contractors sourcing from across the globe, Donald Rumsfeld threatened to recommend a Presidential veto of his own Departmental budget until Hunter backed off.[78]

Conclusions

In this chapter, we sought to develop a conceptual framework to guide analysis of how wars of and on terror are reshaping cities and urban life in the United States. We suggest that a powerful alliance of companies, investors, and neoconservative officials in the Bush administration are creating a genuinely new urban narrative object. This alliance rarely pursues explicit, deliberate, or openly-acknowledged attempts to reshape the American view of cities: but much as earlier conservative coalitions ignored the needs of cities in order to pursue "free-market" economic policies to benefit the wealthy, today's alliance is based on anti-urbanist principles and a solid commitment to an imperial, unilateral American strategy in the "war on terror."[79] As a consequence, the urban is redefined: cities now appear in terms of their *vulnerability to* terrorism, or their propensity to *breed and support* terrorists. The construct of the terror city performs the daily work of justifying the increased militarization of urban life "over here" in order to protect Americans from terrorists "over there," providing a distinctively urban counterpart to America's National Security Strategy doctrine of preventive war.

The ultimate trajectory for the terror city wrapped in the logic of the precautionary principle is toward a paranoid, insular enclave: New York as Pyongyang. The precautionary principle overrides conceptions of the "good life" in cities and urban planning, and gains credence from axioms that cannot be challenged if the imagination of terror is strong enough. Fears of terror underwrite demands for expanded definitions of threats and expanded resources to fight these threats. Imagination becomes the catalyst for incessant accumulation of surveillant knowledge and power. Perfect security is impossible to define (let alone achieve), but public acknowledgment of such realities appears weak, dangerous, or irresponsible in today's Orange-alert climate of intensified fears.

American cities are deeply vulnerable to the dangers inherent in the terror city hierarchy. Longstanding challenges that cities face in competing for people and jobs are now joined with intensified competition to minimize exposure in the new urban system of fear. The virtues of globalization and markets are suddenly rendered conditional upon a passport and a retinal scan. The freedom and entrepreneurial spirit of informal Islamic money transfer networks are recast as weapons of terror; the circulation of capital is now revered only if it can be traced through the GOP donor lists itemizing the assets of billionaire investors and defense contractors, or through the privatized consumer databases that can quickly be pried open under the provisions of the Patriot Act to see what we're buying at the local Wal-Mart. At the intraurban scale, the envelope of security expands insidiously as urbanites adapt to restrictions that soon become natural, reasonable limitations on freedom, movement, anonymity, uncertainty, disorder—all those things that constitute the essence of the urban. Fear takes concrete form in the urban landscape, reshaping the experience of city life and legitimating further restrictions on the freedom of urbanity. At the same time, the wealth and insecurity of the American terror city is defined and sustained by its other—by the world urban system of terror cities under varying degrees of "control" by American force, by imperial ambitions that, in turn, generate new currents of rage that can be defined as part of the terrorist threat. The American city is defined by, and its security restrictions are justified in reference to, the Iraqi villages encircled with barbed wire and guarded checkpoints to contain the insurgent threat. Colonel Nathan Sassaman, a battalion commander serving in Iraq, may well have demonstrated his qualifications for a cabinet-level appointment in a Bush-era U.S. Department of Housing and Urban Development, when he finished encircling an entire village with barbed wire fortifications and told Dexter Filkins of the *New York Times*, "With a heavy dose of fear and violence, and a lot of money for projects, I think we can convince these people that we are here to help them."[80] Assaulted with officially-sanctioned warnings of constant, evolving threats emanating from cities and villages across the globe, residents of American cities may acquiesce to the current logic of the Project for a New American Century: pre-emptive war to eliminate all possibilities of challenges deemed by the American state as unacceptable in a unipolar world. But another scenario is possible, as American urbanites come to understand that city fortifications against "global" threats fail to keep terror out: such measures only succeed in hiding and justifying American state-sponsored terror in Iraq and elsewhere, in bringing new and more virulent forms of insecurity into the American city, and weaving the metropolis into a destabilized, insecure global urban system of risk. Another world is possible, if we can build a foundation of nonviolence, social justice, human rights and engaged, democratic, communicative action—and if cities can remain open, cosmopolitan, connected. A first step is to challenge the terror city construct and the violence it underwrites. After a generation of deindustrialization, American cities were suddenly forced into a competitive niche in manufacturing consent: it is time to shutter these ideological factories, with their just-in-time production runs of fears and stereotypes, and to begin the hard work of building truly emancipatory systems within systems of cities.[81]

Notes

1. We are deeply indebted to Derek Gregory and Allan Pred for their guidance, patience, and critical engagement. We are also grateful for comments, criticisms, and suggestions from Jatinder Dhillon, Nick Blomley, Tom Slater, and members of the Rutgers Brooklyn Group (Bob Lake, Phil Ashton, James Defilippis, Kathe Newman, and Mark Pendras). John Friedmann graciously received our provocation, but we retain all responsibility for the torture we have inflicted on his pioneering scholarship. John is optimistic that the "present aberration" of the terror city is confined to the American Homeland, and in any event will not outlive the present Administration. We do sincerely hope John is correct. John Friedmann, personal communication by electronic mail (Vancouver: January 7, 2005).
2. CNN Wolf Blitzer Reports (Atlanta: CNN, aired December 14, 2004), transcript available at http://edition.cnn.com/TRANSCRIPTS/0412/14/wbr.01.html.
3. Neil Smith, "Scales of Terror: The Manufacturing of Nationalism and the War for U.S. Globalism," in Michael Sorkin and Sharon Zukin (eds.), *After the World Trade Center* (New York: Routledge, 2002), 97–108; Derek Gregory, *The Colonial Present: Afghanistan, Palestine, Iraq* (Oxford: Blackwell, 2004).
4. "The Vulcans were the military generation. Their wellspring, the common institution in their careers, was the Pentagon." James Mann, *The Rise of the Vulcans* (New York: Viking, 2004) p. xiii. Ann Markusen, Peter Hall, Scott Campbell, and Sabina Deitrich, *The Rise of the Gunbelt: The Military Remapping of Industrial America* (New York: Oxford University Press, 1991).
5. Compare Stephen Graham, "In a Moment: On Global Mobilities and the Terrorised City," *City* 5 no. 3 (2001): 411–415; and Peter Marcuse, "Reflections on the Events: All Cities Will Change," online posting to H-Urban discussion listserv, distributed September 24, 2001, available at http://www2.h-net.msu.edu/~urban (reprinted in *City* 5.3 (2001)) with Mike Davis, *Dead Cities and Other Tales* (New York: The New Press, 2002); David Harvey, *The New Imperialism* (Oxford: Oxford University Press, 2003); H. V. Savitch, and Grigoriy Ardashev, "Does Terror Have an Urban Future?" *Urban Studies* 38, no. 13 (2001): 2515–2533 (drafted shortly prior to the attacks of

September 11); and Michael Sorkin and Sharon Zukin, eds., *After the World Trade Center: Rethinking New York City* (New York: Routledge, 2002).

6. Hank V. Savitch, "Does 9-11 Portend a New Paradigm for Cities?" *Urban Affairs Review*, 39, no. 1 (2003): 103–127.

7. John Friedmann, "The World City Hypothesis," *Development and Change* 17, no. 1 (1986): 69–84: 69.

8. Bruno Latour, "Why Has Critique Run Out of Steam? From Matters of Fact to Matters of Concern," *Critical Inquiry* 30, no. 2 (2004): 225–248: 227.

9. Robert A. Beauregard, "Representing Urban Decline: Postwar Cities as Narrative Objects," *Urban Affairs Quarterly* 29, no. 2 (1993): 187–202.

10. Seymour Martin Lipset, "Still the Exceptional Nation?" Wilson Quarterly 24, no. 1 (2000): 31–45.

11. Hans Blix, interviewed in James Bamford, *A Pretext for War: 9/11, Iraq, and the Abuse of America's Intelligence Agencies* (New York: DoubleDay, 2004), 360.

12. An anonymous aide interviewed in Ron Suskind, "Without a Doubt," *New York Times Magazine* (October 17, 2004): 44.

13. Gearóid Ó Tuathail and Timothy W. Luke, "Present at the (Dis)integration: Deterritorialization and Reterritorialization in the New Wor(l)d Order," *Annals of the Association of American Geographers* 84, no. 3 (1994): 381–398: 381.

14. Francis Fukuyama, *The End of History and the Last Man* (New York: Free Press, 1992).

15. Mike Davis, *Dead Cities and Other Tales*, 4.

16. See Brian Knowlton, "U.S. Must Act on 'Murky' Data to Prevent Terror, Wolfowitz Says," *International Herald Tribune*, July 27, 2003; Norman Mailer, *Why Are We at War?* (New York: Random House, 2003); and Peter Marcuse, "Reflections on the Events: All Cities Will Change."

17. Richard V. Ericson and Kevin D. Haggerty, *Policing the Risk Society* (Toronto: University of Toronto Press, 1997), 86.

18. Ericson and Haggerty, *Policing the Risk Society*, 6.

19. Ericson and Haggerty, *Policing the Risk Society*.

20. Ericson and Haggerty, *Policing the Risk Society*.

21. As cited in Karen Dolan, *The Costs of War Hit Home* (Washington, DC: Institute for Policy Studies, Cities for Peace Program, 2003).

22. See, for example: Brian J. L. Berry, "Cities as Systems of Cities Within Systems of Cities," *Papers of the Regional Science Association* 13: 147-163; and Allan Pred, *City-Systems in Advanced Economies* (New York: Wiley, 1977).

23. Scott, Global City-Regions, and Smith, Transnational Urbanism.

24. Ron Scherer and Alexandra Marks, "Gangs, Prison: Al Qaeda Breeding Grounds?" *Christian Science Monitor*, June 14, 2002.

25. U. S. Department of Homeland Security, "Securing the Homeland: Protecting Our States and Cities," press release, April 8, 2003, Washington, DC: Office of the Press Secretary, U.S. Department of Homeland Security.

26. U.S. Department of Homeland Security, "Securing the Homeland."

27. Allocations for metropolitan antiterrorist measures were allocated among 29 different cities in a May, 2003 round of grants, and among 50 cities in a second round announced in November. The latter, totaling $675 million, were led by New York City ($47 million), Chicago ($34), Washington ($29.3), Los Angeles ($28), San Francisco ($26.4), and Philadelphia ($23) (Raymond Hernandez, "New York Gets $64 Million in Federal Aid Against Terror." *New York Times*, November 14, 2003: A20).

New York area mass transit systems were also set to receive $17.5 million to improve security.

28. Eric Lipton, "Big Cities Will Get More in Antiterrorism Grants," *New York Times* (December 22, 2004) p. A14.

29. Savitch, and Ardashev, "Does Terror Have an Urban Future?" 2516.

30. And, of course, the visible yet unstable hierarchy of potential target cities is underlain by the invisible urban system under construction by American defense and intelligence agencies. In part to skirt judicial review, the agencies have established a network of detention centers across the globe, from Afghanistan (Bagram Air Base, Kandahar, Kabul) to Iraq (Baghdad International Airport) and Cuba (Guantánamo Bay) to house prisoners captured in the recent wars.

31. See, for example, Norman J. Glickman, ed., *The Urban Impacts of Federal Policies* (Baltimore: Johns Hopkins, 1980); and Yvonne Scruggs, "HUD's Stewardship of National Urban Policy: A Retrospective View," *Cityscape* 1, no. 3 (1995): 33–68.

32. U. S. Department of Homeland Security, *National Strategy for Homeland Security* (Washington, DC: U. S. Department of Homeland Security, 2002): 7.

33. U. S. Directorate of Central Intelligence, *National Strategy for Combating Terrorism* (Langley, VA: U. S. Central Intelligence Agency, 2003): 8.

34. See, for example: Davis, *Dead Cities and Other Tales*; Gregory, *Colonial Present,* and Harvey, *The New Imperialism.*

35. U.S. Department of Homeland Security, "Securing the Homeland."

36. Glickman, *Urban Impacts.*

37. Peter Hall, *Cities of Tomorrow,* third edition (Oxford: Blackwell, 2002).

38. Marcuse, "Reflections on the Events: All Cities Will Change."

39. See, for example: Lynn A. Staeheli, Janet E. Kodras, and Colin Flint, eds., *State Devolution in America: Implications for a Diverse Society* (Thousand Oaks, CA: Sage Publications, 1997); Jamie Peck and Adam Tickell, "Neoliberalizing Space," *Antipode* 34, no. 3 (2002): 380–404; and Neil Smith, "Scales of Terror: The Manufacturing of Nationalism and the War for U.S. Globalism," in Michael Sorkin and Sharon Zukin, eds., *After the World Trade Center: Rethinking New York City* (New York: Routledge, 2002), 97–108.

40. Neil Smith, "Scales of Terror," 98.

41. Eric Lichtblau, "F.B.I. Scrutinizes Antiwar Rallies," *New York Times*, November 23, 2003: A1, A18.

42. Naomi Klein, "America's Enemy Within," *Guardian* (November 26, 2003): 25.

43. Klein, "America's Enemy Within."

44. Fox Butterfield, "F.B.I. Used Killers as Informants, Report Says," *New York Times*, November 21, 2003: A24.

45. Michael Hardt and Antonio Negri, *Empire* (Cambridge, MA: Harvard University Press, 2000).

46. For example: David Harvey, *The New Imperialism* (Oxford: Oxford University Press, 2003) and Neil Smith, "Scales of Terror."

47. James Howard Kuntsler and Nikos A. Salingaros, "The End of Tall Buildings," *Planetizen.com*, 17 September, 2001, available at http://www.planetizen.com/oped/itme.php?id=30.

48. Kuntsler and Salingaros, "The End of Tall Buildings."

49. Marcuse, "Reflections on the Events: All Cities Will Change."

50. Matthew Farish, "Disaster and Decentralization: American Cities and the Cold War," *Cultural Geographies* 10, no. 2 (2003): 125–148.

51. Ford Motor Company, "Vaulting Into the Urban Future: Ford SYN[US]," http://www.fordvehicles.com/autoshow/concept/synus, accessed January 30, 2005.

52. Ford Motor Company, "Vaulting"; Aaron Naparstek, "The Ford Blade Runner," http://www.naparstek.com/2005/01/ford-blade-runner.php, accessed January 30, 2005.

53. Eduardo Mendieta, "SUVing Through the Slums of Globalizing Neoliberalism," unpublished manuscript (draft, November 2004) forthcoming in *City*; see also Stephen Graham, "Postmortem City: Towards an Urban Geopolitics," *City* 8, no. 2 (2004): 165–196.

54. John Holusha, "More Attention to Security in Designing Buildings," *New York Times*, March 10, 2002, Real Estate section.

55. Holusha, "More Attention to Security in Designing Buildings," and Marcuse, "Reflections on the Events: All Cities Will Change."

56. See, for example, Don Mitchell, "The Annihilation of Space by Law: The Roots and Implications of Anti-Homeless Laws in the United States," *Antipode* 29 (1997): 303–335 and Don Mitchell, *Cultural Geography: A Critical Introduction* (Oxford: Blackwell, 2002).

57. Marcuse, "Reflections on the Events: All Cities Will Change."

58. Guy Halverson, "What Insurance Industry's Surprising Rebound Means for Investors, Consumers," *Christian Science Monitor*, June 3, 2002.

59. Tom Anderson, "Insurers Calculate Terrorism Risk," *Argus Online*, December 18, 2002, available at http://www.theargusonline.com/

60. Howard Kunreuther, "The Role of Insurance in Managing Extreme Events: Implications for Terrorism Coverage," *Risk Analysis* 22, no. 3 (2002): 427–428; Jason Hackworth, "Local Autonomy, Bond-Rating Agencies and Neoliberal Urbanism in the United States," *International Journal of Urban and Regional Research* 26, no. 4 (2002): 707–725.

61. See Risk Management Solutions, Inc., "Latest, Expert View of Evolving Terrorism Threat Incorporated into RMS Terrorism Risk Model," press release, September 9, 2003, Newark, CA: Risk Management Solutions, Inc. and Risk Management Solutions, Inc. *Managing Terrorism Risk in 2004* (Newark, CA: Risk Management Solutions, Inc., 2003).

62. See Risk Management Solutions, Inc., *Managing Terrorism Risk in 2004* and Risk Management Solutions, Inc. *Understanding and Managing Terrorism Risk*, 2003, Newark, CA: Risk Management Solutions, Inc., available at http://www.rms.com.

63. Risk Management Solutions, Inc., *Managing Terrorism Risk in 2004*.

64. Joseph B. Treaster, "Insurance Price Rate Determined for Cities at Risk of Terrorism," *New York Times*, February 2, 2002: C5.

65. The U.S. patent and trademark office received a wave of applications within weeks of the September 11 attacks, with several requests claiming rights over variations of the twin-towers silhouette. U.S. Treasury Secretary Paul O'Neil attended the re-opening of the New York Stock Exchange in an elaborate ceremony in late September, 2001.

66. The Center for Public Integrity has assembled evidence that nine of the thirty members of the Pentagon's Defense Policy Board had links to defense companies securing $76 billion in contracts in the two years prior to the Spring 2003 Iraq War (Charles Lewis, "Press Release Announcing Windfalls of War," October 30, 2003, Washington, DC: Center for Public Integrity).

67. Harvey, *The New Imperialism*.

68. See Davis, *Dead Cities and Other Tales* and Ann Markusen, Peter Hall, Scott Campbell, and Sabina Deitrick, *The Rise of the Gunbelt*.

69. Jim Rutenberg, "Coming Soon to Arab TV's: U.S. Answer to Al Jazeera, Production Values and All," *New York Times*, December 17, 2003: A22.

70. Charles Lewis, "Press Release Announcing Windfalls of War."

71. See Lewis, "Press Release Announcing Windfalls of War."

72. John Schwartz, "Venture to Offer ID Card for Use at Security Checks," *New York Times*, October 23, 2003: C4.

73. Bradford McKee, "Fortress Home: Welcome Mat Bites," *New York Times*, January 22, 2004: D1, D4.

74. David Lyon, 'Technology vs. 'Terrorism': Circuits of City Surveillance Since September 11th,' *International Journal of Urban and Regional Research* 27, no. 3 (2003): 666–678.

75. See Carl Hulse, "Swiftly, Terror Futures Market is a Concept Without a Future," *New York Times*, July 30, 2003: A1, A10 and Eric Schmitt, "Poindexter Will be Quitting over Terrorism Betting Plan." *New York Times*, August 1, 2003: A10.

76. Meanwhile, at the federal level, the Office of Drug Control policy sponsors television ads (often targeted to white suburbanites) to blame teenagers buying marijuana joints for financing terrorists. See Sasha Abramsky, "The Drug War Goes Up in Smoke," *The Nation*, August 18, 2003 and Karen Dolan, *The Costs of War Hit Home* (Washington, DC: Institute for Policy Studies, Cities for Peace Program, 2003).

77. Markusen, Hall, Campbell and Deitrick, *The Rise of the Gunbelt*.

78. Leslie Wayne, "Butting Heads with the Pentagon: Old Friend in House for Military Wants to Force it to 'Buy America'," *New York Times*, July 23, 2003: C1, C9.

79. Indeed, one of the enduring ironies of the 2004 Presidential election was the urban-rural split in voters' reception to Bush's war-on-terror agenda for a second term. Bush gained the strongest support for his steadfast (if carefully parsed) equation of Iraq with September 11 in rural areas, small towns, and other areas with the lowest vulnerability to large-scale attacks.

80. Quoted in Dexter Filkins, "Tough New Tactics by U.S. Tighten Grips on Iraqi Towns," *New York Times*, December 7, 2003: A1, A13.

81. Edward S. Herman, Noam Chomsky, and Dan Frank, eds., *Manufacturing Consent: The Political Economy of the Mass Media* (New York: Pantheon, 2002); Brian J. L. Berry, "Cities as Systems of Cities."

18

Banal Terrorism
Spatial Fetishism and Everyday Insecurity

Cindi Katz

I try not to mourn, I try to organize, in between I make jokes—pointed jokes. Jokes that I wouldn't burden with "resistance" but that at least reframe the familiar as strange, and so undermine the very banality by which hegemony is so often secured. Some of these come to mind as I walk through the public spaces of New York—the train stations, the charged intersections and squares, the marquee buildings—and see the National Guard, dressed in camouflage. They cluster next to clumps of New York cops, collectively alerting us to our need for alertness, their laconic postures surely a pose. I get through these spaces imagining the New Yorker cartoon I could draw, if I could draw: A guy dressed like a fire hydrant or in brick and pizza patterned fatigues tilting back to eye a more traditionally camouflaged soldier in Pennsylvania Station. The caption echoes Marisa Tomei in *My Cousin Vinny* to read, "Oh, and you blend!?!" The cartoon toys with a deadly serious question. Why would dressing for Desert Storm in the midst of New York City reassure residents and visitors of their safety? There is, of course, an exacting science and art of camouflage that surely has anticipated urban warfare. By what form of trifling with the imagination does the security state authorized—but not inaugurated—by September 11 place such inappropriate bodies in New York's and many other public spaces?

Likewise, the explosion of surveillance cameras and other strategies of public vigilance all around the city. Are "we" safer now that all bridge and tunnel entrances are guarded by some combination of cameras, police, and military surveillance? If I concede that inspecting vehicles moving in, out and through the city might offer some shred of protection—though the sheer numbers and sources of this traffic belie this—of what possible use, beyond security charade, is visual vigilance of tunnel entrances, turnstiles, or exit ramps? A couple of my friends got caught in one such breach of security, video-taping the spot where the number 7 subway train emerges from underground in its route from Manhattan to Queens. Within minutes they were confronted by a police officer who demanded their camera as he brusquely told them that all photography of public transportation was forbidden in New York. The filmmaker was madly rewinding the video just shot as they insisted that they had not actually filmed anything yet at that site. As the cop grabbed the camera, my friend hoped that she'd made it past the offending footage. She had, only to have reached an earlier shot. A map. Of the Middle East. Fortune was with them. The cop had been

349

educated in the United States and so was unfamiliar with what was mapped. "What's this a map of?" he demanded. "Europe!" my geographer colleague jumped to reassure him. After a few more questions about where they were from, the cop was mollified and retreated, leaving them with the camera and video intact.

These stories suggest visceral connections between geography and power, but not in a monological sense (Katz 2005). In the first instance, state power is expressed through deliberate geographic illiteracy; camouflage without any landscape referent. In the second, geographical ignorance was artfully manipulated to evade the state's authority. Apart from exposing the intertwinings of geography and power, I recall these vignettes here to reveal two potent instances of what I am calling "banal terrorism." They are everyday, routinized, barely noticed reminders of terror or the threat of an always already presence of terrorism in our midst.

I have developed the idea of banal terrorism through shameless appropriation of Michael Billig's notion of banal nationalism (Billig 1995). Billig provocatively suggests that the ideological foundations of nationalism are produced and reproduced in a banal and everyday way through what he punningly refers to as "flagging," the little, beneath the radar, and even surreptitious things that remind those in established nations of their nationhood. Determined to dislocate nationalism from its ready association with more virulent expressions, as something shared and produced by Serbs, Basques, Eritreans, Armenians, Tamils and other separatists or national liberationists, Billig insists that "we" too are nationalists. His argument is that those in established and even powerful nations are constantly reminded of their nationhood in the course of daily life, and that these banal practices—a lapel pin here, a bumper sticker there, an anthem at the start of a sporting event—produce identities of belonging that incorporate people in reproducing a "homeland" and with it a world of homelands that are themselves naturalized. Among the discursive and material social practices Billig flags as banal nationalism are the "unwaved" flags that, for example, droop everywhere in the United States; and the newspaper and other media accounts that incorporate people in "the" nation through such discursive mechanisms as "the" president, "the" elections, "the" army, which mark the unnamed us of the U.S. and bring us into the body of the nation as Americans. In other words, through the little—but constant—reminders of nationhood, a vigorous national identity is produced. Coursing through this identity is a congeries of beliefs, assumptions, habits, and practices that can be called forth during crises to rally support for national causes, the military, "us," "our" boys, national sacrifice, and the like.

Banal nationalism brings nationalism in from the periphery and makes it a home grown and homespun product. Marianne Gullestad (2001) makes a similar argument regarding Norwegian nationalism, which is *really* homespun. Folkloric and celebratory, it produces a self-congratulatory sense of belonging so powerful (and frequently smug) that Norway rejected membership in the European Union, one of only two western European nations to do so. Banal nationalism also calls forth what I am calling "banal terrorism," which is connected and analogous to it but distinct. Banal terrorism produces a sense of terror and fear in a drivelly and everyday way. The common (non)sense constructed and assumed around terrorism (and terrorists) in all sorts of banal ways can be hailed at moments of crisis to authorize such things as a suspension of civil liberties or an open-ended and clearly never-ending "War on

Terrorism." The material social practices of banal terrorism work at all scales and their intricate circuitry not only enables them to authorize and reinforce one another, but naturalizes their acceptability and seeming common sense. The banality of terrorism and the state of terror it invokes work almost at the capillary level; we've gone from duct tape and the farce of color-coded alerts to talismanic lunacy. I recently saw a license plate that said "fight terrorism." As the fight stoops to smiley face tactics, we are urged—everywhere—to "say something" if we "see something." I see something: Camouflaged soldiers in the midst of all manner of urban spaces. That, of course, is their point. Banal terrorism is sutured to—and secured in—the performance of security in the everyday environment.

Like banal nationalism, banal terrorism embraces a set of themes about "us"—"we" are "threatened," "they" hate/are jealous of "us," "we" share a "homeland"—but it goes a step further as these notions about "us" authorize and propel a common sense notion of "them" as threat. If in Billig's understanding, the very idea of "homeland" is an outcrop of banal nationalism, it is presupposed in banal terrorism, if only as a means to frame a fortress against polymorphous threats. Witness how quickly the term "homeland"—which I don't think I'm alone in associating with Nazism—got called forth in the security state fostered (but not invented) by the events of September 11, 2001. The fact that in the United States a cabinet level Department of Homeland Security was formed, with very little popular objection, as an über security apparatus, despite the many ways it compromises the nation's most sacred myths about itself, exposes the potency of banal nationalism and its obstreperous offspring, banal terrorism. Banal terrorism produces xenophobic discourses around "homeland" that work to narrow the channel of threat and danger. At the same time, its discourses produce themes of the nation as porous and perforated, but ready to be mobilized as a coherent agent against less coherent threats. Likewise, the material social practices of banal terrorism create and perform discursive formations around "duty" and "honor," leading to such things as the Patriot Act, which rallies around and assumes a particular brand of patriotism.[1]

Banal terrorism diffuses, reproduces, and reinforces these themes as common sense through such relatively innocuous mechanisms as the camouflagery, multi-colored security alerts, airport and other forms of screening, the increased presence of explosive sniffing dogs, and the proliferation of background noise and imagery exhorting us—everywhere—to report suspicious activity, people, and things. Banal terrorism also produces and reproduces common sense themes about what constitutes a terrorist. The common sense is predictably racist and also ignorant. It conflates Islam and Arab to embrace all brown men no matter what their national origins or religious beliefs. The working profile largely ignores women and excludes the angry white men of the Oklahoma City bombing as types. Without these home-grown Christian militiamen, the normalized profile of a terrorist is one of an antimodern, angry, jealous zealot; a heartless brainwashed agent living in a "sleeper cell," "who infiltrates and takes advantage of "the freedoms" of "our" everyday life even as he would destroy them. These themes of banal terrorism made supporting the "War on Terrorism" common sense and airbrushed away many of the slippages that authorized its extension into Iraq and its shameful excesses such as Guantánamo or Abu Ghraib.[2]

Here I want to address the spatial fetishism of banal terrorism, or the way particular performances of security in the landscape both create and reproduce a banal notion of terrorism—its paradoxical routinization—at the same time as they obscure and mystify the social, cultural and political-economic relations that propel global terrorism and undergird the security state.

The term "spatial fetishism" is used by critical geographers to describe understandings of space as producing effects; as causal of particular conditions and material social practices rather than as the outcome of specific social relations and practices—space as socially produced. While in a reductive sense this definition is apposite to my purposes in that it suggests a notion of space that obscures social relations and reifies space as having political meaning, I want to draw out the entailments of fetishism in the Marxist and Freudian senses of the term in order to point to both what is being concealed by the appearance of security and what sort of lack or trauma drives its production, reproduction, and ready consumption. Working through these entailments may help to clarify both our interpolation into the security state and its multiple manifestations and effects.

Marx, of course, brilliantly begins *Capital* with a close examination of the commodity, demonstrating that exchange value sets up a relation between things that obscures and mystifies the underlying social relations that both produce that value and make its abstraction possible. Relations between people—in all their unevenness—appear in "fantastic form" as a relation between things. Marx refers to this quintessential mystification of capitalism as commodity fetishism (Marx 1967).

Freud, in a 1927 essay, "Fetishism," bluntly, categorically, and even strangely avuncularly, gets right to his point by declaring that across all of his male cases the meaning and purpose of the fetish was the same—a penis substitute (Freud 1963). He quickly adds that it is not just any chance penis, but the mother's phallus, which young boys believe in and some do not wish to forego, associating the mother's castration with the potential for their own. As Freud delineates, the perception of the lost penis persists interlocked with an energetic action to keep up the denial of it, so that the belief (in the mother's phallus) is simultaneously retained and given up. A compromise is struck within the unconscious wherein a successor to the phallus is produced to absorb the interest that earlier went to the (imagined) penis. The fetish, then, creates what Freud calls a permanent memorial to the horror of castration; a marker of the repression of the knowledge of what has been lost, which of course was never there.

Drawing on these complementary notions of fetishism, I want to explore some instances of the spatial fetishism I associate with banal terrorism first to argue that through them the social relations of terrorism are concealed at the same time as the horror of those social relations are both denied and revisited, and so known viscerally. Second, to delineate what some of these social relations are and thus what is at stake in the reproduction of banal terrorism through the performance of security, spatial fetishism, and other means. Finally, I hope at least to gesture toward a politics that might not only disclose and reveal the social relations that hold these formulations in place across space and scale, but rework them as well.

The camouflaging I marked at the start of this piece is an instance of spatial fetishism that works at the scale of the body and urban space. It is—paradoxically—an obvious performance to produce and reproduce the nexus of terror and security. In urban and other environments we call law enforcement personnel who want to move undetected, undercover, and we know from all manner of cop shows if not personal experience, that these guys "blend." And yet here we have soldiers who have little familiarity with their surroundings cropping up in jungle and desert motifs. They commonly stand near the police, who are already in ample supply. Their camouflage makes them visible—their bodies emblematic of a muscular state. None of this alters a thing regarding the protection of people and the spaces they traverse. This staging of security does nothing so much as authorize a security state and routinize the ever-presence of terrorism in our midst. This routinization engages the popular imaginary and reproduces docility vis à vis the state and its security operations. And this is, of course, the intent of making visible that which is designed for invisibility.

Meanwhile, at a vastly different scale and in wholly other environments, that security state grows unseen. But in part the unseeing, and the willingness not to see, are achieved through everyday performances of terror/security such as those of the camouflaged soldiers in U.S. urban centers. Well camouflaged in the deserts of the southwest, for instance, the military operates in what it calls the "black world." According to the artist-geographer, Trevor Paglen (2005), it is a world that does not exist, cannot be seen, and will not respond no matter what the provocation, even its own employees. In this world of deep secrecy and total camouflage, the military and national security operatives produce billions of dollars of war machinery with unlimited funding and zero accountability. Their operations are enabled, in part, by the militarization of the U.S. state, which, in part, has been enabled and authorized by our everyday seeing of threat-security performed. These stealth landscapes conceal the research and development and manufacture of weapons and material for enduring and globalized warfare (Paglen 2005). Concealed on the other side of the country is the always prepared bunker government, a stealth landscape buried in the mountains of Virginia and elsewhere. Fully operable, these vast bunkered spaces are ready to receive, house, and entertain representatives of state and some of their families in rotating shifts of ninety days (Willis 2003). The readiness of this shadow state is underwritten again in part by our incorporation in particular regimes of seeing and not seeing.

Another example of spatial fetishism is what Peter Marcuse refers to as urban citadelization. Not unconnected to urban camouflaging, these spatial practices exceed embodiment and involve the all too familiar forms of bunkering and fortressing of particular patches of real estate as well as the increased gating of communities; urban, suburban, and otherwise. Gating was an increasingly common practice globally prior to 9/11, but in the years since has been broadly expanded, democratized, and given the patina of a neat alibi. Citadelization performs security, but so selectively that it almost rehearses and reinforces the very vulnerabilities it is staged to counter. For instance, much of the attention is on so-called marquee buildings, prestigious addresses saturated with symbolic value. So the emblematic Empire State Building is surrounded by rampart-planters and bollards along with security guards, and all visitors including workers must pass through metal detectors and have their bags checked upon entering–all of this security is privatized of course, but that is another story. Meanwhile, its neighbors, including, for example, the Graduate Center of the City University of New York where I work, are open and relatively unguarded, to say nothing of the sidewalks and streets that surround the building itself. So again, what is accomplished by these practices? What do such fetishizations of space conceal? What is revealed by even a scratch on their surface?

For one they reveal a stubborn vision of terrorism and a narrow imagination of its space-time. The whole point of terrorism—what makes it terrifying—is its unpredictability, the unexpected, unanticipatable registers of its space-time. The bunkering of marquee buildings may comfort (but more likely just annoys) their occupants, but why would the next attack rehearse the spectacular nature of the September 11 attacks? What if terrorism really does get routine? When quotidian sites like busses, cafes, subway cars become targets and the temporality of attack is humdrum, the relative futility of all manner of "preparedness" is made clear. Bunkering fetishizes the question; at best protecting certain people and targets, inevitably leaving countless others open and vulnerable. Its practices, and the fantasy of producing citadels of safety and security, defy the very meaning and essence of urban life—of open cities—although as Peter Marcuse suggests, these security practices (well underway prior to September 11) are part and parcel of producing divided cities; of walling off haves and have-nots, of invisibilizing the effects of neoliberal disinvestments in social welfare and reproduction (Marcuse 2003). Contemporary ghettos, he notes, are not just "night ghettos" like those of old, where people essential to the production of urban life—an integral part of the fabric of the city—went to sleep. Now we have twenty-four hour ghettos where excessed populations—homeless people, unemployed people—who are only a drag on urban life, are meant to stay (Marcuse 2003). Warehoused (to say nothing of those imprisoned); these populations would only disturb those in the citadels, their presence potentially reminding the privileged or just barely still-integrated of the social costs of their protection and potential vulnerability. Again spatial fetishization does its work of occluding, of repressing, of displacing the pain and price of the neoliberal security state.

Another sort of fetishism is also at work here. The citadelization of particular addresses, of symbolic sites, uncannily rehearses the mirage of the symbolism. These are empty signifiers, quite literally. While corporate headquarters have historically vied for prestigious addresses; needing a real estate claim in one global city or another—often more than one, their operations have been insistently decentralized and globalized over the past several decades. One of the things concealed through the spatial fetishization I am charting is this unhinging of production—material and symbolic—from particular places and all that unhinging allows. This will be addressed below; here I want to mark the largely inconsequential nature of address. This inconsequentiality was seen, as has been commonly noted, in how fast business as usual resumed even for those hardest hit by the September 11 attacks (except, of course, for the loss of life). In less than a week, back office operations and other corporate locations near and far from New York City had absorbed the functions of the spaces that were destroyed or compromised. Even the New York Stock Exchange was back to relatively normal operations a week later, suggesting a different sort of spatial fetishism—prior to and exceeding the security state. The corporate address increasingly had staged a prestigious, powerful presence that obscured its often hollowed out interior or a replicatability of function in the extended spaces of capitalist globalism. Since 9/11 marquee buildings and prestigious addresses have lost some of their allure, even as symbols, as corporate deconcentration (in the name of safety) has continued to so-called edge cities or other less notable locations worldwide (Marcuse 2003). Meanwhile, urban citadels perform the play of safety while spatial divisions, which mark political-economic divisions, harden and expand.

The third and final spatial fetishism I want to address is the fortress nation. Here again there is a performance of bunkering; this time at a national scale. Among its signs are not only the increased border policing north and south, but the construction of an actual wall along a long stretch of the U.S.-Mexico border. The fortress nation is also reflected in airport screening, new harsh visa requirements, and other processes that invoke racial profiling on a world scale, the introduction of biometric fortressing through fingerprint entry requirements, and talk of instating pupil recognition identification modes for crossing borders or clearing security. The last is sure to sharpen the division between a mobile elite and a stalled, queued, interrogated, lumpen-travelariat. But the fortress nation, like the other fetishisms, is a spatial fiction. The nation is porous and perforated. Overlooked illegal immigration is essentially national policy, and millions of undocumented workers and would-be workers are essential to the United States and its globalized political economy. The performance of fortressing is belied everywhere by "wide-shut" borders (to say nothing of the fantastic security threat posed by containerized shipping, which remains essential unencumbered nationally and internationally.)

The contradictions, concealments, and horrors of this form of spatial fetishism are perhaps the starkest of all the ones I've traced. There is the performance of strict security—the reality of which falls on targeted racialized populations from the global south—at the juridical/legal level, while the economy, and therefore corporate leaders and small business owners alike, demands an open flow of immigrants. In another but intersecting realm there is the security state's mobilization of the nation as perforated—the creepy insistence that "they" may be anywhere and are everywhere, sleeper cells ready to be triggered, suicide bombers ready to roll, antimodern zealots hiding in the folds and interstices of "our" freedom. The banality of ever-present terror enables the nation to be mobilized as a coherent whole that is made coherent in part through deployments against less coherent threats. Terror, in other words, is mobilized to solidify a porous nation—the constitutive outside pushed inside and made interstitial; existing as Marx said of the Jews in ancient Poland, in the pores of society. The fortress paradoxically encloses what is in its pores as the always already perforated nation-space calls forth the fortress. Indeed the porosity of the United States is one of the foundational myths of the nation, and attempts to seal it off or solidify it threaten not only the nation's historical understandings of itself, but its vibrancy in the future.

Clearly, we are no safer for these instances of spatial fetishism or performances of security. But in any event, our safety would be at most only a byproduct of these performances. It is, of course, the nature of terrorism to work the interstices, to shock, to enact a repercussive unintelligibility. Its time-space does not conform to expected logics, and that characteristic is key to its success. Terrorists work in a deterritorialized way, puncturing the lull of the routine. If terrorism is inherently unpredictable, terrorism made banal is an attempt to routinize its presence while not addressing the contradictory truths of terrorism made routine. Since September 11, 2001 the U.S.

government has allocated over $18 billion to secure air travel, while appropriating only $250 million for mass transit security (Chan 2005). Not only does this allocation indicate skewed priorities and glaring vulnerabilities, but in the same week as the London underground bombings revealed the quotidian nature of contemporary terrorism, the U.S. Congress reduced next year's allocation for securing mass transit from $150 to $100 million. But then, of course, it's not clear how effective any of these expenditures are. All the camo in Pennsylvania Station wouldn't stop an attack on the numerous subway lines that run beneath it, and its presence should give us pause. As I suggested earlier, under the sign of such performances of security we find the growth and increasing ubiquity of what is known as a "surveillant assemblage," a Deleuzian idea that welds "big brother," whom we've familiarized through decades of fear, with rhizomatic surveillance, the current state of the game, which makes vigilance in every direction and at all scales the new normal.

If terrorism is part of the landscape (and the effects of banal terrorism make that so), then all means to ward it off are sanctioned. People submit to security searches; accept the proliferation of surveillance cameras; and don't mind that their e-mails might be filtered, read, or censored or that other means of seemingly private communication might be scrutinized. Many seem to welcome a military presence in civilian spaces and some call for such formerly objectionable things as national identity cards, even in the form of biometric "smart" cards that would be loaded with all sorts of personal data. The appeal of these cards is that "we" who have nothing to hide will be identified, while others will be flushed to the surface. That binary of false comfort notwithstanding, these cards are only as good as their source materials, and these can be fraudulent. If a forged birth certificate is used in the acquisition of a smart card, it won't be as smart as it seems. But then, we live in a society that in less virulent times took comfort in fences, making them higher in places that seemed more threatening. Yet no matter how tall, fences are almost always breached at the bottom. This obvious fact seems beside the point to those bent on securing particular environments. Likewise, when the banal security of the smart card is achieved through eclipsing its potential flaws of origin.[3]

Much of the state's intent in all this—which is laudable in obvious ways—is to prevent terrorism rather than prosecute it afterward. But prevention requires at once a massive security apparatus and a considered and informed allocation of limited resources. The former has already been deployed in ways that exceed what might reasonably be considered its mandate, often at the expense of the latter. Among the pernicious and extra-legal strategies are racial profiling; blanket surveillance of everyday material social practices long considered to be private; and "anticipatory policing," which, if we ratchet down the scale of its ambit and focus on yesterday's big fear, crime, would call for apprehending criminals before they commit a crime. These contentious policies and practices suggest some of the contradictions at the heart of the state's strategies. Apprehending and holding "terrorists" before they commit a terrorist act, because they fit a profile, for example, puts the state and those it inculcates through the daily practices of banal terrorism on a slippery and dangerous slope. In the UK, "profiling" is already being done among young people whom police consider "likely" to become criminals. Analogous with the U.S.'s unprecedented preemptive strike on Iraq, authorized by an unsubstantiated and fraudulent assertion of their having weapons of mass destruction or the ability to make them anew, policing and security conducted in anticipation of certain people becoming criminals or terrorists is unacceptable, unwarranted, and dangerously erosive to the boundaries of long-standing social and political-economic contracts and conventions.

While some of the security measures that have been implemented in the past few years probably have prevented various attacks on innocent people, they will not, and, indeed, it is the nature of terrorism that they cannot, catch everything. Under these circumstances, it is ever more urgent to question not only the effectiveness of the security state naturalized in the course of the practices associated with banal terrorism, but the huge costs through which it is purchased. Among these is the diversion of state expenditures from the social wage to militarization at home and abroad. Far more people are hurt or killed from the preventable diseases of poverty, from heart disease and cancer, from HIV-AIDS, in automobile accidents, and in the course of everyday violence than in terrorist attacks. Yet state expenditure is wildly skewed toward the latter, which, of course, worsens the mortality and morbidity rates associated with the former. Another cost of banal terrorism is the erosion of civil liberties, authorized, in part, by the discursive construction of otherness; it seems to most Americans that state and other surveillance strategies are more about "them," than "us." But them is always already us, and the failure to recognize this jeopardizes the entire fabric of civil society.

There are perhaps some nonfetishistic means available to reduce the likelihood of future terrorist attacks, and I want to at least gesture toward these, though space prohibits a more detailed discussion. One strategy for thwarting the plans of terrorists, which was deployed in the first weeks after September 11, is to follow the money and cut it off at the source. Here, as is well known, law enforcement and other state agents followed the trail and quickly found themselves, or more accurately and abstractly the state that employs them and the ruling classes of corporate America. There are only so many international banks, and finance capital flows through narrow, well-defined, and quite ugly shared channels; witness the money laundering operations of drug cartels and how all too often they have been off limits in the "war on drugs." Not only are the houses of Bush and Saud intimately linked (Unger 2004), but the central circuitry of capitalist globalism is shared in soberingly similar ways by international terrorist organizations and multinational corporations. Their rhizomes traverse the globe, sprouting (and dying) in this locality or that as if they have local specificity, but the veneer of specificity is purchased through social relations at higher scales. The intertwined nature of these rhizomes seems to have limited the pursuit of many of the financial flows of terrorism. Following the trail of money did not go on for long or get very far, although it might have been quite productive in reducing the extent and number of terrorist attacks. In its place we find another enactment of spatial fetishism in the service of state violence. In the so-called War on Terror the United States and its allies have confronted a number of sovereign states purportedly to rout out various rhizomatic and deterritorialized organizations within their borders. The perpetrators of this war invoke and rely upon a Manichean geography of "good" nations—the "coalition of the willing" —against "bad"—the "axis of evil" or rogue states—to ease their way, attaching the trace of evil or roguishness to individual subjects as an alibi for torture or imprisonment that flouts international law.

Another means for reducing the chances of subsequent terrorist attacks involves intelligence that deserves the name. Evidence suggests that had local law enforcement, intelligence, and customs and immigration agencies shared their knowledge prior to September 11, 2001 they might have seen what was in relatively in plain sight (to say nothing of Bush having attended to his intelligence briefings in the summer of 2001, which indicated that airplanes might be used as weapons in an attack on the United States). Rather than knowledge sharing, however, the U.S. intelligence and law enforcement communities have a bureaucratized and bunkered approach to knowledge, as well as an inexplicable mining approach to its acquisition wherein information is gathered without limits, but not routinely sifted, interpreted, or analyzed. The knowledge exchange strategies of the intelligence community (if not its approach to knowledge formation) suggest the practices of those communities intent on guarding precious knowledge. For instance, at Los Alamos National Laboratories, where the atomic bomb was developed in a startlingly short time during World War II, scientists to this day compartmentalize their knowledge such that no one person knows everything. Through these means and others, the secrets of nuclear weaponry are secured from leakage or theft (McNamara 2001). Los Alamos, as it turned out, mimicked the practices of the Native American pueblos in whose midst they lived and worked. In these communities sacred knowledge was guarded through its compartmentalization and brought together in important ceremonies in a sacred protected site, the kiva. Not only does it take a community to produce and share important knowledge, but no single actor could hold or relay it all. While these strategies of knowledge production and exchange call forth community, they atomize knowledge to protect it. But even under the great web of Homeland Security, those who gather intelligence in the United States do not call forth community, but rather continue to keep their knowledge guarded and discrete, protecting their power and authority as they miss opportunities to put the pieces together and see a more developed picture of any given situation. Commission after commission have made clear that such practices are the opposite of what might be effective in preventing terrorist acts.

Of course, the surest way to thwart terrorism is to go to the roots; not just the shallow space-traversing rhizomes, but the issues that spur particular social actors to see terrorism as viable politics. Here I refer telegraphically to the material social practices of a globalized imperialist, racist, and sexist neoliberal capitalism that is as rhizomatic and mobile as international terrorist organizations. The social relations of production associated with contemporary global capitalism have increasingly separated production from social reproduction and in the process excessed millions of people not only from the promises of secular capitalist modernity but from any semblance of a viable future. The patterns of mobility and cultural production associated with this social formation have rendered these shifts manifest on a world scale. The changes and their wider visibility have provoked what might be thought of as ontological insecurity; an effect of the bleak futurity associated with the contemporary political economy. Ontological insecurity is called forth by the globalization of capitalist production over the past several decades, by the unmooring of previous advances in the social wage associated with the altered relationship between production and social reproduction, and by the construction of new ways of identification and new forms of subjectivity over the past few decades.

Banal terrorism works the circuitry of ontological insecurity, normalizing fear and the responses to it across geographic scale. Among these responses are household bunkering, domestic hypervigilance, gating of neighborhoods and guarding of buildings, all manner of screening in public spaces, and preemptive military strikes on sovereign nations.

Banal terrorism works to evade and mask the real sources of problems in the United States. More broadly, it avoids and tends to diminish the imagined importance of such things as the large and growing gap between rich and poor people, communities, regions, and nations; or the erosion of previously assumed guarantees about the future—that the next generation will be better off than the present one—in other words, the death of futurity. Indeed in the spring of 2004 banal terrorism was absurdly brought to bear on both social reproduction and the assault on the social wage when then Education Secretary Paige actually called the National Educators Association terrorists because of their insistence on providing real funding for President Bush's much vaunted but woefully underfunded No Child Left Behind initiative. In the very absurdity and fact of this utterance, it is easy to see the ways that banal terrorism is inserted in daily life and works a dangerous and suspect terrain.

While the parallels between the contemporary security state and its paranoias and those of the McCarthyist 1950s of the cold war are clear, something different and even more dangerous is going on now. With globalization and without the cold war there is no constitutive outside for either U.S. imperial ambitions or the sorts of solid (if mythic) identifications the nation once afforded its people. These circumstances are ontologically difficult. As the world has been mapped, gridded, and "worlded," and various boundaries—whether between inhabited areas and their surrounding wastelands, woods, wildernesses, or waters that terrified as they protected, or between discrete communities of all scales—have been made porous, the grounds of identity, of sovereignty, of power have shifted sharply over the past few decades prompting what I am calling ontological insecurity. It seems as if an enemy—a threatening evil other—must be conjured and reproduced not just to authorize state violence and militarism, but so that "we" can know ourselves. And here banal terrorism and banal nationalism blur. Banal nationalism makes "us" nationalists (and this is a "we" leftist critics must flag). The nation or "homeland" produced by banal nationalism is assumed and drawn on in the course of banal terrorism not just to call forth particular kinds of conformity, but to exhort "us" to purvey "civilization," order, "freedom" and "democracy" to others constituted as wanting if not abject. But this ordering is at once gloss and alibi. If banal terrorism is the latest apparatus of hegemonic consent, it is important to remember that less banal forms of terror—sponsored by the state— are present in its deployment. The mechanisms of state sponsored terrorism are ready to turn on "us" without warning and without provocation. It is the very banality of the ways terrorism is constructed and confronted in the contemporary United States that opens the door to just a little more of this everyday.

The performance of security in the everyday environment conceals both this rotten heart and the insecurities it provokes. It conceals the invasive social relations of the security state, conceals the militarization of the political economy (and its extraordinary deferred costs), conceals the ascendance of a theocratic authoritarian and possibly fascist state slowly and stealthily occurring around us, and conceals that this antidemocratic, militarized state is being constructed upon a political economy hollowed out by thirty years of neoliberalism, and thus is built at the expense of collective social well-being with a huge mortgage on the future.

In a larger frame, the spatial fetishisms of the security state work in the Marxian sense of fetishism to obscure the social relations associated with ontological insecurity, which is attendant upon all these shifts; shifting our focus instead to the menacing other within and without, and not coincidentally incorporating some of the excessed into the military to wage multiple wars on terrorism. In the Freudian sense of the fetish, these spatializations mark the site of permanent vulnerability (to the impoverishments of the future as it currently stands as much as to terrorism), which we know but produce the fetish of security among other things to deny. But at a deeper level, in rehearsing the vulnerability, these spatial fetishisms repress our knowledge that in the post-cold war world "we" have/are the phallus. If as an imperial and largely unencumbered power the United States can do no better than to instantiate a venal, rapacious capitalism, which builds on and reinforces all of the uneven social relations of its past as if the social, political, economic, cultural, and environmental struggles of the twentieth century had never occurred, the horror is almost beyond comprehension.

This horror—and our implication in its production—can no longer be occluded by the fetishism of security and the routinization of terrorism. Exposing its contours and entailments is only a first step. Redressing its multiple oppressions in their rhizomatic spread and tangle requires a political imagination as geographically lithe and symbolically compelling as global capitalism, and its most viable counter force, Islamic fundamentalism, in the struggle to produce a more just, peaceful, and creative future.

Acknowledgment

I am grateful to audiences at the Futures of American Studies Institute at Dartmouth, the meetings of the Association of American Geographers, and a conference on the critical geopolitics of fear at University of Durham. Thanks as well to Peter Marcuse and Mark Leone for their close readings and suggestions, as well as their own work on similar issues. Thank you to Derek Gregory and Allan Pred who are the best of friends, the most patient of editors, and the most hilarious of subjects and scriveners. This chapter would have been done a lot sooner if I wasn't having so much fun with Eric Lott, but it would have been a lot worse without his critical interventions everyplace along the way.

References

Billig, Michael. (1995). *Banal Nationalism*. London and Thousand Oaks, CA: Sage Publications.

Chan, Sewell. (2005). Easing Anxiety on Mass Transit, *New York Times*, Week in Review. July 17, 4.

Freud, Sigmund. (1963). *Sexuality and the Psychology of Love*. New York: Collier Books.

Gullestad, Marianne. (2001). "Imagined Sameness: Shifting Notions of 'Us' and 'Them' in Norway. In Line Alice Ytrehus (ed.), *Forestillinger om 'den andre'*. Kristiansand: Høyskoleforlaget.

Katz, Cindi. (2005). Lost and Found: Geographical Fictions and the Imagined Geographies of American Studies, *Prospects: An Annual of American Studies*, 30,17-25.

Marcuse, Peter. (2003). On the Global Uses of September 11 and Its Urban Impact. In Stanley Aronowitz and Heather Gautney (eds.), *Implicating Empire: Globalization and Resistance in the 21st Century World Order*. New York: Basic Books, 271-85.

Marx, Karl. (1967). *Capital, Volume I*. New York: International Publishers.

McNamara, Laura. (2001). "Ways of Knowing" About Weapons: The Cold War's End at the Los Alamos National Laboratories. Unpublished Doctoral Dissertation, Department of Anthropology, University of New Mexico.

Paglen, Trevor. (2005). "Goatsucker: Stories from the Stealth Archives," Paper presented at the Annual Meetings of the Association of American Geographers, April 6. Denver.

Unger, Craig. (2004). *House of Bush, House of Saud: The Secret Relationship Between the World's Two Most Powerful Dynasties*. New York: Scribner.

Willis, Susan. (2003). Empire's Shadow, *New Left Review* 22 July/August: 59–70.

Notes

1. There are limits to the reach of banal terrorism even when well orchestrated and inflicted upon a vulnerable and willing population. Many Americans balked at former Attorney General John Ashcroft's and then Secretary of Homeland Security Tom Ridge's proposal for TIPS (Terrorism Information and Prevention System), which sought to incorporate everyone into a domestic spy network. Neighbors were invited to inform on one another and delivery people called upon to report suspicious activities or wall hangings. This fantasy of a volunteer security corps ran aground along with many of the proposals that comprised Patriot Act II.

2. Some of the common sensibility of the War on Terrorism was performed by its predecessors such as the War on Drugs and the War on Crime, and, in another vein, the 1996 Immigration Act, but space precludes attending to these here.

3. The conveniences of bank, credit, and store discount cards; toll transponders; Internet accounts; medical identification cards; and the like have proven their vulnerability to illegitimate use, and the ascendence of identity theft makes clear that these flaws will proliferate, compromising "smart" identification systems at their origins.

19

Situated Ignorance and State Terrorism

Silences, W.M.D., Collective Amnesia,
and the Manufacture of Fear

Allan Pred

[The prisoners held at Guantánamo are] devoted to killing millions of Americans. Vice President Cheney propag(and)ating extreme dread[1]

The first sign of a smoking gun may be a mushroom cloud. President George W. Bush sowing fear and ignorance in his 2003 State of the Union Address[2]

He's unable to connect [the Muslim world] to us in any other way than fear. Thomas Carothers, Carnegie Endowment for Peace scholar, speaking of President Bush[3]

You can fool some of the people all of the time, and those are the ones you want to concentrate on. President Bush "wisecracking" at a Gridiron Club Dinner, Washington DC, March, 2001

To terrify is to frighten greatly, to instill intense fear, to drum up images of horrible disaster, brutal punishment, or death hovering just around the next corner, or the one after that, or at least some proximate corner—out of sight, waiting to pounce, to strike arbitrarily, to perhaps target YOU. To terrify is to subject others to extreme dread, to produce in them an anxiety of the anticipated but unpredictable, to color their minds with shades of trepidation, to pack their mental baggage with images and advance notices—or "threat advisories"—that cause worry and dis-ease, and, consequently, to insist upon their being vigilant. Ever on the alert in the spaces of everyday life. Especially in (un)certain places.

Terrorism consists of those deeds and statements, those material practices and discourses, those enacted policies and pronouncements, which are meant to terrify. Terrorism, as the *Oxford English Dictionary* reminds us, is a "policy intended to strike with terror those against whom it is adopted." It is "government by intimidation," government designed to cow into docility, to render timid or compliant by way of inspiring fear.[4] As a policy, terrorism may be deemed successful even if it does not persistently terrify. Even if the fear it generates is no more than a dully thumping subconscious insecurity that surfaces only when directly prompted, it is successful if it helps steer most into a political coma, into a state of passive or even enthusiastic consent.

[H]istory teaches us that the barbarian is the imperial sovereign's favorite concept, the best friend who can be called to duty in many disguises. Magnus Fiskesjö[5]

Terror may be instilled by way of a variety of strategies. Not all of which require the actual or threatened use of violence. Terrorist policies may also be implemented, fear and compliance may be sought or achieved, through the construction of a collective enemy, through discursively dis-placing threat to one or more distant Others, through scare stories and fear-mongering. Or, as during the persistent moment of danger associated with the invasion and occupation of Iraq, the state may gain public acquiescence to its use of violence against distant "terrorist" Others *and innocent civilians*—as well as its domestic measures of repression—through successfully terrorizing a substantial fraction of its own population by way of menacing images. Through successfully perpetuating "imaginative geographies" of Their Terrorist/Arab/Muslim space and Their uncivilized, subhuman barbarism. Through successfully folding distance into monstrous Difference.[6] Through successfully insisting that They are a pervasive military threat to Our Civilization, to the security of Our way of life. Through avoiding any consideration of our role in precipitating militant radicalism, in provoking the spread of "political Islam in its insurrectional forms."[7] Through successfully implanting a just-below-the-surface sense of fear by way of redundant representations strewn across the paths of everyday life.[8]

> *Our conservative estimate is that Iraq today has a stockpile of between 100 and 500 tons of chemical-weapons agents. … Even the low end of 100 tons of agent would enable Saddam Hussein to cause mass casualties across more than 100 square miles of territory, an area nearly five times the size of Manhattan.… There can be no doubt that Saddam Hussein has biological weapons and the capability to rapidly produce more, many more. … This is evidence, not conjecture. This is true. This is all well documented.* Secretary of State Colin Powell before the United Nations and a global television audience on February 5, 2003[9]

> *There's overwhelming evidence there was a connection between al Qa'ida and the Iraqi government.* Vice President Cheney, attempting to perpetuate ignorance of actual circumstances in a National Public Radio interview, January 22, 2004[10]

> *How can these people be so ignorant?* Tariq Ali, speaking of widespread American ignorance as to why many Iraqis loathe the UN[11]

As of the fall of 2003, 60 percent or more of the U.S. population had been (mis)led to still believe that Saddam was "personally involved" with 9/11, that Saddam cooperated extensively with al-Qa'ida, that Iraq possessed an arsenal of mass-destruction weapons at the time of invasion and that those weapons had actually been found. All subsequently revealed evidence to the contrary, less than three weeks before the 2004 election 84 percent of those preferring Bush believed that Saddam "had strong links with al-Qa'ida," while 58 percent of them believed "Iraq had weapons of mass destruction when the U.S. invaded," and 52 percent of them held that Saddam "helped plan and support the [9/11] hijackers."[12] These remarkably high figures are but one indicator that the discursive promotion of the invasion and occupation of Iraq, and the post-9/11 "War on Terror" more generally, has relied heavily on the production of widespread forms of anxiety-ridden "situated ignorance," on the successful production of fear-filled forms of situated knowledge that are infused with distortions, misrepresentations, and disinformation, and otherwise largely comprised of gaping holes. I employ the term "situated ignorance" because what people do or *do not* know, the discourses they have or *have not* been exposed to, the context-flexible meanings and taken for granted or contested categories that have entered into their subject formation and dispositions to react, can in no way be divorced from the situated practices in which they have participated—or have been excluded from. I employ the term because, even in this age of wireless telecommunications and the Internet, the collective or individual encountering of discourse is always an embodied practice, occurring at dispersed sites whose particular nexus of power relations and other invisible and visible geographies continue to matter. In every instance.

> *Among the privileges enjoyed by rich, fat, superpower America is the power to invent public reality. Politicians and the mass media do much of the inventing for us by telling us stories which purport to unfold a relatively simple reality. As our tribal storytellers, they shape our knowledge and ignorance of the world, not only producing ideas and emotions which influence the way we lead our lives, but also leaving us dangerously unaware of the difference between stories and reality.* Russell Baker[13]

> *Following the attacks of September 11, government at every level began to restrict information available to the public, ... Our newspapers began to read like official gazettes, television news simply gave up and followed the orders of its corporate owners, and the two political parties competed with each other in being obsequious to the White House.* Chalmers Johnson,[14] who recognizes, along with Christian Appy, that "the central lesson of Vietnam [for Reagan and his successors] was not that foreign policy had to be more democratic, but the opposite."[15]

> *In the period before the war US journalists were far too reliant on sources sympathetic to the administration. Those with dissenting views—and there were more than a few—were shut out. Reflecting this, the coverage was highly deferential to the White House. This was especially apparent on the issue of Iraq's weapons of mass destruction—the heart of the President's case for war. Even now [January 29, 2004], papers like the [New York] Times and [Washington] Post seem loath to give prominent play to stories that make the administration look bad.* Michael Massing[16]

> *A democratic politics requires the informed consent of its citizens, and it is hard to see how a war for democracy can be fought on a foundation of falsehoods.* Derek Gregory[17]

If a truly democratic politics requires the informed consent of its citizens, and if the state's leadership has willfully attempted to manufacture fear, or deliberately terrorize, by way of its silences and secrecy, its W(ords of) M(ass) D(istraction) and D(eception), and its construction of collective amnesia, then that leadership, and those echoing elements of the mass media that uncritically disseminated on its behalf until six months beyond the invasion of Iraq (or longer), cannot escape being construed as subverters or corrupters of democracy, as agents who have served (or are still serving) to undermine democracy.[18] However loudly they may sing the glories of Freedom. Of Liberation. And of Democracy itself.

> *How do people make history, starting from conditions pre-established to dissuade them from intervening in it? One of [the] answers [of Guy Debord and the Situationist International] was to engage in continual acts of détournement, which involved the appropriation of [popular] images and artifacts— ... ripping them from their context ...to make them mean something wholly different ... [and in the process] warping them into critique.* Don Mitchell[19]

Here the shackles of conventional textual strategy are tossed aside. With a clatter that is meant to show. Here the (con)fusion(s) of state terrorism and situated ignorance are addressed and undressed by way of a *détournement*. Here the Homeland Security Advisory System is critically warped by way of a montage. A montage in which the 'facts' do not simply speak for themselves, but magnify and illuminate one another by way of their constellation while speaking for (and of) the power relations through which they are constituted.

Homeland Security Advisory System: Code Green—Low Condition.
This condition is declared when there is a low risk of terrorist attacks.[20]

Situated Ignorance Advisory System: Code Green— (Apparently) Low Condition
When nothing is said or heard,
when silence reigns,
when secrecy is maintained by those in power,
the threat level is apparently lowest.
But, all the same, be on the alert!
Appearances are deceiving!
Green may be red!

Silence itself… is less the absolute limit of discourse, the other side from which it is separated by a strict boundary, than an element that functions alongside the things said, with them and in relation to them within overall strategies. … There is not one silence but many silences, and they are an integral part of the strategies that underlie and permeate discourses. Michel Foucault[21]

[T]he real sovereign is the one who can least afford to show his cards. Magnus Fiskesjö[22]

Every discourse has its silences that perform essential work in the production of "truth"(ful ignorance). Silences may be deployed to perpetuate a state of fear through strategic omissions, through deliberately keeping secret matters that ought to be made public, through the failure to state that which might reduce any sense of endangerment, through withholding any information that might reveal that already prevailing images of threat are exaggerated or without substance, through covering up any circumstances which might diminish anxiety. Through, among countless examples, burying pre-invasion intelligence reports that seriously questioned Saddam's possession of weapons of mass destruction and his cooperation with al Qa'ida.[23] And later, when a commission was appointed by President Bush to conduct a CIA-focused probe of "intelligence capabilities," through specifically excluding any examination of the Pentagon's Office of Special Plans, a Defense Department unit created in early 2002 by Wolfowitz and Rumsfeld.[24] A unit established in the belief that the CIA "was out to *disprove* linkage between Iraq and terrorism." A policy-informing unit whose goal was "to put the data under the microscope to reveal what the intelligence community can't see."[25] A neoconservative led unit that "churned out propaganda-style intelligence" that "found its way directly into speeches by Bush, Cheney, and other officials."[26] A unit whose zoom-to-the-top "reports were not to be mingled or shared with the CIA or state department for fear of corruption by skepticism."[27] A "talking point" preparation unit whose leadership "bulldozed internal dissent … and relentlessly pushed for confrontation with Iraq."[28] A unit whose Iraqi-war objectives were fully in keeping with those expressed in the now much hushed up *Rebuilding Ameri-*

ca's Defenses, a "blueprint" for reshaping the military and U.S. global policy authored by Dick Cheney, Donald Rumsfeld, Paul Wolfowitz, Jeb Bush, and Lewis Libby that was issued two month's *before* George W. Bush's election by the neoconservative think tank, Project for the New American Century.[29] Behind the scenes Republicans succeeded in maintaining silence, to prevent any intelligence probe of the Office of Special Plans on the grounds that it is a Pentagon policy unit rather than part of the government's "intelligence community."[30]

> *It wasn't intelligence—it was propaganda. They'd take a little bit of intelligence, cherry-pick it, make it sound much more exciting, usually by taking it out of context, often by juxtaposition of two pieces of information that don't belong together.* Retired Air Force Lt. Colonel Karen Kwiatkowski, former staff member of the Office of Special Plans[31]

Homeland Security Advisory System: Code Blue—Guarded Condition
This condition is declared when there is a general risk of terrorist attacks.

Situated Ignorance Advisory System: Code Blue— (Off) Guarded Condition
When a lot begins to be said and much begins to be heard,
about terrorists both over There and hidden among Us,
when efforts to grab your attention begin to become pervasive,
as a matter of general (risk) principle,
do not allow yourself to be caught off guard,
do not allow yourself to be taken in by W(ords of) M(ass) D(istraction).

Right from the shocking and tragic outset, immediately following the horrendous events of 9/11, discourses pertaining to the "War on Terror," to anthrax mailings and looming additional acts of terrorism, and to the need for Homeland Security, served to obscure the fallout from the latest crises of overcapacity and the workings of global economic restructuring. And to disarm what had been a mounting criticism of the Bush administration's economic and energy policies. For the content of these fear-mongering discourses not only provided an attention-fixing glue that largely prevented sustained perception of other matters. These W(ords of) M(ass) D(istraction) were, moreover, employed to suggest that pre-existing unemployment and economic-decline problems were not pre-existing, but the direct consequence of 9-11 rather than of the periodic breakdowns of capitalism. In the near aftermath the public even was implored to act patriotically, to counter terrorism by way of increased consumption, to undo the deeds of terrorist Others by purchasing "big ticket" items. To counter terrorism by buying the official line. Since then 9/11 and the "War on Terror" have served repeatedly as words of mass distraction, as smokescreens for promoting tax cuts for corporations and the rich, the weakening of environmental regulations, and other items on the Bush agenda.[32] While those very same dread-inspiring words of mass distraction have helped prevent most from recognizing the "War on Terrorism" itself—and its centerpiece invasion of Iraq—as a part of the country's ongoing project of military and capitalistic imperialism.

> [M]ost Americans do not recognize—or do not want to recognize—that the United States dominates the world through its military power. Due to government secrecy, they are often ignorant

of the fact that their government garrisons the globe. They do not realize that a vast network of American military bases on every continent except Antarctica actually constitutes a new form of empire. Chalmers Johnson[33]

But if Arendt is right, then any [global] hegemon, if it is to maintain its position in relation to endless capital accumulation, must endlessly seek to extend, expand, and intensify its power. David Harvey, considering America's growth as a "capitalist imperialist" power[34]

* * * * *

Think about what was going on in Iraq a year ago with people being tortured, rape rooms, mass graves, gross corruption, a country that used chemical weapons against its own people. Defense Secretary Donald Rumsfeld at the 40th Conference on Security Policy, Munich, February 7, 2004 ("forgetting" his previous approval of a program allowing that "male prisoners could be treated roughly and exposed to sexual humiliation," "forgetting" that those brutal interrogation techniques already had been permitted to "spread quickly from use against a few "high-value target" al Qaeda suspects to scores of ordinary Afghans and then hundreds of innocent Iraqis").[35]

I call on all governments to join with the United States and the community of law-abiding nations in prohibiting, investigating, and prosecuting all acts of torture. President Bush in a June 2003 address ("forgetting" the "extraordinary rendition" program of torture by proxy that had been in operation since 2002);[36] "forgetting" that so-called "no-touch" torture techniques and other forms of "Human Resource Exploitation" have been associated with the "US intelligence commmunity" over the past fifty years—at times being put to direct use, [recommencing at Bagram Air Base near Kabul in 2002], at times being "disseminated globally to police in Asia and Latin America through USAID's Office of Public Safety" [1963–75] and the US Army's Mobile Training Teams [Central America during the 1980s]).[37]

Homeland Security Advisory System: Code Yellow—Elevated Condition
An Elevated Condition is declared when there is
a significant risk of terrorist attacks.

Situated Ignorance Advisory System: Code Yellow—Elevated Condition (of Forgetting)
You are advised to be on elevated alert for collective amnesia
when atrocities of the past are repeatedly summoned up,
when tales of pre-war torture and rape are frequently reiterated in detail,
when the horrid consequences of past chemical-
weapon deployment are depicted over and over,
when past crimes against humanity are time and
again catalogued with moral indignation,
but there is no reference to the economic and political support
provided during the period of crime commission,
nor to the simultaneous supply of weapons and chemicals,
nor to other past (in)actions elsewhere in the Middle East
and Afghanistan,
that helped propagate the emergence of "terrorists" prior to invasion—
and continued to do so thereafter.

Repetition ... is inseparable from the modern production of historical amnesia.
Jonathan Crary[38]

Don't forget! Every way of remembering is also a way of forgetting. Don't forget "Remember the *Maine!*"[39] And September 11, 1973.[40] And, and, and...

Don't forget! Collective amnesia also may be constructed to forget that Others also have forms of collective memory. That they too may be called upon to recall past acts of "bravery," "heroism," and "glory." And to act accordingly.

Again, I say, don't forget the Alamo. US forces can kill every rebel in [Fallujah, Najaf, and Karbala] at once. But if those militia represent the heartfelt grievances of besieged Iraqis, then Iraqi history will be written like Texas history some day. Greg Moses[41]

People do not forget. They do not forget the death of their fellows, they do not forget torture and mutilation, they do not forget injustice, they do not forget oppression, they do not forget the terrorism of mighty powers. They not only don't forget. They strike back. Harold Pinter in his 2005 Nobel Prize for Literature address.

* * * * *

War is generally crafted and pursued for political reasons, but the reasons given to the Congress and to the American people for this one were inaccurate and so misleading as to be false. Moreover, they were false by design.

They spent their energy gathering pieces of information and creating a propaganda story line, which is the same story line we heard the president and Vice President Cheney tell the American people in the fall of 2002. ... Much of the phraseology that was in our talking points consists of the same things I heard the president say. Retired Air Force Lt. Colonel Karen Kwiatkowski, speaking of the "fear-peddling" work done by the "talking points" generated in the Office of Special Plans[42]

Homeland Security System: Code Orange—High Condition
A High Condition is declared when there is
a high risk of terrorist attacks.

Situated Ignorance Advisory System: Code Orange—High Condition
(of Deception)
You are advised to be on high alert for W(ords
of) M(ass) D(eception) attacks,
for statements that are grossly misleading or inaccurate,
if not outright lies,[43]
when those who are ultimately responsible
for the discursive sowing of terror,
when those who—
in anti-democratic fashion—
command fear-mongering
and the production of situated ignorance,
are themselves marked by the deepest forms of
situated ignorance regarding Iraq and Islam,
are themselves content to ignore

all but those
who share the same forms of (un)knowing,[44]
and gain comfort in that ignorance
from a belief that the President has been divinely "called" to serve,
from a belief that the nation has a divine mission in global affairs,
from a Manichaeistic conviction that we are engaged in
"a monumental struggle of good versus evil"[45]
and that
"God [is] on America's side"[46]
as "our nation is the greatest force for good in history."[47]

Intelligence gathered by this and other governments leaves no doubt that the Iraq regime continues to possess and conceal some of the most lethal weapons ever devised. President George W. Bush in a national address, March 17, 2003.[48] (Statements such as this contributed to fear-laden situated ignorance not only because of their authoritative forcefulness, but because they were reinforced by way of redundancy, because they time and again came into resonance with previous and subsequent well publicized and uncriticized remarks. Such statements also helped to constitute *situated* ignorance because they were received and filtered through local mass media outlets; because they were directly discussed, commented upon and given meaning at dispersed sites; because any understanding or interpretation of them was dependent upon already held forms of situated knowledge and ignorance, upon situated-practice derived [pre]dispositions to hear and observe in some ways rather than others.)

On September 22, 2003, the Associated Press reported the following: *Bush said he insulates himself from the "opinions" that seep into news coverage by getting his news from his own aides. He said he scans headlines, but rarely reads news stories. "I appreciate people's opinions, but I'm more interested in news," the President said. "And the best way to get the news is from objective sources, and the most objective sources I have are people on my staff [Andrew Card and Condoleezza Rice] who tell me what's happening in the world."*

He is not stupid. He is ignorant. And he is ignorant by design. John W. Dean, former White House counsel to President Richard M. Nixon, speaking of President George W. Bush's unwillingness to inform himself in detail about policy matters and an associated division of labor whereby Bush serves as (figure)head of state, as master of orchestrated public appearances, and Vice President Cheney serves, in behind-the-scenes practice, as head of government.[49] (Other "inside" accounts attest to Bush's refusal to read policy reports, his aversion even to one-page report summaries, his impatience with extensive oral analyses, and his disdain for outside advice, open dialogue or any deliberation of facts that might undercut *faith* in his already reached decisions—decisions often resting on the assumption that reality is actually "what he alone [infallibly] has declared it to be.")[50]

[T]he prime impression one carries away from Woodward's airless pages is of a White House utterly secluded from reality. If Bush had walked out of the front gate to Pennsylvania Avenue, hailed any taxi and asked its driver to give him a briefing on the world situation, he would have done better than with what was served up to him by his staff. All evidence suggests that Bush doesn't want to hear any briefing that might perturb his fixed opinions. Alexander Cockburn, waxing acerbic about the level of (situated) ignorance that prevailed among top administration figures during "the march toward the attack on Iraq"[51]

Announcement from the White (out)House at the height of a shrill and frenzied Orange Alert: "Something big is in the making." (Cartoon printed in Dagens Nyheter [Sweden's largest daily newspaper], July 4, 2002).

What I started to see [in February, 2002] was the man that would emerge over the next year—a Messianic American Calvinist. He doesn't want to hear from anyone who doubts him. Jim Wallis, clergyman whose book, *Faith Works*, had influenced George W. Bush[52]

I trust God speaks through me. Statement attributed to George W. Bush in a private meeting with Amish farmers[53]

God told me to strike al Qaida and I struck them, and then he instructed me to strike at Saddam, which I did. George W. Bush, self-proclaimed "war president," in a June 2003 meeting conversation with then Palestinian Prime Minister Mahmoud Abbas[54]

President Bush said to all of us: "I am driven with a mission from God." God would tell me, "George, go and fight these terrorists in Afghanistan." And I did. And then God would tell me "George, go and end the tyranny in Iraq." And I did. Former Palestinian foreign minister Nabil Shaath recounting the same conversation in a 2005 BBC interview.[55]

George sees this as a religious war. He doesn't have a p.c. view of this war. His view of this is that they are trying to kill the Christians. And we will strike back with more force and more ferocity than they will ever know. Statement attributed to an unspecified Bush family member[56]

[The Nobel-Prize winning Austrian playwright Elfriede Jelinek depicts] a Christianity that is flexibly adaptable to war and aggression because its convenient division between God and Jesus allows one to choose the alternative best suited to one's purpose: the strict and unpardoning [and ruthlessly vengeful] or the forgiving. Lars Ring, characterizing a leading theme in Jelinek's *Bambiland*, a monologue on the US invasion of Iraq[57]

Submerged in ignorance regarding the history of Palestinian dispossession, in April 2004 the Bush administration made concessions to the government of Ariel Sharon, allowing that vast areas of the Palestinian West Bank should become part of Israel. This, like other pro-Israeli moves, was in keeping with the desires of those fundamentalist Christians—among whom the president apparently is to be counted—who insist that the coming of the Messiah cannot occur unless the Jewish people have control over the Temple of the Mount and Jerusalem. In the context of this and other actions in Iraq, Robert Fisk echoed other critics in exclaiming: "What better recruiting sergeant could Bin Laden have than George Bush?"[58] Even before the Abu Ghraib atrocities were revealed.

If this is not evil, then evil has no meaning. President Bush, in his 2004 State of the Union Address, referring to the occurrence of torture and rape during Saddam Hussein's regime

---

Homeland Security System: Code Red—Severe Condition
A Severe Condition reflects a severe risk of terrorist attacks.

Situated Ignorance Advisory System: Code Red—
Severe Condition (of Domestic Repression)
A condition of severe risk of state terrorism exists
when repressive measures are not limited to
those confined at Guantánamo Bay,
when repressive actions are not only arbitrarily taken against aliens
present in the United States,
when efforts are made to surpass the measures of domestic
repression and surveillance contained in the Patriot Act,[59]
when criticism becomes synonymous with treason,
or even heresy,
and the social contract is shredded,[60]
when "the government is daily expanding military operations
into areas of local government and law enforcement
that historically have been off limits,"[61]
when attempts are made to broaden the distribution of
situated ignorance by way of collective muzzling.[62]
Say no more.

This should be a model for homeland defense. Miami Mayor Manny Diaz, speaking after 2,500 law-enforcement personnel from forty local, state, and federal agencies had employed pepper spray and unwarranted violence to "successfully control" activists who were peacefully demonstrating against the Free-Trade Area of the Americas negotiations; speaking after the completion of a "security" operation that received $8.5 million of its funding from the $87 billion special appropriation for Iraq and Afghanistan as a result of having classified the activists as "terrorists" from outside.[63]

The F.B.I. is dangerously targeting Americans who are engaged in nothing more than lawful protest. The line between terrorism and legitimate civil disobedience is [now] blurred. Anthony Romero, executive director of the American Civil Liberties Union, in a *New York Times* article (November 23, 2003) reporting that the F.B.I. "has collected extensive information on the tactics, training and organization of antiwar demonstrators and has advised local law enforcement officials to report any suspicious activity at protests to its counterterrorism squads."

We don't kick the shit out of them. We send them to other countries so they can kick the shit out of them. An unnamed U.S. intelligence official referring—in January 2004—to "extraordinary rendition," a torture-by-proxy program "authorized" by a "secret presidential finding" for use against foreign citizens taken into custody in the United States or elsewhere, for placing civilians taken into U.S. custody beyond the protection of U.S. laws and treating them as subhumans. (In one "extraordinary rendition" case a totally innocent Syrian-born Canadian citizen was apprehended at Kennedy International Airport, denied access to a lawyer, and eventually—with Justice Department approval—delivered to Syria where he was submitted to horrific military intelligence tortures before being released after ten months.) [64] A reference made months before the acts of brutal barbarism committed at Abu Ghraib became public knowledge, months before it was revealed that we physically and psychologically "kick the shit out of them" on our own.[65] A reference made months before it became known that Defense Department lawyers had contended in 2003 that "the president wasn't bound by laws prohibiting torture and that government agents who might torture prisoners at his direction couldn't be prosecuted by the Justice Department."[66] A reference made months before Human Rights First made it known that, in addition to all the foreign locations where "extraordinary rendition" is conducted, the U.S. military and the CIA operates a gulag archipelago of twenty-four facilities—extending from Jordan through Iraq, Afghanistan, Pakistan and Thailand to a number of battleships—where well over 12,400 prisoners are held indefinitely without being charged or being given access to legal representation, where those who literally or figuratively "kick the shit out of them" may do so with impunity.[67]

In February 2003, the Justice Department drafted a piece of legislation that thus far has not become an official proposal. The Domestic Security Enhancement Act provides "that any American who supports the activities (even peaceful ones) of an organization the government designates as terrorist presumptively loses his or her citizenship. The citizen would become an alien."[68] And thus subject to?

In the fall of 2003 President Bush requested that Congress amend the Patriot Act "to let federal agents demand private records, and compel testimony, without the approval of a judge or even a federal prosecutor."[69] As a consequence of widely produced situated ignorance, few people recognized that even without this authority the federal government was already in a position "to tap into and listen to all citizens' phone calls, faxes, and e-mail transmissions" whenever it so chose.[70]

> *What this all boils down to is an attempt to silence criticism of US policy, and put an end to disagreement with the neo-conservative agenda.* Sara Roy, senior research scholar at Harvard's Center for Middle Eastern Studies, referring to House Resolution 3077[71]

> *Some might conclude that perhaps scholars who study the Middle East know something worth listening to. But the neocons already know what they want to hear.... Neocons believe it is better for the government to control teaching and research rather than to allow established policy to be questioned.* Joel Beinin, professor of Middle East History at Stanford University, referring to those who spurred the passage of HR 3077[72]

On October 21, 2003, the House of Representatives unanimously passed HR 3077, the International Studies in Higher Education Act, which, if ever adopted by the Senate, will establish an International Education Advisory Board that will include members from the Department of Defense, the National Security Agency, and Homeland Security.[73] Among other things, the board will determine whether or not "supporters of American foreign policy are adequately represented" in the Middle Eastern

Studies Centers of major universities and thereby worthy of federal Title VI funding. It will, moreover, in conjunction with its "broad investigative powers 'to study, monitor, appraise, and evaluate' [the] activities of area studies centers" be enabled to "recommend ways 'to improve programs … to better reflect the national needs related to homeland security.'"[74] "Inherent in the act is the assumption that if most established experts believe American Middle East Policy is bad, the flaw lies with the experts, not the policy." The legislation is consistent with sentiments repeatedly expressed by neoconservatives since 9/11 that mark academic experts on the Middle East as "a kind of intellectual fifth column" and point to universities, and area studies programs in particular, as a "weak link" in the "war on terror." [75]

One month later, in November 2003, General Tommy Franks stated in an interview that, in the event of a w.m.d.-attack by terrorists, "the Constitution will likely be discarded" and a military government established in order to avoid a repeat attack.[76] Such a claim may be seen as fully in keeping with the fact that ever since the cold war there has been an ongoing "transfer of power from the representatives of the people to the Pentagon and the various intelligence agencies"—a growing fusion of the military and the executive branch, and the emergence of an "imperial presidency," that has been "eroding the democratic underpinnings of our constitutional republic."[77]

Say no more. Say: "No more!"

* * * * *

These people have no respect for the Constitution. The Congress was misled, it was lied to. At a very minimum that is a subversion of the Constitution. Retired Air Force Lt. Colonel Karen Kwiatkowski, once again observing on the basis of her time as a staff member at the Office of Special Plans[78]

They broke our Constitution. They broke Nuremberg. They broke the Geneva Conventions. Everything. And if somebody doesn't say it, does it mean it didn't happen? Somebody has to say it, and I'll say it. I've called George Bush a terrorist. He says a terrorist is somebody who kills innocent people. That's his own definition. So, by George Bush's own definition, he is a terrorist, because there are almost 100,000 innocent Iraqis that have been killed. And innocent Afghanis that have been killed. Cindy Sheehan[79]

Sometimes, despite our own inevitable situated ignorance, we already know enough. Sometimes it is not knowledge we lack. Sometimes "what is missing is the courage to understand what we know and draw conclusions."[80] And to put them into practice.

Such a moment is this. When withdrawal from Iraq is nowhere in the foreseeable future and a number of permanent military bases are under construction in that country. When two much ballyhooed "democratic" Iraqi elections came about only after all the major parties were compelled not to call for any specifically scheduled withdrawal of U.S. occupation forces. When the very results of the first election may well have been manipulated "by U.S. authorities … in order to reduce the percentage of the vote received by the United Iraqi Alliance from 56% to 48%."[81] When the state continues to attempt fear-mongering by issuing misleading data on the number of U.S.-based terrorists it has convicted as well as periodically repackaging old "intelligence" and announcing new threats to the homeland.[82] When Bush is once again president after a campaign that purposefully sought to inspire fear by repeatedly asserting that the defeat of Kerry was necessary to avoid Armageddon. When that campaign set out to psychologically terrorize elements of the voting public by relentlessly referring to the "War on Terror"—without a serious word on what it is that radicalizes occupied Iraqis and enrages Muslims elsewhere, that precipitates extremism and provokes ruthless physical acts of (counter)terrorism. When it is persistently (mis)claimed by Bush and those around him that the war in Iraq must be continued in order to avoid making "the world more dangerous" and "America less safe,"[83]—even though that war is clearly a mega-engine of terrorist production, a conflict which plays into the hands of the most radical strand of Islam, allowing it by means of satellite television and other media to create "a profound sense of collective suffering"[84] among Arabs and Muslims all around the world. When there is no end of statements about "staying the course" and "confronting evil," about a direct connection between the perpetrators of 9/11 and the insurgents being fought in Iraq. When Bush's "use of religion seems designed to remove any doubt—first in his own mind, then in the public's—about his course;" when his ignorance-drenched decisions thereby "become immune from scrutiny" and democracy thereby becomes further undermined.[85] When efforts are being made to convert the FBI into a secret police agency.[86] When the Director of National Intelligence has a history of providing false intelligence to Congress. When, in early 2006, congressional efforts to investigate the "intelligence" activities of the Office of Special Plans remained partly obstructed by the Pentagon. When it has been revealed that another Pentagon unit, the U.S. Special Operations Command, has also been given Ministry-of-Propaganda-like functions, with $300 million allocated to plant press stories and otherwise conduct a "global" campaign "to counter terrorist ideology and sway foreign audiences to support American policies."[87] When, in particular, "the U.S. military [had been] conducting a propaganda campaign to magnify the role of the leader of al-Qaeda in Iraq,"[88] until his death. When evidence of torture by proxy and the use of "extreme interrogation measures" by U.S. intelligence officers accumulates almost daily. When the "War on Terrorism" is becoming even more under Pentagon control and thereby ever more beyond congressional oversight.[89] When the manifestations of anti-democratic state terrorism have been multiple and simultaneous and are once again in evidence with respect to Iran. When, not least of all, tireless reference to 9/11 and Iran's w.m.d. threat is coupled with both the issuing of legislation-nullifying presidential "signing statements" and talk of presidential "unitary powers" to further facilitate, rationalize, and naturalize: extraordinary renditions; the use of torture at Guantánamo and elsewhere; and the National Security Agency's spying on innocent U.S. citizens without court orders. When a former NSA employee has testified before Congress as to the existence of another top-secret "special access" surveillance program that is apparently "violating the constitutional rights of millions of Americans," and when a Halliburton subsidiary has been granted $385 million to construct detention centers for the Homeland Security Department that might "be used to detain American citizens if the Bush administration were to declare martial law."[90] When a Bush addendum to the USA Patriot Act reauthorized in March, 2006, stated "that he did not feel obligated to obey requirements that he inform Congress about how the FBI was using the act's expanded police powers."[91] When an "imperial presidency" is becoming further entrenched by way of merging the "War on Terror" mantra with assertions "that a president can claim power without restriction or supervision by the courts or Congress."[92] When executive orders signed by President Bush enable him, upon declaring a "national emergency" without approval of Congress, to order the secretly formed Northern Command for National Defense "to send troops into American streets, seize control of radio and television stations and networks and impose martial law."[93] When, in short, the Constitution's separation of powers has been decimated and a form of trust-our-strong-leader, "smiley-faced," low-key fascism is being gradually fortified, having already been quietly put partly in place. When, consequently, more than ever, we should be on full spectrum alert for strategically deployed silences, words of mass distraction, the propagation of collective amnesia, words of mass deception, and actual and proposed measures of domestic repression that are meant to gag. When, when, when … . When, if revolution is perhaps too strong a term for the collective action that is necessary, it is still appropriate to close with the following Walter Benjamin aphorism.

> *Marx says that revolutions are the locomotive of history. But perhaps it is quite otherwise. Perhaps revolutions are an attempt by the passengers on this train—namely, the human race—to activate the emergency brake.* Walter Benjamin[94]

Time to reveal the location(s) of the emergency brake.
Time to bring matters to a screeching halt.
Time to counteract situated ignorance.
At multiple sites.
And then?
Time to?

Notes

1. Anthony Lewis, "Un-American Activities," *The New York Review,* October 23, 2003, 16–19 (16).
2. This phrase apparently was taken directly from a now notoriously inept *New York Times* article on aluminum tubes that legitimated ill-founded White House arguments pertaining to Saddam Hussein's pursuit of nuclear weapons (Judith Miller and Michael Gordon, "US Says Hussein Intensifies Quest for A-Bomb Parts," *New York Times,* September 8, 2002; cf. David Barstow, "Skewed Intelligence on Iraq Colored the March to War," *New York Times,* October 3, 2004). As Cindi Katz points out, ("Banal Terrorism," chapter 18, this volume), the mushroom cloud image was repeatedly summoned up in public statements by Bush and others at the top of his administration, perhaps most (in)famously in a speech given by the president in Cincinnati on October 7, 2002. In that same speech Bush confidently declared Iraq possessed a "massive stockpile of biological weapons."
3. George Packer, "A Democratic World," *The New Yorker,* February 16 & 23, 2004, 100–108 (108).
4. *The Shorter Oxford English Dictionary on Historical Principles,* third revised edition (Oxford: The Clarendon Press, 1962), 2155.
5. Magnus Fiskesjö, *The Thanksgiving Pardon, the Death of Teddy's Bear, and the Sovereign Exception of Guantanamo* (Chicago: Prickly Paradigm Press, 2003), 69.

6. See Derek Gregory's expansion of Said's "imaginative geographies" and Agamben's "spaces of exception" in his brilliant analysis of Afghanistan, Iraq, Palestine, and the "War on Terror" (*The Colonial Present* [Oxford: Blackwell, 2004]).

7. Michael Watts, "Revolutionary Islam and Modern Terror," chapter 10, this volume.

8. Cf. Michael Billig, *Banal Nationalism* (London: SAGE Publications, 1995); and Katz, "Banal Terrorism."

9. As Powell's speech received "rapturous reviews from the American press," his charges achieved particular strength through being repeated countless times by other administration figures—even though the accusations were "viewed skeptically by most foreign governments" (Michael Massing, "Now They Tell Us," *The New York Review*, February 26, 2004, 43–49 [47]).

10. In testimony before the Senate Armed Services Committee on March 9, 2004, CIA Director George Tenet rejected Cheney's often made claim. Cheney's insistent position is fully in keeping both with charges—made by former Treasury Secretary Paul O'Neill and others—he "agitated for U.S. intervention [in Iraq] well before the terrorist attacks of September 11, 2001," and with a top-secret document indicating that his Energy Task Force was to consider "actions regarding the capture of new and existing oil and gas fields"(Jane Meyer, "Contract Sport—What did the Vice-President do for Halliburton?," *The New Yorker*, February 16 & 23, 2004, 80–91 [89]).

11. Tariq Ali during an interview by Geov Parrish, available at http://www.workingforchange.com/article.cfm?itemid-16075.

12. PRNewswire, "Iraq, 9/11, Al Qaeda and Weapons of Mass Destruction: What the Public Believes Now, According to Latest Harris Poll," October 21, 2004. Corresponding percentages for those preferring Kerry were 37, 23, and 16.

13. Russell Baker, "The Awful Truth," *The New York Review*, November 6, 2003, 6–12 (8).

14. Chalmers Johnson, *The Sorrows of Empire: Militarism, Secrecy, and the End of the Republic* (New York: Metropolitan Books, 2004), 13.

15. Appy continues: "it had to become ever more the province of national security managers who operated without the close scrutiny of the media, the oversight of Congress, or accountability to an involved public (Christian Appy, *Working-Class War: American Combat Soldiers and Vietnam* (Chapel Hill: University of North Carolina Press, 1993), 5. And Johnson adds: "The result has been the emergence of a coterie of professional militarists who have been appointed to senior positions throughout the executive branch" (*Sorrows of Empire*, 60).

16. Massing, "Now They Tell Us," 43, 49.

17. Gregory, *Colonial Present*,

18. While Fox News, Clear Channel Radio, and other right-wing corporate media outlets relayed "information" generated by the Bush administration with tones of enthusiastic endorsement, other broadcast and print media frequently repeated White House positions on Iraq and the "War on Terror" in an uncritical manner because of "a fear of appearing unpatriotic" or of punitively being denied future access, and related "competitive pressures" (Meilikki Org, "Fears Impacted U.S. Reporting on Iraq," Associated Press, March 19, 2004). Or, as one subsequent study concluded: "Many stories stenographically reported the incumbent administration's perspectives on WMD, giving too little critical examination of the way officials framed the events, issues, threats and policy options" (Susan Moeller, "Media Coverage of Weapons of Mass Destruction," Center for International and Security Studies at the University

of Maryland [http://www.cissm.umd.edu/]). Whatever the case, the press, including the *New York Times* and the *Washington Post*, "did not do their job," and "the
American media did not play the role of checking and balancing the exercise of
power that the standard theory of democracy requires" (John Steinbruner in a fore-
word to Moeller, "Media Coverage;" and Massing, "Now They Tell Us"[for a detailed
analysis of the failures of the *New York Times* and *Washington Post*]). And, not
until May 26, 2004—when the failures of the occupation were multiplying disaster-
ously—did the *New York Times* publicly concede that numerous articles published
before and during the war were all too uncritical, that stories indicating Iraq possessed biological and chemical weapons and was developing nuclear weapons were
based on dubious sources (cf. note 2, above).

19. Don Mitchell, *Cultural Geography: A Critical Introduction* (Oxford: Blackwell Pub-
    lishers, 2000), 165. The initial quote is from Greil Marcus, *Lipstick Traces: A Secret
    History of the Twentieth Century* (Cambridge, MA: Harvard University Press, 1989),
    178.

20. This and all subsequent Homeland Security Advisory System descriptions are
    directly quoted from the Department of Homeland Security's Web site, http://www.
    dhs.gov/dhspublic/display?theme=29.

21. Michel Foucault, *The History of Sexuality*, vol. 1, *An Introduction*, translated by Rob-
    ert Hurley (New York: Vintage Books, 1990 [1976]), 27.

22. Fiskejö, *Thanksgiving Turkey*, 33.

23. On numerous occasions, from well before the invasion of Iraq until well into 2004,
    anonymous U.S. and British career intelligence agents informed journalists of the
    repeated suppression of dissenting intelligence (e.g., Peter Beaumont, Gaby Hinsliff,
    and Paul Harris, "US Officials Knew in May Iraq Possessed No WMD," *The Observer*,
    February 4, 2004; and Massing, "Now They Tell Us"). Such accounts—including
    those referring to the "enormous pressure" exerted by Vice President Cheney and
    the Pentagon to get "the CIA to go along with its version of events"—either went
    totally unmentioned in the mainstream American mass media or were inserted
    within the body of inside-page stories where few would read them (one key excep-
    tion was the Knight Ridder newspapers, which are beyond the national spotlight,
    having no presence in New York or Washington, D.C.; quote from Robert Dreyfuss
    and Jason Vest, "The Lie Factory," *Mother Jones*, February 2004, 34–41 [39]). Even
    when CIA director George Tenet told Congress in October, 2002, that Iraq posed no
    imminent threat it was widely unreported or given no prominence. Tenet's position
    rested on a just received top-secret report on Iraq's arms programs prepared for him
    by the National Intelligence Council, a board of senior analysts. When the White
    House made information from the report public in July, 2003, it systematically
    silenced all portions that were incongruent with its policies, stripping the document
    of "dissenting opinions, warnings of insufficient information and doubts about dis-
    posed dictator Saddam Hussein's intentions," specifically muzzling doubts about
    "whether Saddam was stockpiling biological and chemical weapons and whether
    he might dispatch poison-spraying robot aircraft to attack the United States" (Jona-
    than S. Landay, "Doubts, Dissent Stripped from Public Version of Iraq Assessment,"
    Knight-Ridder, February 10, 2004).

24. The Office of Special Plans was also pushed for by Vice President Cheney. It was
    created by breaking off the "Iraq desk" of the Defense Department's office for Near
    East South Asia (NESA). Considerably expanded, it also absorbed another Defense
    Department unit established weeks after 9/11 to produce anti-Iraq "disinformation"

by way of "scour[ing] reports from the CIA…and other agencies to find nuggets of information linking Iraq, Al Qaeda, terrorism, and the existence of Iraqi weapons of mass destruction" (Dreyfuss and Vest, "Lie Factory," 37, 39).

25. An unnamed Pentagon adviser quoted in Seymour M. Hersh, "Annals of National Security: Selective Intelligence," *The New Yorker,* May 12, 2003, 44–51 (45), emphasis in original. According to Hersch, the highly influential unit not only massaged previously gathered data, but also relied on otherwise disproved Iraqi defectors who had agendas of their own. Based on their sources, Dreyfuss and Vest assert that the Office of Special Plans received a "vast flow of bogus intelligence … [from] Chalabi's Iraqi National Congress group of exiles," intelligence that was "misleading and often faked," intelligence much of which—according to Vincent Cannistraro, a former CIA chief of counterterrorism—involved "telling the Defense Department what they want[ed] to hear" ("Lie Factory," 40–41).

26. Dreyfuss and Vest, "Lie Factory," 40.

27. Sidney Blumenthal, "Bush's Other War: US Intelligence Is Being Scapegoated for Getting It Right on Iraq," *The Guardian,* November 1, 2003.

28. Marc Cooper, "Soldier for the Truth," *L.A. Weekly,* February 20, 2004.

29. The "blueprint" was far from entirely new, as Wolfowitz and others had been repeatedly calling for "regime change" in Iraq since 1992. … Other now highly relevant contents of *Rebuilding America's Defenses* remain enshrouded in silence, such as its chilling proposal for the development of biological weapons "that can target specific genotypes [and] may transform biological warfare from the realm of terror to a politically useful tool." Note, for example, Michael Meacher MP, "This War on Terrorism is Bogus," *The Guardian,* September 6, 2003.

30. Dreyfuss and Vest, "Lie Factory," 41.

31. Dreyfuss and Vest, "Lie Factory," 36. Kwiatkowski, a long-term Republican and self-styled conservative, came to regard the Office of Special Plans as a "nerve center" for a "neo-conservative coup, a hijacking of the Pentagon" (Cooper, "Soldier for the Truth"). However, at least with respect to Iraq, a Democratic administration may well have pushed the Pentagon in the same policy direction given the reasons for promoting an invasion she says were discussed by neo-conservatives within the Special Plans office (cf. Stephen Gowans, "Neo-conservatives Not the Problem," [February 25, 2004], http://www3.sympaticco.ca/sr.gowans/neocons.html). These reasons—kept entirely *silent* in official administration discourse—were as follows: a need to guarantee that "financial benefits" would go to U.S. corporations rather than French, German, and Russian firms once sanctions were ended; a need to terminate the Iraqi practice of selling oil in Euros rather than in already weakening dollars; and, with Saudi Arabia becoming negative about a continued U.S. military presence, a need to establish additional bases in order "to secure energy lines of communication in the region."

32. Cf. Paul Krugman, *The Great Unraveling: Losing Our Way in the New Century* (New York: Norton, 2003).

33. Johnson, *Sorrows of Empire,* 1, emphasis added. As of 2001 the Department of Defense admitted to the existence of 725 military bases outside of the country. However, as Johnson notes (5): "Actually, there are many more, since some bases exist under leaseholds, informal agreements, or disguises of various kinds. And more have been created since the announcement was made."

34. David Harvey, *The New Imperialism* (Oxford: Oxford University Press, 2003), 35.

35. Seymour M. Hersh, "Annals of National Security: The Gray Zone," *The New Yorker,* May 24, 2004, 38–44 (41); and Alfred W. McCoy, "The Hidden History of CIA Torture," *San Francisco Chronicle,* September 19, 2004. Also see note 64, below.

36. See note 64, below, and the text thereto.

37. Alfred W. McCoy, "Comment: Torture at Abu Ghraib Followed CIA's Manual," *Boston Globe,* May 14, 2004; and Duncan Campbell and Suzanne Goldenberg, "Afghan Detainees Routinely Tortured and Humiliated by US Troops," *The Guardian,* June 23, 2004.

38. Jonathan Crary, *Suspensions of Perception: Attention, Spectacle, and Modern Culture* (Cambridge, MA: The MIT Press, 1999), 369.

39. Reference to this rallying cry in support of war with Spain is appropriate—especially if one draws a parallel between Spain's alleged sinking of the USS *Maine* in 1898 and Saddam's alleged possession of weapons of mass destruction—for: "Not since the jingoists of the Spanish-American War have so many Americans openly called for abandoning even a semblance of constitutional and democratic foreign policy and endorsed imperialism" (Johnson, *Sorrows of Empire,* 67). It also should not be forgotten that the war fever encapsulated in the "Remember the *Maine*" slogan helped to obscure the atrocities and war crimes committed by U.S. troops in conjunction with the massacre of at least 200,000 Filipinos.

40. Previous highly repeated discourses have produced collective amnesia regarding 9/11/73, the date on which the democratically elected Chilean government of Salvador Allende was overthrown by General Augusto Pinochet with the considerable assistance of the CIA and the Nixon White House (massive documentary evidence thereof is reproduced in Peter Kornbluh, *The Pinochet File: A Declassified Dossier on Atrocity and Accountability* [New York: The New Press, 2003]).

41. Greg Moses, "Bremer's De-De-Baathification Gambit Legitimates Fallujah Rebels," http://peacefile.org/wordpress (April 25, 2004).

42. Karen Kwiatkowski, "The New Pentagon Papers," http://www.salon.com/opinion/feature/2004/03/10/osp/, and Cooper, "Soldier for the Truth."

43. Since 2003 a stream of books, reports and articles—too numerous to cite—have documented the lies and deceptions propagated by the Bush administration. Nevertheless, all too little has been written about the work such lies and deceptions do in (re)producing fear and compliance, and even eliciting enthusiastic support, among a significant fraction of the population.

44. In Haraway's highly influential book chapter (Donna Haraway, "Situated Knowledges: The Science Question in Feminism and the Privilege of Partial Perspective," in *Simians, Cyborgs, and Women: The Reinvention of Nature* (New York and London: Routledge, 1991), 183–201) it is suggested "that the most appropriate response to the situatedness of knowledge is to reach out and engage others—in conversation/solidarity—so, presumably the flip side of this for situated ignorance is not to reach out at all but to confine oneself to talking with those who (un)know exactly the same as you (hence [the Bush administration's] disparagement of those who disagree—not just France, Germany, and "Old Europe," but the "enemy within": traitors) or, in addition, to reach out not through dialogue but through abuse, rapacity and bluster" (Derek Gregory, personal e-mail correspondence, February 12, 2004).

45. President George W. Bush on September 12, 2001.

46. Joan Didion, "Mr. Bush & the Divine," *The New York Review,* November 6, 2004, 81–86 (85). At a February 2003 address to the Religious Broadcasters in Nashville, on among other occasions, President Bush conflated his administration's policy with

"God's gift to every human being in the world" and confidently claimed the U.S. had been "called" to lead the world to peace (ibid). Whether such public statements are sincerely believed or designed to further bolster support from the religious right, many of those associated with the Office of Special Plans and other Pentagon units concerned with "counterterrorism" speak "the language of a holy war between good and evil" (Kwiatkowski, "New Pentagon Papers").

47. President George W. Bush, speaking at Crawford, Texas, August 31, 2002.

48. Six months earlier, in September 2002, the Bush administration was making the same kind of claims, "daily terrifying the world with statements about Saddam Hussein's clandestine weapons and the need for a preventive invasion of Iraq, [even though] the CIA revealed that there was no national intelligence estimate on Iraq" (Johnson, *Sorrows of Empire*, 10–11).

49. Statement made in an interview with Amy Goodman, "Democracy Now," Pacific Radio network stations, April 6, 2004.

50. Richard A. Clarke, *Against All Enemies: Inside America's War on Terror* (New York: The Free Press, 2004); Nicholas Lemann, "Remember the Alamo: How George W. Bush Reinvented Himself," *The New Yorker*, October 18, 2004, 148–163 (156); Ron Suskind, *The Price of Loyalty: George W. Bush, the White House and the Education of Paul O'Neill* (New York: Simon & Schuster, 2003); Suskind, "Without a Doubt," *New York Times Magazine*, October 17, 2004, 44–51 ff.; and Bob Woodward, *Plan of Attack* (New York: Simon & Schuster, 2004).

51. Alexander Cockburn, referring to Woodward's *Plan of Attack*, in "Stupid Leaders, Useless Spies, Angry World," *The Nation*, May 17, 2004, 8.

52. Suskind, "Without a Doubt," 50.

53. Suskind, "Without a Doubt," 51.

54. Dilip Hiro, *Secrets and Lies: Operation "Iraqi Freedom" and After* (New York: Nation Books, 2004), 383, quoting the Tel Aviv newspaper *Ha'aretz* of June 24. 2003.

55. Ewen MacAskill, "George Bush: 'God Told Me to End the Tyranny in Iraq,'" *The Guardian*, October 7, 2005. Confronted with questions about Shaath's account, Scott McClellan, the president's press secretary, responded: "No, that's absurd. He's never made such comments." Pressed with further questions, McClellan admitted that he didn't know about the June 2003 meeting, but all the same insisted: "I stand by what I just said" ("McClellan's briefing," *San Francisco Chronicle*, October 8, 2005).

56. David Greenberg, "Fathers and Sons: George W. Bush and His Forebears," *The New Yorker*, July 12 & 19, 2004, 92–98 (97-98).

57. Lars Ring, "Raseri och äckel över amerikansk retorik," *Svenska Dagbladet*, May 28, 2004.

58. Robert Fisk, "By Endorsing Ariel Sharon's Plan George Bush Has Legitimated Terrorism," *The Independent*, April 16, 2004.

59. Government surveillance of U.S. citizens has a long history prior to the Patriot Act. See Christian Parenti, *The Soft Cage: Surveillance in America from Slave Passes to the War on Terror* (New York: Basic, 2003).

60. Henry Giroux and Paul Street, "Shredding the Social Contract," available at http://www.zmag.org, September 4, 2003.

61. William M. Arkin, "Mission Creep Hits Home—American armed forces are assuming major new domestic policing and surveillance roles," *Los Angeles Times*, November 23, 2003.

62. Regarding the Patriot Act, repression, and the Justice Department see David Cole, *Enemy Aliens: Double Standards and Constitutional Freedoms in the War on Terrorism* (New York: The New Press, 2003); Cynthia Brown, ed., *Lost Liberties: Ashcroft and the Assault on Personal Freedom* (New York: The New Press, 2003); James Bovard, *Terrorism & Tyranny: Trampling Freedom, Justice and Peace to Rid the World of Evil* (New York: Palmgrave Macmillan, 2003).

63. Naomi Klein, reporting in *The Globe and Mail,* Nov. 25, 2003. In this connection it should be recalled that the "national Security Strategy of September 2002, which announced the Bush Doctrine of pre-emptive war, also included the free market and the FTAA as principles the Pentagon is bound to advance and protect" (Tom Hayden, "Evidence of Things Unseen: The Rise of a New Movement," *AlterNet,* Oct. 21, 2003, available at http://www.alternet.org/story.html?StoryID=1700.0

64. Christopher Pyle, "Torture by Proxy," *San Francisco Chronicle,* section D, January 4, 2004. "Extraordinary rendition" was already put into practice by the Bush administration during 2002 (Dana Priest and Barton Gellman, "'Stress and Duress' Tactics used on Terrorism Suspects Held in Secret Overseas Facilities," *Washington Post,* December 26, 2002). Similar practices were conducted during the Clinton administration, including the delivery of suspects to the Philippine National Police in 1995 (McCoy, "Comment").

65. According to Seymour Hersh, "the roots of the Abu Ghraib prison scandal lie not in the criminal inclinations of a few Army reservists but in a decision, approved [in 2003] by Secretary of Defense Donald Rumsfeld, to expand a highly secret operation, which had been focused on the hunt for Al Qaeda, to the interrogation of prisoners in Iraq." Present and former intelligence officials interviewed by Hersh indicated that "the Pentagon's operation … encouraged physical coercion and sexual humiliation of Iraqi prisoners [often "cabdrivers, brothers-in-law, and people pulled off the streets"] in an effort to generate more intelligence about the growing insurgency in Iraq" (Hersh, "Annals of National Security: The Gray Zone," 38, 42). Also see Hersch, *Chain of Command: The Road from 9/11 to Abu Ghraib* (New York: HarperCollins Publishers, 2004); and Mark Danner, *Torture and Truth: America, Abu Ghraib and The War on Terror* (New York: New York Review Books, 2004).

66. Jess Bravin, "Pentagon Set Framework for Use of Torture: Security or Legal Factors Could Trump Restrictions, Memo to Rumsfeld Argued," *Wall Street Journal,* June 7, 2004. A Justice Department memo prepared in August 2002 also sought to legally justify the use of torture, pointing to, among other things, "the unlimited war-time powers of the president as commander-in-chief." Although the Bush administration attempted to distance itself from the memo once it was leaked, statements subsequently made to the New York Times by "current and former government officials" are clearly readable as a "backhanded" defense of torture (David Johnston and James Risen, "Aides Say Memo Backed Coercion for Qaeda Cases," *New York Times,* June 27, 2004; Joseph Kay, US Government's Unofficial Defense of Torture," available at http://www.wsws.org/articles/2004/jun2004/tort-j30.shtml.

67. Georg Cederskog, "Tusentals fängslas utan åtal," *Dagens Nyheter,* July 4, 2004; Yossi Melman, "Holding Al-Qaida Suspects in Secret Jordanian Lockup," *Haaretz,* October 13, 2004.

68. Lewis, "Un-American Activities," 16.

69. Lewis, "Un-American Activities,"18.

70. Johnson, *Sorrows of Empire,* 78.

71. Sara Roy, "On the Silencing of US Academics," *London Review of Books,* April 1, 2004.

72. Joel Beinin, "Thought Control for Middle East Studies," CommonDreams.org, March 31, 2004.

73. As of this writing, the Senate Health, Education, Labor and Pensions Committee was still considering its own version of HR 3077 for submission to the full Senate.

74. Michelle Goldberg, "Osama University?," available at http://www.salon.com/news/feature/2003/11/06/middle_east/print.html; Beinin, "Thought Control;" and Roy, "On the Silencing." As it currently stands "HR 3077 contains other provisions that are equally outrageous. For example it requires Title VI institutions to provide government recruiters with access to students and student recruiting information. The bill even directs the secretary of education and the advisory board to study—i.e. spy on—communities of US citizens who speak a foreign language, "particularly such communities that include speakers of languages that are critical to the national security of the United States'" (Roy, "On the Silencing").

75. Goldberg, "Osama University?" Such sentiments have gained wide circulation, in among other ways, through the publicity given *Defending Civilization: How Our Universities Are Failing America and What Can be Done about It,* a report issued in November 2001 by the American Council of Trustees and Alumni, an organization established by the vice president's wife, Lynne Cheney and Senator Joseph Lieberman.

76. John O. Edwards, "Gen. Franks Doubts Constitution Will Survive WMD Attack," available at http://www.newsmax.com/archives/articles/2003/11/20/185048.shtml.

77. Johnson, *Sorrows of Empire,* 3.

78. Cooper, "Soldier for the Truth," and Kwiatkowski, "New Pentagon Papers."

79. Tom Englehardt, "Cindy Sheehan, Our Imploding President," TomDispatch.com, December 29, 2005.

80. Sven Lindqvist, *Exterminate All the Brutes* (London: Granta, 1996 [1992]), 2.

81. Mark Jensen, "Scott Ritter Says U.S. Plans June Attack on Iran, 'Cooked' Jan. 30 Iraqi Election Results," United for Peace of Pierce County (WA), February 19, 2005, available at http://www.ufppc.org/content/view/2295 .

82. Dan Eggen and Julie Tate, "In Terror Cases, Few Convictions," *Washington Post,* June 12, 2005.

83. Statement made September 22, 2005.

84. Watts, "Revolutionary Islam and Modern Terror."

85. Greenberg, "Fathers and Sons," 98.

86. "Bush Approves Radical Step toward Creation of a Secret Police Force," *Washington Post,* June 30, 2005.

87. Matt Kelley, "Pentagon Rolls Out Stealth PR," *USA Today,* December 14, 2005.

88. Thomas E. Ricks, "Military Plays Up Role of Zarqawi," *Washington Post,* April 10, 2006.

89. Seymour M. Hersh, "The Coming Wars," *The New Yorker,"* January 24 & 31, 2005.

90. Nat Perry, "Bush's Mysterious 'New Programs,'" *Consortium News,* February 21, 2006, quoting Russell D. Tice and Peter Dale Scott.

91. Charlie Savage, "Bush Shuns Patriot Act Requirement," *Boston Globe,* March 24, 2006.

92. "The Imperial Presidency at Work," editorial, *New York Times,* January 15, 2006.

93. Doug Thompson, "Bush Could Seize Absolute Control of U.S. Government," *Capitol Hill Blue,* January 13, 2006, available at http://www.capitolhillblue.com/artman/publisher/printer_7986.shtml.

94. Walter Benjamin, "Paralipomena to 'On the Concept of History'," [1940] in Howard Eiland and Michael W. Jennings, eds., *Walter Benjamin: Selected Writings,* vol. 4, *1938–1940* (Cambridge, MA.: Harvard University Press, 2003), 401–411 (402).

Contributors

Simon Dalby is Professor of Geography and Political Economy at Carleton University, Ottawa, Canada

Matthew Farish is Assistant Professor of Geography at the University of Toronto, Canada

Jim Glassman is Associate Professor of Geography at the University of British Columbia at Vancouver, Canada

Stephen Graham is Professor of Geography at the University of Durham, UK

Mitchell Gray is a writer and Journalist at Word Merchant Communications, Vancouver, Canada

Derek Gregory is Distinguished University Scholar and Professor of Geography at the University of British Columbia at Vancouver, Canada

Jennifer Hyndman is Associate Professor of Geography at Simon Fraser University, Burnaby, British Columbia, Canada

Cindi Katz is Professor in the Environmental Psychology Program at the Graduate Center, City University of New York, USA

Gerry Kearns is Fellow of Jesus College and University Senior Lecturer in Geography at the University of Cambridge, UK

Philippe Le Billon is Assistant Professor at the Department of Geography and the Liu Institute for Global Issues, University of British Columbia at Vancouver, Canada

Alison Mountz is Assistant Professor of Geography at Syracuse University, USA

Eric N. Olund is Lecturer in Human Geography at the University of Sheffield, UK

Rupal Oza is Assistant Professor of Geography and Director of the Women's Studies program at Hunter College, City University of New York, USA

Ulrich Oslender is Research Fellow in the Department of Geographical and Earth Sciences, University of Glasgow, Scotland, UK

Trevor Paglen is completing his PhD at the Department of Geography, University of California at Berkeley, USA

Allan Pred is Professor of the Graduate School and a member of the Department of Geography at the University of California at Berkeley, USA

Anna J. Secor is Associate Professor of Geography at the University of Kentucky, USA

Nigel Thrift is Vice-Chancellor of the University of Warwick, UK

Michael Watts is Professor of Geography and Chancellor's Professor, University of California at Berkeley, USA

Elvin Wyly is Associate Professor of Geography and Chair of the Urban Studies Program at the University of British Columbia at Vancouver, Canada

Index

9/11 1, 2, 55, 80, 83, 87, 93, 94, 95, 96, 101, 104, 111, 154, 175, 176, 177, 190, 191, 200 n. 50, 07, 225, 226, 256, 295, 297, 300, 301, 303, 310, 311, 324, 329, 331, 332, 333, 336, 337, 338, 339, 347 n. 65, 348 n. 79, 353, 354, 357, 358, 364, 365, 367, 374, 375, 380 n. 40

A

Abjection 46-7, 48, 50, 193, 198, 215
Abu Ghraib 5, 42, 68, 70, 198, 206, 207-8, 209, 210, 211, 218-29, 205, 255, 351, 372, 373, 382 n. 65
Accumulation by dispossession '[primitive accumulation'] 16, 193
Aesthetics 209-10, 276, 277, 280-4, 287, 293 n. 14, 293 n. 20
Affect 274, 275, 276, 279-80, 282, 283, 286, 287, 292 n.7
Afghanistan 4, 55, 58, 62, 63, 68-9, 70, 83, 85, 93, 95, 137, 190, 191, 196, 200 n. 39, 214, 219, 223, 224, 226, 227, 232 n. 33, 300, 297, 300, 301, 304, 306, 310, 329, 341, 369, 371, 373
Africa 3, 133, 136, 137, 138, 139, 141, 142, 143
Agamben, G. 7, 13, 14, 16, 18, 20, 39, 40, 42, 44, 51, 77, 79, 85, 87, 88, 206-7, 208, 210, 231 n. 16, 235 n. 71, 252 n. 36, 253 n. 57, 275, 292 n. 8,
Al Qaeda 62, 69, 70, 94, 95, 96, 97, 133, 135, 137, 140, 147, 176, 177, 178, 179, 180 fn, 185, 186, 187, 188, 189, 190, 191, 197, 200 n. 39, 293 n. 13, 298, 301, 302, 303, 311, 324, 364, 366, 368, 371, 375, 382 n. 65
Aliens, enemy 65, 70, 207
Area 51 4, 238-9, 249
Area studies 2, 250, 260, 261, 262-4, 373-4
Asylum 77-9, 80, 81, 83, 84, 88, 213
Australia 80, 83-4, 85, 86, 87, 88, 90

B

Ban 13, 39, 51
Banal terrorism 349-361
Bare life 4, 5, 7, 8, 14, 16, 17, 18, 20, 23, 26, 30, 66, 206, 210, 231 n. 16, 321
Benjamin, W. 40, 42, 45, 46, 48, 51, 176, 285, 376
Biopolitics 2, 7, 13-18, 56, 57, 64, 70, 71, 215, 226, 275, 276,
Biopower 206, 208, 304
Black sites 5, 226
Black world 2, 239, 244, 245, 246, 248, 249, 250, 353
Bombing 7, 22-3, 24-25, 26, 28, 38, 55, 69, 95, 96, 97, 115-6, 119, 175, 176, 198, 202 n. 73, 237, 240, 248, 253 n. 62, 253 n. 63, 257, 260, 265, 274, 310, 313, 317-8, 319, 320, 356
Border(s) 4, 77, 79, 80, 81, 82, 86, 83, 88, 89, 137, 243, 244, 247, 265

Britain 9, 11, 14-30, 60, 74 n. 73, 83, 87, 155, 156, 187, 208
Bush, George W. 55, 56, 57, 58, 61-3, 64, 67, 68, 70, 75 n. 87, 75 n. 89, 93, 94, 101, 104, 111, 179, 180, 197, 207, 211, 214, 219, 222, 255, 299, 303, 304, 332, 335, 339, 341, 342, 348 n. 79, 358, 359, 363, 364, 366, 367, 368, 370, 371, 372, 373, 374, 375, 376, 376 n. 2, 380 n. 46

C

Camp(s) 7, 56, 65, 88, 89, 208, 210, 212, 213, 252 n. 36, 208
Canada 79, 80, 81, 82, 86, 88, 89, 145-6, 147
Cartography 2, 295-308, 334
Catholics, Catholicism 9, 11, 12, 13, 14, 17, 19, 20, 23, 24, 26, 27, 29, 94, 122, 163, 180, 194, 280, 293 n. 16
Cheney, Dick 101, 218, 221, 332, 363, 364, 366, 367, 369, 378 n. 24
Christianity, Christians 153, 155, 158, 161, 162, 176, 179, 180, 182, 351, 371
CIA 95, 104, 136, 137, 178, 182, 215, 216, 218, 224, 225, 226, 229, 240, 241, 242, 250, 251 n. 21, 260, 281, 293 n. 16, 298, 366, 373, 378 n. 23
Civilians 9, 115, 136, 197, 219, 273, 313, 314, 317, 319, 320, 321, 356
Cold War 2, 101, 243, 249, 256, 257, 258, 269, 262, 263, 297, 332, 338
Collateral damage 8, 55, 71
Colombia 4, 5, 82, 111-132
Colonialism 2, 3, 4, 7, 8, 9, 13, 16, 17, 18, 20, 21, 22, 26, 28, 29, 57, 96, 114, 147, 155, 156, 157, 169 n. 22, 182, 200 n. 41, 206, 209, 211-3, 229, 253 n. 56, 262, 263, 280, 295
Compassion 275, 286-8
Conflict commodities 3, 133-152, 302
Cosumption, politics of 134-6, 138-9, 148, 302
Coup d'état 41, 196

D

De-territorialization 114, 116, 126, 355
Diamonds 133-152, 302
Drug trafficking, trade 100, 111, 118, 130 n. 15, 135, 303, 304, 357, 361 n.2

E

Emergency 4, 18, 21, 29, 37, 39, 40, 41, 43, 44, 51, 53, 88, 97, 176, 207, 243, 265, 305
Enemy, enmity 58, 79, 90, 256, 297, 299, 312-3, 359, 364
Everyday life 5, 113, 115, 289, 296, 309-10, 320, 323, 324, 351, 363, 364

Exception 4, 7, 18, 21, 28, 37, 39-40, 42, 44, 48, 49, 50,
         51, 68, 77, 79, 85, 86, 87, 88, 89, 207, 208,
         209, 226, 229, 232 n. 23, 223 n. 27, 242, 248,
         252 n. 36, 253 n. 57, 292 n. 8, 304
Extra-territorializiation 79, 81, 89, 208-9, 226

F

Famine 4, 7, 9, 13, 15, 16, 17, 23-4
Fear 1, 2, 4, 5, 6, 22, 80, 83, 113, 114, 120, 122, 256,
         275, 296, 297, 324, 330, 332, 343, 350, 364,
         367, 374
Foucault, M. 13, 47, 56, 57, 70, 71 n.2, 206, 207, 251 n.
         4, 257, 275, 292 n. 4, 366

G

Geneva Conventions 28, 207, 214, 215, 217, 219, 222-3,
         224, 225, 374
Geographical imagination 1, 2
Geopolitics 3, 6, 63, 87, 88, 93, 113, 154, 193, 256, 257,
         258, 259, 261, 286, 295, 296, 299, 303, 305,
         310, 316, 320, 323, 330, 332, 338, 341
Globalization 80, 93, 104, 125, 170 n. 37, 197, 281, 297,
         298, 299, 300, 301, 302, 304, 305, 331, 337,
         338, 343, 357, 358, 359
Governmentality 70, 71 n. 2, 214
Groom Lake 237-254
Guantánamo Bay 2, 5, 42, 56, 68, 70, 71, 71, 78, 83, 85,
         205, 207-8, 209, 211-218, 223, 224, 225, 226,
         227, 229, 231 n. 21, 232 n. 26, 232 n. 33, 346
         n. 30, 351, 363, 372, 375
Guerrilla groups, violence, wars 111, 113, 115, 116, 117,
         118, 122, 127, 136, 138
Gujarat 163-7

H

Habeas corpus 4, 18, 21, 23, 27, 69, 207, 214, 216, 232 n.
         25, 232 n. 26
Hamas 187 fn, 191, 277, 278
Hezbollah 187 fn, 188, 192, 277, 279
Hinduism 155, 156, 157, 158, 160, 165, 170 n. 37, 179
Hindus 153, 154, 157, 159, 162, 163, 164, 165, 169 n.
         22, 183
Hindutva 4, 153, 155, 156, 159, 161, 167, 170 n. 37
Homeland security 1, 5, 90, 100, 135, 256, 257, 265,
         296, 324, 329, 333, 334, 335, 337, 351, 358,
         366, 367, 369, 372
Homeland 229, 258, 265, 296, 322, 339, 350, 351, 359
Homo sacer 230

I

Imaginative geographies 2, 3, 5, 121, 135, 142, 145,
         215, 364
Immigrants 6, 77-92
Immigration 225, 336
Imperialism 12-13, 29, 93, 94, 104, 139, 179, 187, 198,
         209, 213, 245, 258, 281, 298, 299, 300, 301,
         302, 367
India 4, 22, 104, 153-173, 277, 298
Indistinction 4, 40, 47-8, 225, 246

Indonesia 2, 80, 94, 96-8, 99, 101, 103, 104, 105, 181
Infrastructural warfare 309-28
IRA 27-9
Iraq 4, 5, 55, 58, 63, 75 n. 87, 83, 85, 86, 87, 93, 130 n.
         21, 135, 137m, 176, 187, 197-8, 203 n. 91, 203
         n. 96, 205, 218, 219, 220, 222, 223, 224, 225,
         229, 255, 278, 280, 281, 297, 298, 299, 300,
         301, 304, 205, 306, 311, 312, 313, 314, 316-
         23, 329, 333, 337, 341, 343, 344, 348 n. 79,
         356, 364, 365, 366, 367, 370, 371, 373, 374,
         375, 376 n. 2, 377 n. 18, 378 n. 23, 279 n. 25,
         379 n. 31, 382 n. 65
Ireland 2, 4, 7-35
Islam 3, 61-2, 97, 103, 104, 160, 165, 170 n. 37, 175-203,
         220, 228, 280, 351, 375; Islam, virtual 189,
         191
Islamicists, Islamicism [political Islam] 3, 41, 48, 49-
         50, 94, 95, 97, 98, 99, 101, 102, 104, 137, 176,
         177, 178, 179, 181, 182, 183, 192, 194, 197,
         210 n. 47, 220, 321, 336, 360, 364
Islamophobia 154
Israel 28, 80, 228, 278, 311

J

Judaism 180, 186

K

Kurds 4, 5, 37, 41-4, 47, 49, 53 n. 4, 84

L

Landscape 4, 120-1, 127, 157, 167, 239, 245, 247, 254
         n. 68, 286, 343, 350, 352, 353, 356; inner
         255-271
Law 4, 7, 12, 13, 14, 15, 17, 18, 19, 20 21, 28, 29, 37, 39,
         40, 41, 42, 43, 44, 45, 46, 47, 48, 50, 51, 58,
         66, 67, 69, 77, 83, 84, 98, 113, 114, 207, 208,
         209, 211, 212, 213, 214, 215, 216, 218, 219,
         223, 225, 226, 227, 230 n. 6, 231 n. 16, 245-6,
         247, 289, 313, 356, 372, 375; Islamic 181,
         182, 185, 186, 202 n. 85

M

Manhattan Project 239-40, 242, 244
Media 4, 147, 188-9, 255, 277, 279, 281-4, 286, 289, 292
         n. 3, 292 n. 14, 293 n. 19, 294 n. 24, 295-6,
         310, 315, 317, 320, 332, 341, 350, 375, 376,
         378 n. 23
Melodrama 283-4, 294 n. 23, 294 n. 24
Microgeographies 84, 119, 122, 124
Military 1, 2, 3, 4, 5, 18, 23, 27, 37, 41, 55, 71, 94, 95, 96,
         97, 98, 100, 101, 102, 103, 111, 113, 116-7,
         118, 122, 137, 130 n. 21, 177, 179, 187, 190,
         198, 222, 238, 240, 242, 245, 249, 257, 260,
         280, 297, 298, 300, 302, 304, 311, 312, 314,
         317, 319, 321, 324, 336, 338, 342, 350, 353,
         356, 357, 360. 367, 372, 374

Muslims 58, 61, 64, 67, 71, 153, 154, 155, 156, 157, 158,
      161, 162, 163, 164, 165, 166, 167, 169 n. 22,
      171 n. 52, 175, 178, 188, 189, 200 n. 35, 210,
      227, 255, 364

N

Narco-terrorism 111, 118, 130 n. 15
Nationalism 3,5, 9, 23, 24, 25, 27, 94, 96, 154, 155, 160,
      163, 164, 179, 188, 193, 194, 197, 228, 256,
      278, 350, 351
Nazis, Nazism 56, 206, 208, 210, 225, 240, 261, 310, 351
Neoconservatism 29, 101, 176, 230 n. 6, 330, 331, 243
Neoliberalism 178, 179, 195, 196, 198, 230 n. 6, 334,
      336, 354, 358, 360
Nevada 2, 4, 237, 241, 246, 247, 249, 250, 265
New York City 1, 19, 142, 176, 177, 178, 209, 265, 329,
      334, 335, 336, 337, 338, 340, 341, 349, 354
Nomos 7, 253 n. 57

O

Oil 3, 135, 177, 184, 193, 194-6, 197, 203 n. 91, 302, 341,
      379 n. 31
Orientalism 154, 155, 156, 176, 177, 178, 179, 228, 336
Osama bin Laden 58, 62, 177, 178, 179, 186, 188, 190,
      191,192, 195, 201 n. 50, 205

P

Palestine 4, 28, 80, 85, 158, 177, 219, 228, 274, 278, 327
      n. 74, 372
Paramilitary groups, paramilitary violence 4, 98, 113,
      114, 115, 118, 119, 120, 122, 126, 127, 136,
      246
Patriot Act 62, 64, 67-8, 74 n. 73, 343, 351, 372, 373,
      375
Peace 26, 113, 125, 288, 324
Pentagon 1, 3, 133, 188, 198, 207, 210, 215, 217, 238,
      239, 240, 255, 295, 296, 297, 298, 301, 304,
      310, 320, 329, 330, 338, 342, 347 n. 66, 366,
      367, 374, 375, 379 n. 31, 381 n. 46, 382 n. 63
Philippines 2, 94-96, 99, 101, 103, 105
Police, policing 27, 40, 41, 43-48, 50, 79, 82, 85, 88, 99,
      100, 138, 144, 161, 337, 349, 353, 375
Political violence 1, 2, 3, 4, 5, 6, 9, 17, 25, 26, 85, 117,
      129 n. 14, 187, 188, 265, 274
Prison(s) 2,5,9, 20, 23, 24, 28, 37, 38, 41, 43, 45, 65, 80,
      175, 184, 185, 205, 206, 211, 213, 218, 220,
      221, 225, 226, 227, 235 n. 71, 342, 346 n. 30
Profiling 1, 68, 83, 356
Protestants, Protestantism 8, 12, 13, 14, 17, 2o, 27, 182
Protestants, Protestantism 8, 9, 11, 12, 13, 14, 20, 22, 27
Psychological warfare 256-7, 260, 262-4 , 312, 320

Q

Qutb, Sayyid 175, 176, 178, 184, 185-6, 193, 194, 197,
      200 n. 50, 200 n. 53, 200 n. 54

R

Racialization 55, 58, 59, 62, 63, 67, 113, 136, 336, 351
Racism 56, 57, 64, 66, 67, 68, 70, 71, 261

Refugees 4, 37, 44, 77-92, 213
Renditions, extraordinary 225-6, 373
Rights, civil 9, 12, 16, 27, 55, 57, 63, 64, 68, 357
Rights, human 7, 28, 41, 49, 79, 98, 100, 125, 126, 136,
      144, 151 n.10, 194, 225, 323
Risk society 332-3
Rumsfeld, Donald 69, 70, 101, 217, 221, 312, 332, 340,
      342, 366, 367, 368, 382 n. 65

S

Saddam Hussein 58, 62, 93, 196, 205, 218, 219, 221, 233
      n. 37, 248, 302, 364, 366, 371, 372, 376 n. 2,
      378 n. 23, 380 n. 39, 381 n. 48
Said, E. 154, 177
Schmitt, Carl 58, 178, 208-9, 215, 253 n. 57, 305
Security 5, 19-20, 37, 41, 53, 77, 78, 79, 80, 81, 82, 86,
      89, 97, 98, 100, 105, 222, 256, 330, 333, 338,
      341, 342, 349, 351, 352, 353, 354, 356, 357,
      359,
Security, ontological 358-60
September 11, 2001 see 9/11
Sexuality 71, 81
Situated ignorance 5, 6, 89, 364-5, 366, 367, 368, 369,
      370, 372, 374, 380 n. 44
Slums 181, 193-4
Sovereign power 7, 40, 45, 71, 77, 82, 85, 88, 206, 207,
      208, 211, 214, 226, 294 n. 32
Space(s) 1, 4, 5, 26, 49, 40, 42, 43, 44, 47, 48, 50, 51, 56,
      58, 68, 70, 77, 78, 79, 82, 83, 84, 87, 89, 113,
      120, 121, 122, 125, 126, 127, 136, 143, 146,
      153, 154, 156, 157, 160, 162, 163, 166, 169
      n. 22, 176, 193, 207, 209, 210, 211, 213, 226,
      229, 242, 244, 246-7, 252 n. 36, 256, 257,
      258, 259, 264, 274, 275, 284, 285, 286, 288,
      289, 324, 329, 336, 339, 349, 352, 355
Spatial fetishism 352-6, 360
Spatial strategy 153, 154, 155, 157, 161, 167
Spectacle 190-1, 311
State 1, 2, 3, 5, 7, 9, 10, 11, 13, 15, 16, 18, 20, 21, 22, 26,
      27, 28 29, 37, 38, 40, 41, 43, 46, 48, 49, 50,
      56, 57, 58, 64, 71, 77, 79, 80, 82, 86, 87, 97,
      119, 126, 142, 147, 164, 166, 176, 179, 181,
      183, 184, 185, 186, 187, 188, 190, 192, 193,
      194, 222, 246, 247, 274, 276, 303, 311, 312,
      324, 349, 350, 352, 353, 354, 356, 257, 359,
      364, 365
Suicide bombing 4, 8, 58, 191, 275, 276, 277-84, 286,
      288, 292 n. 9, 293 n. 10, 293 n. 12, 293 n. 14,
      293 n. 19, 293 n. 20, 311

T

Targets 313-5, 317, 318
Taussig, M. 42, 43, 46, 121, 126, 229
Territory, territorialization 9-13, 17-18, 21, 40, 42, 47,
      48, 57, 58, 64, 71, 77, 80, 87, 114, 115, 120,
      124-5, 127, 153, 157, 160, 208, 209, 212, 214
Terror city hypothesis 329-48

Terror 1, 2, 4, 5, 6, 12, 22, 23, 58, 62, 77, 111, 114, 115,
       116, 119, 120, 121, 122, 125, 126, 133, 135,
       140, 142, 146, 176, 178, 179, 185, 187, 188,
       197, 198, 256, 304, 323, 324, 325, 329, 333,
       340, 343, 344, 351, 353, 355, 364, 369
Terrorism 1, 3, 8, 9, 18, 21, 22, 25, 26, 28, 39, 55, 58, 62,
       68, 69, 70, 78, 83, 86, 89, 93, 94, 95, 96, 97,
       98, 100, 102, 103, 111, 127, 135, 140, 147, 189,
       198, 207, 214, 220, 293 n. 14, 295, 301, 310,
       312, 329, 329, 330, 331, 333, 334, 335, 336,
       338, 339, 340, 350, 351, 352, 354, 355, 356,
       357, 358, 363, 365, 369, 372
Thailand 2, 94, 98-101, 105, 373
Torture 5, 20, 27, 41, 44, 45-7, 56, 68, 71, 81, 175, 185,
       192, 205-6, 211, 215-8, 219, 221, 223, 226,
       228, 255, 368, 373, 375, 383 n. 66
Turkey 4, 21, 37-53, 83, 181, 194, 277, 278

U

United Nations 29, 58, 78, 87, 88, 119, 122, 136, 137,
       139, 141, 220, 318-9, 323, 364
United States 2, 3, 4, 5, 7, 19, 23, 24, 25, 29, 42, 55-75,
       79, 81, 82, 85, 86, 87, 88, 89, 90, 93, 95, 96,
       98, 100, 105, 111, 127, 140, 154, 186, 190,
       191, 196, 207, 209, 212, 213, 214, 215-7, 226,
       227, 231 n. 10, 240, 245, 246, 248, 250, 255,
       257, 258, 298, 299, 300, 303, 310, 311, 312,
       319, 322, 325, 329, 330, 331, 333, 334, 335,
       336, 338, 339, 342, 343, 350, 356, 357, 358,
       359, 360, 368

USSR 212, 240, 249, 259, 263

W

War on terror 1, 7, 56, 57, 58, 62, 63, 67-70, 86, 89, 93,
       95, 96, 97, 98, 99, 100, 101, 105, 111, 127, 135,
       136, 176, 179, 192, 206, 207, 209, 210, 213,
       214, 215, 217, 221, 223, 227, 230, 255, 256,
       258, 295, 296, 299, 301, 303, 304, 306, 324,
       325, 330, 339, 343, 348 n. 79, 350-1, 357, 361
       n. 2, 364, 367, 375, 376
War 2, 4, 5, 10, 13, 26, 27, 42, 56, 57, 58, 60, 64, 66, 67,
       78, 79, 86, 88, 117, 118, 130 n. 21, 133, 134,
       136, 138, 140, 141, 142, 194, 207, 208, 209,
       214, 219, 227, 239, 240, 256, 260, 261, 263,
       265, 273, 277, 281, 285, 286, 288, 293 n. 19,
       295, 297, 301, 302, 303, 304, 305, 306, 310,
       312, 315, 316-9, 320-1, 322, 323, 324, 325,
       329, 340, 344, 332, 359, 369